FILTON COLLEGE

DISCRIMINATION LAW

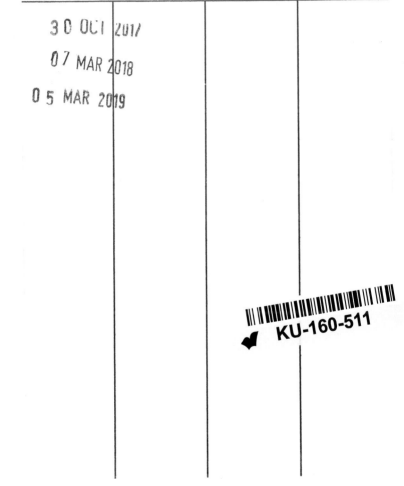

AUSTRALIA
Law Book Co.
Sydney

CANADA and USA
Carswell
Toronto

HONG KONG
Sweet & Maxwell Asia

NEW ZEALAND
Brookers
Wellington

SINGAPORE and MALAYSIA
Sweet & Maxwell Asia
Singapore and Kuala Lumpur

DISCRIMINATION LAW

FIRST EDITION

BY

MICHAEL CONNOLLY

London
Sweet & Maxwell Ltd
2006

Published by
Sweet & Maxwell Limited of
100 Avenue Road, London NW3 3PF
Typeset by J&L Composition, Filey, North Yorkshire
Printed and bound in Great Britain by
William Clowes Ltd, Beccles, Suffolk

A CIP catalogue record
for this book is available
from the British Library

ISBN: 0 421 930 004
9 780 421 930 001

No natural forests were destroyed
to make this product, only farmed timber
was used and re-planted.

PREFACE

Discrimination law is a technical and difficult subject. The matter is compounded by the extensive and rather ad hoc growth in the coverage over recent years, which continues relentlessly. In this book I have attempted to describe the law simply and clearly, using examples and logical organisation. But the law's complexity is no excuse to omit analysis, so I have added comment where appropriate. I have made many comparisons with other jurisdictions, especially with United States federal law. The US Civil Rights Act 1964 was the forerunner of much of the discrimination law in Great Britain and Europe, and the federal courts have years of experience dealing with many issues new to Britain.

Amid all this, I hope the contents demonstrate that discrimination law is a necessary tool inspired by the milk of human kindness to help redress the failings in our societies, and not simply a highbrow philosophical concept.

This edition covers the new Age Regulations, in force in October 2006, and the wide-ranging Equality Act 2006, although I have tried to state the law as it stood on May 31, 2006.

Michael Connolly
London
Summer 2006

CONTENTS

TABLE OF CASES

ix

TABLE OF STATUTES

TABLE OF STATUTORY INSTRUMENTS

CHAPTER 1

THEORIES OF DISCRIMINATION LAW

1. THE MEANING OF DISCRIMINATION

For the general public, an easily-received legal definition of discrimi-   **1–001**
nation is different treatment motivated by prejudice or hostility.[1] For
practitioners of discrimination law, this is too simplistic. The lawyer
knows that discrimination must include, at the least, behaviour that
has an unintended adverse effect on a protected group (normally indirect discrimination), say a customary length of residence requirement
to work in local services. Meanwhile the judiciary, aware of this
professional opinion, are conscious of the public's perception when
defining discrimination. Hence, in *Khan v Chief Constable of West
Yorkshire*,[2] Lord Woolf MR, (as he then was) stated: "To regard a
person as acting unlawfully when he had not been motivated either
consciously or unconsciously by any discriminatory motive is hardly
likely to assist the objective of promoting harmonious racial relations". In *Nagarajan v London Regional Transport*,[3] Lord Browne-
Wilkinson dissented: "To introduce something akin to strict liability
into the Acts which will lead to individuals being stamped as racially
discriminatory . . . where these matters were not consciously in their
minds when they acted is unlikely to recommend the legislation to the

---

[1] Alexander argues strongly not all discrimination should be unlawful, even where it is immoral.
"For example, a person who, in choosing a spouse . . . excludes members of a particular race
solely because of a bias, may be acting within her moral rights even if she is acting immorally."
L. Alexander, "What makes wrongful discrimination wrong? Biases, preferences, stereotypes
and proxies" (1992) 141 Penns UL Rev 149 p.201.
[2] [2000] I.C.R. 1169, at para.14, CA, Discussed, Ch.7, para.7–009.
[3] [2000] 1 A.C. 501, at 510 HL. Discussed, Ch.7, para.7–008.

1

public as being fair and proper protection for the minorities that they are seeking to protect".

The use of public understanding as an interpretive tool is clearly controversial, but for some public understanding is "crucial in a democracy . . . and necessary for the enactment and enforcement of civil rights law".[4] Whatever the merits of that view, the reality is that the legal definition of discrimination will be, to some degree, influenced by the public's understanding of discrimination. So it cannot be ignored in the following discussion.

Even as a simplistic notion of prejudice, discrimination can be attributed with several meanings. Sunstein considers that it encompasses three types of mistake.[5] The first is an incorrect view that people in certain groups possess certain characteristics. The second is a belief that many members of a group have certain characteristics when in fact only a few of them do. Here the error is an extremely over-broad generalisation. The third mistake is a reliance on fairly accurate group-based generalisations when more accurate (and not especially costly) classifying devices are available. Thus even where a group predominantly possesses a particular characteristic, it is possible to identify the relevant individuals, rather than treat the group as a whole. An example arose in *Bohon-Mitchell v Common Professional Examination Board*[6] where those with degrees from outside the British Isles were presumed to be unfamiliar with the British way of life. For Rutherglen, the typical liberal understanding of discrimination is "doubly paradoxical".[7] It appreciates unintentional discrimination, yet at the same time endorses positive action programmes which expressly account for race or sex.

1–002   A new more subtle and challenging definition of *racial* discrimination was brought into the public's consciousness in 1999 by the Macpherson Report (the inquiry into the police response to the murder of the black teenager, Stephen Lawrence). The Report drew together many explanations of the phrase *institutional racism* to produce a widely accepted definition. After making the point that overt racism was not at issue in the inquiry, it identified "unwitting" racism, and "unconscious" racism. The Report then noted the *effect* of actions and police culture as areas for attention: the problem lies not with individual officers, but with the organisation. The Macpherson Report defined institutional racism as:

> "The collective failure of an organisation to provide an appropriate and professional service to people because of their colour,

---

[4] G. Rutherglen, "Discrimination and its discontents" (1995) 81 Virginia L Rev 117, pp.127–128.
[5] C. Sunstein, "Three civil rights fallacies" (1991) 79 California L Rev 751, pp.752–753.
[6] [1978] I.R.L.R. 525, IT. See further, Ch.6, para.6–032.
[7] G. Rutherglen, "Discrimination and its discontents" (1995) 81 Virginia L Rev 117, pp.127–28.

culture, or ethnic origin. It can be seen or detected in processes, attitudes and behaviour which amount to discrimination through unwitting prejudice, ignorance, thoughtlessness and racist stereotyping which disadvantage minority ethnic people."[8]

Discrimination can also be characterised under principles of either *harm* or *unfairness*.[9] The harm principle rests on a strong connection between the stigma and denied opportunity of the different treatment, and social historical factors, such as the forms of second-class citizenship experienced by some racial groups and women. The stigma, degradation and humiliation of slavery, (and the more recent racial segregation), is revived with every modern-day act of racial discrimination. Well into the 20th century, women were legal second-class citizens. They were inferior in marriage, where their legal existence was suspended, domestic violence condoned, and rape lawful. They were denied the vote, and suffered inferior job opportunities, prospects and pay.[10] Consequently, every act of sex discrimination may be seen and felt as an act championing the old arrangements. Two consequences flow from this analysis. The first is that the discriminator is easily stamped as the wrongdoer, which it makes it harder to justify outlawing unintentional (usually indirect) discrimination, which, as *Griggs v Duke Power*[11] illustrates, is necessary to redress the problems associated with second-class citizenship. The second consequence is that arguments for discrimination law to include other groups appear less convincing than those for sex and race.[12] Take, for instance, the latest addition to the British statute book, age discrimination. The Canadian the Supreme Court is more tolerant of age discrimination because it is based on neither feelings of hostility nor intolerance.[13] A study of age discrimination law in the United States revealed that the chief beneficiaries are middle-class white males.[14]

The fairness principle relies on a much weaker link between social **1–003** history and discriminatory practices. History informs us that decision-making based on irrational factors such as race and sex is inherently *unfair*. This view is easier to reconcile with the law of indirect discrimination, as less, or no, blame need be attached to the discriminator. It also makes it easier to explain the inclusion of other grounds (such as age) within the anti-discrimination legal framework. Its weakness is

---

[8] The Stephen Lawrence Inquiry, Report of an Inquiry by Sir William Macpherson, advised by Tom Cook, The Right Reverend Dr John Sentamu, Dr Richard Stone. February 1999. Presented to Parliament by the Home Secretary. Cm 4262–I, London: TSO, at paras 6.1–6.34.
[9] See J. Gardner, "Liberals and unlawful discrimination" (1989) 9 O.J.L.S. 1, pp.2–8.
[10] See S. Fredman, *Women and the Law*, 1997, Oxford: Clarendon Press, Ch.2.
[11] (1971) 401 US 424. See Ch.6, para.6–001.
[12] See further below para.1–009.
[13] *McKinney v University of Guelph* [1990] 3 SCR 229, at 297. The US Supreme Court takes a similar line, see Ch.2, para.2–008.
[14] See G. Rutherglen, "From race to age: the expanding scope of employment discrimination law" (1995) 24 *Journal of Legal Studies* 491, p.495.

that it risks treating "all non-meritocratic preferences as being on all fours with slavery"[15] and "opens up the possibility of white male legal actions which exploit the vulnerability of any legal recognition of race or gender difference ..."[16] The fairness principle is also harder to reconcile with positive action programmes, which inherently discriminate against a dominant but protected group, typically white males. Preferences for women or blacks repeat the same wrong that caused their subjugation in the first place. Positive action is easier to reconcile with the harm principle because here the "wrongs" are not comparable. One is to subjugate a class of persons, the other is to redress subjugation.

2. The Aims of the Law

1–004   Assuming that discrimination is either harmful or unfair, or both, the next question is what should be the overall aim of legal intervention. The single aspiration upon which all interested parties appear to agree is the achievement of "equality". This word appears in discrimination legislation and Human Rights instruments the world over. But it is not free of debate. First, after examination, one learns that its most distinctive feature is its "shifting meaning".[17] Rather like a politician seeking a broad mandate, it reflects whatever meaning the observer wishes it to have. The second problem is that although equality is "virtue word"[18] and as such difficult to criticise, once it is given a firm meaning, it becomes clear that equality is not necessarily a good thing. What follows is a discussion of various models and ideals of equality within discrimination law.

(1) Formal Equality

1–005   Equality has been the underpinning principle of modern anti-discrimination law, beginning in the United States with the Civil Rights Act 1964. The primary goal of that Act was redressing the historic inequalities suffered by the United States' African-American population. The Act made it unlawful to "discriminate" because of such individual's race, colour, religion, sex or national origin.[19] From this, the US Supreme Court developed the disparate treatment (or direct discrimination) model.[20] The logical consequence is that those obligated by the Act must practice same—or *equal*—treatment.

---

[15] See J. Gardner, "Liberals and unlawful discrimination" (1989) 9 O.J.L.S. 1, p.8.
[16] N. Lacey, "From individual to group", in B. Hepple and E. Szyszczak (eds), *Discrimination: The Limits of Law*, 1992, London: Mansell, p.104.
[17] P. Westen, *Speaking of Equality* (1990) Princeton: Princeton University Press, p.xviii.
[18] *ibid.*
[19] e.g. Title VII, s.703(a), codified as 42 USC s.2000e-2.
[20] See e.g. *McDonnell Douglas Corp v Green* 411 US 792 (1973).

Britain too, adopted this model, with, for example, the 1976 Race Relations Act providing that direct discrimination was treating someone "less favourably" on racial grounds, meaning that, on racial grounds, persons should be treated equally.

These models of equality are symmetrical, meaning that the law   **1–006** protects whites as well as blacks, men as well as women, and so on and so forth. In their simplest form, these models represent *formal* equality, that like should be treated as like. (The notable exception here is disability discrimination law, which insists upon *different* treatment.)[21] There a number of problems associated with formal equality.

The first problem is that equal treatment is not necessarily virtuous. At its most general equal treatment is a consequence of the rule of law, by which laws must be enforced equally. But this does not prevent discriminatory laws, such as apartheid, being enacted and enforced equally.[22] A law of equal treatment is a step removed from unequal laws, but its enforcement can have counter-productive or unequal results. In his comment on the French law of vagrancy and theft, Anatole France mocked: "The law, in its majestic equality, forbids the rich as well as the poor to sleep under bridges, to beg in the streets, and to steal bread."[23] In this context, Westen notes the equal treatment handed out in Hitler's concentration camps.[24] The point is that equal treatment can amount to equally *bad* treatment.

In one infamous US case, after a court ordered Mississippi city to abandon its racial segregation policy for its swimming pools (four white-only, one black-only), the city administration responded by closing down all its pools instead. This act did not offend the US constitutional right to equality.[25] In the context of sex discrimination law, employers have defended claims by arguing (successfully) that they treated the claimant and her comparator equally *badly*. This has arisen in the field of sexual harassment, where homophobic abuse of a lesbian was not actionable because a male homosexual would have been equally abused.[26] Similarly, men and women in a factory were treated equally by the display of pornographic pictures of women.[27] In the field of pregnancy, British courts have compared the pregnant woman with a "sick man", allowing employers to prevail if they can

---

[21] See generally, Ch.11, para.11–021. Hugh Collins identified three "deviations" from a simple equal treatment principle. First, different *treatment* is required in some cases, e.g. pregnancy and disability. Second, equal treatment is not permitted where it causes unjustifiable indirect discrimination. Third, affirmative action. See H. Collins, "Discrimination, Equality and Social inclusion" (2003) 66 M.L.R. 16, pp.16–17.

[22] See J. Jowell, "Is Equality a Constitutional Principle?" (1994) 47 *Current Legal Problems* (Pt.2, Collected Papers) 1, pp.4–91.

[23] Anatole France, *Le Lys Rouge* (*The Red Lily*), 1894, quoted in John Bartlett, *Familiar Quotations*, 14th rev. ed. (Boston: Little Brown, 1968) p.802a.

[24] P. Westen, *Speaking of Equality* (1990) Princeton: Princeton University Press, p.xvii.

[25] *Palmer v Thompson* 403 US 217 (1971).

[26] *Pearce v Governing Body of Mayfield Secondary School*, [2003] UKHL 34. See further, paras 3–015 and 8–081.

[27] *Stewart v Cleveland Guest Ltd* [1996] I.C.R. 535 EAT. See further Ch.5, para.5–023.

show that they would dismiss any worker who took a certain amount of time off work for illness.[28] The irony here is that the worse the treatment, the more likely it is that he will be believed. Some industries employing predominantly female or minority workers, may pay poverty wages.[29] In all these cases the solution has been asymmetrical law, requiring no comparator, such as free-standing laws against sexual harassment and pregnancy discrimination, and the National Minimum Wage Act 1998.

1–007   Workers also may be equally victimised for bringing discrimination claims so long as all workers are treated that way, whatever the nature of their claim. Under this meaning of equality, such workers can be denied a reference,[30] or a transfer or grievance proceedings.[31]

The second problem centres on the need of the equal treatment model for a comparator. A claimant cannot insist that she has been treated unequally until she produces a person who would have been treated more favourably. There are technical and philosophical problems associated with the comparator-driven approach. Technical problems arise because this model does not allow for differences between the groups. This most notable case here is pregnancy discrimination. A claimant cannot produce a pregnant male comparator.[32] Similarly, in cases involving religion, claimants will often be seeking *different*, rather than equal treatment. For instance, there is no obviously suitable comparator for a Muslin worker requesting Friday afternoons off work to attend a Mosque. This problem has been recognised overtly in the United States. In *EEOC v Ithaca Industries*[33] the employer was obliged to accommodate a worker's refusal to work on a Sunday for a religious reason, by enquiring if fellow workers would cover that shift. This was because, for cases of religious discrimination, the legislation's equality theory is not disparate treatment or disparate impact, but "reasonable accommodation."[34] This theory was reconciled with a notion of equality by Judge Hall, who noted: "We are convinced that [the legislation] . . . has the primary secular effect of preserving the *equal* employment opportunities of those employees whose moral scruples conflict with work rules . . ."[35]

---

[28] *Hayes v Malleable Working Men's Club and Institute* [1985] I.C.R. 703, EAT. This approach was effectively overruled by the ECJ. See further, Ch.4, para.4–037.

[29] See the discussion on real or hypothetical comparators, Ch.9, para.9–006.

[30] *Khan v Chief Constable of West Yorkshire* [2002] 1 W.L.R. 1947, HL. See further, para.7–009.

[31] *Corneleus v University College Swansea* [1987] I.R.L.R. 141 CA. See further, para.7–006.

[32] See, Ch.4, para.4–037.

[33] 849 F 2d 116 (4th Cir 1988), certiorari denied, 488 US 924 91988).

[34] In 1972, an amendment to Title VII, para.701(j), (codified in 42 USC s.2000e(j)) was enacted with the stated purpose to protect Sabbath observers whose employers fail to adjust work schedules to fit their needs. "The Act thus requires that an employer, short of undue hardship, make reasonable accommodations to the religious needs of its employees." per Judge Hall, *ibid.*, at 118.

[35] *ibid.*, at 119. Emphasis supplied.

The philosophical objection is that, the comparator, when found, **1–008**
"far from being an abstract individual, is in fact white, male,
Christian, able-bodied, and heterosexual."[36] Hence, this approach
provides only *"equality in terms of a norm set by men"* leaving women
with the right only to aspire to be the same as men.[37] Similarly,
Townsend-Smith feared that the law could be used to reinforce male-
based values, such as an ability to work longer hours, have unbroken
and long service, aggression or dynamism. "[I]t is important to see
how deep-rooted is the notion of merit in our society, and that merit
has historically been determined in male terms. The danger is that the
law will accept male definitions of what is meritorious in employment,
and that this will not correspond with the desires or best interests of
many or most women."[38] Likewise, equipment and machinery in the
workplace can have gender connotations: "In a training workshop . . .
it is impossible to get a teenage lad to wipe the floor with a mop,
though he may be persuaded to sweep it with a broom."[39]

Similarly, Lacey argues that, for women, formal equality does not
go far enough as "it has little bite in view of the disadvantages which
women suffer in private areas such as family life, untouched by the
sex discrimination legislation".[40] The problem, she argues, is formal
equality conceptualises problem as *sex discrimination* rather than
discrimination against women, rendering "invisible the real social
problem." This objection applies to other grounds as well as gender. A
benign quality, such as being socially reserved, can be used as a reason
not to hire, even though this quality is characteristic of Indian Hindus
of the Brahmin caste.[41]

The third problem is that in principle, equal treatment prevents
more favourable treatment, and so prevents positive action. It is naive
to believe that positive action is not necessary to redress the effects of
past discrimination, which is a major reason for the legislation in the
first place. Yet it clashes with the basic notion of equal treatment,
especially in the mind of the public. Positive action plans are only
permissible as an exception to the equal treatment model.[42]

The fourth problem with the equal treatment model is that it **1–009**
suggests that everyone is entitled to it, rather than just those groups

---

[36] S. Fredman, *Discrimination Law*, 2001, OUP, p.9.

[37] See T. Ward, "Beyond sex equality: the limits of sex equality in the new Europe", in T. Hervey and D. O'Keeffe (eds), *Sex Equality Law in the European Union*, 1996, Chichester: John Wiley, p.370.

[38] R. Townshend-Smith, *Sex Discrimination in Employment: Law, Practice and Policy*, 1989, London: Sweet & Maxwell, pp.25–26.

[39] C. Cockburn, *In The Way of Women: Men's Resistance to Sex Equality in Organisations*, 1991, Basingstoke: Macmillan, p.38.

[40] N. Lacey, "Legislation against sex discrimination: questions from a feminist perspective" (1986) 14 J.L.S. 411, pp.413–17.

[41] See *Kapoor v Monash University* (2001) VSCA 0247, 4 VR 483, Supreme Court of Victoria, Australia.

[42] Positive, or affirmative, action, is discussed in Ch.12.

specified in dedicated legislation. Other groups, whose political power is not so strong, are as likely to be in need of equal treatment as many covered by the legislation. Further, it is difficult to construct arguments to deny equal treatment to any individual, whether idiosyncratic or conventional.

There is ample evidence that anyone feeling aggrieved will feel entitled to equal treatment. Men,[43] atheists,[44] whites[45] and white racists[46] readily have used the symmetry of the equal treatment model to redress their own grievances. In the UK, before the introduction of dedicated religious discrimination legislation, religious groups argued that they, by coincidence, were also racial groups, so fell within the protection of the Race Relations Act 1976.[47] Many on low wages have tried obtaining a "fair" wage using equal pay law.[48]

People generally may feel entitled to equal treatment because there is little evidence of any single fundamental principle dictating which groups should be singled out. The reasons for inclusion appear to be more capricious than principled. In a relatively short time, the world has moved from a "norm" of treating races and women differently, to specifying religion, disability, sexual orientation, gender reassignment and age (in addition to race and gender) as deserving of equal treatment.

1–010 One explanation is that these groups operated successful political campaigns. Some are embedded in the respective nation's consciousness. President Kennedy was moved by Martin Luther King's "I have a dream" speech to promote the Civil Rights Act of 1964.[49] In the UK, the daughter of the Minister for Disabled People drew huge public support by leading a campaign that embarrassed a reluctant government to introduce the Disability Discrimination Act 1995.[50] But not all groups obtained protection principally through their own political campaigns. The EUs Race Directive was partly, at least, the result of the politicians' fear of Europe's far-right fascists exploiting the

---

[43] *Jepson and Dyas-Elliott v The Labour Party* [1996] I.R.L.R. 116, IT. See further, Ch.12, para.12–002. Cases brought by male claimants under equal pay legislation have been instrumental in the restructuring of pension plans. See e.g. *Barber v Guardian Royal Exchange* C Case-262/88; [1990] I.R.L.R. 240 ECJ.

[44] *EEOC v Townley Engineering* 859 F 2d 610 (1988). See further, Ch.4, para.4–028.

[45] See e.g. *McDonald v Santa fe Trail Transportation Co* 427 US 273 (1976); *Carter v Gallagher* 452 F 2d 315 (CAB 1971) cert denied 406 US 950 (1972).

[46] *Redfearn v Serco* [2006] EWCA 659. There are numerous examples in the US of the Ku Klux Klan invoking equality law. See e.g. *New York ex rel Bryant v Zimmerman (No.2)* 278 US 63.

[47] *Mandla v Dowell Lee* [1983] AC 548 HL (Sikhs recognised as racial group); *Crown Suppliers v Dawkins* [1993] I.C.R. 517 CA (Rastafarians denied recognition).

[48] See e.g. *Strathclyde Regional Council v Wallace* [1988] 2 W.L.R. 259, HL; *Glasgow CC v Marshall* [2000] 1 W.L.R. 333, HL. Discussed Ch.9, para.9–030.

[49] See J. Greenya, "Rites of Passage: The Civil Rights Act of 1964," *Washington Lawyer* March/April 2000 (*www.dcbar.org*, search for "Rites of Passage"); C. Whalen and B. Whalen, *The Longest Debate: a Legislative History of the Civil Rights Act* (1985) Washington DC: Seven Locks Press, 1985.

[50] Respectively, Victoria and Nicholas Scott. See *The Times* May 12, 1994 and May 21, 1994; *The Independent* May 12, 1994.

enlargement from 15 to 25 nations.[51] The EUs equal pay law was enshrined in the original Treaty of Rome at the insistence of the French: as France was the only country with an equal pay law at the time, French *employers* (not workers) campaigned for its inclusion in the Treaty to avoid unfair competition from other member states.[52] Gender was introduced into the Civil Rights Act 1964 as a wrecking amendment, the proposer believing that Congress would never vote for it.[53]

Thus, the reasons why particular groups have been singled out for dedicated anti-discrimination legislation are many and varied. On the other hand, a sense of a principle can be detected from attempts to apply the "equality" rubric contained in human rights or constitutional instruments. The Supreme Court of Canada centres its approach on "human dignity." The US Supreme Court identifies "suspect", "non-suspect", and "residual" classes of persons. The jurisprudence of the European Court of Human Rights is less developed, with a tentative notion of "personal characteristics", but often a simple difference in treatment is enough.[54]

A fifth objection to the equal treatment model is its characteristic of "equality as consistency". Its like-for-like nature is too rigid to address to all forms of inequality.[55] The equal treatment model starts from the position that the claimant and comparator are in the same position, say a woman and man doing work of equal value. Of course they are not like-for-like when the woman is doing work of less value. Yet, theoretically at least, the formal equality dictates that she may be paid 30 per cent less even though her work is only 20 per cent less value. Conversely, a woman doing work of *more* value is only entitled to the same pay. She cannot claim proportionally more money than him.[56] But this problem is less to do with principle and more to do with the

---

[51] In its proposal, the European Commission stated: "[T]he [Race] Directive will provide a solid basis for the enlargement of the European Union, which must be founded on the full and effective respect of human rights. The process of enlargement will bring into the EU new and different cultures and ethnic minorities. To avoid social strains in both existing and new Member States and to create a common Community of respect and tolerance for racial and ethnic diversity, it is essential to put in place a common European framework for the fight against racism." COM/99/0566 final—CNS 99/0253, at p.4, para.[6].

[52] "What is particularly striking about what we know of the debates and manoeuvres which produced Art.119 is the level of abstraction at which they took place. At no time are the interests of women considered even obliquely or the issues of social justice raised. The distance from the reality of work or any real struggle seems complete. However, the potential for a stronger implementation of equal pay was embedded in the history of the article and, paradoxically, in the history of the EC itself. It took activist women to realise these possibilities—and switch the debate from one of economic rationality to a demand for rights." C. Hoskyns, *Integrating Gender,* 1996, London: Verso, p.57.

[53] The proposer was the 80 year-old segregationist Democrat Howard Smith of Virginia. See Greenya, above fn 49.

[54] These approaches are considered further in Ch.2, para.2–007.

[55] See S. Fredman, *Discrimination Law*, 2001, OUP, p.10.

[56] *Evesham v North Hertfordshire Health Authority* [2000] I.C.R. 612, CA. See further Ch.9, para.9–006.

restriction in the equal pay legislation that allows only a real (i.e. not hypothetical) comparator. Once this restriction is disregarded, claims like this can succeed under the equal treatment principle.[57]

(2) Substantive Equality[58]

1–011   These limitations of formal equality have led to moves towards substantive equality. Perhaps the most dramatic shift occurred with the US Supreme Court's change of heart towards the racial segregation policies of the southern States. In 1896, in *Plessy v Ferguson*,[59] the Court held that "separate but equal" segregation in streetcars did not breach the constitutional right to equal protection of the laws. "We consider the underlying fallacy of the claimant's argument to consist in the assumption that the enforced separation of the two races stamps the colored race with a badge of inferiority. If this be so, it is not by reason of anything found in the act, but solely because the colored race chooses to put that construction upon it." In other words, the Court considered that once formal equality had been achieved, how people felt about the result was their problem. However, some 60 years later in *Brown v Board of Education*[60] the Court ruled that segregation in education was inherently unequal and unconstitutional. And so substantive equality demands that social justice and equality is meaningful and real to disadvantaged groups. The shift has been recognised expressly by Canadian Supreme Court Justice (now Chief Justice) Beverly McLachlin:

"It is the belief that if equality is to be realized, we must move beyond formal legalism to measures that will make a practical difference in the lives of members of groups that have been traditionally subject to the tactics of subordination . . . The use of the law to promote substantive equality, the phase we presently find ourselves in, takes two forms. The first is legislated programs whereby government, social and economic institutions are encouraged or, in some cases, required, to include people of under-represented groups. The second is the judicial concept of substantive equality, developed by the courts . . ."[61]

---

[57] See *County of Washington v Gunther* 452 US 161 (Sup Ct 1981). See further Ch.9, para.9–006.
[58] See C. Barnard and B. Hepple, "Substantive equality", (2000) 59(3) C.L.J. 562; For a discussion of EC discrimination law as a substantive rights, or anti-discrimination, model, see M. Barbera, "Not the Same? The Judicial Role in the New Community Anti-Discrimination Law Context" (2002) 31 I.L.J. 82; For a Canadian perspective, see C.D. Bavis, "*Vriend v Alberta, Law v Canada, Ontario v M and H*: the latest steps on the winding path to substantive equality", 37 Alberta L Rev 683.
[59] 163 US 537, at 551 (1896).
[60] 347 US 483 (1954).
[61] B. McLachlin, "The evolution of equality" (1996) 54 Advocate 563, citing *Andrews v Law Society of British Columbia* [1989] 1 SCR 143.

Substantive equality suggests that responsibility for discrimination rests not just with the wrongdoer in court, but the dominant group as a whole which has benefited from society's structuring on racial, gender, and other grounds. This means that the dominant group should bear the cost of change.[62] It arises for example, when "innocent" whites and males lose out to apparently lesser-qualified minorities or women in positive action programmes in employment, education, or housing. Substantive equality also suggests that the State has a role. If it does nothing it is perpetuating discrimination. Thus it has a positive duty to intervene.[63]

Two particular theories are aligned with substantive equality: **1–012** *equality of opportunity* and equality *of results*. Lustagarton described these two notions thus:

"In its purest or most extreme form the first accepts that discrimination has been abolished when all formal and deliberate barriers against blacks have been dismantled. Its concern stops with determining whether the factor of race has caused an individual to suffer adverse treatment. At the furthest point at the other end of the spectrum the unalloyed fair-share approach is concerned only with equality of result, measured in terms of proportionality. Its inherent logic leads to the adoption of quotas as a remedy once a finding of discrimination is made."[64]

The shift from formal equality to equality of opportunity was articulated by Wasserstrom, who suggested that that in a sea of inequalities, it seems pointless, philosophically and practically, to redress just one. As formal equality seeks to reward individual merit (rather than group status), it is the most qualified who deserve the most benefits. Yet, the distribution of these qualifications is dictated by factors beyond the control of the individual, such as the home environment, socio-economic class of parents, and the quality of the schools attended. "Since individuals do not deserve having had any of these things vis-à-vis other individuals, they do not, for the most part, deserve their qualifications. And since they do not deserve their abilities they do not in any strong sense deserve to be admitted because of their abilities . . ."[65] Thus, there can only be true equality if the competitors in a race begin from the same starting point.[66]

---

[62] See S. Fredman, *Discrimination Law*, 2001, OUP, p.129.
[63] *ibid.*
[64] L. Lustgarton, *Legal Control of Racial Discrimination,* 1980, London: Macmillan Press pp.6–7; see also L. Mayhew, *Law and Equal Opportunity*, 1968 Cambridge, Mass., Harvard UP pp.59–74.
[65] R. Wasserstrom, "Racism, sexism and preferential treatment: an approach to the topics" (1977) 24 UCLA L Rev 581, pp.619–20.
[66] K. O'Donovan and E. Szyszczak, *Equality and Sex Discrimination Law*, 1988, Oxford: Blackwells, pp.4–5; S. Fredman, *Discrimination Law*, 2001, OUP, p.14.

1–013   Lacey's criticism of formal equality (above, para.1–008) can be just as relevant here. If the race is one designed by white men, and is one in which they naturally prevail, even an equality of opportunity model fails to address the true problem.[67] Regardless of the merits of that opinion, it is undeniable that equality of opportunity cannot guarantee that society's benefits will be evenly distributed. The *equality of results* approach rests on the patent injustice of unevenly distributed benefits. At the least, this a measure by which the equality of opportunity model can be tested. But even this approach may fall short of expectation: "as one might have suspected from its American antecedents the fair-share approach is in no way compatible with great inequalities of income, wealth and social resources: it merely requires that blacks fit into the existing patterns of inequality in the same proportions as whites."[68]

The pragmatic view of all this is that the undefined slogan *equal opportunities* was able to unite diverse political groups to support anti-discrimination legislation. "How many liberal supporters of the current legislation, for example, would have been content to reflect on the implications of a thorough-going commitment to equality of opportunity in terms of socialisation of childrearing or even genetic engineering?"[69]

(3) Equality, Pluralism and Compassion

1–014   Wasserstrom[70] has presented three alternative goals of "equality" law. The first is the *assimilationist* model. Here, in a non-racist society, a person's race is the "functional equivalent" of their eye colour. This is less easy to present in respect to sex, disability and religion, where there are accepted differences that characterise these groups. The second is diversity. Here genuine differences, say between religions, are a "positive good". It would be a worse society if everyone were a member of one religion. The third is tolerance. Here there is nothing intrinsically positive about diversity, but tolerance outweighs the evils of achieving homogeneity.

The second and third of these goals align with current policy in North America and the EU. But slogans in common use at the moment such as *different but equal* and *equality and diversity*[71] are paradoxical, giving the law the delicate task of achieving both

---

[67] S. Fredman, *Discrimination Law*, 2001, OUP, pp.128–129.
[68] L. Lustgarton, *Legal Control of Racial Discrimination,* 1980, London: Macmillan Press, pp.6–7.
[69] N. Lacey, "Legislation against sex discrimination: questions from a feminist perspective" (1986) 14 J.L.S. 411, p.414.
[70] R. Wasserstrom, "Racism, sexism and preferential treatment: an approach to the topics" (1977) 24 UCLA L Rev 581, pp.585–589.
[71] Current Government documents on discrimination law employ this phrase, e.g. "Equality and Diversity: Age Matters. Age Consultation." (2003); Equality and Diversity: Updating the Sex Discrimination Act" (2003).

equality and diversity. Wasserstrom suggests that this may be achieved with celebration or tolerance. Of course, in reality a dose of both is required. It suggests that the key is psychological, or emotional, rather than formal. Human rights law generally originates, partly at least, from human compassion, or the milk of human kindness. People generally have a sense of compassion, especially for the underdog. This appears at odds with the resistance by ordinary (so presumably decent) people to much discrimination law, especially positive action programmes[72] and the truism that anti-discrimination laws are enacted to combat prejudices in mainstream society. The comments by Lords Woolf and Browne-Wilkinson (above, para.1–001) reveal that the general public's perception is important in defining the law. But in complex societies where so much disadvantage is invisible to an uniformed public, this is no more useful than asking for a jury's opinion after providing it with newspapers instead of the evidence. The notion falls well short of an ideal. This implies that there is a duty on politicians and the judiciary to educate the public in the real disadvantages that exist in their society, so triggering their innate human compassion. The neglect of this duty is most sadly apparent with immigration and asylum. Mainstream politicians commonly and quite comfortably inform the public of problems associated with asylum seekers[73] but rarely explain a traumatic story behind any plea for sanctuary. This breeds cynicism rather than compassion, which in turn feeds into the legal interpretations, as Lords Woolf and Browne-Wilkinson have confirmed.

The judiciary can take a lead as well. For the law to be structured around human compassion is not as fanciful as it first seems. As noted above, the Canadian Supreme Court has developed its human rights jurisprudence around the theme of "human dignity".[74] The US Supreme Court identifies groups for constitutional protection against discrimination by factors such as a history of purposeful and invidious discrimination, based on prejudice or inaccurate stereotypes,

---

[72] In the 2004 general election, in a core Labour constituency, Peter Law resigned from the Labour Party in protest at the selection of a candidate from an all-women short-list. He stood as an independent and overturned the Labour majority of 19,000 votes, winning with a majority of 9,000 (*The Times* April 6, 2004). In 2006 the Labour Party issued an apology to the electorate "for getting it wrong". (*The Independent* May 8, 2006).

[73] There are countless examples. In 2002, the Home Secretary, David Blunkett, observed that the children of asylum seekers were "swamping" some schools (*The Times* April 25, 2002). In 1972 it was observed that the Government's "ambivalent" policy was to proclaim racism wrong whilst declaring that Britain was too small to absorb any more immigrants: "Understandably, few people have grasped the distinction. The more obvious conclusion that has generally been drawn is that if coloured immigration presents a threat to Britain's well-being, so does the coloured minority living in Britain." A. Lester and G. Bindman, *Race and Law*, 1972, Harmondsworth: Penguin, p.13.

[74] For a discussion of dignity in English law, see D. Feldman, "Human dignity as a legal value", see Ch.2, para.2–007 Pt I [1999] PL 682, Pt II [200] P.L. 61.

against a class without political power.[75] These observations about the state of groups in society are as loaded with compassion as they are with intellectual rigour. This attempt at defining legally the underdog shows that positive human emotions can be identified and realised in law.

---

[75] Accordingly racial groups are afforded more protection than age groups (see further, Ch.2, para.2–008). The Supreme Court has not refined the matter much further though, as, somewhat perversely, whites are afforded the same equal protection as other racial groups: *Adarand Constructors v Pena* 515 US 200 (1995), see further Ch.12, para.12–020.

CHAPTER 2

THE SOURCES OF ANTI-DISCRIMINATION LAW

INTRODUCTION

There is nowadays a bewildering range of legislation covering discrimination,[1] having grown piecemeal in recent years. Legislation specifically covers Race, Religion or Belief, Sex, Gender Reassignment, Sexual Orientation, Disability, and Age. The principal domestic legislation consists of the Race Relations Act 1976 (RRA 1976), Sex Discrimination Act 1975 (SDA 1975), which includes gender reassignment, Equal Pay Act 1970 and the Disability Discrimination Act 1995 (DDA 1995). This "scheme" covers discrimination in employment and other fields, such as the provision of goods, facilities and services, education, housing and premises, and public body functions. In addition (deriving from EC law) there are statutory instruments covering employment discrimination only for Religion or Belief (in force December 2, 2003), Sexual Orientation (December 1, 2003), and Age (October 1, 2006).[2]

2–001

Further, Pt 2 of the Equality Act 2006[3] brings the law on Religion or Belief into to line with the "scheme", by extending coverage to the

---

[1] See S. Fredman, "Equality: a new generation?" (2001) 30 I.L.J. 145.

[2] Respectively, Employment Equality (Religion or Belief) Regulations 2003, SI 2003/1660; Employment Equality (Sexual Orientation) Regulations 2003, SI 2003/1661; Employment Equality (Age) Regulations 2006, SI 2003/1031.

[3] Expected in force October 2006.

other fields. Part 3 of the Equality Act 2006 empowers the Secretary of State to make similar regulations for sexual orientation. The relevant enforcement commissions (i.e. the Equal Opportunities Commission, Commission for Racial Equality and Disability Rights Commission) are empowered to issue codes of practice for most activities covered by the sex, race and disability legislation. It is not compulsory to follow a Code of Practice, but a failure to follow a Code may be taken into account in proceedings. Once the new Commission for Equality and Human Rights becomes operational, it may issue codes for the other grounds (such as sexual orientation, religion or belief, and age) as well.[4]

2–002   At the European level, legislation specifically covers equal pay between the sexes (Art.141 EC Treaty), sex discrimination in employment matters[5] (Equal Treatment Directive 76/207/EEC); race discrimination in employment matters, social security and healthcare, education, the supply of goods, services and housing (Race Directive 2000/43/EC); nationality discrimination in employment (Art.39 EC Treaty); and discrimination in employment matters on the ground of religion or belief, disability, age and sexual orientation (Employment Equality (Framework) Directive 2000/78/EC). More generally, Art.13 EC[6] provides the power to "combat discrimination based on sex, racial or ethnic origins, religion or belief, disability, age or sexual orientation." Article 13 has great potential, especially as it is not limited to employment matters. It facilitated the Framework and Race Directives, and more recently, the Equal Treatment in Goods and Services Directive, which extends Community sex discrimination law to the fields of the supply of goods and services,[7] but not media content, advertising or public or private education.[8]

The Directives differ from the pre-existing domestic discrimination legislation (i.e. SDA 1975, RRA 1976, DDA 1995) in many ways. These differences can be subdivided into definitions, procedural rules, and fields covered. The Directives provide a different (broader) defini-

---

[4] SDA 1975, s.56A; RRA 1976 s.47; DDA 1995, s.53A. For the CEHR, EA 2006, ss.14–15. On the role of the commissions, see Ch.13, para.13–029 *et seq.*

[5] Includes self-employment, occupation, vocational guidance and training, advanced vocational training and retraining, including practical work experience, trade organisations and unions (Art.4).

[6] Introduced by the Treaty of Amsterdam, May 1, 1999.

[7] Equal Treatment in Goods and Services Directive 2004/113/EC, due in force by December 21, 2007. Paragraph (11) of the preamble refers to Art.50, EC Treaty for the definition of services, as those: "normally provided for remuneration, in so far as they are not governed by the provisions relating to freedom of movement for goods, capital and persons. 'Services' shall in particular include: (a) activities of an industrial character; (b) activities of a commercial character; (c) activities of craftsmen; (d) activities of the professions." For a definition of goods, the preamble refers the free movement of goods provisions of the EC Treaty, which have been interpreted to cover anything capable of money valuation and of being the object of commercial transactions (*Commission v Italy* (case 7/68)).

[8] *ibid.,* Recital 13, Art.3(3).

tion of indirect discrimination, and new dedicated definitions of harassment and sexual harassment. The Race Directive covers discrimination only on the grounds of "racial or ethnic origin", whilst the RRA 1976, in addition covers "colour" and "nationality". Second, the Directives provide a procedural difference, mandating a shifting burden of proof, which is new to domestic practice. Third, unlike their domestic counterparts, the Directives' coverage for sex and disability discrimination are, for the time being anyway, limited to employment matters. The essential story here is the failure to amend domestic legislation universally when implementing EC law, so to avoid anomalies. This leaves a "residual" class of claims, which fall under the "residual" unreformed law. Hence, these claims must be pleaded under the residual law. The residual class of claims will be a constant theme through the book, with each chapter explaining the current and the residual law. This vast sprawl of legislation, and the anomalies, have, naturally enough, triggered calls for a single equality statute, which will is discussed at the end of this chapter.

In addition the Human Rights Act 1998 incorporated into domestic   **2–003**
law the European Convention on Human Rights, which covers discrimination "on any ground such as sex, race, colour, language, religion, political or other opinion, national or social origin, association with a national minority, property, birth or other status." Note that this list is non-exhaustive. However the Convention only covers discrimination in connection with any of the free-standing rights, such as freedom of association, or the right to respect for private and family life, although freedom of religion is specifically protected by Art.9. The effect is widespread, as the Act imposes upon all public bodies, including the courts, a duty to abide by the Convention.

The judiciary also has a part to play. There is role of the common law in combating discrimination, which has developed very little, if at all. There is also the interpretation of the legislation, which has proved to be particularly important in the development of discrimination law.

1. THE HUMAN RIGHTS ACT 1998[9]

Many cases of discrimination will fall outside of the legislative   **2–004**
scheme. For instance, the age discrimination Regulations are confined to employment matters, and do not extend to activities such as the

---

[9] See N. Foster, "The European Court of Justice and the European Convention for the Protection of Human Rights" (1987) 8 Human Rights LJ 245; Y. Aras "The ECHR and non-discrimination" (1998) 7 *Amicus Curiae*, the *Journal of the Society for Advanced Legal Studies* 6. Generally, B. Clarke (Ed.), *Challenging Racism,* 2003, London: Lawrence and Wishart, in association with the Discrimination Law Association, ILPA, CRE and 1990 Trust; K. Ewing, "The Human Rights Act and Labour Law" (1998) 27 I.L.J. 275.

provision of goods, facilities and services, housing, and education. Further, the grounds of discrimination are strictly limited to those provided by the legislation, which does not cover expressly, say, discrimination on the grounds of social origin, property, birth or other status. These, and any other, gaps in coverage *may* be covered by the European Convention on Human Rights (ECHR), which was incorporated into domestic law by the Human Rights Act 1998 (HRA 1998), which came into force on October 2, 2000.[10]

The Human Rights Act brings into domestic law a model of "higher" law familiar to most western democracies, by which the state and its "ordinary" laws must comply. The United States" Equal Protection Clause of the Fourteenth or Fifth Amendments provides a constitutional guarantee of equal protection of the laws, so state or federal discriminatory laws may be challenged as unconstitutional. Similarly, Canada enjoys the Charter of Rights and Freedoms, by which national and provincial laws must comply. The matter is more complex in the UK, because of the absence of a formal written constitution and a system that facilitates "higher" law. Thus, whilst the Human Rights Act encourages the State, including the courts, to comply with the Convention, where legislation cannot be reconciled with a Convention right, it cannot be struck down by the courts. Note that, although the Convention and the Court of Human Rights (ECtHR) are separate from European Community law, the European Court of Justice (ECJ) will respect the Convention's principles,[11] and so Convention principles can find their way into UK law via Community law.

Of course, much depends on the approach of the judiciary to the Human Rights Act. In 2000 the Master of the Rolls (as he then was) Lord Woolf gave early notice that "judges should be robust in resisting" inappropriate arguments based on the Human Rights Act, and that "counsel will need to show self-restraint if [the HRA 1998] is not to be discredited."[12]

What follows is a discussion of how the Convention deals with discrimination, and how its incorporation may modify and compliment existing discrimination law. Integral to this is how "robust" or otherwise, the judges have been.

---

[10] SI 2000/1851.
[11] See e.g. *R v Kirk* (Case 63/83) [1984] 2 E.C.R. 2689; *Johnston v Chief Constable of the Royal Ulster Constabulary* (Case 222/84) [1986] E.C.R. 1651. See generally, J. Steiner and L. Woods, *Textbook on EC Law* 2003, 8th ed., OUP, paras 7.3–7.5.
[12] *Daniels v Walker* [2000] 1 W.L.R. 1382, at 1388, CA.

(1) Discrimination and the European Convention on Human Rights[13]

(a) The Claim Must Fall Within a Convention Right

The Convention gives no free-standing right against discrimination.[14]   **2–005**
Article 14 provides merely that the rights and freedoms in the
Convention must be "secured" without discrimination. The free-
standing, substantive, rights given by the Convention are, to Life
(Art.2), against Torture (3) and Slavery (4), to Liberty (5) and a Fair
Trial (6), against Punishment Without Law (7), to Respect for Family
and Private Life (8), to Freedom of Thought, Conscience and Religion
(9), to Freedom of Expression (10), Assembly and Association (11),
and to Marry (12), the right to peaceful enjoyment of one's possessions
(1st Protocol, Art.1), the right to education (1P 2) and free elections
(1P 3).

However, there is no need to prove a breach of a substantive right
for claims of discrimination. Were it otherwise, Art.14 would serve no
useful purpose.[15] So long as the activity falls within the "ambit" of one
of the rights, Art.14 is engaged. In *Petrovic v Austria*,[16] the State paid
parental leave allowance to mothers, but not fathers. Mr Petrovic, a
father, challenged this rule under the Convention, for discriminating
on the ground of sex. He relied on Art.8 in combination with Art.14.
The Court held that although Art.8 imposed no obligation upon
States to give financial assistance to parents, the allowance fell within
the ambit of Art.8 and so Art.14 was engaged. The Court's reasoning
is that Art.14 comes into play whenever "the subject-matter of the
disadvantage . . . constitutes one of the modalities of the exercise of
a right guaranteed" or the measures complained of are "linked to the
exercise of a right guaranteed". And so, "By granting parental leave
allowance States are able to demonstrate their respect for family life
within the meaning of Art.8".[17] The case also shows that if States
choose to provide rights or freedoms beyond their Convention
obligations, but within the ambit of a substantive Article, they must
comply with Art.14 when doing so.

---

[13] See M. Connolly, "Discrimination on the ground of sexual orientation outside the workplace:
is it actionable?" [2005] 2 Web JCLI.

[14] The 12th Protocol provides a free-standing right against discrimination. It has been adopted,
but yet ratified and the UK government is not likely to ratify it in the foreseeable future. (To
follow its progress, see *http://conventions.coe.int/Treaty/EN/cadreprincipal.htm*.) For a discussion of the protocol see G. Moon (2000) 1 E.H.R.L.R. 49; J. Schokkenbroek, "Towards a
stronger European protection against discrimination: the preparation of a new additional protocol to the ECHR" and J. Cooper, "Applying equality and non-discrimination rights through
the Human Rights Act 1998" both in *Race Discrimination*, 2000, Oxford: Hart; and V. Khaliq
"Protocol 12 to the ECHR: a step forward or a step too far?" [2001] PL 457.

[15] This point is made in Lester and Pannick, *Human Rights Law and Practice* (2004) London:
LexisNexis, p.418, para.4.14.10.

[16] (1998) 33 E.H.R.R. 307.

[17] *ibid*., at paras 27–29.

It remains unclear precisely what the Court meant by the two definitions given ("modality" and "link"). In the Court of Appeal in *Mendoza v Ghaidan*[18] Buxton, L.J. cited Grosz, Beatson & Duffy, which concluded that "even the most tenuous link with another provision in the Convention will suffice for Art.14 to enter into play".[19] Some judges have doubted this opinion. For instance, in *R. (Erskine) v London Borough of Lambeth*,[20] Mitting, J suggested: "[I]t overstates the effect of the Strasbourg case law."[21] And in *R. (Douglas) v North Tyneside MBC*,[22] Scott Baker, L.J. commented: "For my part I do not read Buxton, L.J. as seeking to extend the ambit of the test as set out in Petrovic's case. The bottom line is that the measures of which complaint is made have to be linked to the exercise of the right guaranteed."[23] Most recently, the House of Lords, in *Secretary of State for Work and Pensions v M*[24] emphatically rejected the "tenuous link" rubric.

2–006   The difference between "link" (*per* Scott Baker, L.J.) and "tenuous link" (*per* Grosz *et al*) is perhaps illustrated in *Douglas*, where it was claimed that the refusal of student loans to over-55 year olds amounted to age discrimination, under Art.2 of the 1st Protocol (right to education) combined with Art.14. The Court of Appeal held that student funding was "one stage removed"[25] from the right to education. This is a convenient rubric, with the attraction of apparent certainty, but its logic is questionable. In *Petrovic* the Court stated that parental leave allowance showed the state's "respect for family life". It is impossible to escape the similarity to student loans demonstrating the state's respect for education.

A similar distinction was relied on in *M*, where the claim centred on the calculations by the Child Support Agency for contributions by absent parents. The scheme treated absent parents who were married more favourably than those living together in a same-sex relationship, with the result that the claimant had to make higher contributions. The House of Lords held that Art.8 was not engaged, distinguishing *Petrovic* on the basis that there was no adverse impact against her in family life with own children, only against her in her same sex relationship, which did not engage Art.8.[26]

---

[18] [2002] 4 All E.R. 1162, affirmed *Godin-Mendoza v Ghaidan* [2004] UKHL 30, although the HL offered no opinion on this matter, at para.12.

[19] Grosz, Beatson and Duffy, *Human Rights: The 1998 Act and the European Convention,* (1999) London: Sweet and Maxwell, p.327.

[20] [2003] EWHC 2479 (Admin).

[21] *ibid.*, at paras 21–22.

[22] [2004] 1 All E.R. 709, CA.

[23] *ibid.*, at para.54.

[24] [2006] 2 W.L.R. 637.

[25] [2004] 1 All E.R. 709, at paras 57 and 60, CA. Distinguished in *S v Special Educational Needs and Disability Tribunal* [2005] EWHC 196 (Admin) where the funding extended beyond the mere facilitating of education to its nature and quality (at para.35).

[26] [2006] 2 W.L.R. 637, at paras 17–18, 85–87, and 124.

In *M* the House of Lords has signalled a retreat from "tenuous link" rubric. Whether it survives an appeal to the European Court is another matter.

(b) Grounds of discrimination covered by the ECHR

Article 14 provides that the Convention rights must be "secured" **2–007** without discrimination "on any ground such as sex, race, colour, language, religion, political or other opinion, national or social origin, association with a national minority, property, birth or other status". Not only are the specific examples far wider than current domestic or European discrimination legislation, it is clear that the use of the words "such as" opens Art.14 to many more grounds than those listed. Among other things, this open-ended formula allows for changing values, and discrimination that was once acceptable may become unacceptable.[27] The basis for identifying other grounds for protection under Art.14 is vague. In *Kjeldsen v Denmark*[28] the Court stated that Art.14 prohibits discrimination based on a "personal characteristic ('status') by which persons or groups of persons are distinguishable from each other."[29] But this is somewhat narrow to be taken as a definitive interpretation, as Art.14 itself lists "property" as a protected ground. Further, Art.14 has been held to include groups as wide-ranging as owners of non-residential (distinct from residential) buildings, owners of a pit bull terriers (distinct from other breeds of dog), and small landowners (distinct from large landowners), coastal (distinct from open sea) fishermen.[30] More conventionally, the ECtHR has recognised sexual orientation, marital status, illegitimacy, trade union status, military rank, and conscientious objection[31] as falling within this residual category.

In recent times, some domestic courts have clung to *Kjeldsen*, holding that Art.14 required discrimination to be by reference to some status analogous with those expressly mentioned, such as sex, race or colour, and held that Art.14 does not include, for example, those charged but not convicted of a criminal offence, those who have commenced legal proceedings, the hunting community, and employees

---

[27] See the different approaches to gender reassignment in *Sheffield & Horsham v UK* (1998) 27 E.H.R.R. 347 and *Goodwin v UK* (2002) E.H.R.R. 447, and more generally, (below para.2–018) the "living tree" school of interpretation.

[28] (1976) 1 E.H.R.R. 711, at para.56.

[29] *ibid.*, at para.56.

[30] Respectively, *Spadea v Italy* (1996) 21 E.H.R.R. 482, at paras 42–46; *Bullock v UK* (1996) 21 E.H.R.R. CD 85, at para.5; *Chassagnou v France* (2000) 7 B.H.R.C. 151, at paras 86–95; *Posti and Rahko v Finland* (2002) 37 E.H.R.R. 158, at paras 79–87.

[31] Respectively, *Salgueiro v Portugal* (2001) 31 E.H.R.R. 47; *Wessels-Bergervoet v The Netherlands* (2004) 38 E.H.R.R. 793; *Sahin v Germany* [2003] 2 F.L.R. 671, at para.94 (including different treatment of parents of children born out of wedlock); *Swedish Engine Drivers Union v Sweden* (1976) 1 E.H.R.R. 617; *Engel v NL* (1979–80) 1 E.H.R.R. 647, at para.72 ("house arrest" for commissioned officers, jail for other servicemen); *De Jong, Baljet and Van den Brink v The Netherlands* (No.1) (1986) 8 E.H.R.R. 20.

working abroad.[32] But it is clear from the instances above, that the ECtHR has not adhered to any strict formula relating to "personal characteristics", and that Art.14 remains very wide. In fact, it seems that a mere difference in treatment (under one of the free-standing Articles) is enough to engage Art.14. Even in the UK, "residing abroad" was recognised recently as a personal characteristic for Art.14.[33] The ECtHR exercises control over claims when deciding if the difference in treatment, is justified.[34]

In Canada, s.15 of the Charter of Rights provides a free-standing prohibition of discrimination, "in particular" on the grounds of "national or ethnic origin, colour, religion, sex, age, or mental or physical disability." The phrase "in particular" allows the courts to add to these "enumerated grounds". In doing this the approach is centred on human dignity.[35] In *Law v Andrews*,[36] the Supreme Court of Canada, stated that this means that an individual or group feels self-respect and self-worth and is concerned with physical and psychological integrity and empowerment. It does not relate to the status of an individual in society, but the manner in which a person legitimately feels when confronted with a particular law. It is harmed by unfair treatment or when individuals and groups are marginalized, ignored, or devalued. The courts look for an "analogous ground" based on a "personal characteristic that is immutable or changeable only at unacceptable cost to personal identity." This includes "constructively immutable" grounds, such as religion,[37] "citizenship",[38] sexual orientation,[39] and age.[40]

2–008   In the United States the Equal Protection Clause of the Fourteenth or Fifth Amendments provides a constitutional guarantee of equal protection of the laws.[41] Unlike the ECHR, or the Canadian Charter, there is no list from which to draw analogous grounds. The Supreme Court has identified three classes of protected groups under the Clause: suspect class; quasi-suspect class; and a residual, "normal,"

---

[32] Respectively, *R. (S) v Chief Constable of the South Yorkshire Police* [2004] UKHL 39, at paras 48–51; *R. (Hooper) v Secretary of State for Work and Pensions* [2005] UKHL 29, at para.65; *R. (Countryside Alliance & others) v Attorney General* [2005] EWHC 1677 (Admin), at paras 196–197; *Botham v Ministry of Defence* UKEAT/0503/04/DM, at para.21 (reversed on other grounds, [2006] 1 All E.R. 823, HL).

[33] *R. (Carson) v Secretary of State for Work and Pensions* [2005] UKHL 37, at para.13.

[34] See below, "(c) Definition of Discrimination under the ECHR".

[35] For a discussion of dignity in English law, see D. Feldman, "Human dignity as a legal value", Pt I [1999] P.L. 682, Pt II [200] P.L. 61.

[36] [1999] 1 SCR 497, at para.53.

[37] *Corbiere v Canada* [1999] 2 SCR 203, para.13.

[38] *Law Society of British Columbia v Andrews* [1989] 1 SCR 143.

[39] See e.g. *Egan v Canada* [1995] 2 SCR 513; *M v H* [1999] 2 SCR 3.

[40] Age is afforded less protection because "There is a general relationship between advancing age and declining ability" and discrimination on other grounds is "generally based on feelings of hostility and intolerance." *McKinney v University of Guelph* [1990] 3 SCR 229, at 297.

[41] The equal protection component of the Fifth Amendment imposes precisely the same constitutional requirements on the federal government as the equal protection clause of the Fourteenth Amendment imposes on state governments: *Weinberger v Wiesenfeld* 420 US 636, at 638 n2 (Sup Ct 1975).

class. Suspect classes are entitled to strict scrutiny of the challenged law. These means that such a law will survive only if it is suitably tailored to serve a compelling state or Government interest.[42] Quasi-suspect classes are entitled to intermediate—or "heightened" scrutiny. Challenged laws will survive this scrutiny if they are "substantially related" to a legitimate state, or Government, interest.[43] Finally, laws that discriminate against a residual class will be subjected to "normal" scrutiny, which means they must be "rationally related to a legitimate state interest."[44]

In deciding if a group qualifies as a suspect class, a court will normally consider three factors.[45] The first is a history of purposeful discrimination.[46] Second, the discrimination embodies a gross unfairness that is "invidious." Considerations here could be a class trait that bears no relation to ability to perform or contribute to society, or that the class has been saddled with unique disabilities because of prejudice or inaccurate stereotypes, or that the trait defining the class is immutable. Third, the group lacks the political power necessary to obtain redress from the political branches of government. The factors necessary to qualify as a quasi-suspect group are less concrete. It has been suggested that a history of past discrimination is relevant,[47] or where the characteristic, beyond the individual's control, bears "no relation to the individual's ability to participate in and contribute to society,"[48] It has been held that groups defined by race, alienage [*sic*], national origin,[49] and sexual orientation[50] are suspect classes. Gender and illegitimacy[51] are quasi-suspect classes, whilst age and disability are residual classes. On age, the Supreme Court noted that (unlike racial groups) this group has not experienced a "history of purposeful unequal treatment or been subjected to unique disabilities

---

[42] *McLaughlin v Florida* 379 US 184, at 192 (Sup Ct 1964); *Graham v Richardson* 403 US 365 (Sup Ct 1971). The Fifth Amendment is used also to attack affirmative action programmes based on race: see further Ch.12, para.12–019 *et seq.*

[43] *Mills v Habluetzel*, 456 US 91, at 99 (Sup Ct 1982).

[44] *City of Cleburne, Texas v Cleburne Living Center* 473 US 432, at 446 (Sup Ct 1985).

[45] See concurring opinion of Norris, Circuit Judge, in *Watkins v US Army* 875 F 2d 699 (9th Cir 1989).

[46] See, e.g., *City of Cleburne, Texas v Cleburne Living Center* 473 US 432, at 441 (Sup Ct 1985); *Massachusetts Board of Retirement v Murgia* 427 US 307, at 313 (Sup Ct 1976).

[47] See Norris, Circuit Judge, *Watkins v US Army* 875 F 2d 699, at 712 n4 (9th Cir 1989), and see generally, Nowak, Rotunda & Young, *Constitutional Law*, Ch.16, para.1, at 593 (2nd edn 1983).

[48] Per J. White, *City of Cleburne, Texas v Cleburne Living Center* 473 US 432, at 441 (Sup Ct 1985), citing *Mathews v Lucas* 427 US 495, at 505 (Sup Ct 1976).

[49] "These factors are so seldom relevant to the achievement of any legitimate state interest that laws grounded in such considerations are deemed to reflect prejudice and antipathy—a view that those in the burdened class are not as worthy or deserving as others." *ibid.*, at 440.

[50] *Watkins v US Army* 875 F 2d 699, at 728 (9th Cir 1989). The case concerned a homosexual and the Court did not discuss whether bisexuality was included.

[51] Respectively, *United States v Virginia* 518 US 515 (1996); *Mathews v Lucas* 427 US 495, at 505 (Sup Ct 1976).

on the basis of stereotyped characteristics not truly indicative of their abilities."[52] On disability, the Supreme Court cited this academic opinion: "[C]lassifications based on physical disability and intelligence are typically accepted as legitimate, even by judges and commentators who assert that immutability is relevant. The explanation, when one is given, is that *those* characteristics (unlike the one the commentator is trying to render suspect) are often relevant to legitimate purposes. At that point there's not much left of the immutability theory, is there?"[53]

(c) Definition of Discrimination under the ECHR

2–009   In order to establish discrimination under Art.14, the applicant has to show treatment different to another person in an analogous situation, or a failure "to treat differently persons whose situations are significantly different."[54] These two phases correspond to direct and indirect discrimination, respectively, although indirect discrimination is at a very early stage of development.[55] The State defendant then has the opportunity to "objectively and reasonably justify" the discriminatory measure. This means that, in contrast to most discrimination schemes, direct discrimination is potentially justifiable.[56] To be justified, the discrimination must pursue a legitimate aim and have reasonable relationship of proportionality between the means employed and the aim sought to be realised.[57] When applying this standard, the Court can be deferential to defendant States, affording them a "margin of appreciation" which will vary according to the circumstances, the subject-matter and its background.[58] In some cases, the Court demands "very weighty reasons" to justify discrimination. These cases include discrimination on grounds of sex, sexual orientation, birth out of wedlock, marital status, and nationality.[59] Without saying as much,

---

[52] *Massachusetts Board of Retirement v Murgia*, 427 US 307, at 313 (Sup Ct 1976).

[53] *City of Cleburne, Texas v Cleburne Living Center* 473 US 432 (Sup Ct 1985), citing, at 443, J.H. Ely, *Democracy and Distrust* (1980) Cambridge: Harvard UP, p.150.

[54] *Thlimmenos v Greece* (2001) 31 E.H.R.R. 14, at para.44.

[55] See *Hugh Jordan v UK* (2001) 37 E.H.R.R. 52, where the Court refused to recognise a case of indirect discrimination based on statistics: "Where a general policy or measure has disproportionately prejudicial effects on a particular group, it is not excluded that this may be considered as discriminatory notwithstanding that it is not specifically aimed or directed at that group. However . . . the Court does not consider that statistics can in themselves disclose a practice which could be classified as discriminatory within the meaning of Art.14." (At para.154.)

[56] For a discussion on whether direct discrimination generally should be justifiable see J. Bowers and E. Moran, "Justification in Direct Discrimination Law: Breaking the taboo" (2002) 31 I.L.J. 307. For a response see T. Gill and K. Monaghan, "Justification in Direct Sex Discrimination Law: Taboo Upheld" (2003) 32 I.L.J. 115.

[57] *Karner v Austria* (2003) 2 F.L.R. 623, at para.37.

[58] *Ünal Tekeli v Turkey* [2005] 1 FCR 663, at para.52.

[59] Respectively *Ünal Tekeli v Turkey* [2005] 1 F.C.R. 663, at 53; *Karner v Austria* (2003) 2 F.L.R. 623, at para.37; *Sahin v Germany* [2003] 2 F.L.R. 671, at para.94 (including different treatment of parents of children born out of wedlock); *Wessels-Bergervoet v The Netherlands* (2004) 38

the Court appears to be dividing cases into "suspect" and "non-suspect" classes, loosely corresponding to the classifications made by the US Supreme Court (above).[60] This suggests that disability and age will be treated less seriously, or as "non-suspect" classes. An example of the Court's scrutiny in a "suspect" class can be seen in *Karner v Austria*.[61] The applicant lived with his partner in a same-sex relationship in his partner's apartment. After his partner died, (designating Karner as his heir), the landlord sought possession relying on the Austrian Rent Act which provided rights of succession only for family members. The Austrian Government argued that the provision in the Rent Act was for the protection of "the traditional family unit". The Court held that whilst the protection of the family could be a weighty and legitimate reason, it had not been shown that the exclusion of same-sex relationships from the benefit of the Rent Act was necessary for that aim.

(2) Liability of Private Parties

Principally, the Convention binds only the State, and it is only the State that can be sued ("vertical effect"). However, there is a grey area where disputes between private parties may involve Convention rights ("horizontal effect"). Article 1 obliges States to "secure for everyone within their jurisdiction the rights and freedoms defined in . . . the Convention". So a state can be liable for a breach arising from a dispute between private parties. In *Young, James & Webster v UK*[62] the Court held that the State could be liable under Art.11 (freedom of association) by legalising the dismissal (by a state or private employer) of workers who refused to join a closed-shop trade union. The Human Rights Act attempts to confine liability to "public authorities", or anyone carrying out public functions. Section 6(1), HRA 1998, provides that a "public authority" must act compatibly with the Convention rights. Section 6(3) defines a "public authority" as any person whose functions are of a public nature. Section 6(5) qualifies this, excluding acts by private parties where the nature of the act is private. Thus, the draftsmen envisaged two classes of "public authority". First, "core" public authorities, which will be liable for Convention breaches, whether the act was public or private. Second, "hybrid" authorities, which may be a private party carrying out some public functions; these bodies can be liable for Convention breaches, but only when carrying out public functions.

2–010

E.H.R.R. 793, at para.49 ("very strong reasons" required); and *Koua Poirrez v France* (2005) 40 E.H.R.R. 34, at para.46.

[60] para.2–008. See De O. Schutter, "The prohibition of Discrimination under European human rights law: Relevance for the EU". ISBN 92–894–9171–X (EN): *http://europa.eu.int/comm/employment_ social/publications/2005/ke6605103_en.html*.

[61] (2003) 2 F.L.R. 623. Followed in *Godin-Mendoza v Ghaidan* [2004] UKHL 30.

[62] (1981) 4 E.H.R.R. 38.

The HRA 1998 does not provide the certainty of a list of public bodies, handing a significant interpretive role to the courts. The House of Lords, in *Aston Cantlow v Wallbank*[63] made it clear that the courts should follow Strasbourg jurisprudence. Lord Hobhouse explained: "The relevant concept is the opposition of the 'victim' and a 'governmental body'. The former can make a complaint; the latter can only be the object of a complaint."[64]

This polarised analysis of victims and governmental bodies suggests that private parties, such as providers of goods, facilities and services, housing landlords and schools, cannot be liable under the HRA 1998. This appears to emasculate s.6, leaving no scope for a hybrid body to be liable. In *Poplar Housing Association Ltd v Donoghue*[65] the Court of Appeal stated that normally private landlords, including housing associations, are carrying out private functions, and so are not bound by the HRA 1998. However, on the facts, the Court found that a private landlord, who took over a property occupied by a tenant with a weekly non-secure tenancy granted by her local authority (pending a decision on whether she was intentionally homeless), was bound by the HRA 1998, because the private landlord's role was "so closely assimilated" to that of the local authority's. This suggests that a private landlord may be bound by the Human Rights Act only when carrying out a *particular* public function on behalf of a local authority. It is arguable that the position is slightly different for education. In *Costello-Roberts v UK*[66] the Strasbourg Court made clear "that the State cannot absolve itself from responsibility by delegating its obligations to private bodies or individuals." Further, "in the United Kingdom, independent schools co-exist with a system of public education. The fundamental right of everyone to education is a right guaranteed equally to pupils in State and independent schools, no distinction being made between the two."[67] The implication is that education is governmental in character and that private schools are bound by the Human Rights Act. At the least, where the State is funding, even partly, a school or a pupil at a school, the school's role relating to the funding could be said to be "so closely assimilated" to the State's role of providing education, it would be bound by the HRA 1998.

2–011   Nonetheless, *Costello-Roberts* provides all victims of discrimination by *private* schools a remedy against the Government. This logic does not extend to the provision of housing, because the Convention only provides, by Art.8, the right to respect for a person's home, not a right

---

[63] [2004] 1 A.C. 546, held, by 4 to 1, that a Parochial Church Council was not a public body.
[64] *ibid.*, at para.87.
[65] [2001] EWCA 595, at paras 59–66.
[66] (1993) 25 E.H.R.R. 112.
[67] *ibid.*, at para.27.

to obtain one.[68] Nor does it apply to the provision of goods, facilities and services where they are of a "social nature".[69]

Notwithstanding s.6 of the Act, private parties, exercising private functions, may find themselves bound by Convention rights, because s.3 provides that, so far as possible, domestic legislation must be interpreted to be compatible with Convention Rights. Failing this a court must issue a declaration of incompatibility (s.4). This makes it possible for parties to call upon Convention rights in a private dispute which is governed by legislation.

The liability of private parties may be affected also by the influence of the Human Rights Act on the common law and statutory interpretation. Each is discussed below.

2. THE COMMON LAW

The common law has not developed a sophisticated principle of equality or non-discrimination. This may be the result of it being reactive in nature and its tradition of freedom of contract.[70] The general attitude of the common law towards specific cases of equality and discrimination was epitomised by the House of Lords in *Roberts v Hopwood*[71] where Poplar Borough Council embarked upon an equal pay policy for its lowest paid workers. The policy was struck down by the House of Lords on the ground that the Council had been misguided "by some eccentric principles of socialistic philanthropy, or by a feminist ambition to secure the equality of the sexes in the matter of wages in the world of labour." In *Scala Ballroom v Ratcliffe*[72] the Court of Appeal observed that a "colour bar" was a policy which the owners of a ballroom "were entitled to adopt in their own business interests".[73] The introduction of discrimination legislation paradoxically reinforced this position, allowing the common law, in deference to Parliament, to wash its hands of discrimination issues whenever the facts fell outside of an activity prescribed by the legislation. So even where there was patent sex discrimination[74] or indirect sex discrimination[75] by the immigration authorities, and the activity fell outside the discrimination legislation, the courts considered themselves powerless

2–012

---

[68] *X v Germany* (1956) 1 YB 202.
[69] *Botta v Italy* (1998) 26 E.H.R.R. 241.
[70] Robilliard, St John A, "Should Parliament enact a Religious Discrimination Act" (1978) *Public Law* 379, p.380.
[71] [1925] A.C. 578, at 599. HL.
[72] [1958] 3 All E.R. 220.
[73] *ibid.*, at 221, but the Court refused an injunction to prevent the musician's union from boycotting the ballroom.
[74] *R. v Entry Clearance Officer Bombay Ex p. Amin* [1983] 2 A.C. 818, HL. See Ch.10, para.10–013.
[75] *Bernstein v Immigration Appeal Tribunal and Department of Employment* [1988] 3 C.M.L.R. 445.

to act: "[S]ex discrimination is not of itself unlawful. It is unlawful only in circumstances proscribed by the [sex discrimination legislation]."[76]

From time to time, it has been suggested that the common law carries some form of equality principle. In *Short v Poole Corporation*,[77] the Court of Appeal suggested that the courts could strike down as ultra vires any decision made by a public body made on "alien and irrelevant grounds", such as a teacher being dismissed "because she had red hair, or for some equally frivolous or foolish reason." Any hope inferred from this pronouncement was immediately crushed when the Court upheld a decision to dismiss a teacher because she was married.

More recently, Lord Hoffman has hinted that there exists an equality principle in the common law of a more substantive nature. In *Matadeen v Pointu*[78] he said "that treating like cases alike and unlike cases differently is a general axiom of rational behaviour", and thus irrational discrimination was subject to judicial review, a remedy against public bodies.[79] In *Arthur J Hall v Simons*,[80] he invoked a "fundamental principle of justice which requires that people should be treated equally and like cases treated alike", as one of his reasons for holding that advocates, like any other professional, should enjoy no immunity from professional negligence claims, a private law matter. Lord Steyn has written that there is a "constitutional principle of equality developed domestically by English courts" which is wider than the "relatively weak" Art.14 of the ECHR.[81] However, arguments (based on these comments) that there exists at common law a general tenet against discrimination have so far found little favour in the courts' decision-making, either being rejected or sidelined: Lord Hoffman's comments do no more than pronounce that irrational discrimination (like any irrational behaviour by a public body) was subject to judicial review in public law;[82] and any principle of equality does not add much, if anything, to a claimant's Convention Rights under Human Rights Act.[83]

2–013   There are some ancient duties placed by the common law upon the likes of innkeepers, common carriers and some monopoly enterprises such as ports and harbours, to accept all travellers and others who are

---

[76] *Bernstein v Immigration Appeal Tribunal and Department of Employment* [1988] 3 C.M.L.R. 445 at para.41.

[77] [1926] Ch.66, at 91.

[78] [1999] 1 A.C. 98, delivering the opinion of the Pricy Council.

[79] *ibid.*, at 109, but Lord Hoffman also highlighted the difficulties of a general principle of non-discrimination, in contrast to specified enumerated grounds, such as sex and race.

[80] [2000] 3 All E.R. 673, at 689, HL.

[81] Lord Steyn, "Democracy through law", [2002] E.H.R.L.R. (Issue 6) 723, at 731–732.

[82] Under the *Wednesbury* ([1948] 1 KB 223) principle; see *Regina (Association of British Civilian Internees: Far East Region) v Secretary of State for Defence* [2003] EWCA Civ 473, at paras 83–86 (also overruling *Gurung v Ministry of Defence* [2004] EWCA Civ 1863 so far as it held (at para.29) that discrimination on the ground of birthplace was irrational).

[83] *R. (Montana) v Secretary of State for the Home Department* [2001] 1 W.L.R. 552 CA, at para.15.

"in a fit and reasonable condition to be received."[84] A rare (if not only) only example of one of these "ancient duties" coinciding racial discrimination arose in *Constantine v Imperial Hotels*.[85] Here, a black West Indian cricketer (and later a member of the Race Relations Board) was refused accommodation for fear of upsetting white American soldiers. The Kings Bench Division awarded Constantine nominal damages for the breach of the innkeepers' duty to receive all travellers.

In the United States, many states have a common law "public policy" exception to the general employment-at-will doctrine. The exception is narrow and applies only to dismissals (not hiring or treatment and opportunities to existing workers) where there is no statutory remedy, and only to protect "fundamental and well-defined" policies, such as illegality or the exercise of statutory rights. Hence there is very narrow scope for discrimination claims at common law.[86] In *Thibodeau v Design Group One Architects*[87] a Connecticut appeal court held that dismissal on the ground of pregnancy was contrary to public policy and so the claimant's action at common law for wrongful dismissal succeeded.

(a) The Common Law and the Human Rights Act 1998

As seen above (para.2–010), s.6, HRA 1998, provides that a public **2–014** authority must act compatibly with Convention rights. According to s.6(3)(a) a public authority includes the courts and tribunals. This broadens the scope of s.6, but also creates some uncertainty as to just how far a court can develop the common law to accord with Convention rights. The particular question here is whether the courts merely should develop existing common law, or to create new law, to accord with Convention rights. This question is particularly relevant for disputes between private parties.

The issue is best understood beyond the usual vertical/horizontal effect dichotomy (equating to state/private party liability), by considering a more subtle analysis, with a further distinction between two types of horizontal effect: direct and indirect. With *direct* horizontal effect, private parties are bound by convention rights and so can be sued for a violation. With *indirect* horizontal effect, a private party may be bound by a convention right, but only through some indirect mechanism. This may arise where a refusal of a remedy would infringe

---

[84] See J. Jowell "Is Equality a Constitutional Principle?" (1994) 47 *Current Legal Problems* (Pt 2, Collected Papers) 1, p.91.

[85] [1944] 1 K.B. 693, KBD.

[86] See e.g. *Kempfer v Automated Finishing* 211 Wis 2d 100, at 105–114 (1996); and M. Wagoner Jn (1996) "Comment: The public policy exception to the employment at will doctrine in Ohio: a need for a legislative approach" 57 Ohio St L.J. 1799.

[87] 260 Conn 691 (2002).

a Convention right.[88] When the Human Rights Bill was going through Parliament, the Government anticipated it would have indirect, but not direct, horizontal effect.[89] The case law so far suggests the judges will take the same line. Under the HRA 1998 the courts have developed the common law breach of confidence into a law of privacy, to accord with Art.8 of the Convention.[90] But in *Campbell v MGM Ltd* Baroness Hale cautioned that: "[T]he courts will not invent a new cause of action to cover types of activity which were not previously covered . . ."[91] This is similar to the position in Canada, where s.32(1) of the Charter of Rights and Freedoms states that the Charter applies to the national and provincial governments and legislatures, but *not* to the courts. The Supreme Court has stated that although courts should "develop the principles of the common law in a manner consistent with the fundamental values enshrined in the Constitution", it cannot be said "that one private party owes a constitutional duty to another." Thus the Canadian Charter of Rights and Freedoms does not afford causes of action or defences between to private parties.[92]

Although the judicial comments so far in Britain amount to much the same thing, there are reasons why the British courts could go further and adopt a "direct" horizontal approach. First, Baroness Hale's pronouncement in *Campbell* is *obiter*. The second reason rejects the notion that human rights instruments are intended only to protect the individual from abuses by the State.[93] The matter is different now because the HRA 1998 has incorporated the Convention into domestic law, which (as the Government spun it) was "bringing rights home". If the law cannot prevent an abuse of those rights, solely on the ground that the abuser is a private party, then the proposition that human rights are fundamental—and have been brought "home"— overstates the position somewhat. It allows also the State to violate rights by proxy. If minded, a government could encourage widespread homophobia by private parties under a political crusade on "family values", or Islamophobia with a "war on terror". Where this has

---

[88] R. Clayton (2000) *The Law of Human Rights,* OUP, at p.225, para.5.76.

[89] The Lord Chancellor stated: "[I]t is right as a matter of principle for the courts to have the duty of acting compatibly with the convention not only in cases involving other public authorities but also in developing the common law in deciding cases between individuals . . . In my view the courts may not act as legislators and grant new remedies for infringement of convention rights unless the common law itself enables them to develop new rights or remedies." (HL Deb cols 783–785 (November 24, 1997)).

[90] See G. Phillipson "Transforming breach of confidence? Towards a common law right of privacy under the Human Rights Act" (2003) 66 M.L.R. 726.

[91] [2004] UKHL 22, at para.133.

[92] *Retail, Wholesale and Department Store Union v Dolphin Delivery Ltd* [1986] 2 SCR 573, at p.593.

[93] Even so, the Strasbourg Court may hold a State liable for not protecting an individual's Convention rights where a private party has infringed a right—see e.g. *Young, James and Webster v UK* (1981) 4 E.H.R.R. 38 and *Costello-Roberts v UK* (1993) 25 E.H.R.R. 112 (see further above paras 2–010—2–011).

occurred beyond the scope of the dedicated discrimination legislation, (such as in the provision of goods, services and housing) there is no obvious legal redress. The most obvious solution is for the courts to develop and create common law in accordance with the Convention, as and when disputes arise.

The third reason is that the restrictive "indirect effect" approach will create anomalies. Take, for example, the provision of housing. Since the 1980s, successive Governments in the UK have encouraged the movement of local authority housing management into the private sector. Under the "indirect effect" rubric a tenant's human rights may depend on something as capricious as the identity of the landlord: state or private.[94] But if the "direct effect" rubric were followed, a court could impose a duty on a landlord, public or private, not to discriminate contrary of the Convention. Further, as legislation must be interpreted to accord with the Convention (see below), some private disputes may turn on whether they are governed by legislation or the common law.

2–015

Of course, as the coverage of the dedicated legislation becomes more comprehensive,[95] the need for Convention rights in the private sphere diminishes. But all this means is that less is being asked of the Human Rights Act. Convention rights should not be withheld on the basis that demand is falling. The Convention is a ready-made instrument that could be used to quell new prejudices in new situations, before they become serious and widespread. The alternative for the victims is to wait in hope for several years (if not decades) for dedicated discrimination law.

It may be that new causes of action are not required to impose Convention rights on the private sector. The ancient common law duties (see above para.2–013) could be developed—by indirect effect— in the areas of the provision of goods, facilities and services, housing and education. As things stood before the HRA 1998, these duties could be used against hoteliers, and perhaps even a yacht club, who refuse admission, or membership, on irrational (including discrimina-tory) grounds. But under the HRA 1998, the courts could develop these duties to prevent discrimination under Art.14 in housing (Art.8) and education (1st Protocol, Art.2), although they could not impose such duties into areas of a "broad and indeterminate social nature", such as the provision some leisure facilities, because the Convention itself does not provide for this.[96]

---

[94] See comments in *Poplar Housing Association Ltd v Donoghue* [2001] EWCA 595, at paras 59–65.
[95] See above, para.2–001.
[96] *Botta v Italy* (1998) 26 E.H.R.R. 241.

3. Judicial Statutory Interpretation[97]

2–016   Although the common law has failed to develop substantive principles of equality and non-discrimination, the judiciary has played a significant part in the development of discrimination law when interpreting the legislation. This is a theme throughout the book. There are many theories of statutory interpretation, from "framer's intent" to "living tree", from "literal" to "purposive". Most cases fall into the literal/purposive dichotomy.

For English judges the literal rule of interpretation has its roots in the constitutional settlement of 1688. Article 9 of the Bill of Rights proclaimed that ". . . the freedom of speech and debates or proceedings in Parlyament ought not to be impeached or questioned in any court or place out of Parlyament." By the Victorian era the deference afforded to statutory words by the judiciary amounted to a rule of interpretation that would do no more than give the words their literal meaning.[98] The consequence is that a judge cannot go behind the face of the statute to discover its meaning and purpose, even if the result frustrates its purpose. In *Perera v Civil Service Commission,*[99] a job specification stated that applicants with British nationality, a good command of English, and experience in the UK would be at an "advantage". The Race Relations Act 1976 at the time prohibited "requirements or conditions" that had a disproportionate impact on a racial group. The Court of Appeal held that as the specification was a "mere preference" and not an absolute bar to the job, it was not a "requirement" and so fell outside the Act. This meant that employers could relegate all their requirements to "mere preferences" and evade the legislation. The phrase "requirement or condition" has since been replaced with "provision, criterion or practice".

A consequence of the literal rule was ever more complex Acts of Parliament with torturous formulas to cover every imagined scenario within the statutes' purpose.[100] In more recent years a shift from this position could be detected. Some judges began to reject the literal approach and gave words their "natural" and "ordinary" meaning.[101] But this was not universal. Another development came in *Pepper v*

---

[97] See M. Barbera, "Not the Same? The Judicial Role in the New Community Anti-Discrimination Law Context" (2002) 31 I.L.J. 82.

[98] See Lord Bramwell, *Hill v E & W India Dock Co* (1884) 9 A.C. 448 HL, at 464–465 and later Lord Loreburn L.C., *London & India Docks v Thames Steam & Lighterage* [1909] A.C. 15 HL, at 19, and Lord Atkinson, *Vacher & Sons v London Soc. of Compositors* [1913] A.C. 107 HL, at 121–122.

[99] [1980] I.C.R. 699 (see further, Ch.6, para.6–050). The classic case of the literal rule frustrating the purpose of the statute is *Fisher v Bell* [1961] 1 Q.B. 394.

[100] Lord Diplock once remarked in *Fothergill v Monarch Airlines* [1980] 3 W.L.R. 209, at 222— that "the current style of legislative draftsmanship" was an "unhappy legacy of this judicial attitude."

[101] See e.g. *Fothergill v Monarch Airlines* [1980] 3 W.L.R. 209, HL, and *Brutus v Cozens* [1973] A.C. 854, HL.

Hart[102] where the House of Lords ruled that in cases of ambiguity a court could look to Parliamentary debates to resolve the meaning of a statute. But this is an exceptional, rather than normal, practice. As shown in *Perera,* ambiguity is not normally the problem.

A third development undermining the literal rule is the increasing **2–017** need for judges to interpret the legislation of the European Community. Community law is entrenched in the "purposive" school of interpretation. Legislation pronounces general principles for the judiciary to develop and apply. This has been the practice of the European Court of Justice. Britain's obligations under EU membership require the judges to give Community legislation and its domestic counterparts a purposive interpretation. Further, Community law requires that domestic legislation is interpreted, so far as possible, to conform to Community law.[103] In *Falkirk Council v Whyte*[104] a job specification that "management training and supervisory experience" was "desirable" adversely affected women. The Sex Discrimination Act 1975 (like the Race Relations Act) prohibited only "requirements or conditions" that had an adverse impact on women. This case differed from *Perera* because at the time sex discrimination law was governed ultimately by the Community law (the Equal Treatment Directive 76/207/EEC). This enabled the EAT to interpret the phrase "requirement or condition" according to the purpose of the legislation: "In many ways this was a classic situation of indirect sex discrimination, with mostly women in basic grade posts, and mostly men in promoted management posts—a vivid example of what the Act and its forerunners in the United States set out to eliminate".[105] Again, this approach is not universal practice. On occasion the courts still use the literal rule when applying European law[106] and elsewhere English judges still employ the literal rule as their basic tool of statutory interpretation.

A fourth development that may change the judges' approach to statutory interpretation, at least so far as human rights are concerned, was the passing of the Human Rights Act 1998, which came into force in October 2000. This Act introduces the European Convention on Human Rights (ECHR) into domestic law. Section 3, HRA 1998, provides: "So far as it is possible to do so, primary legislation and subordinate legislation must be read and given effect in a way which is compatible with the Convention rights". Failing this, by s.4, a court

[102] [1983] 1 All E.R. 42, HL.
[103] *Marleasing SA v La Comercial Internacional de Alimentacion SA* Case C-106/89 [1990] ECR 4135, at 4159.
[104] [1997] I.R.L.R. 560. For a commentary, see M. Connolly, "Discrimination Law: Requirements and Preferences" (1998) 27 I.L.J. 133. The classic case of a purposive interpretation of EC-derived law is *Litster v Forth Dry Dock & Engineering Co* [1990] 1 A.C. 546, HL.
[105] *ibid.*, at 562.
[106] See e.g. *Secretary of State v Spence* [1987] Q.B. 179 CA, approved by Lord Oliver in *Litster Forth v Dry Dock & Engineering Co* [1990] 1 A.C. 546, at 577, HL.

must issue a declaration of incompatibility. Domestic courts are obliged by s.2, HRA 1998 to take into account the case law of the European Court of Human Rights, which takes a purposive, rather than literal, approach, and so ought to adopt a purposive approach when interpreting Act.[107] In the context of discrimination, this means that legislation falling within the ambit of one of the free-standing Convention rights must be interpreted, if possible, so that it does not have a discriminatory effect in violation of Art.14, ECHR. This makes it possible for parties to call upon Convention rights in a private dispute which is governed by legislation.

2–018   In *Godin-Mendoza v Ghaidan*[108] the claimant and Mr Walwyn-Jones lived together in a same-sex relationship in Mr Walwyn-Jones' rented flat. When Mr Walwyn-Jones died, Mendoza claimed from the landlord a right to succeed the statutory tenancy under the Rent Act 1977, which provided (by Sch.1, para.2) that the surviving spouse of the original tenant shall succeed the tenancy. It defined "spouse" as "a person who was living with the original tenant as his or her wife or husband". The Court of Appeal held that "as his or her wife or husband" in para.2 should be read to mean "as if they were his wife or husband".[109] The House of Lords upheld that decision, but significantly, Lord Nicholls reasoned: "The precise form of words read in for this purpose is of no significance. It is their substantive effect which matters."[110] This tells us that courts should not be fettered by an impossibility of a grammatical solution and that s.3 goes further merely than resolving ambiguities in legislation. However, the interpretation should "go with the grain of the legislation"[111] and not be against a fundamental feature of it or amount to a decision better suited for Parliament, for instance, where recognising a male-to-female transsexual as female under the Matrimonial Causes Act 1973 "would have had exceedingly wide ramifications".[112] That said, the Human Rights Act should not commonly affect the interpretation of the dedicated discrimination legislation, for two reasons. First, most of the domestic legislation is subject to Community law, which is not prone to offending the Convention on Human Rights. Second, the Community and domestic concepts of discrimination are far more developed than the Convention concept,[113] and so are less likely to fall short of the Convention.

An alternative analysis to the literal/purposive dichotomy was provided by Lord Browne-Wilkinson who argued that English judges,

---

[107] In *Barclays Bank v Ellis* (Unreported, August 9, 2000 CA) Schiemann, L.J. stated ". . . if Counsel wish to rely on provisions of the Human Rights Act then it is their duty to have available. . .decisions of the European Court of Human Rights upon which they wish to rely or which will help the court in its adjudication."

[108] [2004] 2 A.C. 557.

[109] [2003] 1 F.L.R. 468, at para.35.

[110] [2004] 2 A.C. 557, at para.35.

[111] *per* Lord Rodger, *ibid.*, at para.121.

[112] *per* Lord Nicholls, *ibid.*, at para.33, citing *Bellinger v Bellinger* [2003] UKHL 21.

[113] See above, para.2–009.

when interpreting statutes, merely "seek to ensure that the meritorious triumph and the dirty dogs lick their wounds."[114] The point is that the decision is made on moral grounds, but articulated on legal reasoning. That may explain why there appears to be no single approach. In recent years judges may have simply identified the "dirty dog" and then chosen the reasoning, be it literal, "ordinary", "natural" or purposive as a matter of convenience to justify the decision. The Human Rights Act will change this in two ways, according to Lord Browne-Wilkinson. Judgments on the Act will be made *and* articulated on moral grounds, but this will no longer be the moral standpoint of the individual judge, but the code of morals developed, inter alia, by the European Court of Human Rights and the social and political realities of the day. This approach resembles the "living tree" school of interpretation,[115] which holds that legislation of constitutional nature should be read according to the values of the present day, as opposed to the time it was enacted, or the "framer's intent". The flaw in "framer's intent" school is illustrated in *Dred Scott v Sandford*,[116] where the US Supreme Court denied a black man the right to sue because the Constitution, when drafted, recognised blacks only as "an inferior class of beings" and not US citizens.

In sum, when interpreting domestic discrimination legislation, which falls within the scope of Community law, the courts should take a purposive approach, and if possible, interpret domestic law to accord with Community law. When interpreting domestic legislation which falls outside Community law, courts *ought* to take a purposive approach (to avoid another "*Perera* problem"). Should the legislation fall within the scope of the Human Rights Act, courts should interpret it according to the Convention rights, with the approach shown by *Mendoza*.

4. A SINGLE EQUALITY ACT[117]

The bewildering amount of legislation and anomalies, highlighted during this chapter, and throughout the book, have inevitably led to calls for a single equality act.[118] In 2000, it was estimated that there   **2–019**

[114] B. Markesinis (ed.), *The Impact of the Human Rights Act on English Law*, (1998) OUP, p.22.
[115] *Edwards v A–G of Canada* [1930] A.C. 124 PC, at 136; see B. Wilson, "The Making of a Constitution" [1988] P.L.J. 370. Notable here is the changing attitude towards transsexualism by the ECtHR, seen in *Sheffield & Horsham v UK* (1998) *Goodwin v UK* (2002) E.H.R.R. 447.
[116] 60 US 393 (Sup Ct 1857). For a fine example of the living tree/framer's intent dichotomy, see respectively the dissenting (Lord Scarman) and majority (Lord Denning and Orr, L.J.) speeches in *Ahmed v ILEA* [1978] Q.B. 36, CA.
[117] See, especially, for comparisons with South Africa, S. Fredman, "The Future of Equality in Britain," EOC Working Paper 5 (2002) ISBN, 184206 038 4 or available at *www.eoc.org*.
[118] See B. Hepple, Q.C., M. Coussey and T. Choudhury, *Equality: A New framework Report of the Independent Review of the Enforcement of UK Anti-Discrimination legislation* (2000) Oxford: Hart; J. Harrington, "Making Sense of Equality Law: A Review of the Hepple Report" (2001)

were at least 30 relevant Acts, 38 statutory instruments, 11 codes of practice, and 12 EC Directives and Recommendations directly relevant to discrimination,[119] and within sex discrimination law alone, 15 differences between EC and domestic law.[120] The anomalies are countless. The following examples show how tortuous the statutory "scheme" has become. Sexual harassment recently was made specifically unlawful in employment matters, but this was not extended to other fields. So claims for sexual harassment in the provision for goods or services, for instance, must (for time being) be pleaded as direct sex discrimination, a more technical and sometimes impossible task.[121] A tribunal entertaining a claim for direct race discrimination, based on ethnicity and nationality, would have to divide the hearing procedurally. The new (formalised burden of proof) rules apply to the ethnicity aspect, whilst the old "residual" rules apply to the nationality aspect.[122] Similarly, there are different definitions of indirect discrimination depending upon whether the claim is based on nationality, colour, (residual definition) or racial or ethnic origins (new definition).[123] Under the DDA 1995, the definitions of discrimination differ depending upon whether the claim falls within employment matters, or the one of the other fields, such as the supply of services, or education (see generally Ch.11). In addition, many claims yet to be heard would have arisen before any particular change came into force, and so must be conducted under old definitions or rules.

There are, however, reservations about moving to a single equality act. The Commission for Racial Equality has argued that a single equality statute would blur the focus on specific types of discrimination, with a general concept of equality unable to achieve the "sharp impact" necessary to tackle institutional racism.[124] Further, the proposition of a single equality act assumes that equality is the best vehicle to tackle particular social ills, which are many and varied. Yet the symmetrical nature of the equality principle makes it an inadequate model in the areas of religion, disability, pregnancy, sexual harassment and the historical results of discrimination.[125] There is no doubt that the present state of the legislation is unsatisfactory, and reform is necessary, but reform may be better accomplished with dedicated laws, tailored to their respective goals. It will be seen in the relevant parts of this book, that the law has been refined or adapted already on a rather

---

64 (issue 5) MLR 757 and S. McKay, "Proposing a New Framework to Combat Discrimination" (2001) 30 I.L.J. 133.

[119] *ibid.*, at para.2.1. Since the publication of this report the Government has introduced five sets of Regulations covering race, sexual orientation, religion, age and equal pay.

[120] *ibid.*, at para.2.6. Many anomalies will become apparent throughout this book.

[121] See Ch.5, para.5–022.

[122] See Ch.13, para.13–002.

[123] See Ch.6, paras 6–048 and 6–006.

[124] Hepple *et al*, above, fn 118, at para.2.10.

[125] See generally Ch.1, para.1–005.

ad hoc basis, to lesser or greater degrees, for issues of pregnancy, disability, religion (in the US), and positive discrimination.

The first formal attempt to realise a single equality enactment was launched by the EU Commission, which adopted a proposal[126] to clarify Community sex discrimination law by consolidating the five existing directives. For the UK, the Government has embarked upon a wide-reaching discrimination law review to achieve a clearer and more streamlined framework.[127]

---

[126] Proposal for a Directive of the European Parliament and of the Council on the implementation of the principle of equal opportunities and equal treatment of men and women in matters of employment and occupation (2004/0084/COD).

[127] See *www.womenandequalityunit.gov.uk/dlr* and for an independent, but connected review, *www.theequalitiesreview.org.uk.*

CHAPTER 3

THE PROHIBITED GROUNDS OF DISCRIMINATION

INTRODUCTION

The legislation specifically covers race, religion or belief, sex, gender **3–001** reassignment, sexual orientation, disability and age.[1] The definition of disability is discussed separately in Ch.11.[2] The principal domestic legislation is the Race Relations Act 1976 (RRA 1976) and Sex Discrimination Act 1975 (SDA 1975). In addition, deriving from European directives, there are statutory instruments covering religion or belief, sexual orientation and age. European legislation specifically covers sex (including gender reassignment),[3] racial and ethnic origin,[4] nationality,[5] and religion and belief, disability, age and sexual orientation.[6] However, this European legislation is limited in that most of it extends only to employment matters. The exception is the Race Directive, which, like the RRA 1976 and SDA 1975, extends to other fields such as the provision of services, housing, and education. In addition, the Equality Act 2006 extends the coverage of religion or belief discrimination to other fields,[7] and provides the Secretary of

---

[1] Age discrimination legislation is in force October 1, 2006.
[2] See p.297.
[3] Equal Treatment Directive 76/207 and Art.141 (Equal pay) EC Treaty.
[4] Race Directive 2000/43/EC.
[5] Art.39 EC Treaty.
[6] Equal Treatment in Employment Directive 2000/78/EC.
[7] Expected in force October 2006.

State power to extend similarly the coverage of sexual orientation discrimination. The Human Rights Act 1998, which incorporated the European Convention on Human Rights, covers discrimination on all of the above grounds plus many others, but only in connection with any of the free-standing rights, such as freedom of association, or the right to respect for private and family life, although freedom of religion is protected specifically by Art.9. The coverage of the Convention is discussed in Ch.2.[8]

1. RACE

3–002 First, it is necessary to understand of the complexities caused by the implementation of the Race Directive 2000/43/EC. Section 3, RRA 1976, defines racial grounds to mean "colour, race, nationality or ethnic or national origins". However, this is now a residual definition, because the Race Directive provides a new, slightly narrower definition: "racial or ethnic origin".[9] This new definition of race was accompanied by amendments elsewhere, such as a new definition of indirect discrimination and a formulised shifting burden of proof, which generally favour claimants. Accordingly, there are now two classes of claim under the RRA 1976. Where the claim falls within the scope of the Directive the new definitions apply. However, should a claim fall only within the residual definition of race, it will be heard according to the old definitions elsewhere in the Act.[10]

The new definition covers only "racial or ethnic origin", although there is little doubt that the ECJ would interpret this broadly. Accordingly, the draftsmen have included "*national* origins" in the amendment to reflect the true meaning of the Directive. However, "colour" and "nationality" are excluded from the amendments. Again, there is little doubt that the ECJ would interpret "race" to include most cases of discrimination on the grounds of colour. However, on rare occasions this may not be possible, for instance, where a dark-skinned black person discriminates against a light-skinned black person.[11] However, the ECJ will not interpret the Directive to cover claims under "nationality", as Art.3 of the Directive expressly reserves such matters for EC Treaty, Art.39, which principally is concerned with the free movement of workers. There is no overlap between s.3,

---

[8] See para.2–007.

[9] Race Directive 2000/43/EC, Art.1.

[10] This would not have been the case had Parliament amended the RRA 1976 wholesale along the lines of the Directive. Instead, the Government, using its powers given by the European Communities Act 1972, amended the RRA 1976 by statutory instrument: Race Relations Act 1976 (Amendment) Regulations 2003 SI 2003/1626.

[11] See *Walker v Secretary of the Treasury* 713 F Supp 403 (ND Ga 1989), discussed further *below*, para.3–004.

RRA 1976, and the new provisions, which use the word "race". Section 3 only defines "racial grounds" and "racial group", but not "race". So it is not possible to argue, for instance, that the new definition of indirect discrimination includes "nationality" via the definition in s.3.

(1) The Meaning of Race

Modern opinion is that there is no scientific definition of race which could serve any purpose under discrimination legislation.[12] There is an absence of case law on the issue in Britain. However, there has been much litigation over the definition of race in the United States. In *Saint Francis College v Al-Khazraji*,[13] a case brought under the general equality provision (s.1981) of the Civil Rights Act 1866, the Supreme Court rejected an argument that modern scientific theory placed humans into three major racial groups: Caucasoid, Mongoloid, and Negroid. White, J noted that when passing the Civil Rights Act 1866, Congress referred to the Scandinavian, Chinese, Latin, Spanish, Anglo-Saxon, Jewish, Mexican, black, Mongolian, Gypsy, and German races. He concluded that

3–003

> "Congress intended to protect from discrimination identifiable classes of persons who are subjected to intentional discrimination solely because of their ancestry or ethnic characteristics. Such discrimination is racial discrimination . . . whether or not it would be classified as racial in terms of modern scientific theory . . . It is clear . . . that a distinctive physiognomy is not essential . . ."[14]

The ECJ's purposive approach to interpretation suggests that it also would reject a scientific approach to this question. There is evidence that the British courts also would reject this line as well. In *Mandla v Dowell Lee*,[15] the House of Lords disapproved of the scientific approach made below by the Court of Appeal.

---

[12] See e.g.: J. Solomos, *Race and Racism in Britain*, 2nd edn, 1993, London: Macmillan, pp.8–9, 183–85, 193; R. Miles, *Racism*, 1989, London: Routledge, p.119; J. Solomos and L. Back, *Racism and Society*, 1996, London: Macmillan, pp.210, 216; and the ultimately doomed discussion by the Court of Appeal in *Mandla v Dowell Lee* [1983] Q.B. 1, *per* Lord Denning MR, at 10F, Oliver, L.J., at 15H and Kerr, L.J., at 22D. The Court's approach and conclusion were rejected by the House of Lords [1983] A.C. 548.

[13] 481 US 604 (Sup Ct 1987). For a full review of this and other cases on the issue see *Sandhu v Lockheed Missiles* 26 Cal App 4th 846 (1994).

[14] 481 US 604 (1987), 610 fn 4, and 612–613. The argument that there were only three racial groups for the purposes of the legislation was rejected for another reason by a lower court (the Third Circuit) in this case. It found that the strict "three race" approach would lead to anomalies: "while a white would be able to claim anti-white discrimination under the statute . . . a Mexican-American or an Indian would be unable to make out a claim, unless they contended they were unfairly treated by virtue of being Caucasians." (784 F 2d 505, at 520.)

[15] [1983] A.C. 548, HL. See below, para.3–007 "(5) Ethnic Origins".

(2) Colour

3–004 There has been no litigation over the meaning of "colour" in s.3 of the Race Relations Act. The matter has arisen occasionally in the United States. In *Walker v Secretary of the Treasury*,[16] Ms Walker was a light-skinned black woman who worked in an office of predominantly dark-skinned black persons. She claimed that she was dismissed because of her lighter skin colour and claimed discrimination under Title VII of the Civil Rights Act 1964. Ms Walker, as a black person, could not claim that she was discriminated on grounds of race; this claim was peculiar to colour. The defendants argued that legislative history and case law all pointed towards the statutory word "colour" meaning the same thing as "race", thus it was not possible to bring an action on colour without some proof of a racial element. The District Court discussed the issue at length and dismissed the defendants' argument for two reasons. First, to give two words (i.e. colour and race) in the same phrase a single meaning would make one of those words redundant. The second reason was drawn from the Supreme Court's definition of race in *Saint Francis College v Al-Khazraji*,[17] where White, J. stated that a distinctive physiognomy was not necessary to bring a claim of discrimination based on race. The court in *Walker* extended this logic to cover colour, thus, it was unnecessary for Ms Walker to prove a distinctive physiognomy. Her claim based solely on colour could succeed. It was noted in *Felix v Marquez*[18] that colour may be the "most practical" claim where the victim has mixed heritage.

(3) Nationality

3–005 This category was introduced into the 1976 Act as a result of the House of Lords' decision in *Ealing LBC v CRE*,[19] a case on the 1968 Race Relations Act, which prohibited discrimination on the ground of "national origin", but not "nationality". The House of Lords held that a Polish national, whom the Council had refused to put on their housing list, had no claim under the 1968 Act. Lord Cross stated, "It is not difficult to see why the legislature in enacting the . . . Act used this new phrase 'national origins' and not the word 'nationality' which had a well-established meaning in law. It was because 'nationality' in the strict sense was quite irrelevant to the problem with which they were faced. Most of the people against whom discrimination was being practised or hatred stirred up were in fact British subjects". Section 78 of the 1976 Act provides that, unless the context otherwise

---

[16] 713 F Supp 403 (ND Ga 1989) and 742 F Supp 670 (ND Ga 1990).
[17] 481 US 604 (1987). See above: "(1) The Meaning of Race", para.3–003.
[18] 24 Empl Prac Dec (CCH) para.31,279 (DDC 1980), discussed briefly in *Walker v Secretary of the Treasury* 713 F Supp 403, (1989) at 406–407.
[19] [1972] A.C. 342, see also below, "(4) National origins," para.3–006.

requires, "'nationality' includes citizenship". Consequently Polish, or any other, nationals, or citizens, are protected under the 1976 Act. There is an overlap with EC law here. The EC Treaty recognises that there shall be freedom of movement within the Community for Member State nationals. Consequently, discrimination on grounds of nationality is outlawed in several areas. For instance, Art.39 outlaws discrimination against *workers* on grounds of nationality. The wording of Art.39 reflects its principal purpose, which is to secure free movement, rather than to outlaw irrational discrimination.[20] Consequently, Art.39 does not cover discrimination within a Member State against a national of that State,[21] and should not cover, for example, discrimination in England against a Welsh person.[22]

There is one area where the US courts have been uncharacteristically conservative when recognising racial groups for protection. A fine distinction between "national origin" and "citizenship" is made to deny aliens rights under the Civil Rights Act 1964. In *Espinoza v Farah Manufacturing Co*[23] the defendant company hired only US citizens. Mrs Espinoza was a Mexican citizen and a first generation US immigrant who was married to an US citizen. She was refused a job and the Supreme Court held that the defendant was not discriminating on grounds of "national origin". (In fact 98 per cent of the company's employees were of Mexican origin.) This was discrimination solely based on citizenship and consequently she was not protected under US discrimination law.

(4) National Origins

There are a number of situations where a claim under "national origins", may succeed where a claim under "nationality" would not. For instance, where a nation no longer exists, or at least no longer exists as a nation state (e.g. Scotland).[24] In *Ealing LBC v Race Relations Board*[25] Lord Simon suggested that within Great Britain, Scots, Welsh and English could each be defined by national origins.[26] In *Northern Joint Police Board v Power*[27] the EAT held that an

3–006

---

[20] See G. de Búrca, "The role of Equality in European Community Law" in A. Dashwood and S. O'Leary, *The Principle of Equal Treatment in European Community Law*, 1997, London: Sweet and Maxwell.

[21] *Morsen* and *Jhanjan* Joined Cases 35, 36/82 [1982] E.C.R. 3723 ECJ. See also *R v Saunders* Case 175/78 [1979] E.C.R. 1129, para.10 ECJ.

[22] However, such discrimination should be covered by the RRA 1976, under national or ethnic origins. See below.

[23] 414 US 86 (1973), J. Douglas, dissenting.

[24] On the specific issue of "national" minorities within the UK, see M. MacEwen, "Racial grounds: a definition of identity" (1998) 3 I.J.D.L. 51.

[25] [1972] A.C. 342, HL.

[26] *ibid.*, at 363–364.

[27] [1997] I.R.L.R. 610, EAT. See also *BBC Scotland v Souster* [2001] I.R.L.R. 150 CS (English); and *Griffiths v Reading University Students Union* (1996) unreported, Case No: 16476/96, see 31 DCLD 3 (Welsh).

Englishman could claim that he was discriminated against in Scotland on the ground of his national origin. On this basis Walloons (Belgiums of French origin), Catalans, Basques, Sicilians, Bretons and Cornish should have a claim under "national origins". It is clear they could succeed in the US courts. For instance in *Pejic v Hughes Helicopters*[28] it was held that Serbians were a protected class under by national origin, although Serbia (at the time, in 1988) was no longer an independent State. The Ninth Circuit stated "Unless historical reality is ignored, the term 'national origin' must include countries no longer in existence." In *Roach v Dresser*[29] a District Court went further and held that a Cajun whose ancestry derives from Acadia (now Nova Scotia) fell within the meaning of "national origin" even though Acadia as a nation never existed (it was a colony). The reasoning given was that "Distinctions between citizens solely because of their ancestors are odious to a free people whose institutions are founded upon the doctrine of equality. . .". The US courts may have been more generous here because the legislation[30]—unlike the EC and British versions—does not include "ethnic origins".

(5) Ethnic Origins

3–007 It has been argued (successfully) that Sikhs, Jews,[31] Romany travellers,[32] and (unsuccessfully) that Rastafarians[33] fall within the definition of ethnic origins. Of course, as the legislation specifically addressed to religious discrimination comes into force, what follows applies only to other (non-religion) cases and residual religion cases. The leading case on the definition of ethnic origins in the RRA 1976 is *Mandla v Dowell Lee*.[34] Here, a private school insisted that boys wore the school uniform, including a cap, and kept their hair cut "so as not to touch the collar". The school refused Gurinder Singh admission as a pupil because he would not comply with those rules. As an orthodox Sikh, he was obliged not to cut his hair, and to restrain it by wearing a turban. Singh claimed that he had been indirectly discriminated against as a Sikh, and so argued that Sikhs fell within the RRA 1976, defined by *ethnic origins*. The House of Lords agreed. Lord Fraser's guidance contained two "essential" and five further "relevant" characteristics. The essential characteristics were: a long shared history, of which the group is conscious as distinguishing it from other groups, and the memory of which it keeps alive; and a cultural tradition of its own, including family

---

[28] 840 F 2d 667, at 673 (9th Cir 1988).
[29] *Roach v Dresser Industrial Valve & Instrument Div* 494 F Supp 215, at 218 (D La 1980).
[30] See "Religion or Belief" below, para.3–009.
[31] *King-Ansell v Police* [1979] 2 N.Z.L.R. 531. Decided under similar legislation in New Zealand and approved in *Mandla v Dowell Lee* [1983] A.C. 548, at 562, HL.
[32] *Commission for Racial Equality v Dutton* [1989] Q.B. 783, C.A.
[33] *Crown Suppliers v Dawkins* [1993] I.C.R. 517 CA.
[34] [1983] A.C. 548 HL.

and social customs and manners, often but not necessarily associated with religious observance. The relevant characteristics were: either a common geographical origin, or descent from a small number of common ancestors; a common language, not necessarily peculiar to the group; a common literature peculiar to the group; a common religion differing from that of neighbouring groups or from the general community surrounding it; being a minority, or being an oppressed or a dominant group within a larger community.[35]

This unanimous House of Lords decision in favour of the claimant appeared to settle the meaning of *ethnic origins* in the RRA 1976. But an examination of the speeches reveals some confusion.[36] Lords Brandon and Roskill concurred with the speeches of both Lord Fraser and Lord Templeman whilst Lord Edmund-Davies restricted himself to concurring in the decision. Yet the criteria proposed in each speech differ. Lord Templeman spoke of (a) group descent, (b) geographical origin and (c) group history.[37] Yet only "group history" was stated by Lord Fraser to be an "essential" characteristic. "Group descent" and "geographical origin", said Lord Fraser, were merely "relevant" characteristics. In practice Lord Fraser's test has become fashionable and it is the one usually applied by courts and tribunals.

In *Crown Suppliers v Dawkins,*[38] Dawkins was refused a job as a van driver because he was unwilling to cut his hair. This was because his Rastafarian faith obliged him to keep it in dreadlocks. Dawkins claimed that Rastafarians were a racial group defined by "ethnic origins" within the meaning of s.3, RRA 1976. The Court of Appeal applied Lord Fraser's criteria, and concluded that as Rastafarians did not have a long shared or "group" history (about 60 years' at the time) they did not form a racial group within the RRA 1976, although it failed to suggest how many years were required to qualify.[39] In *Commission for Racial Equality v Dutton,*[40] the Court of Appeal applied Lord Fraser's criteria to Romany travellers and held that they fell within the definition. The Court recognised this ethnic group as having a common descent from Northern India and some distinctive customs. Accordingly, it refused to recognise a wider group of mere "nomads", which would include "didicois, mumpers, peace people, new age travellers, hippies, tinkers, hawkers, self-styled 'anarchists', and others, as well as (Romany) gipsies."[41]

---

[35] *ibid.*, 560–563.
[36] For criticisms of *Mandla* see G.T. Pagone, "The Lawyer's Hunt for Snarks, Religion and Races" [1984] CLJ 218 and H. Benyon and N. Love, "*Mandla* and the Meaning of 'Racial Group'" (1984) 100 Law Quarterly Review 120.
[37] [1983] A.C. 548 HL, 569E.
[38] [1993] I.C.R. 517.
[39] *ibid.*, 526. Since December 2, 2003 religious discrimination in employment matters is covered by the Employment Equality (Religion or Belief) Regulations SI 2003/1660, discussed below, para.3–009.
[40] [1989] Q.B. 783, CA.
[41] *ibid.*, 796.

3–008   The county court judge had found that those few travellers who
satisfied Lord Fraser's two "essential characteristics" had been
absorbed by a larger group of travellers, some of whom had abandoned the nomadic way of life and/or were indistinguishable from the
general public. Although it reversed this decision, the Court of Appeal
implied that there may come a time when the Romany travellers are no
longer sufficiently separate to be entitled to protection under the Act.[42]
This has clearly happened to Celts, Saxons and Danes, who at one
time probably would have satisfied the definition.

A particular issue is whether a racial group can be defined by
language.[43] The matter arose in *Gwynedd CC v Jones,*[44] where the
council required job applicants to speak Welsh. Two Welsh
complainants—who spoke English only—brought a claim of discrimination on grounds of their ethnic origins. The EAT held that it was
"wrong in law" to define a racial group by a language factor alone and
that even if it was a question of fact, such a finding would be "wholly
unreasonable". Sir Ralph Kilner Brown noted:

> "We cannot believe that, for example, a Mrs Jones from
> Holyhead who speaks Welsh as well as English is to be regarded
> as belonging to a different racial group from her dear friend, a
> Mrs Thomas from Colwyn Bay who speaks only English."[45]

The ratio decidendi of *Jones* is that direct discrimination against
English-only-speaking Welsh persons is not unlawful under the RRA
1976. However, the decision, and the statement that language alone
could not be used to define a racial group, implied that Welsh speakers
did not form a racial group. This analysis has been criticised by one
commentator who suggested (Scottish) Gaels at least, fell within the
definition of ethnic origins.[46] There remains an anomaly. An English
woman resident in Wales, who could not comply with a Welsh
language requirement, could bring a claim of *indirect* discrimination
based her national origin.[47] A considerably smaller proportion of

---

[42] Note the Race Relations (Northern Ireland) Order 1997 expressly includes the Irish Traveller
community as a racial group. Art.5(2): "In this Order 'racial grounds'—(a) includes the
grounds of belonging to the Irish Traveller community, that is to say the community of people
commonly so called who are identified (both by themselves and by others) as people with a
shared history, culture and traditions including, historically, a nomadic way of life on the
island of Ireland . . ."

[43] W. McLeod, "Autochthonous language communities and the Race Relations Act, *Web of
Current Legal Issues* [1998] 1 Web JCCI-htm. See also for the United States, I. Locke-Steven,
"Language discrimination and English-only rules in the workplace: the case for legislative
amendment of Title VII", Texas Tech Law Review v.27 1996 pp.33–72.

[44] [1986] I.C.R. 833 EAT.

[45] *ibid.*, 834.

[46] See W. McLeod *above* fn 43.

[47] See above, (4) "National Origins". Of course, such a requirement would be lawful if it were
justified. For the ease of justifying language requirements in see *Groener v Minister of
Education* Case 397/87 [1989] 2 E.C.R. 3967 ECJ.

English, than Welsh, could comply with the requirement. To build on the imagery of Sir Ralf Kilner Brown, of two non-Welsh speaking neighbours, only Mrs Smith enjoys the protection of the Act. Mrs Jones can be discriminated against because she is Welsh.

2. RELIGION OR BELIEF[48]

The Employment Equality (Religion or Belief) Regulations 2003[49] came into force on December 2, 2003. They cover only employment matters. Part 2 of the Equality Act 2006[50] extends the coverage roughly in line with the existing schemes for sex, race and disability discrimination, to include goods, facilities and services, premises, education, and public authorities. It also introduces a slightly broader definition of religion and belief.   **3–009**

Until the 2003 Regulations, there was no express protection for religious discrimination in Great Britain. There has been, since 1976, legislation against discrimination on grounds of "religious or political opinion" in Northern Ireland.[51] Otherwise, the position for religious groups was capricious, and remains so for any residual cases. As seen above, religious groups could claim under the RRA 1976 only if their religion coincided with a racial group by its "ethnic origins", as defined by Lord Fraser's *Mandla* criteria.[52] By this Sikhs,[53] Romany travellers,[54] and Jews[55] will qualify, but Rastafarians will not.[56] The difficulty for Muslims qualifying under the *Mandla* criteria was summarised in *Nyazi v Rymans Ltd*[57]: "Muslims include people of many nations and colours, who speak many languages and whose only common denominator is religion and religious culture." However, it may be possible for a Muslim to claim indirect discrimination under the RRA 1976 where the religion and national origin coincide. So for example, a Muslim of Pakistani origin may rely on her membership of racial group defined by national origin, rather than ethic origins.

---

[48] See generally, B. Hepple and T. Choudhury (2001), "Tackling Religious Discrimination: Practical Implications for Policy-makers and Legislators" Home Office Series 221. London: Home Office; see also P. Cumper, "The Protection of Religious Rights under Section 13 of the Human Rights Act 1998" [2002] PL 254.

[49] Implementing the Employment Equality Directive 2000/78/EC. See L. Vickers, "The *Draft* Employment Equality (Religion or Belief) Regulations" (2003) 32 I.L.J. 23.

[50] Expected in force October 2006.

[51] Fair Employment (Northern Ireland) Act 1976.

[52] *Mandla v Dowell Lee* [1983] A.C. 548 HL, see above "1 (5) Ethnic Origins", para.3–007.

[53] *ibid.*

[54] *Commission for Racial Equality v Dutton* [1989] Q.B. 783 CA.

[55] *King-Ansell v Police* [1979] 2 NZLR 531. Decided under similar legislation in New Zealand and approved in *Mandla v Dowell Lee* [1983] A.C. 548 HL, 562. It was the Government's intention that persons of the Jewish faith be protected under the Race Relations Act 1965. In a debate on that Act the Home Secretary stated that the word "ethnic" would "undoubtedly" include Jews (711 HC Deb May 3, 1965 cols 932–933).

[56] *Crown Suppliers v Dawkins* [1993] I.C.R. 517 C.A. See above "1(5) Ethnic Origins" para.3–007.

[57] EAT/6/88 (Unreported).

Any discrimination against Muslims is also likely to discriminate, indirectly, against Pakistanis.[58]

Regulation 2(1) of the Religion or Belief Regulations 2003 defines "religion or belief" as "any religion, religious belief, or similar philosophical belief". This widens the scope of the Regulations beyond conventional religions. At the least, this should avert detailed in-depth debates over whether, say, Catholicism is a religion or a denomination of Christianity.[59] The inclusion of *philosophical* beliefs suggests that some non-religious beliefs are protected. The symmetrical nature of the legislation means that atheists should be protected as well, in a similar way that men are protected under the Sex Discrimination Act, and whites under the Race Relations Act. This is confirmed by the amended definition, which includes a "lack of religion" or belief.[60] The amended definition ensures that those without a particular belief, such as agnostics, are protected. However, it is less clear if they are covered by the original definition.[61] The Explanatory Notes to the amended definition suggests that it includes Buddhism, Sikhism, Rastafarianism, Baha'is, Zoroastrians and Jains.[62]

3–010   A similarly broad approach has been adopted in the United States, where courts have been interpreting the statutory word "religion" for decades. Organised religions recognised in the US include Sikhs,[63] Tantric Buddhists,[64] Jews,[65] and Rastafarians.[66] Further, in *Frazee v Illinois Department of Employment Security*[67] the Supreme Court held that a man who expressed a Christian belief but belonged to no religious church or sect was protected. Atheists also have been held to come within the definition of "religion".[68] The US courts also have recognised political beliefs that were rooted in a religion. In *Wilson v United States West Communications*[69] a Roman Catholic employee made a religious vow to wear an anti-abortion button displaying a colour photograph of a foetus and two anti-abortion slogans. It was held that this practice came within the meaning of

---

[58] See, for example, *Hussain v Midland Cosmetics Sales*, EAT/915/00 ("Pakistani Muslims"); and *JH Walker v Hussain* [1996] I.C.R. 291 EAT ("Asian Muslims"). See generally, S. Poulter Muslim "Headscarves in School: Contrasting Approaches in England and France" [1997] *Oxford Journal of Legal Studies* 43.

[59] Confirmed by the Explanatory Notes to Equality Act 2006, para.170. Contrast the exception in reg.7(3), which is limited to "religious ethos". See Ch.8, para.8–053.

[60] Inserted by EA 2006, s.77. Expected in force October 2006.

[61] Discussed, Ch.4, para.4–028.

[62] Explanatory Notes to Equality Act 2006, para.170.

[63] See *Bhatia v Chevron* 734 F 2d 1382 (9th Cir 1984).

[64] See *State v Rocheleau* 451 A 2d 1144 (1982).

[65] *Lapine v Edward Marshall Boehm Inc* No 89 C 8420 (ND Ill 990).

[66] Formally known as *The Twelve Tribes of Israel*. See *Whyte v United States* 471 A 2d 1018 (DC App 1984), under the Free Exercise Clause of the First Amendment.

[67] 489 US 829 (1989).

[68] *EEOC v Townley Engineering* 859 F 2d 610 (9th Cir 1988). See also *Young v Southwestern Saving and Loan Association* 509 F 2d 140 (5th Cir 1975), at 144.

[69] 58 F 3d 1337 (1994).

"religion".[70] In *Dorr v First Kentucky*[71] a member of a religious group (called *Integrity*, affiliated to the Episcopal Church) committed to equal rights for homosexual men and women fell within the definition of "religion". In *American Postal Workers Union v Postmaster General*[72] two window clerks refused to handle draft (conscription) papers on the grounds that their religion prohibited them from doing anything to facilitate war. Their employer's refusal to accommodate this was held to be religious discrimination under Title VII of the Civil Rights Act 1964. The limit of this liberal approach was, perhaps, expressed by the Supreme Court when noting that an asserted belief might be "so bizarre, so clearly nonreligious in motivation, as not to be entitled to protection . . .".[73] A distinction is made between religious and political beliefs. In *Bellamy v Mason's Stores*[74] it was held that the Ku Klux Klan were not a religion under Title VII: "[T]he proclaimed racist and anti-semitic ideology . . . takes on a . . . narrow, temporal and political character inconsistent with the meaning of 'religion'".

The definition in the Religion or Belief Regulations 2003 is broad enough to accommodate the approach taken in these cases, even before the amendment.

3. Sex, Gender Reassignment and Sexual Orientation

These three categories are drawn together under one general heading **3–011** because each has a relationship with the definition of "sex" in the Sex Discrimination Act 1975. Apart from the SDA 1975, the relevant legislation is the Equal Treatment Directive 76/207/EEC, EC Treaty, Art.141 (Equal pay), and the Employment Equality Directive 2000/78/EC and the subsequent Employment Equality (Sexual Orientation) Regulations 2003. The SDA 1975 covers discrimination against men as well as women, and discrimination on the grounds of pregnancy.[75] The coverage becomes more complex in relation to gender reassignment. Here, the SDA 1975 covers direct discrimination and harassment, but not, in terms, indirect discrimination. The coverage is restricted also to the field of employment matters.[76] Claims of indirect discrimination should be possible under the Equal Treatment Directive.

---

[70] 58 F 3d 1337 at 1340. Although the evidence showed that the wearing of the badge was within the vow, the *displaying* of it was not, and so outside of the meaning of "religion".

[71] *Dorr v First Kentucky National Corporation; First National Bank of Louisville* 796 F 2d 179 (6th Cir 1986).

[72] 781 F 2d 772 (9th Cir 1986).

[73] *Thomas v Review Board of Indiana Employment Security Div* 450 US 707, at 715 (Sup Ct 1981), a case under the Free Exercise Clause.

[74] 508 F 2d 504, at 505 (4th Cir 1974) affirming 368 F Supp 1025, at 1026 (ED Va 1973).

[75] *Webb v EMO Air Cargo (No.2)* [1994] Q.B. 718 HL.

[76] The coverage should extend beyond employment by December 21, 2007: Equal Treatment in Goods and Services Directive 2004/113/EC, see further Ch.2, para.2–002.

As we shall see, it may possible, with some ingenuity, to extend the SDA 1975 to cover indirect discrimination in *all* fields. Sexual orientation discrimination is covered by the Employment Equality (Sexual Orientation) Regulations 2003.[77] The Regulations extend only to employment matters, although under Pt 3 of the Equality Act 2006 there is power to extend the coverage. Until then, in other fields the SDA 1975 may be used where the discrimination also amounts to *sex* discrimination.

(1) Gender Reassignment

3–012   Gender reassignment is a recognised ground of discrimination. But the law here is so unplanned it is best understood with its recent history. The first major case was *P v S and Cornwall CC*,[78] where the ECJ held that the dismissal of a worker because he intended to undergo gender reassignment amounted to *sex* discrimination under the Equal Treatment Directive. The difficulty for transsexuals being recognised under the heading of "sex" in discrimination claims had been in the comparison. Asking whether a transsexual of the opposite sex would have been treated more favourably will rarely help the claimant. A defendant could normally show that he would have treated a female-to-male transsexual in the same way. But the ECJ sidestepped this question by declaring that "the Directive cannot be confined simply to discrimination based on the fact that a person is of one or another sex," and then stated that the comparison should be with "persons of the sex to which he or she was deemed to belong before undergoing gender reassignment."[79] The logic is questionable. The underlying problem for the claimant was that he could not be recognised, even post-operative, legally as a woman, and so, the claimant being a male throughout, this comparison could only be one between persons of the same sex.[80] That problem has since largely been alleviated by the Gender Recognition Act 2004, under which, transsexuals can apply for legal recognition of their aspired sex if (1) they have or have had gender dysphoria, and (2) have lived in the acquired gender for two years prior to the application, and (3) intend to live permanently in the acquired gender.[81] Note that surgery and/or hormone treatment is not essential for recognition. Whatever its theoretical shortcomings, the decision in *P v S* recognised transsexuals as a protected group under sex discrimination law.

P v S led to SDA 1975, s 2A, coming into force on May 1, 1999, which provides that it is unlawful to treat a person less favourably on

---

[77] SI 2003/1661.
[78] Case C-13/94 E.C.R. I-2143, [1996] I.C.R. 795.
[79] *ibid.*, at paras 20–21.
[80] See L. Flynn, "Case note: *P v S and Cornwall CC*" [1997] C.M.L. Rev. 367, at 375–384.
[81] Gender Recognition Act 2004, s.2.

the ground that that person "intends to undergo, is undergoing or has undergone gender reassignment". However, s.2A (being passed under the European Communities Act 1972) implemented only the *decision* in *P v S*, and so is confined to cases of *direct* discrimination in the field of employment matters only (although, as discussed below, it may be possible to extend the protection beyond that given by s.2A). By expressly identifying gender reassignment as a ground of discrimination, s.2A removes the problem of comparing a male with a female. Instead, the comparator is a non-transsexual.[82] Nevertheless, problems remain for those living in the acquired—but yet to be legally recognised—gender, and wishing to share male- or female-only facilities, such as toilets or changing rooms. In *Croft v Royal Mail*[83] the claimant, a male-to-female pre-operative transsexual who had been diagnosed with gender dysphoria, embarked upon the "the real life test" by "presenting" as a woman. Her employer (with the support of the female staff) refused her permission to use the female toilet and instead allowed her to use the disabled toilet. The Court of Appeal compared the claimant's treatment with that given to a non-transsexual and concluded that as a man would not be allowed to use the female toilet, the claimant had not been treated less favourably on the ground of gender reassignment.[84] The real issue in such cases is the point at which the claimant's acquired sex is recognised under the Equal Treatment Directive and the SDA 1975. Of course, recognition under the Gender Recognition Act 2004 would put the matter beyond doubt. However, the discrimination legislation protects more than just those recognised under the Gender Recognition Act,[85] so this poses a difficult question of fact for tribunals, as the Court of Appeal emphasized in *Croft*. It held that a claimant's sex could not be purely "self-defined",[86] but neither could an employer's refusal to recognise a person's acquired sex "be permanent".[87]

A free standing definition of harassment on the ground of gender **3–013** reassignment was introduced into the SDA 1975 on October 1, 2005 as section 4A(3)[88] in response to the Equal Treatment Amendment Directive 2002/73/EC, but as the Government could not "conceive" of a discriminatory situation not covered by this and the existing prohibition against direct discrimination, no definition of indirect discrimination was included.[89] Nonetheless, it is possible to broaden

---

[82] Strictly speaking, the comparator should be (as the case may be): one who does not intend to undergo gender reassignment; *or* one who is not undergoing gender reassignment; *or* one who has not undergone gender reassignment.

[83] [2003] I.C.R. 1425, CA.

[84] *ibid.*, para.48.

[85] See *A v Chief Constable of West Yorkshire Police* [2005] 1 A.C. 51, HL.

[86] [2003] I.C.R. 1425, at para.39.

[87] *ibid.*, paras 46–47.

[88] Inserted by SI 2005/2467, reg.5.

[89] "Equality and Diversity: Updating the Sex Discrimination Act. Government Response to Consultation". URN 05/1345. See: *www.womenandequalityunit.gov.uk/publications/etadgovresponse.doc*.

the protection beyond ss.2A and 4A(3). In *Chessington World of Adventures v Reed*,[90] an employment case predating s.2A, the EAT held that in light of the decision in *P v S*, the SDA 1975 had to be interpreted to cover discrimination on the ground of gender reassignment. This reasoning is that the word "sex" in the Sex Discrimination Act 1975 can apply to transsexuals. Thus it is arguable that the definitions of direct and indirect *sex* discrimination (in s.1) apply to gender reassignment discrimination. Further, as the Act extends sex discrimination to fields beyond employment, such as the provision of goods, facilities and services, and housing, gender reassignment discrimination in these fields is covered also.

The obstacle to applying s.1 in this way is that s.2A then becomes redundant. The counter argument is that s.2A serves a purpose of "amplifying" s.1(1)(a) (direct sex discrimination). To assess the strength of the arguments, the cases need to be divided into those within employment, and those in other fields. The "amplifying" argument may appear artificial, but, for cases in the employment field, it allows a domestic tribunal to apply the SDA 1975 in accordance with the Equal Treatment Directive. Although the ECJ's decision in *P v S* extended only to direct discrimination, it is inconceivable that the ECJ would restrict the Directive to cover only direct discrimination where the case concerned gender reassignment. As domestic courts and tribunals are obliged to interpret domestic legislation in accordance with EU law, so far as it is possible to do so,[91] this "artificial" argument should be all that is needed to achieve that.

Of course, in the second class of cases—those in a field other than employment—such reasoning cannot be used.[92] What can be said to support the "artificial" argument is that it gives the statutory word "sex" its ordinary meaning, in accordance with *Reed* and *P v S*. This avoids the anomaly of the word "sex" in s.1, SDA 1975 having one meaning for employment cases (assuming the above argument would succeed) and another meaning other fields.

(2) Sexual Orientation

3–014 Sexual orientation discrimination is covered by the Employment Equality (Sexual Orientation) Regulations 2003,[93] which came into force on December 1, 2003. Regulation 2 covers homosexual, hetero-

---

[90] [1997] I.R.L.R. 556, EAT.

[91] The doctrine of indirect effect. Domestic courts should interpret domestic legislation as far as possible to accord with a Directive whether the domestic law in question was enacted *before or after* the Directive: *Marleasing SA v La Comercial Internacional de Alimintacion* Case C 106/89 [1990] 1 C.M.L.R. 305, at para.13.

[92] At least not until the Equal Treatment in Goods and Services Directive 2004/113/EC comes into force, by December 21, 2007, which will extend Community sex discrimination law beyond employment matters into other fields.

[93] SI 2003/1661.

sexual, and bisexual persons. The Regulations were implemented in response to the Employment Equality Work Directive,[94] and so they extend only to employment and vocational training, although under Pt 3 of the Equality Act 2006 there is power to extend the coverage. Until such a time, the result is that outside the field of employment matters, there is no specific protection against such discrimination. However, there are at least three possible alternative paths for such claims to succeed. The first two are under the Human Rights Act 1998 and the developing common law. These are discussed in Ch.2 (para.2–005).

The third is by a conventional claim under the Sex Discrimination Act. Discrimination on grounds of sexual orientation may, by coincidence, amount to sex discrimination, thus falling within the SDA 1975, which applies to the provision of goods, facilities and services, education, and premises (as well as employment matters). The key to success here is making the correct comparison and showing that the claimant was treated less favourably than a comparator of the opposite sex would have been treated, all other circumstances being the same (or "not materially different"; see SDA 1975, s.5(3)). So, for instance, one should look for a homosexual man being treated less favourably than a homosexual woman. This argument succeeded in the Court of Appeal in *Smith v Gardner Merchant*,[95] an *employment* case predating the Regulations, which is why it was brought under the SDA. Paul Smith was harassed at work. A colleague constantly asked personal questions regarding his sexuality and made offensive remarks about him being gay. For example, he probably had all sorts of diseases, and that gay people who spread AIDS should be put on an island. The Court of Appeal held that Smith had been discriminated against on the ground of his sex, but not before some doubt. As Ward, L.J. stated:[96]

> "By focusing on the applicant's homosexuality, the drift of the argument pushes one almost ineluctably – as I myself was carried along – to ask the wrong question: was he discriminated against because he was a man (sex) or because he was a homosexual (sexual orientation)? ... The fault in the argument is that it precludes consideration of a vital question, namely whether or not discrimination against him based upon his homosexuality may not also be discrimination against him as a man."

Thus, when the correct comparison is made—between the treatment given to a male homosexual and a female homosexual—ostensibly homophobic behaviour may be exposed as sex discrimination as well.

3–015

---

[94] 2000/78/EC.
[95] [1999] I.C.R. 134, CA.
[96] *ibid.*, at paras 2 and 4.

If the facts are disposed to this argument, counsel should have no problem persuading a court. The lesson for practitioners is that, when hearing an account from a client, to probe for all the facts and incidents and analyse them carefully, so as not—in the words of the contrite Ward, L.J., to be "carried along" to the wrong question. Other examples might include harassment related specifically to male sexual acts, a gay man's physical strength, competitiveness, or sporting prowess; or adverse commentary regarding lesbian mothers.

The limitation of this approach was illustrated by the House of Lords decision in *Pearce v Governing Body of Mayfield School*.[97] A not unfamiliar story was that of the teacher, Shirley Pearce, who was taunted by pupils at her school because she was a lesbian. The headmaster told her "grit your teeth." Later, her head of department suggested that she either look for another job or join the supply list. Ms Pearce went off sick—for a second time—and, a year later, took early retirement on health grounds. She lost her claim against the school for sex discrimination. Again, although this was an employment case, Shirley Pearce had to rely on the SDA 1975, as the facts predated the 2003 Regulations. The House of Lords held that as the pupils would have subjected a male gay teacher to similar abuse, Ms Pearce was not treated less favourably than a male gay teacher.[98]

In the field of education, the obvious problem is homophobic bullying. Where a school treats this less seriously than, say, sexual harassment, it may be discriminating against the victim on the ground of sex. In a US case, *Nabozny v Podlesny*,[99] a group of schoolboys subjected a pupil who was homosexual to a mock rape. The school did not punish the boys, although it admitted it would punish boys who assaulted or mock-raped a girl. This was held to be *sex* discrimination under the Constitutional Equal Protection Clause. For the provision of goods, facilities and services, as well as housing, the same reasoning applies. So, for instance, a pub landlord who refuses to serve gay men, but admits lesbians, could be liable under the SDA 1975. Other providers such as swimming baths, gyms and sports centres, and landlords letting premises, could be similarly liable.

3–016   The problem will be solved partly with the implementation of the Equal Treatment in Goods and Services Directive 2004/113/EC, due by December 21, 2007. This extends Community sex discrimination law—and with it the free-standing definition of sexual harassment—to the provision of goods and services, including housing, but not

---

[97] [2003] UKHL 34.

[98] A problem with this case is that the House of Lords focussed on the treatment by the pupils, when the defendant was the *employer*. The focus should have been on whether the employer would have treated a man, suffering homophobic abuse from pupils, more favourably. Although, on the facts, the result may have been the same.

[99] 92 F 3d 446, (7th Cir 1996).

education.[100] The definition, covering any conduct of a sexual nature, is not gender specific, and so covers sexual harassment against homosexuals. It will not, however, cover other homophobic harassment, such as adverse commentary regarding lesbian mothers. Of course, many cases will be mixture of the two. If a claim focuses of the sexual aspects of the harassment, it should succeed. Another limitation is that the Directive, excluding education, will not solve the problem of homophobic abuse in schools.

4. MARITAL AND CIVIL PARTNERSHIP STATUS[101]

The SDA 1975 and the Equal Treatment Directive make it unlawful to discriminate on grounds of a person's marital status. The SDA 1975 now specifies that this includes partners in a civil partnership,[102] and the following applies equally to civil partnerships. Section 3 outlaws both direct and indirect discrimination against married people. There are two significant features to the SDA definition. First, it is limited to employment matters only. Second, s.3 is drafted to protect a married person only; discrimination against a single person is lawful under the SDA 1975. This excludes those intending to be married, those living together who are not formally married, and those who have once been married. In some senses, Art.2(1) of the Equal Treatment Directive is more broadly drafted, covering discrimination "in relation to marital or family status". This covers, for example, someone who is dismissed because they intend to marry, or divorce, although these rights could only be against emanations of the State.

3–017

5. AGE

Age discrimination was included in the Employment Equality Directive,[103] although the Government negotiated an extension to October 2006 for implementation.[104] The resulting Employment Equality (Age) Regulations 2006,[105] are of course confined to employment matters. A number of factors distinguish age from other grounds

3–018

---

[100] Art.1 provides: "4. This Directive shall not apply to education nor to the content of media and advertising, in particular advertising and television advertising as defined in Art 1(b) of Council Directive 89/552/EEC." See further, Ch.2, para.2–002, and for harassment, Ch.5, para.5–003.

[101] See M. Bell, "Employment law consequences of the Civil Partnership Act 2004" (2006) I.L.J. 179.

[102] Added by the Civil Partnership Act 2004, s.251(2) (in force December 5, 2005, SI 2005/3175, Art.2(1) and Sch.1).

[103] 2000/78/EC. See generally, H. Meenan, "Age equality after the Employment Directive" (2003) 10(1) *Maastricht Journal of European and Comparative Law* 9.

[104] See H. Desmond (2000) 29 I.L.J. 403.

[105] SI 2006/1031, in force October 1, 2006.

protected from discrimination. First, experience in other jurisdictions suggests that age discrimination carries far less stigma.[106] Thus, employers may be given more leeway when trying to justify any prima facie discrimination. Second, it will often be more difficult to prove age discrimination. It was observed in the US case, *Laugesen v Anaconda Co*,[107] that, even without discrimination, a dismissed older worker will normally be replaced by someone younger.

> "This factor of progression and replacement is not necessarily involved in cases involving the immutable characteristics of race, sex and national origins. Thus, while the principle thrust of the Age Act is to protect the older worker from victimisation by arbitrary classification on account of age, we do not believe that Congress intended automatic presumptions to apply whenever a worker is replaced by another of a different age."

There is a school of thought in the United States that it is inappropriate to analyse a facially neutral practice for indirect age discrimination, because, unlike other forms of discrimination, there are no historical prejudices and lingering effects of prior discrimination; all older workers were once younger and able to make choices about their education, training, and jobs, free from age discrimination.[108] Recently, however, the Supreme Court has ruled age is a ground subject to indirect discrimination analysis.[109] There are no such doubts in the Directive and resulting Regulations, which expressly provide for indirect discrimination.[110]

In the United States age discrimination legislation dates back to the Age Discrimination in Employment Act 1967. It has been gradually amended, and the present model[111] differs from the Directive in two substantial ways. First, the US model is designed to safeguard older persons, and only those aged 40 or above are protected. The Directive, by contrast, has no such limitation. Thus, it will be unlawful to discriminate against *younger* persons, as well as older ones.

3–019   The second difference is that the British model includes some form of upper age limit. An upper limit of 70 years was abolished in the US

---

[106] See, in Canada, for instance, *Gosselin v Quebec (Attorney General)* [2002] 4 SCR 429, at para.68. See also *Large v Stratford (City)* [1995] 3 SCR 733; *McKinney v University of Guelph* [1990] 3 SCR 229. In the US, *Massachusetts Board of Retirement v Murgia*, 427 US 307, at 313 (Sup Ct 1976). See further, Ch.2, paras 2–007—2–008.

[107] 510 F 2d 307, at 312 (6th Cir 1975).

[108] See comment of J. Kennedy in *Hazen Paper Co v Biggins* 507 US 604, at 618 (Sup Ct 1993), citing Krop, PS, (1982) "Age Discrimination and the Disparate Impact Doctrine" 34 Stan L Rev 837, at 854. See also, Pontz, EH, (1995) "Comment, what a difference the ADEA makes: why disparate impact theory should not apply to the Age Discrimination in Employment Act" 74 NC L Rev 299–300. Contrast *Lorillard v Pons* 434 US 575, at 584 (Sup Ct 1978).

[109] *Smith v City of Jackson* 544 US 228 (Sup Ct 2005).

[110] For an example, see Ch.6, para.6–026.

[111] For a general history of the US model, see D. Neumark (2003) 21 Contemporary Economic Policy 297.

in 1986. The British Regulations include a "default retirement age" of 65,[112] thus enabling employers to dismiss workers reaching that age on the ground of retirement.

For cases predating the Age Regulations, it may be possible that an age related requirement or practice amounts to indirect discrimination on another protected ground, such as sex. It has been held that a preference for young workers (aged between 17 and a half and 28) adversely affects women,[113] although an attempt by older workers to show that a compulsory retirement age of 65 could adversely affect men failed.[114] In any case, a defendant may be able to justify the age requirement if it is unrelated to sex.

---

[112] See further, Ch.8, para.8–062.

[113] *Price v Civil Service Commission* [1977] I.R.L.R. 291, EAT.

[114] *Rutherford v Secretary of State for Trade and Industry* (No.2) [2006] UKHL 19. See Ch.6, para.6–014.

Chapter 4

DIRECT DISCRIMINATION

1. Introduction to the Legislation

In its simplest form, direct discrimination arises when a defendant **4–001** expressly links the victim's protected characteristic (say, sex, or race) with his less favourable treatment of her. For instance, a job advertisement may read: "Librarians wanted, no women need apply." As we shall see, most cases are subtler than that. It may be contrasted with *indirect* discrimination, where an apparently neutral practice has a disproportionate impact on the protected group. The advert above could be reworded: "Librarians wanted, applicants must be over six foot tall." This is not direct discrimination; but because it has broadly the same effect, it will be scrutinised as *indirect* discrimination. Unlike indirect discrimination, there is no general defence to direct discrimination,[1] only specific exceptions for a particular field, such as employment, or the provision of goods, facilities, or services.[2] The definitions of direct discrimination across the legislation are broadly the same, although there are some relatively minor differences, which will be highlighted in this chapter when appropriate.

4–002 **Race Directive 2000/43/EC[3]**

Article 2

Concept of Discrimination

2 . . . (a) direct discrimination shall be taken to occur where one person is treated less favourably than another is, has been or would be treated in a comparable situation, on grounds of racial or ethnic origin . . .

4–003 **Race Relations Act 1976**

1(1) A person discriminates against another . . . if:

(a)   on racial grounds he treats that other less favourably than he treats or would treat other persons . . .

4–004 **Sex Discrimination Act 1975**

1(1) . . .a person discriminates against a woman if:

(a)   on the ground of her sex he treats her less favourably than he treats or would treat a man . . .

These definitions in common have two broad elements: (a) "less favourable treatment" and (b) "on the grounds of."

2. Less Favourable Treatment

(1) "Treatment"

4–005 One might think that this part of the definition was straightforward. But the courts have drawn a line between being treated less favourably, and being *considered* less favourably. In *De Souza v Automobile Association*,[4] Maria De Souza, whilst standing outside her manager's

---

[1] For a discussion on whether direct discrimination generally should be justifiable see J. Bowers and E. Moran, 'Justification in Direct Discrimination Law: Breaking the taboo" (2002) 31 I.L.J. 307. For a response see T. Gill and K. Monaghan, "Justification in Direct Sex Discrimination Law: Taboo Upheld" (2003) 32 I.L.J. 115.

[2] These defences are considered in Chs 8 and 10 respectively.

[3] Equal Treatment Directive 76/207/EEC, Art.2, (as amended by 2002/73/EC, Art.1, in force October 5, 2005), and Employment Equality Directive 2000/78/EC, Art.2, are materially the same.

[4] [1986] I.C.R. 514 CA

office, overheard him tell a senior clerk to give some typing to "the wog"; he was referring to Ms De Souza. The Court of Appeal held that for the remark to amount to "treatment" it would have to have been directed at Ms De Souza, or intended to have been overheard by her, or knowing or reasonably anticipating that it would be passed on to her. It held that the manager had not discriminated because he had merely *considered*, rather than *treated* Ms De Souza less favourably.[5] There should be very few cases like this, where there is an insulated comment, and nothing more. First, in most cases, the claimant would have received in addition, less favourable treatment in other forms, say in relation to workload, discipline, or perhaps in the quality of the supply of a service. Here, the comment will be good evidence that the ground of that treatment was a prohibited ground, such as race or sex. Second, it should be possible to argue in a case like *De Souza* that the racist remark would encourage racism, or at least a tolerance of it, in the office. Thus a person making such a remark, especially if a person in authority, ought to anticipate that it would be "passed on" to the claimant, even if in a different form, such as racial stereotyping. In which case, the remark amounts to "treatment." Finally, note that *De Souza* is not an authority that a racial insult cannot amount to less favourable treatment.[6]

(2) "Less favourable"

(a) What is "Less" Favourable?

The treatment must be *less* favourable, rather than unfavourable. In *Macdonald v Advocate General for Scotland*[7] the Royal Air Force had a policy of interrogating, humiliating and then dismissing both male and female homosexuals. The claim of sex discrimination[8] failed because although the treatment for males and females was, in some respects, necessarily different, it was equal, albeit equally bad.

4–006

Although *different* treatment is not in itself actionable, it is enough that the victim perceived—reasonably—that she had been treated less favourably. The key is that there must be some reasonable ground for that perception. In *R. v Birmingham City Council, Ex p. EOC*,[9] the council provided more grammar school places for boys than for girls. It argued that the girls had not been treated *less* favourably because there was no evidence that grammar schools were better than the

---

[5] *per* May, L.J., *ibid.,* at 524E. See also *Westmount Housing Association v Hughes* EAT/0998/00, (Transcript) October 2, 2001 ("that black woman"); and *British Midland Airways Limited v Kinton* EAT/459/93, (Transcript) November 26, 1993.

[6] For unlawful harassment, see Ch.5, p.101.

[7] [2003] UKHL 34.

[8] The case was argued as sex discrimination because it pre-dated the Employment Equality (Sexual Orientation) Regulations 2003.

[9] [1989] A.C. 1155 CA and HL.

other schools. The House of Lords rejected this argument, holding that as the girls were denied a choice—which they, reasonably, valued—they had been treated less favourably than the boys.[10] In *Gill v El Vino*[11] only men were served at the bar of a wine bar. Women were asked to be seated and given table service. The Court of Appeal held that although table service provided an adequate (if not superior) alternative, women were treated less favourably because, unlike the men, they were denied a choice. In *Chief Constable of West Yorkshire v Khan* (a case of victimisation under the Race Relations Act 1976)[12] the House of Lords held that an employer's refusal to give a reference amounted to less favourable treatment, even though that reference would have been negative and *lessoned* the candidate's chances. The candidate, reasonably, would have preferred to have the reference. Accordingly, it is not enough that the claimant simply considered, without reason, that she was treated less favourably. In *Burrett v West Birmingham HA*[13] a female nurse complained that she had to wear headgear, whilst male nurses did not. The EAT held that as both male and female nurses were bound to wear respective uniforms (jacket with epaulettes for men, headgear for women) the claimant could not, reasonably, claim to have been treated *less* favourably.

The Court of Appeal struggled with this issue in *Simon v Brimham Associates*.[14] At a job interview, Mr Simon was asked to disclose his religion. He refused. The interviewer then explained that the job was with an Arab company and stated "If, for instance, you were of the Jewish faith, it might preclude your selection for the job". Mr Simon ended the interview there and then and made a claim for direct discrimination. It was held that as all applicants were asked about their religion, the interviewer had treated Mr Simon no less favourably than he would treat any other applicant. This narrow interpretation carries a serious flaw. It cannot be the law that employers may state to all candidates, for example, that they do not employ homosexuals, or Roman Catholics. Further, what if this employer stated in its job advertisement that "Jews might be precluded"? It is hard to imagine a more blatant, (and offensive), case of direct discrimination. The advertisement, like the interviewer's statement, is made to all. In either case, the result is the same; Jews are not welcome to apply. In either case it is absurd to say that all those who read, or hear, the statement are being treated equally. Quite clearly, Jews are being treated less

---

[10] [1989] A.C. 1193. See also *R. v Secretary of State for Education and Science, Ex p. Keating, The Times* December 3, 1985, (council to run single-sex school for girls held to be treating boys less favourably).

[11] [1983] Q.B. 425, CA.

[12] [2002] 1 W.L.R. 1947. Discussed Ch.7, para.7–009.

[13] [1994] I.R.L.R. 7 EAT. This does not mean that all dress codes necessarily treat men and women equally. See below, para.4–032. The decision on the facts is not above criticism, see fn 132 below, and accompanying text.

[14] [1987] I.C.R. 596, CA. See also below para.4–022.

favourably than non-Jews. Alternatively, if, as the decision suggests, the practice was neutral, Simon could have argued an alternative claim of *indirect* discrimination.

(3) The Comparison

Race Relations Act 1976 4–007

3(4) A comparison of the case of a person of a particular racial group with that of a person not of that group under s.1(1) . . . must be such that the relevant circumstances in the one case are the same, or not materially different, from the other.

The relevant provisions for discrimination on the grounds of sex, age, sexual orientation and religion are materially the same.

(a) The Compulsory Comparison

The first point to make is that a comparison *must* be made. This was illustrated in *Glasgow CC v Zafar*,[15] where an industrial tribunal held that the employer's dismissal procedure had been so seriously defective it constituted unreasonable treatment, and that such unreasonable treatment amounted to less favourable treatment on racial grounds. The House of Lords held that this approach was defective because there had been no comparison with the treatment that would have been afforded to a worker of another race, in the same circumstances. The tribunal wrongly focussed on the *reasonableness* of the employer's treatment of the worker, and *not* whether that treatment included racial discrimination. In fact, the only comparison made was with another *employer*, which is irrelevant. This is not to state that a tribunal cannot infer from the defendant's unreasonable behaviour, that he would have treated a comparator more favourably. The point is that a claimant must bring a comparator into court. Note though, the phrase "or would treat", in the statutory definition (above, para.4–003) makes it clear that the comparator may be a hypothetical person.

4–008

(b) Relevant Circumstances

The domestic legislation (see above) makes it clear that the relevant circumstances of comparator must be materially the same as the claimant. In other words, the comparison must be "like-with-like", the only difference between the two being the protected ground, i.e. sex, race, religion, age, or sexual orientation.

4–009

---

[15] [1998] I.C.R. 120, HL. See further Ch.13, para.13–004.

The "relevant circumstances" for the comparison was discussed at length by the House of Lords in *Shamoon v Chief Constable of the RUC*.[16] Here, a superintendent relieved Inspector Joan Shamoon of her appraisal duties in response to complaints by officers. She brought claim of sex discrimination,[17] using as comparators two male inspectors, who had not been relieved of their appraisal duties. Her difficulty was that no complaints had been made against these inspectors, and she had not proved that she had been treated less favourably than a male inspector would have been, had he received complaints. On these relatively straightforward facts the House dismissed her claim, but stressed she had failed on *both* elements, (*less favourable treatment* and *on the ground of sex*). In doing so the House went further than necessary to resolve the case before it, by insisting that the relevant circumstances must not be altered for both elements. This was based on an interpretation of the equivalent of RRA 1976, s.3(4) (above, para.4–007), that, according to the House, applies to s.1(1) (the definition of direct discrimination), *as a whole*.

4–010   This interpretation is problematic because often it will mean incorporating irrelevant facts into the comparison, making it an unduly complicated and clumsy exercise. It leaves tribunals with an unpalatable choice. They incorporate merely the circumstances "relevant" for the comparison, and risk omitting evidence crucial to the second element, "on grounds of." The alternative, to retain that crucial evidence for the second element, is to incorporate it into the first element and embark upon a clumsy, complicated and artificial exercise of making the comparison with irrelevant factors. This is illustrated using a classic case of direct discrimination, *King v Great Britain-China Centre*.[18] Ms King, who was Chinese but educated in Britain, applied for a post at the China Centre, an organisation established to foster closer ties with China. She met the requirements of fluent spoken Chinese and a personal knowledge of China. A white English person was appointed. The background circumstances were that none of the five Chinese applicants made the short list of eight white candidates, and that no Chinese person had ever been employed in the centre. The Court of Appeal held that the industrial tribunal was entitled to draw the conclusion that King was discriminated against because she did not come from the "same, essentially British, academic background" as the existing staff. If the tribunal had heard the case after *Shamoon,* it would be obliged to incorporate those two background factors into the comparison, when they are irrelevant to the question of less favourable treatment. A simple comparison between King and the equally qualified successful (white) candidate is

---

[16] [2003] I.C.R. 337, HL.
[17] Under the Sex Discrimination (Northern Ireland) Order 1976, which, for this purpose, is materially the same as the SDA 1975.
[18] [1992] I.C.R. 516, CA. See further, Ch.13, para.13–003.

all that was necessary. The short-listing and employment history are irrelevant to the question of whether King was treated *less* favourably, although, of course, they are relevant for the second question of the identifying the ground of the treatment. This interpretation is consistent with the legislation, which demands that the relevant circumstances be materially the same in each case for the "comparison," but makes no such demand for identifying the ground of the treatment. It is true that the ground of the treatment may be identified by a comparison in some instances, (such as *Shamoon*), but for the majority of cases the ground of the treatment will be identified from a variety of circumstantial evidence, (as in *King*).

The problem is aggravated by the House of Lords suggesting that the second question (the ground of the treatment) is subjective, with Lord Roger expressing the logical conclusion of this view, that the relevant circumstances should be those that were taken into account by the defendant.[19] This unduly restricts the circumstances that can be included when asking if the treatment was less favourable. Suppose a variation on *Shamoon*: the complaints against her were based on sex— male officers did not like being appraised by a female superior—but neutral on their face. As the superintendent was unaware that the complaints were based on sex, he could not have taken this into consideration,[20] and so it would be excluded from the comparison. This would mislead a tribunal to the perverse conclusion that the claimant had not been treated less favourably than a man would have been, when she lost her appraisal duties because she was a woman. It is better, simpler, and consistent with the legislation, to keep the comparison discrete from the second element, "on the ground of". The principal goal of the comparison is to see if there was *less* favourable treatment. The comparison then may, or may not, be used, in the second question to help establish whether the treatment was on a protected ground.

(c) Other Problems with the Comparison

It is important that the circumstances of the comparator are not tainted with discrimination on the ground in question, as this can sabotage a good claim. This is illustrated in *Re Equal Opportunities Commission for Northern Ireland's Application.*[21] In Northern Ireland, the Department of Education allocated non-fee paying grammar school places equally to boys and to girls: each group received 27 per cent of the places. That discriminated against the girls because they performed better in the entrance exam. Consequently 422 boys were

4–011

---

[19] [2003] I.C.R. 337, at para.134.
[20] Known in the US as the "cat's paw" theory, discussed below, para.4–021.
[21] [1989] I.R.L.R. 64, NI High Court. A case brought on the Sex Discrimination (Northern Ireland) Order 1976, which is set out in similar terms to the SDA 1975.

awarded places, even though they had achieved lower marks than a group of 555 girls, who were not awarded places. This was held, in a prior case, to be unlawful sex discrimination. However, the Department refused to withdraw the boys' offers out of "fairness", because, unlike the girls, the boys had not had their hopes raised. The EOC challenged this refusal as being discriminatory. The Department argued that the treatment (the refusal) was based, not upon sex, but on "fairness". Hutton, L.C.J. held that it was incorrect to include the "fairness" aspect in the circumstances of the comparators (the 422 boys), as the situation leading to the "fairness argument" was itself caused by sex discrimination. Thus the comparators should remain in the same circumstances as in the prior case (boys offered a place with a lower mark than the claimant girls) and the 555 girls should be awarded places instead of the boys.

It is can be misleading to change the *defendant's* circumstances for the comparison. In *Grieg v Community Industry*,[22] Ms Grieg was refused a job with an all-male decorating team because otherwise it would have "created an imbalance to the composition of the team". The employer defended a sex discrimination claim by arguing that the comparator should be a man refused a job with an *all-women* team. The EAT held that the comparator's circumstances should not include a different job. The correct comparator was a man applying for the *same* job. The "relevant circumstances" would not be the same if the job were changed.

Complications again arise in the comparison where the discrimination is on a prohibited ground of a third party.[23] In *Showboat Entertainment Centre v Owens*,[24] Mr Owens, who is white, was sacked for refusing to obey an order to exclude black youths from an amusement arcade. The EAT held that the comparator should be a man having all the same characteristics as the complainant except his "attitude" to race,[25] or, as the case may be, to sexual orientation or religion.

(d) The Comparison and Gender Reassignment

4–012 For discrimination on the ground of gender reassignment, s.2A(3), SDA 1975 provides in relation to the worker's absence, that a person is treated less favourably if

> "(a) he is treated less favourably than he would be if the absence was due to sickness or injury, or (b) he is treated less favourably than he would be if the absence was due to some other cause and,

---

[22] [1979] I.C.R. 356, EAT.
[23] Discussed below, para.4–024.
[24] [1984] 1 All E.R. 836, see also below, para.4–025.
[25] *per* J. Browne-Wilkinson (as he then was) *ibid.*, at 842 c–g.

having regard to the circumstances of the case, it is reasonable for him to be treated no less favourably."

This is aimed at the situation where the worker is taking time off work in relation to undergoing gender reassignment. It is designed to avoid the comparison used in the analogous situation of pregnancy, where a pregnant woman is *not* normally compared to a sick man (see below, para.4–037).

(e) The Comparison and Married or Civil Partnership Status
For discrimination on the ground of married status, the comparison is **4–013** with an unmarried person *of the same sex* as the complainant, so that the provision applies even to a wholly female, or wholly male, work-force. So it is no defence for an employer to treat all married employees equally badly; if it treats married workers less favourably than unmarried ones, then the employer is liable. This applies equally to civil partnership status.

3. "On the Ground Of"

(1) Mixed Ground Cases
In some cases the defendant would have acted on discriminatory and **4–014** non-discriminatory grounds. For example, in *Owen and Briggs v James*[26] a firm of solicitors refused to employ a black applicant, Ms James. A partner in the firm had stated to the successful candidate: "I cannot understand why an English employer would want to take on a coloured girl when English girls are available." However, race was not the only factor in the decision to reject the applicant. Other reasons were Ms James' lack of employment in the previous three years, and her "unsatisfactory demeanour" at the interview. The firm argued that it was not liable because the rejection of Ms James was not solely motivated by race. The Court of Appeal ruled that for liability, it was sufficient that race was an "important" or "substantial"[27] factor in the decision, and so Ms James' claim for discrimination succeeded. However, the rule announced is quite restrictive because it excludes claims where the discriminatory factor was less than substantial. The rule has been expanded more recently, under the influence of the various European discrimination Directives, most of which[28] mandate that there should be "no discrimination *whatsoever*" on the protected grounds (emphasis supplied). In *Igen v Wong*[29] the Court of Appeal

---

[26] [1982] I.C.R. 618, CA.
[27] *ibid.*, respectively at paras 22 and 35–36.
[28] A notable exception is the Race Directive 2000/43/EC.
[29] *Igen (formally Leeds Careers Guidance) v Wong* [2005] I.C.R. 931.

stated that only if "the treatment was in no sense whatsoever" on the protected ground would the defendant escape liability, but qualified this when stating: "We find it hard to believe that the principle of equal treatment would be breached by the merely trivial."[30] Whether this goes far enough to comply with the Directives is questionable,[31] and may lead to all manner of complex disputes. Of course, as the trier of fact, a court of first instance is entitled to find that the discriminatory element was so trivial that it played no part in the treatment.[32] But once it is found that the discriminatory element was a ground of the treatment, no matter how trivial, a finding of discrimination becomes irresistible, especially in the face of the Directives' demand for no discrimination *whatsoever.*

(2) Discriminatory Motive and the *But For* Test

4–015   The statutory formula requires that the protected ground—i.e. sex, race, religion, age or sexual orientation—was the ground for the less favourable treatment. This is discovered by asking if the defendant so treated the claimant *because of* the protected ground, or perhaps even more simply, by asking if the defendant would have treated the claimant so *but for* the protected ground.[33] The point of this approach is to avoid questions of defendants' discriminatory intent, or motive. Otherwise it would be a good defence for an employer to show that he discriminated against a protected group not because he intended to do so but (for example) because of customer preference, or to save money,

---

[30] *ibid.*, at para.37. See further, Ch.13, para.13–006. The US Supreme Court, in *Price Waterhouse v Hopkins* 490 US 228 (1989) suggested that an employer may avoid liability with an "affirmative defense" of showing that it would have made the same decision absent the discriminatory factor. Congress reversed this by legislating that liability can be established where discrimination was "a motivating factor for any employment practice, even though other factors also motivated the practice" (42 USC s. 2000e–2(m)). However, where the employer makes out an affirmative defense, the remedies are restricted to declarations, injunctions and costs (42 USC s.2000e–5(g)(2)(B)).

[31] In employment cases where the claimant has to prove, in addition, that she suffered a "detriment," the Court of Appeal has recognised the *de minimis* principle: *Jiad v Byford* [2003] I.R.L.R. 232, at paras 34 and 43.

[32] In *Seide v Gillette Industries Ltd* [1980] I.R.L.R. 427, anti-Semitic remarks made to the claimant led to his transfer (about which no complaint was made). He subsequently sought to involve another employee in the dispute, which led to a second transfer in order to minimise disruption, this transfer entailing loss of wages. The EAT held: "It does not seem to us to be enough merely to consider whether the fact that the person is of a particular racial group . . . is any part of the background . . . [T]he question which has to be asked is whether the activating cause of what happens is that the employer has treated a person less favourably than others on racial grounds." (at 431) The EAT held that the industrial tribunal was entitled to find that the first transfer was not a cause of the second transfer. *Cf Din v Carrington Viyella Ltd* [1982] I.C.R. 256, where the EAT observed that it will normally be unlawful to remove the victim from the source of the discrimination, whether or not any loss of pay or status is involved, and even if the motive is simply the avoidance of future unrest. See also, *Kingston v British Railways Board* [1984] I.C.R. 781, CA.

[33] Respectively, *R. v Birmingham City Council, Ex p. Equal Opportunities Commission* [1989] 1 A.C. 1156, at 1194, HL; *James v Eastliegh BC* [1990] 2 A.C. 751, at 774B–C, HL.

or avoid controversy.[34] In *R. v Birmingham City Council, Ex p. Equal Opportunities Commission*,[35] there was a general trend over a number of years to move away from (selective) grammar schools towards (non-selective) comprehensive schools. Small pockets of resistance ensured that a few remained, the majority of which were boys' schools. So the Council found itself in the position of having more grammar school places for boys than for girls. The EOC challenged the Council for discriminating against girls. The Council argued that, for liability, there had to be an *intention* or *motive* to discriminate on the ground of sex, which was absent here. A unanimous House of Lords rejected that argument, stating the council offered less places to girls *because of* their sex.

However, this relatively straightforward element has since been the subject much judicial opinion, especially in the House of Lords. A year or so after the *Birmingham* grammar schools case, in *James v Eastleigh BC*,[36] only a bare majority held the line. Here, the Council's municipal swimming baths admitted free-of-charge persons "of pensionable age". In the United Kingdom, men reach pensionable age at 65 and women at 60.[37] So when Mr and Mrs James, each aged 61, visited the baths, Mrs James was admitted free whilst Mr James was required to pay. Mr James complained that he was receiving less favourable treatment on the ground of his sex. The Council argued that the policy was motivated by a wish to help pensioners, and not by sex. The Court of Appeal agreed with the Council, but a bare majority of the House of Lords reversed, promoting the *but for* test.[38]

The *but for* test has been attacked on several fronts. First, in his dissent in *James*, Lord Lowry[39] offered a meticulous grammatical interpretation of the statutory formula, and pointed out that "ground" was attached to the treatment, which was the act of the discriminator. His fear was that instead of asking "What was the ground of the treatment?" the *but for* test would encourage tribunals to ask, "Did the treatment disfavour her because she belongs to a protected group?" The difference between these questions is illustrated by considering two types of discrimination defined in the legislation: direct and indirect. *Indirect* discrimination was added to catch cases where an apparently neutral practice causes an adverse effect upon a

---

[34] *ibid.*, at 1194. See especially, *R. v Commission for Racial Equality Ex p. Westminster City Council* [1985] ICR 827, CA, below para.4–019.

[35] [1989] 1 A.C. 1156, HL.

[36] [1990] 2 A.C. 751, HL.

[37] The Government plans to raise the women's state pension age to the same as the man's, gradually between 2010 and 2020. See "Equality and Diversity: Age Matters. Age Consultation." (2003), p.23, para.4.13; or *http://www.thepensionservice.gov.uk/planningahead/state-pens.asp.*

[38] [1990] 2 A.C. 751, at 774B–C.

[39] *ibid.*, at 775, specifically endorsing the approach of Browne-Wilkinson, L.J. (as he then was), taken in the Court of Appeal, [1990] 1 Q.B. 61. For a criticism of the Court of Appeal decision, see J. Ross, "Reason, ground, intention, motive and purpose" (1990) 53 M.L.R. 391.

protected group.[40] The distinction is important, for only indirect discrimination allows a general justification defence. Take a classic case of indirect discrimination: an employer's requirement that its workers have a high school diploma adversely affects blacks, who had a history inferior schooling.[41] A black applicant, without a diploma, was disfavoured by the requirement because inter alia he was black; had he been white, he would have had a better chance of meeting the requirement. Now suppose a case of *direct* discrimination: an employer says simply: "No blacks need apply." In *either* case it could be said that that *but for* his race the black applicant would have been recruited. However, more is needed for liability in the latter (direct discrimination) case, otherwise it cannot be distinguished from the high school diploma case of *indirect* discrimination. As Lord Lowry interprets it, the *but for* test cannot distinguish between direct and indirect discrimination. His fear is, of course, is that a claimant may argue: "I belong to a protected group. I was badly treated. Therefore I am a victim of direct discrimination."[42]

4–016   However, this fear is misplaced. It is based upon a slight, and perhaps deft, variation of the *but for* test. The focus should be on the defendant's behaviour (the ground for the treatment) and not the claimant's posture (the ground for the disadvantage). The question to be asked should be: would the defendant have treated him so, but for the protected ground? It is *not*: would the claimant have received unfavourable treatment, but for the protected ground? And so, although Lord Lowry's interpretation of the statutory formula is correct, it is in fact no different from the *but for* test, properly applied. What seems to have driven him to his opinion was his, indeed the whole House's, analysis of the facts of *James*, which they treated as one of direct discrimination, when it was, in fact, a case of *indirect* discrimination. It appears that they lost sight of the basic premise that facially-discriminatory treatment belongs to direct discrimination theory, whilst facially-neutral treatment, which adversely affects a protected group, belongs to *indirect* discrimination theory. "Pensionable age" is a facially-neutral requirement that adversely affected men aged 60 to 65, just as a benefit for "full-time workers" will adversely affect women.[43]

---

[40] For indirect discrimination, see Ch.6.

[41] See *Griggs v Duke Power* 401 US 424 (1971), below, Ch.6, para.6–001. The employer here will have the opportunity to "justify" the requirement, by showing that the diploma was necessary for the job.

[42] See e.g. *Glasgow CC v Zafar* [1998] I.C.R. 120, HL, above, para.4–008 and Ch.13, para.13–004.

[43] More women than men work part-time. See *Jenkins v Kingsgate* Case 96/80 [1981] E.C.R. 911, ECJ, below Ch.9, para.9–032. Indeed, the Labour Government, when introducing the SDA 1975, envisaged a body offering reduced prices for pensioners as an example of indirect discrimination, that could be justified (HL Deb Vol.362, cols. 10116–17 (July 14, 1975)). However, following a challenge in the ECtHR, (*Matthews v UK* Application No 40302/98), the parties settled because the Government legislated that travel concession for the elderly should apply all those aged 60 or over: Travel Concessions (Eligibility) Act 2002.

The second attack on the *but for* test is that it is unsuitable for mixed ground cases.[44] In these cases, where there is more than one cause of the treatment, the *but for* test loses its usefulness. Its theoretical weakness was explained by the US Supreme Court in *Price Waterhouse v Hopkins*:[45]

> Suppose two physical forces act upon and move an object, and suppose that either force acting alone would have moved the object. As the [*but for* test] would have it, *neither* physical force was a "cause" of the motion unless we can show that but for one or both of them, the object would not have moved; apparently both forces were simply "in the air" unless we can identify at least one of them as a but-for cause of the object's movement. . . . Events that are causally overdetermined, in other words, may not have any "cause" at all. This cannot be so.[46]

Its practical weakness is that it could lead a tribunal into far too much speculation as to the proportion, or weight, of the various factors which led to the treatment, as well as what might have been, *but for* the protected ground. If it were applied in the *Owen and Briggs v James* case[47] (which predated the *but for* test), the tribunal would have been drawn into the position of deciding—or speculating—whether Ms James would have been rejected because of her three years of unemployment and/or her "unsatisfactory demeanour".

The third attack on the *but for* test is more subtle, but may prove to be the most effective. There have been a number of judicial statements suggesting a subjective approach: that for liability, a defendant must hold in his mind a discriminatory motive. The first comments arose in two cases on the parallel clause "by reason that" in the victimisation provisions of the discrimination legislation. Dissenting in *Nagarajan v LRT*,[48] Lord Browne-Wilkinson stated courts should not introduce "something akin to strict liability . . . which will lead to individuals being stamped as racially discriminatory . . . where these matters were not consciously in their minds." In *Khan v Chief Constable of West Yorkshire*, Lord Woolf M.R. (as he then was) commented: "To regard a person as acting unlawfully when he had not been motivated either consciously or unconsciously by any discriminatory motive is hardly likely to assist the objective of promoting harmonious racial relations."[49] On appeal, the House of Lords appeared to agree by holding

4–017

---

[44] Described above, para.4–014.

[45] 490 US 228 (1989).

[46] *per* Brennan J. 490 US 228, at 241 (1989). This was a criticism of the conservative minority's dissent, which was using the *but for* test to *restrict* the application of the legislation.

[47] [1982] I.C.R. 618, CA. See above, para.4–014.

[48] [2000] 1 A.C. 501, at 510, HL. Discussed below at Ch.7, para.7–008.

[49] [2000] I.C.R. 1169, CA, at para.14. In spite of this opinion, Lord Woolf felt bound by *James* and the *Birmingham* grammar school case to apply the *but for* test and decide for the claimant.

that the question was "subjective."[50] Most recently, in *Shamoon v Chief Constable of the RUC,*[51] a sex discrimination claim, neither the *but for* test, *James v Eastleigh,* or the *Birmingham* grammar schools case were mentioned. Instead, the judgments asked *why* the claimant was treated so. What few other comments were made on the issue suggested that tribunals should look for discriminatory motive;[52] and that the relevant circumstances for the comparison should be those that the *defendant* took into account,[53] again pointing to a subjective approach.

4–018   These comments undermine the *but for* test, which was designed to avoid questions of the defendant's motive.[54] Further, they appear to controvert the procedural guidelines for employment tribunals provided by the Court of Appeal, and approved by the House of Lords. In *King v Great Britain-China Centre,*[55] Neill, L.J. observed that it was unusual to find direct evidence of discrimination, and that few defendants would even admit to themselves that they had discriminated, instead assuming that the claimant "would not have fitted in." Thus tribunals should make "proper inferences" from the primary facts.[56] This was approved by the House of Lords in *Glasgow CC v Zafar,*[57] where Lord Browne-Wilkinson added: "[T]hose who discriminate on the grounds of race or gender do not in general advertise their prejudices: indeed, they may not even be aware of them." None of this squares with the suggestions that liability should depend upon the subjective view of the defendant, which in most cases will be "innocent".

To understand precisely how far (if at all) the law has shifted away from the *but for* test, it necessary to understand precisely what these judges meant by "subjective" and "discriminatory motive." There is a danger that this analysis could descend into a semantic debate, obscuring, rather than clarifying, the law. So it may be helpful to envisage some concrete categories of direct discrimination claims.

But his *opinion* was vindicated by the reversal of his *decision* by the House of Lords: [2001] UKHL 48. Discussed below, Ch.7, paras 7–008—7–011.

[50] Cited as *Chief Constable of West Yorkshire v Khan* [2001] UKHL 48, at paras 29 and 77. Discussed below, Ch.7, paras 7–008—7–011.

[51] [2003] I.C.R. 337. The facts are set out above, para.4–009.

[52] *per* Lords Hope, *ibid.,* at para.55, and Scott, at para.116.

[53] *per* Lord Roger, *ibid.,* at para.134.

[54] *R. v Birmingham City Council, Ex p. Equal Opportunities Commission* [1989] 1 A.C. 1156, at 1194, HL.

[55] [1992] I.C.R. 513, at 518, CA, (see above, para.4–010). On proving discrimination, see Ch.13, para.13–002.

[56] *ibid.*

[57] [1998] I.C.R. 120, at 126, HL. See further above, para.4–008 and on proving discrimination, Ch.13, para.13–002.

1. *The defendant acted out of prejudice towards the protected* **4–019**
   group. A blatant example would be a "No Blacks" notice. A
   more likely one would be an employer who states: "I cannot
   understand why an English employer would want to take on
   a coloured girl when English girls are available."[58] This category includes stereotyping where the ground of discrimination is explicit.[59] In this category of rare cases, the defendant
   will be liable under the subjective or the *but for* approach.

2. *The defendant treated badly a person from a protected group.*
   These cases are at the other extreme and without more will
   fail under the subjective approach because there is, obviously,
   no discriminatory element to the defendant's act. They will
   also fail under the *but for* test because *but for* the claimant's
   protected group, the treatment would have been the same.

3. *The defendant acts upon discriminatory factors, of which he
   ought to be aware, but is not.* An example of this is *King v
   China Centre-Great Britain* (above, para.4–010). This category
   includes stereotyping where the ground of discrimination is
   not explicit.[60] Here, the defendant does not have the protected
   ground in his mind, which points to no liability under the
   subjective approach, (although there is liability under the *but
   for* test). The difficulty with this conclusion is that excludes
   the vast majority of direct discrimination claims. It is also at
   odds with the policy of the legislation. As the US Supreme
   Court stated in the context of sex discrimination: "An
   employer who objects to aggressiveness in women but whose
   positions require this trait places women in an intolerable and
   impermissible catch 22: out of a job if they behave aggressively and out of a job if they do not."[61] Further, it is most
   unlikely that those judges promoting the subjective approach
   intended to overrule a line of cases specifically approved by
   their most persistent advocate, Lord Browne-Wilkinson.[62]
   Theoretically, the only way to reconcile these cases with the
   subjective approach is with a rather artificial and semantic
   notion that the defendant holds the discriminatory factors in
   his mind, even though he is unaware that those factors are
   discriminatory.

---

[58] See *Owen and Briggs v James* [1982] I.C.R. 618, CA, above, at para.4–014.
[59] e.g. *Alexander v Home Office* [1988] 2 All E.R. 118, CA. See below, para.4–030.
[60] e.g. *Price Waterhouse v Hopkins* 490 US 228 (Sup Ct 1989). See below, para.4–030.
[61] *per* Brennan J. *ibid.*, at 251.
[62] Respectively, in *Zafar v Glasgow CC* [1998] I.C.R. 120, at 126, HL; and dissenting in *Nagarajan
v LRT* [2000] 1 A.C. 501, at 510, "stereotypes provide no excuse for what would otherwise be
racially discriminatory."

4. *The defendant is aware that he is treating a person differently on a protected ground, but discrimination is not his principal motive.* Examples include the *Birmingham* grammar schools case (where there was no "motive"),[63] the "customer preference" cases (where an employer discriminates to please its customers, or other third parties), such as *R. v Commission for Racial Equality Ex p. Westminster City Council*,[64] where the council dismissed a newly-hired black worker because of pressure from the white workforce to revert to the word-of-mouth hiring practice. This category, by principle, should include "benign" motive cases, such as impermissible affirmative action programmes,[65] or for instance, where an employer differentiates out of chivalry,[66] or refuses to hire certain persons to save them from, say, racial, religious, sexual, or homophobic, harassment in the workplace.[67]

4–020

Here, the "discriminatory motive" comments are at their most ambiguous and semantic. Their meaning falls upon the distinction, if any, between "awareness" and "motive". It could be argued that even if a defendant is aware that his action will differentiate on a protected ground, there is no liability because he was not *motivated* by prejudice. This view accords with the House of Lords' decision in *Chief Constable of West Yorkshire v Khan*,[68] a case on the parallel clause "by reason that" in the victimisation provisions in the discrimination legislation.[69] Here, the defendant was aware that the claimant had done the "protected act," (bringing a race discrimination claim) when acting (refusing a reference) for "another" reason (not prejudicing his defence to the race discrimination claim). The House of Lords made it clear that the defendant was not liable for victimisation because he was not motivated by the protected act.

---

[63] [1989] 1 A.C. 1156, HL. See above, para.4–015. It is debatable whether *James v Eastleigh BC* falls into this category. As it was contended (see above para.4–016) that this was in fact a case of *indirect* discrimination, the answer must be no.

[64] [1985] I.C.R. 827, CA.

[65] e.g. *Jepson and Dyas-Elliott v The Labour Party* [1996] I.R.L.R. 116, IT. (An attempt to balance the representation of the sexes in Parliament amounted to direct discrimination. Reversed by legislation with a specific exception: SDA 1975, s.42A, inserted by the Sex Discrimination (Election Candidates) Act 2002, s.1. The provision will expire at the end of 2015, unless renewed by statutory instrument: s.3, SD(EC)A 2002). See also *ACAS v Taylor* (1997) EAT/788/97, (policy of choosing women predominantly for interview for 31 posts, because only 17 per cent of SEOs at ACAS were female, was direct discrimination). See generally, Ch.12, para.12–002.

[66] *Ministry of Defence v Jeremiah* [1980] Q.B. 87, CA. (Women not required to work in dirty part of factory.)

[67] *Greig v Community Industry* [1979] I.C.R. 356, EAT. (Woman denied work with all-male decorating team.)

[68] [2001] UKHL 48. See Ch.7, paras 7–007 and 7–009.

[69] For victimisation, see Ch.7.

If this reasoning were applied to direct discrimination, there would be no liability in cases in this category. This result cannot be squared with existing case law (such as the *Birmingham* grammar schools case, and *Ex p. Westminster City Council*), which was not expressly disapproved by the judges when making their comments. Nor can it be squared with the wording of the legislation, because in this category of cases, the *ground* of the treatment, which is express, was a protected ground. Further, focusing on *why* the defendant acted is to introduce a benign motive defence, which resembles the general justification defence belonging to *indirect* discrimination. The legislation does not permit that. The obvious solution is to confine the *Khan* decision to victimisation, and consider afresh what is meant by "subjective" and "discriminatory motive" in the context of direct discrimination.

Suppose now that "discriminatory motive" includes an awareness that one's action will differentiate on a protected ground.[70] This definition fulfils the policy and wording of the legislation. It will not catch cases where a defendant acts against a member of a protected group for an entirely separate matter (such as dismissal for theft, or non-hire for lack of necessary qualifications), because such an act contains no discriminatory element.

This accords with the case law in the United States, which insists upon a discriminatory motive for liability for direct discrimination (or "disparate treatment"), but recognises "benign motive" cases. For instance, a union was liable for disparate treatment of its black members for failing to challenge their employer's discriminatory practices, even though the union's stance was not based in racial prejudice, but in deference to its white membership, and/or to gain favour with the employer to achieve other goals.[71] Similarly, an employer was held to carry the requisite discriminatory motive when refusing to hire fertile women on health grounds.[72] The Supreme Court stated that: "[D]isparate treatment . . . does not depend on *why* the employer discriminates but rather on the explicit terms of the discrimination . . . The beneficence of an employer's purpose does not undermine the conclusion that an explicit gender-based policy is sex discrimination."[73] Customer preference cases are likewise treated as carrying the

---

[70] Even in the (criminal) law of murder, where the defendant faces far graver consequences, "intent" includes an awareness (barring some unforeseen intervention) that death or serious injury is a "virtual certainty" as a result of his action: *R. v Woollin* [1999] A.C. 82, HL.

[71] *Goodman v Lukens Steel* 482 US 656 (Sup Ct 1987).

[72] *United Automobile Workers v Johnson Controls* 499 US 187 (Sup Ct 1991). (Holding that decisions about the welfare of future children should be left to the parents.)

[73] *per* Blackmun J. *ibid.*, at 199–200. (Emphasis supplied.)

requisite discriminatory intent.[74] In affirmative action cases the Supreme Court has been more forthright, stating that "racial discrimination based on benign prejudice is just as noxious as discrimination inspired by malicious prejudice."[75]

4–021
Finally note that where a benign motive coincides with a specific defence provided by the legislation in any particular field of application (e.g. employment, education, provision of goods, facilities and services), there will be no liability. An obvious example would be employing only men to play male roles in a dramatic performance, the motive being authenticity.[76]

Thus, to accord with the wording and purpose of the legislation, "discriminatory motive" must include an awareness that one's action will differentiate on a protected ground, regardless of any alternative benign motive. As such, it does not differ from the *but for* test.

5. *"Cat's Paw" theory: The defendant acts upon discriminatory factors of which he is* not *aware.* Here an employer treats a worker less favourably in response to discriminatorily motivated, but facially neutral, acts by other workers. The *Shamoon* variation (offered above)[77] is an example of this, where male workers complain about a female supervisor because they do not like being subordinate to a woman, resulting in the supervisor being disciplined. Here there is a difference between the *but for* test and the subjective approach. Clearly the supervisor would not have been disciplined *but for* her sex. Yet there were no discriminatory factors in the employer's mind when acting. In the US, despite the "discriminatory motive" doctrine, courts have developed an "imputed intent" or "cat's paw" theory for cases like this. In *Shager v Upjohn*,[78] Shager's supervisor (aged 38) was hostile to Shager (aged 53) because of his age. The supervisor influenced the hiring committee, who were unaware of Shager's age, to dismiss Shager. He was replaced

---

[74] *Diaz v Pan Am* 442 F 2d 385 (5th Cir 1971), certiorari denied, 404 US 950 (1971). (Preference for (female) air stewardesses.)

[75] *Adarand Constructors v Pena* 515 US 200, at 241 (1995), a constitutional challenge under the equal protection clause of the Fifth Amendment. See further Ch.12, para.12–020.

[76] For (unsuccessful) arguments that a "benign" motive constituted a Bone Fide Occupation Requirement defence under the US legislation, see, *United Automobile Workers v Johnson Controls* 499 US 187 (1991) and *Diaz v Pan Am* 442 F 2d 385 (5th Cir 1971), certiorari denied, 404 US 950 (1971).

[77] See para.4–010.

[78] 913 F 2d 398 (7th Cir 1990); see also *Russell v McKinney Hosp* 235 3 F 3d 219, at 227 (5th Cir 2000); *Griffin v Washington Convention Centre* 142 F 3d 1308, at 1312 (DC Cir 1998); *Burlington Ind v Ellerth* 524 US 742, at 762 (Sup Ct 1998).

with a younger worker. It was held that the committee had acted as a conduit—or "cat's paw"—for the supervisor's prejudice, and so the employer was liable for direct age discrimination. The features of this theory are that the prejudiced subordinate has influence over the decision-maker and so "poisons the well"[79] from which that decision-maker draws his knowledge. It is yet to be seen if this theory takes hold in the UK. The sentiment of the judges' "subjective" comments point to rejection of the theory. But if analysed as imputed intent, or a variation of vicarious liability, it is not such a big leap from that sentiment to be unthinkable, and it would serve the policy of the legislation. The "cat's paw" theory shows that for this category of cases, the *but for* test can be reconciled with the subjective approach. In these cases, the "ground" of the treatment is a protected ground, and as such, defendants should be liable.

6. *Honest, but mistaken, belief.* Where the treatment of a person of   **4–022**
a protected group is for an entirely non-discriminatory reason, (such as standard dismissal for theft, or non-recruitment for lack of necessary qualifications) there is no liability. However, similar cases arise where there is evidence of discrimination, and the defendant held an honest, but *mistaken*, belief that he acted for a separate non-discriminatory reason. This is illustrated by two US cases. In *Pesterfield v TVA*[80] a worker's doctor wrote to the employer stating that the worker had a psychological disorder, but was fit to return to work. The employer misinterpreted the second part of this letter and, thinking he was *unfit* for work, refused to take the worker back. The worker's claim for disability discrimination failed because the employer had acted honestly, albeit mistakenly, for a non-discriminatory reason. In *McKnight v Kimberly Clark*,[81] a worker was dismissed because of an allegation of a sexual assault. There was evidence that the allegation was unfounded, and of hostility in the workplace to older workers, although the allegation was not motivated by age. The claim for age discrimination failed, because even if the allegation were untrue, the employer had acted upon an honest mistake. The US Circuits are divided on whether the employer's belief needs to be honest *and* reasonable, or

---

[79] *Sarate v Loop Transfer Inc* US Dist LEXIS 13170, at 12 (ND Ill 1997). See also the *obiter dictum* of the EAT in *Williams v YKK* [2003] All E.R. (D) 141 (Mar), (EAT/0408/01 AM, see *www.employmentappeals.gov.uk*), at para.23, that an unprejudiced manager's decision may be affected, or tainted, by a report made by a prejudiced supervisor.

[80] 941 F 2d 437, at 443–44 (6th Cir. 1991).

[81] 149 F 3d 1125, at 1129 (10th Cir 1998).

merely honest.[82] The difference between this category and the "cat's paw" cases (above) is that the non-discriminatory reason is not tainted, or "poisoned", with discrimination.

For the purpose of this discussion, these cases are clearer than they appear. There is obviously no discriminatory motive. Further, the *but for* test achieves the same result. Even in *Pesterfield's* case, where the letter and the protected ground were closely tied, it could not be concluded that *but for* his disability, he would have been retained.[83] The evidence suggested that even with his disability, he was "fit for work" and would have been retained. In *McKnight's* case it could not be said that he was dismissed *because of* his age, or *but for* his age he would not have been dismissed. So for these cases, there is no difference between the *but for* test and the subjective approach.

7. *The defendant is unaware that the claimant belongs to a protected group, but, on a protected ground, treats the claimant less favourably.* This category differs from the "honest mistake" cases (above) because the mistake here is not realising that the claimant *belonged* to a protected group. However, he holds a discriminatory motive in his mind. In *Simon v Brimham Associates,*[84] Mr Simon, a Jew, attended an interview with a firm of job consultants. When asked, he refused to disclose his religion. The interviewer then explained that the job was with an Arab company and those of the Jewish faith would not be selected. Mr Simon ended the interview there and then and claimed that he had been discriminated against. The industrial tribunal held that for there to be discrimination, it must be shown that the discriminator was aware of the claimant's race. The Court of Appeal disagreed in part, stating that it was a question of fact in each case and that such knowledge could be a factor. It agreed with the industrial tribunal that there had not been discrimination in this case. With respect to the Court of Appeal, its focus on the interview led it into a rather pointless discussion on whether this "treatment" was on the ground of Mr Simon's religion. The primary fact here is that the defendant would not employ Jews, and it is this treatment that should have been the focus of the discussion. The interview is merely evidence of the "no-Jews" policy. Once that is recognised, it

---

[82] See the discussion in *Smith v Chrysler* 155 F 3d 799 (6th Cir 1998) and R. Michaels "*Legitimate reasons for firing: must they be reasonable?*" 71 Fordham L Rev 2643 (2003).

[83] Under the UK definition of disability, "for a reason which relates to the disabled person's disability" (DDA 1995, s.3A(1)) the employer may have been liable if it could not justify the treatment. See Ch.11, para.11–028.

[84] [1987] I.C.R. 596 CA. See also above, para.4–006.

is clear that there is no difference between the *but for* test and the subjective approach. *But for*, his religion, Mr Simon would have been considered for the job. The employer intended to discriminate against Jews with its "no-Jews" policy. There can few clearer examples of discriminatory motive.

These seven variations of a direct discrimination claim show that the subjective approach can be reconciled with the *but test*, but in some instances, this is a rather artificial exercise. **4–023**

This discussion reveals that the subjective approach is open to variety of meanings. It is likely to cause confusion, especially in employment tribunals, where the panel may not have the benefit of (or the time for) long debates about its precise meaning, and is thus likely to produce more appeals. The *but for* test, properly applied, does not extend the law beyond its intended scope, and is relatively clear and simple. But it carries the risk of being improperly applied and is unsuitable for mixed ground cases. The better view is to stay true to the purpose and wording of the legislation, and ask simply, if the protected ground was a ground of the treatment. This question can resolve, correctly, and relatively simply, all seven of the categories listed above (liability in all but categories two and six). There is no need to venture into new notions and different language to express and resolve this question.

(3) Discrimination on a Third Party's Protected Ground and Perceived Discrimination

These two situations are drawn together because liability rests on the same drafting discrepancies between different grounds of discrimination. There is a broad definition (covering race and sexual orientation), a narrow definition (sex and age) and hybrid one (religion). **4–024**

(a) Race and Sexual Orientation

The legislation covering race and sexual orientation is drafted to outlaw discrimination "on racial grounds" or "on the grounds of" sexual orientation. This definition includes less favourable treatment on a *third party's* protected ground, and on a (mistakenly) perceived protected ground. "Third party" discrimination itself covers two scenarios: instructions to discriminate, and "association discrimination". In *Showboat Entertainment Centre Ltd v Owens*,[85] a white manager of an amusement centre was instructed by his employer to refuse admission to black youths. He declined to obey this order and **4–025**

---

[85] [1984] 1 All E.R. 836 EAT. See also above, para.4–011. Approved in *Weathersfield (t/a Van & Truck Rentals) v Sargent* [1999] I.C.R. 425, CA. (White woman resigned after instruction not to hire vehicles to "coloured and Asians.")

was dismissed. The EAT held that the instruction (plainly amounting to racial discrimination against any excluded black youths) constituted racial discrimination against the (white) manager.

"Association discrimination" occurs against someone for their association with a person from a protected group. Examples would include an employer refusing to hire a white woman because her husband is black,[86] or because her son is gay.

It can happen that a defendant discriminates against a person because he thinks, or perceives, incorrectly, that the person belongs to a protected group. For instance, an employer may reject a Asian, stereotyping her as a non-British national, or a straight man, thinking he is gay. The definition "on grounds of" in the legislation covering race and sexual orientation is broad enough to include these scenarios.

4–026   The broad definition produced an unintended consequence in *Redfearn v Serco (t/a West Yorkshire Transport Service)*,[87] where a driver, whose passengers were 70–80 per cent Asian, was dismissed for being a member of the British National Party (an all-white racist political party). The EAT held that as he was dismissed for his racial views, he was dismissed on racial grounds. The Court of Appeal reversed, but more on policy grounds than a logical interpretation of the Act. The policy objection, according to Mummery, L.J., was that the logical conclusion of Redfearn's argument was that an employer dismissing a worker for serious racial harassment would be treating him less favourably "on racial grounds", which was not the purpose of the Act.[88] This reasoning has force, but there is a difference between conduct at work and publicly held views which are not manifested at work. On the matter of strict interpretation, Mummery, L.J. found that Redferan was *not* dismissed on racial grounds. Instead, "he was dismissed on the ground of a particular non-racial characteristic shared by him with a tiny proportion of the white population, that is membership of . . . a political party like the BNP." He added, perhaps needlessly, that an employer could "apply the same approach to a member of a similar political party, which confined its membership to black people".[89] This is a fragile distinction from *Showboat v Owens*, and would come under further strain should a black worker be dismissed for being a member of an innocuous association, for instance, a Caribbean arts club. Of course, it cannot be the purpose of the statute to come to Redfearn's aid *because* he was an overt racist. And so the result, fulfilling a purposive interpretation, is palatable and correct, but it may save future embarrassments to redraft the definition specifying third party and perceived discrimination in similar

---

[86] See *Wilson v TB Steelwork* (1978) COIT 706/44 (See IDS Employment Law Handbook 48 (1990) p.9) IT.
[87] [2006] EWCA 659.
[88] *ibid.*, at 43.
[89] *ibid.*, at 47–49.

terms to religion or belief discrimination in the Equality Act 2006 (see below).

(b) Sex and Age

In contrast, the definition of direct discrimination in the Sex Discrimination Act 1975 and the Age Discrimination Regulations 2006[90] is drafted less generously, outlawing discrimination on the ground of *her* sex, gender assignment, marital status, or age, as the case may be. This excludes discrimination on the ground of a third party's protected ground and so does not cover, for example, a manager being disciplined for refusing to obey an instruction not to employ women, or married or older persons. However, if a person complains that he has been instructed to discriminate, he has effectively made an allegation of discrimination,[91] and if he has been less favourably treated because of this complaint, he may have an action under the victimisation provisions of the legislation.[92] But the victimisation provisions cannot be used in cases of "association discrimination", because, simply, there is no unlawful act about which to complain. And if there were, the complaint, coming after the act, would not be the cause of the less favourable treatment. Take for example an applicant refused a job because his brother is transsexual. The refusal itself, being "association discrimination", is not unlawful, and so any complaint about that could not attract the protection of the victimisation provisions.[93] And even if it could, the provisions only cover a *reaction* to the complaint, which of little use when the problem was the job refusal.

Whilst it is unlikely that a defendant will be mistaken over whether a victim is male or female, he may incorrectly perceive that a person is a transsexual, and discriminate on that basis. Such treatment falls outside of the statutory definition.

It is doubtful that the limited statutory definition is compatible with the relevant Directives, which employ the broader phrase "on grounds of" sex, or age.[94] When amending the SDA 1975, in response to the Equal Treatment Amendment Directive 2002/73/EC, the Government stated that there was no need to amend the domestic definition, for

4–027

---

[90] In force October 1, 2006.

[91] This is only because an instruction to discriminate is unlawful under s.39, although enforceable only by the Equal Opportunities Commission (s.72) or when operational (expected October 2007) the Commission for Equality and Human Rights (EA 2006, s.25). For instruction to discriminate, see Ch.5, para.5–029.

[92] See Ch.7. In addition, where an employee discloses unlawful discriminatory behaviour in certain circumstances, there may be protection under the Public Interest Disclosure Act 1998, the Act designed to protect whistleblowers.

[93] *Waters v Commissioner of Police of the Metropolis* [1997] I.C.R. 1073, CA, discussed Ch.7, para.7–005.

[94] Respectively, Equal Treatment Directive 76/207/EEC, Art.2(2); Employment Equality Directive 2000/78/EC, Art.2(2)(a).

two reasons. The first was that the Government "did not consider" that the phrasing of the Equal Treatment Directive was chosen deliberately. For this, it relied on "some other language versions" that used the possessive adjective—"en raison de son sexe" in the French version for example.[95] As the Government state, only some versions took this line, which means others did not,[96] and makes it just as likely that the French and UK versions are wrong. The second reason was that those who are instructed to discriminate may have an action for victimisation.[97] But this does not account for those who cannot use the victimisation provisions,[98] and falls short of the Directive's general edict that there shall be no discrimination "whatsoever" on the ground of sex. This is also a rather clumsy way of implementing Art.2(4) or either the Equal Treatment or Employment Equality Directive 2000/78/EC, which outlaws expressly "instructions to discriminate". Victimisation focuses on the employer's *retribution*, rather than the instruction itself.

(c) Religion or Belief

4–028 The third, hybrid, definition, arises in religion or belief discrimination. The problem for the draftsman was that the standard formula (on the grounds of religion or belief) had the potential to cover the scenario where an employer discriminates because of his *own* religion and consequently, for instance, refuses to hire homosexuals (a matter appropriate for the Sexual Orientation Regulations 2003). Thus the original version contained a rider excluding the discriminator's religion or belief (Religion or Belief Regulations 2003, reg.3(2)). The problem with this rider is that it may exclude discrimination against all non-adherents to the employer's religion, for instance a Christian business refusing to employ all non-believers.[99] An applicant who does not adhere to the employer's religion because of his own religion or belief should be covered, even if his belief is atheism. However, where an applicant has no particular belief it seems there is no liability, and so for instance, an employer with a strongly held religious belief would not be liable for discriminating against an agnostic. This is because the victim has no "belief" and the discrimination is on the ground of the employer's religion.

---

[95] See the Government's consultation paper, "*Equality and Diversity: Updating the Sex Discrimination Act*", 2005 (URN 05/503) p.41, para.131. Available at *www.dti.gov.uk/publications*.

[96] See e.g., the Polish, Dutch, Italian and Spanish versions.

[97] "Equality and Diversity: Updating the Sex Discrimination Act. Government Response to Consultation", 2005 (URN 05/1345) p.30, para.13.6. Available at *www.dti.gov.uk/publications*.

[98] Discussed Ch.7.

[99] See M. Rubenstein, *Is lack of belief protected?* (2004) 128 EOR. In the US case *EEOC v Townley Engineering* 859 F 2d 610 (9th Cir 1988) the employer made "a covenant with God" that the company would be a "would be a Christian, faith-operated business" and insisted that employees attend a weekly devotional service. It was held that this discriminated against an atheist, but there was no discussion on whether such an employer would be similarly liable to an agnostic.

A new version, introduced by the Equality Act 2006[100] resolves this by including expressly a "lack of" religion or belief within the protection, and reformulating the definition of direct discrimination thus:

> [A] person ("A") discriminates against another person ("B") if— on the grounds of the religion or belief of B or of any other person except A (whether or not it is also A's religion or belief) A treats B less favourably than he treats or would treat other persons.

Either formula covers "third party" discrimination, so, for instance, it is unlawful to dismiss a worker because her father is a Muslim convert. But for perceived discrimination, there exists a further discrepancy, this time between the amended formula for employment matters the one for other fields. The latter includes a provision for perceived discrimination: "a reference to a person's religion or belief includes a reference to a religion or belief to which he is thought to belong or subscribe".[101] This has not been done for the amended formula for employment matters. So the amendments, as they stand, mean that it is unlawful for a shopkeeper to refuse to serve a customer because the shopkeeper mistakenly perceives the customer to be of a certain religion. However, it is *lawful* for an employer to dismiss an Asian thinking (incorrectly) that he is a Muslim, or to dismiss a gentile, thinking (incorrectly) that he is a Jew.

4. DIRECT DISCRIMINATION AND STEREOTYPING

(1) Stereotyping and Less Favourable Treatment
It must not be assumed that stereotyping alone is enough for liability.   **4–029**
It must operate to treat the claimant *less* favourably than the comparator. It is possible, theoretically at least, for a defendant to stereotype both claimant and comparator, and thus treat them equally. This is illustrated vividly in the dress code cases, discussed below.[102] Another example might be an employer insisting that male workers are aggressive, and females feminine. However, where the employer, in addition, demands, say, aggressiveness for a particular post, it is treating women less favourably.[103]

---

[100] Inserted by EA 2006, s.77. For fields other than employment, see: EA 2006, ss.44–45, expected in force October, 2006.

[101] EA 2006, s.45(2), expected in force October, 2006.

[102] See below para.4–032.

[103] See the US case *Price Waterhouse v Hopkins* 490 US 228 (1989), below, para.4–030.

(2) Stereotyping on the Protected Ground

4–030   Less favourable treatment based upon a stereotype can be unlawful where the stereotype relates to a protected ground. In *Alexander v Home Office*[104] a prisoner was refused (preferable) work in the prison kitchen. The prison assessment stated: "He displays the usual traits associated with people of his ethnic background being arrogant, suspicious of staff, anti-authority, devious and possessing a very large chip on his shoulder . . . that seems too common in most coloured inmates." The trial judge held that the prisoner had been treated not as an individual, but as a racial stereotype. Other examples of racial stereotyping amounting to direct discrimination include: a refusal to let out a hall for a Pakistani wedding, because of problems over payment from previous Asian hirers;[105] a garage refusing to re-spray a car for a black person because the proprietor thought that black people always haggled over the price;[106] and a ban on West Indians from the Hammersmith Palais, following a brawl involving some black youths. In this last case, the judge stated that the licensee ". . . has to bring his judgment to bear upon the individuals as such as distinct from being of a particular colour, race or ethnic origin."[107]

Although these were race discrimination cases, the principle applies to other protected grounds. The leading US case is *Price Waterhouse v Hopkins*[108] where Ann Hopkins, a successful senior manager, was refused a partnership, a position that required aggressiveness. However, partners were on record describing her as "overly aggressive" and "macho", and one advised her to "walk more femininely, talk more femininely, dress more femininely, wear make-up, have her hair styled, and wear jewelry."[109] The Supreme Court held that that stereotyping such as this could be evidence that the refusal was based on sex.[110] In Australia, it was held that a bar on those aged over 28 to become military pilots was based on a stereotype that older candidates would not be fit enough, and as such amounted to age discrimination.[111]

4–031   Claims will encounter a technical problem where defendants have stereotyped *some*, but not all, of the protected group, because of an additional factor. An example would be a refusal to recruit women with young children, on the assumption that they are unreliable. The

---

[104] [1988] 2 All E.R. 118, at 120h, CA.

[105] *Hussain v Canklow Community Centre* CRE Report 1980, p.85, Leeds County Court.

[106] *Race Relations Board v Botley Motor Vehicle Repairs* CRE Report 1977, p.118 Westminster County Court.

[107] *Race Relations Board v Mecca Ltd (Hammersmith Palais)* RRB Report 1974 p.39, Westminster County Court (Judge Ruttle).

[108] 490 US 228 (1989).

[109] *ibid.,* at 235.

[110] Accordingly, some lower courts have held that stereotyping gay men can amount to discrimination on the ground of their *sex* (Federal law does not expressly cover sexual orientation): *Nichols v Azteca* 256 F 3d 864 (9th Cir 2002). Similar logic was used in the sexual harassment case, *Smith v Gardener Merchant* [1999] I.C.R. 134 CA, discussed at paras 3–014 and 5–023.

[111] *Commonwealth of Australia v Human Rights and Equal Opportunity Commission* (Bradley) 60 ALD 157 (1999) Fed Ct of Aus.

protected ground is sex; the additional factor is having young children. Defendants may argue that as they have made assumptions about only *some* women, the refusal to hire only those women was not based on sex. However, the approach taken by the courts is to include the additional factor in the comparison, and so defeat the argument. In *Horsey v Dyfed CC*,[112] Mrs Horsey was obliged by her job with a county council in Wales to take a course at any British University, and then return to work for at least two years. She chose Kent University so that she may reside with her husband, who had just obtained work in nearby London. The Council refused her request, assuming that she would not return to work in Wales, preferring to be with her husband. The EAT held this was discrimination because the refusal was based on a stereotype that women follow their husbands' jobs, and not vice versa. Browne-Wilkinson, J. stated: "In our view . . . the tribunal has to compare the treatment of Mrs Horsey with the treatment which would have been afforded to a married man."[113] The evidence that the council would have treated a man differently was its assumption that Mr Horsey would refuse to follow his wife back to Wales.[114] In *Hurley v Mustoe*[115] the employer dismissed Mrs Hurley, who had four young children, because in his experience women with young children were unreliable. Again, this was held to be less favourable treatment. In *Skyrail v Coleman*[116] a female worker became engaged to a worker at a rival travel agents. The two employers, both of whom were worried about the leaking of confidential information, got together and decided that the female worker should be dismissed after the marriage, on the basis that she was not the "breadwinner." The Court of Appeal held that "the dismissal of a woman based on an assumption that men are more likely than women to be the primary supporters of their spouses and children can amount to discrimination under the Act of 1975."[117] In the United States, this approach has been conceptualised as "sex-plus" theory, where the sex of the claimant, plus a factor, is the cause of the less favourable treatment.[118]

Finally note that employers who assume that women are unable, or less able, to perform jobs with physical demands will directly discriminate if they refuse bluntly to employ women for such jobs. Such an

---

[112] [1982] I.C.R. 755, EAT.

[113] *ibid.*, at 761.

[114] In fact, the council had overlooked that Mr Horsey had in the past twice followed his wife's job.

[115] [1981] I.C.R. 490, EAT.

[116] [1981] I.C.R. 864.

[117] *ibid.*, at 871.

[118] See *Phillips v Martin Marietta Corp* 400 US 542 (1971) where an employer hired fathers with pre-school age children, but rejected mothers with pre-school age children. Otherwise, it hired workers of either sex, without discrimination. The Supreme Court found this could amount to direct discrimination despite the employer showing that 75–80 per cent of recruits were women. The unlawful discrimination was based on sex *plus* the factor of being the parent of a young child.

employer should instead identify the physical demands and specify the requirements in the job description. If the specification has a disproportionate impact on women, it may be challenged as *indirect* discrimination, giving the employer the opportunity to justify the specification. So it is essential that the employer can show that the need for the requirements is legitimate, and the requirements are appropriate and necessary to meet that need.[119]

5. Dress Codes for Men and Women at Work

4–032 Challenges to dress codes that treat male and female workers differently have been treated as special cases. Tribunals appear reluctant to interfere with a business's choice of image, yet they are bound by statute to compare the treatment afforded to each sex by a dress code. Courts have managed to give employers a large measure of discretion by taking a "package" approach to the comparison. Appearance codes are compared as a package, and not on an item-by-item basis. In *Smith v Safeway*,[120] a delicatessen assistant was dismissed because his pony-tail became too long to be contained under his hat. The rule for male employees insisted on: "Tidy hair not below shirt collar length. No unconventional hair styles or colouring." For women the equivalent provision stated: "Shoulder-length hair must be clipped back. No unconventional hair styles or colouring." The rule was not based on hygiene. Of course, Mr Smith's objection was that only women could keep long hair. But the Court of Appeal compared the hair codes as a whole (tidiness, styling, colouring, as well as length) and ruled that that as the code applied conventional standards even-handedly, Safeway did not treat Mr Smith less favourably.[121]

A similar approach is taken in the United States.[122] Only if the requirements, taken as a whole, place an "unequal burden" upon one of the sexes, will it be challengeable. In *Jespersen v Harrah's Operating*

---

[119] See *FM Thorn v Meggit Engineering Ltd* [1976] I.R.L.R. 241 IT. In the US Supreme Court case, *Dothard v Rawlinson* 433 US 321 (1977), height and weight requirements designed to measure strength were used in the recruitment of prison officers, but excluded 41 per cent of women in contrast to under one per cent of men. The employer had no evidence that the requirements were related to job performance, and so the claim of indirect discrimination succeeded. On indirect discrimination, see Ch.6.

[120] [1996] I.C.R. 868.

[121] The only UK exception to this approach appears to be *McConomy v Croft Inns* [1992] I.R.L.R. 561 where the High Court of Northern Ireland held that a ban by a bar on male customers wearing earrings was unlawful sex discrimination, under the equivalent of SDA 1975, s.29 (see Ch.10, para.10–009). Although the bar operated a "smart" dress code for both sexes, the court did not adopt a "package" approach. The case pre-dates *Smith v Safeway*, and perhaps more significantly, was not an employment complaint, suggesting that for dress codes the courts may be more generous to employers than to providers of goods, facilities, or services.

[122] On US dress codes see, K. Bartlett, "*Only girls wear barrettes*" 92 Mich L Rev 2541; K. Klare, "*Power/Dressing: Regulation of employee appearance*" 26 New Eng L Rev 1395.

Company[123] a casino required staff to be "well groomed, appealing to the eye, be firm and body toned, and be comfortable with maintaining this look while wearing the specified uniform" and in addition, women had to wear stockings and coloured nail polish, and wear their hair "teased, curled, or styled," whilst men were barred from wearing makeup or coloured nail polish, and were required to keep short hair-cuts and neatly trimmed fingernails. Ms Jespersen's complaint that having to wear make-up was discriminatory was rejected as the code placed an equal burden on men and women.

This approach is open to criticism on two fronts. First, technically, it is questionable. Second, its application has been over-generous to employers. First, it is unlikely in other cases of direct discrimination that the courts would entertain the package approach. If say, in *Gill v El Vino*[124] the wine bar served only men at the bar, but gave *only* women table service, Ms Gill's claim of sex discrimination still would have succeeded. She was deprived of a choice which she, reasonably, valued. Similarly, if a sports centre offered free swimming only to women, but free badminton only to men, a man could claim direct discrimination: that men get free badminton is no consolation to man who wishes to swim.[125] It is also a striking departure from the established approach to equal pay claims, where pay and benefits must be compared on an item-by-item basis, and *not* as a package. It is no defence to say that a women does just as well as her male comparator because although her pay is less, her dinner breaks are longer.[126] There is, of course, a distinction between these examples and the dress code cases, where relevant differences between men and women may be a factor for appearances. But differences between men and women has not prevented the courts, albeit via a torturous route,[127] from concluding that pregnancy discrimination *is* sex discrimination.[128] An item-by-item approach for dress codes need not lead to absurd results, such as compulsory cross-dressing. For instance, a code requiring men to wear a smart shirt and trousers, and women to wear a smart blouse and skirt, may be treating them *differently*, but could not be said to be treating men *less favourably* than women.

Second, although the package approach favours employers, it should not give them unfettered discretion. The codes, as a whole, should treat the sexes even-handedly, or, in the statutory language, no "less favourably" than each other. Unfortunately, tribunals have been

4–033

---

[123] 392 F 3d 1076 (9th Cir 2004).

[124] [1983] Q.B. 425, CA. See above, para.4–006.

[125] This point was made by Wintemute: see R. Wintemute, "*Recognising new kinds of direct sex discrimination: transsexualism, sexual orientation and dress codes*" (1997) 60 M.L.R. 334, pp.354–55.

[126] See *Hayward v Cammell Laird (No 2)* [1988] A.C. 894 HL (discussed below, Ch.9, para.9–041).

[127] See *Hayes v Malleable Working Men's Club* [1985] I.C.R. 703, where an EAT compared the treatment afforded to a pregnant woman, to that afforded to a sick man, which is itself, a form of "package" approach. See further, below, para.4–037.

[128] *Webb v EMO Cargo* Case C-32/93, [1994] E.C.R. I-3567, ECJ.

very slack with this question. Two examples will suffice to illustrate this. In *Schmidt v Austicks Bookshops Ltd*[129] the claimant was required to wear a skirt at work, and while serving the public, to wear overalls. The only restriction on men was a ban on tee-shirts. The EAT dismissed the overalls complaint as too trivial to amount to a "detriment" within s.6,[130] and held (on the skirt issue) that Schmidt had been treated no less favourably than male workers. In *Cootes v John Lewis Plc*[131] female sales staff were required to wear a uniform of a polyester blue suit with a green blouse, whilst male equivalents had to wear a dark suit and tie. The EAT held that the codes treated the sexes even-handedly, despite Ms Cootes' arguments that: (1) she objected to the polyester; (2) the male suits marked men out as more senior; and (3) the uniform marked her out in public (commuting and at lunchtimes) as a member of the sales staff.

It is clear in both these cases that the codes treated women less favourably than the men. Tribunals avoid this seemingly obvious result by applying *Smith v Safeway's* test: did the code apply conventional standards even-handedly? Exchange the word "conventional" for "stereotypical" and the test is debunked. At their heart, both decisions are based on stereotypes of women in the workplace. One commentator noted: "*Schmidt* permits employers to reinforce, through dress codes, the very stereotypes of 'male' (serious, responsible, mature) and 'female' (decorative handmaidens) which disadvantage women at work."[132] Further, allowing employers this amount of discretion is, in many cases, pandering to customer preference, a notion ordinarily rejected in direct discrimination.[133] Some courts in the United States have held codes based on stereotypes to amount to direct discrimination. In *Carroll v Talman Federal Savings and Loan Association of Chicago*[134] female staff were obliged to wear a uniform, whilst equivalent males only had to wear customary business attire, which could be a suit, a sport jacket and trousers, or even a "leisure suit", as long as it was worn with a shirt and tie. The court held that this different treatment was demeaning to women because it suggested that the men were more senior. Moreover, the code suggested that only men were able to choose suitable business attire, which was an "offensive stereotype."[135] Similarly, in *Frank v United*

---

[129] [1978] I.C.R. 85, EAT.

[130] A necessary ingredient for this employment claim. See Ch.8, para.8–015.

[131] EAT/1414/00, (Transcript) February 27, 2001.

[132] A. McColgan, *Discrimination Law*, 2005, Oxford: Hart, p.483. See also *Burrett v West Birmingham HA* (EAT/1414/00, (Transcript) 27 Feb 2001) where a female nurse complained (unsuccessfully) that a rule that female nurses wear headgear, whilst male nurses wear a jacket with epaulettes, stereotyped the sexes.

[133] See *R. v Birmingham CC Ex p. EOC* [1989] 1 A.C. 1155, *per* Lord Goff, at 1194, discussed above, para.4–015.

[134] 604 F 2d 1028 (7th Cir 1979), certiorari denied 445 US 929 (1980).

[135] *ibid.*, at 1033. In fact, the employer argued: "the selection of . . . clothing on the part of women is not a matter of business judgment. It is a matter of taste, a matter of what the other

Airlines[136] a policy of subjecting women to more onerous weight requirements than men was held to be a discriminatory appearance code. Accordingly, the Court in *Jespersen* (above) suggested that if an appearance code imposed an unequal burden on women because of the expense and time in buying and applying make-up, it could be unlawful.[137]

In both the UK and US, challenges by men required to keep their **4–034** hair short have repeatedly failed.[138] Although the British courts characterise such a requirement as imposing no more than "conventional" standards, they are just another stereotype, this time, that men with long hair—but not women—do not appear either authoritative, smart, presentable, or hygienic, as the case may be. Further, by adhering to the "conventional standards" rubric, courts are, at best, applying a purely objective test, which is a departure from the usual approach, which is to ask whether the *claimant*, reasonably, perceived the treatment as less favourable.[139] Unlike most dress codes, short hair is an appearance that the worker must take home with him into his private and social life.[140] Just as a person reasonably may value a poor job reference,[141] a grammar school place,[142] or service at the bar,[143] he may, just as reasonably (at the least), value his choice of appearance in his private and social life.

In dress code cases, the approach should be to make an item-by-item comparison, and ask whether a particular sex has been treated *less* favourably (rather than just differently). Consideration should be given to the complainant's reasonably held perception, and exclude unnecessary complications of conventions and stereotypes. This approach will not lead to absurdities (such as men being required to wear skirts or blouses), nor will it inhibit employers from presenting a

---

women are wearing, what fashion is currently. When we get into that realm . . . problems develop. Somehow, the women who have excellent business judgment somehow follow the fashion, and the slit-skirt fashion which is currently prevalent . . . They tend to follow those (fashions) and they don't seem to equate that with a matter of business judgment." (*ibid.*)

[136] 216 F 3d 845 (9th Cir 2000).

[137] Ms Jesperson produced academic evidence of the expense to women of the make-up requirement, but no evidence of the expense to men of their requirements, so no comparison could be made: 392 F 3d 1076, at 1081 (9th Cir 2004).

[138] See *Smith v Safeway* [1995] I.C.R. 472 CA (above); *Fuller v Mastercare Service & Distribution* EAT/0707/00, (Transcript) September 24, 2001. In the US, see *Willingham v Macon Telegraph Publishing Co* 507 F 2d 1084 (5th Cir 1975) (hair length not immutable); and more recently see *Harper v Blockbuster* 139 F 3d 1385 (11th Cir 1998) certiorari denied 525 US 1000 (1998), and the cases cited within.

[139] See "What is 'Less' Favourable" above, para.4–006.

[140] *Quaere* is such an interpretation of the SDA 1975 an interference with a man's private life and thus incompatible with the ECHR, either under Art.8 alone (right to a private life), or in combination with Art.14 (rights must be secured without discrimination)? *Cf Kara v UK* 27 E.H.R.R. CD 272, where a claim that a "cross-dressing" ban breached Arts 8, 10 and 14 was ruled inadmissible by the Commission. On the ECHR and discrimination, see Ch.2, para.2–005.

[141] *Chief Constable of West Yorkshire v Khan* [2002] 1 W.L.R. 1947, HL

[142] *R. v Birmingham City Council Ex p. EOC* [1989] A.C. 1155, CA and HL. See para.4–006, above.

[143] *Gill v El Vino* [1983] Q.B. 425, CA. See para.4–006.

particular image of their choice, so long as it is not based on sexual stereotypes.

6. DIRECT DISCRIMINATION AND SEGREGATION—RACE ONLY

4–035 Section 1(2) of the Race Relations Act 1976 (RRA 1976) provides that "segregating a person from other persons on grounds of race is treating him less favourably than they are treated." There are no parallel provisions for the other protected grounds. In the White Paper *Racial Discrimination* the Government adopted the observation of the Race Relations Board that "[F]or a time segregation may represent a form of accommodation acceptable to all, but if it hardens into patterns, tensions and conflicts will occur when pressures to change that pattern arise."[144] The inspiration for this is was the US Supreme Court's seminal decision in *Brown v Board of Education,*[145] holding that "separate but equal" segregated schooling was unconstitutional.

In *Pel Ltd v Modgill*[146] a paint shop in a factory was staffed solely by Asians. Originally, there had been white workers there as well. However, over the years as vacancies arose they were filled by friends or relatives of the Asians through word of mouth; the personnel department did no recruiting. The paint spray work was the dirtiest in the factory and the Asians complained of segregation under the RRA 1976. The EAT held that in the absence of a policy to segregate, there was no segregation unlawful under the Act. In effect, the EAT is holding that there must be a *positive* act of segregation by the defendant, to fall within the statutory definition. In this case, the employer merely *acquiesced* in the segregation. As well as being contrary to the sentiment expressed in the White Paper, this interpretation of the Act carries technical problems. On the face of it, the word employed by the Act "segregating" is a verb, suggesting that there must be some positive act by the defendant. However, s.78 provides that for the purposes of the RRA 1976, an act includes a deliberate omission. And clearly, in this case, segregation arose as a result of the company's deliberate omissions. The simple "non-intervention" of the personnel office is a powerful weapon in the workplace.[147]

Note that all parties in this case referred to the job of working in the paint shop as "the dirtiest in the factory". That should not matter when s.1(2) provides that segregating, *in itself* amounts to less favourable treatment.

---

[144] Cmnd 6234, para.62.
[145] 347 US 483 (1954).
[146] *Ftatu v Modgill; Pel Ltd v Modgill* [1980] I.R.L.R. 142, EAT.
[147] For the difficulties of analysing cases of large scale "passive" segregation, see the US case *Wards Cove v Atonio* 490 US 642 (1989), discussed in Ch.8, para.6–008.

Since the introduction of a new definition of indirect discrimination, the *Pel* decision, on its facts, may become obsolete. Under the new definition, indirect discrimination can occur when an apparently neutral "provision, criterion, or practice" (replacing "requirement or condition") has a discriminatory effect. Hence, where it puts the claimant's group at a disadvantage, word-of-mouth hiring may challengeable as a discriminatory practice. Word-of-mouth hiring as indirect discrimination is discussed Ch.6 at para.6–011.

7. DIRECT DISCRIMINATION AND PREGNANCY

The main issues relating to pregnancy discrimination have arisen in the employment field. European Community employment rights law is now dominant here. There are two strands of this law. The first holds that adverse treatment on the ground of pregnancy amounts to direct sex discrimination under the Equal Treatment Directive 76/207/EEC, or in some cases under EC Treaty, Art.141 (equal pay). The second provides rights to pregnant workers, irrespective of discrimination. These rights include maternity leave, pay, and special health and safety measures.[148] **4–036**

(1) Pregnancy Discrimination as Direct Sex Discrimination

Section 3A, Sex Discrimination Act 1975, was recently inserted to codify the case law on pregnancy discrimination in employment and vocational training. It provides that it is unlawful, during her pregnancy and maternity leave[149] to treat less favourably a woman on the ground of her pregnancy, or maternity leave entitlement. The notable feature is that the treatment must be on the ground of pregnancy, not sex. Thus, there is no need for a male comparator. Any comparison should be with a non-pregnant person. As such, this is a departure from the *sex* discrimination model and a recognition that pregnancy is itself a protected ground. The history of the case law that brought about this position is tortured and complex. **4–037**

The heart of the problem is that *sex* discrimination law is unable to address properly *pregnancy* discrimination. The equal treatment model, being symmetrical, demands a comparison between the treatment given to the woman, and that which would have been given to a man in the same circumstances.[150] Of course, as men do not get pregnant, this comparison is impossible for these cases. Accordingly, back

---

[148] For an example of pregnancy discrimination being contrary to common law in the US, see *Thibodeau v Design Group One Architect,* 260 Conn 691 (2002), and further, Ch.2, para.2–013.
[149] See below, para.4–041.
[150] See above Ch.1, para.1–005.

in 1980, the EAT in *Turley v Allders Department Stores Ltd*,[151] held that a claim of sex discrimination on the ground of pregnancy must inevitably fail, for want of a comparator. The next stage in the evolution of this law came in 1985, when the EAT in *Hayes v Malleable Working Men's Club and Institute*[152] used a "sick man" as a comparator. Apart from the obvious absurdity of this proposition, it carries practical problems. Employers may escape liability by showing that they treat their sick male workers equally *badly,* for instance, with a policy of dismissing workers after four weeks' absence. This defence becomes truly poisonous to discrimination law if used by typical sweatshop employers with an all-female workforce. These employers cannot bring a real comparator into court, only a hypothetical one. A tribunal will have the somewhat dubious task of deciding how a sweatshop employer might treat male workers; the evidence being how badly it treats its female workers.

   The law was salvaged in 1991 by the ECJ, when in *Dekker*[153] it held that as only women become pregnant, discrimination on the ground of pregnancy is direct sex discrimination. No comparison with a man is necessary. This rather crude approach ignores the niceties of symmetry, but achieves the purpose of the legislation. What sets apart pregnancy cases from other cases of direct discrimination is (1) that there is no requirement for a comparison, and (2) to a certain degree, at least, the treatment need only be *related* to the pregnancy.[154]

4–038   Since *Dekker* the story has been about the circumstances in which an employer can escape liability when the different treatment was for a reason *related to* the pregnancy, such as absence, or illness. The first issue is whether the treatment is on the ground of pregnancy or unavailability. In *Webb v EMO Air Cargo (UK) Ltd*[155] the claimant—who was hired on an indefinite basis, but initially to replace a worker on maternity leave—was dismissed because *she* became pregnant a few weeks into the job. The ECJ held that this was direct sex discrimination.[156] When the case returned to the UK, Lord Keith suggested that

---

[151] [1980] I.C.R. 6, EAT. In the US Supreme Court a majority held that a distinction "between pregnant and nonpregnant persons" was not one based on sex, as there were "nonpregnant" women. (*General Electric v Gilbert* 429 US 125 (1976), 134–135). The position was remedied by the (non-symmetrical) Pregnancy Discrimination Act 1978, which amended s.701, Title VII with a new subs.(k), (USC s.2000e(k)).

[152] [1985] I.C.R. 703.

[153] *Dekker v Stichting Vormingscentrum voor Jonge Volwassen (VJV-Centrum) Plus* Case C-177/88, [1990] E.C.R. I–3941.

[154] It has been argued that pregnancy discrimination is better viewed as a species of indirect sex discrimination. See R. Wintemute, "When is pregnancy discrimination indirect sex discrimination?" (1998) 27 I.L.J. 23. In response, it was argued that it is *neither* direct or indirect sex discrimination, and that there should be a separate Pregnancy Discrimination Act, as well as legislation providing pregnant women positive benefits: S. Honeyball, (2000) 29 I.L.J. 43.

[155] Case C-32/93 [1994] I.R.L.R. 482, ECJ.

[156] Thus in *Abbey National v Formoso* [1999] I.R.L.R. 222, the EAT held that a dismissal of a woman unable to attend her disciplinary hearing because she was on maternity leave, amounted to sex discrimination.

this left an exception whereby an employer could refuse to hire pregnant women for a short-term fixed contract where she would unavailable for the duration of that contract.[157] However, the ECJ went some way to denying that possibility in *Tele Danmark v Brandt-Nielson.*[158] It ruled that it makes no difference whether the contract was fixed or indefinite. "In either case the woman's inability to perform her contract of employment is due to pregnancy."[159] The question for the ECJ was whether the woman's inability to perform a *substantial part* of the contract made any difference. Unfortunately for the sake of clarity, the ECJ did not extend its answer beyond this to the situation where a woman is unavailable to perform the *whole* of the contract, because of her pregnancy. However, the ECJ underpinned its ruling by noting that there were no exceptions for fixed-term contracts in the relevant legislation and that fixed-term contracts may be terminated, renewed or extended, thus resembling indefinite contracts.[160] This observation— that it is not possible to predict the length of an employment contract—suggests that there cannot be such an exception, but the question remains undecided.

The next issue, which is related to the last one, is whether there is liability when the worker fails to disclose that she is pregnant at the time of her recruitment. Here the ECJ has been trenchant and held that women are under no obligation to disclose their pregnancy at recruitment, even if she knows that she will not be able to perform a substantial part of the contract.[161] The ECJ took the same view where a woman requested an early return from parental leave, knowing that her (new) pregnancy would prevent her from performing her all her duties.[162] In these cases, the ECJ reasons, dismissal is because of the pregnancy, and as such amounts to direct sex discrimination.

The third issue is whether adverse treatment for a pregnancy-related illness amounts to discrimination. The ECJ has held that *dismissal* for unavailability (caused by the pregnancy-related illness) during the pregnancy and any period of subsequent maternity leave, amounts to discrimination on the ground of pregnancy, and so amounts to direct sex discrimination.[163] However, if the pregnancy-related illness persists beyond the maternity leave, or if the illness during pregnancy or maternity is *not* pregnancy-related, then the dismissal must be compared with the treatment that would have been afforded to a male

---

[157] *Webb v EMO Air Cargo (UK) Ltd (No.2)* [1995] I.R.L.R. 645, at 647–648, HL.
[158] *Tele Danmark v HK (acting for Brandt-Nielson)* Case C-109/00, [2001] ECR I-6993, ECJ.
[159] *ibid.*, at para.31.
[160] *ibid.*, at para.32.
[161] *ibid.*, at para.34.
[162] *Busch v Klinikum Neustadt GmbH* Case C-320/01, [2003] I-02041, ECJ.
[163] *Brown v Rentokil* Case C-399/96 [1998] I.C.R. 790, at para.26. Nowadays, Art.10, Pregnant Workers Directive 92/85/EEC, moves the emphasis towards the protection of pregnant workers, by prohibiting their dismissal from the start of the pregnancy to the end of the maternity leave, *save in exceptional circumstances not connected with her condition.*

comparator.[164] It follows from the Court's reasoning, that any less favourable treatment short of dismissal (except in relation to pay, see below),[165] during pregnancy or maternity leave, because of a pregnancy-related illness, also will amount to sex discrimination. This has been confirmed by an amendment to the Equal Treatment Directive.[166]

4–039   It is clear from the above that there can liability for discrimination *related* to pregnancy. This resembles disability-related discrimination established by the Disability Discrimination Act 1995.[167] It suggests that that where the pregnancy is one step removed from the employer's act, the employer can be liable when he is unaware of the pregnancy. In a disability discrimination case, Heinz *v Kendrick*[168] Lindsay, J. suggested obiter:

> "If a woman was, for example, sacked for repeatedly falling faint one morning over the machinery at which she worked or over her food production line, would she not, objectively regarded, have been dismissed for 'a reason *connected with* her pregnancy' if she was able to demonstrate at the hearing that it had been her pregnancy that had made her faint, even if both she and the employer had thought at the time that she had fainted because she had been out clubbing too late the night before?"

Another scenario might be absenteeism because of a pregnancy related illness, where the women may not be telling her employer of her pregnancy for fear of dismissal. In *Ramdoolar v Bycity Ltd*[169] a pregnant women was dismissed because she was unable to carry out routine tasks and occasionally was late for work. The employer was unaware that she was pregnant. The worker claimed using the Maternity and Parental Leave Regulations 1999,[170] which specify that a dismissal "connected to" a worker's pregnancy is an automatically unfair dismissal. The EAT declined to follow Lindsay, J.'s opinion and held that for liability the employer has to know of the pregnancy.

---

[164] *Larsson v Fotex Supermarket* Case C-400/95 [1997] E.C.R. I-2757, at paras 22–26. In *Caledonia Bureau v Caffrey* [1998] I.C.R. 603, a Scottish EAT held that post-natal depression arising during maternity leave, but persisting beyond that, was an illness related to pregnancy, so that the dismissal amounted to sex discrimination on the ground of pregnancy. This decision goes beyond the boundaries set in *Larsson, Brown,* and the Pregnant Workers Directive, and so cannot be supported by EC law.

[165] See para.4–042.

[166] Art.2(7): "Less favourable treatment of a woman related to pregnancy or maternity leave within the meaning of [the Pregnant Workers] Directive 92/85/EEC shall constitute discrimination within the meaning of this Directive." (Inserted by Art.1, Equal Treatment Amendment Directive 2002/73/EC, due in force October 5, 2005.)

[167] Discussed Ch.11, para.11–028.

[168] [2000] I.C.R. 491, at para.24, EAT.

[169] [2005] I.C.R. 368, at paras 23–24.

[170] SI 1999/3312, reg.20. There is a small employer (less than six workers) exemption (reg.20(6)), which the Government plan to abolish in April 2007: "Equality and Diversity: Updating the Sex Discrimination Act. Government Response to Consultation", 2005 (URN 05/1345) p.30, para.4.22. Available at *www.dti.gov.uk/publications*.

Further, it was stated that an employer who was aware of the symptoms could not be fixed liability even if he *ought* to have known she was pregnant, (although an employer who *suspects* she was pregnant may be liable if he dismisses her to get her off the books before it is confirmed). This is going too far. It does not square even with the conventional view of direct discrimination, which holds that employers can be liable where they *ought* to have been aware that they were acting on discriminatory factors.[171]

4–040 The next issue is how far an employer may act to protect a pregnant, or breastfeeding, woman on health and safety grounds. Of course, the law here moves further away from the equal treatment model. It specifically *prohibits* employers from obliging these workers to do certain tasks.[172] More generally, the Equal Treatment Directive, Art.2(7) expressly allows employers to derogate from the discrimination principle for "the protection of women . . . particularly as regards pregnancy and maternity." The Pregnant Workers Directive 92/85/EC, passed ostensibly on health and safety grounds, requires employers to assess the risks to these workers, and make temporary adjustments to their work, or if not feasible, move them to another job, or if that is not feasible, grant them leave. A worker cannot be dismissed because it would be unsafe or unhealthy for her to do her work whilst pregnant or breastfeeding.[173] Within that limit, the rubric is proportionality.

An employer may not derogate merely out of a public concern for women's safety. In *Johnston v RUC*[174] the police force of Northern Ireland dismissed female police officers, to protect them from being assassination targets, even though both men and women were at risk. The ECJ held that the derogation must be specifically related to the "biological condition and the special relationship which exists between a woman and her child" which this was not.[175]

Finally, some employers may consider the *circumstances* of the pregnancy, rather than the pregnancy itself, as a reason to adversely treat a worker.[176] In *O'Neill v Governors of St Thomas More Roman Catholic School*[177] a school teacher of religious education and "personal relationships" became pregnant as the result of a relationship with a local Roman Catholic priest. When this became public, she was dismissed. The school argued that it was the paternity of the child

---

[171] See *King v Great Britain-China Centre* [1992] I.C.R. 516, CA, above, para.4–010, and the discussion at para.4–019.

[172] See e.g. Pregnant Workers Directive 92/85/EC, Art.6 (risk of specified exposure), Art.7 (night work).

[173] See *Silke-Karin Mahlburg v Land Mecklenburg-Vorpommern* Case C-207/98 2000 E.C.R. I-549, ECJ.

[174] Case 222/84, [1987] 1 Q.B. 129.

[175] *ibid.*, at para.40. But the ECJ held it was possible to derogate under Art.2(2) (now 2(6)) in special circumstances in Northern Ireland at the time.

[176] For a case on pregnancy or misconduct, see *Shomer v B and R Residential Lettings Ltd* [1992] I.R.L.R. 317, CA.

[177] [1997] I.C.R. 33, EAT.

and the adverse publicity that made her job untenable, and *not* her pregnancy *per se*; had the pregnancy occurred in other circumstances, she would not have been dismissed. The EAT rejected this argument, holding that the dismissal was related to the pregnancy and so amounted to discrimination on the ground of pregnancy, which was of course, direct sex discrimination.

It is clear from this case law that the ECJ has sanctioned a variation on the definition of direct discrimination, by recognising less favourable treatment *related to*, (rather than *on the ground of*) pregnancy. Unfortunately, SDA 1975, s.3A, employs the phrase *on the ground of*. The consequences are as follows. First, pregnancy-related illness is still covered because SDA 1975, s 3A(3)(b), includes this as a "ground". Second, domestic courts should give the phrase a broad interpretation in to accord with the paramount ECJ approach.[178] Third, this will cause some confusion as the single phrase *on the ground of* will have different meanings across the discrimination legislation, and even within the SDA 1975. Fourth, where the ECJ has yet to regulate, domestic courts may feel free to give the phrase *on the ground of* a narrower meaning, especially in accordance with the current trend, which is focusing on the defendant's *motive*.[179] For instance, if *O'Neill* were heard now, under s.3A, a court could be tempted to hold that the dismissal was *on the ground* of morality, and not pregnancy, even though it was *related to* the pregnancy.

(2) Specific Protection: Sections 99 and 47C, Employment Rights Act 1996

4–041 The Pregnant Workers Directive 92/85/EEC provides a right to at least 14 weeks maternity leave. The domestic legislation goes further, providing compulsory (two weeks), ordinary (a further 24 weeks), and additional (a further 26 weeks) maternity leave.[180] Of course, an abuse of these rights may lead to a discrimination claim.[181] However, a parallel cause of action is provided for employment claims by the Employment Rights Act 1996. Section 99 stipulates that if the reason or principal reason for a dismissal is pregnancy, childbirth, or maternity leave, the dismissal is automatically unfair. As with sex discrimination claims, no qualifying period of employment is required: it applies from day one. Any detriment short of dismissal is made unlawful by s.47C. These are specific *employment* rights. Damages for

---

[178] This was the Government's view: "Equality and Diversity: Updating the Sex Discrimination Act. Government Response to Consultation", 2005 (URN 05/1345) p.30, para.4.5. Available at *www.dti.gov.uk/publications*.

[179] See the discussion above, "(2) Discriminatory Motive and the *But For* Test" para.4–015, esp para.4–017.

[180] Respectively, ERA 1996, ss.72, 71 and 73 (SI 1999/3312, regs 7 and 8). Women must satisfy qualification conditions.

[181] See especially Equal Treatment Directive 76/207, Art.2(7).

unfair dismissal, but not for a detriment short of a dismissal, are capped, at the time of writing, to £56,800.[182]

The drafting of these provisions require simply that the *reason* for the treatment is pregnancy-related. Thus, the woman does not have to inform her employer of her pregnancy at the time of recruitment.[183] Of course, the employer must be informed at some time before the dismissal, otherwise pregnancy could not be the "reason" for the dismissal or detriment. The drafting of ss.47C and 99 allows for the situation where the employer acts because it has discovered the pregnancy by a third party.[184]

(3) Pregnancy, Pay and Benefits

As well as stipulating a right to maternity leave, the Pregnant Workers **4–042** Directive 92/85/EEC instructs Member States to establish a right to maternity pay to accompany the leave. The level of pay need only be the level of State sick pay in the Member State concerned. This is a minimum. As with sick pay, employers are free to pay more than the legal minimum. Nonetheless, under the Pregnant Workers Directive, a pregnant woman may receive less pay than she would have done if she were not pregnant, either by comparison with her employer's sick pay or her normal salary. This raises the question of whether she could claim direct discrimination under the equal pay legislation (EC Treaty, Art.141). In *Gillespie v Northern Health and Social Services Board*[185] women on maternity leave received full weekly pay for the first four weeks, nine-tenths for the next two weeks and then one-half for 12 weeks. The ECJ held that although maternity pay comes within Art.141, this did not amount to discrimination because women on maternity leave were "in a special position which requires them to be afforded special protection, but which is not comparable either with that of a man or with that of a woman actually at work."[186]

The "*Gillespie* ruling" by the ECJ is essentially pragmatic. An alternative decision in effect would force employers to provide full pay, or at least their normal sick-pay (where it is above the State level), thus rendering this part of the Directive redundant. As Advocate General Léger noted in *Gillespie*, to give full protection to pregnant women on

---

[182] ERA 1996, s.124(1). The figure is normally raised in accordance with the retail prices index each February (Employment Relations Act 1999, s.34). The figure of £56,800 was inserted by the Employment Rights (Increase of Limits) Order 2004, SI 2989, Sch, and applies to events (giving rise to the action) that took place after February 1, 2005. For claims of sex discrimination by those dismissed by the armed forces for pregnancy see Ch.13, para.13–021.

[183] See also under EC law, *Tele Danmark v HK (acting for Brandt-Nielson)* C-109/00, [2001] ECR I-6993, ECJ, *Busch v Klinikum Neustadt GmbH* Case C-320/01, [2003] 2003 I-02041 ECJ. (Noted above, para.4–038.)

[184] For liability elsewhere where the employer is unaware of the pregnancy at the time of treatment, see the discussion of *Heinz v Kendrick* and *Ramdoolar v Bycity Ltd,* above, para.4–039.

[185] Case C-342/93, [1996] I.C.R. 498, ECJ. For commentary on this case and its implications see, M. Wynn, "Pregnancy Discrimination: Equality, Protection or Reconciliation?" (1999) 62 M.L.R. 435.

[186] *ibid.,* at para.17.

maternity leave "would threaten to upset the balance of the entire social welfare system."[187] The theoretical weakness of this decision is illustrated in *Hoj Pedersen*[188] where *before* maternity leave was due, a women unavailable for work because of a pregnancy-related illness was given only half-pay, whilst other workers (this includes women), absent for a non-pregnancy related illness, were given full pay. The ECJ held that this was discrimination on the ground of pregnancy, and so amounted to sex discrimination, (under Art.141). This claim succeeded because, arising as it did before the maternity leave was due, it fell outside of the maternity leave and pay provisions of the Pregnant Workers Directive. Had the half-pay fallen within the maternity period, and thus the Pregnant Workers Directive, the claim would have failed.[189]

The implications of the *Gillespie* ruling were realised in the following cases. In *Boyle v EOC*[190] the Civil Service paid the same amount for either sick pay or maternity pay, save that to qualify for maternity pay, the woman had to return to work for at least a month. Following the logic of *Gillespie,* the ECJ refused to compare the maternity pay with the sick pay, and held the condition did not amount to sex discrimination. In *Todd v Eastern Health and Social Services Board* [191]the Northern Ireland Court of Appeal held that *contractual* maternity pay, which was lower than the *contractual* sick pay, could not be challenged as discriminatory.

4–043   However, benefits or detriments *related to* maternity pay may be challenged as discriminatory. In *Alabaster v Woolwich Plc*[192] the claimant's maternity pay was related to her salary. However, the formula pinned maternity pay to the salary some time before her leave began. Thus, a pay rise awarded after this time was not reflected in her maternity pay. The ECJ held that this was sex discrimination, under Art.141, as pregnant women did not receive the benefit of the pay rise, expressed in their maternity pay, because they were pregnant. The Court stated that so far as maternity pay is related to salary, any pay rise from the calculation date to the end of maternity leave must be reflected in the maternity pay.[193] The distinction between pay and pay-related detriments becomes even more delicate in cases of bonus payments. In *Green v GUS Home*

---

[187] Case C-342/93, [1996] I.C.R. 498, ECJ at para.48 of the A-G's Opinion. For discussion of the complicated interaction between pregnancy rights and sickness benefits, see S. Cox, "Maternity and sex discrimination law: where are we now?" (1997) 75 EOR 23, pp.26–28.

[188] *Hoj Pedersen v Faellesforeningen for Danmarks Brugsforeninger and Dansk Tandlaegeforening* Case C-66/96, [1998] E.C.R. I-7327, ECJ.

[189]   *ibid.*, paras 38–39.

[190] Case C-411/96 1998 E.C.R. I-6401. See E. Caracciolo di Torella, "Recent developments in pregnancy and maternity rights" [1999] 28 I.L.J. 276.

[191] [1997] I.R.L.R. 410, NICA.

[192] Case C-147/02, [2004] ECR I-0000. Upon its return, the CA implemented this ruling through the Equal Pay Act 1970, by disapplying the Act's requirement for a comparator: *Alabaster v Barclays Bank (No.2)* [2005] EWCA 508.

[193] *ibid.*, at para.50.

Shopping[194] the EAT held that depriving a woman of a loyalty bonus—dependant upon "goodwill"—because she was absent through pregnancy, was unlawful sex discrimination. Yet more recently, in *Hoyland v ASDA* [195] the EAT held that a bonus dependant on profits and attendance constituted "pay", and so a women on maternity leave was not entitled to a bonus related to that period of absence.[196] The EAT observed that *Green* was decided on "unusual" facts and its value as a precedent was "slight."[197] In *Green* the bonus was discretionary and not expressly dependant on attendance. Other cases may feature an inseparable mix of subjectively and objectively judged factors, such as loyalty, performance, attendance, and so on. These will be even more difficult to decide.

Detriments which are not pay, but are related to maternity leave, fall outside the *Gillespie* ruling, and should be challengeable as sex discrimination, or under the specific protection afforded by ss.99 and 47C, Employment Rights Act 1996.[198] This includes detriments flowing from the maternity leave that affect the pay *outside of the maternity leave period*. For instance, in *Land Brandenburg v Ursula*[199] the wage scale was decided by length of service. A woman was not upgraded on the wage scale because her employer failed to incorporate into this calculation her time off on maternity leave. The ECJ held that amounted to sex discrimination, this time under the Equal Treatment Directive 76/207/EEC. Likewise in *CNAVTS v Thibault*[200] the ECJ held that to deprive a woman on maternity leave of her annual assessment, and the resulting possibility of promotion, was discrimination under the Equal Treatment Directive.

The Pregnant Workers Directive gives Member States some leeway. States may set conditions of eligibility, including up to 12 months continuous employment, and the level of pay need only be the level of State sick pay in the Member State concerned.[201] Accordingly, the UK provides that to be eligible, the worker must qualify for sick pay, by minimum national insurance contributions (this excludes low-paid workers), and must have at least 26 weeks' continuous service. In *Gillespie*, the ECJ commented that the level of maternity pay should not be set "so low as to undermine the purpose of maternity leave."[202]

---

[194] [2001] I.R.L.R. 75 EAT.

[195] [2005] I.C.R. 1235, EAT, affirmed, [2006] CSIH 21.

[196] Save for two weeks compulsory maternity leave.

[197] [2005] I.C.R. 1235, at paras 21–22, EAT.

[198] See above, para.4–041.

[199] Case C-284/02, [2004] E.C.R. I-00000.

[200] *Caisse nationale d'assurance vieillesse des travailleurs salaries (CNAVTS) v Evelyne Thibault.* C-136/95, [1998] E.C.R. I-2011, [1998] I.R.L.R. 399. In *Athis v Blue Coat School* [2005] All E.R. (D) 53 (Aug), the EAT stated it could be discriminatory for a school not to inform a teacher on maternity leave that she could make representations regarding decisions about her performance-related pay.

[201] Council Directive 92/85/EEC, Art.11 (3) and (4).

[202] Case C-342/93, [1996] I.C.R. 498, at para.20, ECJ.

In *Banks v Tesco*[203] the claimant, earning just £56 per week, fell below the threshold (of £57) to be eligible for State sick pay, and thus for maternity pay. The EAT held that the domestic rules did not breach either the Pregnant Workers Directive, nor Art.141, and was in accordance with this comment in *Gillespie*, which was confined to the *level* of pay, rather than the separate question of eligibility.

---

[203] *Banks v Tesco & Sec of State for Employment* [1999] I.C.R. 1141 EAT.

CHAPTER 5

HARASSMENT AND OTHER UNLAWFUL ACTS

INTRODUCTION

This chapter covers legal *definitions* of harassment, whilst chapter 8 covers an employer's liability for harassment in the workplace.[1] It also rounds together other acts made unlawful by the legislation: aiding discrimination, instructions to discriminate, discriminatory practices and advertisements.

    5–001

    Dedicated statutory provisions now outlaw sexual harassment and harassment on any of the principal protected grounds. The new provisions cover sexual and sex harassment[2] in the field of employment and vocational training from October 1, 2005, and in the fields

---

[1] At para.8–081.
[2] There is no specific provision for harassment on the ground of marital or civil partnership status, although the latter may be covered by harassment on the ground of sexual orientation.

of goods and services by December 21, 2007;[3] racial (not including purely colour or nationality) harassment in employment, vocational training, trade organisations and unions, social security and health-care, education, the supply of goods, services and premises, from July 19, 2003; sexual orientation harassment in employment from December 1, 2003;[4] age harassment in employment from October 1, 2006; and religion or belief harassment in employment from December 2, 2003.[5]

Before these provisions came into force, victims of harassment had to fashion their claims as sex or race discrimination, ("discriminatory harassment" cases), which is an overly technical and sometimes impossible task. The domestic definitions derive from EC Directives, and as such, their coverage is limited to the scope of the Directives, which is sometimes narrower than the existing domestic legislation. Further, as these specific provisions are fairly recent, many claims arising before the new provisions came into force have yet to be heard. This leaves a residual class[6] of complainants, whose claims either predate the relevant provision, and/or fall outside the scope of the parent Directives.

5–002   In both the UK and United States, the first major pieces of discrimination legislation[7] did not include a concept of harassment. Consequently, courts developed the law of harassment as a form of direct discrimination,[8] (although, as will be seen, the US courts have been more adventurous). The major problem with this is the need for a comparison with how somebody not from the claimant's group would have been treated. It follows that the employer who harasses all races, or both sexes, equally *badly*, can escape liability. Direct discrimination legitimises arguments such as "In this office both whites and blacks get racial abuse", or, "The factory is full of sexual innuendo, in the presence of both men and women".[9] Claims of sexual harassment are the most vulnerable, because conduct of a *sexual* nature, per se, was beyond the scope of *sex* discrimination legislation. Hence, most litigation, innovative arguments, and consequential developments, have arisen from sexual harassment complaints. It so happened that the first major US federal case to formulize harassment as a form of direct discrimination was brought on racial grounds. *Rogers v EEOC*[10] established that a

---

[3] Equal Treatment in Goods and Services Directive 2004/113/EC. See further Ch.2, para.2–002.
[4] Pt 3 of the Equality Act 2006 empowers the Secretary of State to extend this into other fields. (Expected in force October 2006).
[5] No specific definition is included in Pt 2 of the Equality Act 2006, which extends religion or belief discrimination to goods, facilities, services, premises, education and public services. (Expected in force October 2006).
[6] See Ch.2, para.2–002.
[7] Sex Discrimination Act 1975 (UK), and Civil Rights Act 1964 (US).
[8] The publication of C. Mackinnon *Sexual Harassment of Working Women*, 1979, New Haven: Yale UP, was a key development in the legal recognition of sexual harassment.
[9] See *Stewart v Cleveland Guest (Engineering)* [1996] I.C.R. 535, EAT, (below para.5–023)
[10] 454 F 2d 234 (5th Cir 1971). See further, below, para.5–024.

"working environment heavily charged with discrimination" could discriminate against a Hispanic worker. In 1980, the US enforcement agency, the Equal Opportunities Employment Commission, published guidelines for sexual harassment, which included this definition:

> Unwelcome sexual advances, requests for sexual favors, and other verbal or physical conduct of a sexual nature constitute sexual harassment when (1) submission to such conduct is made either explicitly or implicitly a term or condition of an individual's employment, (2) submission to or rejection of such conduct by an individual is used as the basis for employment decisions affecting such individual, or (3) such conduct has the purpose or effect of unreasonably interfering with an individual's work performance or creating an intimidating, hostile, or offensive working environment.[11]

This definition, which the Supreme Court adopted wholesale,[12] is designed to cover two scenarios. First, where sexual favours are sought in return for employment advantages (quid pro quo). The second is where the conduct causes a hostile environment[13] (which is relevant to other unlawful grounds of harassment). Much of the language has found its way into the new EC, and consequential domestic, statutory definitions. Hence, even though the US law remains rooted in discrimination, it is instructive for both the old and the new forms of harassment in Britain.

1. STATUTORY HARASSMENT[14]

The British legislation now defines three forms of harassment: harassment on a protected ground, sexual harassment, and (for sexual and sex harassment only) less favourable treatment based on a person's rejection of, or submission to, unwanted conduct.

5–003

(1) Harassment on a Protected Ground

According to the statutory definition, a person harasses another if on grounds of race or ethnic or national origins, [or sexual orientation, religion or belief, age, gender reassignment, her sex] he engages in unwanted conduct which has the purpose or effect of violating that

5–004

---

[11] Para.1604.11(a). (See *www.eeoc.gov*, and click on "sexual harassment", and then "The regulations".)

[12] See e.g. *Meritor Savings Bank v Vinson* 477 US 57 (1986).

[13] Adopted from the analysis of C. Mackinnon, *Sexual Harassment of Working Women*, 1979, New Haven: Yale UP, at 32.

[14] See L. Clarke, "Harassment, sexual harassment, and the Employment Equality (Sex Discrimination) Regulations 2005", (2006) 35 I.L.J. 161.

other person's dignity, or creating an intimidating, hostile, degrading, humiliating or offensive environment for him.[15]

(a) "On grounds of"

5–005 The formula requires that the conduct is "on the ground of" the protected ground. The choice of this seemingly straightforward phrase will in fact cause problems of one sort or another. The parent Directives employ the phrase "related to", and the Government, when transposing this, stated that "there was no material difference between the two formulations."[16] This is misleading. It is clear from the natural language and context of the formulas, that "on the ground of" carries a more limited meaning than "related to". This is illustrated by case law under the Disability Discrimination Act 1995 (DDA 1995), which employs the phrase "related to". It has been interpreted to cover, for example, dismissal for absenteeism, and a restaurant's ban on dogs or those who have difficulty eating.[17] Such (facially neutral) treatment is *related to* the victim's disability, but not necessarily "on grounds of" it. Elsewhere in the legislation, the phrase "on grounds of" is sufficient, because it is accompanied by its natural counterpart, *indirect* discrimination. Thus, once facially discriminatory conduct ("No blacks") becomes facially neutral ("Applicants must have a high-school diploma")[18] it falls into the definition of indirect discrimination and can be dealt with accordingly. The harassment provisions have no such counterpart. It is arguable that, for instance, harassing people because they are short, slow, physically weak, effeminate or masculine may be conduct *related to* a protected ground (respectively, race/sex, age, sex/age, sexual orientation), but not necessarily *on grounds of* the victim's protected status. Such harassment could be unlawful only if the phrase *on the ground of* were afforded an exceptionally wide interpretation.

The matter is complicated further because elsewhere the statutory phrase *on the ground of* is increasingly being loaded with an element of discriminatory motive. The precise implication of this is yet unclear because the precise meaning of discriminatory motive is still unclear.[19] But arguments of motive will arise in harassment cases where the defendant pleads that he did not realise that his conduct was on a

---

[15] SDA 1975, s.4A (in force October 1, 2005); RRA 1976, s.3A (July 19, 2003); Sexual Orientation Regulations 2003, reg.5 (December 1, 2003); Religion or Belief Regulations 2003, reg.5 (December 2, 2003); Age Regulations 2006, reg.6 (October 1, 2006).

[16] "Equality and Diversity: Updating the Sex Discrimination Act. Government Response to Consultation." 2005 (URN 05/1345) p.9, para.3.11. Available at *www.dti.gov.uk/publications*.

[17] See *Clark v Novacold* [1999] I.C.R. 951, CA, at 964–966.

[18] *Griggs v Duke Power* 401 US 424. See further Ch.6, para.6–001.

[19] Discussed at length in Ch.4, para.4–015.

protected ground.[20] This becomes particularly pertinent where the conduct was merely related to the protected ground, as shown in the examples above. By contrast, the phrase *related to* has been interpreted to cover "unconscious discrimination", where the defendant did not even know that the victim belonged to a protected group.[21]

Examples of harassment given by the Government suggest that the phrase *on the ground of* should be given the broader meaning attributed to the phrase *related to* in the DDA 1995. For instance, men placing items on high shelves, out of reach of most women, and "derogatory comments *relating to* the person's gender".[22] Thus, tribunals have a dilemma. Either they enforce the policy of the harassment provisions and give the phrase *on grounds of* an especially broad meaning (out of step with the phrase's meaning elsewhere in the legislation), and create an anomaly; or give it a meaning consistent with its interpretation elsewhere, and frustrate the purpose of the legislation as well as risk not implementing fully the parent Directives. The supremacy of the Directives suggests that eventually the former option must prevail. So better to start with it and endure the anomaly.

(b) "Her Sex"

For sex (including gender reassignment) only, the definition includes the possessive adjective "her", requiring the conduct to be on the ground of the claimant's sex. The definition of direct sex discrimination employs the same formula. This excludes two scenarios: discrimination on the ground of a third party, and mistaken or "perceived" discrimination. These restrictions are unlikely to limit the law of harassment, except in cases of gender reassignment. For instance, a worker may be harassed because he has a close relative or friend who is transsexual, or a manager, on an incorrect assumption, may harasses a worker for being transsexual. Such cases fall outside the definition.

5–006

(c) Same-Group Harassment

Harassing a person of the same protected group should be actionable. Some examples from the United States, where harassment must amount to discrimination on a protected ground, illustrate this. In

5–007

---

[20] Note that formula does not require that the harasser is aware of the consequences of his conduct. It simply requires that the conduct has a particular "effect" (of violating the victim's dignity, or creating a hostile environment). This narrows the scope of any discriminatory motive required. It only need relate to the conduct itself, and not its consequences.

[21] *per* Lindsay J., *Heinz v Kenrick* [2000] I.C.R. 491, at para.25, although lack of awareness may be relevant to justification. See Ch.11, para.11–031.

[22] "Changes to Sex Discrimination Legislation in Great Britain: Explaining the Employment Equality (Sex Discrimination) Regulations 2005." 2005 (URN 05/1603), pp.7 and 10 respectively (emphasis supplied). Available at *www.dti.gov.uk/publications*.

Oncall v Sundowner Offshore Services[23] the Supreme Court emphasized that the harassment must be because of the victim's sex, but
illustrated, for cases where the harassment is not *sexual*, a carefully
argued claim could succeed. For instance, a female worker may harass
a female colleague in sex-specific derogatory terms because of hostility
towards the woman's presence in the workplace. Accordingly, it can be
unlawful harassment for a black supervisor to call a black worker
"black boy" and "nigger": the treatment is on the ground of the
victim's race.[24] In theory, so long as the conduct is based on the
victim's protected ground, the harasser's group should not matter.

(d) Conduct

5–008   The conduct may take any form, such as oral, written, the displaying
of pictures or symbols,[25] or even dressing up.[26] The Government
provided the following examples of harassment on the ground of sex,
none of which amount to sexual harassment.

(i)   Male workers placing tools on a high shelf, out of the reach
of the female workers.[27]

(ii)   A manager makes humiliating and embarrassing remarks to
a female subordinate and in one incident depicts her as
"brash", which a tribunal finds to be insensitive and to have
gender undertones—it being more frequently applied to a
woman than a man.

(iii)   In a predominantly female workplace, a male complains
about the climate and culture, caused by e.g. belittling
remarks.

(iv)   Derogatory remarks relating to the person's gender, e.g.
"Don't worry your pretty little head about it"; "she's not
thinking straight today—it must be the time of the month";
and "you're looking a bit fat—do you have a bun in the
oven?"

(v)   A pregnant worker suffers derogatory comments, such as she
will no longer be up to the job.

---

[23] 523 US 75, at 80 (1998).

[24] *Ross v Douglas County, Nebraska* 234 F 3d 391 (8th Cir 2000).

[25] In the US case *Harris v International Paper* 765 F Supp 1509 (1991) *vacated in part* 765 F Supp
1529 (1991) the symbol "kkk" (representing the Ku Klux Klan) was written on the (black)
victim's work materials.

[26] In *Harris v International Paper* (*ibid*), colleagues dressed up in white clothes and pranced
around the black victim to recall Ku Klux Klan events.

[27] "Changes to Sex Discrimination Legislation in Great Britain: Explaining the Employment
Equality (Sex Discrimination) Regulations 2005." 2005 (URN 05/1603), p.7. Available at
www.dti.gov.uk/publications.

(vi)   A sole woman on a team is always asked to take notes and make the tea, because it's considered women's work.[28]

Other examples may include derogatory remarks about women's driving skills, emotional rationality, grasp of political affairs, or other gender (but non-sexual) stereotypes.

(e) "Unwanted" Conduct

Issues of proof aside, the courts must decide precisely what is meant **5–009** by "unwanted." It could range from merely that the conduct was not invited, to a requirement that the claimant overtly expressed her aversion to such conduct. The only case history on this point concerns *sexual* harassment. It was discussed by Morison, J. in *Reed v Stedman*[29] under a discriminatory (sexual) harassment case, where it is not an element, but rather one of the circumstances that may decide whether there was discrimination. He noted that some conduct, such as touching a woman in a sexual manner, if not expressly invited, would properly be regarded as unwelcome. At the lower end of the scale, unduly sensitive people should indicate their disapproval. Less is required of the victim in the United States, where *unwanted* (or *unwelcomeness*) is an element for sexual harassment, (but not any other type of harassment). In those cases, the rule is that the "conduct must be unwelcome in the sense that the employee did not solicit or incite it, and in the sense that the employee regarded the conduct as undesirable or offensive".[30] This approach, as far as possible under the element, favours the claimant. So long as the claimant considered the conduct unwelcome, he need not show any outward sign of his disapproval. Only if he solicited or incited it, would the element become an issue. The US approach, being based upon *unwanted* as an element of harassment, is more authentic, and so may become the norm here, especially under the formal shifting burden of proof rules.[31]

(f) Assessing Whether there has been Harassment or Sexual Harassment

The following rules are common to both harassment on a protected **5–010** ground and sexual harassment. The statutory definitions are accompanied by the same formula for assessing whether the conduct has had the effect of violating a person's dignity, or creating a hostile environment: "Conduct shall be regarded as having [that] effect . . . only if,

---

[28] *ibid.*, at p.9.
[29] [1999] I.R.L.R. 299, at 302, EAT.
[30] *Henson v City of Dundee* 683 F 2d 897, at 903 (11th Cit 1982). For a "welcome conduct defence" in US sexual harassment claims, see below, para.5–018.
[31] See Ch.13, para.13–002, esp. 13–005.

having regard to all the circumstances, including in particular the perception of the woman, it should reasonably be considered as having that effect."

(i) Objective or subjective?

5–011 The standard by which the conduct is judged is a mix of objective and subjective. The formula mandates an objective test, but allows the claimant's (subjective) perception to contribute to the objective test. In conventional cases of direct discrimination the House of Lords, in *R. v Birmingham City Council, Ex p. EOC*[32] has held that it is enough that victims considered—reasonably—that they had been treated less favourably, even in the face of objective evidence to the contrary. There must be some reasonable ground for that perception; it is not enough that the claimant simply considered that she was treated less favourably.[33] However, in *Driskel v Peninsula Business Services*[34]—a discriminatory (sexual) harassment case—Holland, J. stated that "the ultimate judgment" is an objective assessment of all the facts. In doing so, tribunals should consider the victim's subjective perception and the understanding, motive and intention of the harasser. He noted that if the claimant was "hypersensitive", and the harasser "reasonably" did not realise his behaviour was to her detriment, there could be no liability.

The Government expressly endorsed the *Driskel* approach in the *pre-consultation* Explanatory Notes to the Regulations on Sexual Orientation and Religion or Belief, and the amendment regulations to the Disability Discrimination Act.[35] It impliedly did so in various documents accompanying the introduction of harassment into the Sex Discrimination Act 1975. For instance, that the "ultimate judgement is an objective assessment",[36] and that the formula "reflects case law".[37] So it appears that the Government considered that the statutory formula codified *Driskel*. At the same time, however, the Government appeared to jettison at least one part of *Driskel*, by stating that sexual harassment "clearly . . . includes unintentional behaviour".[38] This correctly interprets the new formula, which prohibits conduct having the "purpose or *effect*" of violating dignity, or creating a hostile environment (emphasis supplied). At the least,

---

[32] [1989] A.C. 1155, HL. See Ch.4, para.4–015.
[33] *Burrett v West Birmingham HA* [1994] I.R.L.R. 7 EAT, see Ch.4, para.4–006.
[34] [2000] I.R.L.R. 151, at 155, EAT.
[35] See e.g. Explanatory Notes to the *pre consultation draft Disability Discrimination Act 1995 (Amendment) Regulations 2003*, at para.40.
[36] "Equality and Diversity: Updating the Sex Discrimination Act. Government Response to Consultation." 2005 (URN 05/1345) p.9, para.3.17. Available at *www.dti.gov.uk/publications*.
[37] "Changes to Sex Discrimination Legislation in Great Britain: Explaining the Employment Equality (Sex Discrimination) Regulations 2005." 2005 (URN 05/1603), p.7. Available at *www.dti.gov.uk/publications*.
[38] *ibid.*, at p.8.

any suggestion based on *Driskel* that for liability the defendant must have intended to violate the claimant's dignity or create a hostile environment, is wrong.

The statutory formula carries several potential problems. First, for racial harassment, mixing the subjective and objective does not reflect the recommendation of the Lawrence Inquiry to define a racist incident (criminal and non-criminal) as "any incident which is perceived to be racist by the victim or any other person."[39] Second, it affords courts some leeway on how much weight to ascribe to the claimant's perception. By giving tribunals so much discretion with the subjective and objective, it creates uncertainty which may lead to some inconsistent decisions. For instance, in sexual harassment cases, one tribunal may adopt the view of the victim, whilst, on near identical facts, another may adopt the view of the defendant. Another may adopt the view of a male bystander, or a female bystander. Each approach could be critical to the outcome. Third, it is likely that harassment cases will expose a tension between the subjective and objective. For instance, a normal sensitivity of a black person may appear to be a hypersensitivity to a white person. *Driskel* suggests that in such cases, ultimately, tribunals should adopt the view of the white onlooker. On this approach, liability may depend on the race, sex, religion, age, or sexual orientation, of a tribunal panel, which of course, should not be the case.

The US Supreme Court appears to have adopted a "reasonable victim" approach, stating that "the objective severity of the harassment should be judged from the perspective of the reasonable person in the plaintiff's position, considering all the circumstances."[40] This is similar to the standard given in *R. v Birmingham City Council, Ex p. EOC* (above).[41] Lower Federal courts in the United States have expanded on this standard. In the context of racial harassment, its logic was explained thus: In a society ingrained with cultural stereotypes, blacks regularly face negative attitudes, often unconsciously held. As a result, even "an inadvertent racial slight unnoticed either by its white speaker or white bystanders will reverberate in the memory of its black victim." Accordingly, the trier of fact must "walk a mile in the victim's shoes" to understand the effects.[42] In the context of sexual

5–012

---

[39] The Stephen Lawrence Inquiry, Report of an Inquiry by Sir William Macpherson, advised by Tom Cook, The Right Reverend Dr John Sentamu, Dr Richard Stone. February 1999. Presented to Parliament by the Home Secretary. Cm 4262–I, London: TSO, Ch.47 paras 12–13. See also Ch.1 para.1–002.

[40] *Oncale v Sundowner Offshore Services* 523 US 75, at 81 (1998).

[41] [1989] A.C. 1155, HL.

[42] *Harris v International Paper* 765 F Supp 1509, at 1515–1516 (vacated on other grounds 765 F Supp 1529) (1991), citing: Lawrence, "The id, the ego, and equal protection: reckoning with unconscious racism", 39 Stan L Rev 317 (1987); Matsuda, "Public response to racist speech: considering the victim's story", 87 Mich L Rev 2320, 2326–35 (1989); Williams, "Alchemical notes: reconstructing ideals from deconstructed rights", 22 Harv CR-CL L Rev 401, 406–13 (1987) (explaining why black and white apartment-seekers assume different perspectives on the formalities of renting an apartment).

harassment, it was observed that the "sex-blind reasonable person standard tends to be male-biased" and that if only an objective view is considered, a court "would run the risk of reinforcing the prevailing level of discrimination."[43] For example, "A male supervisor might believe . . . that it is legitimate for him to tell a female subordinate that she has a 'great figure' or 'nice legs.'"[44] Of course, the same logic applies to cases of age, religion, and sexual orientation.

The better approach is to adopt this logic and simply continue with the House of Lords' "reasonable victim" model from *R. v Birmingham City Council, Ex p. EOC.* It fulfils the policy of the harassment provisions and provides some consistency throughout the legislation.

(ii) "Having regard to all the circumstances"

5–013 This part of the definition reflects the US Equal Opportunities Employment Commission (EEOC) guidelines for sexual harassment cases, which provide that the court should "look at the record as a whole and at the totality of the circumstances".[45] These may include: the frequency of the discriminatory conduct; its severity; whether it is physically threatening or humiliating, or a mere offensive utterance; and whether it unreasonably interferes with an employee's work performance.[46] Other factors such as the victim's provocative speech or dress may be used to show that the conduct of a sexual nature was welcome.[47] It also allows a court to consider the context of the conduct: a coach may smack a football player's buttocks as he heads onto the field, but should not do the same to the secretary (male or female) back at the office.[48]

Where the conduct is verbal, one US court quoted this saw of Oliver Wendell Holmes: "[A] word is not a crystal, transparent and unchanged" but "is the skin of a living thought and may vary greatly in color and content according to the circumstances and the time in which it is used."[49] Thus, there may be liability where a white super-

---

[43] *Ellison v Brady* 924 F 2d 872, at 878–880 (9th Cir 1991), citing, Ehrenreich, "Pluralist Myths and powerless men: the ideology of reasonableness in sexual harassment law", 99 Yale LJ 1177, at 1207–1208 (1990) (men tend to view some forms of sexual harassment as "harmless social inter-actions to which only overly-sensitive women would object"); Abrams, "Gender discrimination and transformation of workplace norms", 42 Vand L Rev 1183, at 1203 (1989) (the characteristically male view depicts sexual harassment as comparatively harmless amusement).

[44] *Lipsett v University of Puerto Rice* 864 F 2d 881, at 898 (1st Cir 1988).

[45] Para.1604.11(b). (See *www.eeoc.gov*, and click on "sexual harassment", and then "The regulations".) Approved by the Supreme Court in *Meritor Savings Bank v Vinson* 477 US 57, at 69 (1986).

[46] *Harris v Forklift Systems* 510 US 17, at 23 (Sup Ct 1993).

[47] *ibid.*, at 69. See *Mclean v Satellite Technology* 673 F Supp 1458 (ED Mo 1987), below para.5–018.

[48] *per* J. Scalia *Oncale v Sundowner Offshore Services* 523 US 75, at 81 (1998).

[49] *Towne v Eisner*, 245 US 418, at 425 (1918), cited in *Horney v Westfield Gage* 211 F Supp 2d 291, at 309 (2002). See also, R. Kennedy *Nigger: The Strange Case of a Troublesome Word*, (2002) New York: Pantheon Books.

visor uses code words such as "another one", "one of them" and "poor people" when referring to black workers.[50] The circumstances may be particularly pertinent in one-off incidents of sexual harassment. This is illustrated by *Insitu Cleaning v Heads*,[51] a discriminatory harassment case. Here a director's son and company manager, said to a much older female supervisor, "Hiya, big tits". The EAT stated that liability for one-off incidents was "a question of fact and degree." It noted that for a bosses' son to make such a comment to a female worker nearly twice his age would cause distress, and this was compounded by his status and his aggressive, arrogant and dismissive attitude. In these circumstances the defendant was found liable. It has been suggested in the United States that liability for one-off incidents is more likely if the author was a workplace superior, rather than a colleague.[52]

(iii) When does the conduct become unlawful?
A tribunal must decide whether the conduct was serious enough to have the effect of violating a person's dignity, or creating a hostile environment. In cases predating the statutory definitions, tribunals had to decide (1) if the conduct was less favourable, and (2) (for employment cases), if it caused the victim a detriment. Of course, these requirements no longer apply, but older cases on the meaning of "detriment" are instructive when deciding if there has been a violation of dignity, or the creation of a hostile environment. "Detriment" means no more than putting under a disadvantage;[53] there is no need for a physical or economic consequence,[54] nor a change to the victim's working conditions.[55] Thus one-off comments such as "We used to buy you when you were slaves",[56] or "Get this typing done by the wog",[57] can amount to a detriment.

5–014

For hostile environment claims in the United States, the bar is set slightly higher. The standard is that that the conduct must be "sufficiently severe or pervasive to alter the conditions of the victim's employment".[58] In practice, this "working-conditions" standard has

[50] *Aman v Cort Furniture* 85 F 3d 1074, at 1083 (3rd Cir 1996).
[51] [1995] I.R.L.R. 4.
[52] See the dicta in *Brooks v City of San Mateo* 229 F 3d 917, at 927 n9 (9th Cir 2000). (No liability where a male forcibly fondled a colleague's breast.)
[53] *per* Brandon, L.J., *Ministry of Defence v Jerimiah* [1980] Q.B. 87, at 99, CA. See also Ch.8, para.8–015.
[54] *Shamoon v Chief Constable of the RUC* [2003] I.C.R. 337, at para.35, HL. Lord Hoffmann pointed out in *Chief Constable of W Yorks Police v Khan* [2001] I.C.R. 1065, at para.52, HL, that employment tribunals have jurisdiction to award compensation for injury to feelings whether or not compensation is due under any other head: RRA 1976, s.57(4).
[55] *Thomas v Robinson* [2003] I.R.L.R. 7, at para.24, EAT.
[56] *Commission for Racial Equality v United Packing Industry Ltd*, CRE Report, 1980 p.20, IT.
[57] *De Souza v Automobile Association* [1986] I.C.R. 514, CA.
[58] *Harris v Forklift Systems* 510 US 17, at 21 (Sup Ct 1993).

meant that two racial comments (interracial marriage was "disgusting"; blacks get "lynched" in this area) within a month did not create a hostile environment;[59] neither did one racial comment ("Nigger you're suspended") in response to the claimant's persistent interruptions of a meeting.[60] Further, this law "does not reach genuine but innocuous differences in the ways men and women interact", and "requires neither asexuality nor androgyny in the workplace."[61] Moreover, it seems, that some "one-off" serious instances may not amount to sexual harassment: a male forcibly fondling a colleague's breast,[62] and a State governor making sexual advances to an employee, including stroking her leg and exposing himself to her.[63] However, the environment need not be so hostile to affect the victim's mental or physical health,[64] and victims do not have to show an "economic" or "tangible" loss.[65] Examples of working conditions being altered are: a supervisor continually demeaning a worker before his colleagues because of the worker's professed religious views;[66] six instances of harassment of a Jew;[67] and five to ten references to a worker as "nigger".[68]

Under the new provisions on harassment, British courts may follow the "working-conditions" standard from the United States, especially as the "hostile environment" concept was drawn from the US EEOC guidelines.[69] This is a logical approach and certainly reflects the ordinary meaning of the word "harassment", suggesting as it does, more aggressive or persistent conduct than causing a mere disadvantage. This standard would exclude from the harassment provisions many one- or two-off situations, such as those as described in the preceding paragraph. But adopting this standard is not as straightforward as first appears. First, the US model is restricted to the working-conditions standard because it has been developed entirely from the statutory definition of discrimination, which must be related to "compensation, terms, conditions, or privileges of employment."[70] The new free-standing models of harassment in the UK are not restricted so, using

---

[59] *Logan v Kautex Textron* 259 F 3d 635, at 639 (7th Cir 2001).
[60] *Sanders v Village of Dixmoor* 178 F 3d 869, at 870 (7th Cir 1999).
[61] *Oncale v Sundowner Offshore Services* 523 US 75, at 81 (Sup Ct 1998).
[62] *Brooks v City of San Mateo* 229 F 3d 917 (9th Cir 2000). However, the court suggested a one-off incident by a workplace *superior*, rather than a colleague, might be severe enough to be actionable (at 927 n9).
[63] *Jones v Clinton* 990 F Supp 657 (ED Ark 1998), appeal dismissed 161 F 3d 528 (8th Cir 1998).
[64] *Terry v Ashcroft* 336 F 3d 128, at 148 (2nd Cir 2003).
[65] *Meritor Savings Bank v Vinson* 477 US 57, at 64 (Sup Ct 1986).
[66] *Compston v Borden* 424 F Supp 157, at 160–161 (SD Ohio 1976).
[67] *Shanoff v Illinois Dept of Human Services* 258 F 3d 696, at 698–699 (7th Cir 2001).
[68] *Rodgers v Western Southern Life Ins* 12 F 3d 668, at 673 (7th Cir 1993).
[69] See above, para.5–002.
[70] Title VII, s 703(a) (codified as 42 USC s.2000e-2).

the looser phrase "in relation to employment".[71] Second, the UK legislation allows for damages for injury to feelings, whether or not compensation is due under any other head.[72] Third, adopting the working-conditions standard would create the anomalous situation where victims of harassment who had suffered a disadvantage short of a change in working conditions, but which amounted to a "detriment", may be able to bring a case of direct discrimination instead. Provisions dedicated to harassment would be bypassed because they offered *less* protection than the existing law of direct discrimination. To avoid the anomaly, and to keep the law as simple as possible, the courts may prefer to maintain the standard ascribed to "detriment" for harassment claims. If so, the rule will be that conduct violating a person's dignity, or creating a hostile environment for a person, to such a degree that it causes that person a "detriment", becomes unlawful harassment.

(2) Sexual Harassment

Section 4A(1)(b) of the Sex Discrimination Act 1975 now provides that a person sexually harasses another if "he engages in any form of unwanted verbal, non-verbal or physical conduct of a sexual nature that has the purpose or effect—(i) of violating her dignity, or (ii) of creating an intimidating, hostile, degrading, humiliating or offensive environment for her".

5–015

(a) "Conduct of a Sexual Nature"

This removes the obstacle to many sexual harassment claims under the discrimination route. There is no need to show that the conduct was related to the victim's sex, only that it was sexual. Thus it is no defence that that the sexual harassment treats male and female, gay and straight, (or should it occur, Christian and Muslim, old and young,) claimants equally badly. This effectively reverses the House of Lords decisions in *Pearce v Governing Body of Mayfield Secondary School* and *Macdonald v A-G for Scotland*,[73] and removes any arguments that, say, pictures of naked or semi-naked women in the workplace treats both males and females equally.[74]

5–016

---

[71] The phrase is used elsewhere in the discrimination legislation (e.g. RRA 1975, s.4(1), SDA 1975, 6(1)) and has not been restricted to claims of discrimination in the *terms* of employment: see "(4) Detriment" below, para.5–027. In other fields, the same, or similar, phrasing is used: e.g. a local education authority may not harass *when carrying out its functions* (RRA 1976, s.18(1)); it is unlawful for a provider *in relation to* the provision of goods, facilities or services to harass (RRA 1976 s.20(3)).

[72] A point made by Lord Hoffmann in *Chief Constable of W Yorks Police v Khan* [2001] I.C.R. 1065, at para.52, HL.

[73] [2003] I.C.R. 937. See below, para.5–023.

[74] *Stewart v Cleveland Guest (Engineering)* [1996] I.C.R. 535, EAT, see further below, para.5–024.

5–017   The conduct may take any form, such as oral, written, or the displaying of pictures.[75] The Government provided the following examples of sexual harassment.[76]

(i)   A provincial newspaper provides short unpaid work experience placements for journalism students of local colleges. The editor wishes to run a feature on a dispute between residents and a strip club. He wants to send a female work experience student with the photographer to take pictures inside the club during its opening hours. The student makes it clear that she feels very uncomfortable with the idea of this, but the editor says it will be good experience and insists that she accompany the photographer, despite her objections. The student reluctantly agrees, but finds the experience distressing and humiliating. In such a case, a tribunal is likely to find that sexual harassment has occurred.

(ii)   A barmaid in a pub is subjected to unwelcome sexual overtures, inappropriate physical behaviour by her boss and is offered money for sex.

(iii)   A colleague making derogatory sexual comments to the claimant and making sexual remarks to other service users about the claimant.

(iv)   On three occasions, male colleagues working in the same room as the claimant downloaded pornographic images onto a computer screen. Viewed objectively, the behaviour complained of clearly had potential to cause affront to a female employee working in close proximity to the men and was thus to be regarded as degrading or offensive to her as a woman. The fact that the claimant did not complain to her employer was irrelevant, given the obviously detrimental effect that the behaviour had in undermining her dignity at work.

(v)   A model subjected to repeated unwanted sexual advances from X who was employed by the same company and was responsible for engaging models for photographic shoots for advertising purposes. The model claimed that during a shoot, X came to her hotel room and attempted to kiss her. The model rebuffed her advances. X also sent the model text messages and invited her to visit a sex shop.

---

[75] See the US case, *Horney v Westfield Gage* 211 F Supp 2d 291 (2002) (pictures of naked and semi-naked women displayed in workplace).

[76] "Changes to Sex Discrimination Legislation in Great Britain: Explaining the Employment Equality (Sex Discrimination) Regulations 2005." 2005 (URN 05/1603), p.10. Available at *www.dti.gov.uk/publications*.

(vi) A city worker (of either gender) required to go on team outings to strip clubs.

(b) "Unwanted" Conduct and the "Welcomeness Defence"
The claimant must prove that the conduct was "unwanted". First, it **5–018** has been argued that this element is unnecessary: conduct which violates dignity, or creates a hostile environment, without more, amounts to harassment.[77] On the other hand, this element is necessary to "ensure that sexual harassment charges do not become the tool by which one party to a consensual relationship may punish the other."[78]

Although the issue of whether conduct is unwelcome has been discussed under the old discriminatory harassment cases, it was not an element for liability, but rather one of the circumstances that may decide whether there was discrimination. However, *unwanted* (or *unwelcomeness*) is an element for sexual harassment in the United States. So the case law there is more instructive.[79] The rule is that the "conduct must be unwelcome in the sense that the employee did not solicit or incite it, and . . . that the employee regarded the conduct as undesirable or offensive".[80] This approach, as far as possible under the element, favours the claimant. No express, or even implied, gesture showing an aversion to the conduct is required.

However, what amounts to "soliciting" has been the subject of some controversy in the United States, following comments by the Supreme Court in *Meritor Savings Bank v Vinson*,[81] where Rehnquist, J. stated that a claimant's sexually provocative speech or dress is "obviously relevant" as a matter of law in determining whether she found particular sexual advances unwelcome.[82] In *Mclean v Satellite Technology*[83] the claimant had "displayed her body through semi-nude photos or by lifting her skirt to show her supervisor an absence of undergarments" and had made salacious comments to colleagues, customers and competitors. It was held that, because of her "character" she may have welcomed any alleged sexual advances made to her by a superior. Thus her claim of sexual harassment failed. This suggests that there is a "welcomed conduct" defence, which has been criticised as implying sexual attraction is a motive for harassment, ignoring that harassment is often a manifestation of power, stereotyping female sexual conduct,

---

[77] C.J. Wood, "'Inviting sexual harassment': The absurdity of the welcomeness requirement in sexual harassment law", 38 Brandeis L.J. 423 (1999–2000).
[78] Brief for the EEOC as Amicus Curiae, in *Meritor Savings Bank v Vinson* 477 US 57 (1986), (No.84–1979).
[79] See above, para.5–002.
[80] *Henson v City of Dundee* 683 F 2d 897, at 903 (11th Cit 1982).
[81] 477 US 57 (1986).
[82] *ibid.*, at 69.
[83] 673 F Supp 1458 (ED Mo 1987).

and being evocative of attempts in rape cases to blame the victim for the crime.[84]

5–019   *Meritor* also established an important principle regarding the claimant's behaviour. In that case Ms Vinson alleged that her supervisor fondled her in front of other employers, and had followed her into the ladies lavatory and exposed himself to her. During this period, it was contended, she had voluntary sexual intercourse with him some 40 to 50 times. The District Court held that voluntary nature of the sexual relationship showed that Ms Vinson welcomed the supervisor's conduct at work. The Supreme Court held that this approach was mistaken: "The correct inquiry is whether respondent by her conduct indicated that the alleged sexual advances were unwelcome, not whether her actual participation in sexual intercourse was voluntary."[85] In other words, consent to a sexual relationship does not amount to consent to sexual harassment at work. By the same principle, a woman who takes part in sexual banter,[86] or appears to enjoy it,[87] or uses foul language,[88] does not necessarily welcome sexually explicit comments. In an opinion relevant to all this behaviour, Judge Posner, in *Galloway v General Motors*[89] stated that the use of foul language "may be defensive; may be playful rather than hostile or intimidating; may be colored by tone or body language; [or] . . . may be done in a placating, conciliatory, or concessive manner in an effort to improve relations with hostile or threatening coworkers."

(c) Assessing Whether there has been Sexual Harassment

5–020   See the discussion above, para.5–010 *et seq.*

(3) Consequences of Rejecting or Submitting to Unwanted Conduct

5–021   For sex (including gender reassignment) harassment and sexual harassment only, there is a further provision. A person also harasses another if "on the ground of her rejection of or submission to [sexual or sex harassment], he treats her less favourably than he would treat her had she not rejected, or submitted to, the conduct".[90] The usefulness of this provision is for the situation where, for instance, a person who rejects a sexual advance suffers retaliation, which does not necessarily amount harassment or sex discrimination, such as a denial of an

---

[84] Bull, CA, "The implications of admitting evidence of a sexual harassment plaintiff's speech and dress in the aftermath of *Meritor Savings Bank v Vinson*", 41 UCLA L Rev 117, at 119 (1993).

[85] 477 US 57, at 68 (1986).

[86] *Van Jelgerhuis v Mercury Finance* 940 F Supp 1344, at 1361 (SD Ind 1996).

[87] Carr *v Allison Gas Turbine* 32 F 3d 1007, at 1011 (7th Cir 1994).

[88] *Horney v Westfield Cage* 211 F Supp 2d 291, at 309 (D Mass 2002).

[89] 78 F 3d 1164, at 1167 (7th Cir 1996), (abrogated on other grounds, *Nat Rail Passenger Corp v Morgan*, 536 US 101, at 105–107).

[90] SDA 1975, s.4A(1)(c), and (for gender reassignment) s.4A(3)(b).

expected pay rise, or promotion. The retaliation will be actionable under this provision.

2. The Old Law—Discriminatory Harassment

Before the dedicated harassment provisions were enacted, cases of harassment were argued as a form of direct discrimination. As will be seen below, direct discrimination is an unnatural home for harassment. Harassment claims—shoehorned into the definition of direct discrimination—triumphed or fell upon unduly technical arguments.[91] The cases have been predominantly concerned with sexual harassment at work. The new statutory harassment provisions, deriving from European Directives, cover only certain classes and fields of discrimination. Consequently, as elsewhere, there will be "residual" cases, which will be argued under this old law, as direct discrimination. These residual cases will include harassment on the ground of purely colour[92] or nationality, or sexual or sex harassment in the field of education (but not vocational training), or any claims of racial, sexual, or sex harassment, predating the respective provisions. These residual cases are governed by the pre-existing case law. What follows is a review of the elements of harassment developed under case law as a form of direct discrimination, prior to the statutory provisions. For liability for direct discrimination, there must be less favourable treatment on the claimant's protected ground.

5–022

(1) The Comparison—"Less Favourable"
Here lies the major difference between the old case law and the new statutory provisions. Less favourable treatment entails a comparison with how someone else (not belonging to the protected group in question) was, or would have been, treated. This is a major obstacle to sexual harassment cases, where the distinction between sexual behaviour and conduct based on a person's gender becomes vital. The House of Lords made this point emphatically in the joint case of *Pearce v Governing Body of Mayfield Secondary School* and *Macdonald v A-G for Scotland*.[93] In *Pearce*, the claimant, a lesbian, was regularly called "lesbian", "dyke", "lesbian shit", "lemon", "lezzie" or "lez". She went off sick for a second time and took early retirement. Her claim of sexual harassment, which had to be argued as sex discrimination, failed. The House of Lords compared the

5–023

---

[91] For an argument that discrimination law is the wrong legal home for sexual harassment, see J. Dine and B. Watt, "Sexual harassment: moving away from discrimination" (1995) 58 M.L.R. 343.

[92] For a rare case of colour discrimination, see *Walker v Secretary of the Treasury* 713 F Supp 403 (ND Ga 1989) and 742 F Supp 670 (ND Ga 1990); see Ch.3, para.3–004.

[93] [2003] I.C.R. 937.

complainant to a homosexual male and concluded that the comparator would have suffered a "comparable campaign," albeit using different language. In *Macdonald* both male and female military staff were subjected to abusive and demeaning interrogation about their sex lives. The decision in this case was made all the easier by the existence of a real comparator, and so, inevitably, the House found that there was no discrimination on the ground of the claimant's sex. The House was clearly wary of finding homophobic harassment actionable under *sex* discrimination legislation when the ECJ has held that the Equal Treatment Directive 76/207/EEC (the EC principal Sex Discrimination Directive) does not cover sexual orientation discrimination.[94] This logic was taken to an absurd conclusion in *Stewart v Cleveland Guest (Engineering)*[95] where the EAT found no error of law in an industrial tribunal's finding that the display of nude female pin-ups in a factory treated both male and female workers equally, and so did not amount to sex discrimination.

That said, the House of Lords in *Pearce* noted that less favourable treatment on the ground of sex may "readily be inferred" where a male worker subjects a female colleague to persistent unwelcome sexual overtures.[96] The reasoning behind this observation is that sometimes sexual harassment may amount also to conduct on the ground of the victim's sex. Victims of harassment should emphasize this aspect of the facts, even though this means a straightforward harassment claim becomes a technical discrimination one. The result of a carefully argued claim was shown in *Smith v Gardner Merchant*,[97] where a worker was subjected to offensive remarks about him being gay. These included comments that he probably had all sorts of diseases and that gay people who spread AIDS should be put on an island. The Court of Appeal accepted that this amounted to direct sex discrimination under the SDA 1975: a male homosexual must be compared with a female homosexual, and it was clear that a lesbian would not have been subjected to the abuse suffered by the claimant. This logic explains several successful harassment claims pleaded as discrimination: a campaign to oust a female worker including suggestive remarks and brushing up against her;[98] a director's son and manager, saying to a much older female supervisor "Hiya, big tits";[99] and advice from a male head of department, prior to a promotion interview, that the female candidate should wear a short skirt and a see-through blouse

---

[94] *Grant v South West Trains* Case C-249/96 [1998] I.C.R. 449 (see especially [2003] I.C.R. 937, paras 159–163).

[95] [1996] ICR 535. Contrast the approach in the US cases of *Horney v Westfield Gage* 211 F Supp 2d 291 (2002) and *Robinson v Jacksonville Shipyards* F Supp 1486 (MD Fla 1991).

[96] [2003] I.C.R. 937, at para.17. For a brief discussion of this issue under US Federal law see *Henson v Dundee* 682 F 2d 897, at 904 (11th Cir 1982).

[97] [1999] I.C.R. 134, CA. See also, Ch.3, para.3–014.

[98] *Porcelli v Strathclyde Regional Council* ([1986] I.C.R. 564).

[99] *Insitu Cleaning v Heads* [1995] I.R.L.R. 4, EAT See above para.5–013.

showing plenty of cleavage.[100] By the same reasoning, a claim of sex (not *sexual*) harassment succeeded where a male apprentice showed that he would not have been physically assaulted (mainly with an "apprentice correction stick") had he been female.[101]

By contrast, in racial harassment cases, the courts have not made a comparison. For instance in *Commission for Racial Equality v United Packing Industry Ltd*[102] a Pakistani worker was told "We used to buy you when you were slaves." In *De Souza v Automobile Association*,[103] a worker overheard her office manager refer to her as "the wog." And in *Burton v De Vere Hotels*[104] two black female waitresses were the butt of a comedian's racist jokes at an all-male dinner. In these cases, no attempt was made to substitute an equivalent insult to a white person. In *Pearce*, Lord Nicholls disapproved of that approach and insisted that a comparison should be made.[105] In these cases, a comparison would have made no difference to the outcome because upon the facts, it was rather obvious that a white person would not have been treated as badly, which might explain why no comparison was made.

In the United States, where harassment remains a form of direct **5–024** discrimination under Federal law, the courts are bound to make a comparison, although the courts have adopted liberal approach. Thus, a doctor's practice of segregating Hispanic patients created a discriminatory working environment for a Hispanic employee, because of his race;[106] where a male supervisor seeks from a female subordinate sexual favours in exchange for employment advantages (quid pro quo cases), he does so because she is female;[107] where a male manager makes towards a female subordinate sexual innuendos, asks her to pick up objects that he drops, and to remove coins from his trouser pockets, he does so because she is female;[108] and harassing a gay man for being effeminate is done because he is male.[109] On the other hand, if a bisexual supervisor sought sexual favours from male and female subordinates, he would not be doing so on the ground of their sex.[110]

---

[100] *Driskel v Peninsula Business Services* [2000] I.R.L.R. 151, EAT.
[101] *Riley v Base t/a GL1 Heating* (2005) Unreported UKEAT/0092/05/ZT. Available at *www.employmentappeals.gov.uk.*
[102] Commission for Racial Equality Report, 1980 p.20, IT.
[103] [1986] I.C.R. 514, CA.
[104] [1997] I.C.R. 1, EAT.
[105] [2003] I.C.R. 937, at para.30.
[106] *Rogers v EEOC* 454 F 2d 234 (5th Cir 1971).
[107] *Williams v Saxbe* 413 F Supp 654 (DDC 1976); *Barnes v Costle* 561 F 2d 983 (DC Cir 1977).
[108] *Harris v Forklift Systems* 510 US 17 (Sup Ct 1993).
[109] *Nichols v Azteca* 256 F 3d 864 (9th Cir 2001). Federal discrimination law (Title VII) does not cover sexual orientation, and so such cases can only succeed under sex discrimination law. *Cf Smith v Gardner-Merchant* and *Pearce* (above).
[110] *Barnes v Costle* 561 F 2 d 983, at 990 n55 (DC Cir 1977).

(2) Treatment

5–025   In *De Souza v Automobile Association*,[111] Maria De Souza overheard her office manager refer to her as "the wog," whilst she was standing outside his office. The remark was not directed towards her and not intended to have been overheard by her. It was held that the office manager had not discriminated against Ms De Souza. May, L.J. explained that although she had been "considered" less favourably, she had not been "treated" less favourably.[112] Of course, this is not an authority that a racial insult cannot amount to less favourable treatment. Nor is this part of the case relevant under the new provisions, which prohibit conduct having the "purpose or *effect*" of violating dignity, or creating a hostile environment (emphasis supplied). The new definition no longer requires the conduct to be directed at the claimant.

(3) Assessing Whether There Has Been Harassment

5–026   In conventional cases of direct discrimination the House of Lords, in *R. v Birmingham City Council, Ex p. EOC*[113] has held that it is enough that the victim considered—reasonably—that they had been treated less favourably, even in the face of objective evidence. There must be some reasonable grounds for that perception; it is not enough that the claimant simply considered that she was treated less favourably.[114] However, for a claim of harassment as direct discrimination, a slightly different approach was taken in *Driskel v Peninsula Business Services*[115] where Holland, J. stated that "the ultimate judgment" is an objective assessment of all the facts. In doing so, tribunals should consider the victim's subjective perception and the understanding, motive and intention of the harasser. He noted that if the claimant was "hypersensitive", and the harasser "reasonably" did not realise his behaviour was to her detriment, there could be no liability.

(4) Detriment

5–027   It is possible then, that harassment can amount to discrimination, outside of the new statutory provisions. Consequently, a claimant must show that the discrimination occurred in one of the fields covered by the relevant legislation. Nearly all claims will be in the field of employment. Section 6, SDA 1975, provides that it is unlawful for an employer to discriminate against a woman in recruitment, access to promotion *etc*, dismissal *or by subjecting her to some other detriment.*

---

[111] [1986] I.C.R. 514 CA.
[112] *ibid.*, at 524E
[113] [1989] A.C. 1155, HL. See Ch.4, para.4–006.
[114] *Burrett v West Birmingham HA* [1994] I.R.L.R. 7 EAT.
[115] [2000] I.R.L.R. 151, at 155 EAT. For a discussion of this approach, see above, para.5–011.

Unless the harassment causes dismissal,[116] or some other specified disadvantage in s.6, a claimant has the further burden of showing that the harassment caused a "detriment." This has been held to mean no more than putting under a disadvantage.[117] There is no need for a physical or economic consequence,[118] nor a change to the victim's working conditions.[119]

A tribunal will consider all the circumstances when deciding this point. For instance, in *Thomas v Robinson*[120] the EAT suggested that where a worker made a racial slur against another, but afterwards, the two socialised together and appeared to get on well, the claimant may not have suffered a detriment. The EAT suggested also that there was no "detriment" where in "some work environments . . . racial abuse is given and taken in good part by members of different ethnic groups."[121] This view will be of limited application because, as the EAT itself noted, "working in an environment where racist remarks are tolerated may itself be a detriment."[122]

Other "residual" cases (those unaffected by the European derived free-standing definition of harassment), will include the provision of goods, facilities and certain services under the Sex Discrimination Act.[123] Section 29, SDA 1975, provides that it is unlawful to discriminate "by refusing or deliberately omitting to provide . . . goods, facilities or services of the like quality, in the like manner and on the like terms as are normal in his case in relation to male members of the public . . ." This section does not employ the phrase "any other detriment." Sexual harassment in the provision of services is most likely fall foul of s.29 because the service was not provided "in the like manner" as is "normal."

3. Other Unlawful Acts

(1) Aiding Unlawful Acts
Section 42, SDA 1975, s.32, RRA 1976, reg.23 of either the Religion or Belief, or Sexual Orientation, Regulations, reg.26 of the Age   **5–028**

---

[116] Which of course is most likely to be constructive dismissal.

[117] *per* Brandon, L.J., *Ministry of Defence v Jerimiah* [1980] Q.B. 87, at 99, CA. See also Ch.8, para.8–015.

[118] *Shamoon v Chief Constable of the RUC* [2003] I.C.R. 337, at para.35, HL. Lord Hoffmann pointed out in *Chief Constable of W Yorks Police v Khan* [2001] I.C.R. 1065, at para.52, HL, that employment tribunals have jurisdiction to award compensation for injury to feelings whether or not compensation is due under any other head: RRA 1976, s.57(4).

[119] *Thomas v Robinson* [2003] I.R.L.R. 7, at para.24, EAT.

[120] *ibid.*

[121] *ibid.*, at para.25.

[122] *ibid.*, at para.24.

[123] The statutory definition of harassment in the provision of goods and services is due in force by December 21, 2007: Equal Treatment in Goods and Services Directive 2004/113/EC, Art.17(1).

Regulations,[124] and s.73 of the Equality Act 2006[125] provide that a person who "knowingly" aids another person to do an act of unlawful discrimination will be treated as if he did the act himself, unless he relied, reasonably, on a statement by the primary discriminator that the act was lawful. It does not matter that the party who aids was in fact the "prime mover" of the discriminatory act. Thus in *Anyanwu v South Bank Student Union*,[126] where the university made allegations against student union employees, which ultimately led to their allegedly discriminatory dismissal, the university could be liable for aiding the union's act.

(2) Instructions and Pressure to Discriminate

5–029   All the discrimination Directives, by Art.2(4), deem that an instruction to discriminate against persons on grounds of racial or ethnic origin, sex, sexual orientation, religion or belief, or age amounts to unlawful discrimination.

In domestic law the situation is more complex. The Sex Discrimination Act 1975 and the Race Relations Act 1976 prohibit instructions and pressure to do any act made unlawful by this legislation.[127] In *CRE v Imperial Society of Teachers of Dancing*,[128] a secretary of the Society telephoned the local school to recruit a person as a filing clerk. She stated that she would rather the school did not send anyone "coloured" as that person would feel out of place because there were no other coloured employees. It was held that this did not amount to an instruction to discriminate, as the secretary had no authority over the school. However, it amounted to pressure to discriminate because of the implication that the Society may cease to deal with the school should the request not be met.

These provisions in the sex and race Acts can be enforced only by the relevant Commissions.[129] An individual remedy may be available under the Race Relations Act, as it is unlawful to treat a person less favourably on the ground of another's race.[130] So if there is some less favourable treatment (including constructive dismissal)[131] of a person who refuses to the obey an instruction to discriminate, or who protests about the instruction, an individual claim may be possible. By contrast under the SDA 1975, the less favourable treatment must

---

[124] In force October 1, 2006.
[125] Religion or Belief discrimination in other fields. Expected in force October 2006.
[126] [2001] I.C.R. 391, HL.
[127] SDA 1975, ss.39, 40; RRA 1976, ss.30, 31.
[128] [1983] I.C.R. 473, EAT.
[129] See Ch.13, para.13–029.
[130] *Showboat Entertainment Centre v Owens* [1984] ICR 65, EAT (see above Ch.4, para.4–025).
[131] *Weathersfield (t/a Van & Truck Rentals) v Sargent* [1999] I.C.R. 425, CA. (White woman resigned after instruction not to hire vehicles to "coloured and Asians." Employer liable for direct discrimination).

be on the ground of the sex of the complainant. It might be possible to argue that there has been victimisation under s.4(1)(c) or (d). If a person complains that he has been instructed to discriminate, he has effectively alleged that an unlawful act has been committed.[132] For these individual remedies the instruction or pressure *per se* is not enough: the claimant must have been treated less favourably. It is thus arguable that these domestic provisions, especially the SDA 1975, do not reflect fully the parent Directives. One solution could be for the courts to hold that an instruction to discriminate without more amounts to "less favourable treatment" (and in employment cases, "detriment").

There are no specific provisions for instructions or pressure to discriminate under the Religion or Belief and Sexual Orientation, Regulations (which cover employment matters). However, as with the Race Relations Act 1976, an individual action should be available for less favourable treatment the ground of another's religion, belief or sexual orientation, as the case may be.   **5–030**

Regulation 5 of the Age Regulations 2006,[133] in line with the parent Employment Equality Directive 2000/78/EC, outlaws instructions to discriminate, but only where the person was less favourably treated because he refused to comply with the instruction, or complained about it. In substance, this adds nothing to current position for religion or belief, and sexual orientation.

Section 55 of the Equality Act 2006 (religion or belief discrimination in other fields)[134] provides that it is unlawful to instruct, cause or induce (or attempt to cause or induce), either directly or indirectly, another to unlawfully discriminate. It will be enforceable only by the Commission for Equality and Human Rights (see Ch.13, para.13–039).

(3) Discriminatory Practices

Section 37, SDA 1975, or 28, RRA 1976, define discriminatory prac-   **5–031**
tices as the application of a provision, criterion or practice, or requirement or condition, which results in an act of discrimination, *or which would be likely to* result in such an act of discrimination if the persons to whom it is applied were not all of one sex, or race, as the case may be. The formula resembles indirect discrimination, where an apparently neutral practice has an adverse impact on a protected group. The Government stated that these sections were aimed at unintended discrimination which is "so deeply entrenched or so overwhelmingly effective that it is practically invisible, and therefore, may not give rise to any single individual complaint."[135] Similarly, s.53 of the Equality

---

[132] For victimisation generally, see Ch.7.
[133] In force October 1, 2006.
[134] Expected in force October 2007.
[135] *per* John Fraser, Under-Secretary of State for Employment, 906 HC Debs (4 March) 1976 col 1430.

Act 2006[136] makes it unlawful "to operate a practice which would be likely to result in unlawful discrimination if applied to persons of any religion or belief". So even where there is no apparent victim, action may be taken, but only by the relevant Commissions.[137]

(4) Advertisements[138]

5–032   Under s.29, RRA 1976, it is unlawful to publish or to cause to be published an advertisement which "might reasonably be understood as indicating" an intention by a person to do an act of discrimination. Some exceptions are provided for permissible discrimination,[139] and for advertising for particular nationalities for work outside of Great Britain. Section 38, SDA 1975, is substantially the same. In addition it provides that job descriptions "with a sexual connotation (such as 'waiter', 'salesgirl', 'postman' or 'stewardess') shall be taken to indicate an intention to discriminate, unless the advertisement contains an indication to the contrary."

Section 54 of the Equality Act 2006 (religion or belief discrimination in other fields)[140] similarly makes it unlawful to publish, or cause to be published, an advertisement that indicates (expressly or impliedly) an intention by any person to discriminate unlawfully in fields other than employment.

There is an important difference between the RRA and the other provisions. The RRA covers (subject to a number of exceptions) advertisements even where the apparent discrimination is in fact lawful. For instance, advertising accommodation with a nationality requirement, appears discriminatory, but may be lawful under the small premises exception. In the White Paper, the Government said "the public display of racial prejudices and preferences is inherently offensive and likely to encourage the spread of discriminatory attitudes and prejudices."[141]

The phrase in any of these sections, *publish or to cause to be published*, implies that both the publisher and the advertiser may be liable. However, there is a publisher's defence, where it relied, reasonably, on a statement by another. It is a criminal offence knowingly or recklessly to make such a statement that is in a material respect false or misleading.

---

[136] Religion or Belief discrimination in other fields. (Expected in force October 2007).

[137] See below, Ch.13, para.13–029.

[138] See also the discussion of advertisements in recruitment, Ch.8, para.8–010 *et seq.*

[139] The provision does not apply to an advertisement if the intended act would be lawful by virtue of any of ss.5 (GOQs in employment, *but not* employment GORs in s.4A), 6 (employment outside GB), 7(3) and (4)(GOQs and employment outside GB, re contract workers), 10(3)(GOQs for partnerships), 26 (exempt associations), 34(2)(b) (charities), 35 to 39 (special cases re training, education, welfare and sport), and 41 (acts done under statutory authority).

[140] Expected in force October 2007.

[141] *Racial Discrimination* Cmnd 6234, p.19.

The SDA and RRA offer offer a common extensive definition of an **5–033** advertisement:

> "Advertisement" includes every form of advertisement or notice, whether to the public or not, and whether in a newspaper or other publication, by television or radio, by display of notices, signs, labels, showcards or goods, by distribution of samples, circulars, catalogues, price lists or other material, by exhibition of pictures, models or films, or in any other way, and references to the publishing of advertisements shall be construed accordingly.[142]

This definition is broad enough to cover a notice in a house window "For sale to English family"[143] and a notice at a public house "No travellers."[144] There are no parallel provisions for Religion or Belief, Sexual Orientation or Age.

These advertisement provisions can be enforced only by the relevant Commissions.[145]

---

[142] SDA 1975, s.82; RRA 1976, s.78.
[143] *Race Relations Board v Relf,* County Ct, RRB Report 1975, p.56.
[144] *CRE v Dutton* [1989] Q.B. 783, CA. See further Ch.3, para.3–007, and Ch.6 para.6–054.
[145] *Cardiff Women's Aid v Hartup* [1994] IRLR 390, EAT. See also Ch.8, para.8–011. For the Commissions, see Ch.13, para.13–029.

CHAPTER 6

INDIRECT DISCRIMINATION

INTRODUCTION

"Librarians required: no women need apply". This job specification **6–001**
expressly, or directly, discriminates against women. Much the same
effect could be achieved by rewording it to read: "Librarians required:
applicants must be over six feet tall". This indirectly discriminates
against women (as well as some racial groups) because of its adverse
impact on the group. This rather simple example shows that a law

against direct discrimination is not enough to achieve the aims of discrimination law.

The modern concept of indirect discrimination originates from the US case *Griggs v Duke Power*,[1] which was highly influential in the development of indirect discrimination law in both the US and the UK. Duke Power's Station in North Carolina was divided into five departments: Labour, Coal Handling, Operations, Maintenance, and Laboratory and Test. Work in the Labour Department was the dirtiest and lowest paid. A high school diploma and/or the passing of an intelligence test was necessary to gain employment in, or promotion to, any of the four other Departments. Duke Power employed 95 workers at the Station, 14 of whom were black; these 14 were employed in the Labour Department. They sued Duke Power under the Civil Rights Act 1964, Title VII, which prohibited, inter alia, classifying an employee in any way which would adversely affect his status as an employee, because of his race, colour, religion, sex, or national origin. Statistics revealed that 34 per cent of whites completed high school, in contrast to 12 per cent of blacks. Research showed that 58 per cent of whites, in contrast to six per cent of blacks, passed the Intelligence Tests used by Duke Power. Duke Power showed they had not *intended* that the requirements would discriminate, but failed to show that the requirements were related to job performance. A unanimous Supreme Court found Duke Power liable, based on the following reasoning, given in the famous speech of Burger, C.J., who invokes Aesop's fable of the stork and the fox:

> "Congress has now provided that tests or criteria for employment or promotion may not provide equality of opportunity merely in the sense of the fabled offer of milk to the stork and the fox. On the contrary, Congress has now required that the posture and condition of the job-seeker be taken into account. It has—to resort again to the fable—provided that the vessel in which the milk is proffered be one all seekers can use.
>
> The Act proscribes not only overt discrimination but also practices that are fair in form but discriminatory in operation. The touchstone is business necessity. If an employment practice which operates to exclude [black people] cannot be shown to be related to job performance, the practice is prohibited . . .
>
> Congress directed the thrust of the Act to the *consequences* of employment practices, not simply the motivation. More than that, Congress has placed on the employer the burden of showing that any given requirement must have a manifest relationship to the employment in question."[2]

---

[1] 401 US 424 (1971). For an argument that *Griggs* was wrongly decided, see M. Gold, "Griggs" folly: An essay on the theory, problems and origin of the adverse impact definition of employment discrimination and a recommendation for reform." 7 Indus Rel L J 429 (1985).

[2] *ibid.*, at pp.429–32.

This speech established that indirect discrimination is based upon two broad limbs: the prima facie case and justification. First, the claimant must show that an apparently neutral practice has led to an adverse impact on a protected group, for example, where a high school diploma is a condition of employment and a larger proportion of whites than blacks complete high school. Second, the burden shifts to the defendant to justify the practice by showing it was *necessary* to achieve the (non-discriminatory) aim, for instance, by showing that a high school diploma was necessary to perform the job. Indirect discrimination is also known as disparate impact (commonly used in the US), adverse impact, and adverse effect.

1. Theoretical Basis of Indirect Discrimination Law

Although the Supreme Court in *Griggs v Duke Power*[3] provided the foundation of the modern law of indirect discrimination, the Court was less clear about its precise theoretical basis.[4] Of course, many have been offered. From time to time, there have been suggestions that purpose of indirect discrimination is to prevent unscrupulous employers from evading the conventional direct discrimination law, simply by introducing an apparently neutral practice as a pretext.[5] This "pretext theory" carries an ingredient of discriminatory intent for liability. There has been more confusion than necessary on this issue. In 1988, in the Court of Appeal, Staughton, L.J. suggested that neutral criteria that adversely affect a racial group, should not arouse liability if they were invoked upon a whim. Without discriminatory intent, he said, the definition of indirect discrimination would have "an extraordinarily wide and capricious effect".[6] More generally, in 1999, in the House of Lords, Lord Browne-Wilkinson stated courts should not introduce "something akin to strict liability . . . which will lead to individuals being stamped as racially discriminatory . . . where these matters were not consciously in their minds."[7] In 2000, the Master of the Rolls (and later Lord Chief Justice), Lord Woolf commented: "To regard a person as acting unlawfully when he had not been motivated either consciously or unconsciously by any discriminatory motive is hardly likely to assist the objective of promoting harmonious racial relations."[8] These statements overlook

6–002

---

[3] 401 US 424 (1971).

[4] B. Landsberg "Race and the Rehnquist Court" 66 Tul L Rev 1267, at 1281 (1992).

[5] G. Rutherglen "Disparate impact under Title VII: an objective theory of discrimination" (1987) 73 Virginia L Rev 1297, pp.1310–11.

[6] *Meer v London Borough of Tower Hamlets* [1988] I.R.L.R. 399, at 403 CA. Discussed below at para.6–051.

[7] Dissenting in *Nagarajan v LRT* [2000] 1 A.C. 501, at 510 HL. Discussed below, Ch.7, para.7–008.

[8] *Chief Constable of West Yorkshire v Khan* [2000] ICR 1169, at para.4, CA, Discussed below, Ch.7, para.7–009.

the express rejection in *Griggs* of discriminatory intent as an element and incorrectly portray the British position. Nothing in the UK statutes suggest that discriminatory intent is necessary for liability for indirect discrimination. Indeed, for the purpose of remedies, the legislation distinguishes between intentional and unintentional discrimination.[9]

This shows that indirect discrimination has potential beyond pretext cases. In *Griggs,* Burger C.J., said that the legislation was concerned with the consequences of employment practices, suggesting a societal or ethical dimension. The most extreme expression of this purpose is to allocate benefits (such as jobs) in proportion to group membership in the general population, regardless of merit. This could only be achieved only by quotas. Among other things, this has been labelled a "pure disparate impact model".[10] The image of hiring purely by quota is politically and judicially unthinkable nowadays.[11] In one of the most controversial discrimination cases in the United States, the Supreme Court rejected a claim of indirect discrimination by native Alaskan and Phillipino workers at an Alaskan salmon cannery factory who found themselves predominantly in the worst jobs, which carried lowest pay, separate dining facilities and accommodation, and which, according to a dissenting Justice, resembled a plantation economy.[12] Yet the claimants could not show that this scenario was caused by any particular recruitment practice, and a majority rejected the claim, because otherwise employers would be forced to hire by quota. The mere mention of the "Q" word, it seems, was justification enough for the decision, such is its evocative power. In addition, there is a legal objection to quotas and most positive action programmes, as they offend the equality principle, which is symmetrical in nature, and so protects whites as well as blacks, men as well as women, and so on. The US Supreme Court's attitude is trenchant: "[G]overnment-sponsored racial discrimination based on benign prejudice is just as noxious as discrimination inspired by malicious prejudice. In each instance, it is racial discrimination, plain and simple."[13] Less trenchant, but equally effective, was the decision of a British industrial

---

[9] See e.g. SDA 1975, s.65; RRA 1976, s.57; Sexual Orientation Regulations 2003, reg.30; Religion or Belief Regulations 2003, reg.30; Age Regulations 2006, reg.38. In *Draehmpaehl v Urania Immobilien Service ohg* Case-180/95 [1997] I.R.L.R. 538, the ECJ held that damages could not be withheld because the discrimination was unintentional.

[10] See S. Willborn, "The disparate impact model of discrimination: theory and limits" (1985) 34 American UL Rev 799, pp.801–03; M. Carvin "Disparate Impact Claims Under the New Title VII" 68 Notra Dame Law Rev 1153, who calls this a "pure" standard (at 1154); L. Lustgarten, (1980) *Legal Control of Racial Discrimination,* (1980) London; Macmillan Press, who names this "unalloyed" in contrast to the "compromised" statutory theory (at p.54).

[11] See generally, see Ch.12, p.353.

[12] *per* Stevens, J. *Wards Cove Packing Co v Atonio* 490 US 642, at 663 (1989).

[13] *per* Thomas, J. in *Adarand Constructors v Pena* 515 US 200, at 241 (1995). (Striking down a policy that five per cent per annum of all government contracts should be awarded to certified small business concerns owned and controlled by socially and economically disadvantaged individuals.) See further below, para.12–020.

tribunal to declare unlawful, as discriminating against men, the Labour Party's policy of all-women short lists for parliamentary candidates, despite the gross under-representation of women, seen (or heard!) in the Westminster Parliament.[14] Thus politically and legally quotas are out of the question,[15] whether or not indirect discrimination theory encompasses them.

There is a more inherent reason why indirect discrimination does not encompass quotas, and that is its element of justification. The Court in *Griggs* noted that employers would not be liable if they showed that their practice was job-related. In *AMAE v State of California*[16] Afro-American, Hispanic, and Asian groups established that higher proportions of their groups, compared to whites, failed schoolteacher entrance exams. Without more, the "pure" model would bring them success. With that in mind the school governors would have long since abolished the exams and hired by quota. Instead, the element of justification allowed them to show that the exams were necessary for the job. The element of justification means that indirect discrimination theory does not envisage quotas. With this in mind, it is arguable that in fact, the justification element completes a "pure" model of indirect discrimination (rather than compromising it), by identifying the cause(s) of any adverse impact.

6–003

In any case, the existing model lies somewhere between the extremes of the discriminatory-intent and quota models. Theories within this scope include "functional equivalency". This goes beyond the pretext theory, because it covers unintentional discrimination. Its premise is that the purpose of indirect discrimination law is to prohibit practices, adopted without discriminatory intent, that have the functionally equivalent effect as intentional discrimination. Hence, the law addresses not only formal recruitment criteria (as in *Griggs*), but informal or subjective decision-making that, say, perpetuates an imbalanced workforce profile.[17] This reveals that indirect discrimination is more concerned with the *effects* of any behaviour, rather than the nature of the behaviour itself.[18] Thus there is liability even for "innocent" causes (such as accident of history, or unforeseen consequences) of an adverse effect, unless they are work-related and proportionate. Another dimension is that indirect discrimination is more group-orientated, benefiting protected groups even where some

---

[14] *Jepson and Dyas-Elliott v The Labour Party* [1996] I.R.L.R. 116, IT. Effectively reversed by SDA 1975, s.42A, inserted by the Sex Discrimination (Election Candidates) Act 2002, s.1. The provision will expire at the end of 2015, unless renewed by statutory instrument: s.3, SD(EC)A 2002.

[15] For legitimate positive action programmes in the UK, EU and US, see Ch.12.

[16] 231 F 3d 572 (9th Cir 2000).

[17] See e.g. O'Connor, J. in *Watson v Fort Worth Bank* 487 US 977, at 987 (Sup Ct 1988). Subjective decision-making is discussed below, para.6–007.

[18] S. Fredman argues that the law does not aim to achieve equality of results, rather, it focuses on a disproportionate effect merely to "diagnose" a discriminatory act. See S. Fredman, "Equality: a new generation" (2001) 30 I.L.J. 145, at 162.

of the group were unaffected by a particular discriminatory practice (for instance, in *Griggs*, black applicants with a high school diploma).

Elsewhere, indirect discrimination theory in employment matters is seen as an economic tool, equating discriminatory decision-making with inefficient decision-making.[19] This chapter will show, especially with the case law, that there is no consensus on the precise theory of indirect discrimination law.

2. History of Indirect Discrimination Legislation

6–004 The British indirect discrimination legislation has its origins in the United States' Civil Rights Act of 1964 and the Supreme Court's landmark decision in *Griggs v Duke Power Co*, set out above.[20] The Civil Rights Act 1964 contained many Titles outlawing discrimination in such areas as voting rights, public accommodation, facilities and education, and federally assisted programmes. Title VII covered employment. The Act contained no specific definition of *indirect* discrimination, but the Supreme Court recognised indirect discrimination and developed the "disparate impact" theory to outlaw it.[21] The inclusion of indirect discrimination in Britain's legislation is a direct result of the Home Secretary's (the late Roy Jenkins) discovery of *Griggs* whilst on a trip to the United States. Mr Jenkins, upon his return, introduced s.1(1)*(b)* (defining and outlawing *indirect* discrimination) in a late amendment to the 1975 Sex Discrimination Bill. That explains why the White Paper[22] that preceded the Bill contained no indication of the Government's understanding of, and policy towards, indirect discrimination. In fact, the average politician of the day had no understanding of the concept of indirect discrimination. The Conservative Opposition objected to the amendment because:

> . . . we do not know what it means. Secondly we do not think the Government knows what it means; and, thirdly, if we did know

---

[19] See e.g. P. Caldwell, "Reaffirming the disproportionate effects standard liability in Title VII Litigation" 46 U Pitt L Rev 555 (1985); S. Greenberger "A Productivity approach to Disparate Impact and the Civil Rights Act of 1991" 72 Oregon Law Rev 253 (1993). *Cf* R. Epstein, *Forbidden Grounds: The Case Against Employment Discrimination Laws* (Cambridge: Harvard University Press 1992), esp pp.226–229.

[20] 401 US 424 (1971). See para.6–001.

[21] In the years that followed, the Supreme Court developed the disparate impact theory in accordance with the basic tenets of *Griggs*. However, in the late 1980s this was checked by judicial and political divisions. The Supreme Court upset many well-established principles of the theory. Most notable was the bare-majority decision in *Wards Cove Packing Co v Atonio* 490 US 642 (1989) which followed the plurality decision in *Watson v Fort Worth Bank & Trust* 487 US 977 (1988). In response Congress passed the Civil Rights Act 1991. Although this statute re-established some of the earlier principles, it also codified some parts of the *Wards Cove* decision. See further below, paras 6–008 and 6–033.

[22] *Equality for Women* Cmnd 5724, 1974, London: HMSO.

what it meant, we do not think that we would like it, but we cannot be sure.[23]

Nonetheless, the Government added to the Bill a formula defining indirect discrimination and that became law. A year later Parliament used the same formula in the Race Relations Act 1976. This time the respective White Paper on Race Relations[24] included *some* indication of the Government's aims in introducing indirect discrimination laws. However, the imprecise use of language reflected the Government's less than full appreciation of the concept that it was introducing.[25] From its inception in Britain, the legislators have offered very little guidance about their aims and ambitions for indirect discrimination law. Consequently the judges had only the statutory words as guidance.

When the *Griggs* two-limbed theory of indirect discrimination[26] was introduced into British legislation, (i.e. Sex Discrimination Act 1975 and Race Relations Act 1976) some detail was added. There were seven elements contained in the British statutory scheme (six belonging to the first limb). During the 1980's and 1990's, whilst the judges were wrestling with the statutory formula, the ECJ was developing a concept of indirect discrimination from the basic tenets of equal treatment enshrined Community legislation. In time, tension developed between Community and British law where the British definition was narrower, or given a narrower interpretation, than its EC counterpart. This began with the Equal Pay Act 1970[27] and then the Sex Discrimination Act 1975.[28] Eventually a series of Directives forced the broader definition into domestic law, but only in areas of EC competence. The new definition took effect in the Sex Discrimination Act on October 12, 2001, but only for employment matters,[29] and in the Race Relations Act in July 2003 in all fields, but only for discrimination on the grounds of race or ethnic or national origins (not colour or nationality). Consequently there remains a class of residual cases that either predate or fall outside the scope of the parent Directives. The Sexual Orientation, Religion or Belief, and Age Regulations contained the new definition from their outset. A more detailed account of the new Directives can be found at the start of Ch.2.

Essentially, the new version substitutes the phrases "requirement or condition" with "provision, criterion or practice"; and "considerably

6–005

---

[23] *per* Ian Gilmour, Standing Committee B (22 April 1975), col. 36.
[24] *Racial Discrimination* Cmnd 6234, 1975, London: HMSO.
[25] See further below, para.6–050.
[26] Prima facie case and justification. See above, para.6–001.
[27] See *Enderby v Frenchay HA* [1991] I.C.R. 382 EAT and [1994] I.C.R. 112 CA and ECJ, below paras 6–031 and 9–033.
[28] See *Falkirk Council v Whyte* [1997] I.R.L.R. 560, Ch.2, 2–017.
[29] This was achieved by the Burden of Proof Directive 97/80/EC. This definition was further amended on October 1, 2005 by Art.2, Equal Treatment Amendment Directive, 2002/73/EC. It is due to be extended to the provision of goods and services by General Sex Equality Directive 2004/113/EC, due in force by December 12, 2007. See further, Ch.2, para.2–002.

smaller" with "particular disadvantage". It also provides a more detailed definition of justification. What follows is an account of the elements of the new law. The residual law is covered at the end of the Ch.2.

3. THE ELEMENTS OF INDIRECTION DISCRIMINATION

Race Relations Act 1976

1 (1A) A person also discriminates against another if . . . he applies to that other a provision, criterion or practice which he applies or would apply equally to persons not of the same race or ethnic or national origins as that other, but—

(a) which puts or would put persons of the same race or ethnic or national origins as that other at a particular disadvantage when compared with other persons,
(b) which puts that other at that disadvantage, and
(c) which he cannot show to be a proportionate means of achieving a legitimate aim.

The same formula is used in the Sex Discrimination Act 1975, and the Sexual Orientation, Religion or Belief, and Age Regulations. The formula consists of the following elements: (1) the application of a provision, criterion or practice, which (2) causes ("which puts"); (3) an adverse, or disparate, impact ("particular disadvantage") to the claimant's protected group; and (4) causes disadvantage to the claimant; and (5) cannot be justified (paragraph (c)). As with *Griggs*, the first four complete the claimant's prima facie case, after which the burden shifts to the defendant to justify the challenged practice. Identifying a *protected group* is covered in Ch.3, and *disadvantage to the claimant* requires no further discussion, because it is merely to ensure a claimant has *locus standi* (a right to sue).[30] What follows is a discussion of the elements in a slightly rearranged order, starting with (1) the "provision, criterion or practice", (2) proving the particular disadvantage, (3) causation, and (4) justification.

(1) Provision, Criterion or Practice

6–006 A broad range of requirements can be attacked as indirectly discriminating against a protected group. For instance, maximum age requirements may adversely affect women,[31] and nepotistic requirements for

---

[30] See e.g. 893 HC 1491–2 June 18, 1975.
[31] See e.g. *Price v Civil Service Commission (No.2)* [1978] I.R.L.R., IT 3; *Jones v University of Manchester* [1993] I.C.R. 474, CA.

membership in associations or trade unions may adversely affect or exclude certain racial groups.[32] The relatively new statutory phrase *provision, criterion or practice* (replacing *requirement or condition*) has significantly broadened the reach of indirect discrimination law in the UK. British case law on the new formula is still thin, so cases from the United States (where since its inception in 1964, the legislation used the phrase "employment *practice*") are particularly instructive. The new formula should cover not just strict requirements, but also mere *preferences*, such as job criteria which state that local experience, or management experience, or British nationality, is "desirable".[33] It should also cover the situation where points are awarded to candidates fulfilling each of a number of criteria, such as experience in a certain country, in line with the approach taken by the ECJ.[34] Accordingly, the new definition reverses the effect of *Brook v Haringey LB*,[35] that a last-in-first-out selection procedure (that adversely affected women) was not a "requirement" for the purpose of the old definition because it was not the sole criterion.

The new definition has the potential to encompass two other practices: subjective decision making and word-of-mouth recruitment and promotion.

(a) Subjective Decision Making

This takes many forms. For instance, the final decision for job candidates who meet the minimum requirements may be a subjective evaluation of the candidates' previous work and potential. This may disfavour those groups who have suffered discrimination in the past, indeed it may perpetuate it.[36] This can occur in recruitment, promotion and redundancy, for instance, in the US case *Caron v Scott Paper*[37] the claimants were allowed to challenge a redundancy procedure as adversely affecting older workers. Workers were evaluated

6–007

---

[32] See *Handsworth Horticultural Institute Ltd v CRE* (unreported) Birmingham County Court; see "Ruled Out", F Invest 1992, ISBN 1 85442 0887, (all-white social club in area of just 40 per cent white population required that new members were sponsored by two members and approved by committee); and the US case, *Local 53, Asbestos Workers v Vogler* 407 F 2d 1047 (5th Cir 1969), (membership of trade union restricted to sons or close relatives of existing members, who were predominantly white).

[33] See respectively, *Meer v London Borough of Tower Hamlets* [1988] I.R.L.R. 399 CA; *Falkirk Council v Whyte* [1997] I.R.L.R. 560, EAT; *Perera v CSC* [1983] I.C.R. 428, CA. See below, paras 6–050—6–052.

[34] *Ingetraut Scholz v Opera Universitaria di Cagliari* Case C-419/92 [1994] E.C.R. 1-507 (if the German candidate had experience *in Italy* (rather than Germany) she would have amassed enough credit to have been chosen).

[35] [1992] I.R.L.R. 478, EAT, followed *Hall v Shorts Missile Systems* [1996] NI 214, NICA.

[36] See E. Bartholet, "Application of Title VII to jobs in high places" (1982) 95 Harv L Rev 947, pp.955–58, 978–80.

[37] 834 F Supp 33 (D Me 1993). See also *Graffam v Scott Paper* 870 F Supp 389, at 395 (D Me 1994) affirmed 60 F 3d 809 (1st Cir 1995), and *District Council 37 v New York City Department of Parks* 113 F 3d 347, at 351 (2nd Cir 1997) (subjective choice of job titles for redundancy may adversely affect those aged over 40).

using six subjective factors and one objective factor. The subjective factors used were: job skills; leading change skills; interpersonal skills; self-management; performance; and versatility. The only objective factor was length of service. The US Supreme Court, in *Watson v Fort Worth Bank*,[38] confirmed that the indirect discrimination theory developed in *Griggs* (see above)[39] could apply to "an employer's undisciplined system of subjective decision making", although it noted that where some personal qualities, for example, common sense, good judgment, originality, ambition, loyalty and tact, cannot be measured accurately by objective testing, the decision-making may be easier to justify.[40] It maybe more difficult to justify other subjective recruitment practices, such as delegation to managers or supervisors who simply favour those "whose face fits", or who "go on gut reactions" to the applicants;[41] or advertising in areas that happen to be predominantly white.[42]

In many cases, there is mixture of these practices. Here are two examples from US case law. In *Rowe v General Motors*,[43] the following promotion/transfer procedure was identified:

(1)   The foreman's recommendation was the indispensable single most important factor in the promotion process.

(2)   Foremen were given no written instructions for the qualifications or qualities necessary for promotion.

(3)   Those standards which were determined to be controlling were vague and subjective.

(4)   Hourly employees were not notified of promotion opportunities nor were they notified of the qualifications necessary to get jobs.

(5)   There were no safeguards in the procedure designed to avert discriminatory practices.

6–008   It was held that this "procedure" amounted to an employment practice which discriminated against blacks, who predominantly occupied the "Hourly" jobs. Similarly, in *Montana Rail Link v Byard*[44] it was held that the following amounted to a discriminatory employment practice:

---

[38] 487 US 977 (1988).

[39] At para.6–001.

[40] 487 US 977 (1988), at 999.

[41] *Green v US Steel* 570 F Supp 254, 269 (ED Pa 1983), certiorari denied 498 US 814.

[42] *US v City of Warren, Michigan* 138 F 3d 1083 (6th Cir 1998).

[43] 457 F 2d 348, at 358–359 (5th Cir 1972)

[44] 260 Mont 331, at 352 (1993). Decided under the Montana Human Rights Act under Title VII disparate impact principles.

(1)   The impression made on the interviewers by the applicants was the single most important factor in the hiring process, although the applicants were not told of this.

(2)   Those responsible for making hiring decisions followed no written instructions for the qualifications necessary for hiring.

(3)   The standards which were determined to be controlling were vague and subjective.

(4)   The applicants were not properly informed, and indeed may have been misled about the qualifications necessary to get jobs and about the procedures they had to follow to be hired.

(5)   There are no safeguards in the hiring procedure designed to avert discriminatory practice.

(6)   A "word of mouth" recruitment campaign was instigated by the employer.

(7)   Interviews for some applicants were no more than "informal chats".

(8)   Some applicants hired were not interviewed at all.

There comes a point where an employer's decision-making becomes so informal that it is impossible to pinpoint any specific criterion that causes an adverse impact. This is frustrating for claimants where statistics reveal a significant disparity in the workforce. Whether such situations are challengeable under indirect discrimination law has been the subject of fierce debate in the United States. It was triggered by the case of *Wards Cove Packing Co v Atonio*.[45] Wards Cove ran salmon canneries in Alaska. Three practices were identified. It recruited its skilled workers using its offices in Washington and Oregon. Second, there was no promotion from the unskilled to the skilled positions; all skilled jobs were filled solely through the Washington and Oregon offices (many unskilled workers testified that they possessed the necessary skills to fill some of the skilled jobs). Third, the skilled and unskilled workers were accommodated in separate dormitories and mess halls. The statistics showed that the skilled workers were mainly white and the unskilled ones mainly Filipino or native Alaskan. A class of non-white unskilled workers brought a case of indirect discrimination, heavily based on the statistics.

A bare majority of the Supreme Court rejected the claim, holding **6–009** that it was necessary to isolate each specific employment practice and show it caused a disparity, something the claimants could not do. The

---

[45] 490 US 642 (Sup Ct 1989).

reasoning of the majority was clear, with White, J. stating that an alternative result would mean that any employer with a racially imbalanced workforce could be "haled into court" to justify to the situation.[46] This would force employers to adopt quotas. The decision caused uproar and confusion. Congress acted to clarify the law and passed s.105 of the Civil Rights Act 1991, which endorsed *Wards Cove* by providing that complainants must show that "each particular challenged employment practice causes a disparate impact . . ." but qualified it by stating that where the decision-making process is not capable of separation for analysis, it may be treated as one employment practice. The Act provided an example: in *Dothard v Rawlinson,*[47] height and weight requirements designed to measure strength were used in the recruitment of prison officers but discriminated against women. According to the exception, these requirements could not be separated for analysis and so could be taken as a whole when linking them to the adverse impact.

Section 105 appears to restore matters to the pre-*Wards Cove* position, emphasizing that there must be a causal link between the practice, or groups of practices, and the disparity. In a case following the 1991 Act, *Butler v Home Depot,*[48] statistics showed that over a four-year period, women made up just 6.4 per cent of the new recruits, whereas women made up some 36–39 per cent of the labour market qualified for the jobs. The employer's recruitment policy consisted of delegating decisions to store managers who based their decisions on their own subjective judgments, with virtually no written criteria. It was held that the recruitment practices were not capable of separation and could be analysed as a whole. It was then relatively easy for the claimants to show that the practice caused the disparity and establish a prima facie case.[49]

The position in the US now appears to be that where a decision-making process is so vague that it is impossible to pinpoint a specific criterion causing a disparate impact, the process may be treated as a whole, making proof of causation much more straightforward. This should not lead to the adoption of quotas, as feared in *Wards Cove*. First, any significant imbalance should alert the employer that something is wrong. An investigation will identify a cause, which should be eradicated, refined or justified. If the employers in say, *Butler v Home Depot,* had taken that action, there would have been no expensive litigation. Second, if instead the employer panics and adopts quotas, it will face *direct* discrimination claims from those intentionally disadvantaged under the quotas.[50]

---

[46] 490 US, at 652.
[47] 433 US 321 (Sup Ct 1977). See also below, paras 6–027 and 6–040.
[48] No C-94-4335 SI, C-95-2182 SI, (ND Cal. August 29, 1997).
[49] *ibid.,* at 47–48.
[50] In the US, intentional discrimination will attract higher damages. For permitted affirmative action, see Ch.12, below, p.353.

This American experience suggests that the new statutory phrase **6–010**
provision, criterion or practice can be interpreted to cover even the
most vague decision making processes, where they can be combined to
show that, as a whole, they cause a disparate impact. However, *Wards
Cove*, and the subsequent Congressional reform, make it clear that
some offending practice must be identified. No case can be brought on
statistics alone. Again, the reason behind this is the fear that such
claims would force employers into adopting quotas. As noted above,
this would not necessarily be the case. Further, an absolute bar on
such claims may prove unjust in rare cases. Take the following
example. A factory in a predominantly black area employs a predominantly white workforce. The jobs are low-skilled, making it unlikely
that the cause of the disparity is a skills shortage amongst the local
population. The employer uses a heavily disguised recruitment
process, which claimants are unable to identify. Here, the recognition
of a claim based on statistics would, at the least, force the employer to
expose its recruitment policy to scrutiny. The key to recognising a
prima facie case in these circumstances is making an inference from
the statistics that the employer is using a discriminatory employment
practice.[51]

(b) Word-of-Mouth Recruitment
Like some subjective decision-making, word-of-mouth recruitment **6–011**
(or promotion) has a tendency to perpetuate an imbalanced workforce
or membership (be it predominantly male, or white, or Protestant,
Muslim and so on), and so should fall within the purpose of the legislation. To date, there are no British cases on the issue under the new
formula, although the EOC's Code of Practice suggests that where it
precludes members of one sex from applying, word-of-mouth recruitment should be "avoided".[52] When word-of-mouth recruitment or
promotion forms part of a decision making process, and this process
is analysed as a whole (see above), it becomes subject to scrutiny, albeit
only in a loose sense. This should be incentive enough for employers
and others to avoid the process. However, where the word-of-mouth
recruitment or promotion is the only process, it is less clear if it is challengeable as indirect discrimination. In the United States, in the
absence of a Supreme Court ruling on the matter, the courts are

---

[51] The ECJ is taking this line in equal pay claims when there is a disparity in wages and the pay
structure is not transparent. See further Ch.9, para.9–029.
[52] See *www.eoc.org.uk*, click on "The Law". In *Coker v Lord Chancellor* [2002] I.C.R. 321, the
Court of Appeal noted *obiter* "It is possible that a recruitment exercise conducted by word of
mouth, by personal recommendation or by other informal recruitment method will constitute
indirect discrimination." (At para.57.) Discussed further below, para.6–025. Word-of-mouth
hiring was challenged, unsuccessfully, as a form of racial segregation in *Pel Ltd v Modgill*
[1980] IRLR 142 EAT, discussed above, Ch.4 para.4–035. The CRE Code of Practice (in force
April 6, 2006) makes no mention of word-of-mouth recruitment.

divided. Some Circuits recognise word-of-mouth recruitment as an employment practice,[53] others do not.[54] The reason given for rejecting such claims is that "passive reliance on employee word-of-mouth recruiting" is not "affirmative" enough to amount to an employer's *practice*.[55] However, there seems to be no reason or principle why an employer's acquiescence in a discriminatory practice by its workers should escape the law. On general tort principles, an omission amounts to an act. Indeed, in the US the Supreme Court has held that inaction by an employer, who did not more than rely on the subjective judgment of supervisors in recruitment, can be challenged under indirect discrimination law.[56] Similarly, the British legislation stipulates that for the purpose of the legislation, an act includes a deliberate omission.[57] Accordingly, word-of-mouth recruitment or promotion, even where the defendant has merely acquiesced in it, should be challengeable under the new statutory phrase *provision, criterion or practice* where it causes a disparate impact on a protected group.

(2) Proving a Particular Disadvantage

6–012   The next stage involves selecting the appropriate pool for analysis. The pool is analysed to see if the protected group has been put at a particular disadvantage. Some methods of analysis will dictate the content of the pool, so Pts (a) and (b)(i) below, especially need to be digested as one.

(a) Choosing the Pool

6–013   **The Race Relations Act 1976**

> 3(4) A comparison of the case of a person of a particular racial group with that of a person not of that group . . . must be such that the relevant circumstances in the one case are the same, or not materially different, from the other.

All domestic discrimination legislation (save disability) carries this rubric, adapted for the ground in question. Although it appears only to apply to direct discrimination (referring to a comparison of

---

[53] *United States v Georgia Power* 474 F 2d 906, at 925–926 (5th Cir 1973).
[54] *EEOC v Chicago Miniature Lamp Works* 947 F 2d 292 (7th Cir 1991). This division has not proved critical in the US, because an employer who *ought* to have known that its word-of-mouth recruitment policy had a discriminatory effect, can be liable for intentional *direct* discrimination, the word-of-mouth recruitment being a mere pretext: *Domingo v New England Fish Company* 727 F 2d 1429 at 1435–36 (9th 1984).
[55] See e.g. *ibid.*, at 298–299.
[56] *Watson v Fort Worth Bank* 487 US 977 (1988), see above para.6–007.
[57] SDA 1975, s.82; RRA 1976, s.78; Sexual Orientation Regulations 2003, reg.2; Religion or Belief Regulations 2003, reg.2; Age Regulations 2006, reg.2.

persons and not groups), it has been held to apply also to indirect discrimination.[58]

The pool consists of a set of persons in the same circumstances as the claimant, save for the challenged factor, which should be irrelevant. In *Jones v University of Manchester,*[59] the job requirement was to be a graduate aged 27–35. The claimant argued that the age requirement indirectly discriminated against women. She argued that the pool should be of graduates who had obtained their degree as mature students, i.e. aged at least 25. This was rejected as the age factor should be was disregarded. The correct pool was *all* graduates. (Then the proportion of female graduates within the age requirement was compared with the proportion of male graduates within the age requirement.)

In another sex discrimination case, *Allonby v Accrington &* **6–014** *Rossendale College,*[60] where part-time lecturers were dismissed and rehired through an agency on inferior terms, the part-time factor was disregarded providing a pool of *all* the College's teaching staff. (The comparison was between the proportions of female full-timers and male full-timers (i.e. those not dismissed), which was 21 and 38 per cent respectively.) In *McCausland v Dungannon DC*[61] the claim, under the Fair Employment (Northern Ireland) Act 1989, (outlawing discrimination on grounds of religious belief or political opinion), was that a job requirement to be an existing member of staff indirectly discriminated against Catholics. The other (unchallenged) requirement was a "standard occupational classification" (SOC) of 1, 2 or 3. The pool consisted of anyone from the whole Northern Ireland workforce with a SOC 1, 2 or 3. (The comparison was between the proportions of Catholics and Protestants from the pool who could comply with the requirement to be an existing member of staff.)

This approach has been thrown into doubt by the majority's pronouncements in the recent House of Lords case *Rutherford v Secretary of State for Trade and Industry (No.2).*[62] In this case, predating the Age Regulations 2006, Mr Rutherford was dismissed at the age of 67. By s.109 of the Employment Rights Act 1996, those over 65 cannot claim for unfair dismissal. Mr Rutherford argued that s.109 adversely affected men and so was contrary to EC sex discrimination law. The majority compared men and women over 65 who were in work, and concluded that there was no adverse impact *at all*, because s.109 treated these workers equally, irrespective of sex. Notable in this methodology is the inclusion of the challenged factor (age) in deciding the pool. This seems to have come about because the

---

[58] *Allonby v Accrington & Rossendale College* [2001] I.C.R. 1189, CA, see further below, and para.6–034.

[59] [1993] I.C.R. 474, CA.

[60] [2001] I.C.R. 1189, CA, see further below, para.6–034.

[61] [1993] IRLR 583, NICA. See further below, para.6–019.

[62] [2006] UKHL 19.

majority struggled to equate an age limit with a condition, such as that for two-years' service for unfair dismissal rights in *Seymour-Smith*.[63] The claimant's case was relatively simple: that as men have a greater tendency to work beyond 65, they are disproportionately affected by s.109. Disregard the age factor and the pool (crudely) is the nation's entire workforce,[64] with the comparison between the proportions of men and women who cannot meet the condition (to be under 65). In the event, as the minority found, this did not show a significant enough difference to suggest that that s.109 adversely affected men.[65] The majority's approach compared only those in the disadvantaged group, with the inevitable result of no adverse impact. Indeed, the impact was *precisely* the same on men and women, a sure sign that there is something wrong with the test. The chances of a neutral requirement having precisely the same impact on two groups are low. *Rutherford* was decided under the old definition, which demands a "requirement or condition" and can be conveniently distinguished on that basis.

Section 3(4) should not be used to include factors of defendant's objective justification. In *Spicer v Government of Spain*[66] a Spanish state school based in London paid teachers seconded from the Spanish civil service (all Spanish) more than teachers recruited in England (some English, some Spanish). The claim was for indirect discrimination on the ground of nationality, under the RRA 1976. The employer argued that the secondees should not be in the pool, as they were paid more because they were Spanish civil servants, and so their relevant circumstances differed from the other teachers. The Court of Appeal rejected this argument, holding that the correct pool consisted of all the teachers at the school. This is undoubtedly correct. Effectively, the employer was arguing that those favoured by the challenged practice should be excluded from the pool. As the Court of Appeal noted, if that were allowed, no claim of indirect discrimination could succeed.[67] The matter of *why* the secondees were paid more was a matter for objective justification.

6–015   Sometimes the pool is dictated by the choice of analysis. For example, a dismissal selection procedure (the challenged practice) may

---

[63] See below para.000. In *Rutherford*, Lord Scott said: "But where the provision in question does not constitute a condition for obtaining a benefit that some employees are able to satisfy and some are not but imposes a disadvantage on those who remain in employment after a specified age, the situation produced presents a rather different picture." (*ibid.*, at para.15.) Contrast *Price v Civil Service Commission* [1978] I.C.R. 27, below, paras 6–018 and 6–054.

[64] Conceivably this could be refined with factors such as the (then) two-year qualification period for unfair dismissal and unemployed persons who wish to work. But this would make no difference to the outcome.

[65] *per* Lords Nicholls and Walker, affirming the view of the EAT ([2002] I.C.R. 123, EAT) and CA, ([2004] EWCA Civ 1186).

[66] [2005] I.C.R. 213.

[67] *ibid.*, at para.28. See also the discussion in relation to direct discrimination, Ch.4, at paras 4–009—4–011.

dictate that the pool is the entire workforce, as in *Allonby*. This is commonly so in employment cases when the challenged practice applies only to existing workers, so making the logical pool the whole (or perhaps a class) of the workforce. Normally, where national legislation is being challenged as being contrary to EC discrimination law, the pool is drawn from the entire population. In *R. v Secretary of State for Employment, Ex p. Seymour-Smith*,[68] the extension of the qualification period for Unfair Dismissal rights to two years was challenged as indirectly discriminating against women, who are more transient in the workforce than men.[69] The pool chosen was the UK's total workforce.

Choosing a pool can be complex and less certain in other cases. This is especially so in recruitment. To compare the success rate of male and female, or black and white, or Catholic or Protestant, *applicants* is attractive because it measures precisely the impact of the challenged practice. However, this may be misleading as it omits persons deterred from applying in the first place. It does not account for those deterred by say, an employer's reputation for nepotism or discrimination, or a discriminatory factor in the job description, such an unnecessary academic qualification or minimum height requirement. It may also be distorted where an employer has promoted enthusiastically its equal opportunities policy so that a disproportionately high number of minorities or women apply. If the pool is not restricted to applicants, a geographical pool may be used. Here, there are a number of factors to consider. In job recruitment, for instance, an appropriate labour market must be chosen, identifying those otherwise qualified for the job (see *McCausland v Dungannon DC*, below, para.6–019). In sex discrimination cases, normally women and men with any given qualifications are evenly distributed throughout the nation, so any statistics are unlikely to be distorted by a limited or extended geographical pool. However, other protected groups, especially racial groups, are less likely to be evenly distributed. Other factors may be incorporated to measure more accurately the impact on the claimant's group. The nature of the job may be important. People will relocate readily for many jobs (academics for instance), suggesting the pool could be geographically wide, perhaps the whole nation. Where the job is likely to be taken only by local people, the pool becomes geographically smaller, although perhaps denser. This may be especially so for low-skilled jobs, where potential applicants are unlikely to relocate or commute over long distances, whilst at the same time, there is likely to be a large proportion of qualified persons in the locality.

---

[68] [2000] I.C.R. 244, HL. See further below, para.6–024. See also *Rutherford v Secretary of State for Trade and Industry (No.2)* [2005] I.C.R. 119, affirmed [2006] UKHL 19 see above, para.6–014.

[69] It was reduced to one year where the effective date of termination is after June 1, 1999: Unfair Dismissal and Statement of Reasons for Dismissal (Variation of Qualifying Period) Order 1999, SI 1999/1436.

Parallel or similar arguments may apply in other fields, such as membership of associations, or access to services or education.

(b) Proving a Particular Disadvantage

6–016 The old definition of indirect discrimination demanded that there had to be a "considerable difference" between the proportion of claimant's group who could comply, and proportion of the other group who could comply. Note that the *proportions*, not numbers, are compared. The new definition requires that the challenged practice puts the claimant's group at a "particular disadvantage". This liberates the old law in two ways. First, there is no longer a need to look for a considerable difference—other methods of analysis can be used. Second, the analysis is no longer confined to comparing the positive figures, representing only those who were *advantaged* by the requirement; now the negative figures, representing those *disadvantaged* by the practice, may be used. Finally, the scenario of appointing from a circle of family, friends or acquaintances requires special consideration.

(i) Choosing the appropriate analytical model [70]

6–017 There are five established models available: (a) intrinsically liable; (b) considerable difference; (c) small but persistent difference; (d) the four-fifths rule; and (e) the probability of chance.

(i)(a) Intrinsically liable

6–018 The new definition of indirect discrimination was not intended to mandate that statistical proof was the only method of proving a case. In the absence of available statistics, it is enough if the challenged practice is intrinsically liable to adversely affect a protected group. The draft Race Directive referred to *O'Flynn v Chief Adjudication Officer* [71] as its model for indirect discrimination. [72] In *O'Flynn* the UK Government granted means-tested social security payments for funeral expenses incurred by all workers (including migrant workers), but only if the burial or cremation took place in the UK. An Irish national brought an action of discrimination on the ground of nationality (under Regulation 1612/68, Art.7(2)), arguing that the restriction infringed the Community principle of free movement of workers by indirectly discriminating against migrant workers. The Government argued that there was no statistical evidence that its rule adversely

---

[70] See T. Sugrue and W. Fairley, "A case of unexamined assumptions: the use and misuse of the statistical analysis of *Castenada/Hazlewood* in discrimination legislation" (1983) 24 Boston College L Rev 925; M. Garaud, "Legal standards and statistical proof in Title VII litigation: in search of a coherent disparate impact model" (1990) 139 Penns UL Rev 455, p.474.

[71] Case C-237/94, [1996] E.C.R. I-2617, ECJ.

[72] COM (1999) 566 Final 1999/0253 (CNS)/0655) p.6, fn 8.

affected foreign nationals in the UK. The ECJ held that it was not necessary to prove that the restriction did in practice adversely affect migrant workers. It was sufficient that it was "intrinsically liable" to have such an effect. In cases such as the present, it was above all the migrant worker who may, on the death of a member of the family, have to arrange for burial in another Member State, in view of the links which the members of such a family generally maintain with their State of origin.[73] Thus, where the challenged practice by its nature, or is intrinsically, liable to adversely affect a protected group, a prime facie case is made out. This approach was adopted by the Court of Appeal in *Secretary of State for Work and Pensions v Bobezes*[74] where child allowance payments were withheld from a migrant worker because his child spent time with its grandparents in Portugal. Citing *O'Flynn*, Lord Slynn noted that "It was enough in cases of discrimination based on nationality that the effect of the provision is 'essentially' 'intrinsically' 'susceptible by its very nature' 'by its own nature' liable to be discriminatory."[75] It was disappointing that Lord Slynn restricted these comments to nationality discrimination. There is no reason why it should not apply to any ground where the challenged practice intrinsically, or by its nature, will adversely affect any particular protected group, especially where there is an absence of statistics, or their use would escalate the costs of litigation beyond the reach of many claimants, or for that matter, defendants (such as small employers). Measures disadvantaging part-time workers intrinsically discriminate against women; uniform requirements of hats, or skirts, intrinsically discriminate against some racial groups. The sense in this approach was shown in *London Underground Ltd v Edwards (No.2)*[76] where the claim was that a new rostering system would adversely affect single parents. The tribunal was happy to conclude that that it was "common knowledge" that more women than men were single parents. In *Price v Civil Service Commission,*[77] where an age limit of 17–27 adversely affected women because of family responsibilities, the EAT based its finding of adverse impact on "Knowledge and experience".[78]

The courts appear to be stricter in the United States. Disparate impact will not be assumed simply because it is logical or likely. In *Thomas v Metroflight*[79] a rule barred the employment of spouses. The effect of this was that when two workers married, one was dismissed. If the couple did not choose who should quit, the one with less

[73] Case C-237/94, [1996], at paras 20–22.
[74] E.C.R. I-2617, [2005] 3 All E.R. 497, CA. Applied in *R. (Elias) v Secretary of State for Defence* [2005] I.R.L.R. 788 Q.B.D.
[75] *per* Lord Slynn, *ibid.*, at para.24.
[76] [1997] I.R.L.R. 157, EAT. See further below, para.6–038.
[77] [1978] I.C.R. 27. See further below, para.6–054.
[78] *ibid.*, at 32.
[79] 814 F 2d 1506 (10th Cir 1987).

seniority would be fired. When Thomas married she was dismissed as the least senior. She claimed that the rule adversely affected women because logically, women were more likely to be less senior than any man they might marry. Thomas was the second person to be dismissed under the rule, the first also being a women. The court held that the sample of two women was too small to be statistically significant and it could not assume that the rule adversely affected women (even though it admitted it suspected it did) and dismissed Thomas' claim.

(i)(b) Considerable difference

6–019   Where statistics are appropriate, there are a number of models available. A fairly conventional model (especially under the old definition), of comparing the proportions of the positive figures for a considerable difference, is illustrated in *McCausland v Dungannon DC*.[80] The claim, under the Fair Employment (Northern Ireland) Act 1989, (outlawing discrimination on grounds of religious belief or political opinion), was that a job requirement for a chief works manager to be an existing worker in local government, indirectly discriminated against Catholics. The other (unchallenged) requirement was a "standard occupational classification" (SOC) of 1, 2 or 3. The pool chosen was the whole Northern Ireland workforce with the SOC 1, 2 or 3. The number of SOC 1, 2 or 3 workers in Northern Ireland consisted of 28,159 Catholics and 50,170 Protestants. The number of SOC 1, 2 or 3 workers in local government consisted of 423 Catholics and 1,039 Protestants. The comparison was between the proportion of Catholics, and the proportion of Protestants, who could comply with the requirement to be in local government. The proportions were 1.5 per cent and 2.1 per cent respectively. The ratio reveals a considerable difference. The Catholic percentage (1.5) is just 71 per cent of the Protestant percentage (2.1). Hence (roughly) for every ten Protestants who qualified, there were seven Catholics, (a ratio of 10:7).

(i)(c) Small but persistent difference

6–020   A deviation from the considerable difference rubric was made by the ECJ in *R. v Secretary of State for Employment, Ex p. Seymour-Smith*.[81] Domestic legislation extended the qualification period for Unfair Dismissal rights to two years.[82] Ms Seymour-Smith challenged this as being contrary to Art.119 (now 141) EC Treaty because it discrimi-

---

[80] [1993] I.R.L.R. 583, NICA.
[81] Case C-167/97, [1999] I.C.R. 447. See M. Connolly "Commentary, *R. v Secretary of State for Employment, Ex p. Seymour-Smith*" [2000] 05/2 Jo Civ Lib 212, pp.217–219.
[82] The Unfair Dismissal (Variation of Qualifying Period) Order 1985, SI 1985/782. It has since been reduced to one year where the effective date of termination is after June 1, 1999: Unfair Dismissal and Statement of Reasons for Dismissal (Variation of Qualifying Period) Order 1999, SI 1999/1436.

nated against women, who are more transient in the workforce than men. Both sides accepted the Annual Labour Force Surveys from 1985 to 1991 (when Ms Seymour-Smith was dismissed) as evidence of the impact of the two-year requirement. These are surveys of the UK's total workforce. They reveal that in 1985, for example, the total workforce in the UK was 18.73 million. If the two-year requirement were neutral in its effect, some 8.48 million men and 5.44 million women would have qualified under the two-year rule. However, the survey revealed that, in fact, only 5.07 million women qualified. So some 370,000 women were adversely affected. That was the situation expressed as *numbers*; the disparity was eight-and-a-half percentage points. That means, roughly, for every ten men who qualified for Unfair Dismissal rights, only nine women did so. That figure remained roughly constant until 1991. In a nutshell, the problem was whether a "small" difference, established and constant over a number of years, was enough to show a prima facie case of sex discrimination. The ECJ held that case could be brought where "the statistical evidence revealed a lesser but persistent and relatively constant disparity over a long period."[83]

(i)(d) Four-fifths rule

An alternative is to compare the success rates of candidates. **6–021**
Guidelines issued by the US Equal Employment Opportunity Commission state that an inference of adverse impact should not be made unless the rate of recruitment of the victim's group is less than four-fifths (or 80 per cent) of the rate at which the group with the highest rate is selected.[84] In *Bushey v New York State Civil Service Commission*[85] a written examination was used for the post of Captain in the State prisons. Two hundred and forty three whites and 32 non-whites took the test. One hundred and nineteen (49 per cent) of the whites and 8 (25 per cent) of the non-Whites, passed the test. As the pass rate for non-whites was approximately 50 per cent that of whites, a prima facie case was made out.

(i)(e) Probability of chance

A variation on the four-fifths rule is the "probability of chance" **6–022**
model. Here, unless a disparity in the test results occurs by chance, an adverse impact can be inferred. In *Bridgeport Guardians v City of Bridgeport*[86] tests used in the promotion of police officers to the rank

---

[83] Case C-167/97, [1999] I.C.R. 447, at para.61.
[84] 29 CFR 1607.4(D) (1978) revised July 1, 2000. Or see *www.eeoc.gov*.
[85] 733 F 2d 220 (2nd Cir 1984), certiorari denied, 469 US 1117 (1985).
[86] 933 F 2d 1140 (2nd Cir 1991).

of sergeant were challenged. One hundred and seventy persons applied for nineteen posts. The results were as follows:

Race of candidate	Number taking exam	Number passing	Per cent passing	Highest rank
White	115	78	68%	1–19
Black	27	8	30%	20
Hispanic	28	13	46%	22

6–023   Two things can be seen from these results. First, a substantially lower proportion of non-whites passed the test. Second, that each of the nineteen best performers was white. And so the nineteen vacancies were filled by whites. Statistical analysis was presented which showed that the disparity between the whites' and blacks' results would occur by chance once in 10,000 times and the disparity between the white's and Hispanic's would occur twice in 10,000. The Court relied on the "rule of thumb" that anything less than one in twenty could not be put down to chance, and held that the statistics raised an inference adverse impact.

Courts in the United States are not bound by these models and are at liberty to reject a statistical model. In *Bushey* (see above) the category of non-whites included four Hispanics, two of whom passed the test. Thus their pass rate (50 per cent) was comparable to the whites'. It was held that in the case of the Hispanics, no prima facie case could be made out. In *New York City Transit Authority v Beazer*[87] the employers refused to employ anyone enrolled in a drug rehabilitation programme. The claimants produced evidence that of those in public rehabilitation, 63 per cent were black or Hispanic. This statistic was rejected because it did not account for those in *private* rehabilitation, and further, there was no evidence of how many of those in rehabilitation were otherwise qualified for the job. In *Connecticut v Teal*[88] a two-stage entrance test was used. The first screened out 46 per cent of the black applicants, but only 20 per cent of the white ones. However, 22.9 per cent of the initial black applicants passed the second test, compared to just 13.5 per cent for the white applicants. The employer argued a "bottom line" defence, that ultimately, the testing had not adversely affected the black applicants. The US Supreme Court rejected this argument, and held that the focus should be on the initial screening test (which was discriminatory).

[87] 440 US 568 (Sup Ct 1979).
[88] 457 US 440, at 452 (1982).

(ii) Positive or negative figures?

A second feature of the new definition of indirect discrimination is **6–024**
that it no longer confines the comparison to positive figures. The old
formula in the domestic legislation required the comparison between
those who *can* comply with the requirement or condition, thus
mandating the use of positive figures only. The new formula requires
that the provision, criterion or practice "puts" the protected group "at
a particular disadvantage", which suggests a comparison of the negative figures, but is open enough to permit the use of positive figures as
well. This can occur where positive figures help establish the "disadvantage". The significance of the different comparisons was illustrated
by an argument advanced in *Seymour-Smith*.[89] By comparing the
"negative" figures, (i.e. the proportions of those who *cannot* comply),
the result can look quite different. In 1985, for example, 22.6 per cent
of women could *not* meet the two-year requirement. The figure for
men was 31 per cent. Thus for every ten women disadvantaged, there
were only seven men. By contrast, the "positive" figures revealed that
for every ten men who qualified, only nine women did so, an apparently narrower margin. However, the House of Lords based its decision on the "positive" figures, and in the event, by a majority, the
result was the same, there was an adverse impact. What the example
demonstrates is that it may be advisable to make both comparisons as
a check.

(iii) Appointing from within a circle of family, friends, or personal
    acquaintances

In *Coker v Lord Chancellor*,[90] the Lord Chancellor appointed a white **6–025**
male as his special advisor. The requirements were inter alia, a
commitment to New Labour, knowledge of politics and the law, and
to be of "sufficiently high quality". The post was never advertised,
and the Lord Chancellor had not looked outside his circle of
acquaintances when making the appointment. An employment
tribunal[91] upheld Ms Coker's claim of indirect discrimination,
finding that the Lord Chancellor had applied a requirement that the
successful candidate must be personally known to him. As this class
of persons were predominantly white males, it indirectly discriminated on the grounds of sex and race. However, the EAT and the
Court of Appeal found for the Lord Chancellor. Assuming the pool
consisted of all the persons qualified for the job, save being personally known to the Lord Chancellor, the Court of Appeal reasoned

---

[89] See [1995] I.C.R. 889, at 904, CA. The details are set out above, para.6–020. See also the
    example given by Lord Walker in *Rutherford v Secretary of State for Trade and Industry* [2006]
    UKHL 19, at para.67.
[90] [2002] I.C.R. 321, CA.
[91] [1999] I.R.L.R. 396.

that there can only be a disparate impact if a significant proportion of the pool can comply with the requirement. Hence, the practice of appointing from within a circle of family, friends, or personal acquaintances is unlikely to amount to indirect discrimination. This reasoning is rather fragile, and cannot disguise a rather blatant case of nepotism, the antithesis of equal opportunities. There is no reason why the proportion of qualifiers should be "significant" (by which the Court of Appeal appeared to mean "large"). The legislation required that the proportion of qualifiers from the claimant's group was "considerably smaller" than the proportion of qualifiers from the comparator's group. In *McCausland v Dungannon DC*[92] the court compared a small proportion of Protestant qualifiers—2.1 per cent— with an even smaller proportion of Catholic qualifiers—1.5 per cent. Thus Catholic qualifiers were 71 per cent of Protestant qualifiers, and it was held that the Catholic proportion was considerably smaller than the Protestant proportion. If the pool consisted of those qualified for the post, save for being personally known to the Lord Chancellor, it might contain, say, 50 persons, half of whom were women. The proportion of male qualifiers (i.e. the lone appointee) would have been one in 25 (4 per cent), whilst the proportion of female qualifiers would have been zero.[93] This is a significantly greater disparity than that in *McCausland*. Further, the new definitions no longer require a comparison of those *advantaged* by the challenged practice and hence can no longer be used to the support the notion that the practice must favour a "significant proportion" of the pool. Finally, it is arguable that Ms Coker would prevail under the Equal Treatment Directive which provides "that there shall be no discrimination *whatsoever* on the grounds of sex . . .".[94] The issue in cases like this should be whether the requirement to be personally known is objectively justifiable.

---

[92] [1993] I.R.L.R. 583, NICA. See further, above, para.6–019.

[93] Even under the old definition, a claim can succeed if the proportion of the claimant's group who can comply is zero. In *Greencroft Social Club v Mullen* [1985] I.C.R. 796, only members were entitled to a disciplinary hearing. Women were not admitted as members, so the proportion of women who were entitled to the disciplinary hearing was zero. The EAT found that the disciplinary hearing rule adversely affected women. In his commentaries to *Coker* in the IRLR, Michael Rubenstein noted, "The prohibition of discrimination in selection arrangements—a concept which lies at the heart of discrimination law—can be circumvented by the simple expedient of not having any selection arrangements." ([2001] I.R.L.R. 116, at 115) and "[T]he Court of Appeal seems to be answering the wrong question of whether it was indirectly discriminatory to appoint Mr Hart rather than whether the tribunal was right to find the arrangements for selection were indirectly discriminatory. The applicants were not challenging the appointment of Mr Hart as such—the reduction of the 'elite pool . . . to a single man'. They were challenging the selection arrangements whereby the potential candidates were confined to an 'elite pool'. The statutes rightly treats these as separate and distinct causes of action." ([2002] I.R.L.R., at 3)

[94] 76/207/EC, Art.2. (Emphasis supplied.)

(iv) Age discrimination

There is a school of thought in the United States that it is inappro-   **6–026**
priate to analyse a facially neutral practice for indirect age discrimination, because, unlike other forms of discrimination, there are no
historical prejudices and lingering effects of prior discrimination; all
older workers were once younger and able to make choices about their
education, training, and jobs, free from age discrimination.[95] Recently,
however, the Supreme Court has ruled (by a five to three majority)
that age is a ground subject to indirect discrimination analysis,
although with a modified defence.[96]

An example of how facially neutral factors can have a disparate
impact on a particular age is shown in the US case *Caron v Scott
Paper*.[97] The claimants challenged a redundancy procedure by which
they were evaluated by a team of co-workers using seven factors: job
skills; leading change skills; interpersonal skills; self-management;
performance; versatility; and length of service (the only objective
factor). The comparison was made between the victim's group (those
over 50) and the others (those 40–50). This revealed that the redundancy process retained 61.5 per cent of the victim's group and 91.5 per
cent of the others, which is clearly significant enough to raise a prima
facie case.

(3) Causation

The statutory definitions require that the challenged practice "puts"   **6–027**
the claimant's group "at a particular disadvantage". This causative
element demands a connection between the challenged practice and
the claimant's sex, race, religion or belief, or sexual orientation, or age,
as the case may be.

Where there are tangible challenged practices, causation is unlikely
to be an issue. It goes without saying that, for instance, entrance
exams, last-in-first-out selection for redundancy, or length of service
benefits, will have a tangible impact on those who, respectively, fail the
exam, are selected for redundancy, or have inferior service records. In
such cases the issue will be whether that impact falls disproportionately upon a protected group, which is a separate matter. In the US
case, *Dothard v Rawlinson*,[98] minimum height and weight requirements

---

[95] See comment of Kennedy, J. in *Hazen Paper Co v Biggins* 507 US 604, at 618 (Sup Ct 1993), citing
Krop, P.S., (1982) "Age Discrimination and the Disparate Impact Doctrine" 34 Stan L Rev 837,
at 854. See also, E.H. Pontz (1995), "Comment, What A Difference The ADEA Makes: Why
Disparate Impact Theory Should Not Apply To The Age Discrimination In Employment Act"
74 NC L. Rev. 299–300. Contrast *Lorillard v Pons* 434 US 575, at 584 (Sup Ct 1978).

[96] *Smith v City of Jackson* 544 US 228 (Sup Ct 2005), see further below, para.6–046. A similar
result was achieved by the Federal Court of Australia using that nation's adoption of the ILO
Discrimination (Employment and Occupation) Convention 1958: *Commonwealth of Australia
v Human Rights & Equal Opportunity Commission (Hamilton)* 63 ALD 641, at paras 27–45.

[97] 834 F Supp 33 (D Me 1993).

[98] 433 US 321 (Sup Ct 1977). See also above, para.6–009, and below para.6–040.

combined with statistics showing the likely impact of such a measure on women was enough, without more, to prove a causal link between the two. This was because the practices were clearly defined and the disparity so great that it would offend common sense to come to any other conclusion.[99]

As noted above,[100] the new definition opens the way to challenges to subjective employment practices. Where these practices are vague, statistics are likely to play an important part in the claim. It is when the practices are vague that causation will be an issue. Once again, the experience in the United States offers some guidance on how the law may develop here.

6–028   A connection between a practice and the victim's group became an express and detailed element of the US scheme following the *Wards Cove* decision. Congress codified this requirement by legislating that a plaintiff must link any disparate impact to a specific practice. In cases of subjective decision-making, there may be an identified suspect practice (e.g. nepotism in recruitment) and evidence of some racial disparity (e.g., amongst successful applicants). Yet there is no tangible link between the two. The question is in what circumstances, if at all, can proof of the practice and disparity without more be used to prove a causal link between the two. The US courts have held that "Statistical evidence may be probative where it reveals a disparity so great that it cannot be accounted for by chance"[101] and "statistical disparities must be sufficiently substantial that they raise . . . an inference of causation."[102] The loose term *sufficiently substantial* alludes to the courts' practice of not adhering to a particular formula when deciding whether there has been a disparate impact. There is nothing more precise than that.

It would seem from *Bushey v New York State Civil Service Commission*[103] and *Bridgeport Guardians*[104] that where the "four-fifths" or "probability of chance" formulas are used,[105] an inference of causation will be made from a simple finding of an adverse impact. There are other cases where causation was proved without these formulas. For instance, in *Butler v Home Depot*[106] the claimants presented statistics that showed a 20 per cent disparity between the women in the qualified labour market and those within the workforce. The Court held simply that the statistical evidence was "of a *kind* and *degree*

---

[99] National statistics showed that the requirements would exclude over 40 per cent of the female population but less than 1 per cent of the male population. The main issue was whether the employer could justify the requirements.

[100] See para.6–007.

[101] *Bridgeport Guardians v City of Bridgeport* 933 F 2d 1140, at 1146 (2nd Cir 1991).

[102] *Watson v Fort Worth Bank* 487 US 977, at 995 (Sup Ct 1988).

[103] 733 F 2d 220 (2nd Cir 1984), certiorari denied, 469 US 1117 (1985). See above, para.6–021.

[104] 933 F 2d 1140, at 1146. See above, para.6–022.

[105] See above paras 6–021—6–022.

[106] No C-94-4335 SI, C-95-2182 SI, (N.D. Cal. August 29, 1997). See above, para.6–009.

from which causation may reasonably be inferred."[107] From this, it would seem that even if the disparity falls below 20 per cent, it is at least *conceivable* that a court may find that there is causation, should it find that disparity to be "sufficiently substantial".

(4) The Defence of Objective Justification

Once the claimant has established a prima facie case, the burden shifts to the defendant to "objectively justify" the provision, criterion or practice. So, for instance, an employer requiring candidates to have a maths "A" level (which adversely affected women) would have to show that the requirement was necessary to perform the job. If it does so, there is no liability. This section is sub-divided into two discussions. First, there is an attempt to establish the precise meaning of the defence, and second, a review of the defence being used in a variety of circumstances.

6–029

(a) The meaning of the justification defence[108]

There are three issues to explore here. First, the differences between the EC and British definitions, second, where the defence itself is based upon discrimination, and third, the US "alternative practice" doctrine.

The new generation of discrimination Directives state that a defendant may "objectively justify" the challenged provision, criterion or practice by showing a *legitimate aim*, and that *the means of achieving that aim are appropriate and necessary*. This formula codifies ECJ case law, especially *Bilka-Kaufhaus v Weber von Hartz*,[109] which itself is rooted in the Community law principle of proportionality,[110] and is generally known as the "*Bilka* test". The means of achieving the legitimate aim must be appropriate, meaning at the least, that there must be a causal connection between the aim and the method employed to achieve it, and that the means must not be tainted with discrimination.[111] "Necessity" encapsulates two elements. The defence should not succeed where there exists a less discriminatory alternative. In addition, a court may have to balance any discriminatory effect of the challenged practice against the benefits of achieving the legitimate aim.

The test has been transposed into the domestic legislation as "a proportionate means of achieving a legitimate aim".[112]

6–030

---

[107] *ibid.*, at 49. Emphasis supplied.

[108] See R. Townshend-Smith, "Justifying indirect discrimination in English and American law: how stringent should the test be?" (1995) 1 I.J.D.L. 103.

[109] Case 170/84, [1987] I.C.R. 110, (see below, Ch.9, para.9–032).

[110] See the *Cassis de Dijon* case, C-120/78 (*Rewe-Zentral AG v Bundesmonopolverwaltung für Branntwein*) [1979] E.C.R. 649.

[111] See "Defences based on discrimination", below, para.6–034.

[112] A different formula of "reasonably justify" is used by the Equality Act 2006 (expected in force October 2006) for religion or belief discrimination in fields other than employment. See below, para.6–044.

(i) Domestic and EC definitions contrasted

6–031   Until recently, the British legislation used the more open-ended phrase, "justifiable irrespective of" sex or race, as the case may be.[113] The courts generally have held this to mean that the reasonable needs of the defendant should be weighed against the discriminatory effect of the challenged practice. This is known as the "*Hampson* balancing test".[114] As the influence of EC law grew, domestic courts were forced to reconcile this approach with the EC model, which they felt able to do, by holding that the *Hampson* balancing test reflects the EC's model of proportionality.[115] Conveniently, the new domestic legislative formula defines justification as being a "proportionate means of achieving a legitimate aim". Thus it appears that EC law, domestic case law, and the new and old domestic statutory formulas are at one: they all reflect the model of proportionality. If this is right, then the new legislative formula should not alter the *Hampson* test.

However, a closer examination reveals that there exists an important difference between domestic and EC law. In short, the *Hampson* test dilutes the question of a less discriminatory alternative, one aspect of the "necessary" ingredient.[116] A brief history helps explain this. In the early years of the British legislation, tribunals (influenced by US case law, upon which our legislation was based),[117] spoke of "necessity". For example, in *Steel v Union of Post Office Workers*[118] Phillips, J., President of the EAT, said that the practice must be inter alia "genuine and necessary". In 1982, however, the Court of Appeal in *Ojutiku v Manpower Services Commission*[119] contrasted "necessary" with the statutory word "justifiable"; Kerr, L.J. stated that "justifiable ... clearly applies a lower standard than ... necessary".[120] Eveleigh, L.J., considered it to mean "something ... acceptable to right-thinking people as sound and tolerable."[121] Balcombe, L.J., in *Hampson v Department of Education,*[122] drew back from this loose interpretation and created the *Hampson* test, which has been approved and applied ever since.[123] This history shows that the *Hampson* test is rooted in a

---

[113] For cases under EC competence only, this definition was replaced in the RRA 1976 on July 19, 2003, and in the SDA 1975 on October 1, 2005.

[114] *Hampson v Department of Education* [1989] I.C.R. 179, at 196F, CA.

[115] See e.g. *Barry v Midland Bank* [1999] I.C.R. 859, at 870, HL; *Hardys v Lax* [2005] I.C.R. 1565, at para.32, CA

[116] See M. Connolly, "Discrimination Law: Justification, Alternative Measures and Defences Based on Sex" (2001) 30 I.L.J. 311.

[117] Described above paras 6–004—6–005.

[118] [1978] I.C.R. 181, at 187 EAT.

[119] [1982] I.C.R. 661 CA. In Parliament, the Government resisted amendments to the Sex Discrimination Bill that would have replaced "justifiable" with "necessary". Lord Harris stated that where a body offered reduced fares for pensioners, the policy might be justifiable, but not necessary (362 HL Deb July 14, 1975 cols 10116–17).

[120] *ibid.*, at 670.

[121] *ibid.*, at 668.

[122] [1989] I.C.R. 179, CA.

[123] See e.g. *Allonby v Accrington and Rossendale College* [2001] I.C.R. 1189, at para.24, CA; *Hardys v Lax* [2005] ICR 1565, at para.59, CA.

theory that justification requires a lower standard than "necessary". That is contrary to the EC proportionality principle, *Bilka*, and the definition now provided in the Directives, and by extension, the subsequent domestic legislation. The reconciliation of *Hampson* with EC law has been more about language than substance, although the Court of Appeal is now brazen enough to note that it has "reformulated" the EC model to mean "*reasonably* necessary", a clear dilution.[124] In practice, recent Court of Appeal decisions may have moved a little closer to the EC model, stating that a defendant cannot justify a measure simply by showing it was one of "a band of reasonable responses which a reasonable employer would adopt",[125] and that a tribunal, when applying the balancing test, should consider "fairly obvious alternatives."[126] However, a defendant was not bound to show that its practice was the only possible one available.[127] This language of compromise over-complicates the matter, and most importantly, glosses over the legislative policy to find the least discriminatory way to achieve the legitimate aim.

Three examples will highlight this difference. In *Enderby v Frenchay Health Authority*[128] the defendant Health Authority was trying to justify a difference in pay between speech therapists (98 per cent female) and pharmacists (63 per cent female). The pharmacists were paid about 40 per cent more than the speech therapists. As women were over-represented in the lower paid group the Health Authority were obliged to justify the difference. It argued that market forces caused the difference. But the evidence was that only an extra ten per cent pay was needed to recruit a sufficient number of pharmacists. Thus there existed a less discriminatory alternative of paying the pharmacists a ten per cent premium. The EAT applied the *Hampson* test and weighed the 40 per cent difference in pay against the need for sufficient pharmacists. Given that stark choice, the EAT held that the difference in pay was justified. But the ECJ held that the pay difference could only be justified to the proportion that market forces required (ten per cent). The existence of the less discriminatory alternative meant that the practice (a 40 per cent pay difference) could not be justified. For the ECJ, proportionality means *no more than* necessary.

Second, there is an early British case of discrimination under the **6–032** RRA 1976, predating *Hampson*. In *Bohon-Mitchell v Common Professional Examination Board*[129] it was the defendant's policy that persons with a degree in a subject other than law were required to take

---

[124] *Hardys v Lax* [2005] I.C.R. 1565, at para.32, CA; *Cadman v Health and Safety Executive* [2004] EWCA 1317, at paras 30–31, CA, citing *Barry v Midland Bank* [1999] I.C.R. 319, at 336, CA.

[125] *ibid.*, at paras 31–32, CA.

[126] *Allonby v Accrington and Rossendale College* [2001] I.C.R. 1189, at para.28, CA.

[127] *Hardys v Lax* [2005] I.C.R. 1565, at para.32, CA.

[128] [1991] 1 CMLR 626, at 663 and 668, EAT; Case C-127/92, [1994] I.C.R. 112, ECJ.

[129] [1978] I.R.L.R. 525.

a course in academic law to qualify to take the Bar finals. This was normally a 12-month course. However, those with a non-British or non-Irish degree were required to complete a 21 month course. In 1978 Ms Bohon-Mitchell, who had been living in England (except for one year) since 1972 and was married to an Englishman, applied to take her Bar finals. When she was informed that, as an American graduate, she would have to sit the 21-month course, she complained of discrimination on grounds of nationality or national origin. The defendant tried to justify that requirement on the grounds that barristers needed a wide knowledge of the English way of life, and the simplest way of identifying those without such experience was by their degrees. The industrial tribunal held that the requirement to sit a 21-month course was not justified because it was not *necessary* to achieve the aim. Instead, each candidate's familiarity with the English way of life could be assessed on a case by case basis.[130] If the tribunal had gone straight to the "objective balance" *Hampson* approach, it may well have concluded that the requirement was justified. The evidence was that just eight out of 191 applicants with a non-law degree had "overseas" degrees. Probably fewer than that eight had been resident in Britain and were therefore "familiar with the English way of life." In any case the discriminatory effect was relatively minor. If this discriminatory effect were weighed against the administrative costs of changing the system, a court may well find that defendant's administrative needs justified the practice. In other words discrimination could be allowed to continue because that would be more convenient for the defendant.

Finally, take a hypothetical example of an entrance exam, or tests for a job, which are not updated. Here the tests might adversely affect a minority group simply because white candidates are more familiar with the test through their links with the predominantly white workforce. In other respects, the test may be a valid indicator of job performance. A simple balancing test weighs the discriminatory effect against the need to predict job performance and would conclude that the testing is justified. But if the inquiry asked also if the tests were necessary, it would it find them unjustified, because a less discriminatory alternative exists (most obviously, regular updating).

This does not mean that the difference between the domestic and the EC definitions merely is a matter of degree. It is a fundamental difference. The compromise in the domestic approach test upsets the theory of indirect discrimination. Where a practice having a disparate impact is shown to be absolutely necessary to achieve a genuine non-discriminatory goal, then the cause of the disparate impact lies elsewhere. No action lies against the defendant. The cause(s) of any disparate impact can be identified only if the courts impose a strict

---

[130] [1978] I.R.L.R., at 530, para.29.

test of necessity. A lesser standard allows defendants leeway to discriminate and blurs the causes of a disparate impact.

Logically, this difference should disappear with the new domestic statutory definition, which expressly includes "proportionate." Yet the Court of Appeal has shown itself perfectly willing to persist with the illusion of harmony, by "reformulating" the EC definition.   **6–033**

A similar uncertainty has dogged American case law. In the seminal US Supreme Court case *Griggs v Duke Power*,[131] Burger, C.J. stated: "The touchstone is business necessity. If an employment practice which operates to exclude [black people] . . . cannot be shown to be related to job performance, the practice is prohibited." However, later he said: "Congress has placed on the employer the burden of showing that any given requirement must have a manifest relationship to the employment in question."[132] Here we have two standards ("business necessity" and "manifest relationship") in the same speech. Subsequent Supreme Court pronouncements have vacillated between the two, giving for instance, "significant correlation" and "necessary".[133] This uncertainty was codified by the Civil Rights Act 1991, which stated that a practice must be "job related for the position in question and consistent with business necessity."[134] However, different standards of justification in the United States matter little where less discriminatory alternatives exist because the Supreme Court has developed a separate "alternative practice" doctrine.[135]

(ii) Defences based upon discrimination

It is implicit in the *Bilka* test that the justification must not be related to the ground of discrimination in question. In *Jenkins v Kingsgate*[136] the ECJ stated the factors used as a defence should be objectively justified and be "in no way related to any discrimination based on sex." This was expressed in the original Sex Discrimination Act 1975 and Race Relations Act 1976 (e.g. "justifiable irrespective of sex"), but was not restated in the new domestic definitions. However, it should come under the general expressed principle of proportionality, and it is inconceivable that the new definitions, based upon EC law, differ in substance on this matter.[137] The issue is likely to arise where employers respond to a law giving rights to a protected group, by manoeuvring that group into a position where those rights are not applicable. This   **6–034**

---

[131] (1971) 401 US 424.

[132] *ibid.*, at 431–432.

[133] Respectively *Albemarle Paper v Moody* 1975 422 US 405, at 431 (1975) and *Dothard v Rawlinson* 1977 433 US 321, at 331 (1977).

[134] 42 USC s.2000e-2, (k)(1)(A)(i).

[135] See below, para.6–036.

[136] [1981] I.C.R. 592, at para.11. See below, Ch.9, para.9–032. See also *Bilka* [1986] 2 CMLR 701, at para.37.

[137] In any case, the Directives' non-regression principle prevents them being used to reduce existing rights.

appeared to be the case in *Allonby v Accrington & Rossendale College.*[138]

Accrington & Rossendale College employed 341 part-time lecturers on successive one-year contracts. In 1996 legislation came into force obliging employers to afford part-time workers equal benefits to those given to full-time workers.[139] The purpose of the legislation was to prevent indirect sex discrimination, as part-time workers are predominantly women. Faced with the extra expense the College responded by dismissing all its part-time lecturers and re-employing them as subcontractors, through an agency. Consequently the part-timers were paid less and lost a series of benefits (e.g. sick pay). Ms Allonby, a part-time lecturer, brought several actions against the College, including one for indirect sex discrimination, as the dismissals fell disproportionately upon women (who made up two-thirds of the part-time lecturers, but only one-half of the full-time lecturers). On appeal, Ms Allonby argued that the College had failed to justify the dismissals because, inter alia, although the primary aim was to save money, they were rooted in the legislation designed to prevent discrimination against women. The Court of Appeal allowed her appeal chiefly because the tribunal failed to consider any "fairly obvious" alternatives or apply an "objective balance" (*Hampson*) test. On this failure Sedley, L.J. said that: "In particular there is no recognition [by the tribunal] that if the aim of the dismissal was itself discriminatory . . . it could never afford justification."[140] But the judge said no more than that on the issue.

Ms Allonby cited *R. v Secretary of State, Ex p. Equal Opportunities Commission* and *R. v Secretary of State, Ex p. Seymour-Smith.*[141] In *Ex p. EOC* (the case that led to the Regulations) Lord Keith held that existing Regulations that afforded lesser benefits to part-time workers constituted a "gross breach of the principle of equal pay and could not be possibly regarded as a suitable means of achieving an increase in part-time employment."[142] In *Seymour-Smith* the ECJ, when giving a ruling on justification, stated that a Government measure "cannot have the effect of frustrating the implementation of a fundamental principle of Community law such as that of equal pay . . ."[143]

6–035 Those cases concerned Government measures made in pursuance of a social policy, where a Government is allowed a "broad margin of

---

[138] [2001] I.C.R. 1189, CA. For a commentary, see M. Connolly, "Discrimination Law: Justification, Alternative Measures and Defences Based on Sex" (2001) 30 I.L.J. 311.

[139] Although not specified by the EAT or the CA this was presumably the Employment Protection (Part-Time Employees) Regulations 1995, passed in response to *R. v Sec of State for Employment, Ex p. EOC* [1994] 1 All E.R. 910, where the House of Lords held that existing legislation prescribing inferior rights to part-time workers was incompatible with Community sex discrimination law.

[140] [2001] I.C.R. 1189, at para.29.

[141] Respectively [1995] 1 AC 1, HL; [1999] I.C.R. 447, ECJ.

[142] *ibid.*, at 30.

[143] [1999] I.C.R. 447, at para.75. Discussed below, at para.6–043.

discretion".[144] No such discretion is afforded in ordinary employment cases and so the College should be under a stricter duty to justify. The express aim of the College's arrangement was to give (predominantly female) part-time lecturers less benefits and pay, which appears also to be a "gross breach of the principle of equal pay" and accordingly should never be justified. On this point alone Ms Allonby should have prevailed.[145]

There lies in such cases a related line of argument. In *Orphanos v Queen Mary College*[146] the plaintiff challenged a requirement to be ordinarily resident within the European Community for three years, so to be exempt from full overseas student fees. The immediate goal of the requirement was to curtail public expenditure on education. The House of Lords held that the requirement was "so closely related" to nationality that it could not be justified and amounted to indirect racial discrimination.[147] In *Allonby* the dismissals of a predominantly female group were inspired by Regulations passed to provide equal benefits to women. It is at least arguable that the requirement is "so closely related" to sex that it should not be justifiable.

(iii) The US alternative practice doctrine

In the United States, the Supreme Court developed the alternative practice doctrine. Should a prima facie case be met with a proper business necessity defence, the plaintiff may still win by proposing an alternative business practice which has a less discriminatory effect. This has since been recognised in the Civil Rights Act 1991.[148] The rubric generally used was set in *Albermarle Paper Co v Moody*[149] where the Court stated that the alternative should "also serve the employer's legitimate interest in 'efficient and trustworthy workmanship.'"[150]

6–036

An example of a successful demonstration of an alternative practice can be seen in *Bridgeport Guardians v City of Bridgeport*[151] where tests used in the promotion of police officers to the rank of sergeant were challenged. One hundred and seventy persons applied for nineteen posts and the results showed that the tests had a disparate impact on blacks and Hispanics, with only 30 per cent and 46 per cent respectively

---

[144] See e.g. *Seymour-Smith, ibid.*, at para.74, and below, para.6–041.

[145] The justification issue was remitted to an employment tribunal for a further hearing, whilst other issues were referred to the ECJ: (C256/01) [2004] I.C.R. 1328.

[146] [1985] A.C. 761, HL.

[147] *ibid.*, at 772–773. See also *R. (Elias) v Secretary of State for Defence* [2005] EWHC 1435, where it was held that a requirement to be born in the UK, or have a parent or grandparent born in the UK, to qualify for a £10,000 "debt of honour" for imprisonment in Hong Kong by the Japanese in WW2, was so closely related to nationality that it could not be justified (at paras 86–90).

[148] Section 105, codified as 42 USC s.2000e-2(k)(1), which also provides that the alternative practice doctrine should be applied according to pre-*Wards Cove* principles (see above, para.6–009).

[149] 422 US 405 (1975).

[150] *ibid.*, at 425 citing *McDonnell Douglas Corp v Green* 411 US 792, at 802 (Sup Ct 1973).

[151] 933 F 2d 1140 (2nd Cir 1991). See also above, para.6–022.

passing in comparison with 68 per cent of whites. But the real impact was worse than that because the nineteen best performers were selected, leaving no minorities with promotion. The employer successfully justified the tests as a reliable and accurate predictor of job performance. However, what the results table[152] did not reveal was that, of all those passing, the marks were extremely close. The plaintiffs put forward evidence that the difference between a few marks was insignificant. Accordingly the plaintiffs suggested that the marks should be banded: that is, marks within, say, eight per cent of each other, placed in a single band. Then the successful candidates could be selected from those bands, using other (non-discriminatory) factors to decide. In this way the best performers were selected without a disparate impact. The Court found that the use of banding would alleviate the disparate racial effect of the examination without imposing any significant burden on the defendants whilst serving their legitimate interests.[153]

The doctrine has not been adopted by the EC or British schemes. However, a strict test of proportionality should achieve the same result. If a claimant can identify a less discriminatory alternative means of achieving the same aim, the justification should fail for being disproportionate.

(b) Examples of the Defence

(i) Part-time workers and family responsibilities

6–037   It is now so established that less favourable treatment of part-time workers adversely affects women, that dedicated legislation has been passed to protect part-time workers. The Part-time Workers (Prevention of Less Favourable Treatment) Regulations 2000[154] provide that less favourable treatment of a part-time worker is unlawful unless "objectively justified."[155]

These Regulations protect those who are already working part-time. They do not extend to the situation where a female full-time worker wishes to switch to part-time, or more child-centred hours. Section 80F of the Employment Rights Act 1996 gives parents of children under the age of six (18 if the child has disability) the right to request flexible working. The employer may refuse a request if "he considers"

---

[152] 933 F 2d, at 1143. The results table is set out above, para.6–022.

[153] *ibid.*, at 1145 and 1148.

[154] SI 2000/1551, came into force, July 1, 2000, implementing Directive 97/81/EC. For a commentary concluding that the protections given by the regulations are too few and too narrow, see A. McColgan "Missing the Point? The Part-time Workers (Prevention of Less Favourable Treatment) Regulations 2000 (SI 2000/1551)" (2000) 29 I.L.J. 260. See, also, M. Schmidt, "The right to part-time work under German law: progress in or a boomerang for equal employment opportunities?" (2001) 30 I.L.J. 335.

[155] Justification of inferior pay for part-time workers is discussed in Ch.9 under "Economic Reasons", para.9–032.

one or more of specified grounds applies. These grounds are: (1) the burden of additional costs, (2) detrimental effect on ability to meet customer demand, (3) inability to re-organise work among existing staff, (4) inability to recruit additional staff, (5) detrimental impact on quality, (6) detrimental impact on performance, (7) insufficiency of work during the periods the employee proposes to work, (8) planned structural changes".[156]

The employer also must provide an explanation.[157] An employee may complain to an employment tribunal only if the decision is based on "incorrect facts"[158] or the employer has not followed the prescribed procedure.[159] The subjective element "he considers" means the employee cannot challenge the business ground(s) given by the employer. The remedy is compensation capped to a maximum of eight weeks' pay, with a week's pay itself capped at £290.[160] This imposes an obligation upon an employer to do no more than "consider" the request and give reasons for its denial. Beyond that, women in this situation may rely on discrimination law, where a refusal may have to be *objectively* justified.

An employer refusing a request by a woman to switch to part-time   **6–038** or flexible hours is likely to indirectly discriminate against women, unless the refusal is justified. In *Home Office v Holmes*[161] the EAT rejected an argument that a refusal was justified simply because the bulk of British industry, and its civil service, was organised around full-time working. An employer has to justify the refusal on the particular circumstances of the claimant's job. This was the case in *Greater Glasgow Health Board v Carey*[162] where a health visitor asked to switch to a two-and-a-half, or three day week. Her employer refused and instead offered her five half-days per week. This was because the nature of the work was not task orientated, but on a personal-contact basis with patients; personal discussions with patients and personal observations were not all apt to put on record. This meant that it was important that each health visitor was available for patients and other agencies, such as doctors and social workers, every day of the week. The EAT held that the refusal was justified. The justification may be also economic, where a switch to part-time by, say, a manager would inevitably mean that the post becomes shared. This may involve a duplication of many tasks, such as interviews and meetings, and extra time spent communicating and record keeping. Such an employer

---

[156] ERA 1996, s.80G (b).

[157] Flexible Working (Procedural Requirements) Regulations 2002, SI 2002/3207, reg.5(b)(2).

[158] ERA 1996, s.80H (1)(b).

[159] ERA 1996, s.80H (1)(b), and Flexible Working (Eligibility, Complaints and Remedies) Regulations 2002, SI 2002/3236, reg.6.

[160] ERA 1996, s.227, inserted by Employment Rights (Increase of Limits) Order 2005 SI 2005/3352, Art.3 of the Schedule in force February 1, 2006. It is normally raised each February in line with retail prices.

[161] [1984] I.C.R. 678.

[162] [1987] I.R.L.R. 484.

would argue that job-sharing here would make the business less competitive.[163]

Those cases involved a switch from full-time to part-time work. It is possible to challenge a requirement to change the pattern of work. In *London Underground v Edwards (No.2)*[164] the employer implemented a new flexible shift pattern, where duties were to begin at 4.45 am. Ms Edwards, a single mother with a young child, had been working daytime hours so to be at home mornings and evenings. She objected to the new shift pattern and requested to continue working her daytime shifts. Her employer refused and she resigned, claiming indirect discrimination. On the issue of justification, the evidence was that the employer could have accommodated her request without damaging its business plan, and that the employer originally was willing to accommodate her request but changed its mind following pressure from the predominantly male workforce. Accordingly, the EAT held that the refusal was not justified.

Logically, if employers can be liable for denying a switch from full- to part-time work, or for forcing inflexible hours upon staff, they should equally be vulnerable when refusing to *hire* on a part-time or flexible basis.

(ii) Testing and educational qualifications[165]

6–039 Using tests or qualifications for employment decisions such as recruitment, promotion or redeployment has the merit of being objective, but carries the risk of operating as "built in headwinds"[166] against minority groups and women. They can adversely affect any of those groups, for, say, cultural or historic reasons. In *Griggs v Duke Power*,[167] the requirement to pass an intelligence test (or have a high school diploma), adversely affected blacks because of the history of segregated education. Tests for promotion may favour those with long work experience and so disfavour women, who generally would have entered the workplace more recently.[168] Such tests must be justified as necessary for the job. The Commission for Racial Equality's

---

[163] See *Hardys v Lax* [2005] I.C.R. 1565 CA, where such an argument failed mainly because the tribunal considered the employer's evidence was "exaggerated" (at paras 40–49).

[164] [1997] I.R.L.R. 157. The decision was upheld by the Court of Appeal [1998] I.R.L.R. 364, but there was no appeal on the justification issue. On the issue of the refusal having an adverse impact on women, see above, para.6–018.

[165] See also the discussion on causation, above, para.6–027, and the alternative practice doctrine, above para.6–036. See R. Wood, "Psychometrics should make assessment fairer." (1996) 67 EOR 27; M. Pearn, R. Kandola and R. Mottram *Selection Tests and Sex Bias: the Impact of Selection Testing on the Employment Opportunities of Men and Women*, 1987, Manchester: EOC; *Towards Fair Selection: a Survey of Test Practice and Thirteen Case Studies*, 1993, London: Commission for Racial Equality.

[166] *Griggs v Duke Power* 401 US 424, at 432 (Sup Ct 1971). See further, above, para.6–001.

[167] *ibid.*

[168] See *R. v London Borough of Hammersmith and Fulham Ex p. Nalgo* [1991] I.R.L.R. 249, Q.B.D.

Code of Practice advises employers that tests should validated by "professionals in assessment" and be consistent with the employer's equal opportunities policy. In particular, the tests should correspond to the job requirements and special care must be taken where there are candidates whose first language is not English.[169]

In UK and Community law, there is no legal requirement that tests are validated, but of course validation will greatly improve the chance of justifying them. As with other challenged practices, employers must show that the tests meet the *Bilka* test. Equally, qualifications which have only a vague relationship to the job (as in *Griggs*), or which over-state the true requirement ("excellent English" when good English is appropriate) are unlikely to be an appropriate and proportionate means of achieving a legitimate aim.

In the United States, courts will demand that challenged tests are validated "by professionally acceptable methods, to be predictive of or significantly correlated with important elements of work behaviour".[170] There, the courts afford "great deference"[171] to the Equal Employment Opportunity Commission Uniform Guidelines, which classifies three types of test. "Content validity" tests replicate major tasks required by the job, such as typing speed for a computer operator. "Criterion" or "predictive validity" tests use empirical data to predict work job performance and potential. Third, "Construct validity" demonstrates which candidates have identifiable characteristics which have been determined to be important for successful job performance. Accordingly, general intelligence tests, such as those used in *Griggs*, are unlikely to be justified.

(iii) Physical and health & safety justifications

A requirement by an employer for physical strength or stamina is not **6–040** exempt under the Sex Discrimination Act 1975 as "a genuine occupational qualification."[172] So it is unlawful (as direct discrimination) to exclude *all* women from a job on the basis that few will be able to meet the relevant strength requirement. Employers must instead impose a standard common to both male and female applicants, and (assuming it would adversely affect women or another protected group) justify it. The most well known US case on this matter is *Dothard v Rawlinson*[173] where minimum height and weight requirements for employment as a

---

[169] "Code of Practice on Racial Equality in Employment" (2005) London: CRE, (in force April 6, 2006), ISBN 1 85442 570 6, at paras 4.23 to 4.26. The Code refers employers to the British Psychological Society and its Psychological Testing Centre, at *www.psychtesting.org.uk*.

[170] *Albermarle Paper v Moody* 422 US 405, at 431 (Sup Ct 1975), citing the Uniform Guidance issued by the EEOC, 29 CFR 1607. See *www.eeoc.gov* and click on "EEOC Regulations".

[171] *ibid.*

[172] SDA 1975, s.7(2)(a).

[173] 433 US 321 (1977), see further above paras 6–009 and 6–027.

prison guard was not justified because the employer produced no evidence that the requirements were related to the goal that prison officers needed to be physically strong. Instead, the Supreme Court noted, the employer could have used specific strength tests.[174]

In *Singh v British Rail Engineering Ltd*,[175] the employer introduced a requirement that workers wear "bump caps" when working under raised railway carriages. This requirement indirectly discriminated against Sikhs (orthodox Sikh men being obliged to wear a turban) but was held to be justified. It should be noted that employer's arguments were less than watertight. The first ground was the fear of civil and criminal liability, should a worker not wearing a bump cap be injured. But as it had supplied and recommended the wearing of the caps, the risk of civil liability was extremely low, in the face of a worker's refusal. Further, British Rail could not specify the criminal risk. Employers should be obliged under the *Bilka* standard to be more specific than pronouncing a vague unsubstantiated risk. The second ground was that making an exception for Sikh workers would cause the other workers to disobey the requirement. This amounts to imposing a discriminatory requirement out of fear of the reaction of the workers to what they perceive as special treatment for a racial minority. It parallels cases where employers directly discriminate because of pressure from the workforce, which is no defence.[176] In the context of justifying indirect discrimination, this cannot be accepted as a legitimate aim. A Sikh man cannot be blamed for management's failure to supervise properly its workforce. The legitimate aim in this case is safety. The proper question is whether the requirement to wear a bump cap (instead of a turban enveloping his unshorn hair) was necessary in pursuit of that aim. One contribution to that issue was made by Mr Singh, when he pointed out that Sikh men were not obliged to wear helmets when fighting (for Britain) in the two world wars, or when employed as policemen.

An even less convincing justification was accepted in *Singh v Rowntree Mackintosh*,[177] where a ban on beards (again indirectly discriminating against Sikhs) in a confectionery factory to reduce the risk of contamination by facial hair was held to be justified, despite evidence that the "no beards" policy was not adopted in their other

---

[174] 433 US 321, at 331–332.
[175] [1986] I.C.R. 22, EAT. Followed in *Dhanjal v British Steel* (unreported) EAT/66/94. Sikhs enjoy statutory exemptions from wearing safety helmets on construction sites (Employment Act 1989, s.11) and crash helmets on motorcycles (Road Traffic Act 1988 s.16).
[176] See *R. v Commission for Racial Equality Ex p. Westminster CC* [1985] I.C.R. 827, CA, discussed Ch.4, para.4–019.
[177] [1979] I.C.R. 554 EAT. See also *Panesar v Nestle* [1980] I.R.L.R. 60, EAT; affirmed [1980] I.C.R. 44 (note); [1980] I.R.L.R. 64, CA; *Knag v Brookes* 40 Equal Opportunities Review Discrimination Case Law Digest 2 (ban on Sikh bracelet in food factory justified).

factories, that "moustaches and side-whiskers" were not banned, and that there existed an alternative of beard-masks.

(iv) Social policy justifications

Where a defence is based on social policy, the *Bilka* test is modified. **6–041** Defendants must still show that the practice reflects a necessary aim of its social policy and is suitable and necessary for achieving that aim, but at the same time, they are afforded a broad margin of discretion in choosing the appropriate means to achieve that policy. But the margin of discretion is not so broad to have the effect of frustrating the implementation of the fundamental principle of equal treatment. Mere generalisations will not suffice. This was restated by the ECJ in *R. v Secretary of State for Employment, Ex p. Seymour-Smith*.[178] The defence is used normally by Governments defending a domestic measure against superior Community discrimination law, although it should be possible for a private party defendant to justify a social aim, or for a tribunal to summons the relevant government minister to justify the challenged legislation.

It is possible that the recent raft of Directives, which effectively codify the *Bilka* test, will trigger a stricter test, so that a social policy defence no longer enjoys the broad margin of discretion.[179] These recent Directives do not apply to all grounds of discrimination prohibited by Community law, such as nationality, and if a stricter test were not applied in these areas as well, the result would be a duel standard. Since the new Directives came into force, beginning with the Burden of Proof Directive 97/80/EC in 2001 (codifying the definition of indirect sex discrimination), the case law is inconclusive. In *Nikoloudi*[180] the ECJ appeared to apply a stricter test, omitting to mention the broad margin of discretion. However a few months later in *Mangold v Helm*,[181] when applying the objective justification test for age discrimination under the Employment Equality Directive 2000/78/EC, the Court stated, without reference to *Nikoloudi*, that Member States "undoubtedly" had a broad discretion.

Where a margin of discretion is appropriate, the cases show that encouraging more employment is a common and legitimate aim, that the more serious the adverse impact the stronger the justification

---

[178] Case C-167/97, [1999] I.C.R. 447, ECJ, at paras 69–77. See further above paras 6–020 and 6–024.

[179] See C. Barnard and B. Hepple, "Substantive equality" (2000) 59(3) CLR 562, at 575. For a brief description of legislative scheme, see Ch.2, para.2–001.

[180] *Nikoloudi v Organismos Tilepikoinonion Ellados AE* Case C-196/02 (2005), especially at para.48, ECJ.

[181] Case C-144/04 [2006] I.R.L.R. 143, at para.63 ECJ. See further below, para.6–046 and Ch.8, para.8–058. Advocate-General Ruiz-Jarabo Colomer also stated that Member States had a "broad discretion" with social policy in *Vergani v Agenzia delle Entrate, Ufficio di Arona* Case C 207-04, at para.52 (2005).

needs to be, and that generally defendants should put forward some fairly detailed and objective evidence in support of their arguments.

6–042   Domestic measures disfavouring part-time workers, and thus adversely affecting women, appear to be the hardest to justify, mainly because the adverse effect is so well recognised and severe. In *R. v Secretary of State for Employment, Ex p. Equal Opportunities Commission*,[182] the British Government's reason for restricting or excluding unfair dismissal and redundancy pay rights for part-time workers was no more than a statement asserting this would encourage employers to hire more part-time workers. As no objective evidence was produced to support this, the House of Lords held that the policy was not justified. In *Steinicke*[183] German law for public sector workers provided that those over 55 could convert to part-time work, *if they had worked full-time for three of the five preceding years*. The German Government stated that the policy was for "budgetary reasons" and to encourage part-time work and save costs. The ECJ held that the rule in fact discouraged part-time work, as it acted as a disincentive to enter part-time work in the first place. It added that if budgetary considerations were allowed to justify indirect discrimination, the principle of equal treatment would vary with the state of public finances. In *Rinner-Kuhn*[184] the German Government's justification for excluding those who worked up to ten hours per week from a right to sick pay from their employers, was that these workers were "not integrated in and connected with the undertaking in a way comparable with other workers." The ECJ rejected this as a "generalised statement" which did not amount to objective justification. However, in *Nolte*,[185] the challenge was to the exclusion of those who worked less than 15 hours per week ("minor employment") from the *State* sick pay scheme. Here the German Government advanced more detailed arguments: (i) the policy corresponded to a structural principle of the German social security scheme; (ii) the only way the foster the demand for minor employment was within this structure; and (iii) that otherwise there would be an increase in unlawful employment and circumventing devices (e.g. false self-employment). The ECJ held the policy was justified, noting the State's broad margin of discretion.

In *Hockenjos v Secretary of State for Social Security*[186] an enhanced Jobseeker's Allowance ("JSA") was given to parents in receipt of Child Benefit, to account for the extra expense of child care. Where the parents were separated, the Child Benefit, and consequently the enhanced JSA, was usually paid to the mother. Consequently, Mr

---

[182] [1995] 1 A.C. 1. See also above, para.6–034.

[183] *Steinicke v Bundesanstalt fur Arbeit* Case C-77/02, [2003] I.R.L.R. 892, at paras 61–69.

[184] *Rinner-Kuhn v FWW Spezial-Gebäudereinigung GmbH and Co KG* Case 171/88, [1989] I.R.L.R. 493, at 496. See also *Nikoloudi v Organismos Tilepikoinonion Ellados AE* Case C-196/02, at para.52.

[185] *Nolte v Landesversicherungsanstalt Hannover* Case C-317/93, [1996] I.R.L.R. 225.

[186] [2004] EWCA 1749 (Civ).

Hockenjos, a separated father, received only the lower amount of JSA, despite sharing a proportion of the child care duties. The Child Benefit link adversely affected men and Hockenjos challenged it at as contrary to Equal Treatment in Social Security Directive 79/7/EEC. The Government argued that the Child Benefit link was justified to "ensure consistency" and avoid the "obvious problems when two parents put forward conflicting claims of responsibility". The Court of Appeal stated that where a policy frustrates the fundamental principle of equal treatment, deference to its the margin of discretion is no longer possible, and held that as the Government had not considered less discriminatory alternatives, the Child Benefit link was not justified.[187]

A notable departure from this pattern was made by the House of Lords when hearing *Seymour-Smith*[188] upon its return from the ECJ. Here, legislation which in 1985 extended the qualification period for Unfair Dismissal rights to two years' continuous employment,[189] was challenged as it adversely affected women, who are more transient in the workforce than men.[190] The Government's argument was that the legislation would encourage recruitment, although it offered no evidence that, after six years, it had made any impact. The House of Lords held that the Government had justified the legislation. Lord Nicholls cited the part of the ECJ's ruling on justification which omitted the word "necessary". That was enough for him to conclude that the burden on the Government was not "as heavy as previously thought."[191] Read as a whole the ECJ's judgment clearly envisaged that the measure must be "necessary" to achieve an aim.[192] Even on Lord Nicholls' less stringent test, the decision was surprising. After all, although the ECJ held that encouraging recruitment was a legitimate aim, it observed that "Mere generalisations concerning the capacity of a specific measure to encourage recruitment are not enough ..."[193] The decision might be explained by the marginal adverse effect of the legislation (about eight per cent less women than men qualified for unfair dismissal rights). But on a national scale, it meant that for no good reason, for some fourteen years, hundreds of thousands of British women worked without the protection of Unfair Dismissal rights.

6–043

---

[187] *ibid.*, *per* Scott Baker, L.J. at paras 28, 44, 47 and 71 and Ward, L.J., concurring 177.

[188] [2000] I.C.R. 244. See above, paras 6–020 and 6–024. See M. Connolly "Commentary, *R. v Secretary of State for Employment, Ex p. Seymour-Smith*" [2000] 05/2 Jo Civ Lib 212.

[189] Unfair Dismissal (Variation of Qualifying Period) Order 1985, SI 1985/782. The period is now one year where the effective date of termination is after June 1, 1999: Unfair Dismissal and Statement of reasons for Dismissal (Variation of Qualifying Period) Order 1999, SI 1999/1436.

[190] The statistics are set out above, para.6–020.

[191] [2000] I.C.R. 244, at 261.

[192] See e.g. [1999] I.C.R. 447, at para.65.

[193] *ibid.*, at paras 71 and 76.

As noted above, generally the defendant in these cases will be a Member State, arguing that a domestic measure is compatible with Community discrimination law. However, there is nothing in the domestic or EC legislation that limits to this defence only to Governments. Accordingly, in *Hlozek v Roche Austria Gesellschaft mbH*[194] Advocate-General Kokott stated that a private employer should be able use this defence, and enjoy equally the broad margin of discretion afforded to Member States. Some years earlier, in *Greater Manchester Police Authority v Lea*,[195] the EAT held that there had to be a link between the function of the employer and the objective justification. Accordingly, the employer's policy of not hiring those with occupational pensions (adversely affecting men) to favour the unemployed was not justified, as the aim was not linked to the employer's function. The EAT based its reasoning on the *Hampson* balancing test, which requires that the discriminatory effect of the challenged practice is balanced against the reasonable needs of the *employer*.[196] However, no damage is done to this test if the employer's "reasonable needs" is substituted for its "legitimate social policy". Thus, under domestic law, an employer should be able to use a social policy as a defence, and *Lea* should not be followed. Under Community law, there seems no reason to doubt that Advocate-General Kokott's opinion is correct.

Where an employer follows a domestic measure that apparently contravenes the equal treatment principle in Community law, a problem arises. The claimant is suing the employer, but challenging the validity of the Government's measure, which it introduced in pursuit of a social policy. Unless the case proceeds by judicial review, the employer may be in the position of defending the Government's social policy. Where the case progresses to the ECJ a Member State may make representations.[197] For domestic courts the issue arose in *Harvest Town Circle Ltd v Rutherford (No.1)*.[198] In this case, predating the Age Regulations 2006, Mr Rutherford, aged 67, was dismissed. By s.109 of the Employment Rights Act 1996, those over 65 cannot claim unfair dismissal. Mr Rutherford argued that s.109 adversely affected men and so was contrary to EC sex discrimination law. As Harvest Ltd produced no evidence to justify s.109, the tribunal concluded that the exclusion was not justified. The EAT held this to be an error of law. A tribunal could not come to a proper decision without hearing the Government's argument, and therefore it should invite or if neces-

---

[194] Case C-19/02, [2005] 1 CMLR 28, at paras AG57–58. The case was decided by the Court on other grounds.
[195] [1990] I.R.L.R. 372, EAT.
[196] See above, para.6–031.
[197] See e.g., *Jenkins v Kingsgate*, C-98/80, [1981] ECR 911, *Barber v Guardian Royal Exchange* C-262/88, [1990] E.C.R. I-1889.
[198] [2002] I.C.R. 123, EAT.

sary *summons* "against his will" the appropriate minister to put its case.[199]

(v) Religion or Belief Discrimination
For religion or belief discrimination in employment cases, different **6–044** considerations may apply to the application of the justification test. This is because it will be common for workers to seek *different*, rather than equal, treatment, typically, time off for religious observances and practices, or dispensation from an appearance rule (such as "no beards", or "short skirts"). As such, these claims resemble those brought under disability discrimination law which imposes a positive duty of "reasonable accommodation". As the legislation provides no express duty of reasonable accommodation, these cases will be decided under the indirect discrimination model. Claimants must allege that the failure to accommodate was a discriminatory practice (having an adverse impact), which the employer must justify. The main problem to arise is likely to be where workers take time off for religious observances and practices. The failure to accommodate is likely to materialise into a positive act when the worker is disciplined for ignoring the rule. And so these cases will turn on the employer's justification of the rule.

In the United States, the law recognises this scenario. For religious discrimination in employment, the law is not centred on the "business necessity" defence,[200] but rather on a duty to "reasonably accommodate" a worker's "religious observance or practice without undue hardship on the conduct of the employer's business".[201] This places a positive duty on employers to take steps to accommodate the religious needs of their workers. For instance, an employer is be obliged to accommodate a worker's request to be absent on Sundays by inquiring if fellow workers would cover that shift.[202] In *Ansonia Board of Education v Phillbrook*[203] the Supreme Court held that giving the right to unpaid leave plus three days paid leave, for religious holidays, was a reasonable accommodation. The "undue hardship" element affords the courts some flexibility to weigh the business needs against the

---

[199] [2002] I.C.R. 123, at paras 28–29. Harvest Ltd later became insolvent, leaving the Government liable for any unfair dismissal compensation payable, conveniently making it an interested party and a defendant in the proceedings. However, the House of Lords resolved the claim on basis that there was no adverse impact, and so justification was not required: *Rutherford v Secretary of State for Trade and Industry (No.2)* [2006] UKHL 19. Discussed, above para.6–014.

[200] See above, para.6–033.

[201] Title VII, para.701(j), (codified in 42 USC s.2000e(j)). This amendment was inserted in 1972 with the stated purpose to protect Sabbath observers whose employers fail to adjust work schedules to fit their needs (see e.g. *EEOC v Ithaca Industries* 849 F 2d 116, at 118 (4th Cir 1988)).

[202] *EEOC v Ithaca Industries* 849 F 2d 116 (4th Cir 1988), certiorari denied, 488 US 924 (1988).

[203] 497 US 60 (1986).

accommodation sought. In *Trans World Airlines v Hardison*[204] the Supreme Court held that the employer, which had pared its weekend staffing to a minimum and had asked for voluntary cover, was not obliged to pay premium rates to attract weekend staff nor upset its seniority system, to allow a worker Saturdays off for his Sabbath. It further stated that that any cost to the employer above *de minimis* was an undue hardship.[205]

6–045   An English employment tribunal took a similar—if slightly stricter—approach to this question in *JH Walker Ltd v Hussain*,[206] which was heard under the old, and arguably less strict, test of justification.[207] In this case 18 workers were disciplined for taking a day off work to celebrate Eid, a Muslim holy day, in breach of a new rule that holidays could not be taken during the company's busiest time. The workers brought a claim of indirect racial discrimination (as the facts arose before the Religion of Belief Regulations 2003). The absence of half the production staff for a day caused a loss of profit, but this could have been reduced to a "minimum" had the employer made appropriate arrangements in advance and exploited the workers' willingness to put in extra hours. The tribunal weighed the competing interests and held that the rule was not justified.

In fields other than employment, the defence is drafted less strictly. Section 45(3)(d) of the Equality Act 2006[208] provides that the defendant must "reasonably justify" the challenged provision, criterion or practice "by reference to matters other than [the relevant] religion or belief."

(vi) Age Discrimination

6–046   In addition to the standard defence for indirect discrimination, the Employment Equality Directive 2000/78/EC, Art.6(1), allows Member States to legislate for exceptions specific to age, providing that they are objectively and reasonably justified by a legitimate aim, and if the means of achieving that aim are appropriate and necessary. "Legitimate aims" include employment policy, labour market and vocational training objectives. The significance of this exception is that direct, as well as indirect discrimination may be objectively justified.

In other jurisdictions, courts have taken a less strict line with age discrimination, considering it a less serious social evil than say, race or sex discrimination.[209] In the US, instead of the standard "business necessity" test, employers are required merely to show "reason-

---

[204] 432 US 63 (1977).
[205] *ibid.*, at 84.
[206] [1996] I.C.R. 291, at 295–296, EAT. See also Ch.13, para.13–025.
[207] See above, para.6–031.
[208] *Expected in force October 2006.
[209] See para.6–026 and Ch.2, paras 2–007—2–008.

able factors other than age."[210] Art.6(1) reflects this less strict approach, but in *Mangold v Helm,*[211] a case of a Member State invoking Article 6(1) to justify direct age discrimination, the ECJ applied the objective justification test as rigorously as it has for other grounds of discrimination.

(vii) Seniority, Merit, and Bonus Systems
These are covered in Ch.9, paras 9–035—9–037.   **6–047**

4. RESIDUAL LAW

As noted above[212] there remains a class of residual cases that either   **6–048**
predate or fall outside the scope of the new definitions, and must
be brought under the original domestic definition of indirect
discrimination.

Race Relations Act 1976   **6–049**

1(1) "A person discriminates against another . . . if— . . .

> *(b)* he applies to that other a requirement or condition which
> he applies or would apply equally to persons not of the
> same racial group as that other but—
> (i) which is such that the proportion of persons of that same
> racial group who can comply with it is considerably
> smaller than the proportion of persons not of that racial
> group who can comply with it, and
> (ii) which he cannot show to be justifiable irrespective of the
> colour, race, nationality or ethnic or national origins of
> the person to whom it is applied; and
> (iii) is to the detriment of that other because he cannot
> comply with it.[213]

Essentially, this formula is the same as the new one. Claimants must
establish a prima facie case by showing that a requirement adversely
affected their racial or gender group. The burden then shifts to the
employer to justify the requirement, irrespective of race, or sex, as the
case may be. The formula appears narrower than the new one
(although, as seen below, this can be remedied with a purposive interpretation). The significant differences are the elements "requirement

---

[210] *Smith v City of Jackson* 544 US 228 (Sup Ct 2005).
[211] Case C-144/04 [2006] I.R.L.R. 143. See further Ch.8, para.8–058.
[212] See above para.6–005.
[213] The same formula is used in SDA 1975, s.1(1)*(b)*.

or condition" and "can comply". *Detriment* in para.(iii) is included merely to ensure a claimant has *locus standi* (a right to sue),[214] and requires no further discussion.

(1) Requirement or Condition

6–050   The legislation demands that for prima facie discrimination to be proved, the discriminator must have applied a *requirement or condition* to the victim that adversely affects the victim's group. Often that will not be a problem. For example, a job advertisement might read: "Librarians wanted. Applicants must be over six feet tall". That would adversely affect many groups. However, what if the advertisement were amended to read: "Librarians wanted. Applicants who are at least 6 feet tall will be *preferred*"? Does the exchange of the word *preferred* for *must* take this job advertisement out of the scope of the formula? Particular racial groups remain disadvantaged by the modified criterion, yet it is arguable that, strictly speaking, it falls outside of the statutory words *requirement or condition*. Thus, the judges felt that they had a choice of giving the words a strict literal interpretation or—to serve the purpose of the legislation—a liberal one. Confusion in the White Paper on Racial Discrimination has not helped.[215] For example, it stated that *direct* discrimination laws alone could not address the "practices and procedures which have a discriminatory effect" and "practices which are fair in a formal sense but discriminatory in their operation and effect". Further on one finds "requirement and condition".[216] The legislation used the phrase "requirement or condition".

If the judges prefer the strict interpretation, they create a loophole in this law. Employers could evade the legislation simply by relegating any discriminatory requirements to "mere preferences". Consequently, with this element in particular, the role of the judges is critical. The cases show that in the early days tribunals wavered between strict and broad interpretations. However, since 1983, the judges, with some minor exceptions, have supported the strict one. First, a line of EAT cases indicated a willingness to give the Act a broad and purposive interpretation.[217] For instance in *Watches of Switzerland v Savell*[218] the EAT found that the ". . . vague, subjective, unadvertised promotion procedure which does not provide . . . any adequate mechanisms to prevent subconscious bias unrelated to the merits of the candidates . . . for the post . . ." amounted to a *requirement or condition* within the meaning of s.1(1)*(b)*.[219]

---

[214] See e.g. 893 HC 1491–2 June 18, 1975.
[215] *Racial Discrimination* Cmnd 6234, 1975, London: HMSO.
[216] *ibid.*, respectively paras 35 and 55.
[217] e.g., *Clarke v Eley (IMI) Kynoch* [1983] I.C.R. 165, at 171, *Home Office v Holmes* [1984] I.C.R. 678, at 684.
[218] [1983] I.R.L.R. 141.
[219] Ms Savell's claim only failed because that procedure did not adversely affect women.

The Court of Appeal came to the matter for the first time in *Perera v Civil Service Commission (No.2)*.[220] Here, an advertisement for a legal assistant stated that candidates with a good command of the English language, experience in the UK and with British nationality would be at an advantage. It was held that these "mere preferences" did not amount to a *requirement or condition* within the meaning of the s.1(1)*(b)*. To come within the Act, the Court stated, an employer should elevate the preference to a requirement or "absolute bar" which *has* to be complied with in order to qualify for the job. Stephenson, L.J. justified the decision thus:

> . . . a brilliant man whose personal qualities made him suitable as a legal assistant might well have been sent forward . . . in spite of being, perhaps, below standard on his knowledge of English . . .[221]

That comment reveals the problem. If a candidate has to be "brilliant" to compensate for a racially based "weakness" then he is at a disadvantage because of his race. A "brilliant" black person will obtain a post otherwise suitable for an "average" white person. The Court of Appeal also rejected Mr Perera's strongest argument, that several "preferences" which could not be complied with added up to an absolute bar. If a candidate lacked a good command of the English language, experience in the UK and British nationality he stood no chance of being selected. Nonetheless, the Court of Appeal followed *Perera* in *Meer v London Borough of Tower Hamlets*.[222] Here, the employer attached twelve "selection criteria" to an advertised post. One of these was experience in the Tower Hamlets district. That put persons of Indian origin at a disadvantage because a higher than average proportion of them were new to the area. The Court of Appeal rejected Meer's claim of indirect discrimination holding that the criterion (or "mere preference") of Tower Hamlets experience did not amount to a *requirement or condition*. Staughton, L.J. explained his decision by stating first, that otherwise s.1(1)*(b)* "would have such an extraordinarily wide and capricious effect". Secondly, an employer would be liable to claims "whether or not he had the slightest intention to discriminate on racial grounds". Staughton, L.J. illustrated this point with an example of an employer, who, on a "whim" favours applicants whose surname begins with the letter "A". There will be a risk that a person from a racial group whose surnames begin with "A" less predominantly will have applied, and having been rejected, brings a claim.[223]

6–051

---

[220] [1983] I.C.R. 428
[221] *ibid.*, at 437H–438A
[222] [1988] I.R.L.R. 399, CA.
[223] *ibid.*, at 403.

Two observations are necessary. First, liability is not dependant on discriminatory intent.[224] Second, this employer's "whim" could conceivably amount to discrimination if a higher than average proportion of a protected group were affected by it. For instance, excluding those whose name begins with the letter "P", would exclude all Patels, who make up a significant part of the Indian population. Staughton, L.J. failed to appreciate the *effect* of the "whim", one which almost certainly could not be justified as related to job performance.

It is clear from the facts of these two cases that mere preferences can amount de facto to race or sex discrimination. Yet the decisions hold that anti-discrimination law is not applicable to mere preferences. This reveals the loophole. A bigot could simply reclassify his job conditions as "preferences", so that his job advertisement might read:

> Librarians wanted. Candidates would be at an advantage if they: had an excellent command of English,[225] were clean shaven,[226] were over six feet tall, had a Home Counties accent, were under 30 years old,[227] and had lived in the area all their lives.[228] Free lunch (roast pork) will be provided to those interviewed.

6–052 If the reasoning of the Court of Appeal in *Perera* and *Meer* were extended to this advertisement, those criteria would not infringe s.1(1)*(b)*, even though they would disadvantage and in many cases effectively bar most ethnic minorities and women.

So far, the debate has been on policy grounds. There are also technical reasons to question the *Perera* decision. The Court of Appeal felt that the statutory words could only be read to mean an absolute bar *to the job*.[229] However, there is no reason why they could not cover an absolute bar to *gaining an advantage in the job selection procedure*. This interpretation in no way distorts the statutory words and accords with the purpose of the legislation. There is support for this view in Australia, where under similarly worded legislation, the Federal Court of Western Australia refused to follow *Perera,* holding that "mere preferences" that disadvantaged women, were within phrase "requirement or condition."[230]

---

[224] This is implied by s.57(3), RRA 1976, which provided that no damages shall be payable in cases of unintentional indirect discrimination (discussed Ch.13, para.13–025). See, for example, *Orphanos v Queen Mary College* [1985] A.C. 761 (above para.6–035).

[225] *Perera v Civil Service Commission (no.2)* [1983] I.C.R. 428.

[226] *Panesar v Nestle Co Ltd* [1980] I.C.R. 144 and *Gilbert v United Parcel Service* (Unreported) April 26, 1996 CA.

[227] *Price v Civil Service Commission (No.2)* [1978] I.R.L.R. 3. See below para.6–054.

[228] *Meer v London Borough of Tower Hamlets* [1988] I.R.L.R. 399.

[229] e.g. *ibid.,* at 403.

[230] *Secretary of Department of Foreign Affairs and Trade And: Styles* (1989) 88 ALR 621, see also *Waters v Public Transport Corporation* (1991) 173 CLR 349, High Court of Australia; *Australian Iron & Steel Pty Ltd v Banovic* (1989) 168 CLR 165 at 185 & 195–7, High Court of Australia. Contrast *Commonwealth of Australia v Hamilton* (2000) 63 ALD 641.

Short of this, or an appeal to the House of Lords, *Perera* may be **6–053** avoided if a tribunal finds, *as a question of fact*, that the practice amounted to a requirement, or absolute barrier. In *Jones v University of Manchester*[231] a job advertisement stated that the successful candidate would be "a graduate, preferably aged 27–35 years".[232] An industrial tribunal found that although the advertisement expressed age as a *preference*, in practice the employer had applied the age limit as a *requirement*. The Court of Appeal had doubts over the tribunal's interpretation of the evidence,[233] but refused to interfere with their finding of fact that the employer had applied a "requirement" for the purposes of s.1(1)*(b)* of the Sex Discrimination Act 1975.

Another solution exists for some employment cases of nationality discrimination (which is excluded from the Race Directive 2000/43/EC). Claimants may invoke the lesser known Art.39 (ex 48) EC Treaty, outlawing discrimination on the grounds of nationality against a national of a Member State in the field of employment contrary to the principle of the free movement of workers. Here, these "residual" cases can be drawn under the EC umbrella, and be decided according to ECJ jurisprudence, which recognises indirectly discriminatory practices and preferences.[234]

(2) Causation and "Can Comply"

This is a causative element, demanding a connection between the challenged practice and the claimant's sex or race, as the case may be. The **6–054** definition demands that "the proportion of women who *can comply* [with the requirement] is considerably smaller than the proportion of men who *can comply* with it".[235]

An argument put many times is that the literal meaning of *can comply* excludes anyone who could physically comply with the requirement. Fortunately for the policy of the legislation, these arguments have failed. In *Price v Civil Service Commission*[236] the employer required applicants to be aged between 17 and 28, which indirectly discriminated against women because many women in that age group were unavailable for work for family reasons. The EAT rejected an argument that because women were not obliged to have families they could choose to comply with the requirement, on the basis that it was

---

[231] [1993] I.C.R. 474.

[232] See also *Price v Civil Service Commission (No. 2)* [1978] I.R.L.R. 3, below.

[233] See for instance Ralf Gibson, L.J., [1993] I.C.R. 476, at 490G–491E.

[234] *Ingetraut Scholz v Opera Universitaria di Cagliari* Case C-419/92 [1994] ECR 1-507 (credit given for experience in Italy indirectly discriminated against German national). This is unlikely to cover discrimination, say, against an English person in Wales: see the discussion in Ch.3, para.3–006.

[235] Or "that the proportion of persons of [the claimant's] racial group who *can comply* with [with the requirement] is considerably smaller than the proportion of persons not of that racial group who *can comply* with it". (Emphasis supplied.)

[236] [1978] I.C.R. 27, at p.32

"wholly out of sympathy with the spirit and intent of the Act". In *Mandla v Dowell Lee*[237] a Sikh boy could not wear the school cap because of his turban. The Court of Appeal held he could *physically* comply by simply cutting his hair, removing the turban, and fitting the school cap.[238] Kerr, L.J. suggested that as he had decided that the definition of a racial group is based upon unalterable characteristics, "cannot comply" must be equated with impossibility: "It was not intended to be measured against criteria of free will, choice, or conscience."[239] The House of Lords reversed. Lord Fraser stated: "The word 'can' . . . must . . . have been intended by Parliament to be read not as meaning 'can physically', so as to indicate a theoretical possibility, but as meaning 'can in practice' or can consistently with the customs and cultural conditions of the racial group."[240]

A more technical solution has been to rule that the question depends only on whether the claimant can comply at the time when the requirement or condition is applied. In *Clarke v Eley (IMI) Kynoch Ltd*,[241] Browne-Wilkinson, J. stated that the relevant point in time at which the ability of a part-time worker to comply with the requirement of being full-time was at the date the detriment was imposed—in this case the date she was made redundant. It was irrelevant that she could previously have become a full-time worker, in which event she might have been able to comply. Similarly, in *Commission for Racial Equality v Dutton*,[242] a landlord, who displayed "no travellers" signs at the entrances of his public house, argued that Romany travellers *could* comply with that requirement and remain Romany by giving up the nomadic way of life after seeing the sign, and returning as "non-travellers". The Court of Appeal held that the time of compliance with the requirement was when it was invoked i.e. when a person stood outside the public house wishing to enter.

(3) Proving a Considerable Difference

6–055 Under this formula, the comparison must be between the proportions of those who *can* comply with the requirement. The comparison must reveal a "considerable difference" for an adverse impact to be established. Any—bar the first ("intrinsically liable")—of the analytical methods discussed above[243] under the new definition are suitable, so long as they are based on a "requirement or condition", positive figures are used, and the difference was "considerable."

---

[237] [1983] 1 Q.B. 1, CA; [1983] 2 A.C. 548, HL. The facts are set out in Ch.3, para.3–007.
[238] *ibid.*, at p.16.
[239] *ibid.*, at p.24D-E. See, also, Oliver, L.J. *ibid.*, at p.16F.
[240] [1983] 2 A.C. 548, at p.565.
[241] [1983] I.C.R. 165, EAT.
[242] [1989] Q.B. 783. See also Ch.3, para.3–007.
[243] See para.6–017 *et seq.*

(4) Justification

Once the prima facie case is established, the burden shifts to the defen- **6–056**
dant to justify requirement or condition. The legislation demands that
the challenged requirement is "justifiable irrespective of sex", or race,
as the case may be. The courts have interpreted this to mean that the
reasonable needs of the defendant should be weighed against the
discriminatory effect of the challenged requirement. This is known as
the "*Hampson* balancing test".[244] It is arguable that the EC derived test
is stricter, although domestic courts have always denied this, holding
the domestic and EC tests to be the same.[245] This denial can now
favour claimants, who can assert that courts should maintain this
denial and in doing so, quietly abandon *Hampson* and effectively
apply the EC-derived test (now in the domestic legislation) to these
residual cases.

---

[244] *Hampson v Department of Education* [1989] I.C.R. 179, at 196F, CA.
[245] See the discussion above, para.6–031.

VICTIMISATION

INTRODUCTION

It is not enough that the legislation proscribes direct and indirect **7–001**
discrimination, and harassment. In addition, those who use the legislation, or assist others to do so, need protection against retaliation
for so doing. One survey of 106 unsuccessful claimants revealed that
over a half had suffered a detriment of some sort following a
discrimination claim.[1] The legislation seeks to remove deterrents
with the inclusion of provisions for victimisation, creating a fourth
instance of discrimination.[2]

In recent times, European legislation also has provided for victimisation. For instance, Art.9 of the Race Directive[3] provides that
member States shall "protect individuals from any adverse treatment
or adverse consequence as a reaction to a complaint or to proceedings aimed at enforcing complying with the principle of equal
treatment".

---

[1] (1990) 30 EOR 23.
[2] "Whistle blowers" may gain protection also from the Public Interest Disclosure Act 1998. The
issue of discrimination after "the relationship has come to an end" is discussed in Ch.8 (vic-
timising ex-workers) para.8–017, and Ch.10, para.10–004 (other fields).
[3] 2000/43/EC. See also, Equal Treatment Directive, 76/207/EEC (amended by the Equal treatment Amendment Directive (2002/73/EC), from October 5, 2005), Art.7; Equality Employment
Directive 2000/78/EC, Art.11.

The domestic statutory definition is as follows:

Race Relations Act 1976

7–002   **2 Discrimination by way of victimisation[4]**

(1) A person ("the discriminator") discriminates against another person ("the person victimised") in any circumstances relevant for the purposes of any provision of this Act if he treats the person victimised less favourably than in those circumstances he treats or would treat other persons, and does so by reason that the person victimised has—

(a)   brought proceedings against the discriminator or any other person under this Act; or

(b)   given evidence or information in connection with proceedings brought by any person against the discriminator or any other person under this Act; or

(c)   otherwise done anything under or by reference to this Act in relation to the discriminator or any other person; or

(d)   alleged that the discriminator or any other person has committed an act which (whether or not the allegation so states) would amount to a contravention of this Act,

or by reason that the discriminator knows that the person victimised intends to do any of those things, or suspects that the person victimised has done, or intends to do, any of them.

(2) Subsection (1) does not apply to treatment of a person by reason of any allegation made by him if the allegation was false and not made in good faith.

7–003   Paragraphs (a) to (d) define what have become known generally as "protected acts". It is necessary to prove that (1) there has been a protected act, (2) the defendant treated the complainant less favourably, and (3) that the less favourable treatment was *by reason that* the complainant did the protected act.

The principal Federal legislation in the United States makes it unlawful to retaliate against a person because he has "opposed" any unlawful discriminatory practice, or "because he has made a charge, testified, assisted, or participated in any manner in an investigation, proceeding, or hearing" in a discrimination case.[5] In the former,

---

[4] Similar definitions are provided in the parallel legislation: SDA 1975, s.4; Religion or Belief Regulations 2003, reg.4; Sexual Orientation Regulations 2003, reg.4, Age Regulations 2006 (in force October 1, 2006), reg.4; Equality Act 2006, s.45(4) (religion or belief discrimination in fields other than employment, expected in force October 2006)

[5] Civil Rights Act 1964, Title VII, (42 USC s.2000e–3(a)).

"opposition" cases, which include allegations short of formal proceedings made by the victim or any other party, the courts afford the person limited protection. An employee is protected from retaliation even if the allegation is false, so long as it was made in good faith.[6] But the courts will balance the interests of the employee and employer. The employee is not protected if he "violates the legitimate rules and orders of his employer, disrupts the employment environment, or interferes with the attainment of his employer's goals."[7] On the other hand, the protection given to one who "participates" in any manner in formal proceedings is comprehensive, covering even malicious and false statements contained in a discrimination charge.[8] The limit seems to be absence from work without good cause.[9]

1. THE PROTECTED ACTS

Paragraph (1)(a) covers those bringing a claim of discrimination, even where the victimiser is not the defendant: where a person brings a racial discrimination claim against a shopkeeper for refusing to serve him, the shopkeeper's brother, who happens to be the employer of the claimant, victimises him; or where an employer rejects a job applicant because of previous actions of discrimination (even if unsuccessful) brought by the applicant against *another* employer.

7–004

Paragraph (b) covers those giving evidence in a discrimination claim. The broadly worded para.(c) has been held to cover a job centre worker reporting that employers were encouraging the job centre to discriminate when supplying staff;[10] and the making of secret tape recordings in an attempt to establish discrimination by a taxi cab association.[11]

Paragraph (d) is worded more narrowly, requiring that the behaviour alleged actually was a breach of the Act. Apart from the most obvious cases, in practice, there will be very few protected acts falling under para.(d). This is because the paragraph requires, as a prerequisite, proof of the breach of the Act. None of the other paragraphs require this, so long as the allegation was not false, and made in good faith. The difficulty of pleading a case under para.(d) was illustrated in *Waters v Commissioner of Police of the Metropolis*.[12] Miss Waters, a police officer, alleged that she was the victim of rape and buggery by a fellow officer while they were off duty. No action was taken against the alleged assailant. She testified that as a result of making the complaint she was: aggressively treated, ostracised by colleagues and

7–005

---

[6] *Love v RE/MAX of America* 738 F 2d 383, at 385 (10th Cir 1984).
[7] *Booker v Brown & Williamson Tobacco* 879 F 2d 1304, at 1312 (6th Cir 1989).
[8] *Pettway v American Cast Iron Pipe Co* 411 F 2d 998, at 1007 (5th Cir 1969).
[9] *Booker v Brown & Williamson Tobacco* 879 F 2d 1304, at 1312 (6th Cir 1989).
[10] *Kirby v Manpower Services Commission* [1980] I.C.R. 420, EAT. See further, below, para.7–006.
[11] *Aziz v Trinity Street Taxis Ltd* [1989] Q.B. 463, CA. See further, below, para.7–006.
[12] [1997] I.C.R. 1073, CA.

senior officers, transferred to civilian duties, denied proper time off, refused placements, told she should leave, subjected to pornography by colleagues, threatened with violence by her chief superintendent, and required to take a psychological analysis to verify she was fit for duty. Further, her complaints were not properly investigated and confidences were broken. The Court of Appeal rejected her claim of victimisation because the alleged assailant was acting outside the course of his employment, so she had not alleged that the Act had been breached.[13]

In many cases, at the time of the original complaint, and right up to a final tribunal or court ruling, neither the victim nor victimiser will know whether the allegation contained a "a breach of the Act". The policy should be to protect allegations whether or not they necessarily turn out to be well grounded, especially as the vast majority will never be brought to court. However, only para.(d) requires that the principal allegation is well grounded. So the solution, it seems, is to plead such cases under para.(c) (anything done by reference to the Act). In these cases there remains protection from spurious claims as subs.(2) excludes from protection allegations which are "false and not made in good faith".[14] Had Miss Waters pleaded her case under para.(c) the issue would have been whether her principal allegation of rape and buggery was false and made not in good faith, rather than the more technical question of whether such conduct could amount to a breach of the Act.[15] In the United States, the courts would protect from retaliation a person in Miss Waters' situation. She would have been afforded the limited protection given to an "opposer", which covers allegations made in good faith that do not amount to a breach of the statute.[16]

2. TREATED LESS FAVOURABLY

(1) The Comparison—Treated Less Favourably Than Whom?

7–006   The phrase "he treats *or would treat* other persons" in subs.(1) (emphasis supplied) allows the comparator to be real or hypothetical. The proper comparison is between the treatment of alleged victim and the treatment that was, or would have been, given to another, who had not done *any* element of the protected act. It has proved rather too easy for tribunals to assume that the comparator has done part of the protected act as well, with disastrous results. For instance, in *Kirby v Manpower Services Commission*,[17] an employee at a job centre was

---

[13] Waters did not appeal against this aspect of the decision, but won her appeal to the House of Lords that management's response had been negligent. See [2000] I.C.R. 1064, HL.
[14] Applies to all the parallel provisions. See fn 4, above.
[15] See generally R. Townshend-Smith (1996) 2 I.J.D.L. 137.
[16] *Love v RE/MAX of America* 738 F 2d 383, at 385 (10th Cir 1984).
[17] [1980] I.C.R. 420, EAT.

moved to less desirable work because he disclosed confidential information regarding suspected discrimination by some employers. The EAT rejected his claim of victimisation because any person disclosing confidential information of *any nature* would have been moved to other work. Thus the EAT held that that treatment was not less favourable. The Court of Appeal in *Aziz v Trinity Street Taxis*[18] overruled *Kirby* and held that the comparison should *not* include any element of the protected act.

In *Aziz,* the complainant was an Asian taxicab proprietor and a member of an association of taxicab operators. When the association required him to pay £1,000 to have a third taxi admitted to its radio system, he felt he was being unfairly treated on racial grounds. He recorded secretly conversations with other taxi drivers, and made an unsuccessful complaint to a tribunal about the additional fee. The recordings were revealed during the hearing of that complaint. As a result, he was expelled from the association on the ground that the making of the recordings was an unjustified intrusion and a serious breach of the trust that had to exist between members. Aziz complained of victimisation. The association argued that as any member making secret recordings would be expelled, Aziz was not treated less favourably. The Court of Appeal rejected this argument, noting that if the protected act itself constituted part of the comparison all complaints of victimisation would "necessarily fail" if the defendant could show he would treat all those who did the protected act equally badly; "an absurd result."[19] The comparison was to be made with a non-Asian member of the taxi association who had *not* made secret tape recordings. Under this test it is obvious that Aziz was treated less favourably than this comparator.

This is the correct approach, first, for the reason given in *Aziz*, and second, if one removes only the race[20] element from the protected act, a tribunal is then effectively trying to identify *racial discrimination*, rather than victimisation, which would render the provisions on victimisation redundant. Nonetheless, since the law apparently was settled in *Aziz*, back in 1988, defendants consistently have advanced the "*Kirby* comparator". They may have been encouraged by the reluctance of the Court of Appeal in *Aziz* to overrule its own decision on this element in *Cornelius v University College of Swansea*.[21] In that case it was held that an employer's refusal to grant a transfer request or allow the grievance procedure, after the claimant had issued sex discrimination proceedings, was not less favourable treatment, because the employer would have treated any worker bringing *any* proceedings, in the same way. Since then, in a number cases, counsel for the defendant has cited

---

[18] [1989] Q.B. 463, CA.

[19] *per* Slade, L.J., *ibid.*, 483. Aziz lost his claim on the third element, *by reason that*. See below.

[20] Or, as the case may be, sex, sexual orientation, religion or belief, or age.

[21] [1987] I.R.L.R. 141. Discussed [2000] 29 I.L.J. 304.

Cornelius in support of using a *Kirby* comparator, only for the Court of Appeal to reject *Kirby* but merely "distinguish" *Cornelius*. This occurred in *Khan v Chief Constable of West Yorkshire*,[22] *Brown v TNT Express Worldwide*,[23] as well as *Aziz*.

This uncertainty was not helped by the sentiment expressed by some of judges in the appeals in *Chief Constable of West Yorkshire v Khan*.[24] In the House of Lords, for instance, Lord Nicholls commented, when favouring the *Aziz* approach, that "There are arguments in favour of both approaches."[25] This is not the language to put a bad case to death. In fact, only Lords Scott and Hoffman rejected the *Kirby* comparator unequivocally.[26] In the court below, the then Master of the Rolls, Lord Woolf, stated:[27] "I would like to look favourably on [the] submission that you should ask whether the respondent was treated any differently from anyone else who brought proceedings." But he "felt driven" by precedent and his interpretation of s.2 of the Race Relations Act 1976 ("RRA 1976") to reject the *Kirby* comparator. All the same, it must be assumed that now the House of Lords has rejected *Kirby*, no matter how reluctantly, the *Kirby* comparator, as used in *Cornelius*, is bad law.

(2) What is "Less Favourable"?

7–007   On the face of it, deciding if the treatment itself was less favourable is straightforward. In some cases though, a victim may perceive the treatment differently from the defendant. In *Chief Constable of West Yorkshire v Khan*,[28] the Chief Constable refused to give a reference to Detective Sergeant Khan in support of a job application with the Norfolk Police, because Khan was pursuing a claim of racial discrimination against the Chief Constable, as his current employer. Nonetheless, the Norfolk Police invited Khan for an interview, but failed to appoint him. It was common ground that had a reference been given, containing the Yorkshire Police's low assessment of Sergeant Khan's managerial skills, he would have stood *less* chance of being short-listed for an interview. Accordingly, in Khan's action for victimisation, the Chief Constable argued that Khan had been treated *more*, not less, favourably. The House of Lords rejected that argument. Lord Scott concluded: "It cannot . . . be enough for s.2(1) purposes simply to show that the complainant has been treated differently . . . I think it suffices if the complainant can reasonably say that he would

---

[22] [2000] I.C.R. 1169, CA, at para.28. The House of Lords' decision is discussed below.
[23] [2001] I.C.R. 182, at para.33.
[24] [2000] I.C.R. 1169, CA; [2001] UKHL 48. See further, below, paras 7–007 and 7–009.
[25] *ibid.*, at para.27.
[26] *ibid.*, respectively at paras 72 and 48.
[27] [2000] I.C.R. 1169, at para.24, CA.
[28] [2001] UKHL 48. See further, below, para.7–009.

have preferred not to have been treated differently."[29] This approach echoes the direct sex discrimination case *R. v Birmingham City Council, Ex p. EOC,*[30] where it was held that the denial of a grammar school place (to a girl) was less favourable in spite of evidence that the education standards of grammar and comprehensive schools were comparable. It would seem that the courts should not be too pedantic about this element. There must be more than just *different* treatment, but it is enough if the complainant perceives—reasonably—that she has been treated less favourably.

3. "By Reason That"

The third element in proving a case of victimisation centres on the link between the protected act and the less favourable treatment, or in the statutory language, the less favourable treatment must be *by reason that* the victim did the protected act. This element is essential to prevent fanciful claims where a person who has performed a protected act is treated less favourably for an entirely separate reason, for instance, where a worker who has made a claim of sexual harassment is dismissed for theft. However, there is a class of cases where the matter cannot be so clearly cut. In these cases, (the "general policy" cases), the defendant treats the "victim" less favourably, by reason that she did the protected act *irrespective of* its discrimination ingredient, because, under a general policy, anybody who does the protected act *minus the discrimination element* would still be treated in that way. For example, an employer has a policy to suspend any worker who brings a legal action against it. It then suspends a worker for bringing a racial discrimination claim against it. The discrimination factor in the protected act was irrelevant to the employer's reason. In other words, the defendant was not *motivated* by the racial discrimination factor. Courts sympathetic to defendants in these cases generally have accepted this argument. In *Aziz*[31] it was held that the defendants were motivated by the breach of trust, even though the tape recordings were part of the protected act. By adopting this approach however, the courts were introducing an ingredient of motive, or intent, into this element, which in the past, the House of Lords has refused to do. In *Nagarajan v London Regional Transport*[32] the claimant, a man of Indian origin, was interviewed for a job with London Regional Transport (LRT), against whom, he had in the past brought several complaints of racial discrimination. LRT did not offer Mr Nagarajan

7–008

---

[29] *ibid.*, at para.76.
[30] [1989] 1 A.C. 1156. See Ch.4, para.4–015. The statutory definition of direct discrimination also uses the phrase "treats less favourably."
[31] See above, para.7–006.
[32] [2000] A.C. 501.

a job and he won a claim of victimisation in the industrial tribunal, which based its decision on three findings. First, all three members of the interviewing panel were aware of the previous proceedings. Second, Mr Nagarajan was given one out of ten for "articulacy" [*sic*] by the panel, despite him having been a transport information assistant for four months without complaint; the mark was "plainly ridiculous and unrealistically low", the tribunal found. Third, one of the panellists considered that Mr Nagarajan was "very anti-management". The tribunal concluded that the interviewers "were consciously or subconsciously influenced by the fact that the applicant had previously brought industrial tribunal proceedings against LRT".[33] LRT appealed on the basis that a defendant must be shown to have been "consciously motivated" by the protected act: as the tribunal failed to distinguish between *conscious* and *subconscious* motivation, no case of *conscious* motivation had been made out. A majority of the House of Lords dismissed LRT's appeal,[34] following the "objective and not subjective",[35] or "straightforward",[36] approach, applied to the parallel element *on the ground of* in the definition of direct discrimination, in *EOC v Birmingham City Council*,[37] and again in *James v Eastleigh BC*,[38] where Lord Goff specifically applied the *but for* test. In *Nagarajan*, Lord Nicholls concluded "I can see no reason to apply a different approach to s.2."[39] Thus, it seemed, the correct approach was to ask: "*but for* the protected act, would the claimant have been less favourably treated?"

7–009   However, the House of Lords took a different approach when faced with a "general policy" case some two years' later. In *Chief Constable of West Yorkshire v Khan*,[40] the employer, who refused to give a reference to a worker who had brought a discrimination claim, (the details are set out above, para.7–007), argued that as he would refuse a reference to anyone with an existing claim, whatever its nature, he was not motivated by the racial discrimination aspect of this claim. The Court of Appeal[41] followed *Nagarajan* and found for the claimant, on the basis that *but for* Khan's outstanding proceedings, the Chief Constable would have given him a reference. A unanimous House of Lords reversed.[42] This decision, made within two-and-a-half years of *Nagarajan*, has thrown into doubt the precise meaning of the phrase

---

[33] *ibid.*, at 516.
[34] Lords Nicholls, Steyn, Hutton and Hobhouse. Lord Browne-Wilkinson dissented.
[35] So described by Lord Bridge in *James v Eastleigh BC* [1990] AC 751, at 765.
[36] *per* Lord Steyn, [2000] 1 A.C. 501, at 521.
[37] [1989] 1 A.C. 1156, HL. Discussed Ch.4, para.4–015.
[38] [1990] A.C. 751, HL. Discussed Ch.4, para.4–015.
[39] [2000] 1 A.C. 501, at 512.
[40] [2001] UKHL 48.
[41] [2000] I.C.R. 1169, CA, at para.28.
[42] Contrast the US position: an employer refusing to give a reference for fear of creating evidence damaging to its defence of the discrimination charge will be liable for victimisation: *Sparrow v Piedmont Health* 593 F Supp 1107, at 1119 (MD NC 1984).

by reason that. Clarity was not helped by the various interpretations of this element. Lord Nicholls said is not causative, whilst Lord Hoffman said that it was. Lord Hutton's position is unclear because he concurred with *both* Lord Nicholls and Lord Hoffman. Meanwhile Lord Scott said the phrase was one of "not strict causation".[43]

The appeal in *Nagarajan* turned on whether it was enough that the employer's motivation (in reacting to previous proceedings) was *sub*conscious. The House of Lords, applying the "straightforward" *but for* test, held that it was. In fact, nothing said in *Khan* upsets the ratio decidendi of *Nagarajan*, which was that motivation could be either conscious or subconscious. But the speeches in *Khan* at best side-stepped, and at worst ignored, the wider statements in *Nagarajan* concerning the phrase *by reason that.* Nevertheless, a unanimous House of Lords clearly rejected the *but for* approach for cases of victimisation. And so, following *Khan*, that is what the law is *not.* It is less easy to say what the law *is.*

The key to understanding that, so far as it is possible, lies in the decision of the whole House depending upon a fine distinction, between the *bringing* and *existence* of proceedings. To this end Lords Nicholls, Hoffman and Scott drew support from *Cornelius v University College of Swansea*,[44] noting a feature of that case was that the College had acted on the *existence*, rather than the *bringing* of proceedings. This fine distinction shows a drift away from the straight-forward approach adopted by the House of Lords in *Nagarajan*, where Lord Nicholls himself said "in the application of this legislation legalistic phrases, as well as subtle distinctions, are better avoided so far as possible".[45] This distinction becomes even less credible if one accepts that Sergeant Khan may have by-passed it by adding a second protected act to his pleadings, that under s.2(1)*(c)*, RRA 1976, he had "otherwise done anything under or by reference to this Act". As well as having *brought* proceedings, he was "otherwise" *maintaining* them in existence.

Thus far it could be ventured that the ratio decidendi of *Khan* is that a defendant who acted by reason of the *existence*, and not the *bringing*, of the proceedings cannot be liable under s.2(1)*(a)*, RRA 1976, (by reason that the person has "brought proceedings . . ."). Standing alone, this proposition sabotages the purpose of the House's own rejection of the *Kirby* comparator (see above)[46] for establishing less favourable treatment. Employers could simply argue that they responded to all proceedings in this way, whatever their nature. So long as the employer acted after the proceedings were brought, virtually no claim

7–010

---

[43] [2001] UKHL 48, respectively, at paras 29, 54 and 77. See M. Connolly, "The House of Lords retreat from the causative approach announced *Nagarajan* and leave claimants in a 'Khan's Fork'" (2002) 31 I.L.J. 161, at 166.

[44] [1987] I.R.L.R. 141. The facts are set out above, para.7–006. Discussed [2000] 29 I.L.J. 304.

[45] [2000] A.C. 501, at 512.

[46] Under the element of less favourable treatment, above, para.7–006.

of victimisation could succeed under s.2(1)*(a)*. However, the House added a further dimension, noting that the employer had acted "reasonably and honestly"[47] and "in accordance with perfectly understandable advice,"[48] and had not "singled out" a worker for less favourable treatment.[49] It is now possible to qualify the *ratio* as being that there is no liability under s.2(1)*(a)*, RRA 1976, where the defendant acted, *reasonably and honestly*, by reason of the existence, and not the bringing, of proceedings.

This qualification carries a series of problems. First and most obviously, there is no such requirement in the legislation that for liability, the defendant acted unreasonably and dishonestly. Second, focussing on the predicament of the "reasonable and honest" employer undermines the policy of the provisions, which is the removal of deterrents to enforcing the anti-discrimination legislation. Third, this "extra element" of acting reasonably and honestly does little to save the decision from sabotaging the purpose of rejecting *Kirby*. In most cases employers will prove that they acted "reasonably and honestly" by showing that the company normally treats in the same way, any worker who brings *any* proceedings. Indeed, that was the defence in *Khan*. Accordingly, employers can escape liability (once again) when, for example, suspending a worker on full pay, or refusing a transfer, promotion, access to a grievance procedure, or denying the usual—but discretionary—incremental pay rise or bonus. So long as all workers are equally "victimised" pending the outcome of proceedings, a claim of victimisation will fail and the rejection of the *Kirby* comparator is rendered impotent. Fourth, the "reasonable and honest" requirement carries a suggestion that tribunals should identify an *intention* to victimise—or simple vengeance—by the employer, for liability. Take for instance, a case where several months into discrimination proceedings the employer announces, "I've had enough of this trial, it's gone on far too long. All the claimant's transfer requests are to be refused." Such an employer would rely on *Khan* stating that he reacted to the *existence*, not the *bringing*, of proceedings. If a tribunal then demanded honest and reasonable behaviour, it must find the employer liable. Yet this example is indistinguishable from *Khan*, save for the element of vengeance, which should not be an ingredient for liability.

This danger was realised in *Derbyshire v St Helens Metropolitan BC*,[50] where the Court of Appeal applied *Khan* to conduct that went beyond a "general policy". Here, 510 catering staff brought an equal pay claim. Most compromised, but 39 persisted. The council then wrote directly to every member of staff stating that should the claim succeed, the resulting cost was likely to cause mass redundancies. For

[47] *per* Lord Nicholls, [2001] UKHL 48, at para.31.
[48] *per* Lord Mackay, *ibid.*, at para.44.
[49] *per* Lord Scott, *ibid.*, at para.80.
[50] [2006] I.C.R. 90.

the 39 litigants this induced fear and pressure to compromise the claim. In their consequent claim for victimisation, the Court of Appeal agreed that they had been treated less favourably (it was "usual" to correspond with their trade union or solicitors), but a majority, applying *Khan*, held that the council had acted "honestly and reasonably" in trying to settle the proceedings.[51] In effect, the majority has held that even though the treatment was less favourable, and out of the ordinary, so long as the employer acted honestly and reasonably, it did not matter that this treatment clearly was "by reason that" the claimants were pursuing proceedings. At the time of writing an appeal was due in the House of Lords. If the appeal fails, employers will be free to deter litigation using any means, so long as it is "honest and reasonable", which on the facts of *Derbyshire*, appears to be a rather elastic phrase.

Khan, Cornelius and *Aziz* are can be understood by reducing them **7–011** to the salient facts. As such, they are "general policy" cases. The decisions in these cases amount to a dividing of the protected act, which is contrary to the wording and the policy of the legislation. Further, if the case is reduced to requiring a defendant to be motivated by the (racial, or other) discriminatory ingredient of the protected act, it becomes a case of discrimination per se (be it race, sex or another protected ground), leaving the provisions on victimisation redundant. Whilst both the employer and the worker will find themselves in a difficult position, the provisions on victimisation are not aimed at resolving the employer's predicament. On the contrary, as Lord Steyn pronounced in *Nagarajan* "victimisation was as serious a mischief as direct discrimination."[52] It is now inconceivable, one hopes, that a tribunal would embark on such a diversion from the statutory wording and purpose in a case of direct discrimination, no matter how "reasonably and honestly" the defendant had acted.

None of this is to say that intention, or motivation, per se should not be a factor. After all, the defendant is part of the causal chain, or link, between the protected act and the less favourable treatment. What goes through the defendant must, presumably, go through his mind. But the proper issue is: motivated by *what*? Once it is understood that the protected act cannot be divided (or distinguished as suggested in *Khan* and *Cornelius*), the issue becomes much simpler: was the defendant motivated by the (undivided) protected act? Thus, a factor of motivation per se need not curtail the straightforward *but for* approach expressed in *Nagarajan* and *James v Eastleigh*. So long as the cause of the less favourable treatment is the protected act, taken without division or fine distinctions, motivation is a harmless

---

[51] *ibid., per* Parker, L.J. at para.58, *per* Lloyd, L.J., at paras 78–82. In addition, Parker, L.J., used the distinction between the bringing and existence of proceedings (at para.53).
[52] [2000] A.C. 501, at 521.

ingredient. This does not impose some open-ended liability on defendants. There remains a link between the less favourable treatment and
the protected act. So, for example, the employer who, aware of a
complaint of sexual harassment, dismisses the complainant for an
entirely separate incident of theft, would not liable for victimisation.

CHAPTER 8

DISCRIMINATION IN EMPLOYMENT

1. Definition of Employment

8–001   Claimants using the employment provisions of the domestic discrimination legislation must be in employment at an establishment in Great Britain.

(1) Employment

8–002   The definition in the domestic discrimination legislation is broad. It is intended to cover the self-employed, as well as ordinary employees. Thus, under the legislation, "employment" means "employment under a contract of service or of apprenticeship or a contract personally to execute any work or labour".[1] The definition is wider than that found in most employment legislation, such as the law of unfair dismissal, which covers only employees who work under a contract of employment.[2] In *Quinnen v Hovells*[3] Waite J. said that "those who engage, however cursorily, the talents, skills or labour of the self-employed" must ensure there is no discrimination in their appointment, terms or dismissal.

There is no exemption for small employers. In the United States, the Federal discrimination law, Civil Rights Act 1964, Title VII, applies only to employers with 15 or more workers, although state legislation may offer more protection.

The position of purely commercial contracts—where a sole trader or practitioner, or partner of a firm, agrees to provide services—is less certain. Here the requirements seem to be (a) a contractual relation-

---

[1] SDA 1975, s.82(1); RRA 1976, 78(1); and (omitting the words "or labour") Age Regulations 2006 (in force October 1, 2006), reg.2; Religion or Belief Regulations 2003, reg.2; Sexual Orientation Regulations 2003, reg.2; and ("subject to any prescribed provision"), DDA 1995, s.68. For Community law level the ECJ stated "The essential feature of an employment relationship . . . is that for a certain period of time a person performs services for and under the direction of another person in return for which he receives remuneration." (*Lawrie-Blum v Land Baden-Wurttemberg* Case 66/85 [1986] ECR 2121, at para.17. Applied *Perceval-Lance v Department of Economic Development* [2000] I.R.L.R. 380, NICA.)
[2] Employment Rights Act 1996, s.230(1).
[3] [1984] I.C.R. 525, at p.532, EAT.

ship, (b) an obligation to carry out the work personally, which is (c) the "dominant purpose" of the contract.[4]

(a) Contractual Relationship

An appointment that is not overtly contractual should not obscure any underlying contractual nature to the arrangement. In *Percy v Church of Scotland Board of National Mission*[5] the appointment of a minister of the Church of Scotland to an "ecclesiastical office", in other words, to act as a parish minister, was for a five-year term, with a minimum stipend, a manse, holidays, and travelling expenses. The House of Lords held that holding an ecclesiastical office and the existence of a contract to provide services were not mutually exclusive, and the arrangement, which contained the ingredients for a contract, was contractual. Further, the fragmented arrangement of the Church, which made it difficult to pin down precisely who is the employer, should not stand in the way of otherwise well-founded claims.[6]

8–003

(b) To Carry Out the Work Personally

The obligation must be that the person to the contract carries out work personally. In *Patterson v Legal Services Commission*[7] a sole principal in a law firm (which employed several staff) claimed racial discrimination against the Legal Services Commission in relation to its awarding of a legal aid franchise. The Court of Appeal held that Ms Patterson was not employed by the Commission because she was not obliged to carry out any of the work—under the arrangement she was entitled to delegate all of the work to her staff.[8] Likewise, a motorcycle recovery driver, who contracted with a dealer to collect motorcycles using his own vehicle, but could delegate some or all of the work, was not "employed".[9] Neither was a sub-postmaster who was required to provide premises and ensure that the post office work was carried out either by himself or his staff;[10] nor a taxi driver who supplied his own car and paid a taxi firm £75 per week for a radio and access to its customers, but was not obliged to take any work at all.[11]

8–004

---

[4] *Mirror Group Newspapers Ltd v Gunning* [1986] I.C.R. 145, at 151, CA.

[5] [2005] UKHL 73.

[6] Now that "office-holders" are expressly included in the SDA 1975 by s.10B (in force October 1, 2005), a minister of religion is protected either as an employee or an office-holder. See further below, para.8–078.

[7] [2004] I.C.R. 312.

[8] The Commission was held to be a "qualifying body" for the purpose of RRA 1976, s.12. See below, para.8–076.

[9] *Hawkins v Darken (tla Sawbridgeworth Motorcycles)* [2004] EWCA Civ 1755, (for the DDA 1995).

[10] *Tanna v Post Office* [1981] I.C.R. 374, EAT, (for the RRA 1976).

[11] *Mingeley v Pennock* [2004] I.C.R. 727, CA, (for the RRA 1976).

(c) The Dominant Purpose

8–005 In *Loughran & Kelly v Northern Ireland Housing Executive*[12] the housing executive invited applications from firms of solicitors to sit on a panel to defend public liability claims, stating that from each firm either one or two solicitors "would be mainly responsible for carrying out panel work." It rejected the applications from Loughran and Kelly, who brought claims of discrimination under the Fair Employment (Northern Ireland) Act 1976, which carries the same definition of "employment" as the other discrimination legislation. The House of Lords, by a bare majority in each case, held that claimants were "employed" for the purposes of the Act. Loughran was a sole principal of his firm and the majority held that the dominant purpose was work by him, even though he may delegate some of it to an assistant solicitor and a secretary. Kelly was a partner in a two-partner firm and whilst Lords Steyn and Slynn found that *the partnership* was contracted to do most of the work, Lord Griffiths found that just Kelly was so responsible. So although Kelly prevailed, there was no majority to say that firms or companies can come under the definition of "employment".

By contrast, in *Mirror Group Newspapers Ltd v Gunning*,[13] the contract in question was to distribute a Sunday newspaper on terms that the contractor would exercise "day-to-day supervision" of the operation. The Court of Appeal held that the dominant purpose of this contract was to distribute the newspapers, and the requirement of day-to-day supervision was not enough to make it a contract of employment under the Sex Discrimination Act 1975.

(d) Illegal Employment Contracts

8–006 The general rule is that the courts will not enforce an illegal contract, such as one operating to defraud the inland revenue. Accordingly, the illegality of an employment contract will undermine a wrongful dismissal claim (that is, for breach of contract).[14] However, in *Leighton v Michael and Charalambous*[15] the EAT held that an employee under an illegal contract was entitled to sue for sexual harassment. This was approved by the Court of Appeal in *Hall v Woolston Hall Leisure*.[16] The reasoning is that discrimination is a statutory tort, and the right arises separately from the employment contract, although the ille-

---

[12] [1999] 1 A.C. 428.

[13] [1986] I.C.R. 145.

[14] *Napier v National Business Agency* [1951] 2 All E.R. 264, CA. The Court of Appeal, in *Hewcastle Catering v Ahmed and Elkanah* [1991] I.R.L.R. 473 allowed a claim of *unfair* dismissal to succeed, despite the claimant workers participating, but not profiting, in the employer's tax fraud. The special circumstances were that the workers were sacked for giving evidence against the employer regarding the fraud.

[15] [1995] I.C.R. 1091.

[16] [2001] I.C.R. 99.

gality could be of such a nature it would be against public policy to enforce the action.

(2) In Great Britain

In addition to being "in employment", the general rule is that a claimant must be employed at an establishment in Great Britain, a requirement that is fulfilled "if the employee does his work wholly or partly in Great Britain."[17] This question is decided by regarding the whole of the employment period, not just the place of commencement, or the place where the complaint arose.[18] The legislation may not apply where work is done in Great Britain unexpectedly. In *Deria v The General Council of British Shipping*[19] a requisitioned ship was ordered unexpectedly by the Government to dock in Southampton. The Court of Appeal held that the worker is not covered because it was not anticipated at the outset that any work would be in Great Britain. The basis of the decision was that the parties should be certain at the outset of the voyage whether the legislation applied. This decision may be explainable on its facts, but where a worker who finds himself working unexpectedly in Great Britain for some length of time, such a decision would be much harder to justify, not least because it would become impossible to deny that he worked "partly" in Great Britain.[20]

8–007

Under Art.39 (ex 48) EC, it is unlawful for an employer to discriminate on the ground of nationality against a national of the European Union. Hence, where say, an employer refuses to recruit an EU national for work not "wholly or partly in Great Britain" on the ground of his nationality, the domestic definition may have to be disapplied in deference to Community law.[21]

The general rule does not apply to seaman recruited abroad for discriminatory pay on ground of nationality.[22] This is to enable the British shipping industry to compete in a market where third-world wages commonly are paid.

The exception to the general rule is that work wholly outside Great Britain is covered if:

(a)   the employer has a place of business at an establishment in Great Britain,

---

[17] SDA 1975, s.10; RRA 1976, s.8; Religion or Belief Regulations 2003, reg.9; Sexual Orientation Regulations 2003, reg.9; Age Regulations 2006, reg.10 (in force October 1, 2006); DDA 1995, s.68.

[18] *Saggar v Ministry of Defence* [2005] I.C.R. 1073, CA

[19] [1986] I.C.R. 172. Decided under the earlier definition: unless work is done "wholly or mainly outside Great Britain."

[20] See also the careful distinguishing of *Deria* by the Court of Appeal in *Saggar v Ministry of Defence* [2005] I.C.R. 1073, at para.35.

[21] *Bossa v Nordstress Ltd* [1998] I.C.R. 694, EAT.

[22] RRA 1976, s.9.

(b)   the work is for the purposes of the business carried on at that establishment, and

(c)   the employee is ordinarily resident in Great Britain—

(i)   at the time when he applies for or is offered the employment, or
(ii)   at any time during the course of the employment.[23]

2. Unlawful Employment Discrimination

(1) Discrimination in Recruitment

8–008   Section 4(1) of the Race Relations act 1976 provides:

It is unlawful for a person, in relation to employment by him at an establishment in Great Britain, to discriminate against another—

(a)   in the arrangements he makes for the purpose of determining who should be offered that employment; or
(b)   in the terms on which he offers him that employment; or
(c)   by refusing or deliberately omitting to offer him that employment.

The parallel provisions in the other legislation are materially the same.[24] It is also unlawful to harass a person who has applied for employment.[25]

(a) Arrangements for Recruitment

8–009   Paragraph (a) covers all aspects of the recruitment process leading to the appointment and the terms of that appointment. This will include for example, the drawing up of the job specification, the taking up of references and the short-listing process. In *Ministry of Defence v Fair Employment Agency*[26] it was held discriminatory (under the Fair Employment (Northern Ireland) Act 1976) to require a security check only for the Roman Catholic candidate.

---

[23] SDA 1975, s.10(1) and (1A) (in force October 1, 2005); RRA 1976, s.8(1) and (1A); Religion or Belief Regulations 2003, reg.9(1) and (2); Sexual Orientation Regulations 2003, reg.9(1) and (2); Age Regulations 2006, reg.10(1) and (2) (in force October 1, 2006); DDA 1995, s.68(2) and (2A). This exception, deriving from Community law, applies to the Race Relations Act 1976 only so far as discrimination on the ground of race or national or ethnic origins, or harassment. See generally, Ch.2, para.2–002.

[24] SDA 1975, s.6(1); Religion or Belief Regulations 2003, reg.6(1); Sexual Orientation Regulations 2003, reg.6(1); Age Regulations 2006, reg.7(1) (in force October 1, 2006).

[25] SDA 1975, s.6(2A); RRA 1976, s.4(2A); Religion or Belief Regulations 2003, reg.6(3); Sexual Orientation Regulations 2003, reg.6(3); Age Regulations 2006, reg.7(3) (in force October 1, 2006).

[26] [1988] 11 NIJB 75, NICA. (The Fair Employment (NI) Act 1976 outlaws discrimination on the ground of religion or political belief.)

The word "person" in the provisions means "employer".[27] Thus, the provisions do not refer to any particular person in the recruitment process, but simply the arrangements made by the *employer*. In *Brennan v JH Dewhurst Ltd*,[28] the defendant advertised for a butcher's assistant, and appointed (in a non-discriminatory manner) a local manager to carry out the "first-filter" interviews, the final decision being with the district manager. The local manager interviewed a female candidate in a discriminatory manner, making it clear that he did not want a woman appointed. The EAT held that the local manager's interview was part of the selection arrangements, and so the defendant was liable. The employer could not disassociate itself from the *effect* of its arrangement. Further, it did not matter that in the event, no one was appointed to the post. This case also demonstrates that a discriminatory intent in the making of the arrangements is not necessary for liability.

Word-of-mouth hiring should come within the "arrangements",[29] although this has not been tested in the courts.[30] It was accepted, *obiter*, in *Coker v Lord Chancellor*[31] that word-of-mouth hiring could amount to unlawful discrimination, although it was held in that case that creating a job for a member of the family, a friend, or a personal acquaintance was not discriminatory. This logic prompted the comment: "The prohibition of discrimination in selection arrangements—a concept which lies at the heart of discrimination law—can be circumvented by the simple expedient of not having any selection arrangements."[32]

Logically, advertising forms part of the "arrangements" for recruitment.[33] However, enforcement of unlawful discriminatory advertising seems to be reserved for the enforcement commissions.[34] Discriminatory advertising is specifically outlawed by the Sex Discrimination Act 1975 and the Race Relations Act 1976, but not as of yet by the Sexual Orientation, Religion or Belief, or the Age Regulations.[35]

8–010

---

[27] *Nagarajan v LRT* [2000] 1 A.C. 501, at 514 HL. The more recent legislation (the Sexual Orientation, Religion or Belief, or Age Regulations) uses the word "employer" instead.

[28] [1984] I.C.R. 52, EAT.

[29] Especially as the definition of indirect discrimination is now less restrictive: see Ch.6, paras 6–006 and 6–011.

[30] The US Circuits are divided on this issue: see *United States v Georgia Power* 474 F 2d 906, at 925–926 (7th Cir 1993) and *EEOC v Chicago Miniature Lamp Works* 947 F 2d 292 (7th Cir 1991). Discussed Ch.6, para.6–011

[31] [2002] I.C.R. 321, at para.57, CA. Discussed, Ch.6, para.6–025.

[32] Michael Rubenstein, commentaries to *Coker* in the I.R.L.R., [2001] I.R.L.R. 116, at 115.

[33] *Brindley v Tayside Health Board* [1976] I.R.L.R. 364, IT.

[34] See Ch.13, para.13–029.

[35] DDA 1995, s.16B provides for discriminatory advertising in a similar way to the SDA 1975 and RRA 1976. See further, Ch.5, para.5–032. Equality Act 2006, s.54, outlaws discriminatory advertising for religion or belief in fields other than employment (expected in force October 2007).

Section 29(1) of the RRA 1976 makes it unlawful to publish "an advertisement[36] which indicates, or might reasonably be understood as indicating, an intention by a person to do an act of discrimination" even if any subsequent act happens to be lawful. The parallel provision of the SDA 1975, s.38(1), is limited to advertisements which "indicate an intention" to do an unlawful act. Generally, both sections do not apply where one of the exceptions, such as a Genuine Occupational Requirement, applies.[37] Under the SDA, s.38(3) states that job descriptions with a sexual connotation (such as waiter, salesgirl, postman or stewardess) indicate an intention to discriminate "unless the advertisement contains an indication to the contrary."[38]

8–011 As well as facially discriminatory advertisements, it is conceivable that advertisements which indirectly discriminate are unlawful, such as those placed in men's or women's magazines, or distributed only in predominantly white areas,[39] or displayed in part of the workplace frequented predominantly by men.

As noted above, enforcement under these sections lies exclusively with the enforcement commissions. This led the EAT in *Cardiff Women's Aid v Hartup*[40] to hold that job advertisements did not fall with the "arrangements" for recruitment with the result that individuals could not bring an action based on a discriminatory advertisement. This polarised analysis hardly helps those who, say, have been deterred from applying for a job by the advertisement's content, or did not even know about the post because of where it was placed. However, despite the EAT's reasoning, the claim in *Hartup* was brought by a person who had never held the desire or intent to apply for the job, in other words a person without *locus standi*. Hence, those who are deterred from applying, or those unaware of the job, should be able to distinguish *Hartup* on that basis. As a matter of policy *Hartup* is a poor decision. So long as a claimant has *locus standi* there are no policy reasons to prevent victims from challenging discriminatory advertisements. Indeed, it would be a welcome deterrent, especially within small and medium businesses, where the enforcement commissions are unlikely to become aware of, or have the resources to investigate, internally advertised posts. The matter becomes more bizarre after considering the Sexual Orientation, Religion or Belief,

---

[36] Ss.82, SDA 1975, and 78, RRA 1976, offer a common broad definition of an advertisement: "'Advertisement' includes every form of advertisement or notice, whether to the public or not, and whether in a newspaper or other publication, by television or radio, by display of notices, signs, labels, showcards or goods, by distribution of samples, circulars, catalogues, price lists or other material, by exhibition of pictures, models or films, or in any other way, and references to the publishing of advertisements shall be construed accordingly".

[37] Not always the case under the RRA 1975, see Ch.5, para.5–032.

[38] In *Equal Opportunities Commission v Robertson* [1980] I.R.L.R. 44 an industrial tribunal held that the words "craftsman", "ex-policeman or similar", "bloke", "manageress" each had sexual connotations, but "manager" and "carpenter/handyman" did not.

[39] See the US case, *US v City of Warren, Michigan* 138 F 3d 1083 (6th Cir 1998).

[40] [1994] I.R.L.R. 390.

and Age legislation, which, as of yet, carries no specific parallel provisions on advertising. If *Hartup* stands as a precedent for the meaning of "arrangements", then job advertisements that discriminate on the grounds of Sexual Orientation, Religion or Belief, or Age are unchallengeable *by any party.*

(b) The Terms Offered

The job offer must not be on discriminatory terms, such as lower pay   **8–012**
for a woman, a company car for a man, or a probationary period for a black person. For sex discrimination cases, once the offer becomes part of the employment, the matter comes under the Equal Pay Act 1970, rather than the SDA 1975. The relationship between these two pieces of legislation is explained in Ch.9.[41]

(2) Discrimination During Employment

Section 4(2) of the Race Relations Act 1976 provides: **8–013**

> It is unlawful for a person, in the case of a person employed by him at an establishment in Great Britain, to discriminate against that employee—
>
> (a)   in the terms of employment which he affords him; or
> (b)   in the way he affords him access to opportunities for promotion, transfer or training, or to any other benefits, facilities or services, or by refusing or deliberately omitting to afford him access to them; or
> (c)   by dismissing him, or subjecting him to any other detriment.

The parallel provisions in the other legislation are materially the same.[42] It is also unlawful for an employer to harass an employee.[43]

(a) Discriminatory Dismissals

Dismissal in the discrimination legislation includes constructive   **8–014**
dismissal, that is where the employer's conduct, amounting to a serious breach of contract, entitles the innocent party to resign from

---

[41] See below, para.9–002.
[42] SDA 1975, s.6(2), (save that paragraph (a) ("terms") is covered EqPA 1970, s.1); Religion or Belief Regulations 2003, reg.6(2), Sexual Orientation Regulations 2003, reg.6(2); Age Regulations 2006, reg.7(2), (in force October 1, 2006).
[43] SDA 1975, s.6(2A); RRA 1976, s.4(2A); Religion or Belief Regulations 2003, reg.6(3); Sexual Orientation Regulations 2003, reg.6(3); Age Regulations 2006, reg.7(3) (in force October 1, 2006).

the contract.[44] Accordingly, in *Weathersfield Ltd (Trading As Van & Truck Rentals) v Sargent*[45] the Court of Appeal applied the established contract principles of acceptance of a repudiatory breach. Here Mrs Sargent, a white European, was appointed as a receptionist by the defendant. On her first day she was told not to hire out vehicles to "any coloured or Asians." She was stunned and a few days later resigned, without giving her reason. She brought a claim of racial discrimination, claiming constructive dismissal on the ground of race.[46] One issue was whether she could claim constructive dismissal without having given her reason for leaving. The Court of Appeal held that it was not necessary in law to state the reason for leaving and so found for Ms Sargent. "[T]he more outrageous or embarrassing are the instructions given to them, or suggestions made to them, the less likely they may be to argue the point there and then . . . Moreover, there is no suggestion in this case that the employers would have changed their policy had she asked them to do so."[47] However, the Court warned that when no reason was given at the time, it will be more difficult to show that the employer's conduct was the true reason for leaving.

Often, claims for discriminatory dismissal will overlap with unfair dismissal claims (provided by the Employment Rights Act 1996). But there are some important differences between unfair dismissal and discriminatory dismissal. The first is that for unfair dismissal only, there is a general one-year qualification period.[48] This applies equally to full-time and part-time employees. Second, unfair dismissal compensation remains subject to a statutory maximum limit on compensation, at the time of writing, £58,400.[49] There is no cap on the compensation available for unlawful discrimination. Typically, this will benefit highly paid workers,[50] or those whose career has been terminated by a discriminatory dismissal.[51] Third, the definition of an

---

[44] SDA 1975, s.82(1A)(b); RRA 1976, s.4(4A); Religion or Belief Regulations 2003, reg.6(5)(b); Sexual Orientation Regulations 2003, reg.6(5)(b); Age Regulations 2006, reg.7(5)(b) (in force October 1, 2006).

[45] [1999] I.C.R. 425.

[46] It is possible to be discriminated against on the grounds of another's race: *Showboat v Owens* [1984] 1 W.L.R. 284, CA. See further, Ch.4, para.4–025.

[47] [1999] I.C.R. 425, at 433.

[48] ERA 1996, s.108(1). There are some exceptions to this rule.

[49] Employment Rights Act 1996, s.124. As from February 1, 2006: Employment Rights (Increase of Limits) Order 2005 SI 2005/3352, Sch, Art.3. It is normally raised each February in line with retail prices.

[50] In *Chaudhary v BMA* UKEAT/1351/01/DA and UKEAT/0804/02/DA, (Transcript) the EAT upheld an award of £800,000 to a doctor whose career was damaged by racial discrimination. In *Bower v Shroder Securities* (2002) an employment tribunal awarded £1.4m to a city worker who was forced to resign because of sex discrimination (reported *www.eoc.org.gov* and *The Times* January 11, 2002). On the lifting of the cap in discrimination claims, see Ch.13, para.13–020.

[51] Such as those women dismissed form the armed forces for pregnancy. See, e.g., *Ministry of Defence v Cannock* [1994] I.C.R. 918, EAT; A. Arnull, "EC law and the dismissal of pregnant servicewomen" (1995) 24 I.L.J. 215; and now the Sex Discrimination Act 1975 (Application to Armed Forces, etc) Regulations 1994 SI 1995/3276. Discussed below, Ch.13 para13–021.

employee is much broader in the discrimination legislation, covering the self-employed. Unfair dismissal rights are available only to employees who work under a contract of employment. Fourth, unlike unfair dismissal, there is a right under discrimination law to damages for injury to feelings.[52]

It is possible to combine the two allegations in a single case. As a matter of law it does not necessarily follow that an employer has acted unreasonably for the purpose of unfair dismissal (a question which involves considering the employer's conduct on the basis of factors known to him at the time he takes his decision) just because he has dismissed an employee as a result of an indirectly discriminatory condition.[53] Thus a "fair" dismissal may have been discriminatory and vice versa.[54]

Note finally that a dismissal of a person aged 65 or over on the ground of retirement may be lawful as an exemption under the Age Regulations 2006.[55]

(b) Any Other Detriment

Should the facts not fall within any of the specified circumstances (such as access to promotion or dismissal) a claim may still succeed if the employee suffered "any other detriment". In *Shamoon v Chief Constable of the Royal Ulster Constabulary*[56] the House of Lords stated the question was: "Is the treatment of such a kind that a reasonable worker would or might take the view that in all the circumstances it was to his detriment?" It was not necessary to demonstrate some physical or economic consequence.

8–015

In *Shamoon* a police inspector carried out as one of her duties appraisals of officers. Following complaints by officers, she was relieved of the appraisal duty. She brought a claim of discrimination under the Sex Discrimination (Northern Ireland) Order 1976. Article 8(2)(b) is set out in identical terms to s.4(2)(b), RRA 1975 (set out above). The Northern Ireland Court of Appeal[57] held that Ms Shamoon had not suffered a detriment because she had no right to carry out appraisals and there was no accompanying loss of rank or financial loss. The House of Lords reversed, and held that the loss of

---

[52] *Vento v Chief Constable of West Yorkshire Police* [2003] I.C.R. 318, CA. *Cf Dunnachie v Kingston-upon-Hull City Council* [2005] 1 A.C. 190, HL.

[53] *per* Browne-Wilkinson, J. (as he then was), *Clarke v Eley (IMI) Kynoch Ltd* [1983] I.C.R. 165, at 177, EAT.

[54] In *Claydon House v Bradbury* Unreported (2004) UKEAT/0315/04/MAA, (Transcript) (available at *www.employmentappeals.gov.uk*), the claimant was dismissed for a fair reason (gross misconduct), although the reason for her "misconduct" (absenteeism) was a disability.

[55] See further, below para.8–062.

[56] [2003] I.C.R. 337, at para.35, citing *Ministry of Defence v Jeremiah* [1980] Q.B. 87, at p.104, CA.

[57] [2001] I.R.L.R. 520 at 522.

the appraisal work was a detriment simply because it would reduce her standing amongst colleagues.[58]

8–016   In *Chief Constable of West Yorkshire v Khan*[59] the House of Lords held that an employer's refusal to give a reference amounted to a detriment, even though in the event a reference would have been negative and *lessoned* the candidate's chances. The candidate, reasonably, would have preferred to have the reference.

An unjustified sense of grievance cannot amount to "detriment". In *Barclays Bank plc v Kapur (No.2)*[60] workers were not given pension rights in respect to their previous service for their employer in Kenya, because they had been given a compensation package. As they were no worse off financially, the Court of Appeal held they had suffered no detriment. Less convincing is *Schmidt v Austicks Bookshops*,[61] where female, but not male, workers in a bookshop were required to wear overalls when in public areas. The EAT held that this was not serious enough to amount to a detriment. It is unlikely that this decision can survive the approach taken in *Shamoon*. A reasonable worker may well feel demeaned at having to wear overalls in public, which gives the impression that she is of a different status to any male worker.

(3) Discrimination After Employment

8–017   The most common form of discrimination against ex-workers is the failure to provide a reference because that worker had previously brought a complaint of discrimination. Section 27A of the Race Relations Act 1976 provides that it is unlawful for an employer to discriminate against, or harass, an ex-worker where the discrimination or harassment "arises out of and is closely connected to" the previous employment. The parallel provisions in the other legislation are materially the same.[62] The provisions were inserted to implement Community law, and so are not strictly relevant to residual cases (for instance, discrimination solely on grounds of colour or nationality, or acts of discrimination or harassment predating the provisions).[63]

These provisions codified the case of *Coote v Granada*.[64] Here, Mrs Coote sued her employer following her dismissal for being pregnant. Subsequently, and after those proceedings were dead, the employer refused to give her a reference and Mrs Coote sued again, this time for

---

[58] [2003] I.C.R. 337, at para.37. However, she lost appeal because she was treated no less favourably than a male inspector would have been in the same circumstances. See further Ch.4, para.4–009.

[59] [2001] I.C.R. 1065. See further, Ch.7, para.7–009.

[60] [1995] I.R.L.R. 87.

[61] [1978] I.C.R. 85, at 88. See also Ch.4, para.4–033.

[62] SDA 1975, s.20A, (in force for discrimination July 19, 2003, for harassment October 1, 2005); Religion or Belief Regulations 2003, reg.21; Sexual Orientation Regulations 2003, reg.21; Age Regulations 2006, reg.24 (in force October 1, 2006).

[63] See Ch.2, para.2–002.

[64] Case C-185/97, [1999] I.C.R. 100, ECJ.

victimisation. An industrial tribunal ruled that s.6(2) of the Sex Discrimination Act 1975 ("It is unlawful for a person, in the case of a woman employed by him . . . to discriminate against her")[65] extended discrimination only so far as persons *employed* by the defendant. As Mrs Coote no longer worked for Granada when they refused the reference, she was not protected by the Act. The ECJ, applying the Equal Treatment Directive 76/207/EC, took a different view, holding that "Fear of such measures . . . might deter workers who considered themselves the victims of discrimination from pursuing their claims . . . and would consequently . . . seriously . . . jeopardise implementation of the aim pursued by the Directive."[66] Following the ECJ's ruling, the Employment Appeal Tribunal held that s.6(2) covered ex-workers.[67]

However, the position for residual cases is much the same. In *Relaxion v Rhys-Harper*[68] the House of Lords held that either s.6(2) of the SDA or s.4(2) of the RRA related to benefits and obligations arising from the employment relationship, irrespective of whether that relationship had ended.[69]

3. Employment Exemptions

At Community law level, the Directives provide a general rubric **8–018** known as a "Genuine Occupational Requirement" (GOR) for each of the grounds of discrimination covered, which allows employers to discriminate when the job determines. Under this, the law may develop and recognise specific jobs where discrimination is permissible, so long as they comply with the rubric. In addition, the Directives allow Member States to provide some specific exceptions, say for the armed forces, depending on the ground. The Sex Discrimination Act 1975 and Race Relations Act 1976 predate their respective parent Directives. These statutes carry an exhaustive list of specific types of job where it may be a Genuine Occupational *Qualification* (GOQ) to be a particular sex or race. Of course, nowadays, these must comply with the GOR rubric from the respective Directive. For discrimination on the ground of gender assignment, the SDA 1975 has been amended with a number of GOQ exemptions and specific exemptions, which must comply with the Equal Treatment Directive 76/207/EC. For

---

[65] RRA 1976, s.4(2) is materially the same, and set out above, para.8–013.

[66] Case C-185/97, [1999] I.C.R. 100, at para.24.

[67] *Coote v Granada Hospitality Ltd (No.2)* [1999] I.C.R. 942.

[68] The collective appeals of *Rhys-Harper v Relaxion Group plc, D'Souza v Lambeth LBC, Jones v 3M Healthcare Ltd* [2003] I.C.R. 867, overruling *Post Office v Adekeye* [1997] I.C.R. 110, CA.

[69] Thus there is no liability where the act complained of does not arise from the employment relationship, such as a refusal to implement an employment tribunal's reinstatement order for which there was a free-standing remedy (under the Employment Rights Act 1996, ss.112, 113, 114 and 117): *ibid.*, in the case of *D'Souza*, at paras 49–53, 124–125, 159–160, 205 and 221. This interpretation was given also to the DDA 1995, s.4(2).

sexual orientation, religion or belief, and age, the respective Regulations carry the general GOR rubric, as well as some specific exceptions.

(1) Gender—Genuine Occupational Requirement and Qualification

8–019 Until October 5, 2005 Art.2(2) of the Equal Treatment Directive 76/207/EEC provided a general exception where the employment activities "by reason of their nature or the context in which they are carried out, the sex of the worker constitutes a determining factor." The amended version is stricter. Now, Art.2(6) still relates to the "nature" and "context" of the job, but operates only where sex "constitutes a genuine and determining occupational requirement, provided that the objective is legitimate and the requirement is proportionate." Further, the amended version can be used only for "access to employment".[70]

All exceptions in domestic law must comply with this general rubric and so the Sex Discrimination Act 1975 and its interpretation, must comply with the Equal Treatment Directive. Where it does not, workers in the public sector may claim simply under the direct effect of the Directive,[71] whilst those in the private sector may use the indirect effect principle that the domestic legislation must be interpreted as far as is possible to accord with the Directive.[72]

Section 7 of the Sex Discrimination Act 1975 carries an exhaustive list of specific exemptions, known as Genuine Occupational Qualification, or GOQ, exemptions. Unlike the Directive, it does not allow new exceptions to be developed by the courts under a general principle. The non-regression principle means that Parliament cannot use the general definition in the Directive to introduce new exceptions where this would reduce the protection against sex discrimination.[73]

8–020 Before looking at the specific GOQ exemptions, there are some common principles to note. Under s.7(3), a GOQ defence can be raised where only *some* of the job duties require a man or a woman.[74] However, by s.7(4), the defence will fail where other employees are "capable of carrying out the duties" and that it would be reasonable to employ them on such duties, and where this can be done without

---

[70] See Equal Treatment (Amendment) Directive 2002/73/EC. Contrast GOR exemptions for other grounds, and especially the GOQ exemptions for gender reassignment (below para.8–035).

[71] *Marshall v Southampton and SW Hants AHA* Case 152/84 [1986] 1 Q.B. 401, ECJ.

[72] *Marleasing SA v La Comercial Internacional de Alimentacion SA* Case C106/89, [1992] E.C.R. I-4135, ECJ.

[73] Equal Treatment Directive 76/207/EEC, Art.8e (2).

[74] SDA 1975, s.7(3). See *Tottenham Green Under Fives' Centre v Marshall* [1989] I.C.R. 214, EAT, and *(No.2)* [1991] I.C.R. 320, EAT, decided under the parallel provision, RRA 1976, s.5(3).

undue inconvenience.[75] This coincides with the proportionality principle in the parent Directive and means that is unlikely that an
employer can reserve a job for, say, a woman, because one of the job's
minor duties must be carried out by a woman, when there exists other
female employees who could perform that duty. The "other
employees" must exist at the time, and so s.7(4) will not apply for
example, where the employer was recruiting workers for a new all-
women's health club which had not yet been opened; thus, the GOQ
exemption "to preserve decency or privacy" applied even though it
might well fail once other employees had been hired.[76] However, if an
employer used this as tactic to avoid s.7(4), say by recruiting senior
staff first (all men) and then filling the remaining posts with a mix of
men and women, a question must arise as to the compliance of this
lacuna in s.7(4) with the Directive.

The defence can only be used in relation to the arrangements for
recruitment, the decision to offer the job, or to transfer, training or
promotion.[77] It cannot be used to dismiss a worker. Thus it is not
possible to hire a person and then apply a GOQ retrospectively and
dismiss her. However, where a redundancy situation arises and a
remaining job is revised, a GOQ may be used when selecting the
person for the revised job. In *Timex v Hodgson*[78] a reorganisation
reduced the need for three supervisors to one. Timex decided to retain
the woman supervisor (and dismiss the two male ones) so that she
could (i) deal with the personal and private problems of the female
workers; (ii) accompany women to the first aid room, (iii), deal with
the supply of sanitary towels in the women's lavatory and pills for
period pains, and (iv) sometimes take urine samples from women who
worked toxic materials. The EAT held that "the correct analysis is that
the employers discriminate against the man by selecting the woman to
do the revised job, not in dismissing the man who is not selected for
the revised job." Thus, this was a discriminatory omission to offer the
man a job, rather than a dismissal of the man, and so the GOQ could
apply.

What follows is a description of each GOQ exemption specified in
the Sex Discrimination Act 1975. Note that the statutory definitions
use the terms "man" and "woman" interchangeably.

---

[75] Applied *Etam plc v Rowan* [1989] I.R.L.R. 150, EAT (sixteen other (female) employees in ladies' fashion store could cover fitting room duties). *Cf Lasertop Ltd v Webster* [1997] I.C.R. 828, EAT (unduly inconvenient for man selling membership of a women-only health club to hand over to a woman when showing potential customers the changing area).

[76] *Lasertop Ltd v Webster* [1997] I.C.R. 828, EAT.

[77] Respectively, claims under SDA 1975, ss.6(1)(a), or (c), or 6(2)(a). See above, para.8–008 and para.8–013.

[78] [1082] I.C.R. 63, at 67.

(a) Physiology and Authenticity

8–021　Section 7(2)(a), SDA 1975, provides a GOQ exemption where "the essential nature of the job calls for a man for reasons of physiology (excluding physical strength or stamina) or, in dramatic performances or other entertainment, for reasons of authenticity, so that the essential nature of the job would be materially different if carried out by a woman".

The physiology exception would apply to wet-nursing and the sex industry. The authenticity exception has a potentially wide range, applying not only to "drama", but also to "entertainment". Of course, for dramatic authenticity, it is permissible to cast female and male roles to their respective sexes. For entertainment, where the essence of the work is to entertain members of the opposite sex, such as a dance troupes to entertain at hen nights, or vice versa, it should be permissible to hire only men, or women, as the case may be.[79] Beyond that, cases may be harder to decide. In the US case, *Wilson v Southwest Airlines*[80] an airline promoted its female cabin crews to attract male business travellers and accordingly hired only women. It was held that as the essence of an airline was safe travel, not entertainment, no "bona fide occupational qualification" (BFOQ) could apply: "Sex does not become a BFOQ merely because an employer chooses to exploit female sexuality as a marketing tool, or to better insure profitability". Identifying the nature of the job will not always that straightforward. For instance, a restaurant or bar may employ all-female, or all-male,[81] serving staff, to accord with a theme.[82] Further, as Pannick has noted, "There is a thin but important line between sex as a GOQ where the essential nature of the job requires a woman, and the case where the job can more effectively be performed by a woman because of customer reaction."[83] In the US case, *Diaz v Pan American*[84] it was held that customer preference (for female airline cabin crew) could not support a BFOQ.

(b) Privacy or Decency

8–022　Section 7(2)(b) provides a defence "where the job needs to be held by a man to preserve privacy or decency" because either (i) it is likely to

---

[79] In *Cropper v UK Express Ltd*, (1992), unreported, (ET case no 25757/91; see *www.eoc.org.uk*) an employment tribunal held that sex was a GOQ for working on a telephone sex chat-line.

[80] 517 F Supp 292, at 303 (ND Tex 1981).

[81] See the *EEOC v Joe's Stone Crab* litigation (220 F 3d 1263 (11th Cir 2000)) where male serving staff were used to evoke an "Old World" ambiance.

[82] It was suggested in *Cross v Playboy Club*, Appeal No 773, Case No CFS 22618–70 (New York Human Rights Appeal Board, 1971) that being female is a BFOQ to be a Playboy Bunny, female sexuality being reasonably necessary to perform the essential purpose of the job which is to entice and entertain male customers. Cited in *Wilson v Southwest Airlines* 517 F Supp 292, at 302 (ND Tex 1981).

[83] D. Pannick, *Sex Discrimination Law*, 1985, Oxford: OUP, p.238.

[84] 442 F 2d 385 (5th Cir 1971) *certiorari denied* 404 US 950 (1971).

involve physical contact . . . where men "might reasonably object to its being carried out by a woman"; or (ii) the holder of the job is likely to do his work in circumstances where men might reasonably object to the presence of a woman because they are in a state of undress or are using sanitary facilities".

The "physical contact" exception will arise, say, where customers require measuring for clothing.[85] The second part of this *privacy or decency* defence arises where the jobholder is in a state of undress or is using sanitary facilities. In *Sisley v Britannia Security Systems Ltd*,[86] the EAT held that a jobholder's work encompassed "all matters reasonably incidental to it". Here the employer operated a security control station, described as a confined "building within a building". The (all-female) staff worked up to 12-hour shifts. The employer provided a folding bed and the staff were in the habit of sleeping during breaks in their underwear, so as not to crease their uniforms. The GOQ defence succeeded here even though the "state of undress" was a matter merely incidental to the work. For that reason, this decision has been criticised as being incompatible with the Equal Treatment Directive.[87]

(c) Work in a Private Home

Section 7(2)(ba) provides a GOQ exemption where the job is likely to involve the job holder working or living in a private home and "objection might reasonably be taken to allowing" a person of the opposite sex having the degree of physical or social contact with a person living in the home, or the knowledge of intimate details of such a person's life, which is likely because of the nature or the circumstances of the job.

8–023

This could cover, for instance, personal companions or nurses. It is not necessary that the employee works with the employer, so long as it is with a person in the home. The "intimate details" of that person surely must be confined to personal matters, and not those of a more general nature, such as financial or career matters.

(d) Live-in Jobs and Single Sex Accommodation

Section 7(2)(c) provides a GOQ exemption where it is impracticable for the job holder to live elsewhere than in premises provided, which are normally occupied by persons of one sex and which do not have separate sleeping and sanitary facilities for the other sex. It must be

8–024

---

[85] See *Etam plc v Rowan* [1989] I.R.L.R. 150, EAT. (Fitting room duties in ladies' fashion store could support a GOQ, but the defence failed because there were enough other staff to cover.)

[86] [1983] I.C.R. 628.

[87] D. Pannick, *Sex Discrimination Law*, 1985, Oxford: OUP, p.250.

unreasonable to expect the employer to provide such facilities.[88] It does not apply where workers might rest on the premises during a break in their duties.[89] The EOC offers this example of a genuine defence: "An animal sanctuary in a remote location that by law requires two employees on call 24 hours a day, and where the accommodation does not have separate sleeping facilities."

(e) Single-Sex Establishments

8–025 Section 7(2)(d) provides a GOQ exemption where the job is in a single-sex hospital or prison (or other establishment for persons requiring special supervision or attention) and it would not be reasonable having regard to the essential character of the establishment for a member of the opposite sex to do the job. This applies equally to any part of a single-sex establishment. This GOQ exemption has been criticised for being unnecessary. The problems encountered in prisons and hospitals are catered for by the GOQ exemptions of either "privacy and decency" (s.7(2)(b)), "single-sex accommodation" (s.7(2)(c)), or "personal services" (s.7(2)(e)). The argument that inmates need to be dealt with by a person of their own sex (not for reasons of privacy, decency or personal services) "badly smells of the offensive sex stereotyping that the 1975 Act aims to eradicate".[90] In *Secretary of State for Scotland v Henley*[91] a woman's application to become the Assistant Prison Governor of an all-male prison was rejected because a woman could not cope with a riot situation and that the existing governor was a woman. The employer relied on inter alia s.7(2)(d). The EAT rejected these arguments holding that the "riot" argument was purely hypothetical and based on a general assumption, and in any case, the employment of the female governor ruled out using the defence. By contrast, in the US case *Dothard v Rawlinson*[92] the Supreme Court held that it was a BFOQ to be a man to work as a prison guard in an Alabama all-male prison which had no segregation and was characterised by "rampant violence" and a risk of sexual assault upon women by sex offenders.

---

[88] In *Wallace v P and O Steam Navigation Co* (unreported, ET/31000/79, (1979), see *www.eoc-law-scotland.org.uk*) the claimant was refused a job as cinema projectionist on board a ship because the two cabins allocated to projectionists were in an all-male part of the ship. The tribunal found that although there was no suitable accommodation when she applied, it was reasonable to expect the respondents to adapt their premises to accommodate both sexes.

[89] In *Sisley*, (above), it was held that "live" meant to "dwell", rather than exist, and so the defence required actual residence rather than the use of rest facilities: [1983] I.C.R. 628, at 635, EAT.

[90] D. Pannick, *Sex Discrimination Law*, 1985, Oxford: OUP, p.256.

[91] Unreported, EAT/95/83 (1983), see *www.eoc-law-scotland.org.uk*.

[92] 433 US 321 (1977).

(f) Personal Services

Section 7(2)(e) provides a GOQ exemption where the holder of the job provides individuals with personal services promoting their welfare or education, or similar personal services, and those services can most effectively be provided by a man.[93]

8–026

(g) Duties to be Performed Abroad by Men or by Women

Section 7(2)(g)[94] provides a GOQ exemption where a job involves the performance of some duties outside the UK[95] "in a country whose laws or customs are such that the duties could not, or could not effectively, be performed by a woman". There are two criticisms of this exemption.[96] First, in Parliament, the Government did not specify which countries or which jobs were envisaged by this exception, and so no one knows precisely what is being validated.[97] Second, it is a concession to prejudice in other countries, which would not be tolerated under the Race Relations Act 1976. The EOCs Code of Practice[98] suggests that this exemption may be used in countries where women are forbidden to drive. Whilst this example may stand, it does not represent the scope of the exception, which submits to "customs" as well as laws.

8–027

(h) Married Couples and Civil Partners

Section 7(2)(h) provides a GOQ exemption where the job is one of two to be held by a married couple or by a couple who are civil partners of each other.[99] It was intended originally to cover jobs which require a husband and wife team, such as running a pub. This exception has been criticised as having the potential to allow employers to specify stereotypical jobs for the respective male and female spouses, such as caretaker and cleaner.[100]

8–028

---

[93] For a discussion on the parallel GOQ in the RRA 1976, see below, para.8–045. For a transsexual person being excluded from providing personal services, see below, para.8–039.

[94] Section 7(2)(f) is now repealed.

[95] If the work is wholly outside the UK, the SDA 1975 does not apply. See s.10, discussed above, para.8–007.

[96] Discussed by D. Pannick, *Sex Discrimination Law*, 1985, Oxford: OUP, pp.266–269.

[97] The Government stated that this exception was "to deal with what one might call the Middle East problem" (Standing Committee B, Fourth Sitting (May 1, 1975) col 173) and gave Saudi Arabia as an example (363 HL 984 (July 29, 1975, Report Stage).

[98] See *www.eoc.org.uk*, click on "The Law".

[99] The civil partnership exception was added by the Civil Partnership Act 2004, s.251(4) (in force December 5, 2005, SI 2005/3175, Art.2(1) and Sch.1).

[100] D. Pannick, *Sex Discrimination Law*, 1985, Oxford: OUP, p.270.

(2) Gender—Specific Exceptions

(a) National Security

8–029 Section 52(1), SDA 1975, provides that nothing in the legislation "shall render unlawful an act done for the purpose of safeguarding national security."

At one time s.52(2) further provided that a certificate signed by a government minister was conclusive proof that an act was done for the purpose of national security. The ECJ in *Johnston v Chief Constable of the Royal Ulster Constabulary*[101] held that the conclusive nature of such a certificate was contrary to Article 6 of the Equal Treatment Directive, which gives a right to "all persons who consider themselves wronged by failure to apply . . . the principle of equal treatment . . . to pursue their claims by judicial process." As a result, the "ministerial certificate" can no longer be used under the SDA 1975 in cases of employment or vocational training.[102]

(b) Statutory Authority for the Protection of Women

8–030 Section 51, SDA 1975, allows for specific legislation to provide for the protection of women for the purpose of pregnancy, maternity, or "other circumstances giving rise to risks specifically affecting women". This exception is permitted by Art.2(7) of the Equal Treatment Directive.

(c) The Police and Prison Services

8–031 Section 17(2)(a) of the SDA 1975 permits discrimination between men and women police officers "as to requirements, relating to height, uniform or equipment . . ." This permits different height requirements, and prevents a claim that different uniforms are discriminatory.

In contrast to the police exceptions, s.18, specifically permits only height requirements in the prison service. Clothing requirements should be challengeable as direct discrimination, although at present employers enjoy a broad discretion to impose different dress requirements.[103]

(d) Organised Religions—Married Persons and Civil Partners

8–032 The "religious conscience" provision in s.19, SDA 1975, permits discrimination on the ground of sex, and of being married or in a civil partnership, by an employer or a qualifying body[104] for the

---

[101] Case 222/84, [1987] Q.B. 129. See further Ch.4, para.4–040.
[102] SI 1988/249, Art.2. For a similar collapse of this rule in the RRA 1976, see below, para.8–046.
[103] Discussed above, Ch.4, para.4–032.
[104] See below, para.8–076.

purposes of an organised religion. The discrimination must be for "requirements" applied "so as to comply with the doctrines of the religion" or "because of the nature of the employment and the context in which it is carried out, so as to avoid conflicting with the strongly-held religious convictions of a significant number of the religion's followers". This exception can apply to lay-workers, such as typists and cleaners, as well as the clergy, and applicants for ordination. However, the phrase *organised religion* (as opposed to *religious organisation*) means it is unlikely that it could be applied for employment in religious-related organisations, such as a teacher in a faith school.[105]

(e) Armed Forces

Community law has limited application to the armed forces. On the **8–033** one hand, the ECJ has held that it does not apply to decisions of military organisation for internal and external security. On the other, in connection with employment, sex discrimination law cannot be "completely excluded". Hence in *Dory v Germany*[106] it was held that the Equal Treatment Directive did not apply to a rule of voluntary military service for women and compulsory service for men. However, in *Kreil v Germany*[107] the ECJ held a complete exclusion of women from military service breached the Directive.

Until *Johnston v Chief Constable of the Royal Ulster Constabulary*[108] was decided by the ECJ in 1986, the Sex Discrimination Act 1975 carried a blanket exemption for the armed forces. Nowadays the Act, by s.85, expressly is stated to apply to the armed forces as it applies to employment by a private person, but exempts acts "done for the purpose of ensuring the combat effectiveness" of the armed forces.[109] In *Sirdar v Secretary of State for Defence*[110] the Royal Marines did not permit women to serve in any capacity, because of their "interoperability" rule. Hence, Ms Sirdar was rejected when applied to be a chef in the Marines. The Ministry argued that the Marines were a small force, intended to be the first line of attack, and all members, including chefs, are required to serve as frontline commandos. The ECJ endorsed the exemption in s.85 *only so far* as it was necessary, with a margin of discretion, to guarantee public security, and found for the Ministry of Defence.

---

[105] See, in relation to the parallel provision in the Sexual Orientation Regulations 2003, *AMICUS v Secretary of State for Trade and Industry* [2004] EWHC 860, at para.116.

[106] Case C-186/02, [2003] 2 CMLR 26, at para.35, ECJ.

[107] Case C-285/98 [2002] 1 CMLR 36, at para.25.

[108] Case 222/84 [1987] Q.B. 129, ECJ. See above para.8–029 and Ch.4, para.4–040.

[109] Sex Discrimination Act 1975 (Application to Armed Forces, etc) Regulations SI 1994/3276.

[110] Case C-273/97, [2000] I.C.R. 130, ECJ.

(f) Insurance and Actuarial Calculations

8–034 Section 45, SDA 1975, permits "reasonable" reliance on data suggesting different risks for men and women in relation to "an annuity, life insurance policy, accident insurance policy, or similar matter involving the assessment of risk".[111] Employers also are able to take advantage of this exception, which is discussed in Ch.10, para.10–016.

(3) Gender Reassignment—Genuine Occupational Qualification

8–035 Sections 7A and 7B, of the Sex Discrimination Act 1975 provide GOQ exemptions relating to gender reassignment. Neither of these sections can apply once a person has obtained a full gender recognition certificate (recognising their acquired sex) under the Gender Recognition Act 2004.[112] So it may possible to apply a GOQ to a post-operative transsexual person, but only until that person obtains a gender recognition certificate. There are two further specific exceptions for national security and organised religions. Unlike the GOQ exemptions for sex discrimination in s.7(2), all these exemptions may apply to dismissal, as well as to the arrangements for recruitment, the decision to offer the job, or to transfer, training or promotion. This allows for the situation where a gender reassignment issue arises after recruitment.[113]

Sections 7A and 7B, SDA 1975, provide a two-limbed approach to GOQ exemptions. The first "single-sex GOQ" exemptions are provided by section 7A, which in effect, applies the GOQ exemptions for sex discrimination (see above). This operates where a sex GOQ exemption (in s.7(2)) permits a job to be done only by person of a particular sex, *and* it is reasonable to prevent a transsexual person from doing that job. Section 7B then provides four further "supplementary" GOQ exemptions specifically for cases of gender reassignment, although the final two are only "temporary", operable only for the period that someone is *undergoing* gender reassignment.

(a) Intimate Searches

8–036 Section 7B(2)(a) provides the first GOQ exemption, which may apply where the job is likely to entail intimate physical searches authorised by statute. This will apply to the police and some medical staff, say, under the Police and Criminal Evidence Act 1984. Where a duty requires that a person is searched by someone of the same sex, an employer may refuse to employ a transsexual person. This exemption can only be applied if it is reasonable to do so. This incorporates

---

[111] At a Community law level, the ECJ has approved the use of actuarial tables in some forms of pension arrangements: *Neath v Hugh Steeper* Case C-152/91, [1994] I.C.R. 118.
[112] Respectively ss.7A(4) and 7B(3).
[113] Respectively, ss.7A(3), 7B(1)(c), 19(1).

the concept of proportionality, and means that where there are non-transsexual persons available to cover this duty, the transsexual person cannot be excluded.[114]

(b) Work in a Private Home

Section 7B(2)(b) provides a GOQ exemption where the job is likely to involve the jobholder working or living in a private home. It applies when "objection might reasonably be taken to allowing" a person who is undergoing or has undergone gender reassignment having the degree of physical or social contact with a person living in the home, or the knowledge of intimate details of such a person's life, which is likely because of the nature or the circumstances of the job.

8–037

(c) Decency and Privacy—Shared Accommodation

Section 7B(2)(c) provides a GOQ exemption where workers would have to share accommodation with a person undergoing gender reassignment. It applies where "reasonable objection" could be taken—for the purpose of preserving decency and privacy—to the holder of the job sharing accommodation and facilities with either sex. The further requirements are (i) the nature or location of the establishment makes it impracticable for the holder of the job to live elsewhere than in premises provided by the employer, and (ii) it is not reasonable to expect the employer either to equip those premises with suitable accommodation or to make alternative arrangements. This is a temporary GOQ exemption, operable only for the period that someone is *undergoing* gender reassignment.

8–038

(d) Personal Services

Section 7B(2)(d) provides a GOQ exemption where the holder of the job provides vulnerable individuals with personal services promoting their welfare, or similar personal services, and in the reasonable view of the employer those services cannot be effectively provided by a person whilst that person is undergoing gender reassignment.

Where the *sex* of the person is the determining factor, and the employer wishes to exclude a transsexual person, a slightly broader "single-sex GOQ" exemption may be available under s.7A, using the *personal services* gender GOQ exemption from s.7(2)(e) (above).

Again, s.7B(2)(d) provides only a temporary GOQ exemption, operable only for the period that someone is *undergoing* gender reassignment. This means that when hiring, say, a rape victims' counsellor, this exemption cannot be invoked to disallow a male-to-female transsexual

8–039

---

[114] SDA 1975, s.7B(4) & (5). The reasonableness element was added by SI 2005/2467, reg.9, in force October 5, 2005.

person who has been recognised under the 2004 Act. In Canada, the British Columbia Human Rights Code provides an exception for non-profit organizations with a primary purpose the promotion of the interests and welfare of an identifiable group. The exception allows them to operate "a preference to members of the identifiable group."[115] In *Vancouver Rape Relief Society v Nixon*[116] the Society only engaged as counsellors women with a lifetime experience of "male oppression" and accordingly refused to appoint as a voluntary trainee a male-to-female transsexual person whose birth certificate had been amended to show that she was female. It was held that the refusal fell within the exception because there was "a rational connection between the preference and the [Society's] work."

(4) Gender Reassignment—Specific Exceptions

(a) Organised Religions and Religious Conscience

8–040 Section 19, Sex Discrimination Act 1975, permits discrimination on the ground of gender reassignment, by an employer or a qualifying body[117] for the purposes of an organised religion. It allows "requirements" to be applied "so as to comply with the doctrines of the religion" or "because of the nature of the employment and the context in which it is carried out, so as to avoid conflicting with the strongly-held religious convictions of a significant number of the religion's followers". This exception can apply to lay-workers, such as typists and cleaners, as well as the clergy, and applicants for ordination. Further, it is not "temporary" and so can be applied even to a person who has obtained a full gender recognition certificate (recognising their acquired sex) under the Gender Recognition Act 2004. However, the phrase *organised religion* (as opposed to *religious organisation*) means it is unlikely that it could be applied for employment in religious-related organisations, such as a teacher in a faith school.[118] An example suggested by the Government is a small evangelical church wishing to appoint a new elder and for religious reasons, only wants to consider applicants who are not undergoing and have not undergone gender reassignment.[119]

---

[115] Human Rights Code (RSBC 1996, c 210) s.41: "If a charitable, philanthropic, educational, fraternal, religious or social organization or corporation that is not operated for profit has as a primary purpose the promotion of the interests and welfare of an identifiable group or class of persons characterized by a physical or mental disability or by a common race, religion, age, sex, marital status, political belief, colour, ancestry or place of origin, that organization or corporation must not be considered to be contravening this Code because it is granting a preference to members of the identifiable group or class of persons."

[116] [2006] BCD Civ J 8 (BC Court of Appeal), at paras 58 and 77.

[117] See below, para.8–076.

[118] See, in relation to the parallel provision in the Sexual Orientation Regulations 2003, *AMICUS v Secretary of State for Trade and Industry* [2004] EWHC 860, at para.116.

[119] "Changes to Sex Discrimination Legislation in Great Britain: Explaining the Employment Equality (Sex Discrimination) Regulations 2005." (2005) URN 05/1603, at p.22. (See

(b) National Security

Section 52(1), SDA 1975 provides that nothing in the legislation "shall render unlawful an act done for the purpose of safeguarding national security."[120]

8–041

(5) Race—Genuine Occupational Requirement and Qualification

Article 4 of the Race Directive 2000/43/EC provides a general principle for a "genuine and determining occupational requirement" (GOR):

8–042

> Member States may provide that a difference of treatment which is based on a characteristic related to racial or ethnic origin shall not constitute discrimination where, by reason of the nature of the particular occupational activities concerned or of the context in which they are carried out, such a characteristic constitutes a genuine and determining occupational requirement, provided that the objective is legitimate and the requirement is proportionate.

This was implemented on July 19, 2003 by s.4A, Race Relations Act 1976, which repeats broadly this formula and applies it to arrangements for recruitment or decisions to hire, promotion or transfer to, or training for, any employment, as well as dismissal. It covers the job, and the *context* of the job. The employer may apply a GOR to a person who does not meet it, *or to a person whom he is "reasonably satisfied" does not meet it*. As it is implementing the Race Directive, s.4A applies only to discrimination "on grounds of race or ethnic or national origins".[121] In other words, it does not apply to discrimination purely on the grounds of nationality or colour.

Section 5 of the Race Relations Act 1976 has always carried an exhaustive list of specific Genuine Occupational *Qualification* (GOQ) exemptions. Unlike the general formula in the new s.4A, this has not allowed new exceptions to be developed by the courts.

It is clear that the new formula carried in s.4A applies to claims based on race or ethnic or national origins, and that it cannot be used for a claim based purely on nationality or colour, where s.5 remains applicable. However, it is less clear if s.5 can be used in a claim based on grounds of race or ethnic or national origins. Section 5 is stated to apply "where section 4A does not apply". This could be read in two ways. First, that the phrase "where section 4A does not apply" means that where the *claim* is not based on race or ethnic or national origins. As such the two sections are mutually exclusive and that an employer

8–043

---

www.womenandequalityunit.gov.uk.) The elder would be paid, and therefore could fall within the new provision on office-holders. See below, para.8–078.

[120] See further, above, para.8–029.
[121] See Ch.2, para.2–002.

defending a claim based on race or ethnic or national origins cannot rely on the s.5 GOQ exemptions. The second interpretation is that the phrase "where section 4A does not apply" relates only to the *GOR defence*, and triggers s.5 when the employer cannot claim a GOR under s.4A. Thus s.5 provides an employer with *additional* defences. In practice, this should matter little. Even if the sections are mutually exclusive, courts are still likely to use the existing the GOQ exemptions in s.5 as a list of specific examples of the GOR rubric. They can be interpreted to accord with the principles of proportionality as the GOQ exemptions cannot in any case be used where it is reasonable to use existing employees to cover the "GOQ" duties.[122]

There is another dimension to this issue. When implementing the Race Directive, the draftsmen did not create a separate definition of direct discrimination. Instead they utilised the existing definition, so far as it covers race or ethnic or national origins. This leaves no residual path for those claiming on those grounds and as such, all these claims are now bound to face the GOR defence in s.4A. However, s.4A is wider than the s.5 GOQ exemptions because (i) it applies to employment dismissals, (ii) it could allow a defence in a factual situation outside those listed in s.5, (iii) the GOR can apply to a person whom the employer is "reasonably satisfied" does not meet it, and (iv) it applies to the *context* of the job, as well as the job itself.[123] Many claims that could have been brought before the Directive was implemented can now be met with a broader s.4A GOR defence. This means that the implementation of the Directive has reduced the protection against discrimination and that s.4A is in breach of the non-regression principle in Art.6(2). To avoid this result, courts should interpret s.4A so strictly so as not to breach the non-regression principle. This will mean that that the only defences that can used are the pre-existing GOQ exemptions in s.5. Further, these GOQ exemptions must now be interpreted within the bounds of the general principle espoused in s.4A, and so courts should ensure that the existing GOQ exemptions meet the proportionality principle.

It would have been better to take the approach used by the more recent amendments to the Sex Discrimination Act (see above para.8–019) and simply ensure that the existing GOQ exemptions met the proportionality principle and retain them as an *exhaustive* list of examples of the Directive's GOR principle. In effect, to avoid breaching the parent Directive, this is what the courts must do with the Race Relations Act 1976.

---

[122] See, under the parallel provision in the SDA 1975, *Etam plc v Rowan* [1989] I.R.L.R. 150, EAT, above, para.8–020.

[123] See *London Borough of Lambeth v CRE* [1990] I.C.R. 768, CA (below, para.8–045). McColgan noted that the draft CRE Code of Practice suggested the GOR would cover "the post of a manager of a sexual health clinic for Pakistani women as well as the post of a counsellor" (para.2.38 b). See A. McColgan, *Discrimination Law, Text Cases and Materials*, 2005, 2nd edn, Hart: Oxford, at 557.

Finally, there are a couple of minor issues with the transposition. **8–044**
First, s.4A omits the word "legitimate" from the Directive. However, as it is implicit in the proportionality principle, this should not present a problem.[124]

Second, s.4A provides that the GOR can apply to a person whom the employer is "reasonably satisfied" does not meet it. This added phrase allows an employer to discriminate because he made a mistake over the race or ethnic or national origin of the candidate. Such mistakes can come about by, say, a white person's stereotyped perception of characteristics typical to any particular racial group. Discrimination based on "honest mistakes" and stereotyping is clearly contrary to the policy of the legislation.[125] In *AMICUS v Secretary of State for Trade and Industry*[126] the Government argued (successfully) that the basis of the same phrase in the parallel provisions in the Sexual Orientation Regulations 2003 was to enable employers to reject a person who refused to disclose his sexual orientation, "without having to impinge on the applicant's privacy unnecessarily". Whatever its credibility in that context, the argument is barely relevant when applied to racial discrimination. As such, there is risk that this added phrase will breach the Race Directive. Much will depend on the application of the word "reasonably": was the employer's perception reasonable by the standards of mainstream society, or by the standards of legislation intended to combat the prejudices that exist in mainstream society? To minimise the risk, tribunals should opt for the latter.

(a) The Race GOQ Exemptions

Section 5(2) of the Race Relations Act 1976 specifies four GOQ **8–045**
exemptions. By s.5(3) they may apply even where only some of the job's duties require a person of a particular racial group.[127] However, by s.5(4), the defence will fail where other employees are "capable of carrying out the duties", and that it would be reasonable to employ them on such duties, and where this can be done without undue inconvenience.[128] This accords with the proportionality principle in the Race Directive. The "other employees" must exist at the time. The defence can only be used in relation to the arrangements for recruitment, the decision to offer the job, or to transfer, training or

---

[124] See, *AMICUS v Secretary of State for Trade and Industry* [2004] EWHC 860, at paras 69–70, on the same issue arising from the implementation of the Employment Equality Directive 2000/78/EC.

[125] See Ch.4, paras 4–015 *et seq.* and 4–029, and generally Ch.5 on Harassment.

[126] [2004] EWHC 860.

[127] *Tottenham Green Under Fives' Centre v Marshall* [1989] ICR 214, EAT, and *(No.2)* [1991] I.C.R. 320, EAT.

[128] See, under the parallel provision in the SDA 1975, *Etam plc v Rowan* [1989] IRLR 150, EAT, discussed above, para.8–020.

promotion.[129] It cannot be used to dismiss a worker. Thus it is not possible to hire a person and then apply a GOQ retrospectively and dismiss her.[130]

The first three GOQ exemptions relate to "authenticity" for dramatic performances or entertainment, modelling, and catering in "a particular setting." This allows the employment of a person of any race or nationality in all parts of the entertainment industry. Thus a theatre director may decide that only a black person can convincingly play the part of Dr Martin Luther King, while a painter working on a scene from the Mahabharata may ask an employment agency to send only Indian models.[131]

The fourth GOQ exemption, provided, by s.5(2)(d), applies where "the holder of the job provides persons of that racial group with personal services promoting their welfare, and those services can most effectively be provided by a person of that racial group."

The *personal services* defence is based essentially on "customer preference", a factor not normally permitted in discrimination law.[132] It differs slightly from the parallel exemption in the SDA 1975, with its purpose being "welfare" rather than "welfare or education", although little may turn on this. The service must be "personal". In *London Borough of Lambeth v Commission for Racial Equality*[133] The council advertised two jobs in the housing benefit department, one for the assistant head and the other for group manager. The advertisement stated that candidates should be Afro-Caribbean or Asian. This was because more than half of tenants dealt with by the department were of Afro-Caribbean or Asian origin. The Court of Appeal held that the *personal services* GOQ envisaged "direct contact between the giver and the recipient—mainly face-to-face or where there could be susceptibility in personal, physical contact."[134] Thus, it could not be used for management posts which had little contact with the public. The Court also noted that the provider of the service did not have to be from precisely the same ethnic or racial group as the recipient. What mattered was who could give the service "most effectively".[135] This suggests that in some cases where a particular skill is required (e.g. to speak Caribbean patois), the matter should be analysed as *indirect* discrimination, which the employer may be able justify.[136]

---

[129] Respectively, claims under ss.4(1)(a), or (c), or 4(2)(b). See above, para.8–008 and 8–013.

[130] For a discussion of the parallel provision in the Sex Discrimination Act 1975, see above para.8–020.

[131] Examples from the CRE Code of Practice, 2005, CRE: London, ISBN 1 85442 570 6, or see *www.cre.gov.uk*, App.1, p.92, Example T.

[132] See for example Ch.4, paras 4–019 to 4–020.

[133] [1990] I.C.R. 768.

[134] *ibid.*, at 776.

[135] *ibid.*, at 777.

[136] Although the requirement may be met by some white persons, it is likely to have an adverse impact on white persons. For justifying adverse impact, see Ch.6, para.6–029 et al.

(6) Race—Specific Exceptions

(a) National Security

Section 42(1), Race Relations Act 1976, provides that nothing in the **8–046** legislation "shall render unlawful an act done for the purpose of safeguarding national security, if the doing of the act was justified by that purpose."

At one time, s.69(2)(b), RRA 1976 further provided that a certificate signed by a government minister was conclusive proof that an act was done for the purpose of national security. The Fair Employment (Northern Ireland) Act 1989 had a similar defence, which was condemned by European Court of Human Rights in *Tinnelly v UK*.[137] Here, complaints by builders, that they was refused public contracts because of they were Roman Catholic, were blocked by a ministerial certificate "on the ground of national security". No reasons were given. This was in breach of the Convention because it deprived the claimants of their right to "a fair and public hearing . . . by an independent and impartial tribunal" under Art.6 of the European Convention on Human Rights. As a result, the "ministerial certificate" can no longer be used under the RRA 1976, although a new s.67A allows rules of procedure to be made in national security cases.[138]

(b) Statutory Authority

This general defence now only applies to residual cases, i.e. those **8–047** outside of EC competence. In this context these will be cases brought purely on grounds of nationality or colour under the Race Relations Act 1976.[139] For residual cases only s.41(1), RRA 1976, provides that nothing shall render unlawful any act of discrimination done in pursuance of any Act, Order in Council or statutory instrument; or in order to comply with any condition or requirement imposed by a minister of the Crown by virtue of any enactment.

Section 41(1) is capable of a wide or narrow interpretation. The wide interpretation would include acts done in the exercise of a power conferred by legislation. The narrow interpretation includes only acts compelled to be done by an express obligation in legislation. In *Hampson v Department of Education and Science*[140] the House of Lords opted for the narrow construction. In this case, a Hong Kong Chinese woman trained as a teacher for three years, but with an eight-year gap between her second and third years. She taught during this period. The

---

[137] *Tinnelly & Sons Ltd and Others & McElduff and Others v UK* Cases 20390/92;21322/93, (1998) 27 E.H.R.R. 249.
[138] Race Relations (Amendment) Act 2000 repealed s.69(2)(b) (by Sch.3 para.1) and added s.67A (by s.8). For a similar collapse of this rule in the SDA 1976, see above, para.8–029.
[139] RRA 1976, s.41(1A). See generally, Ch.2 para.2–002.
[140] [1991] 1 A.C. 171.

Education (Teachers) Regulations 1982 listed the required qualifications to teach in schools in England and Wales and provided the Education Minister a discretion to decide if other qualifications were comparable. The Minister rejected Ms Hampson's application to teach in England because she did not take her qualification over three consecutive years and it was not of "sufficient quality". The House of Lords held that the Minister's decision, being an exercise of power conferred by legislation, did not come within s.41(1) and so was not immune from the general provisions of the Act. As it indirectly discriminated on the ground of nationality, the Minister was bound to justify it.

(c) Crown and Certain Public Bodies

8–048   Section 75(5) of the Race Relations Act 1976 provides an exemption in relation to employment in the service of the Crown or certain public bodies. They are permitted to restrict employment "to persons of a particular birth, nationality, descent or residence." The only public bodies covered are listed in the Race Relations (Prescribed Public Bodies) (No.2) Regulations 1994.[141]

(7) Sexual Orientation—Genuine Occupational Requirement[142]

8–049   The Employment Equality Directive 2000/78/EC provides by Art.4 the standard EC formula for a Genuine Occupational Requirement, which must be based on "a characteristic related to" sexual orientation by reason of the nature or context of the particular activities of the job. The characteristic must be a genuine and determining requirement for the job. The objective must be legitimate and the requirement proportionate.

Regulation 7 of the Sexual Orientation Regulations 2003[143] implements generally the formula, and then provides one specific exception in relation to organised religions. Regulation 7 applies to recruitment, promotion, transfer, training and dismissal. An example where a GOR might apply given in the Government's Explanatory Notes is the job of leadership of an organisation concerned with advising gay men and lesbians about their rights, or promoting those rights. Here the job's credibility may require a gay or lesbian person. However, the post of *advising* people of these rights is unlikely to warrant a GOR.[144] The

---

[141] SI 1994/1986. Sch.1 lists: Bank of England, Board of Trustees of the Armouries, British Council, House of Commons, House of Lords, Metropolitan Police Office, National Army Museum, National Audit Office, Natural Environment Research Council, United Kingdom Atomic Energy Authority. See (1994) 54 EOR 7.

[142] See H. Oliver, "Sexual Orientation Discrimination: Perceptions, Definitions and Genuine Occupational Requirements" (2004) 33 I.L.J. 1.

[143] Employment Equality (Sexual Orientation) Regulations 2003, SI 2003/1661.

[144] The *DTI* (not statutory) Explanatory notes to Employment Equality (Sexual Orientation) Regulations 2003 and the Employment Equality (Religion or Belief) Regulations 2003, at para.75.

proportionality principle absorbs the rule from the sex and race GOQ exemptions, that the defence will fail where other employees are "capable of carrying out the duties" requiring a person of a particular sexual orientation.[145]

The drafting of the domestic GOR formula raises two questions of compatibility with the parent Directive. First, the domestic formula omits the word "legitimate" from the Directive. However, as it is implicit in the proportionality principle, this should not present a problem.[146]

Second, para.7(2)(c)(ii) provides that the GOR can apply to a person whom the employer is "reasonably satisfied" does not meet it. So as well as operating where the person is not of a required sexual orientation, it also applies where the employer *perceives* (reasonably) that he is not. It was held in *AMICUS v Secretary of State for Trade and Industry*[147] that this phrase was compatible with the Directive. The High Court endorsed the Government's argument that the basis of the phrase was to enable employers to reject a person who refused to disclose his sexual orientation, "without having to impinge on the applicant's privacy unnecessarily".[148] The danger here is that employers will make stereotypical presumptions based on candidates' appearance and/or demeanour. Much will depend on the application of the word "reasonably": was the employer's perception reasonable by the standards of mainstream society, or by the standards of legislation intended solely to combat a prejudice of mainstream society? To minimise the danger, tribunals should opt for the latter.

8–050

The specific example of a GOR is a "religious conscience" exemption, similar to that provided by s.19, SDA 1975.[149] Regulation 7(3) (but not the Directive) expressly allows an employer "for the purposes of an organised religion" to "apply a requirement related to sexual orientation". The purpose must be either "to comply with that religion's doctrines" *or* (because of the nature and context of the employment) "to avoid conflicting with the strongly held religious convictions of a significant number of the religion's followers".

This GOR exemption can apply to lay-workers, such as typists and cleaners, as well as the clergy.[150] However, the phrase *organised religion* (as opposed to *religious organisation*) means it is unlikely that it could be applied for employment in religious-related organisations, such as a teacher in a faith school.[151] The GOR may be *related* to sexual orientation, which allows the employer to specify *behaviour*, rather than orientation. So, for instance, a church may employ a

---

[145] See above, para.8–020.
[146] *AMICUS v Secretary of State for Trade and Industry* [2004] EWHC 860, at paras 69–70.
[147] *ibid.*
[148] *ibid.*, at para.72.
[149] See above paras 8–032 and 8–040.
[150] DTI Explanatory notes, above fn 144, at para.91.
[151] *AMICUS v Secretary of State for Trade and Industry* [2004] EWHC 860, at para.116.

homosexual priest, but apply a GOR that he must be celibate. The broadest part of this specific exception is the permitting of discrimination where the only objection comes from *some* of the congregation.[152] So, for instance, even where a religion's doctrines and leaders have no objection to homosexuality, discrimination may persist, or in some cases, *commence,* lawfully under this limb of reg.7(3). The Government suggested that a legitimate aim here could be for a minister to have the confidence of the followers.[153] In most areas of discrimination law, as a matter of principle, "customer preference" is no defence.[154] It is hard to maintain in circumstances where the religion itself has no objection that the (contrary) view of the some of the congregation can amount to anything but prejudice. As such, this limb of the exception does not represent a legitimate aim. In *AMICUS v Secretary of State for Trade and Industry*[155] it was held that this limb would be "a far from easy test to satisfy in practice" and as such was compatible with the Directive. But this misses the point. Once the test is satisfied, this limb legitimises prejudice unrelated to a religion's doctrines or leadership.

(8) Sexual Orientation—Specific Exceptions

(a) National Security

8–051 Regulation 24 provides that nothing in the legislation "shall render unlawful an act done for the purpose of safeguarding national security, if the doing of the act was justified by that purpose."

(b) Benefits Dependent on Marital or Civil Partnership Status

8–052 Originally, reg.25 exempted benefits (such as a survivor's pension rights) dependant on marital status. Since the Civil Partnership Act 2004 came into force on December 5, 2005,[156] this has been amended to cover "the conferring of a benefit on married persons and civil partners to the exclusion of all other persons." The effect of this is to preserve the original exemption so far as is relates to service prior to December 5, 2005.

---

[152] A similar formula is used by SDA 1975, s.19.
[153] DTI Explanatory notes, above fn 144, at para.96.
[154] See Ch.4, paras 4–019—4–020.
[155] *AMICUS v Secretary of State for Trade and Industry* [2004] EWHC 860, at para.117.
[156] SI 2005/2114, Art.1.

(9) Religion or Belief—Genuine Occupational Requirement[157]

The Employment Equality Directive 2000/78/EC, and the consequent domestic Regulations provide two GORs for Religion or Belief. The first is for any employer and the second is only for employers with an ethos based on religion or belief. The first, provided by Art.4(1), is the standard EC formula for a Genuine Occupational Requirement, which is available to any employer and must be based on "a characteristic related to" religion or belief by reason of the nature or context of the particular activities of the job. The characteristic must be a genuine and determining requirement for the job. The objective must be legitimate and the requirement proportionate. The second, provided by Art.4(2), is a special exception for organisations with an ethos based on religion or belief. The characteristic must be a requirement for the job, but not a *determining* (i.e. decisive) one, having regard to the organisation's ethos. This exception cannot be used to justify discrimination on any other ground save religion or belief.

8–053

Articles 4(1) and 4(2) have been transposed into the Religion or Belief Regulations 2003[158] as regs 7(2) and 7(3) respectively. Both GORs apply to the nature and the context of the job. Thus, the *nature* of the job of a counsellor of people with long-term illnesses in a Christian support group may not require a Christian, but the *context* may determine that he or she is a Christian, because the purpose of the job is to provide advice from a Christian perspective.[159] An example of a reg.7(2) ("any employer") GOR might be a hospital employing a chaplain to minister to patients, where almost all the patients and staff are Christian.[160]

Under reg.7(3) ("employer with a religious ethos") a Christian hospice might show that it was a requirement for its chief executive to be Christian, because of the role of leadership in relation to maintaining and developing the religious ethos. It is unlikely that the GOR could be applied to a nurse in the hospice if the job did not go beyond the medical care of patients. Similarly, a GOR could not be applied to the job of a shop assistant in a bookshop with a religious ethos, merely on the preference of the employer or customers, if the job is does not go beyond the normal duties for any bookshop assistant.[161]

---

[157] See generally, B. Hepple and T. Choudhury, "Tackling Religious Discrimination: Practical Implications for Policy-makers and Legislators" 2001, Home Office Series 221. London: Home Office; L. Vickers, "The *Draft* Employment Equality (Religion or Belief) Regulations" (2003) 32 I.L.J. 23.

[158] Employment Equality (Religion or Belief) Regulations 2003, SI 2003/1660.

[159] DTI Explanatory notes, above fn 144, at para.72.

[160] *ibid.*, para.76.

[161] *ibid.*, at para.87. A requirement to have knowledge of say, Christian, or Muslim, literature, may have to be justified where it indirectly discriminates. For justification of indirect discrimination, see Ch.6, para.6–029 *et seq.*

The statutory right[162] of church schools to favour teachers of the school's religion is preserved by reg.39.

8–054   The drafting of the domestic GOR formulas raises two questions of compatibility with the parent Directive. First, the domestic formulas omit the word "legitimate" from the Directive. However, as it is implicit in the proportionality principle, this should not present a problem.[163]

Second, sub-paras 7(2)(c)(ii) or 7(3)(c)(ii) provide that the GOR can apply to a person whom the employer is "reasonably satisfied" does not meet it. So as well as operating where the person is not of a required religion or belief, it also applies where the employer *perceives* (reasonably) that he is not. This added phrase allows an employer to discriminate because he made a mistake over the religion or belief of the person. Discrimination based on "honest mistakes" and stereotyping is clearly contrary to the policy of the legislation.[164] In *AMICUS v Secretary of State for Trade and Industry*[165] the Government argued (successfully) that the basis of the same phrase in the parallel provisions in the Sexual Orientation Regulations 2003 was to enable employers to reject a person who refused to disclose his sexual orientation, "without having to impinge on the applicant's privacy unnecessarily". Whatever the weight of that argument, different considerations apply to discrimination on the ground of religion or belief, not least because the manifestation of a person's religion is rarely a private matter.

The law takes a different approach in the United States. For religious discrimination in employment, the law is centred on a duty to "reasonably accommodate" a worker's "religious observance or practice without undue hardship on the conduct of the employer's business".[166] This places a positive duty on employers to take steps to accommodate the religious needs of their workers, unless this would cause "undue hardship". Some examples are given in Ch.6, para.6–044.

(10) Religion or Belief—Specific Exceptions

8–055   *(a) National Security*
Regulation 24 provides that nothing in the legislation "shall render unlawful an act done for the purpose of safeguarding national security, if the doing of the act was justified by that purpose."

---

[162] Education (Scotland) Act 1980, s.21 or (for England and Wales) School Standards and Framework Act 1998, s.60.
[163] *AMICUS v Secretary of State for Trade and Industry* [2004] EWHC 860, at para.69–70.
[164] See Ch.4, paras 4–015 *et seq.* and 4–029, and generally Ch.5 on Harassment.
[165] [2004] EWHC 860.
[166] Title VII, para.701(j), (codified in 42 USC s.2000e(j)).

(b) Sikhs Wearing Turbans

Regulation 26 provides an exception for Sikhs wearing turbans, instead of safety helmets, on construction sites. Thus an employer treating Sikhs differently from other religions on this matter will not breach the Regulations. Technically, this is a specific justification for indirect discrimination against Sikhs, and is included here for completeness.

8–056

(11) Age Defences

The Employment Equality Directive 2000/78/EC provides two defences for age discrimination. The first is the standard GOR formula. The second allows "objective justification" even for direct age discrimination.

8–057

The first defence, provided by Art.4(1), is the standard EC formula for a Genuine Occupational Requirement, which is available to any employer and must be based on "a characteristic related to" age by reason of the nature or context of the particular activities of the job. The characteristic must be a genuine and determining requirement for the job. The objective must be legitimate and the requirement proportionate.

Second, Art.6(1) the Directive provides an extra defence allowing Member States to legislate for exceptions specific to age, providing that they are objectively and reasonably justified by a legitimate aim, and if the means of achieving that aim are appropriate and necessary. "Legitimate aims" may include employment policy, labour market and vocational training objectives.

Article 6(1) provides a non-exhaustive list of three examples. The first allows the setting of special conditions for young people, older workers and persons with caring responsibilities in order to promote their vocational integration or ensure their protection. The second allows the fixing of minimum conditions of age, professional experience or seniority in service. The third allows the fixing of a maximum age for recruitment which is based on the training requirements of the post in question or the need for a reasonable period of employment before retirement.

8–058

In *Mangold v Helm*[167] German law exempted from regulation fixed-term employment contracts for any worker over 52. The purpose was to help unemployed older workers back to work. The ECJ held that the German Government should have a "broad margin of discretion" to implement this social policy,[168] but as it was not tailored for those *unemployed* older workers it could not be deemed "necessary" to achieve the goal. This shows that the ECJ will take the same approach to age discrimination as it does to any other ground.

[167] Case C-144/04, [2006] I.R.L.R. 143.
[168] Discussed Ch.6, para.6–041.

(a) Age—General Occupational Requirement

8–059 Regulation 8 repeats the standard formula, used in other domestic regulations for Sexual Orientation, Race and Religion of Belief. The Government suggested that GOR exemptions would arise in "very few cases". One example given is for acting jobs.[169]

The drafting of the domestic GOR formula raises two questions of compatibility with the parent Directive. First, the domestic formulas omit the word "legitimate" from the Directive. However, as it is implicit in the proportionality principle, this should not present a problem.[170]

Second, subpara.8(2)(c)(ii) provides that the GOR can apply to a person whom the employer is "reasonably satisfied" does not meet it. So as well as operating where the person is not of a required age, it also applies where the employer *perceives* (reasonably) that he is not. This added phrase allows an employer to discriminate because he made a mistake over the age of the person. Discrimination based on "honest mistakes" and stereotyping is clearly contrary to the policy of the legislation.[171] In *AMICUS v Secretary of State for Trade and Industry*[172] the Government argued (successfully) that the basis of the same phrase in the parallel provisions in the Sexual Orientation Regulations 2003 was to enable employers to reject a person who refused to disclose his sexual orientation, "without having to impinge on the applicant's privacy unnecessarily". In this context the issue of privacy carries less weight, not least because the age of a successful candidate should eventually be revealed to an employer for many administrative purposes, such as pensions, the national minimum wage and insurance.

(b) Age—Objective Justification

8–060 The Government opted to provide a general defence of objective justification for both direct and indirect discrimination. The standard formula is provided with the definitions of discrimination in reg.3(1), and states that the defendant employer must show that the treatment or practice must be a proportionate way of achieving a legitimate aim. In *Mangold v Helm* (above) the ECJ applied the objective justification test to a directly discriminatory state measure. The same approach should apply here. The concept of objective justification is rooted in indirect discrimination, and is discussed at length in Ch.6.[173]

---

[169] "Equality and Diversity: Coming of Age" (July 2005), at para.4.2.8. DTI/Pub 7851/3k/07/05/NP. URN 05/1171.
[170] *AMICUS v Secretary of State for Trade and Industry* [2004] EWHC 860, at paras 69–70.
[171] See Ch.4, paras 4–015 *et seq.* and 4–029, and generally Ch.5 on Harassment.
[172] *ibid.*
[173] At para.6–029 *et seq.*

(c) Age—Specific Exemptions

Article 6(1) empowers Member States to specify exemptions. The **8–061**
Regulations provide seven.

(i) Default retirement age

Regulation 30 provides perhaps the most contentious exemption, a **8–062**
default retirement age for those aged 65[174] or over.[175] This is an
exemption for discrimination against those most vulnerable to it, and
probably those who had had the highest expectation from age
discrimination law. It permits employers to dismiss workers who have
reached 65, so long as they follow a complex procedure, set out in
sch.6 of the Regulations. Should employers agree to keep on a worker
beyond 65, save for retirement, the general principle against age
discrimination will apply. So, for instance, discriminatory discipline,
pay, harassment, and job classification would remain unlawful.

The exemption can only be applied to a narrower class of workers
than those normally covered by discrimination legislation, applying to
"employees" within the meaning of the Employment Rights Act
1996,[176] those in Crown employment, and House of Lords and House
of Commons staff. To obtain exemption, the employer must comply
potentially with two procedures. The first is compulsory. The
employer must give the worker at least six months notice of the retirement. However, the notice must be within one year of the retirement.
The second procedure may arise because workers have a "right to
request" not to be retired. If this right is exercised, the employer has a
corresponding "duty to consider" the request. The employer must
inform the worker of its decision, but there are no more demands than
that: the employer need not give reasons for its decision. Hence, an
employer could sit through a meeting to discuss the retirement with a
closed mind and simply confirm his decision at the end.

It is questionable whether this default retirement age can be squared
with the parent Directive. The Government has two grounds for argument. First, Recital 14 suggests a blanket exemption for "retirement
ages". Second, the exemption could be objective justified.

Recital 14 of the preamble, states: "This Directive shall be without **8–063**
prejudice to national provisions laying down retirement ages." The
meaning of this is unclear. The legislative history provides no enlight-
enment and a reading of the face of the Directive suggests that it is
anomalous.

---

[174] Or the "normal retirement age", if higher.

[175] The Government has said that it aspires abolish the default age after five years: Written statement to Parliament, House of Commons Hansard Written Ministerial Statements for
December 14, 2004 (pt 4), Columns 127WS-130WS; or Lords Hansard Text for December 14,
2004 (241214-41), Columns WS78-WS81.

[176] An individual who "works under . . . a contract of employment", ERA 1996, s.230(1). See
above, para.8–002.

The most obvious problem is that Recital 14 conflicts with the fundamental principle of equal treatment stated in Art.2(1), which states that there "shall be no discrimination *whatsoever*" on the grounds set out, including age. (Emphasis supplied.) Further, unlike other recitals, Recital 14 has no corresponding exemption in the main body. There are two specific age-discrimination exceptions contained in the main text, provided by Art.6. It would be anomalous to put a third exception solely in preamble. All this points to the Recital having little meaning, and certainly not one allowing a blanket retiring age. The deciding factor must be that if Recital 14 were read to permit a blanket default retirement age, it would be incompatible with the substantive text of the Directive, especially the fundamental principle of equal treatment in Art.2. In which case, the rule is that the preamble has no legal force and the substantive text must prevail.[177] Accordingly, the default retirement age can only be made under Art.6(1), and so must be objectively justified.

To achieve this, the Government would be bound to show that the default age was introduced in pursuit of a legitimate aim, appropriate and necessary. It may suggest that the indiscriminate effect of the default retirement age is mitigated by giving employees a "right to request" deferred retirement. However, as this right carries no substance (the employer may simply reject the request without reasons, and there is no specific remedy for a failure to "consider"),[178] it cannot help.

8–064 The Government have put forward two reasons to objectively justify the default retiring age. It mentioned that in consultation a "significant" number of employers use a set retirement age as a necessary part of their workforce planning.[179] But a more proportionate solution here is to allow individual employers to set a retirement age where this is, as the Government put it, "necessary". A national default retirement age appears a rather disproportionate response to the needs of this "significant" number of employers.

Second, the Government stated that its consultation showed that without a default retirement age there was risk to the stability of pensions,[180] but again produced no detailed evidence.[181] On the face of it, pension schemes should not suffer if workers carry on working and

---

[177] *Gunnar Nilsson, Per Olov Hagelgren and Solweig Arrborn* Case C-162/97, 1998 ECR I-7477, ECJ, at para.54. See also Opinion of A-G Tizzano in *R. v Sec of State for Trade and Industry ex p BECTU*, Case C-173/99 [2001] ECR I-4881, at para.39.

[178] There are remedies for a failure to give proper notice and a denial of the right to be accompanied at the "meeting" to request not to be retired: Age Regulations, Sch.6, paras 11 and 12, respectively.

[179] "Equality and Diversity: Coming of Age" (July 2005), at para.6.1.14. (DTI/Pub 7851/3k/07/05/NP. URN 05/1171.) See also "Notes on the Regulations" (*www.dti.gov.uk/er/equality*), at para.100.

[180] *ibid.*, at para.6.1.15. Notes on the Regulations, *ibid.*, para.101.

[181] e.g. No extended reasons were given in the Government's Regulatory Impact Assessments (*www.dti.gov.uk/er/equality*).

either draw their pensions, or defer entitlement and continue to contribute to the scheme. This is especially so with the increasingly common "defined contribution" schemes, where the payout is governed by the size of the fund, rather than external factors, such as the final salary, used for "defined benefit" schemes.

Even when combined, these arguments appear weak. Weighed against them, as noted above, the default retirement age exempts those most vulnerable to age discrimination, and will hit hard the low paid (predominantly women in segregated occupations and ethnic minorities), who may be in greater need to continue working beyond the age 65.[182]

The ECJ signalled in *Mangold v Helm*[183] that it will take the same approach to age discrimination as it does to any other ground, with a strict view of proportionality. So this exemption should enjoy no exceptional discretion by a tribunal or court. This contrasts with other jurisdictions, where courts have taken a more lenient approach to age discrimination, at least under constitutional challenges. Under US constitutional law age is neither a *suspect*, nor a *quasi-suspect* group for scrutiny, because the aged "have not experienced a history of purposeful unequal treatment or been subjected to unique disabilities on the basis of stereotyped characteristics not truly indicative of their abilities."[184] The Canadian Supreme Court similarly takes a less stringent approach to age discrimination because unlike discrimination on other grounds, it is not "generally based on feelings of hostility and intolerance."[185] In *McKinney v University of Guelph*[186] s.9(a) of the Ontario Human Rights Code 1981 went further than the British exemption by excluding those aged over 65 from *all* protection under the Code's age discrimination law. By a majority of five to two, the Supreme Court held that s.9 did not violate the non-discrimination tenet in s.15(1) of the Charter of Rights and Freedoms, principally on the basis that a general retirement age of 65 was necessary to preserve the stability and integrity of pension schemes.

(ii) Benefits related to length-of-service

As noted above, Art.6 suggests an exemption allowing for the fixing of minimum conditions of age, professional experience or seniority in service. This covers pay and other benefits, such as a company car. Regulation 32 provides a blanket exemption for length-of-service benefits relating to the first five years of service. Gaps in service are not counted for this purpose. So, for instance, a woman who after

8–065

---

[182] See e.g. the dissent of Wilson, J. in *McKinney v University of Guelph* [1990] 3 SCR 229, at 415–416 (Sup Ct of Canada).

[183] Case C-144/04 [2006 I.R.L.R. 143. See above, para.8–058.

[184] *Massachusetts Board of Retirement v Murgia*, 427 US 307, at 313 (Sup Ct 1976).

[185] *McKinney v University of Guelph* [1990] 3 SCR 229, at 297.

[186] *ibid.*

three years' service takes a year off, will return and begin her fourth year of service for the purpose of this exemption. After five years' service, a length-of-service benefit is exempted only if "it reasonably appears" to the employer that it "fulfils a business need of his undertaking (for example, by encouraging the loyalty or motivation, or rewarding the experience, of some or all of his workers)."

It is questionable whether the five-year blanket exemption could survive a challenge in the ECJ. It allows most obviously, direct and indirect age discrimination, as well as indirect sex discrimination. The question of whether length-of-service benefits that discriminate against women need to be objectively justified is not entirely settled in the ECJ, but recently the Advocate-General has advised that they do.[187] If the Court agrees, then the blanket exemption in reg.32 becomes vulnerable to EC sex discrimination law, and by extension, to any age discrimination claim.

The exemption in reg.33 applies to employers who make redundancy payments based on the statutory scheme (presumably considered exempt by reg.27, see below) but who are more generous than the statutory scheme requires them to be.

Regulation 34 exempts employers when providing life assurance cover to workers, typically by not providing schemes to older workers because of cost.

(iii) National minimum wage

8–066 The National Minimum Wage Act provides two bands for younger workers (16–17 and 18–21). Accordingly, employers are exempted by reg.31 when paying lower wages to these younger persons.

(iv) Occupational pensions

8–067 The Directive covers occupational pension schemes and occupational invalidity benefits. Personal pension schemes are not covered, save where the employer contributes to one. Article 6(2) provides an exemption for the fixing of ages for entry or entitlement, and of age criteria in actuarial calculations (provided this does not result in sex discrimination). Schedule 2, Pt 2, of the Age Regulations provides a detailed list of exempted age-related rules.

(v) Statutory authority

8–068 Regulation 27 provides that an employer may discriminate on the ground of age "in order to comply with a requirement of any statutory provision." The aim here is to give a blanket exemption for age

---

[187] *Cadman v Health and Safety Executive* Case C-17/05, at paras 33 and 66. The matter is discussed in Ch.9, para.9–037.

criteria used in other legislation, such serving alcohol or driving, and thus allow employers to discriminate where other legislation requires.

Article 2(5) of the parent Directive allows for "measures laid down ... which ... are necessary for public security, for the maintenance of public order and the prevention of criminal offences, for the protection of health and for the protection of the rights and freedoms of others". Any statutory measures falling outside of these areas should have to be "objectively justified" in accordance with Art.6(1), and so reg.27 may prove to have been drafted too wide to comply with the Directive.

(vi) National security

Regulation 28 provides that nothing in the legislation "shall render unlawful an act done for the purpose of safeguarding national security, if the doing of the act was justified by that purpose." **8–069**

(vii) The armed forces

Article 3(4) of the Employment Equality Directive 2000/78 expressly allows derogation from the age provisions for the armed forces. This has been taken up in Great Britain and reg.44(4) states that the Age Regulations "do not apply to service in any of the naval, military or air forces of the Crown". This wholesale derogation seems unnecessary, as many age requirements are convenient shorthand for mental and physical fitness, which can be—and often are—independently measured. In an Australian case, the army required trainee pilots to be aged between 19 and 28. This age limit was based on the Army's "inherent requirements" for the job, which were stated to be: (i) an ability to be properly trained for the job of a military line pilot (including an ability to "unlearn" habits and skills acquired in civilian life, and the ability to adapt to the environment of military aviation); (ii) an ability to integrate into the Aviation Regiments; and (iii) an ability to maintain a high level of medical fitness for the duration of the six-year period of appointment. It was held that age was not "tightly connected" to these requirements and so the age limit was not justified. In particular, the physical fitness requirement could not be allowed to "have the effect of damning individuals over 28 years by reference to a stereotypical characteristic (less physical fitness) of their age group."[188] There seems to be no reason to exempt the armed forces in Great Britain from having to justify any age requirements as a Genuine Occupational Requirement in a similar way. **8–070**

---

[188] *Commonwealth v Human Rights & Equal Opportunity Commission (Bradley)* (1999) 95 FCR 218 Federal Court of Australia, at para.41. See also *Commonwealth of Australia v Hamilton,* (2000) 63 ALD 641.

4. DISCRIMINATION BY OTHER BODIES

(1) Contract Workers

8–071   The *employer* of contract workers is liable in the normal way. However, workers employed by a third party who supplies them to a "principal" under a contract are protected from discrimination or harassment by the principal.[189] This would cover, for instance, discrimination by a building company against an electrician working for a sub-contractor, or discrimination by a hospital against a nurse supplied by an agency.[190]

A contract worker may compare her treatment with that given to another contract worker, or a person *employed by the principle*.[191] In practice, this will not lead to a harmonising of the respective worker's terms as normally most of the contract worker's terms will be set by the employer. However, it may be that the principal treats its contract workers differently, for example by providing inferior canteen or washroom facilities, or by not providing professional indemnity insurance or career development support.[192] If this difference in treatment is also discriminatory (say where contract workers were predominantly female, or black, in comparison to the employees) the principal may be liable.

8–072   A principal is a person who makes work available for individuals. In *Harrods Ltd v Remick*[193] the employers had concessions to sell goods in the Harrods department store. The employers installed their own staff, who had to be approved by Harrods, and wore the Harrods' uniform. Otherwise, the employer had control over these staff. It was held that Harrods was a principal for the purposes of the Race Relations Act 1976, which was not limited to situations where the principal had direct control over the work being done.

The employer must supply the workers "under a contract made with the principal". However, there is no need for the employer to have a *direct* contractual relationship with the principal. In *Abbey Life v Tansell*[194] the Court of Appeal held that a worker, who was employed by a company wholly owned by him, which in turn supplied him to an agency, which in turn supplied him to Abbey Life, was a "contract worker" within the parallel provisions in s.12 of the Disability Discrimination Act 1995. This was even though there was no contract between the company employing the worker (that is, his own

---

[189] SDA 1975, s.9; RRA 1976, 7; Religion or Belief Regulations 2003, reg.8, Sexual Orientation Regulations 2003, reg.8; Age Regulations 2006, reg.9 (in force October 1, 2006).

[190] See the *DTI* (not statutory) Explanatory notes to Employment Equality (Sexual Orientation) Regulations 2003 and the Employment Equality (Religion or Belief) Regulations 2003, at para.97.

[191] *Allonby v Accrington and Rossendale College* [2001] I.C.R. 1189, at 1202, CA.

[192] *ibid.*

[193] [1997] I.R.L.R. 583, CA.

[194] *Abbey Life Assurance Co Ltd v Tansell (MHC Consulting Services Ltd v Tansell)* [2000] I.C.R. 789, at 798–799, CA.

company) and Abbey Life. It was enough that the worker was supplied to the principal (Abbey Life) under a contract.

Discrimination by the principal is not limited to when the contract worker is actually doing work for the principal. It includes decisions on selection. In *BP Chemicals v Gillick and Roevin Management Services Ltd*[195] the EAT held that a principal could be liable for sex discrimination for refusing to allow a contract worker to return to the same job following her maternity leave.

(2) Employment Agencies

An employment agency is defined as "a person who for profit or not, **8–073** provides services for the purpose of finding employment for workers or supplying employers with workers". It is unlawful for these agencies to discriminate against a person in relation to its services and "the way in which it provides any of its services".[196] It is also unlawful to harass a person to whom it provides services, or who has requested the provision of such services. The agency has a defence if the employer states that job falls within one of the statutory employment exemptions (such as a sex GOQ) and it is reasonable for the agency to rely on that statement. It is an offence for an employer knowingly or recklessly to make such a statement which is false or misleading.

(3) Partnerships

For this purpose a partnership includes a limited liability partnership. **8–074** By parallel with the standard provisions on employment, the law covers arrangements for who should be offered a partnership, the actual offer, its terms, expulsion from a partnership, or any other detriment.[197] The genuine occupational requirement/qualification defence applies by analogy. By s.10, RRA 1976, small partnerships (those with less than six partners) were exempt from the Act. But this exemption no longer applies where the discrimination comes within Community law competence,[198] which will be in most cases. However, the s.10 exemption may still be used for residual cases, where for instance the harassment or discrimination is purely on grounds of colour, or nationality.[199] Otherwise, there are no exemptions for small partnerships.

---

[195] [1995] I.R.L.R. 128, EAT. Applied by the NICA in *Patefield v Belfast CC* [2000] I.R.L.R. 664.
[196] SDA 1975, s.15; RRA 1976, 14; Religion or Belief Regulations 2003, reg.18; Sexual Orientation Regulations 2003, reg.18; Age Regulations 2006, reg.21 (in force October 1, 2006).
[197] SDA 1975, s.11; RRA 1976, 10; Religion or Belief Regulations 2003, reg.14; Sexual Orientation Regulations 2003, reg.14; Age Regulations 2006, reg.17 (in force October 1, 2006).
[198] RRA 1976, ss.10(1A) and (1B), inserted by reg.12, SI 2003/1626, in force July 19, 2003.
[199] See Ch.2 para.2–002.

(4) Trade Organisations

8–075 These are defined in all the legislation as "an organisation of workers, an organisation of employers, or any other organisation whose members carry on a particular profession or trade for the purposes of which the organisation exists."[200] The law covers access to and conditions of membership—as opposed to employment—as well as benefits, facilities and services conditional upon such membership, and expulsion and the imposition of any other detriment. The provisions extend to discrimination and harassment. Trade organisations are permitted to engage in limited forms of positive action, which are discussed in Ch.12.[201]

Trade unions may face a dilemma where an allegation of harassment or discrimination is made by one union member against another. This occurred in *Fire Brigades Union v Fraser*.[202] The union's policy was to support the claimant (of whichever sex) and not the accused. Accordingly, it supported a women who had complained of harassment and gave the accused, Mr Fraser, no assistance or representation in the disciplinary hearing. The Court of Session held that as the policy was conduct-related, rather than gender-related, it did not infringe s.12, Sex Discrimination Act 1975, and so the accused lost his claim against the union for sex discrimination.

The phrase "organisation of workers" includes an organisation of "professionals", as the label "profession" does not prevent an occupation from being work for these provisions. Hence, an indemnity and advice society for the medical profession was an "organisation of workers".[203] These provisions also apply to employers' organisations, though these are bodies which may have a far looser relationship with their members than trade unions. In *National Federation of Self-Employed and Small Businesses Ltd v Philpott*,[204] it was held that the Federation was "an organisation of employers", even though it was partly a campaigning group and not all its members were employers. As a result, the tribunal had jurisdiction to hear a claim by a person who was expelled from the organisation.

(5) Qualifying Bodies

8–076 The provisions[205] deal with discrimination and harassment by bodies which confer authorisation or qualification necessary for entry into employment. In parallel with the basic employment provisions, the

---

[200] SDA 1975, s.12; RRA 1976, 11; Religion or Belief Regulations 2003, reg.15, Sexual Orientation Regulations 2003, reg.15; Age Regulations 2006, reg.18 (in force October 1, 2006).
[201] At paras 12–004—12–008.
[202] [1998] I.R.L.R. 697, CS.
[203] *Sadek v Medical Protection Society* [2004] I.C.R. 1263. CA.
[204] [1997] I.C.R. 518, EAT.
[205] SDA 1975, s.13; RRA 1976, s.12; Religion or Belief Regulations 2003, reg.16; Sexual Orientation Regulations 2003, reg.16; Age Regulations 2006, reg.19 (in force October 1, 2006).

sections cover the grant of the relevant qualification, its terms, and its withdrawal. This covers bodies as wide ranging as the Council for Legal Education[206] and the Law Society to sporting bodies such as the British Boxing Board of Control.[207] In *British Judo Association v Petty*[208] the Association refused to grant Ms Petty a certificate to referee in men's judo competitions, arguing that their duty was to uphold refereeing standards rather than to award a qualification. The EAT held that the matter was one of substance and not form. The issue was whether the Association's activities in fact controlled entry into refereeing. In *Patterson v Legal Services Commission,*[209] the Court of Appeal held that the provision of a legal aid franchise to a sole practitioner solicitor "facilitated" her entry into, and continuing, practice, and so came within s.12, RRA 1976. However, in *Tattari v Private Patients Plan Ltd*[210] the Court of Appeal held that the rejection by the defendants, who underwrite private health care, of the plaintiff's application to be added to their list of accredited specialists, fell outside of s.12. The defendants were not authorising her to practise in her profession. They simply required that those wishing to enter commercial agreements with them should have a recognised UK qualification.

Some litigation has arisen over whether these provisions cover the selection of candidates by a political party for election. In *Jepson and Dyas-Elliott v The Labour Party,*[211] an industrial tribunal held that it was. Consequently, the Labour Party's policy of all-women short-lists was held to be unlawful. Recently, the effect of the decision was reversed by the introduction of s.42A into the SDA 1975,[212] allowing for arrangements "adopted for the purpose of reducing inequality in the numbers of men and women elected, as candidates for the party." This applies for elections to the UK, European and Scottish parliaments, as well as the Welsh Assembly and local government. However,

---

However, these provisions, in line with the relevant GOR, do not apply to a requirement related to sexual orientation by a professional or trade qualification for purposes of an organised religion, to comply with its doctrine or the strongly held religious convictions of a significant number of its followers (Sexual Orientation Regulations, reg.16(3)). See above, para.8–050.

[206] *Bohon-Mitchell v Common Professional Examination Board* [1978] I.R.L.R. 525, IT. See further Ch.6, para.6–032.

[207] Refusing a women a licence to box professionally was held to be unlawful in *Couch v British Boxing Board of Control*, unreported, IT, (1998) *The Guardian*, March 31, 1998 or see *www.eoc.org.gov*. However, it is sometimes permissible to segregate a particular sport by gender or nationality. See further, Ch.10, para.10–023.

[208] [1981] I.C.R. 660, EAT.

[209] [2004] I.C.R. 312, at paras 63–79, CA.

[210] [1998] I.C.R. 106, CA.

[211] [1996] I.R.L.R. 116.

[212] Inserted by the Sex Discrimination (Election Candidates) Act 2002, s.1. The provision will expire at the end of 2015, unless renewed by statutory instrument: SD(EC)A 2002, s.3.

the Court of Appeal, in *Triesman v Ali*,[213] without referring to *Jepson*, decided that the nomination of candidates for local government elections was *not* a matter within s.12, RRA. This was because, first, the Labour Party was not a body "which can confer a qualification or authorisation," and second, in this case the nomination of a candidate did not, in any meaningful sense, confer any status on the nominee, whose name merely went into a pool for selection. However, the Court did state that a claimant might have a case under s.25, RRA, regarding associations.[214]

Finally note that, for the Sex Discrimination Act 1975 only, s.13(2) provides that where a qualifying body is required by law to satisfy itself as to an applicant's good character, that requirement shall be taken to impose on the authority or body a duty to have regard to any evidence tending to show that the applicant (or any of his employees, or agents) has practised unlawful discrimination in the past.

(6) Vocational Training Bodies

8–077 Section 14, SDA 1975, s.13, RRA 1976, and reg.17 of either the Religion or Belief, or Sexual Orientation, Regulations, and reg.20 of the Age Regulations[215] deal with discrimination by bodies which offer vocational training. By analogy with the situation of employers, discrimination is prohibited in relation to offers, terms, terminations and any other detriments. In addition, discrimination in the arrangements made for determining to whom training is offered is outlawed by the Sex Discrimination Act and the Age Regulations only. Vocational training is defined as training that would help the person fit any employment. In addition, for all the grounds save race, it includes practical work experience and "vocational guidance".

The provisions should be read in conjunction with the exceptions for positive action, which permit specifically discrimination on the grounds of sex or race to remedy under-representation, or to compensate for disadvantages related to sexual orientation, religion or belief, or age.[216] The provisions also make it unlawful for the provider of the training to harass a person who is doing, or seeking to do, vocational training.

(7) "Office-holders"

8–078 All the legislation now covers workers who technically are not in employment, but whose position may be similar to that of

---

[213] [2002] I.C.R. 1026, CA, reversing *Sawyer v Ahsan* [1999] I.R.L.R. 609, EAT. Applied *Carter v Ahsan (No.1)* [2005] I.C.R. 1817, CA.

[214] See below, Ch.10, para.10–011.

[215] In force October 1, 2006.

[216] See Ch.12, paras 12–004—12–008.

employees.[217] These workers are known as "office-holders". They include a person appointed or recommended by a Minister or government department (paid or unpaid), or a person appointed to discharge functions personally for pay (not just expenses or compensation) and is subject to the direction of another person. Government appointments covered include the chairs/members of some non-departmental public bodies, judges, members of tribunals or special advisory committees. Other office holders will include some ministers of religion. Political appointments or politically elected positions, such as local councillors are not covered. The GOR and/or GOQ exemptions apply as they would apply to employment. The provisions account for the situation where a person may be appointed by one party (e.g. a tribunal appointment body), and employed by another (the tribunal body). Each body can be liable for discrimination or harassment at the relevant stages.

5. Special Provisions for Certain Employments

(1) The Police

Section 16, now repealed, of the Race Relations Act 1976, provided **8–079** that a constable was an employee, whilst s.32 provides that "Anything done by a person in course of his employment shall be treated . . . as done by his employer as well . . ." In *Chief Constable of Bedfordshire Police v Liversidge*[218] the Court of Appeal held that, ss.16 and 32 combined did *not* make the Chief Constable, as employer, vicariously, or constructively, liable for discrimination by one police officer to another. Ironically, the Court was influenced by concurrent passing of the Race Relations (Amendment) Act 2000, which expressly remedied this problem. For the Court of Appeal, the new Act was evidence that Parliament had not intended the old definition to cover such situations. Of course, for those police officers complaining of racial discrimination or harassment from colleagues, there is now a remedy.[219] More recently, the Sex Discrimination Act has been amended in the same way.[220] There is also a remedy under reg.11(2) of either the Sexual Orientation, or Religion or Belief, Regulations, or reg.13(2) of the Age Regulations.[221]

---

[217] SDA 1975, ss.10A and 10B; RRA 1976, ss.76 and 76ZA; Religion or Belief Regulations 2003, reg.10; Sexual Orientation Regulations 2003, reg.10; Age Regulations 2006, reg.12, (in force October 1, 2006).

[218] [2002] I.C.R. 1135, CA.

[219] The 2000 Act replaced s.16 with ss.76A and 76B.

[220] Sex Discrimination Act 1975 (Amendment) Regulations 2003 SI 2003/1657, reg.2 inserting s.17(1A) into the SDA 1975. In force July 19, 2003.

[221] In force October 1, 2006.

(2) Barristers and Advocates

8–080 At one time, barristers fell outside the legislation because they work neither under a contract nor under a partnership agreement. To remedy this, the SDA 1975 and RRA 1976 were amended with new ss.35A and 35B, and 26A and 26B, respectively.[222] These apply rules similar to the employment provisions to barristers, advocates and pupils. Regulations 12 and 13 of either the Sexual Orientation, or the Religion or Belief, Regulations, and regs 15 and 16 of the Age Regulations[223] cover barristers, advocates and pupils in the same way. For example, it is unlawful for a barrister or barrister's clerk to discriminate against a pupil or tenant in the arrangements for recruitment, or by "pressure to leave the chamber" or by any other detriment. It is also unlawful for a barrister or barrister's clerk to harass a pupil or tenant. Finally, it is unlawful, in relation to instructing a barrister, for any person to discriminate or harass.

6. EMPLOYER AND INDIVIDUAL LIABILITY

(1) Liability of Employers and Principals

8–081 All the provisions[224] make liable an employer for anything done by its workers in the course of their employment, and a principal for any thing done by his agent within his (actual or subsequent) authority. An employer can be liable even if the act was done without its knowledge or approval, although it has a defence if it took "reasonably practicable" steps to prevent the worker from acting as he did. Generally, employers are not liable for the discriminatory acts (including harassment) of third parties.[225]

Although it may appear so from the wording (especially "in the course of their employment") these provisions do not represent the common law doctrine of vicarious liability. In *Jones v Tower Boot Co*[226] the claimant was of mixed race, 16 years old, and in his first job. His co-workers subjected him to serious racial harassment. Among other incidents, they burnt his arm with a hot screwdriver, threw metal bolts at his head, and repeatedly called him derogatory names such as "chimp," "monkey" and "baboon". The claimant resigned and sued the employer for racial discrimination. The EAT applied the traditional and well-known test of vicarious liability in tort and concluded, predictably, that the employers were not liable, as the acts of harassment were committed outside the course of employment. The Court

---

[222] Inserted by the Courts and Legal Services Act 1990, ss.64 and 65.
[223] In force October 1, 2006.
[224] SDA 1975, s.41; RRA 1976 s.32; Religion or Belief Regulations 2003, reg.22; Sexual Orientation Regulations 2003, reg.22; Age Regulations 2006, reg.25 (in force October 1, 2006).
[225] *Pearce v Governing Body of Mayfield Secondary School* [2003] I.C.R. 937, HL. Discussed below.
[226] [1997] I.C.R. 254, CA.

of Appeal reversed, holding that the phrase in the provisions (in this case s.32, Race Relations Act 1976) "in the course of employment" should be given a broad interpretation, regardless of the common law doctrine of vicarious liability. Otherwise, "the more heinous the act of discrimination, the less likely it will be that the employer is liable."[227]

In general, an employer cannot be liable to its workers for discriminatory acts by third parties. In *Burton and Rhule v de Vere Hotels*[228] two black waitresses were subjected to racist and sexist jibes by a guest speaker at an all-male private dinner party. The EAT held that a "reasonable" employer would have foreseen the problem and withdrawn the two waitresses, and so found the defendant employer liable to the waitresses for the harassment. However, *Pearce v Governing Body of Mayfield Secondary School*[229] the House of Lords disapproved of *Burton*. In *Pearce*, pupils at a school regularly taunted a schoolteacher, who was a lesbian, with names such as "lesbian", "dyke", "lesbian shit", "lemon", "lezzie" or "lez". The teacher sued her employer for sexual harassment. It was stated *obiter* that the employer could not be liable for the acts of the (third party) pupils. The basis of this approach is twofold. First, the legislation outlaws specific forms of discrimination, committed either by a worker, for which his employer may be liable, or by the employer itself. In this case, it was neither the employer nor the staff who harassed the teacher. In particular, whether the employer acted unreasonably is irrelevant. What matters is whether it committed an unlawful act of discrimination. Second, where it is lawful for a third party to discriminate (as with pupils harassing a teacher, or an entertainer harassing a waitress), the employer of the victims cannot be put in a worse position than the perpetrator and be made liable for something which was otherwise lawful.

This in contrast to the approach in the United States, where the law **8–082** of agency is used to impose tortuous liability on employers for their own negligence.[230] Thus where an employer *ought* to have known a third party would harass a worker, (as in *Burton*) it should take preventative steps.[231]

Employers (but not principals) have a defence if they prove that they "took such steps as were reasonably practicable to prevent the

---

[227] *ibid.*, at p.264. See R. Townshend-Smith, "Case note" (1996) 2 I.J.D.L. 137, pp.139–40. For development of the argument, see R. Townshend-Smith, "Harassment as a tort in English law: the boundaries of *Wilkinson v Downton*" (1995) 24 Anglo-Am LR 299; J. Dine and B. Watt, "Sexual harassment: moving away from discrimination" (1995) 58 M.L.R. 343, fn 3.

[228] [1997] I.C.R. 1, EAT.

[229] [2003] I.C.R. 937, at paras 29–37, 96–103, 105, 120–124 and 200–205. see further, Ch.5, para.5–023.

[230] See *Faragher v City of Boca Raton* 524 US 775, at 799–800 (Sup Ct 1998); D. Oppenheimer, "Exacerbating the exasperating: Title VII liability of employers for sexual harassment committed by their supervisors", 81 Cornell L Rev 66 (1995).

[231] See EEOC guidelines 29 CFR s.1604.11(e) (*www.eeoc.gov*) and e.g. *Lockard v Pizza Hut* 162 F 3d 848 (10th Cir 1998).

employee from doing that act, or from doing in the course of his employment acts of that description." In *Canniffe v East Riding of Yorkshire Council*[232] the EAT appeared to suggest that employers should take all reasonably practicable steps to prevent the discriminatory act, even where these steps would not have prevented the act. In this case the claimant was sexually assaulted by a colleague, and argued that their employer had not responded adequately to her prior complaints about the colleague's sexual harassment. The employment tribunal found that a better implementation of its personal harassment policy would not have prevented this serious criminal behaviour, any more than widespread advice about honesty would prevent theft. On that basis the tribunal dismissed the complaint. The EAT held that this was the wrong approach: whether reasonably practicable further steps would have made a difference should not be "determinative either way." The case was remanded for a rehearing. However, the Court of Appeal in *Croft v Royal Mail*[233] disapproved of that approach, holding that the "reasonably practicable" phrase made it "permissible to take into account the extent of the difference, if any, which the action is likely to make." In *Croft* the claimant, a victim of sexual harassment by colleagues, argued that her employer failed to respond properly to her complaints. The employment tribunal noted the employer's existing policy and practice, and found that further actions would not "have had more than at most a marginal effect" on the harassment.[234] The Court of Appeal upheld this approach.

The existence of the defence suggests that it is possible for an act of discrimination by a co-worker to take place whilst the employer has done all that was "reasonably practicable" to prevent it. The approach in *Croft* suggests that the more heinous the discrimination (such as a serious sexual assault) the less likely it is that the employer will be liable, which conflicts with the spirit adopted in *Jones v Tower Boot Co,* (above).[235]

In contrast to employer liability, the references to *principal* and *agent* in the provisions should bear their common law meaning. In *Yearwood v Commissioner of Police of the Metropolis*[236] the EAT noted that at common law an agent may be appointed to do any act on behalf of the principal which the principal might do himself, and held that an investigating officer appointed to carry out disciplinary hearings was not an agent of the chief of police because his task, by its nature, was independent of any control by the chief.

---

[232] [2000] I.R.L.R. 555.
[233] [2003] I.C.R. 1425, at para.61.
[234] Reported *ibid.*, at para.59.
[235] It is arguable that this defence is incompatible with the parent Directives, which do not specify such a defence. The matter was raised, but not considered in *Canniffe* (at para.24). See also *UP and GS v N and RJ*, unreported, IT, Case No: 10781/95, see 35 DCLD 11.
[236] [2004] I.C.R. 660.

(2) Individual Liability

By a rather circular route an individual can be liable for his act of **8–083** discrimination against a co-worker. Section 42, SDA 1975, s.32, RRA 1976, reg.23 of either the Religion or Belief, or Sexual Orientation, Regulations, and reg.26 of the Age Regulations[237] provide that a person who "knowingly" aids another person to do an act of unlawful discrimination will be treated as if he did the act himself, unless he relied, reasonably, on a statement by the primary discriminator that the act was lawful. Where a principal is liable for the act of his agent under the legislation (see above), the agent will be deemed to have aided his principal. Equally, where an employer is liable for an act of a worker under the legislation (see above), the worker will be deemed to have aided the employer. This applies notwithstanding that the employer may have a "reasonably practicable" steps defence (see above) and ultimately is exonerated from liability.[238] This means that, say, employees who harass a co-worker can be personally liable to that co-worker.[239] It does not matter that the party who aids was in fact the "prime mover" of the discriminatory act. Thus in *Anyanwu v South Bank Student Union*[240] where the university made allegations against student union employees, which ultimately led to their allegedly discriminatory dismissal, the university could be liable for aiding the union's act.

---

[237] In force October 1, 2006.
[238] Applied in *Yeboah v Crofton* [2002] I.R.L.R. 634, CA.
[239] *ibid.*
[240] [2001] I.C.R. 391, HL.

CHAPTER 9

EQUAL PAY

INTRODUCTION

The Equal Pay Act 1970 (EPA 1970) enables a woman to claim **9–001** equality with a man where she is engaged on "like work," work "rated as equivalent" under a job evaluation scheme, or where her work is of equal value with that of her male comparator. The employer has a defence where the difference in pay is "genuinely due to a material factor which is not the difference of sex." The Act applies to employees, the self-employed[1] and the Crown service.[2]

---

[1] EPA 1970, s.1(6)(a): "'employed' means employed under a contract of service or of apprenticeship or a contract personally to execute any work or labour."

[2] EPA 1970, s.1(8).

243

Article 141 (ex 119), EC Treaty, guarantees the application of "the principle of equal pay for male and female workers for equal work or work of equal value." This is directly effective and so public and private employers are bound.[3] Article 141 is amplified by the Equal Pay Directive 75/117. Both domestic and European schemes apply equally to men and women. So it is possible to mount a claim based on Art.141 even if the claim falls outside the provisions of the EPA 1970, and vice versa. Both the Equal Opportunities Commission and the European Commission have issued Codes of Practice on equal pay.[4]

1. THE RELATIONSHIP BETWEEN THE EQUAL PAY ACT 1970 AND THE SEX DISCRIMINATION ACT 1975

9–002 The two pieces of legislation took effect on the same date in 1975. While it is clear that as far as possible they are complementary and should be construed as one Code, the relationship between them is unnecessarily complex, and sometimes uncomplimentary and confusing. But it is notable that in the UK, the EU, and the United States, equal pay is provided by separate dedicated statutes.

The Equal Pay Act governs the "terms (whether concerned with pay or not) of a contract under which a woman is employed".[5] It follows that a claim may be brought for inequality in any matter which is regulated by the contract of employment, such as hours, holidays, and fringe benefits. The Sex Discrimination Act 1975 (SDA 1975) deals with matters not regulated by the contract, such as job offers, promotions and transfers, dismissals and victimisation. It is therefore important for claimants to know whether or not each particular complaint is contractual. This is made all the more the difficult where the contract is not in writing (it does not have to be to exist, although written particulars should be given)[6] and where terms may be incorporated from an external source, typically a collective agreement between the employer and a trade union. If, for some reason, the EPA 1970 does not apply, a claim may still be brought under the SDA 1975 *except* where the benefit consists of the payment of money.[7] An offer of a contractual term is governed by the SDA 1975, but the EPA 1970 will apply once that offer is accepted and becomes part of the contract.[8]

---

[3] *Defrenne v Sabena* Case 43/75, [1976] ICR 547; *Jenkins v Kingsgate (Clothing Productions) Ltd* Case 96/80, [1981] I.C.R. 592.

[4] Respectively, "EOC Code of Practice on Equal Pay", (2003), EOC, ISBN 1 84206 094 5; *A Code of Practice on the Implementation of Equal Pay for Work of Equal Value for Women and Men*, Commission of the European Communities COM(96) 336 final, see (1996) 70 EOR 43.

[5] EPA 1970, s.1(2).

[6] Employment Rights Act 1996, ss.230(2) and 1.

[7] SDA 1975, ss.6(2), 6(5).

[8] SDA 1975, s.8(3).

The chief distinctions between the statutes are that under the EPA 1970 the comparator must be real, and a showing of a mere *difference* in pay can raise a rebuttable presumption of sex discrimination.[9] It should be noted here though that these differences are in the future likely the blur somewhat because the Equal Treatment Amendment Directive[10] removed the barrier between the legislative schemes, allowing, for instance, an equal pay claim to be brought as a claim of conventional sex discrimination under the Equal Treatment Directive 76/207/EC.

What follows are discussions of the meaning of pay, the choice of comparator, the meaning of like work, work rated as equivalent and work of equal value, and the employer's defence.

2. The Meaning of Pay

Article 141 states that "pay" means the ordinary wage or any other consideration whether in cash or in kind which the worker receives, directly or indirectly, in respect of his employment from his employer. Further, the worker may receive it, "albeit indirectly, in respect of his employment from his employer. It does not matter whether the worker receives it under a contract of employment, by virtue of legislative provisions or on a voluntary basis." It covers also any future pay.[11]

9–003

Thus, pay includes overtime,[12] performance-related pay and piece rates,[13] sick pay[14] and maternity pay.[15] Payment for time off to attend training courses is covered, even if the employer may not benefit from the training (such as obligatory trade union activities).[16] This is particularly relevant to part-time workers (predominantly women), who may be paid only up to their normal working hours (say 20 per week), even though they spend more time (say 30 hours) on the training course. All fringe benefits are covered, including removal expenses,[17]

---

[9] See below, respectively "(3) Real or Hypothetical Comparator?", para.9–006; and "(3) Fair Pay and Equal Pay", para.9–030.

[10] 2002/73/EC, in force October 5, 2005.

[11] *Arbeiterwohlfahrt der Stadt Berlin Ev v Botel* Case C-360/90, [1992] I.R.L.R. 423, at para.12.

[12] *ibid.*, at para.27.

[13] *Handels-og Kontorfunktionaererernes Forbund i Danmark v Dansk Arbejdsgiverforening (acting for Danfoss)* Case 109/88, [1991] I.C.R. 74, ECJ; *Royal Copenhagen* Case C-400/93 [1996] I.C.R. 51, ECJ.

[14] *Rinner-Kuhn v FWW Spezial-Gebäudereinigung*, Case 171/88, [1989] ECR 2743.

[15] Although this is largely theoretical, as the ECJ in *Gillespie v Northern Health and Social Services Board* Case C-342/93 [1996] I.C.R. 498, and *Boyle v EOC* Case C411/96 [1998] I.R.L.R. 717 held respectively, that no comparison could be made with either a man at work, or a man on sick leave. Hence it is not discriminatory to cease paying normal salary, or to provide benefits inferior to sick pay, to a woman on maternity leave. But see also *Alabaster v Woolwich plc* Case C-147/02, [2004] ECR I-0000, below, para.9–006.

[16] *Arbeiterwohlfahrt der Stadt Berlin Ev v Botel* Case C-360/90 [1992] I.R.L.R. 423, ECJ; *Davies v Neath Port Talbot BC* [1999] I.R.L.R. 769, EAT.

[17] *Durrant v North Yorkshire HA* [1979] I.R.L.R. 401, EAT.

mortgage interest allowance,[18] and voluntary Christmas bonuses.[19] Further, pay covers these benefits where they are given to third parties, such as travel concessions for the whole family.[20] This shows that even non-contractual benefits are covered. Where benefits such as concessions may not be "pay" under the domestic Equal Pay Act 1970, a claim the claim will fall instead under the Sex Discrimination Act 1975.

Occupational pensions and contracted out non-contributory pensions (that, in part, replace the state scheme) also fall within Art.141,[21] but the position is somewhat complicated. The ECJ ruled, in *Barber v Guardian Royal Exchange*,[22] that Art.141 applied to discriminatory pension *payments.* The ECJ accepted that this decision was unexpected, so to avoid an enormous upset to the pension industry it further held that no claims (bar existing ones) could be made relating to pension payments attributable to service before the date of its judgment, May 17, 1990.[23] This does not affect an earlier ruling, in *Bilka*,[24] that a discriminatory exclusion from *membership* of an occupational pension falls under Art.141.[25] Typically, low paid and part-time workers have been excluded from pension schemes. Where these were predominantly women, a retrospective claim may be made under Art.141.[26]

Article 141 also covers statutory and contractual redundancy payments,[27] as well as compensation and awards for statutory unfair dismissal.[28]

3. Choosing a Comparator

(1) Who Chooses the Comparator(s)?

9–004 The general rule is that the claimant chooses her comparator, and the tribunal cannot substitute another it considers more appropriate. In *Pickstone v Freemans*[29] Mrs Pickstone was one of many "warehouse operatives"; all but one were women. They were paid £77.66 per week. However, a "*checker* warehouse operative"—a Mr Phillips—was paid

---

[18] *Sun Alliance and London Insurance Ltd v Dudman* [1978] I.C.R. 551, EAT.

[19] *Lewen v Denda* Case C-333/97, [2000] I.C.R. 648, ECJ.

[20] *Garland v British Rail Engineering* Case C-12/81 [1983] 2 A.C. 751, ECJ.

[21] *Bilka-Kaufhaus v Weber von Hartz* Case C-170/84, [1987] I.C.R. 110, ECJ; *Barber v Guardian Royal Exchange* Case C-262/88, [1991] 1 Q.B. 344, ECJ.

[22] Case C-262/88, [1991] 1 Q.B. 344, ECJ.

[23] This temporal rule is now contained in Protocol 2 of the Maastricht Treaty.

[24] *Bilka-Kaufhaus v Weber von Hartz* Case 170/84, [1987] I.C.R. 110, ECJ.

[25] See *Vroege v NCIV Institut voor Volkshuisvesting BV and Stichting Pensioenfonds NCIV* Case C-57/93, [1995] I.C.R. 635, ECJ.

[26] See below, Ch.13, para.13–018.

[27] *Barber v Guardian Royal Exchange* Case C-262/88, [1991] 1 Q.B. 344, ECJ, at para.13.

[28] *R. v Secretary of State for Employment Ex p. Seymour-Smith* Case C-167/97, [1999] I.C.R. 447, ECJ, at paras 27–29. See further Ch.6, paras 6–024 and 6–043.

[29] [1988] I.C.R. 697, HL.

£81.88 per week. Mrs Pickstone did work of equal value to Mr Phillips and so chose him as her comparator. Freemans argued that as Mrs Pickstone was paid same as the lone male warehouse operative (who did "like work") she could not "have it both ways" and make an alternative "equal value" claim. The House of Lords held that the claimant was entitled to use any appropriate comparator, and so Mrs Pickstone prevailed. The benefit of this approach is that prevents an employer using a token male worker in a predominantly female occupation to avoid equal-value claims, for instance, a supermarket employing a lone male on the checkouts, whilst paying more to the predominantly male shelf-stackers who are doing work of equal value.

However, doubt has been raised over this as an absolute rule where there is no sex discrimination and the claimant chooses an anomalous comparator. In *McPherson v Rathgael Centre for Children*[30] five out of six instructors were male. All six were paid the same. The lone female brought an equal pay claim using as a comparator a newly recruited (seventh) male instructor, who was put on higher pay by mistake. Whilst her appeal succeeded on the point that a mistake is no justification, Hutton, L.C.J. (as he then was) doubted that *Pickstone* should be applied in cases such as this, where clearly there was no sex discrimination (the majority of the lower-paid instructors were men).[31] There is support for this sentiment in the ECJ, which has stated Art.141 only prohibits different pay exclusively based on the difference in sex of the employees concerned.[32] In *Glasgow City Council v Marshall*[33] the claim was by special-school instructors who were doing the same work as teachers for less pay. Seven female instructors compared themselves with a male teacher. At the same time, a *male* instructor compared himself with a female teacher. However, there was no sex disparity between the two groups (females made up about 96 per cent instructors and 97 per cent teachers).[34] The quandary was expressed by Lord Nicholls: "It is a curious result in a sex discrimination case that, on the same facts, claims by women and a claim by a man all succeed."[35] The House of Lords rejected the claim, but rather than disturbing *Pickstone*, it resolved the matter under the material factor defence: as the difference in pay "is not the difference of sex", no further justification was necessary.[36] Thus, where there is no sex discrimination, an anomalous choice of comparator will be allowed (the *Pickstone* rule

---

[30] [1991] I.R.L.R. 206, NICA.

[31] *ibid.*, at para.40. The House of Lords stated that the mistake point was wrongly decided: *Strathclyde Regional Council v Wallace* [1998] I.C.R. 205, at 214–215. See further below, para.9–039.

[32] *Brunnhofer v Bank der Österreichischen Postsparkasse* Case C-381/99, [2001] I.R.L.R. 571, at para.40; *Jenkins v Kingsgate* Case 96/80, [1981] I.C.R. 592, at para.10.

[33] [2000] I.C.R. 196. See also *Strathclyde Regional Council v Wallace* [1998] I.C.R. 205, HL.

[34] A separate argument comparing instructors and teachers from *all* schools was not taken up for being introduced too late.

[35] [2000] I.C.R. 196, at 203.

[36] Discussed further below, para.9–030.

survives), but the claim will fail on the "material factor defence" element. Accordingly, there is nothing to prevent a claimant bringing several (appropriate) comparators into court.[37] In *Hayward v Cammell Laird Shipbuilders Ltd (No.2)*,[38] Ms Hayward, a canteen cook in a shipyard, used a painter, a decorator and a thermal insulation engineer as comparators.

The US courts are divided over this issue. In *Sowell v Alumina Ceramics*[39] it was held that a woman could not establish a prima facie case where she was paid the same as, or more than, at least some male workers doing like work. Conversely, it has also been held that where a woman produces just one male comparator on higher pay, her prima facie case should proceed.[40] However, in these cases, rather like in *Marshall*, the courts have held that there remains a further issue of whether or not the difference in pay was due to sex discrimination.[41]

(2) Predecessors and Successors as Comparators

9–005 In *Macarthys Ltd v Smith*[42] the ECJ held that it was possible to use predecessor in the same job as a comparator. In *Diocese of Hallam Trustee v Connaughton,*[43] Miss Connaughton, an organist, was paid £11,138 per annum at her time of leaving in September 1994. Her male successor was paid £20,000 per annum from January 1995. The EAT held that whilst using a predecessor posed evidential problems it did not preclude Miss Connaughton's claim. Although the successor was appointed some four months' later, it was on near double her salary. Equally, in the United States, claimants may use successors or predecessors as comparators.[44]

(3) Real and Hypothetical Comparators

9–006 Hitherto, although predecessors or successors may be used, the Equal Pay Act 1970, unlike the Sex Discrimination Act 1975, demands that the comparator must be a real person. As the SDA 1975, s.6(6), prevents most equal pay claims being brought under the SDA,

---

[37] But note the House of Lords' caution against this as abuse in equal value claims: *Leverton v Clwyd CC* [1989] A.C. 706, at 751–752. See further below, fn 104 and accompanying text.

[38] [1988] A.C. 894, HL.

[39] 251 F 3d 678, at 684 (8th Cir 2001).

[40] *Hutchins v International Brotherhood of Teamsters*, 177 F 3d 1076 (8th Cir 1999). (A different panel from that in *Sowell* heard this case.)

[41] e.g. in *Hutchins, ibid.* the court stated that the defendant bears the burden "to prove that the disparities complained of were based on . . . a factor other than sex" (at 1080–81). For a discussion of the conflicting authority see *Hennick v Schans Sales Enterprises* 168 F Supp 2d 938, at 947 (ND Iowa 2001).

[42] Case C-129/79, [1980] I.C.R. 672, ECJ.

[43] [1996] I.C.R. 860, EAT.

[44] See *Gandy v Sullivan County* 24 F 3d 861 (6th Cir 1994).

claimants must use a real comparator, which can restrict the claim in some situations. First, the problem is starkest in segregated occupations. As the law stands, female cooks in a shipyard may compare their jobs to painters, whilst cleaners at a coal mine may compare themselves to clerical staff, and seamstresses in a motor factory compare themselves to repair workers.[45] But where these occupations are segregated fully, a comparison for equal pay is impossible. So the cook or the cleaner working for an all-female outside contractor,[46] or the seamstress in an all-female sweatshop, has no claim to equal pay. The sweatshop's seamstress may see her neighbour working for Vauxhall or Ford, being paid a lot more for the same work. As such, the National Minimum Wage legislation has done more for these workers than the Equal Pay Act.[47]

Second, discriminatory pay can operate beyond different pay for equivalent work. Although a woman can compare herself to man doing *inferior* work, and achieve the same level of pay as him,[48] she cannot claim for proportionally *more* pay than he receives.[49] Relative pay differences between different grades of workers may be discriminatory. In the US case *County of Washington v Gunther*,[50] male prison officers had more onerous duties than female prison officers. However, a job evaluation study recommended that the women's pay should be 95 per cent of the men's. The men were paid their worth in full, whilst the women were paid just 70 per cent of the men's pay. In the US, just as in the UK, the Equal Pay Act 1963 demands a real comparator. However, the Supreme Court ruled that the female prison officers could make a claim of sex discrimination using Title VII (the loose equivalent of the Sex Discrimination Act 1975), which does not demand a real comparator.[51]

---

[45] See, respectively, *Hayward v Cammell Laird Shipbuilders (No.2)* [1988] A.C. 894, HL; *British Coal v Smith* [1996] I.C.R. 515, HL; *Neil v Ford* [1984] I.R.L.R. 339, IT (unsuccessfully), *The Independent* May 14, 1991, *The Guardian* March 11, 1991 (successfully).

[46] *Lawrence v Regent Office Care* Case C-320/00, [2003] I.C.R. 1092, ECJ discussed below, para.9–013; see also *Allonby v Accrington & Rossendale College* Case C-256/01, [2004] I.C.R. 1328, ECJ, (college lecturers) see below para.9–013.

[47] In 1998, the government calculated that the proposed minimum wage rate of £3.60 would benefit 1.4 million women and 1.3 million part-time workers. (Department of Trade and Industry Press Release, P/98/489, June 18, 1998, London: DTI.) See further, M. Connolly, *Townshend-Smith Discrimination Law: Text, Cases and Materials* (2004) London: Cavendish, pp.40–41.

[48] *Murphy v Bord Telecom Eireann* Case 157/86, [1988] I.C.R. 445, at para.10 ECJ; contrast *Waddington v Leicester Council for Voluntary Service* [1977] I.C.R. 266, at 270–271 EAT. Discussed below, para.9–017.

[49] *Evesham v North Hertfordshire Health Authority* [2000] I.C.R. 612, CA.

[50] 452 US 161 (1981) Supreme Court.

[51] In fact, the claimants used Title VII because, at the time, the Equal Pay Act did not cover municipal workers: but the point (that Title VII can be used without a comparator) stands. It has been argued that discrimination in collective bargaining and in resulting collective agreements is unlawful under the SDA 1975 irrespective of the position under the EPA 1970: A. Lester, D. Rose, "Equal value claims and sex bias in collective bargaining" (1991) 20 I.L.J. 163.

Finally, although pregnancy discrimination has been held to amount to *sex* discrimination,[52] discrimination in *pay* on the ground of pregnancy may escape liability because the female claimant can find no male comparator. In *Alabaster v Woolwich plc*[53] the claimant's maternity pay was related to her salary. However, the formula pinned maternity pay to the salary some time before her leave began. Accordingly, a pay rise awarded after this time was not reflected in her maternity pay. The ECJ ruled that this was sex discrimination under Art.141, as pregnant women did not receive the benefit of the pay rise because they were pregnant. When the case returned to the UK, the Court of Appeal implemented this ruling by disapplying s.1 of the EPA 1970, so that Alabaster's claim could proceed without the need for a comparator.

The Equal Treatment Amendment Directive 2002/73 provided that the Equal Treatment Directive 76/207 should apply to discriminatory pay claims. However, when the UK implemented the amendments, on October 1, 2005, it omitted to repeal the express bar to pay claims under the SDA 1975 (s.6(6)). Had it done so, claims for equal pay without a real comparator could be brought under the SDA 1975. As things stand, victims of discriminatory pay who cannot produce a real comparator, should call upon EC law and request that the tribunal disapplies s.1 of the EPA 1970 (as in *Alabaster*).

(4) Comparing Part-time to Full-time Workers

9–007   Under equal pay legislation, part-time (predominantly female) workers can compare themselves to full-time workers.[54] It is now so established that less favourable treatment of part-time workers adversely affects women, that dedicated legislation has been passed to protect part-time workers. The Part-time Workers (Prevention of Less Favourable Treatment) Regulations 2000[55] provide that less favourable treatment, including pay, of a part-time worker is unlawful unless "objectively justified." Regulation 1(2) provides that comparisons can be made on a pro rata basis, so that the level of pay for part-time worker is proportionally the same as the full-time worker's. In *Elsner-Lakeberg*[56] both part-time and full-time teachers were obliged to work

---

[52] *Dekker v Stichting Vormingscentrum voor Jonge Volwassen (VJV-Centrum) Plus* Case C-177/88, [1990] E.C.R. I-3941. See further Ch.4, para.4–037.

[53] Case C-147/02, [2004] E.C.R. I-0000. Upon its return, the CA implemented this ruling through the Equal Pay Act 1970, by disapplying the Act's requirement for a comparator: *Alabaster v Barclays Bank (No.2)* [2005] EWCA 508.

[54] *Bilka-Kaufhaus v Weber von Hartz* Case C-170/84, [1987] I.C.R. 110, ECJ. See further paras 9–003, 9–026 and 9–032.

[55] SI 2000/1551, in force July 1, 2000, implementing Directive 97/81/EC. See further Ch.6, para.6–037.

[56] *Elsner-Lakeberg v Land Nordrhein-Westfalen* Case C-285/02, E.C.R. [2004] I-05861. See also *Kowalska v Freie und Hansestadt Hamburg* Case C-33/89, [1992] I.C.R. 29, at para.19, ECJ.

three hours extra per month for no extra pay. The ECJ held that this placed an unequal burden on the part-timers, and raised a prima facie case under Art.141.

Part-time workers cannot compare their overtime pay to that of full-time workers, until the part-time overtime hours reaches a set threshold, say 38 hours per week. So, whilst a full-time worker may be paid at double rates for hours worked in excess of 38 per week, a part-time worker may paid at her standard rate for her extra hours up to 38 per week.[57] However, where the full-timers are paid a bonus for some of their contractually obliged hours, then a comparison can be made.[58]

(5) The Scope of the Comparison

Under the Equal Pay Act 1970 the comparator must be in the "same employment", however, s.1(6) provides an expansive definition of this, allowing a claimant to chose a comparator who works for an "associated employer". Community law, by Art.141 EC, appears to go further than that. In *Defrenne v Sabena (No.2)*,[59] the ECJ stated that it allowed a comparator who is in the same establishment or "service", whether public or private, and whose terms originate from the same legislative provisions or collective agreement. The direct effect of Art.141 allows claimants to try either route in domestic tribunals.

9–008

(a) Section 1(6) EPA 1970

Under the EPA 1970, a comparator (i) must work for the same or an "associated" employer *and* (ii) be employed at the same establishment, or if at a different establishment, on terms and conditions common to both establishments.

9–009

(i) "Associated employer"

Under s.1(6), two employers are to be treated as "associated" if one is a company of which the other (not necessarily a company) has control, or where both employers are companies under the control of a third person (not necessarily a company). Local authorities and public bodies (such as the EOC), as statutory bodies corporate, are not "companies" within this definition.[60]

9–010

---

[57] *Stadt Lengerich v Helmig* Case C-399/92 [1994] E.C.R. I-5725; [1996] I.C.R. 35, ECJ, codified by Part-Time Workers (Prevention of Less Favourable Treatment) Regulations 2000, reg.5(4)).

[58] *James v Great North Eastern Railways* Unreported, (2004) UKEAT/0496/04/SM (Transcript), (available at *www.employmentappeals.gov.uk*).

[59] Case C-43/75, [1976] I.C.R. 547, at para.40, ECJ.

[60] *Merton LBC v Gardiner* [1981] Q.B. 269, at 287, CA; *Hasley v Fair Employment Agency* [1989] I.R.L.R. 106, at para.12, NICA.

(ii) Cross-establishment comparisons

9–011   If the comparator works at the same establishment, there is no need for him to work under common terms and conditions.[61] If the comparator works (for the same or associated employer) at another establishment, then s.6(1) stipulates that he must do so under terms and conditions common to both establishments which are observed "either generally or for employees of the relevant classes." In *Leverton v Clwyd CC*[62] Lord Bridge explained the purpose of this formula:

> An employer operates factory A where he has a long standing collective agreement with the ABC union. The same employer takes over a company operating factory X and becomes an "associated employer" of the persons working there. The previous owner of factory X had a long standing collective agreement with the XYZ union which the new employer continues to operate. The two collective agreements have produced quite different structures governing pay and other terms and conditions of employment at the two factories. Here ... section 1(6) will operate to prevent women in factory A claiming equality with men in factory X and vice versa.

9–012   Of course, if the interpretation were too strict and only comparators who worked on identical terms could be used, the result would be paradoxical: a claimant on identical terms to her comparator would have no need for an equal pay claim. Thus "the terms and conditions do not have to be identical, but on a broad basis to be substantially comparable."[63] In *Leverton* a nursery nurse compared her pay with 11 male clerical officers employed in other establishments by the County Council on terms derived from the same collective agreement, although the comparators worked longer hours and had shorter holidays. In *British Coal Corporation v Smith*[64] canteen workers and cleaners compared themselves with surface mineworkers and one clerical worker. The claimants were employed at 47 different establishments, whilst their comparators were at 14. Both the claimants and comparators worked under a single national agreement, but with some variations, such as concessionary coal and locally operated incentive bonuses. In both *Leverton* and *Smith* the House of Lords applied the "broad" comparison and held that the comparators worked under common terms and conditions.

As these cases demonstrate, where there is a centralised agreement, some variations will not prevent a claim. However, where there is plant bargaining, or a fragmented management structure, or no collective

---

[61] *Lawson v Britfish Ltd* [1987] I.C.R. 726, EAT.
[62] [1989] A.C. 706, at 746, CA and HL.
[63] *per* Lord Slynn, *British Coal v Smith* [1996] I.C.R. 515, at 531, HL.
[64] [1996] I.C.R. 515, HL.

bargaining at all, cross-establishment comparisons may not be possible under the EPA 1970. In these cases, claimants may instead try to claim under Art.141 (discussed below).

By contrast, the US Equal Pay Act 1963 requires the comparator to work for the same employer at the same establishment, although the courts have given this a liberal interpretation. So where there is central control and administration of different job sites, those sites may be considered as a single establishment.[65] A significant "functional relationship" between the work of employees in different locations suggested a single establishment, with geographic considerations being merely one factor in the question.[66]

(b) Article 141

Article 141, as interpreted in *Defrenne v Sabena*,[67] has broader application than s.6(1). First, there is no restriction that one of the associated employers must be a "company". Unlike s.1(6), Art.141 covers the situation where both the claimant's and comparator's employers are *not* companies. This facilitates public sector claims, as *Morton* (below) illustrates. But Art.141 only applies where the claimant and comparator share a single source of pay (such as legislation or a collective agreement), which curbs its impact on contracted-out workers, and by extension, perhaps, "departmentalised" workers.

9–013

The broad application of Art.141 was illustrated in *South Ayrshire Council v Morton*,[68] a case of two separate public sector employers, operating under the same collective agreement. In Scotland, the salary scales for primary school head teachers (75 per cent women), was lower than it is for secondary school head teachers (25 per cent women). Both salary scales were set by the Scottish Joint Negotiating Committee, a quasi-autonomous body set up by the Education (Scotland) Act, 1980 under the general control of the Secretary of State. There were 32 local authorities in Scotland and each was obliged to implement the salary scale, but each had autonomy, as an employer, on how to do this. It was held that Ms Morton, a primary school head teacher, employed by South Ayrshire Council, could use as a comparator a male secondary school head teacher, employed by Highland Council.

The limit of Art.141 was demonstrated when contracted-out workers tried to compare their pay with a male worker of the principal employer. In *Lawrence v Regent Office Care*[69] North Yorkshire County

---

[65] *Brennan v Goose Creek Consolidated Independent School District* 519 F 2d 53 (5th Cir 1975), (13 schools formed a single establishment).

[66] *American Federation of State, County and Municipal Employees v County of Nassau* 609 F Supp 695, at 706 (EDNY 1985).

[67] Case C-43/75, [1976] I.C.R. 547, ECJ.

[68] [2002] I.C.R. 956, CS.

[69] Case C-320/00, [2003] I.C.R. 1092, ECJ.

Council, in some districts, contracted out its school cleaning and catering services. In other districts, the council carried on providing the service itself. The workers affected by the contracting-out were made redundant and re-employed by Regent, who paid them less than the Council's rates. These workers brought a claim of equal pay, using an existing Council worker as a comparator. The ECJ held that such a claim was not possible because the pay could not be attributed to a single source, and so there was no body responsible for the inequality and which could restore equal pay. A similar situation arose in _Allonby v Accrington and Rossendale College_[70] where the college dismissed all its part-time lecturers and rehired them through an agency, for less pay. Ms Allonby tried to compare herself with a full-time male lecturer (who earned more pro rata). The ECJ again rejected her claim.

9–014   A perhaps logical extension of these ECJ decisions suggests that Art.141 has no application where a single employer has a fragmented management structure, leaving its workers "departmentalised". In _Robertson v DEFRA_[71] civil servants working in the Department for Environment Food and Rural Affairs brought equal pay claims using comparators from the Department of the Environment, Transport and the Regions. The claimants and comparators shared the same employer, the Crown. However, since 1995 the terms of employment had been individually negotiated within each civil service department, with the result that the claimant worked under different terms from their comparators (a reason why they could not use the EPA 1970). The Court of Appeal rejected their claim under Art.141, because the difference in pay could not be attributed to a single source.

The decisions in _Lawrence, Allonby_, and _Robertson_ have been criticised on a number grounds, but _Robertson_ requires special attention. First, the decisions essentially are fault-based. As the ECJ in _Lawrence_ noted, there was no one body responsible for disparity in pay. This may be a practical and even laudable sentiment, but as Fredman has observed, it does not explain why the loss should fall on those least at fault.[72] In _Robertson,_ Mummery, L.J. suggested a further dimension to the fault-based notion in these cases when observing that the change from central to departmental pay negotiations and agreements was "genuine" and not made in order to avoid the equal pay legislation.[73] If this stands as a reason for the decision, it will compel tribunals to determine the motive behind the fragmentation, a process loaded with problems of proof, causation and the definition of intent: it may have been _one_ of the motives, or a "background" motive, or an inevitable

---

[70] Case C-256/01, [2004] I.C.R. 1328, ECJ.

[71] [2005] I.C.R. 750, CA. At the time of writing an appeal was due in the House of Lords. Followed in _Armstrong v Newcastle_ [2006] I.R.L.R. 124, CA.

[72] S. Fredman, "Marginalising Equal Pay Laws", (2004) 33(3) I.L.J. 281, at 283.

[73] [2005] I.C.R. 750, at para.35.

though unintended consequence. In *Robertson* one motive was to value workers according to the needs of particular departments. Yet the fragmentation had the obvious consequence of avoiding the harmonising effects of equal pay, and so the distinction between the declared motive and a discriminatory motive is substantially one without a difference.[74] The declared motive should only become relevant at the objective justification stage, where inter alia it can be weighed against its discriminatory effect. Employers should be aware though that where there is sex discrimination in pay, it cannot be justified on the ground that the inequality was the result of separate collective bargaining.[75]

Another apparent reason for the decision in *Robertson* was the "flood-gates" argument. Mummery, L.J., noted that there were about half a million civil servants and that if the departmental barriers were ignored, to reveal a single employer (the Crown), the "the extravagant consequence" would be "that every civil servant would be entitled to compare himself or herself with any other civil servant of the opposite sex, subject only to objective justification by the employer of differences in pay." This was not "sensible or practical".[76] That reason carries two problems. First, the enthusiasm to avoid the "extravagant" spectacle of numerous "fair pay" claims (where men and women doing equal work use anomalous non-typical comparators to achieve a pay rise) is misplaced, because the matter was addressed some time before in *Glasgow City Council v Marshall*,[77] when the House of Lords ruled that such claims should founder at the "genuine material factor" defence stage because any difference in pay was not due to sex. Second, it ignores the possibility that there may be large scale sex discrimination across departmental pay, as shown in *Morton*. Mummery, L.J.'s reasoning erects a barrier to *both* "fair-pay" and genuine claimants, when *Marshall* had already produced a refined solution of allowing the comparison, and then sifting out the "fair-pay" claims at a later stage.

9–015

The strongest part of the decision in *Robertson* is its reliance on the "same source" tenet from *Lawrence*. But even that is not watertight. *Lawrence* and *Allonby* were cases with separate employers. The ECJ did not speculate on the position where there is a single employer. Further, the concept of "single source" becomes somewhat blurred where there is separate bargaining but undoubtedly a single ultimate source of the payment, the employer. In the context of *Robertson*, it was observed that there is a "trend encouraged by the current government of movement of civil servants between

---

[74] This point was made by I. Steele, "Tracing the Single Source: Choice of Comparators in Equal Pay Claims" (2005) 34(4) I.L.J. 338, at 343.

[75] *Enderby v Frenchay HA* Case C-127/92, [1994] I.C.R. 112, at para.23, ECJ. See further below, paras 9–026 and 9–033.

[76] [2005] I.C.R. 750, at para.29.

[77] [2000] I.C.R., see below, para.9–030. 196. See also *Strathclyde Regional Council v Wallace* [1998] I.C.R. 205, HL.

departments, which reinforces the view of the Civil Service as a single amorphous entity."[78] Where private sector employers do this, but retain some control over its workers, by say the use of mobility clauses, the distinction between the autonomous establishment and the ultimate employer becomes even more blurred. The ECJ in *Lawrence* was concerned that it could not identify a body responsible for the inequality which could restore equal pay. No such problem exists in single-employer cases.

The most obvious effect of *Robertson* (should it survive appeal) will be to encourage private employers to follow their Government's lead and create separate establishments, each with autonomous management, with the consequence of avoiding the equal pay legislation operating across those establishments.[79] As noted above, after many battles, female cooks in a shipyard could compare their jobs to painters, whilst cleaners at a coal mine may compare themselves to clerical staff, and motor factory seamstresses may compare themselves to repair workers.[80] At its worse, *Robertson* suggests that an employer may locate its cooks, cleaners and seamstresses in separate establishments with separate bargaining, and then restore these predominantly female occupations to inferior pay, turning back the clock some 30 years and frustrating the harmonising ambition of Art.141.

4. LIKE WORK—SECTION 1(2)(*a*)

9–016 Section 1(4) EPA 1970 provides that:

> A woman is to be regarded as employed on like work with men if, but only if, her work and theirs is of the same or a broadly similar nature, and the difference (if any) between the things she does and the things they do are not of practical importance in relation to terms and conditions of employment; and accordingly in comparing her work with theirs regard shall to be had to the frequency or otherwise with which any such differences occur in practice as well as to the nature of the differences.

Tribunals should approach this question in two stages. First, they should decide if the comparator's work is the same, or of a "broadly similar nature". Second, they should consider if any differences are of "practical importance".

---

[78] I. Steele, "Tracing the Single Source: Choice of Comparators in Equal Pay Claims" (2005) 34(4) I.L.J. 338, at 343.

[79] Steele suggests that *Robertson* may be distinguished on the ground that the departmentalisation in the civil service was created by statute. See above fn 78, (2005) 34 I.L.J. 338, at 344.

[80] See, respectively, *Hayward v Cammell Laird Shipbuilders (No.2)* [1988] A.C. 894; *British Coal v Smith* [1996] I.C.R. 515; *The Independent* May 14, 1991, *The Guardian* March 11, 1991.

(1) "Broadly Similar"

"Broadly similar" simply means that a tribunal "should not be **9–017** required to undertake a too minute an examination"[81] of the respective jobs. In *Capper Pass v Lawton*,[82] Ms Lawton cooked 10 to 20 lunches per day for managers and directors and worked a 40 hour week. Her comparator cooked 350 meals per day in the staff canteen and worked a 45½ hour week. The EAT held that Ms Lawton did like work to her comparator.

Perversely, back in 1977, the EAT suggested that was not possible for a woman to compare herself to man doing *inferior* work for more pay.[83] However, the ECJ, in *Murphy v Bord Telecom Eireann*[84] stated (in an equal value case), that such logic should not prevail, because otherwise it would "be tantamount to rendering the principle of equal pay ineffective and nugatory. . . . an employer would easily be able to circumvent the principle by assigning additional or more onerous duties to workers of a particular sex, who could then be paid a lower wage." This logic applies equally to like-work cases, and so s.1(4) be given a purposive interpretation.

(2) Differences of "Practical Importance"

The point of the second stage is to remove spurious or theoretical **9–018** differences, when the jobs are, in reality, broadly the same. In *Shields v Coomes Holdings*,[85] male workers in a betting shop were paid more because they had special responsibility for security in shops considered particularly vulnerable to robbery, aggravation and hassle. The Court of Appeal held that this difference was of no practical importance. First, in fact no such problems ever arose, so the men's extra duties were theoretical. Second, the men had no special qualifications to deal with trouble. They were given these responsibilities simply because they were men. As Lord Denning, MR observed, women could be just as capable of dealing with trouble, rather as a barmaid might deal with trouble differently from a barman. Alternatively, a woman may carry a strong physical presence, whilst "a small nervous man . . . could not say 'boo to a goose.'"[86]

Under Art.141 the ECJ—in the Vienna Area Health Fund case[87]— has taken a similar, and perhaps slightly narrower approach, apparently suggesting that persons doing similar tasks, but with different

---

[81] *per* Phillips, J., *Capper Pass v Lawton* [1977] Q.B. 852, at 857, EAT.

[82] *ibid.*

[83] Unless the difference is of no practical importance: *Waddington v Leicester Council for Voluntary Service* [1977] I.C.R. 266, at 270–271.

[84] Case 157/86, [1988] I.C.R. 445, at para.10.

[85] [1978] I.C.R. 1159, CA.

[86] *ibid.*, at 1172.

[87] *Angestelltenbetriebsrat der Wiener Gebietskrankenhasse v Wiener Gebietskrankenkasse* Case C-309/97, [1999] I.R.L.R. 804.

qualifications, were not comparable. The persons were qualified doctors and qualified psychologists working alongside each other as psychotherapists, save that the doctors could be called upon to perform other tasks in an emergency. It was not clear from the case whether the Court considered this "emergency" duty real or theoretical. If theoretical, then the Equal Pay Act (according to *Shields v Coomes*) goes further than Art.141.

9–019   Of course, where the difference is real, there is a practical difference for the purpose of the Equal Pay Act 1970. The difference may of supervision, responsibility, or skills. In *Eaton v Nuttall*[88] Phillips, J. gave the example of "two book-keepers working side by side doing, so far as actions were concerned, almost identical work, where on an examination of the importance of the work done it could be seen that one was a senior book-keeper and another a junior book-keeper." In *Eaton v Nuttall* the claimant was a production scheduler responsible for ordering supplies of 2,400 items up to a value of £2.50 each. Her male comparator was also a production scheduler who looked after 1,200 items worth between £5 and £1,000. The EAT held that that as a mistake by the man could prove more expensive, he had more responsibility, and this practical difference meant that he was not doing like work. In *Baker v Rochdale HA*[89] a male district nurse was paid more because he assumed a teaching, training and advisory role in catheterisation (withdrawal of fluid from the body's natural orifices). He had gained the extra experience which enabled him to do this because of a rule that nurses may only administer catheters to persons of the same sex, and as he was just one out of many female nurses he administered far more than any single female nurse. The EAT found the male nurse did not do like work and could not be used as a comparator.

The time when work is performed is not relevant to comparison. In *Dugdale v Kraft Foods*[90] female quality control inspectors compared themselves with male quality control inspectors from another department, who were paid a higher basic wage. Unlike the women, these men worked night shifts every third Sunday, (and received a separate premium for doing so). The EAT held that the men were doing like work, the only difference being the time at which it was done, which was not a practical difference.[91] It may be that the nature of the night work carries extra burdens and so is not like work to its daytime counterpart. In *Thomas v National Coal Board*[92] female daytime canteen workers used a male night-time canteen worker as a comparator. Here

---

[88] [1977] I.C.R. 272, at 277, EAT.
[89] EAT/295/91 (unreported).
[90] [1977] I.C.R. 48.
[91] Approved by Lord Denning, M.R. in *Shields v Coomes Holdings* [1978] I.C.R. 1159, who also noted that this was required by Art.141 EC Treaty (at 1171). The position is the same in the United States, see *Corning Glass Works v Brennan* 417 US 188 (Sup Ct 1974).
[92] [1987] I.C.R. 757, EAT.

it was found that the night work inherently carried extra responsibility because with less people on duty the night staff would have to deal with emergencies.

Of course it will be more difficult to recruit for unsocial hours and nightshifts, and if the law prevented a pay difference, recruitment would be near to impossible. Thus, the law allows employers to pay a separate premium to account for the undesirable hours, but this premium must be objectively justified. This is discussed below, at para.9–035.

5. Work Rated as Equivalent—Section 1(2)(*b*)[93]

Where an employer has carried out a job evaluation scheme, a woman may use the results of that scheme to bring claim of equal pay. So where her job was rated as equivalent to the job of a male employee, she may use that employee as her comparator. He does not have to be doing like work, so long as the work was rated as equivalent under the scheme, for instance, a shipyard cook could be rated as doing equivalent work to a shipyard painter. A scheme may also be used by employers when defending an equal pay claim.[94] The scheme can be relied on for a claim even if it has not been implemented,[95] but the parties who agreed to carry out the study must have accepted its validity.[96]

9–020

(1) Validity of the Scheme

The Equal Pay Act 1970 demands that the scheme is "analytical" and free from sex discrimination.

Section 1(5), EPA 1970, provides:

9–021

> A woman is to be regarded as employed on work rated as equivalent with that of any men if, but only if, her job and their job have been given an equal value, in terms of the demand made on a worker under various headings (for instance effort, skill, decision), on a study made with a view to evaluating in those terms the jobs to be done by all or any of the employees in an undertaking or group of undertakings, or would have been given an

[93] See generally: A. Ghobadian, "Job Evaluation: Trade Union and Staff Association Representatives' Perspectives," Employee Relations, Vol.12, Iss 4, (1990) Emerald; D. Biman and A. Garcia-Diaz, "Factor selection guidelines for job evaluation: A computerised statistical procedure," Computer and Industrial Engineering, Vol.40, Iss 3, p.259 (2001), Elsevier Science Ltd; A Lofstrom, "Can job evaluation improve women's wages?" Applied Economics, Vol.31, Iss 9, p.1053 (1999), Routledge.

[94] EPA 1970, s.1(2)(c). See below, paras 9–024—9–025.

[95] *O'Brien v Sim-Chem Ltd* [1980] I.C.R. 573, HL. (Scheme not implemented because of Government pay policy).

[96] *Arnold v Beecham Group* [1982] I.C.R. 744, at 752, EAT.

equal value but for the evaluation being made on a system setting different values for men and women on the same demand under any heading.

(a) "Analytical"

9–022 The evaluation must be analytical. This means that the jobs of each worker should be valued in terms of the demand made on the worker under various headings, such as training, responsibility and skill. A more expansive definition was given in *Eaton v Nuttall*[97] where the EAT stated that the scheme should be:

> . . . thorough in analysis and capable of impartial application. It should be possible by applying the study to arrive at the position of a particular employee at a particular point in a particular salary grade without taking other matters into account except those unconnected with the nature of the work. It will be in order to take into account such matters as merit or seniority, etc, but any matters concerning the work (e.g. responsibility) one would expect to find taken care of in the evaluation study. One which does not satisfy that test, and requires the management to make a subjective judgment concerning the nature of the work before the employee can be fitted into the appropriate place in the appropriate salary grade, would seem to us not to be a valid study for the purpose of subsection (5).

In *Bromley v Quick*[98] a job evaluation study measured some of the jobs by the demands on the worker, and attributing a value (or weighting) to each demand. The factors used were: skill/training/experience (43 per cent); mental demands (37 per cent); responsibility (10 per cent); physical environment (7 per cent); and external contacts (3 per cent). After the calculations were done, these jobs were ranked. Then other jobs not covered by the study were "slotted in" using a subjective judgment of how the job, *as a whole,* compared with those ranked in by the study. The Court of Appeal held that the scheme was analytical and objective but for the last stage ("slotting in"), which was a fatal flaw, and for that reason it did not comply with s.1(5). Further, it was not saved by a right to appeal given by the employer. However, the court appreciated that any objective scheme inherently will involve some subjective, or value, judgments, such as the weightings accorded to the job factors.[99]

---

[97] [1977] I.C.R. 272, at 278–279.
[98] [1988] I.C.R. 623, CA.
[99] *ibid.*, at 632.

(2) Sex Discrimination

The final phrase to s.1(5) ("or would have been given an equal value **9–023** but for the evaluation being made on a system setting different values for men and women on the same demand under any heading") gives a power to tribunals to adjust the results where the scheme directly discriminates on the ground of sex. Where the scheme contains some indirect sex discrimination (such as according disproportionate weighting to typically male qualities, e.g. physical strength), an equal value claim should be brought. The discrimination inherent in the scheme will prevent the employer relying on it as a defence. (See below, "(1) Job Evaluation Schemes and Sex Discrimination" para.9–025).

6. Equal Value—Section 1(2)(c)[100]

Section 1(2)(c) entitles a woman to compare herself with a man doing **9–024** a different job, so long as it is work of equal value (rather than just "like work"). In *Hayward v Cammell Laird Shipbuilders Ltd (No.2)*,[101] Ms Hayward, a canteen cook in a shipyard, was able to compare her work to that of a painter, a decorator and a thermal insulation engineer. The claimant may also compare herself to a man doing work of a lesser value.[102] A claimant is *reasonably* free to choose her comparator. In *Pickstone v Freemans*[103] the House of Lords held that a woman could use a comparator doing different work (of the same value) for more money, even though there was another man doing the same work, for the same money. The policy behind this decision is to prevent employers using a token male worker in a predominantly female occupation to avoid "equal value" claims: for instance, a supermarket employing a lone male on the checkouts, whilst paying more to the predominantly male shelf-stackers who are doing work of equal value. This also makes sense in more complex cases. Equal value claims can be fraught with evidential difficulties, and at an early stage, a woman may suspect that she is doing work of equal value to several men, each in a different job on different pay. The quandary for the claimant is that if she plumps for a comparator very obviously doing work of equal or lesser value, the resulting pay increase is likely to be minimal. If she opts for the man on the highest pay, her chances of proving that he is doing work of equal value are likely to be reduced. To achieve an optimal result, a claimant may bring several comparators into court. But she may face hostility from the tribunal, inspired by this observation made by the Lord Bridge:

---

[100] See J. Gregory, "Dynamite or damp squib—an assessment of equal value law" (1997) 2 I.J.D.L. 167.

[101] [1988] A.C. 894, HL.

[102] *Murphy v Bord Telecom Eireann* Case 157/86, [1988] I.C.R. 445, ECJ, see further above para.9–017.

[103] [1988] I.C.R. 697, HL. See further, above para.9–004.

"I think that industrial tribunals should, so far as possible, be alert to prevent abuse of the equal value claims procedure by applicants who cast their net over too wide a spread of comparators. To take an extreme case, an applicant who claimed equality with A who earns £X and also with B who earns £2X could hardly complain if an industrial tribunal concluded that her claim of equality with A itself demonstrated that there were no reasonable grounds for her claim of equality with B."[104]

This "extreme case" is not a helpful guide for tribunals when deciding if claimants have "cast their net too wide". All that can be taken from this dictum is that too many comparators may amount to an abuse of process. Tribunals are well familiar with abuse of process principles and should have no trouble applying them in this context.

At the hearing a tribunal may either proceed with the case, or request a report from an independent expert evaluating the claimant's and comparator(s) jobs.[105] The most obvious obstacle to a claim at the early stage is the existence of a job evaluation study already carried out by the employer, which places the claimant below the value of her comparator(s). This will defeat a claim[106] unless the tribunal has reasonable grounds for suspecting that it is not valid or it was made on a system that discriminates of the ground of sex. So, to defeat a claim the scheme must (a) place the claimant's job on lesser value than her comparator(s); (b) be valid;[107] and (c) not be tainted with direct or indirect sex discrimination.

(1) Job Evaluation Schemes and Sex Discrimination

9–025 Where the scheme contains direct sex discrimination, it may be ruled invalid under s.1(5).[108] In any case s.2A(2A)(3) provides that an evaluation in a study discriminates "where a difference, or coincidence, between values set by that system on different demands under the same or different headings is not justifiable irrespective of the sex of the person on whom those demands are made." This deals with direct and indirect sex discrimination.

What does, and does not, amount to sex discrimination in job evaluation schemes was shown in *Rummler v Dato-Druck GmbH*,[109] where the ECJ stated that so far as the nature of the work allows, factors should

---

[104] *Leverton v Clwyd CC* [1989] A.C. 706, at 751–752, HL. The House concurred in Lord Bridge's speech.
[105] EPA 1970, s.2A(1). The option of striking out a claim for showing "no reasonable grounds" that the work was of equal value was repealed by the Equal Pay Act 1970 (Amendment) Regulations 2004, SI 2004/2352, reg.2, in force, October 1, 2004.
[106] See EPA 1970, s.1(2)(c).
[107] Discussed above, under "(1) Validity of the Scheme", para.9–021.
[108] *ibid.*
[109] Case 237/85, [1987] I.C.R. 774.

be attributed to it which do not discriminate on the ground of sex. So factors generally favouring women or men can be used where the nature of the job demands it. In *Rummler*, the pay scale in the printing industry was divided into seven grades. The factors used were previous knowledge required, concentration, effort and exertion, and responsibility. According to the scheme, Grade II jobs could be performed with little previous knowledge and a short training period, a low level of precision, a slight to medium muscular effort, and a slight to medium level of responsibility. Grade III jobs could be performed with a medium previous knowledge and training period, a medium level of precision, a medium to high muscular effort, and a low to medium level of responsibility. Grade IV jobs required previous knowledge gained through task-specific training or, on occasion, lengthy experience on the job, a medium level of precision, medium to high levels of exertion of various kinds, and a medium level of responsibility.

The case centred on the use of physical exertion as a factor. The claimant, a woman classified as Grade II, was required to pack parcels weighing in excess of 20 kg, which *for her* was heavy (rather than medium to heavy) physical work. Accordingly she argued that she should be placed on (a higher) Grade VI. The ECJ rejected this argument, as it would in effect introduce a subjective factor (the strength of the individual, rather than that required by the job). Given that generally men have more physical strength, this would amount to positive sex discrimination.

The general principle of proportionality in European law means that in addition, each factor should be given a proportionate weighting in the overall scheme. If say, a job required tactful customer relations (favouring females) and physical strength (favouring males), the scheme should not give a disproportionate weighting to the physical strength factor.

7. The Defence of Objective Justification

Once the claimant has established a prima facie case, the burden shifts **9–026** to the defendant to "objectively justify" the difference in pay. The formula for justification was provided by the ECJ in *Bilka-Kaufhaus v Weber von Hartz*,[110] which itself is rooted in the Community law principle of proportionality,[111] and is generally known as the "*Bilka* test". The employer must show (1) there was a legitimate aim, and that the means of achieving the legitimate aim were (2) appropriate, and (3) necessary.

---

[110] Case 170/84, [1987] I.C.R. 110 (discussed paras 9–003 and 9–032).
[111] See the *Cassis de Dijon* case, C-120/78 (*Rewe-Zentral AG v Bundesmonopolverwaltung für Branntwein*) [1979] E.C.R. 649.

"Necessity" encapsulates two stages. The defence should not succeed where there exists a less discriminatory alternative. For instance, in *Enderby v Frenchay Health Authority*[112] the employer paid pharmacists (63 per cent female) 40 per cent more than speech therapists (98 per cent female). There was a need to attract a sufficient number of pharmacists (the "legitimate aim"), so they were paid more (an appropriate means), but only a 10 per cent premium was *necessary* to achieve that aim, so only 10 per cent of the pay difference could be justified. In other words, there existed a less discriminatory alternative of paying pharmacists a 10 per cent premium. In addition, a court may have to balance any discriminatory effect of the challenged practice against the benefits of achieving the legitimate aim. For instance, in *R. v Secretary of State for Employment, Ex p. Equal Opportunities Commission*[113] Lord Keith held that Regulations that afforded lesser benefits to part-time workers constituted a "gross breach of the principle of equal pay and could not be possibly regarded as a suitable means of achieving an increase in part-time employment."

(1) Legitimate Factors in the Defence

9–027 The domestic version of the defence is set out in s.1(3) of the Equal Pay Act 1970, and provides that the employer must prove that the variation is genuinely due to a material factor which is not the difference of sex, and (a) (for claims of like work or work rated as equivalent) that must be a material difference between the woman's case and the man's, or (b) (in equal value claims) may be such a material difference.

This wording requires some explanation. When the Act was introduced the defence was intended to allow for factors such as "length of service, merit, output and so on . . . provided that the payments are available to any person who qualifies regardless of sex."[114] These factors are limited to those which are part of the "personal equation" between the woman and her comparator.[115] However, the ECJ in *Bilka* stated that "economic reasons" could used to defend a claim of indirectly discriminatory equal pay, by part-time (predominantly female) workers. And so paragraph (b) was added with the key word "may", which broadens the defence beyond just personal factors in equal value claims.

Another feature of the original draft is that the factors appear to be ones not used when comparing the jobs of the claimant and comparator. Job evaluation schemes, for instance, must be objective, and measure the *demands* of the job, rather than the personal attributes of worker. The defence allows these personal attributes to justify a differ-

---

[112] Case C-127/92, [1994] I.C.R. 112, ECJ.
[113] [1995] 1 AC 1, at 30, HL.
[114] Secretary of State for Employment, Barbara Castle, 795 HC Debs, 920, February 9, 1970.
[115] *Clay Cross (Quarry Services) Ltd v Fletcher* [1979] I.C.R. 1, at 6 and 10, CA.

ence in pay. But in *Christie v Haithe*[116] the EAT held that factors used in the job evaluation could also be relied on as factors for the objective justification. The comparators' work was slightly more heavy and dirty. Nonetheless, the tribunal found their work to be of equal value. But then it held the pay difference was justified because the comparators were doing slightly heavier and more dirty work. Not only is the reasoning perverse, it clouds this already difficult process. All litigants would benefit if they knew there were clear boundaries between the factors available to the comparison and the defence. If the tribunal in *Christie v Haithe* considered the comparators' work significantly more demanding, then it should not have held it was work of equal value. If it considered the work insignificantly more demanding, then it should not have considered it significant for the defence. If it considered the work was of equal value because of other counter-balancing factors in favour of the claimant, such as responsibility, then it was perverse to include only some of the factors in question of justification. For these reasons it is better to keep factors for the comparison (objective demands of the job) and factors for the defence, mutually exclusive.

The US Equal Pay Act 1963, specifies three examples: seniority, merit, and quality or quantity of work as legitimate factors to defend a claim. In addition it allows for any other "factor other than sex." The legislative history suggests that this includes:

9–028

> "among other things, shift differentials, restrictions on or differences based on time of day worked, hours of work, lifting or moving heavy objects, differences based on experience, training, or ability would also be excluded. It also recognizes . . . 'red circle rates.'"[117]

In addition "salary retention" policies to attract or retain certain workers are recognised as a legitimate factor.[118]

(2) Transparency

Some pay structures and levels have often developed piecemeal and it may be difficult or impossible for the employer to show the extent to which particular factors contribute to overall pay. Nonetheless, the employer caries the onus of explaining any pay difference. In *Danfoss*,[119] the ECJ held that if a female worker establishes, in relation to a relatively large number of employees, that the average pay for

9–029

---

[116] [2003] I.R.L.R. 670, applying *Davies v McCartneys* [1989] I.C.R. 707, EAT.
[117] House Comm on Equal Pay Act of 1963, HR Rep No.309 (1963), reported *Taylor v White* 321 F 3d 710, at 718 (8th Cir 2003).
[118] *Taylor v White* 321 F 3d 710, at 718–719 (8th Cir 2003).
[119] *Handels-og Kontorfunktionaerernes Forbund i Danmark v Dansk Arbejdsgiverforening (acting for Danfoss)* Case 109/88, [1989] I.R.L.R. 532, at para.16. See also *Barton v Investec* [2003] I.C.R. 1205, EAT, below para.9–035.

women is less than that for men, and the employer's system of pay is "totally lacking in transparency," it is for the employer to prove that his pay system is not discriminatory.

(3) Fair Pay and Equal Pay

9–030 In *Glasgow City Council v Marshall*[120] special-school instructors were doing the same work as teachers for less pay. Seven female instructors compared themselves with a male teacher. At the same time, a *male* instructor compared himself with a female teacher. However, there was no sex disparity between the two groups (females made up about 96 per cent instructors and 97 per cent teachers). The House of Lords held that by showing a difference in pay, the claimants raised a rebuttable presumption of sex discrimination.[121] The House then applied the "genuine material factor" defence of the Equal Pay Act, and held simply that as the employer had shown there "is not the difference of sex", it was not required to justify the difference in pay.

Marshall seems to have been understood to mean that employers are only obliged to justify a difference in pay in cases of indirect discrimination (i.e. where a facially neutral factor adversely affects a higher proportion of women than men): where there is no adverse effect upon women generally, and the cause is a facially neutral factor (say performance-related pay), there is no onus on the employer to justify any difference in pay. Hence in *Parliamentary Commissioner for Administration v Fernandez*[122] the EAT held that an employer did not have to justify performance-related pay in any sense, (i.e. show that the extra pay was proportionate and that any discriminatory effect was outweighed by its need). Judge Peter Clark based this decision on *Marshall.* This clearly is inconsistent with ECJ jurisprudence. In *Brunnhofer*[123] the ECJ stated that the principle of equal pay "prohibits comparable situations from being treated differently unless the difference is objectively justified." This statement, referring to different treatment, obviously is not confined to cases of indirect discrimination. The facts support this. A female bank worker was paid less than a male doing the same work, ostensibly because his work was of a higher standard. The ECJ held that the pay difference had to be objectively justified.

The confusion flows from a basic difference between equal pay law and conventional discrimination law. In conventional discrimination claims, the claimant must show either a difference in treatment based

[120] [2000] I.C.R. 196.
[121] *ibid.,* at p.203.
[122] [2004] I.C.R. 123. Followed in *Villalba v Merrill Lynch & Co* (2006) unreported, UKEAT/0223/05/LA (see *www.employmentappeals.go.uk*). Contrast *Sharp v Caledonia Group Services Ltd* [2006] I.C.R. 218. At the time of writing *Fernandez* was due in the CA.
[123] *Brunnhofer v Bank der Österreichischen Postsparkasse* Case C-381/99, [2001] I.R.L.R. 571, at para.28.

on sex (direct discrimination) or that the same treatment caused a disparate impact upon women (indirect discrimination). For straightforward equal pay claims, the claimant need show no more than a difference in pay with that of her comparator, to establish a prima facie case. And by establishing a prima facie case, the claimant raises a presumption of sex discrimination, which the employer must rebut.[124] This begs the question: what is meant by sex discrimination under equal pay law? Claims can be analysed as three kinds. First, there is direct discrimination, where the employer pays a woman less because she is a woman. This cannot be justifiable where the difference is based entirely on sex. Second, there is indirect discrimination, where a facially neutral factor (such as inferior pay for part-timers) adversely affects a higher proportion of women than men. Here the adverse impact must be objectively justified. In addition, there is a third class, peculiar to equal pay law. Here, a claimant shows that she is paid less than her comparator for doing equal work, but without having to show the reason why. No one else in the workplace bar the claimant and her comparator comes into this equation. *Fernandez* and *Brunnhofer* are such examples. What distinguishes this class from the first two is that there are no significant statistics to show a disparate impact on women generally, and there is not necessarily an apparent reason for the pay difference. Assuming that the cause is *not* a facially discriminatory one, the relevant question for the present purpose is whether there can be sex discrimination when there are only two persons in the equation, one woman and one man. The history of equal pay confirms that the answer is yes.[125]

Thus where a prima facie case is raised, such as in *Fernandez* (and indeed *Marshall*), the employer must at the least be obliged to rebut the presumption of sex discrimination. In *Marshall* this was done by showing that the two-person equation was facade. Where this is not done, rebuttal means more than just showing that the cause was a neutral factor (*Brunnhofer*). But in *Fernandez* the employer did no more than this. Further, the employer was not compelled to make its pay policy transparent, a requirement under Art.141.[126] For these reasons *Fernandez* must be considered wrong in principle and contrary

9–031

---

[124] "The scheme of the [Equal Pay] Act is that a rebuttable presumption of sex discrimination arises once the gender-based comparison shows that a woman, doing like work or work rated as equivalent or work of equal value to that of a man, is being paid or treated less favourably than the man. The variation between her contract and the man's contract is presumed to be due to the difference in sex." *per* Lord Nichols, giving the judgment in *Glasgow City Council v Marshal* [2000] I.C.R. 196, at 203 HL. See also above, para.9–004.

[125] e.g. *Capper Pass v Lawton* [1977] Q.B. 852, EAT, see above 9–017; *Pickstone v Freemans* [1988] I.C.R. 697, HL, see above para.9–004; *Barton v Investec* [2003] I.C.R. 1205, EAT, see below, para.9–035.

[126] *Handels-og Kontorfunktionaerernes Forbund i Danmark v Dansk Arbejdsgiverforening (acting for Danfoss)* Case 109/88, [1989] I.R.L.R. 532, at para.16 (above para.9–029); *Barton v Investec* [2003] I.C.R. 1205, EAT, below para.9–004. See also EOC Code of Practice on Equal Pay, 2003, EOC, ISBN 1 84206 094 5, at para.70.

to Community law. The case has escaped much criticism, mainly because the claimant was a *man,* so easily labelled a "fair-pay" claim

The fear seems to be that *Brunnhofer* could be used to force employers to justify all *differences* in pay between men and women and open the door to "fair pay" claims.[127] But as *Marshall* demonstrates, fair pay claims can be defeated using the genuine material factor defence. It should not be misused to brand automatically claims of this third class as "fair pay" cases.

(4) The Defence in Operation

(a) Economic Reasons

9–032 In *Jenkins v Kingsgate (Clothing Productions) Ltd,*[128] the ECJ held that lower pay (measured pro-rata) for (predominantly female) part-time workers could be justified by economic factors, which were in this case encouraging full-time work to achieve better utilisation of the employer's machinery and to discourage absenteeism. An "economic reason" was also approved in *Bilka,*[129] where a department store wanted to discourage part-time work (by excluding part-time workers from its pension scheme), because part-time workers generally refuse to work late afternoons and Saturdays.

(b) Market Forces

9–033 In *Rainey v Greater Glasgow Health Board*[130] in order to establish a new NHS prosthetic service, 20 existing private-sector prosthetists were recruited on their private-sector wage. All 20 were men. Subsequent recruits were paid on the lower Whitley scale, a national agreement for ancillary health service staff. A newly recruited female prosthetist claimed equal pay with the higher paid men. The House of Lords held that the pay difference was justified by the need to attract from the private sector in order to establish the service. The law was refined in *Enderby v Frenchay Health Authority*[131] where the employer paid pharmacists (63 per cent female) 40 per cent more than speech therapists (98 per cent female), apparently to attract a sufficient number of pharmacists. But the evidence was that only a 10 per cent premium was necessary to achieve that aim, so only a 10 per cent pay difference was justified. Thus, employers must be able to show with

---

[127] See e.g., Elias, J. (President) in *Villalba v Merrill Lynch & Co* (2006) unreported, UKEAT/0223/05/LA (see *www.employmentappeals.go.uk*) at para.183.

[128] Case 96/80, [1981] E.C.R. 911, para.12 (ECJ), applied by the EAT [1981] I.C.R. 715, esp at pp.723–724.

[129] *Bilka-Kaufhaus v Weber von Hartz* Case 170/84, [1987] I.C.R. 110, at para.36, ECJ.

[130] [1987] A.C. 224. See "Market forces and the equal value material factor defence" (1986) 5 EOR 5.

[131] Case C-127/92, [1994] I.C.R. 112, ECJ.

some precision that *all* the difference can be attributed to the market forces.

In principle a defence of market forces is questionable. As Lord Denning M.R. observed in *Clay Cross (Quarry Services) Ltd v Fletcher*:[132] "An employer cannot avoid his obligations under the Act by saying: 'I paid him more because he asked for more,' or 'I paid her less because she was willing to come for less.' If any such excuse were permitted, the Act would be a dead letter. Those are the very reasons why there was unequal pay before the statute." In *Clay Cross* the claimant sales clerk sought equal pay with a male sales clerk appointed on higher pay, to match his previous wage. The Court of Appeal held that this market forces factor fell outside of the "personal equation" between the claimant and the comparator. The House of Lords in *Rainey* stated that this was "unduly restrictive",[133] but at the same time approved of Browne-Wilkinson, J.'s, observation in *Jenkins v Kingsgate* that market forces reasons should not include obtaining "cheap female labour."[134] This suggests that not all market forces factors can be used, and the *decision* of *Clay Cross* has survived *Rainey*. In *Ratcliffe v North Yorkshire CC*[135] school catering assistants claimed equal pay with men in jobs such as road sweepers and gardeners, with whom they had been rated as equivalent under the local government revaluation scheme. Their pay was lower to compete with private contractors for the supply of school meals. The House of Lords rejected this defence. The feature of *Ratcliffe* was lower wages for a predominantly female occupation, and whatever the technical difficulties with the decision, it is supportable on policy grounds.

(c) Collective Bargaining

In *Enderby* (see above) the pay difference between the speech therapists and the pharmacists came about (in part, at least) as a result of separate collective bargaining. The ECJ held that an employer could not justify a discriminatory pay difference on the ground that it was the result of separate collective bargaining.

9–034

(d) Merit and Bonus Payments

In principle these are permissible, so long as the system is transparent, and the payments are proportionate. In *Danfoss*[136] a collective agreement allowed the employer to make additional payments to individuals within a grade on the basis of the employee's "flexibility", which

9–035

---

[132] [1979] I.C.R. 1, at 6, CA.
[133] [1987] A.C. 224, at 235.
[134] *ibid.*, at 237, citing [1981] I.C.R. 715, at 727, EAT.
[135] [1995] I.C.R. 837.
[136] *Handels-og Kontorfunktionaerernes Forbund i Danmark v Dansk Arbejdsgiverforening (acting for Danfoss)* Case 109/88 [1989] I.R.L.R. 532.

was defined as including an assessment of their capacity, quality of work, autonomy of work and responsibilities. In addition, pay could be increased on the basis of the employee's vocational training and seniority. But the workers were only informed of the amount of their increased wages. They could not determine the relationship of any particular criterion to the increases. Thus workers were unable to compare their additional payments even against workers within the same grade. The average pay of women was 6.85 per cent less than that of men. The ECJ held that once the claimant had shown lower average wage for women, the "total lack of transparency" meant that it was for the employer to show that the system was not discriminatory. The Court further noted first, that payments for higher quality work were gender-neutral, but at the same it was "inconceivable" that the women's work was of generally lower quality. So if the difference in pay shows that a gender neutral criterion had been *applied* in a discriminatory manner, it was not justifiable. Second, that a criterion of "flexibility" in the sense of being able to work various times, or at different locations, may operate to the disadvantage of women who will generally find it more difficult to organise their working time in a flexible manner. This, of course, will prove much more difficult to justify. Third, employers may justify rewarding specific vocational training by demonstrating that that training is of importance for the performance of the specific duties entrusted to the worker.

This approach was taken up by the EAT in *Barton v Investec Henderson Crosthwaite Securities*.[137] The claimant was a City fund manager. She earned the same basic salary (£105,000) as her comparator, and was awarded 7,500 share options. Other firms tried to poach the comparator, and to avoid the prospect of him being head-hunted, his salary was raised to £150,000, he was given a "long-term incentive" payment of £75,000, and awarded 12,000 share options. The employer produced no evidence as to the basis upon which bonuses could be paid, disclosing only the payments made to the claimant and her comparator. The employment tribunal found that the difference in pay was justified, stating that "it is a vital component of the City bonus culture that bonuses are discretionary, scheme rules are unwritten and individuals' bonuses are not revealed," and that "the cultural reason for this is that invidious comparisons would become inevitable. If such comparisons were generally possible the bonus system would collapse."[138] The EAT held that the tribunal was in error to endorse this lack of transparency and that it was for the employer to prove that sex was not a reason for difference in pay.

Where the bonus or premium is unrealistic, disproportionate, or even a sham, the tribunal should adjust the wages so that the premium

---

[137] [2003] I.C.R. 1205, EAT.
[138] Reported *ibid.*, at para.10.

does no more than properly reflect its legitimate aim. Most litigation on this issue has arisen with premiums paid for working undesirable hours. In *National Coal Board v Sherwin*[139] the industrial tribunal heard evidence that inconvenient hours should attract a 20 per cent premium and adjusted the wage structure accordingly. The EAT approved. The difficulty with this is that it resembles wage-setting, a task beyond a tribunal's jurisdiction. Nonetheless, in *Enderby v Frenchay AHA*[140] the ECJ took a similar line, but with the rider that where it is not possible to determine how much of the pay difference is due to market forces, it must decide if market forces can justify the whole difference. This rider appears to encourage a lack of transparency in premiums. However, as the ECJ stated in *Danfoss*[141] a prima facie case of equal pay will force an employer to make it wage structure transparent, otherwise it will not be able to show that the difference is not due to sex. Thus, if an employer comes to court stating that premiums are paid to recruit night workers, but without any evidence of how much extra is required for this recruitment, it runs the risk of the whole premium being ruled as discriminatory.

In the US case *Shulzt v First Victoria National Bank*[142] the male comparators were paid extra because of their participation in training programmes which were "informal, unwritten, and, if not imaginary, consisted of little more than the recognition of the ability of employees to work their way up the ranks." Not surprisingly, these training programmes were held not to be "factors other than sex", and so could not be used to defend the equal pay claim.

(e) Seniority and Length of Service Benefits

A seniority system may allocate to workers ever-improving employ- **9–036** ment rights and benefits (such as priority for promotion), improved pay, pension entitlements, or other perks. Such a system also may be used when selecting for redundancy, especially when on a "last-in, first-out" basis.

Seniority systems based on experience may indirectly discriminate against women and some racial groups. This is because part-time workers (predominantly women) gather less experience in hours worked, or that more women than men have an interrupted career and/or have entered the labour market later in their lives. This latter feature will also affect recent immigrants. Where the seniority system adversely affects part-time workers, and in doing so, adversely affects women, it has to be justified, requiring objective justification based

---

[139] [1978] I.C.R. 700.
[140] Case C-127/92, [1994] I.C.R. 112. See further paras 9–026 and 9–033.
[141] *Handels-og Kontorfunktionaerernes Forbund i Danmark v Dansk Arbejdsgiverforening (acting for Danfoss)* Case C-109/88, [1989] I.R.L.R. 532, at paras 11–16. See further above para.9–029.
[142] 420 F 2d 648, at 654–655 (5th Cir 1969).

"on all the circumstances of each case."[143] Seniority systems may depend upon length of service, or duration of service (calculated pro rata, say on the basis of hours worked), or a mix of the two. The ECJ is strict here. Even where the system depends purely on the amount of time spent at work, it must be justified if it adversely affects part-timers. In *Kording*[144] the requirement to be exempt from an exam to qualify as a tax advisor was 15 years full-time service, or extended on a pro-rata basis for part-time workers. In other words, part-timers would need more than 15 years' service to accumulate the equivalent number of hours. The ECJ held that this had to be justified. (Ms Kording argued that in her 15 years' part-time service she handled the same quality of material as any full-timer, just less volume. Further, the 15 year rule was imposed solely to discourage workers from entering private practice.) In *Nimz*,[145] the pro rata system meant that part-timers had to work twice as many years as a full-timer to achieve the same grading. The defendant argued that full-time workers acquire their skills more quickly. The ECJ held that as a mere generalisation about a class of workers, this was not enough to justify the system, and that the employer should identify criteria specific to the job.

9–037   By extension, a seniority system that adversely affects women or racial groups by penalising full-time workers who have an interrupted and/or shorter career should be objectively justified as well. However, in *Danfoss*[146] the ECJ held that where a length-of-service criterion for higher pay adversely affected women in full-time work, it did *not* have to be justified, "since length of service goes hand in hand with experience and since experience generally enables the employee to perform his duties better, the employer is free to reward it without having to establish the importance it has in the performance of specific tasks entrusted to the employee." This suggests that the ECJ distinguishes between full-time and part-time workers. *Danfoss* predates *Kording, Nimz* and many other cases (that happened to involve part-time workers) where the Court has consistently rejected defences based on mere generalisations. Further, in *Hill v Revenue Commissioners*[147] the Court proclaimed that "Community policy in this area is to encourage and, if possible, adapt working conditions to family responsibilities. Protection of women within family life and in the course of their professional activities is . . . a principle . . . recognised by Community

---

[143] *Nikoloudi v Organismos Tilepikoinonion Ellados AE* Case C-196/02 (2005), at para.55, citing *Gerster v Freistaat Bayern* Case C-1/95, [1997] E.C.R. I-5253, at para.39; *Kording v Senator fur Finanzen* Case C-100/95, [1997] E.C.R. I-5289, at para.23; and *Nimz v Freie und Hansestadt Hamburg* Case C-184/89 [1991] ECR 1–297, at para.14. See also *Hill v Revenue Commissioners* Case C-243/95, [1999] I.C.R. 48, at para.43.

[144] *Kording v Senator fur Finanzen* Case C-100/95, [1997] E.C.R. I-5289, at para.23. See also *Nikoloudi, ibid.*

[145] *Nimz v Freie und Hansestadt Hamburg* Case C-184/89 [1991] E.C.R. 1-297.

[146] *Handels-og Kontorfunktionaerernes Forbund i Danmark v Dansk Arbejdsgiverforening (acting for Danfoss)* Case 109/88, [1991] I.C.R. 74, at para.25, ECJ.

[147] Case C-243/95, [1999] I.C.R. 48, at para.42.

law." *Danfoss* is so clearly out of line on these two points that its credibility as special rule for full-time workers is very weak. But until the ECJ expresses this, doubt remains. The opportunity will arise in *Cadman v Health and Safety Executive.*[148] In a challenge to a seniority system that adversely affected full-time female workers, the EAT felt bound to follow *Danfoss.* The Court of Appeal referred the matter to the ECJ, where the Advocate-General advised that the system had to be justified.[149] At the time of writing, the Court had yet to decide the matter.

In the United States, "bona fide seniority systems" are insulated from discrimination claims by a statutory exception.[150] The main ground of dispute has been where the system perpetuates past (lawful or unlawful) discrimination. In *International Brotherhood of Teamsters v United States*[151] the system divided drivers into two classes: local and intercity. Local drivers could not utilise their seniority within the class to attain intercity work. The local drivers were predominantly black because of (lawful) segregation practised before the Civil Rights Act 1964 came into force, and so the system perpetuated the segregation. The Supreme Court held that but for the statutory exception, the system would have been held unlawful. In *United Air Lines v Evans*[152] a female worker lost time on the seniority scale because she was (unlawfully) dismissed for being married and reinstated some years later. The Supreme Court held that even where it perpetuated past unlawful discrimination, the system could not be challenged. It seems that a system can only be challenged where it was created or applied in bad faith, thus disclosing intentional discrimination. In *Lorance v A & T Technologies*[153] a new seniority system, agreed with the trade union, reclassified the workforce into skilled (predominantly male) and semi-skilled (predominantly female) workers, so that the unskilled workers received many less benefits. This "conspiracy" to preserve the skilled jobs and attendant benefits to men was not a bona fide system and so could not be protected under the statutory exception.

(f) Red-circling

A person who is unable to continue with a job because of illness or redundancy, may be able to take an alternative job in the workplace. He may be retained and paid at his existing rate, and in some cases, continue to receive the customary pay rises due under his old job. Such workers are "red-circled" and cannot be used as comparators, because

9–038

---

[148] [2004] I.C.R. 378, EAT; [2005] I.C.R. 1546, CA. ECJ ref: Case C-17/05.
[149] Case C-17/05, at paras 33 and 66.
[150] Civil Rights Act 1964, s.703(h), 42 USC s.2000 e–2(h).
[151] 431 US 324 (1977).
[152] 431 US 553 (1977).
[153] 490 US 900 (Sup Ct 1989).

their pay is personal, and not related to the particular work that they do now. However, where their higher pay is rooted in sex discrimination, the red circle protection should not apply. In *Snoxell v Vauxhall Motors*[154] the employer decided that men and women machine-part inspectors were incorrectly graded, and so put them on a lower grade. The men's pay, having been arranged on a separate scale, was protected, and so the men, but not the women, were "red-circled" and paid at the previous higher rate. Some years later female inspectors made a like-work claim, using these men as comparators. The EAT held that the employer could not rely on the red-circling as a defence because past discrimination had contributed to the present difference in pay. This applies whether the cause was direct or indirect sex discrimination. Finally, where the red circling was not in any way tainted with sex discrimination, there was no reason why it should not continue "ageing and wasting until eventually it vanishes."[155]

(g) Mistakes

9–039 Where the comparator is paid more because of a genuine mistake, it seems that the employer is not obliged to justify the difference. In *Yorkshire Blood Transfusion Service v Plaskitt*[156] a male laboratory officer was appointed on point 23 of the Whitley wage scale by mistake (the rules allowed appointments up to point 21). An existing female laboratory officer on point 19 brought an equal pay claim. The EAT held that the mistake was genuine and not tainted with discrimination and so the employer was not obliged to justify the pay difference. It came to this result by holding that only in cases of indirect discrimination did the employer have to justify a pay difference.[157] Conversely, in *McPherson v Rathgael Centre for Children*[158] a female instructor brought an equal pay claim using as a comparator a newly recruited male instructor, who was put on higher pay by mistake. The Northern Ireland Court of Appeal held that any difference in pay had to be objectively justified, noting that it is not enough for the employer to show that it had no discriminatory intent.[159] However, the House of Lords in *Strathclyde Regional Council v Wallace*[160] stated that *McPherson* was wrongly decided, and approved of the *Plaskitt* decision.

---

[154] *Snoxell v Vauxhall Motors Ltd; Charles Early and Marriott (Witney) Ltd v Smith and Ball* [1978] 1 Q.B. 11.
[155] *ibid.*, at 32.
[156] [1994] I.C.R. 74.
[157] *ibid.*, at 81.
[158] [1991] I.R.L.R. 206, NICA.
[159] *ibid.*, at para.25.
[160] [1998] I.C.R. 205, at 214–215.

(h) Social Policy
Social policy justifications for equal pay and other discrimination **9–040**
claims are considered together Ch.6, para.6–041.

8. THE EFFECT OF THE EQUALITY CLAUSE

Section 1(1), EPA 1970 provides that if "the terms of a contract under **9–041**
which a woman is employed . . . do not include . . . an equality clause
they shall be deemed to include one". Section 1(2) provides that any
term of the contract which is less favourable than the man's is modified to provide equivalence, and where there is no such equivalent
term, such term effectively will be created by the tribunal's decision. A
new or modified term introduced to accord with the equality clause
remains part of the contract in the normal way. So, for example, it
cannot be "undone," should the comparator cease to do like work.[161]
   This means that the comparison must be on a term-by-term basis.
So, for example, basic pay, cash bonuses, perks (such as company car)
and sickness benefits, are not lumped together, so as to compare the
overall package each worker receives. Differences between pay pack-
ages occur more often in equal value claims, where the comparator,
doing different work, is likely to have been recruited on different
terms. The criticism of this approach is that can lead to mutual
enhancement, or leap-frogging. The woman without a car, gets one
because the man has one. Then the man, with inferior holiday rights,
gets them improved to match the woman's. She in turn, claims an
improved bonus scheme, to match the man's, and so on and so forth.
This argument was raised in *Hayward v Cammell Laird Shipbuilders
Ltd*,[162] where a female canteen cook in a shipyard was doing work of
equal value to a painter, a joiner and a thermal insulation engineer.
Whilst conceding that Ms Hayward received less basic pay than her
comparators, the employer argued that there was no obligation to
raise her basic pay to match the men's, because she had a paid meal
break, additional holidays and better sickness benefits which resulted
in her being *better* off than her comparators. Lord Goff rejected this
argument, reasoning that first, the genuine material factor defence
would prevent some mutual enhancement, and second, the wording of
the Act demanded a term-by-term approach, thus it was for
Parliament to make any amendment.[163]
   The same approach was taken by the ECJ in *Landsting*[164] where the
comparison was between the basic salaries of midwives and a clinical

---

[161] *Sorbie v Trust House Forte Hotels* [1976] 371 EAT.
[162] [1988] A.C. 894, HL. See E. Ellis, "A Welcome Victory for Equality" (1988) 51 M.L.R. 781.
[163] *ibid.*, at 908–909.
[164] *Jämställdhetsombudsmannen v Örebro Läns Landsting* Case C-236/98, [2001] I.C.R. 249. See
    also *Brunnhofer v Bank der Österreichischen Postsparkasse* Case C-381/99, [2001] I.R.L.R.
    571, ECJ.

technician; the "unsocial-hours" payment to the midwives was excluded from this comparison.

Despite the mutual enhancement fears, this is the correct approach. Comparing contracts as a whole would prove very difficult and contentious in practice, and there has been no evidence of a problem of leap-frogging since *Hayward*. Of course, the problem is minimised where employers to operate a transparent unified pay system.

CHAPTER 10

DISCRIMINATION IN FIELDS OTHER THAN EMPLOYMENT

1. EDUCATION

(1) Types of Education Covered

The Sex and Race discrimination legislation applies to state, inde-   **10–001**
pendent, and special schools, as well as further and higher education
colleges and universities.[1] The Religion or Belief, Sexual Orientation,

---

[1] See respectively tables in SDA 1975, s.22 and RRA 1976, s.17.

277

or Age Regulations cover only further and higher education.[2] The Equality Act 2006, Pt 2, covers religion or belief discrimination in schools,[3] and by Pt 3, empowers the Secretary of State to extend this to sexual orientation discrimination.

Where the coverage falls short of education, there may be other remedies.[4] The first Protocol (Art.2) of the European Convention on Human Rights provides a right to education, and combined with Art.14, this right must be "secured" without discrimination. The Convention was incorporated into English law by the Human Rights Act 1998.[5] Thus schools, as an emanation of the State,[6] cannot discriminate unjustifiably against pupils on grounds such as sexual orientation or religion.

A specific problem that falls outside the legislation to date is homophobic bullying at school. However, the school's treatment of this problem coincidently may amount to unlawful *sex* discrimination under the Sex Discrimination Act 1975 (SDA 1975). In the US case, *Nabozny v Podlesny*,[7] a group of schoolboys subjected Jamie Nabozny, a pupil who was homosexual, to a mock rape. The school did not punish the boys, although it admitted it would punish boys who assaulted or mock-raped a girl. In fact, the Principal responsible for school discipline told Jamie that "Boys will be boys." This was held to be *sex* discrimination under the Equal Protection Clause of the 14th Amendment. Such treatment should also amount to sex discrimination. The advantage of this course over the Human Rights Act is that the SDA 1975 does not allow the defendant a general defence to justify direct discrimination and there may be better damages.

(2) Unlawful Discrimination in Education

(a) Discrimination and Harassment

10–002   Some forms of discrimination depend on whether the activity falls under Community law, which is limited to employment matters, save for the Race Directive 2000/43/EC, which applies to all education. However, "employment" at a Community level includes vocational training, which is often provided by further and higher educational

---

[2] Age Regulations in force October 1, 2006.

[3] Expected in force October, 2006.

[4] See M. Connolly, "Discrimination on the ground of sexual orientation outside the workplace: is it actionable?" [2005] 2 Web JCLI.

[5] See further, Ch.2, para.2–004.

[6] Victims of discrimination by private schools have a remedy either against the school or the State: *Costello-Roberts v UK* (1993) 25 E.H.R.R. 112, especially at para.27. In *R (Begum) v Governors of Denbigh High School* [2006] 2 All E.R. 487, the House of Lords held (3 to 2) that a school's refusal to a allow a pupil to wear her orthodox jiljab did not infringe her right to freedom of religion provided by Art.9. The minority held the infringement was justified.

[7] 92 F 3d 446 (7th Cir 1996). See also *Smith v Gardener Merchant* [1999] I.C.R. 134, CA, Ch.3, para.3–014.

institutions. Thus some EC employment-derived definitions will apply to education when it is providing vocational training. In other cases, the domestic provisions (Religion or Belief, Sexual Orientation and Age Regulations) simply equate further and higher education with vocational training.

All the domestic provisions provide that it is unlawful to discriminate in terms of admission or by refusing or deliberately not accepting an application. It is also unlawful to discriminate against existing students or pupils in the access to benefits, facilities or services, or by their exclusion from the establishment, or by any other detriment.[8] In addition, the Sex Discrimination 1975 only, by s.22(1), covers the arrangements made for selection in further and higher education.

Harassment is specifically outlawed by Race Relations Act 1976 (RRA 1976) and the Religion or Belief, Sexual Orientation, or Age Regulations,[9] although the statutory definition of racial harassment is restricted to grounds of race, ethnic or national origins. Religious harassment is not covered expressly by the Equality Act 2006, Pt 2, but may coincide with racial harassment. Harassment and sexual harassment is specifically outlawed by the SDA 1975 for further and higher education, but not for schools.[10] However, the courts recognise harassment as a form of sex or religious direct discrimination, as the case may be, although there are some limitations to this approach.[11]

It is now established that the EC Treaty covers financial assistance to students. In *Bidar v London Borough of Ealing*[12] the ECJ held that a residency rule to qualify for subsidised student loans could discriminate on the ground of nationality contrary to Art.12, EC Treaty (discrimination on ground of nationality). The Court stated that a qualification rule of three years' residency in the UK could be justified if it were to ensure that assistance to students from other member states did not become an unreasonable burden which might affect the overall level of assistance provided by the state. In this case, Bidar, a French national, had lived with his grandmother in England for over three years, during which time he attended secondary school. However, the residency rule would not account for a person's time in the UK whilst he was in receipt of education, and so Bidar was refused a

---

[8] SDA 1975, s.22; RRA 1976, s.17; Religion or Belief Regulations 2003, reg.20; Sexual Orientation Regulations 2003, reg.20; Age Regulations 2006, reg.23 (in force October 1, 2006); EA 2006, s.49 (does not carry the "deliberately not accepting" element", Expected in force October, 2006.

[9] RRA 1976, s.17(2); Religion or Belief Regulations 2003, reg.20(2); Sexual Orientation Regulations 2003 reg.20(2); Age Regulations 2006 reg.23(2) (in force October 1, 2006).

[10] Education is expressly excluded from the forthcoming Equal Treatment in Goods and Services Directive 2004/113/EC (due in force by December 12, 2007), which extends EC sex discrimination law (including free-standing definitions of harassment) to goods and services: Recital 13, Art.3(3). See further Ch.2, para.2–002.

[11] See generally, Ch.5, para.5–022 et al.

[12] Case C-209/03, [2005] Q.B. 812, especially paras 56–63.

student loan for his university course. The ECJ ruled that this aspect of the rule was disproportionate and so could not be justified.

(b) Other Discrimination by Education Authorities

10–003   Sections 18 to 18D, RRA 1976 cover local education authorities, further education and higher education funding councils, the Scottish Further and Higher Education Funding Council and the Training and Development Agency for Schools. It is unlawful for these authorities to discriminate or harass whilst carrying out their functions. Sections 23 to 23D, SDA 1975, repeat these duties, but without the express reference to harassment. Section 51 of the Equality Act 2006,[13] repeats these duties for religion or belief, but for local education authorities only, and again, without the express reference to harassment.

These provisions, applying specifically to education authorities, demand non-discriminatory administration of the institutions under their control. This means, for instance, a claimant may compare one school with another when challenging a policy under these provisions. The obligation includes a duty to take corrective measures, where say historic practices have caused present-day discrimination, as occurred in *Birmingham CC v EOC.*[14] Here, small pockets of resistance kept a few (selective) grammar schools open, the majority of which happened to be boys' schools. In *R. v Secretary of State for Education & Science, Ex p. Keating,*[15] the education authority's policy of closing an all-boys' school, whilst maintaining two all-girls' schools was held to be unlawful. In *R. (R) v Leeds City Council*[16] it was held lawful for the Leeds education authority to refuse to fund transport to a Jewish school (45 miles away in Manchester) because it was outside of its boundary. Wilkie, J stated *obiter* that although s.18 (and s.17), RRA 1976, may apply to school admissions, it did not apply to the funding of transport to school. This goes too far. In the circumstances, the decision may have been correct (either as not being direct discrimination, or being justified indirect discrimination), but it may be wholly different if an education authority bussed pupils to nearby Christian schools, but refused to do the same for pupils at Muslim schools.

(c) Discrimination after Education

10–004   All the provisions, bar the Equality Act 2006, outlaw discrimination or harassment after "the relationship has come to an end" where it

---

[13] Expected in force October, 2006.
[14] [1989] A.C. 1155, HL. See further, Ch.4, para.4–015. See also C. Bourn and J. Whitmore, *Anti-Discrimination Law in Britain*, 3rd edn, 1996, London: Sweet & Maxwell, p.271.
[15] [1985] LGR 469 Q.B.D.
[16] [2005] EWHC 2495, at paras 48–50.

"arises out of and is closely connected to that relationship".[17] Typically, this will cover the refusal to give a reference to a former student because the student had once made a complaint of discrimination. This statutory definition, deriving from EC Directives, has limited reach. For instance, in the SDA 1975 it covers only employment matters, and so impinges on the Education provisions only so far as they apply to vocational training.[18] The statutory definition in the RRA 1976 does not extend to discrimination purely on the ground of colour or nationality. However, case law suggests that these residual cases will be treated in much the same way. The House of Lords held, in *Relaxion v Rhys-Harper*,[19] that the phrase "whom he employs," in s.6 of the *employment* provisions of the SDA 1975, extended to discrimination against ex-workers, where the act complained of related to the employment relationship. A case under the education provisions of the SDA 1975 will turn on the parallel phrase in s.22(c)(ii), "where she is a pupil,"[20] and is likely to be given an equally broad interpretation.

(3) Exemptions

(a) General Occupational Requirements—Religion or Belief, Sexual Orientation and Age

The Religion or Belief, Sexual Orientation, and Age Regulations make **10–005** available their respective Genuine Occupational Requirement defences to providers of further and higher education, so far as they provide vocational training.[21]

A number of specified sixth-form colleges with a religious ethos are exempted from the Religion of Belief Regulations "so far as it is necessary for an institution to give preference in its admissions to persons of a particular religion or belief in order to preserve that institution's religious ethos." This exemption does not include vocational training.[22]

(b) Religion or Belief Discrimination by Schools

Section 50(1) of the Equality Act 2006 exempts "faith schools"— **10–006** maintained or independent—from its provisions, save in relation to excluding pupils, and subjecting them "to any other detriment".

---

[17] SDA 1975, s.20A (in force for harassment October 1, 2005); RRA 1976, s.27A; Religion or Belief Regulations 2003, reg.21; Sexual Orientation Regulations 2003, reg.21; Age Regulations 2006, reg.24 (in force October 1, 2006). See further Ch.8, para.8–017.

[18] SDA 1975, s.1(3)(c).

[19] The collective appeals of *Relaxion Group plc v Rhys-Harper, D'Souza v Lambeth LBC, Jones v 3M Healthcare Ltd* [2003] UKHL 33, overruling *Post Office v Adekeye* [1997] I.C.R. 110, [1997] I.R.L.R. 105, CA. Discussed briefly, above, Ch.8, para.8–017.

[20] Or RRA 1976, s.17(c), or EA 2006, s.49: "where he is a pupil."

[21] For a discussion of these GOR's, see Ch.8 paras 8–049, 8–053, and 8–057.

[22] Religion or Belief Regulations 2003, reg.20(4A) and Sch.1B.

Section 50(2) exempts schools in relation to the curriculum and acts of worship, save in relation to excluding pupils. Section 50(3) empowers the Secretary of State to extend or reduce these exemptions.

(c) Sex Discrimination by Schools

10–007   Section 26 of the SDA 1975 provides an exception for a single-sex educational establishment, even if it takes in "comparatively small" numbers of the opposite sex and confines them to particular courses or classes, or takes in members of the opposite sex exceptionally. Section 26(2) further provides that a co-educational school may offer boarding facilities to one sex only. Section 27 is in place to facilitate a transition from single-sex to co-educational education or boarding. It allows an establishment to apply for a "transitional exemption order" authorising discriminatory admissions during the transitional period specified in the order.

A further general exception to the Act is provided by s.44 which is relevant to schools. It applies to games, sports and other activities of a competitive nature "where the physical strength, stamina or physique of the average woman puts her at a disadvantage to the average man." It permits "any act related to the participation of a person as a competitor in events involving that activity which are confined to competitors of one sex."

This allows for teaching a sport in single-sex groups (e.g. athletics), but does not appear to sanction teaching of a particular sport to just one sex, typically football for boys and hockey for girls. The exemption is for "events", rather than sports. Section 28, which provided a further exception for physical education courses in FE and HE only, was repealed in 2005.[23]

(d) Race: Education and Training

10–008   This exemption is closely associated to positive action.[24] Section 35 provides a defence "for any act done in affording persons of a particular racial group access to facilities or services to meet the special needs of persons of that group in regard to their education, training or welfare . . .". This permits, for example, help with literacy for immigrant groups. Section 36 permits the provision of education or training to people not ordinarily resident in Great Britain and who do not intend to remain afterwards; language schools are the obvious example. However, s.36 applies nowadays only to residual cases, for instance, discrimination purely on the ground of nationality or colour.

---

[23] SI 2005/2467, reg.23(1)(a).
[24] RRA 1976, ss.37, 38. Discriminatory training is also permissible on other protected grounds. See below, Ch.12, paras 12–005 to 12–008.

It no longer applies to discrimination on grounds of race or ethnic or national origins.[25]

2. Goods, Facilities, Services and Clubs

Section 29 of the Sex Discrimination Act, s.20 of the Race Relations Act, and s.46 of the Equality Act 2006[26] (religion or belief) each outlaws discrimination in the provision (whether for payment or not) of goods, facilities or services "to the public or a section of the public". Providers may not discriminate by refusing "or deliberately omitting" to provide goods, facilities or services, or by failing to provide them "of the like quality, in the like manner or on the like terms as are normal". The Equality Act 2006, Pt 3, empowers the Secretary of State to extend these provisions to sexual orientation discrimination.

10–009

Harassment is unlawful specifically by s.20(3), RRA 1976, but yet to be outlawed specifically by the SDA 1975,[27] and is not outlawed expressly by the Equality Act. Religious harassment may coincide with racial harassment. Further, the courts recognise harassment as a form of sex or religious direct discrimination, as the case may be, although there are some problems associated with this approach.[28] Harassment will most likely fall within the phrase (above) "in the like manner." It might be easier to succeed in a claim than in the employment context, especially where the harassment concerns a single incident, as there is no requirement that the harassment be to the complainant's detriment, although that will clearly be relevant in assessing the degree of injury to feelings.

(1) "The Public or a Section of the Public" and Private Clubs

It is not the policy of the legislation to regulate essentially private behaviour. So the law has to distinguish between public and private activities.[29] It attempts to do so by confining these provisions to "the public or a section of the public". The liability of clubs or associations has turned on the interpretation of this phrase.

10–010

The leading cases arose under the Race Relations Act 1968, which used the same formula. In *Charter v Race Relations Board*,[30] the House of Lords held that a Conservative club operated a genuine process for

---

[25] Race Relations Act 1976 (Amendment) Regulations, SI 2003/1626, reg.34.

[26] Expected in force October, 2006.

[27] This should be remedied when the Equal Treatment in Goods and Services Directive 2004/113/EC, due in force December 21, 2007, is implemented. See further Ch.2, para.2–002.

[28] See generally, Ch.5, para.5–022 *et seq.*

[29] See J. Gardner, "Private activities and personal autonomy: at the margins of anti-discrimination law", in B. Hepple and E. Szyszczak (eds), *Discrimination: The Limits of Law*, 1992, London: Mansell, Ch.9.

[30] [1973] A.C. 885.

selection of members and so it was not open "to a section of the public." Similar reasoning was applied in *Dockers Labour Club and Institute Ltd v Race Relations Board*,[31] where Lord Diplock set the test: "Would a notice, 'Public Not Admitted' exhibited on the premises . . . be true?" These decisions meant that clubs such as these lawfully could operate a colour bar.

10–011   In response, s.25, RRA 1976 (but not other legislation), specifically outlawed discrimination by such clubs with 25 or more members. Section 25, RRA 1976 applies to "to any association of persons (however described, whether corporate or unincorporate, and whether or not its activities are carried on for profit)" if (a) it has 25 or more members; and (b) it is *not* open to a section of the public within the meaning of s.20(1); and (c) it is not a trade organisation.[32] There is no need for the association to provide goods, facilities or services: s.25 outlaws discrimination in relation to *membership*. (There is no specific harassment provision.) In some ways then, s.25 is wider than s.20, as there is no need to show that the association provides a service, goods or facilities. In another way it is the inverse of s.20, as it only applies to private associations, defined as *not* being open to "a section of the public". Consequently, claimants may be arguing in *favour* of the narrow interpretation given to that phrase in the *Charter* and *Dockers Labour Club* cases. This occurred in *Treisman v Ali*,[33] where, pending a disciplinary investigation, the Labour Party suspended Ali. As a result, Ali could not be nominated for re-selection as a candidate in the local elections. He could not claim under s.20 because the Labour Party obviously did not provide goods or services. Instead, he used inter alia s.25. Noting Lord Diplock's "*Public Not Admitted* notice" test, the Court of Appeal held that s.25 was "capable" of applying to the Labour Party. It was a question of fact for the County Court.[34]

Membership rules may directly or indirectly discriminate. Indirect discrimination typically arises where applicants are required to be nominated by an existing member, thus perpetuating the existing racial profile of the club.[35]

Section 26 provides an exception from s.25 if the main object of the association is to enable the benefits of membership to persons of a particular racial group, defined otherwise than by reference to colour. This enables organisations to offer membership to groups defined

---

[31] [1976] A.C. 285, at 297G.
[32] Typically trade unions or employers' organisations. See RRA 1976, s.11, discussed Ch.8, para.8–075.
[33] [2002] I.C.R. 1026, CA. The issue was discussed at paras 38–52.
[34] *ibid.*, at paras 51–52.
[35] The CRE issued a non-discrimination notice (see Ch.13, para.13–034) to a social club, whose rules stated that new members had to be sponsored by two members and approved by committee. No non-white had ever applied for membership in an area of just 40 per cent white population: *Handsworth Horticultural Institute Ltd v CRE* (1992, unreported). See *Ruled Out*, F Invest 1992, App.C, London: CRE, ISBN 1 85442 154 9.

by, say, nationality, such as a London Bangladeshi association, a Birmingham Irish society, and so on.

(2) "Goods, Facilities or Services"

The provisions give some examples: hotel accommodation; banking, **10–012** insurance, grants, loans, credit or finance; facilities for education; entertainment, recreation or refreshment;[36] transport or travel; and the services of any profession or trade, or any local or other public authority.

The provisions expressly include "any local or other public authority." The Race Relations (Amendment) Act 2000 introduced ss.19B to 19F into the Act. Section 19B provides simply that it is unlawful for a public authority in carrying out any of its functions to do any act which constitutes racial discrimination or harassment. Among others, this covers the police.[37] Moreover, "public authorities" includes private companies carrying out public functions, such as running prisons.[38] In line with this theme, public authorities have no liability under the section if "the nature of the act is private."[39] Section 21A of the Sex Discrimination Act 1976,[40] and s.52 of the Equality Act 2006[41] (religion of belief) are set out in broadly similar terms.

The reasons behind the need for these amendments was the diffi- **10–013** culty in deciding what functions by a public authority amount to a "service". In *Savjani v Inland Revenue Commissioners*,[42] the Court of Appeal held that the Inland Revenue provided a service when giving tax relief, repayments or advice. This was the case, suggested Templeman, L.J., even though it does not provide a service when carrying out its "duty" of collecting taxes. Accordingly, a prison officer's primary duty may be to detain the inmates, whilst providing a service to prisoners when allocating work or privileges.[43] Shortly after *Savjani*, the House of Lords gave this analysis a further dimension. In

---

[36] *James v Eastleigh BC* [1990] 2 A.C. 751, HL (public swimming baths). See further Ch.4, para.4–015; *McConomy v Croft Inns Ltd* [1992] I.R.L.R. 561, High Ct of NI (public house barring male customers wearing earrings); *Gill v El Vino Co Ltd* [1983] Q.B. 425, CA (Wine bar served men at bar and women at table). See further Ch.4, para.4–032.

[37] Decisions not to prosecute are exempted by s.19F. Further, in practice, liability may be difficult to prove because investigations that may lead to a decision to prosecute are specifically exempted (contrary to the MacPherson recommendation) from the Freedom of Information Act 2000 (s.30)(1).

[38] Exempted public authorities include: Either House of Parliament; the Security and Secret Intelligence services, Government Communications Headquarters (s.19B(3)) and, for grounds of nationality, national or ethnic origins only, Immigration and Nationality officials (s.19D).

[39] RRA 1976, s.19B(4).

[40] In force, April 6, 2007, SI 2006/1082, Art.4.

[41] Expected in force October, 2006.

[42] [1981] Q.B. 458, at 467. Approved by Lord Fraser in *R. v Entry Clearance Officer Bombay Ex p. Amin* [1983] 2 A.C. 818, at 834, HL.

[43] See *Alexander v Home Office* [1988] I.C.R. 685, at 691, CA; J. Gardner "Section 20 of the Race Relations Act 1976: 'facilities' and 'services'" (1987) 50 M.L.R. 345, at 346.

R. v Entry Clearance Officer Bombay, Ex p. Amin[44] a British passport holder resident in India challenged a voucher scheme for entry into the UK. Applications could only be made by the head of the household, who were presumed to be men. Accordingly, the claimant, being a woman, could not apply. She challenged the scheme under s.29 of the Sex Discrimination Act 1975. A bare majority rejected her challenge. Lord Fraser gave two reasons why the immigration officers were not providing a service. First, s.29 applied to the direct provision of facilities or services, and not to the mere grant of permission to use facilities.[45] This is difficult to reconcile with "private sector" cases such as *James v Eastleigh BC*,[46] where the "service" was the granting of permission to use a swimming pool through the issue of a ticket, rather than, say, ensuring that the water was warm and germ-free.[47] The second and more enduring reason was that the only acts covered were those of a private nature, that is those that would be done by a non-public body.[48] This reason has been heavily criticised, not least because no logical basis was provided for it. It produces the absurdity that liability may depend on the existence a private-sector comparator, which, say, in the case of prisons was unthinkable at one time, and nowadays commonplace.[49] Further, it is very difficult to apply with any certainty. For instance, in some respects the granting permission to reside in the UK is similar to a private landowner granting a licence to a person to enter his land, whilst in other respects it is peculiar to Government.[50]

The theme persisted in *Farah v Commissioner of Police for the Metropolis*,[51] where white teenagers with a dog set upon a Somali refugee and her 10-year old cousin. She called the police, who arrested *her*, for affray and causing suffering to the dog. The police offered no evidence and she was acquitted. She sued the police, inter alia, under the RRA 1976 and the Court of Appeal found her claim fell within s.20, but, as the Court made clear, only because the police duties of giving assistance and protection were capable of being carried out by a private security company.

The Commission for Racial Equality urged a reversal of *Amin*: "It is very particularly in areas such as the exercise of police powers, immigration controls, the treatment of prisoners and the licensing and enforcement functions of local authorities that discrimination can

---

[44] [1983] 2 A.C. 818.
[45] *ibid.*, at 834.
[46] [1990] A.C. 751, HL. See further, Ch.4, para.4–015.
[47] This criticism was made by Richard Townshend-Smith. See M. Connolly, *Townshend-Smith on Discrimination Law: Text, Cases and Materials*, (2nd edn), 2004 London: Cavendish, at p.369.
[48] [1983] 2 A.C. 818, at 835.
[49] *per* Richard Townshend-Smith, above, fn 47.
[50] See J. Gardner, "Section 20 of the Race Relations Act 1976: 'facilities' and 'services'" (1987) 50 M.L.R. 345, at 351.
[51] [1997] 1 All E.R. 289, CA.

cause the greatest damage to race relations."[52] The catalyst for change was the Stephen Lawrence Inquiry, which recommended that the police become fully subject to the Race Relations Act.[53] The change that followed opened the scope of the Act to all public authorities. Until April 6th 2007 (see above para.10–012), *Amin* remains good law for the Sex Discrimination Act.

(3) Exemptions

(a) Race Only—Care of Persons
Section 23(2), RRA 1976, provides that s.20 does not apply to anything done by a person who "takes into his home, and treats as if they were members of his family, children, elderly persons, or persons requiring a special degree of care and attention."[54] This exception cannot absolve discrimination by a local authority unless it was in response to the declared wishes of the carer (typically a couple wishing to foster or adopt a child requesting it be of their racial group).[55]

10–014

(b) Sex and Religion or Belief—Specific Skills
Under the Sex Discrimination Act, s.29(3) allows discrimination "where a particular skill is commonly exercised in a different way for men and for women". This allows, say, a ladies' hairdresser not to serve men, or to charge them a different rate, although there must be a fundamental difference in the service being provided.

Similarly, under the Equality Act 2006, s.46(3), allows discrimination "Where a skill is commonly exercised in different ways in relation to or for the purposes of different religions or beliefs". This might allow, say, to serve food only in accordance with a religious doctrine.

10–015

(c) Sex Only—Insurance and Actuarial Calculations
For the Sex Discrimination Act only, s.45 permits "reasonable" reliance on data suggesting different risks for men and women in relation to "an annuity, life insurance policy, accident insurance policy, or similar matter involving the assessment of risk".[56] Employers also are

10–016

---

[52] *Reform of the Race Relations Act 1996: Proposals from the Commission for Racial Equality*, 1998, London: CRE, p.12.

[53] *The Stephen Lawrence Inquiry, Report of an Inquiry by Sir William Macpherson, advised by Tom Cook, The Right Reverend Dr John Sentamu, Dr Richard Stone*. February 1999. Presented to Parliament by the Home Secretary, Cm 4262-I. London: HMSO, especially para.46.32, and Recommendations 9–11.

[54] Reversing the effect of *Applin v Race Relations Board* [1975] A.C. 259, HL.

[55] See *Conwell v Newham LBC* [2000] I.C.R. 42, EAT. See also for religion or belief, below, para.10–031.

[56] At a Community law level, the ECJ has approved the use of actuarial tables in some forms of pension arrangements: *Neath v Hugh Steeper* Case C-152/91, [1994] I.C.R. 118.

able to take advantage of this exception. The "reasonable" element allows courts to question the validity of the statistics and the decisions based upon them. However, in the only case known to date, *Pinder v Friends Provident Life Office*,[57] a county court held that it was reasonable for the defendants to charge a female self-employed dentist 50 per cent more than men for permanent health insurance, based on 1963 statistics. It is hard to imagine that a court nowadays would give such deference to a provider.

Statistics tend to show that women are more prone to illness than men, but live longer. Accordingly women are charged more for health insurance and annuities (a lump sum payment in return for a regular income), and less for life insurance. In the *Los Angeles Department of Water and Power v Manhart*[58] the US Supreme Court roundly rejected the employer's plan, (based on statistics showing that women lived longer than men) for women to pay more than men into a pension fund. The Court gave several reasons for its decision. First, statistics revealed *past* patterns, which may have been due to cultural or social factors, as well as genetic ones. For instance, men may have died sooner because they tended to be heavier smokers. So the statistics did not account for social or cultural changes and are not a reliable guide to future patterns. Second, even presuming that statistics were an accurate predictor, decisions made upon them treated persons as a class, rather than as individuals, something which is not permissible in other areas of discrimination law: "If height is required for a job, a tall woman may not be refused employment merely because, on the average, women are too short. Even a true generalization about the class is an insufficient reason for disqualifying an individual to whom the generalization does not apply." Third, the Court observed that insurers could just as easily use life-expectancy statistics based on race. That is unlawful because it is so repugnant, yet there is no difference in principle between race and sex in this context. Fourth, the defendant argued that insurance is different because it is concerned with risk. However, the Court ruled that risk was "a characteristic of many employment decisions." Employers take risks with, say, individual performance, which they are not allowed to predict with sex-based classifications. So risk was not a reason to exempt insurance.

Finally, note that Art.5 of the Equal Treatment in Goods and Services Directive 2004/113/EC, due in force by December 21, 2007,[59] provides that "the use of sex as a factor in the calculation of premiums and benefits for the purposes of insurance and related financial services shall not result in differences in individuals' premiums and bene-

---

[57] (1985) *The Times*, December 16. See also C. Bourn and J. Whitmore, *Anti-Discrimination Law in Britain*, 3rd edn, 1996, London: Sweet & Maxwell, p.279.

[58] 435 US 702 (1978), at 708–710. For a lengthy discussion of this case and s.45, see D. Pannick, *Sex Discrimination Law*, 1985, Oxford: OUP, pp.189–195.

[59] See further Ch.2, para.2–002.

fits." However, Member States may legislate to "permit proportionate differences in individuals' premiums and benefits where the use of sex is a determining factor in the assessment of risk based on relevant and accurate actuarial and statistical data." If the Government opts for this it must ensure that the statistics are compiled, published, regularly updated and accurate. Further, it must review the option in December 2012. If the Government takes this option, s.45 may survive in some amended form. It is clear from the language of the Directive and ECJ jurisprudence, terms like *accurate*, *determining*, and *proportionate*, will be applied far more strictly than the term *reasonable* was applied by the county court in *Pinder.*

(d) Sex Only—Political Parties

Section 33, SDA 1975, provides an exemption from s.29 for political parties (defined as those with an aspiration the UK Parliament) or its affiliates, allowing special provisions for persons of one sex only in their constitution, organisation or administration. This allows political parties to have special women's groups and reserved places on committees. More recently, s.42A[60] has extended the exemption to the selection of candidates for election.

10–017

(e) Special Facilities or Services

Section 35(1) SDA 1975 provides an exemption from s.29 for (a) hospitals (or parts of), places for persons requiring special care, supervision or attention, or (b) places used by an organised religion, and (c) facilities which are single-sex for privacy where otherwise a person is likely to suffer "serious embarrassment" or "might reasonably object" if they were mixed-sex.

10–018

By s.35(2), a person may provide facilities or services to one sex only, say women, if physical contact between the users is likely, and a woman "might reasonably object" if another user were a man. The EOC observed that the provision of women-only sports and leisure sessions does not fall clearly within the defences provided by ss.35(1)(c) or 35(2), as the degree of embarrassment may not be "sufficiently substantial", although many women might not be willing to participate in mixed sessions. The reason for the embarrassment may vary depending on different cultural and religious traditions.[61]

---

[60] Inserted by the Sex Discrimination (Election Candidates) Act 2002, s.1. See further, Ch.12, para.12–002.
[61] *Equality in the 21st Century: a New Approach*, 1998, Manchester: EOC, paras 64–65.

3. Housing and Other Premises

10–019   Under s.21 of the Race Relations Act 1976,[62] it is unlawful to discriminate in the disposal of premises: in the terms on which they are offered, or by refusing an application, or in the treatment of persons on a waiting list. It is also unlawful for someone managing a premises to discriminate against an occupier "in the way he affords him access to any benefits or facilities, or by refusing or deliberately omitting to afford him access to them; or by evicting him, or subjecting him to any other detriment." Section 30 of the Sex Discrimination Act and s.47 of the Equality Act 2006[63] (religion or belief) are set out in broadly similar terms. The Equality Act 2006, Pt 3, empowers the Secretary of State to extend these provisions to sexual orientation discrimination.

Sections 24 RRA 1976 and 31 SDA 1975, extend the coverage to a landlord's consent for sub-letting, so that say, a landlord may not withhold consent for a tenant to sub-let because the sub-tenant is Asian. Section 47(3), Equality Act 2006 simply provides "It is unlawful for a person to discriminate against another by refusing permission for the disposal of premises to him."

10–020   These provisions are designed to protect purchasers or tenants from discrimination by property owners or managers. The sections for the provision of goods, facilities and services cover other parties who might become involved, such as estate agents. Section 21(2A) RRA 1976, specifically outlaws harassment on grounds of race or ethnic or national origins. There is no equivalent in the SDA 1975, and is not outlawed expressly by the Equality Act. Religious harassment may coincide with racial harassment. Further, the courts recognise harassment as a form of sex or religious direct discrimination, as the case may be, although there are some problems associated with this approach.[64]

Until legislation is passed to cover sexual orientation discrimination in this field, where the discrimination relates to a person's home, a claim may be available under the Human Rights Act 1998, by combining Arts 8 (right to one's home) and 14 (rights must be secured without discrimination).[65]

It is unlawful by s.19A, RRA 1976, for a planning authority to discriminate. This section was inserted in response to the *Amin*[66] case (ruling that public bodies were liable only for functions of private nature) and prevents local authorities discriminating against minori-

---

[62] A revised Code of Practice for Housing (rented and owner-occupier) is due in October 2006. See *www.cre.gov.uk/gdpract/housing.html*.

[63] Expected in force October, 2006.

[64] See generally, Ch.5, para.5–022 et al.

[65] See e.g. *Godin-Mendoza v Ghaidan* [2004] UKHL 30 and the discussion in Ch.2, paras 2–005 and 2–018.

[66] See above, para.10–013.

ties in response to public pressure, by say, withholding planning permission to Romany travellers.

(1) Exemptions—Sex, Colour and Nationality Only

There are two exemptions, which were partly repealed in deference to the Race Directive.[67] Accordingly, what follows only applies under the SDA, the Equality Act, and the residual race cases[68] outside the scope of the Directive, for instance, discrimination purely on the ground of colour or nationality.

10–021

The first exemption allows owner-occupiers[69] to discriminate when disposing (typically, selling or renting) of their premises,[70] unless they do so either through an estate agent or by advertising. Note that here, even a notice in the window indicating that the property is for sale, or to let, amounts to an advertisement.[71] Accordingly the exemption is a narrow one, allowing, say, letting by word-of-mouth.

This leaves open the question of whether discriminatory covenants (e.g. restricting the letting or resale of a property) are lawful under the legislation. In the US case *Shelly v Kraemer*,[72] 30 out of 39 property owners in a single street made covenants that for fifty years their properties could not be occupied "by any person not of the Caucasian race". The expressed intention was to exclude "people of the Negro or Mongolian Race". This was challenged as being contrary to the Equal Protection Clause of the 14th Amendment. The Supreme Court held that although the 14th Amendment applied only to state actions, the local court, being a state body, could not enforce such a covenant, even if created by private parties. In the same way, nowadays, a British court should refuse to enforce such a discriminatory covenant (which is in principle contrary to Arts 8 and 14 of the ECHR), because of its obligation as a public body under the Human Rights Act 1998.[73]

The second exemption, for "small dwellings", is provided by either s.22, RRA 1976, s.32, SDA 1975,[74] or s.48, Equality Act 2006. Discrimination is allowed if the occupier is the owner or a close relative and there is not normally residential accommodation on the

---

[67] Council Directive 2000/43/EC, implemented by the Race Relations Act (Amendment) Regulations 2003, in force July 19, 2003.

[68] See further, Ch.2, para.2–002.

[69] Someone who "owns an estate or interest in the premises".

[70] RRA 1976, s.21(3); SDA 1975, s.30(3); EA 2006, s.48(3).

[71] See *Race Relations Board v Relf*, County Ct, RRB Report 1975, p.56, Ch.5, para.5–033.

[72] 334 US 1 (1948).

[73] For the relationship between the European Convention on Human Rights, the Human Rights Act 1998, and discrimination, see Ch.2, paras 2–004 and 2–014. For a discussion on whether racist covenants are otherwise unlawful, see S. Cretney (1968) 118 N.L.J. 1094; J.F. Garner (1972) 35 M.L.R. 478; J.D.A. Brooke-Taylor (1978) 42 Conv(ns) 24.

[74] These also exempt liability under RRA 1976 s.20, and SDA 1975, s.29 ("Goods, facilities & Services").

premises for more than six persons in addition to the occupier and any members of his household. Section 48(1), Equality Act 2006 provides a varied definition: the premises are of a size where no more than two households, or six individuals, can live in the premises in addition to the landlord or a near relative.

4. GENERAL EXEMPTIONS

(1) Sex, Race and Religion or Belief

(a) Charities

10–022   Section 34, RRA 1976, permits charitable instruments to discriminate unless the ground of the discrimination is colour, in which case it will have effect as if "the restriction by reference to colour is disregarded". This will effectively bar discrimination on the ground of race, but permit discrimination on the ground nationality or religion. The latter is confirmed by s.58, Equality Act 2006. The exemption in the RRA 1976 was further eroded by s.34(3A)[75] which does not allow charities to discriminate on the grounds of race or ethnic or national origins in relation to employment and contract workers.

A parallel exception for charitable instruments that benefit members of one sex only is provided by s.43, SDA 1975.[76] However, under s.78 or 79, the trustees of an educational charity (England and Wales) or the governing body of an educational endowment (Scotland) may apply to the Secretary of State to have the restriction removed or modified so to "conduce to the advancement of education without sex discrimination".

A further exemption from religion or belief discrimination is provided by s.60, Equality Act 2006. Here, charities may ask members or prospective members to assert their acceptance of a religion or belief as a requirement of membership of the charity. But this exception is only valid for charities which first imposed this requirement before May 18, 2005 and have continued to do so ever since.

(b) Sports

10–023   Section 44, SDA 1975, applies to games, sports and other activities of a competitive nature "where the physical strength, stamina or physique of the average woman puts her at a disadvantage to the average man." It permits "any act related to the participation of a person as a competitor in events involving that activity which are confined to competitors of one sex." This allows for the organising of some "physical" sports into single-sex categories. Visible examples

---

[75] Inserted by SI 2003/1626, reg.33, in force July 19, 2003.
[76] See *Hugh-Jones v St John's College Cambridge* [1979] I.C.R. 848, EAT.

include athletics, rugby and football. This does not sanction barring women from playing a particular sport. In *Couch v British Boxing Board of Control*[77] it was held unlawful to refuse a licence to a female boxer to fight other women.

Section 39, RRA 1976, permits a sport to segregate on the basis of nationality, place of birth or residency, if done to select players to represent a "country, place or area, or any related association". This of course facilitates international competition in sports such as rugby and football, as well as allowing teams such as *London Welsh*, or *London Irish* to draw on particular nationalities.

(c) National Security

Section 52(1), SDA 1975, provides that nothing in the legislation **10–024** "shall render unlawful an act done for the purpose of safeguarding national security." Section 52(2) further provides that a certificate signed by a government minister is conclusive proof that an act was done for the purpose of national security. The ECJ in *Johnston v Chief Constable of the Royal Ulster Constabulary*[78] held that this was contrary to Art.6 of the Equal Treatment Directive 76/207/EEC, which covers employment and vocational training only. As a result, the "ministerial certificate" can no longer be used under the SDA 1975 in cases of employment or vocational training,[79] but can be used in other fields. It is likely to be repealed further when the Equal Treatment in Goods and Services Directive 2004/113/EC (due in force by December 21, 2007) is implemented.[80]

The parallel provision, s.42(1), RRA 1976, has been modified similarly for all fields, so that a ministerial certificate cannot be used.[81] In line with this, s.63, Equality Act 2006, exempts acts which can be "justified" for the purpose of national security.

(d) Statutory Authority

This general defence now only applies to cases outside the ambit of **10–025** Community law, that is residual race cases, (such as discrimination purely on the ground of colour or nationality),[82] or sex discrimination cases in fields other than employment and vocational training, or religion or belief discrimination under the Equality Act 2006. Sections 41(1), RRA 1976, 51A, SDA 1975, or 56, EA 2006, provide that nothing shall render unlawful any act of discrimination done *under*

---

[77] Unreported, IT, (1998) *The Guardian*, March 31, 1998, *The Times* April 28, 1998, or see *www.eoc.org.gov*.
[78] Case 222/84, [1987] Q.B. 129. See further Ch.8, para.8–029 and generally, Ch.4, para.4–040.
[79] SI 1988/249, Art.2.
[80] See further Ch.2, para.2–002.
[81] See further Ch.8, para.8–046.
[82] See further Ch.2, para.2–002.

compulsion of [83] any legislation, or requirement imposed by a minister of the Crown by virtue of any enactment.

(2) Race and Religion or Belief

(a) Education, Training or Welfare

10–026   Section 35 provides a defence "for any act done in affording persons of a particular racial group access to facilities or services to meet the special needs of persons of that group in regard to their education, training or welfare". It is closely associated to positive action,[84] and permits, for example, help with literacy for immigrant groups, or social security care arrangements recognising the special needs of ethnic minorities. In *R. (Stephenson) v Stockton-on-Tees BC*[85] the local authority would not compensate disabled persons for home-care costs provided by a family member, unless it was provided for "cultural reasons", that was where some ethnic minority groups required family members to prepare food or provide intimate care. It was held that this "cultural reasons" exemption was permitted by s.35.

Section 36 legitimised the provision of education or training to people not ordinarily resident in Great Britain and who do not intend to remain afterwards; language schools are the obvious example. However, this exemption applies nowadays only to residual cases, such as discrimination purely on the ground of nationality or colour. It no longer applies to discrimination on grounds of race or ethnic or national origins.[86]

In addition, s.57, Equality Act 2006, provides an exemption for meeting special needs for education, training or welfare of persons of a religion or belief, or providing ancillary benefits in that connection

(3) Sex Only

(a) Voluntary Bodies

10–027   Under s.34 of the SDA 1975, non-statutory, non-profit-making bodies are exempt from ss.29 (goods, facilities or services) and 30 (housing and premises) so far as restricting their membership to persons of one sex only, and providing those members with benefits, facilities or services. This covers bodies not sufficiently "private" enough to avoid

---

[83] See *Hampson v Department of Education and Science* [1991] 1 A.C. 171, HL, discussed above, Ch.8, para.8–047.
[84] RRA 1976, ss.37, 38. Discriminatory training is also permissible on other protected grounds. See below, Ch.12, paras 12–005 to 12–008.
[85] [2004] EWHC 2228, at paras 27–28, reversed on other grounds: [2005] EWCA Civ 960, CA.
[86] Race Relations Act 1976 (Amendment) Regulations, SI 2003/1626, reg.34.

being caught by s.29.[87] Thus a centre for victims of domestic violence may restrict its service and facilities to women.[88]

(b) Communal Accommodation
Section 46 of the SDA 1975 provides an exemption from Pts II (Employment) and III (Other Fields) of the Act in the provision communal accommodation, so long as "the accommodation is managed in a way which, given the exigencies of the situation, comes as near as may be to fair and equitable treatment of men and women".

10–028

(4) Religion or Belief Only

(a) Religious Organisations
Section 57, Equality Act 2006, exempts religious or belief organisations, whose main purpose is not commercial, from discriminating in membership, participation in activities, the provision of goods facilities or services, or the use or disposal of premises (which it owns or controls), if the discrimination is for either the purposes of that organisation, or to avoid causing offence to members of the relevant religion or belief.

10–029

(b) Faith Schools
Section 59, Equality Act 2006, exempts an "educational institution established or conducted for the purpose of providing education relating to, or within the framework of, a specified religion or belief", from discriminating in the provision of goods facilities or services, or the use or disposal of premises, if the discrimination is for either the purposes of that institution, or to avoid causing offence to members of the relevant religion or belief.

10–030

(c) Care Within a Family
Section 62, Equality Act 2006 provides an exemption from the whole of Pt 2 where a person takes into his home, and treats as a member of his family, a person requiring a special degree of care and attention, by reason of being elderly, or a child, or otherwise.

10–031

---

[87] See discussion above, para.10–010.
[88] For preferences in staff, see *Vancouver Rape Relief Society v Nixon* [2006] BCD Civ J 8 (BC Court of Appeal), above, Ch.8, para.10–039.

(d) Power to Vary or Create Exemptions

10–032   Section 62, Equality Act 2006 empowers the Secretary of State to make new exemptions for public authority liability (under s.52(1)) or vary any other exemption. Before doing so, the Secretary of State must consult the Commission for Equality and Human Rights.

CHAPTER 11

DISABILITY DISCRIMINATION

INTRODUCTION

11–001 The anti-discrimination principle was extended to disability through the Disability Discrimination Act 1995.[1] The Act is similar in some ways to the other discrimination legislation. Its procedural and remedial provisions are similar, and are discussed as one in Ch.13, whilst positive action is collected together with the other grounds in Ch.12. Its distinctive features are the complex rules for identifying those protected under the Act, (the definition of disability), and the conceptually different definitions of discrimination. Here, the anti-discrimination principle is not rooted in symmetry. Whilst the conventional direct/indirect discrimination framework plays a part, the substantial and tailored concepts are disability-related discrimination and positive duties to make reasonable adjustments. Underlying this exceptional approach is the simple reality that there is no point in identifying the protected group as a single class because disabilities vary in form and severity. When this is coupled with the need of most persons with a disability for *different* treatment, it becomes easy to appreciate why the equal treatment model plays only a minor role. The many forms of disability make it difficult to deal with all cases through primary legislation. So much of the law is given in Regulations or Guidance.

The result is technical and complex legislation, as noted by Mummery, LJ in *Clark v TGD t/a Novacold*:[2]

[I]t is without doubt an unusually complex piece of legislation which poses novel questions of interpretation. It is not surprising that different conclusions have been reached at different levels of decision.

This state of affairs should not be taken as a criticism of the Act or of its drafting or of the judicial disagreements about its interpretation. The whole subject presents unique challenges to legislators and to tribunals and courts, as well as to those responsible for the day-to-day operation of the Act in the workplace.

The Act covers a wide range of activities, including employment matters, the provision of goods, facilities and services, transport, premises and education. Although the definition of disability remains constant throughout the Act, the definitions of discrimination vary slightly, depending on the activity. Since 1995 the Act has been amended several times. The Employment Equality Directive 2000/78/EC brought about many EC-derived definitions into the employment provisions, which were extended into post-16 education.

---

[1] See B. Doyle, "Enabling legislation or dissembling law? The Disability Discrimination Act 1995" (1997) 60 M.L.R. 64.
[2] [1999] I.C.R. 951, at 954, CA.

As a result the Act now carries a definition of direct discrimination. Further amendments were introduced in stages by the Disability Discrimination Act 2005, extending the coverage in most areas.

1. The Definition of Disability

In general, the Act adopts the "medical" model of disability. This contrasts with the "social" model, which identifies the infrastructure of society and social barriers as the cause of disability, rather than a condition or impairment of the claimant. Whatever the model chosen, the task of drawing the line is not easy. "The definition of disability must be both inclusive and exclusive: embracing individuals outside the limited popular perception of 'disability,' yet excluding idiosyncrasies, human traits and transient illness. A distinction must be drawn between chronic or handicapping conditions and temporary or minor maladies."[3]

11–002

Some conditions are "deemed" as disabilities under the Act, irrespective of whether they cause the person an impairment. The deemed conditions are certified blindness or partial sightedness,[4] HIV infection, multiple sclerosis, or cancer, although provision may be made to exclude certain types of cancer.[5] Otherwise, the statutory definition is provided by the Disability Discrimination Act 1995 (DDA 1995), s.1, as amplified by Sch.1. The meaning is further expanded by Regulations[6] and Guidance[7] on matters to be taken into account in interpreting the definition.

Disability Discrimination Act 1995

Section 1(1)

Subject to the provisions of Sch.1, a person has a disability for the purposes of this Act if he has a physical or mental impairment which has a substantial and long term adverse effect on his ability to carry out normal day-to-day activities.

11–003

---

[3] B. Doyle "Employment rights, equal opportunities and disabled persons: the ingredients of reform" (1993) 22 I.L.J. 89, p.91.

[4] "Guidance on matters to be taken into account in determining questions relating to the definition of disability", 2006, para.A10. Issued by the Secretary of State under DDA 1995, s.3, with effect from May 1, 2006. (SI 2006/1005.) See *www.drc.org.uk*, click on "The Law" and "legislation, codes, regulations and guidance".

[5] DDA 1995, Sch.1, para.6A. On HIV generally, see B. Napier, "AIDS, discrimination and employment law" (1989) 18 I.L.J. 84, and *Watt v High Quality Lifestyles* (2006), unreported, UKEAT/0671/05/ZT (see *www.employmentappeals.gov.uk*).

[6] Disability Discrimination (Meaning of Disability) Regulations 1996 SI 1996/1455.

[7] See above, fn 4.

There are four criteria which must be satisfied. There must be (a) a physical or mental impairment, which (b) affects the ability to carry out everyday activities, and such effect is both (c) long-term and (d) substantial.[8]

Before looking at each in turn, it is worth appreciating the general approach adopted by the courts. The Rules of Procedure state that the tribunal "shall make such enquiries of persons appearing before . . . it and of witnesses as . . . it considers appropriate and shall otherwise conduct the hearing in such manner as . . . it considers most appropriate for the clarification of the issues and generally for the just handling of the proceedings."[9] In *Goodwin v The Patent Office*[10] Morison, J. emphasised the inquisitorial element, which he said should used to avoid a "Catch-22" situation in DDA claims: "Some disabled persons may be unable or unwilling to accept that they suffer from any disability; indeed, it may be symptomatic of their condition that they deny it." In such cases, he suggested, the tribunal should offer claimants "direct assistance". However, Morison's, J. enthusiasm was quelled by the Court of Appeal, which has made it clear that that employment tribunals should be neither inquisitorial nor proactive.[11] Morison, J.'s suggestion was developed into another strand of argument by counsel in *Woodrup v London Borough of Southwark*.[12] He argued that, in providing a service to the public, tribunals were obliged under Part III of the DDA 1995, to make "reasonable adjustments" when dealing with disabled people. However, the Court of Appeal called this notion "far fetched."

(1) Impairment

11–004 "Impairment" must be given its ordinary meaning[13] and so it is not necessary that the impairment is a clinically recognised disability. Accordingly, tribunals need not assess the question by reference to a recognised "illness": an amputee, for example, does not have an "illness" but clearly has an impairment.[14] In *Millar v Inland Revenue*, the claimant, after a fall, experienced drooping of his left eyelid, which he associated with sensitivity to bright light, and headaches. The

---

[8] In *Navas v Eurest Colectividades SA*, Case C-13/05, Advocate General Geelhoad advised (at para.85) that, save in exceptional cases, an illness must have "long term or permanent functional restrictions" to qualify as a disability under the Directive 2000/78/EC. An illness *per se* is not enough.

[9] Employment Tribunals (Constitution and Rules of Procedure) Regulations 2004, SI 2004/1861, Sch.1, r.14(3).

[10] [1999] I.C.R. 302, at 307, EAT. The facts are set out below, para.11–015.

[11] *McNicol v Balfour Beatty Rail Maintenance* [2002] I.C.R. 1498, at para.26, citing *Morgan v Staffordshire University* [2002] I.C.R. 475, EAT, at para.20.

[12] [2002] EWCA Civ 1716, at para.16.

[13] Guidance, above, fn 4, para.A3. *per* Mummery, L.J., *Rugamer v Sony Music, McNicol v Balfour Beatty Rail Maintenance*, [2002] I.R.L.R. 711, at para.17, CA.

[14] *per* Lord Penrose, *Millar v Inland Revenue Commissioners* [2005] I.R.L.R. 112, at para.23, Court of Session.

Court of Session held that these conditions could amount to an impairment, even though a consultant neurologist and a consultant ophthalmologist could find no abnormalities or cause of the conditions. In *College of Ripon & York St John v Hobbs*[15] it was held that a claimant with muscle-twitching and cramps, and who could walk only with the aid of a stick, had an impairment, even though expert evidence showed no underlying organic disease. At one time the Act took a more restrictive approach to mental impairments, requiring any mental illness to be a "clinically well-recognised illness." This requirement was repealed on December 5, 2005,[16] and so now the same approach applies to mental and physical impairments.

The Guidance offers a non-exhaustive list of impairments,[17] but cautions that not all impairments are readily identifiable, there being many which are not immediately obvious.[18] Further, there may be adverse effects which are both physical and mental in nature and the effects of a mainly physical nature may stem from an underlying mental impairment, and vice versa.[19]

Addictions, save those resulting from medical treatment, are excluded from the Act.[20] So addictions to alcohol, tobacco, or other drugs are excluded. Where a person suffers such a condition, its effects may amount to an impairment under the Act. So liver disease can be an impairment under the Act, even if it arose from alcoholism.[21] Accordingly, where an impairment (say depression) is accompanied by an addiction (say alcoholism), the correct approach is to assess the depression irrespective of the alcoholism, and decide if amounts to an impairment.[22] The Australian Disability Discrimination Act 1992 contains no exclusion for addictions.[23] The Americans with Disabilities Act 1990 includes alcoholism (past and present) and rehabilitated illegal drug addicts, but current illegal drug users are not protected.

---

[15] [2002] I.R.L.R. 185, EAT.

[16] Disability Discrimination Act 2005, Sch.2, para.1. (In force SI 2005/2774.)

[17] Above fn 4, para.A6: "sensory impairments, such as those affecting sight or hearing; impairments with fluctuating or recurring effects such as rheumatoid arthritis, myalgic encephalitis (ME)/chronic fatigue syndrome (CFS), fibromyalgia, depression and epilepsy; progressive, such as motor neurone disease, muscular dystrophy, forms of dementia and lupus (SLE); organ specific, including respiratory conditions, such as asthma, and cardiovascular diseases, including thrombosis, stroke and heart disease; developmental, such as autistic spectrum disorders (ASD), dyslexia and dyspraxia; learning difficulties; mental health conditions and mental illnesses, such as depression, schizophrenia, eating disorders, bipolar affective disorders, obsessive compulsive disorders, as well as personality disorders and some self-harming behaviour; produced by injury to the body or brain."

[18] Above fn 4, para.A5.

[19] Above fn 4 24, para.A7.

[20] Disability Discrimination (Meaning of Disability) Regulations 1996 SI 1996/1455, reg.3.

[21] Guidance, above, fn 4 para.A8.

[22] *Power v Panasonic* [2003] I.R.L.R. 151, EAT, at para.12. See also *Hutchison 3G UK Ltd v Mason* (2003) unreported, EAT/0369/03/MAA: depression accompanied by cocaine addiction.

[23] *Marsden v Human Rights and Equal Opportunity Commission and Coffs Harbour and District Ex-Servicemen and Women Memorial Club Ltd* [2000] FCA 1619 confirmed that drug addicts could utilise the Act. Following this there was an unsuccessful attempt to amend the Act to exclude addicts.

11–005   Other excluded conditions are: (a) a tendency to set fires; (b) a tendency to steal; (c) a tendency to physical or sexual abuse of other persons; (d) exhibitionism; and (e) voyeurism.[24] A problem that has arisen here is where the excluded condition is caused by a legitimate impairment, say a tendency to violence caused by schizophrenia, or indecent exposure caused by depression. In *Murray v Newham Citizens Advice Bureau*,[25] the EAT held that for an impairment to be an excluded condition, it had to be "free-standing", in the sense that it was not caused by a legitimate impairment. This was criticised because (a) the more severe the tendency, the more likely it is to be caused by a legitimate impairment, and (b) it means that employers are under a duty to make reasonable adjustments for those with a tendency to setting fires, theft, or physical or sexual abuse.[26] In *Nuttall v Butterfield*[27] the EAT commented that the "free-standing" approach was "not helpful" and ruled that the proper approach was to identify the cause of the less favourable treatment: if it were the legitimate impairment, there is a prima facie case, if it were the excluded condition, there is not.

In *Butterfield*, the employer discovered that the claimant had two convictions for indecent exposure, and subsequently dismissed him, on the ground that such behaviour could bring the company's reputation into disrepute. The claimant's exhibitionism was caused by his depression, which was an impairment. The EAT's approach meant that the cause of the dismissal was the claimant's exhibitionism, and not his impairment, which was irrelevant.

11–006   The criticism of *Murray* is rather alarmist, as it overlooks the utility in these cases of the justification defence, which affords a more flexible approach. For instance, where the tendency last manifested some time ago, and appears to be under control, a dismissal will be harder to justify. On the other hand, where the tendency is severe, and not apparently under control, dismissal becomes much easier to justify. Accordingly, the approach in *Butterfield* gets no nearer to a solution. Here the judge leapt from the statutory question, was the treatment *related to* the disability? to a new one, what was the reason for the treatment? Quite clearly the dismissal was *related* to the legitimate impairment (depression), although not for that immediate reason, which was the excluded condition (exhibitionism).

A similar difficulty was encountered by the High Court of Australia in *Purvis v New South Wales*.[28] Here, a pupil who had been brain-

---

[24] Note also that "seasonal allergic rhinitis" (e.g. hay fever) is not an "impairment", although it can be taken into account where it aggravates the effect of another condition: Disability Discrimination (Meaning of Disability) Regulations 1996 SI 1996/1455, reg.4(2) and (3).

[25] [2003] I.C.R. 643. See further below, para.11–033.

[26] I.R.L.R. "Highlights" June 2003.

[27] [2006] I.C.R. 77, at para.29.

[28] *Purvis (on behalf of Hoggan) v New South Wales (Department of Education and Training)* 202 A.L.R. 133 (2003) High Ct of Australia.

damaged when a baby, was as a result violent at school. His foster parents challenged the decision to exclude him under the Australian Disability Discrimination Act 1992. The extra difficulty for the court was that the definition of disability includes, by s.4(g), "a disorder, illness or disease that affects a person's thought processes, perception of reality, emotions or judgment or *that results in disturbed behaviour*." (Emphasis supplied). Thus, the violent behaviour was inseparable from the brain damage. The majority resolved the matter with the artificial analysis that the comparator should be an equally violent schoolboy without the disability, and so the pupil had been treated no less favourably.[29] The minority endowed the comparator with violent behaviour and so found that there was less favourable treatment. This allowed them to examine school's efforts to accommodate the pupil's disability, which in the event were insufficient to justify the treatment.

In both *Purvis* and *Butterfield,* the result was to exclude from any scrutiny less favourable treatment of "offensive behaviour". It was achieved by using a distorted model of "less favourable treatment".

(2) Ability to Carry Out Normal Day-to-Day Activities

The DDA 1995 demands that the impairment has an adverse effect on the claimant's ability to carry out normal day-to-day activities. This is otherwise known as the *functional requirement*. It is a variation on the Americans with Disabilities Act 1990, which demands that the impairment "limits one or more of [the person's] major life activities."[30] The American definition is potentially wider by including those who are restricted in just one activity, but narrower, because it demands the activity is *major*, or "of central importance to most people's daily lives".[31] The US Equal Employment Opportunity Commission (EEOC) suggests that major life activities include "functions such as caring for oneself, performing manual tasks, walking, seeing, hearing, speaking, breathing, learning and working".[32] In *Toyota v Williams*[33] the Supreme Court held that gardening, housework, and playing with children were not major life activities. In *Chenoweth v Hillsborough County*[34] it was held that driving was not a major life activity, on the logic that it would be "an oddity that a major life activity should require a license from the state . . . and deprivation of being self-driven to work cannot be sensibly compared to inability to see or to learn." But both models are in marked contrast to the Australian Disability

11–007

---

[29] Contrast the UK approach, *Clark v Novacold* [1999] I.C.R. 951, CA, see below para.11–029.
[30] 42 USC s.12102(2)(A).
[31] *Toyota v Williams* 534 US 184, at 198 (Sup Ct 2002). But see the limiting construction given by the Supreme Court in *Sutton v United Air Lines* 527 US 471 (1999) below, para.11–010.
[32] 29 CFR s.1630.2(h)(2)(i) (2002). See *www.eeoc.gov*, click on "Disability".
[33] *Toyota v Williams* 534 US 184, at 198 (2002)
[34] 250 F 3d 1328, at 1329–1330 (11th Cir 2001), certiorari denied 534 US 1131 (Sup Ct 2002).

Discrimination Act 1992, which has no demand for a limitation of activities. It requires only an impairment.[35] For the purposes of the DDA 1995, day-to-day activities can be adversely affected *only* via one of the following capacities: (a) mobility; (b) manual dexterity; (c) physical co-ordination; (d) continence; (e) ability to lift, carry out or otherwise move everyday objects; (f) speech, hearing or eyesight; (g) memory or ability to concentrate, learn or understand; or (h) perception of the risk of physical danger.[36] Each of these capacities should be considered in relation to both physical and mental impairments. Mental impairments are not confined to the obvious "memory and ability to concentrate" capacity. For instance, a mental impairment may affect a person's mobility, because of a fear of travelling in cars or buses. Conversely, a physical impairment, such as pain or fatigue, may affect a person's ability to concentrate.[37]

The Guidance provides examples of day-to-day activities corresponding to each of these capacities, and suggests which examples it would be reasonable to regard as having a substantial adverse effect, and which it would not. For instance, under "Mobility", the Guidance suggests that a "total inability to walk, or difficulty walking other than at a slow pace or with unsteady or jerky movements", or "difficulty in travelling a short journey as a passenger in a vehicle, because, for example, it would be painful getting in and out of a car, or sitting in a car for even a short time" would be substantial enough. On the other hand, "experiencing some tiredness or minor discomfort as a result of walking unaided for a distance of about 1.5 kilometres or one mile", or "experiencing some discomfort as a result of travelling in a car for a journey lasting more than two hours", if *considered alone,* would not be.[38] These are examples, not a definitive list. As Morison, J. stated in *Goodwin v The Patent Office*,[39] "What is a day-to-day activity is best left unspecified: easily recognised, but defined with difficulty."

11–008 An impairment also may indirectly affect how a person carries out day-to-activities. For instance, a man with chronic fatigue syndrome may have the physical capability to walk and to stand, but find these very difficult to sustain for any length of time because of the over-

[35] By the Australian DDA 1992, s 4, "Disability" means: "(a) total or partial loss of the person's bodily or mental functions; or (b) total or partial loss of a part of the body; or (c) the presence in the body of organisms causing disease or illness; or (d) the presence in the body of organisms capable of causing disease or illness; or (e) the malfunction, malformation or disfigurement of a part of the person's body; or (f) a disorder or malfunction that results in the person learning differently from a person without the disorder or malfunction; or (g) a disorder, illness or disease that affects a person's thought processes, perception of reality, emotions or judgment or that results in disturbed behaviour; and includes a disability that: (h) presently exists; or (i) previously existed but no longer exists; or (j) may exist in the future; or (k) is imputed to a person."
[36] DDA 1995, Sch.1, para.4.
[37] Guidance, above fn 4, para.D2.
[38] Guidance, above fn 4, para.D20.
[39] [1999] I.C.R. 302, at 309 EAT. See further below, para.11–015.

whelming fatigue he experiences. Or a person, on medical advice, may refrain from an activity that otherwise he could do.[40]

A particular problem in assessing this question was highlighted by Morison, J. in *Goodwin*. He observed that persons with a disability often will adjust their lives to cope. "Thus a person whose capacity to communicate through normal speech was obviously impaired might well choose, more or less voluntarily, to live on their own. If one asked such a person whether they managed to carry on their daily lives without undue problems, the answer might well be 'yes', yet their ability to lead a 'normal' life had obviously been impaired."[41]

The activities affected should be assessed as a whole, and not in isolation. In *Ekpe v Commissioner of Police of the Metropolis*[42] Mrs Ekpe was moved by her employer to a job which involved keyboard duties. She felt that she could not do such a job because she had a physical impairment, which consisted of a wasting of the intrinsic muscles of her right hand. The evidence was that Mrs Ekpe could not carry heavy shopping, scrub pans, peel, grate, sew or put rollers in her hair. She said that sometimes she had to apply her make-up, and feed herself, with her left hand. The employment tribunal concluded that the Mrs Ekpe's impairment did not have a substantial adverse effect on her ability to carry out normal day-to-day activities because, inter alia, she was only unable to cope with heavy shopping; she could cook normally and could still apply make-up with her left hand. Further, applying make-up and putting in hair-rollers were not normal day-to-day activities because "they are activities carried out almost exclusively by women".[43] The EAT allowed Mrs Ekpe's appeal because the tribunal had erred in law by focussing on each activity, rather than making an overall assessment.

11–009

The focus should not be on what a claimant *can* do. In *Leonard v Southern Derbyshire Chamber of Commerce*[44] the EAT criticised an employment tribunal for concentrating on what the claimant (with clinical depression) could do—such as being able to eat, drink and catch a ball—and weighed them against what she could not do—such as negotiate a pavement edge safely. Mr Justice Nelson stated that whilst tribunals should consider matters "in the round", it "must concentrate on what the applicant cannot do or can only do with difficulty rather than on the things that they can do."

---

[40] Guidance, above fn 4, para.D11.
[41] [1999] I.C.R. 302, at 309 EAT.
[42] [2001] I.C.R. 1084.
[43] The Guidance, above fn 4, (paras D5 and D6) states that although activity cannot be one which is normal only for a small group of people, it need not be one carried out by the majority of population, especially so to exclude activities carried out predominantly by one sex.
[44] [2001] I.R.L.R. 19, para.27. Applied *R. (Mr and Mrs H) v Chair of The Special Educational Needs Tribunal and R School* [2004] EWHC 981, para.33.

(a) Work as a Day-to-Day Activity

11–010 As the impairment must affect a person's capacity to carry out *normal* day-to-day activities, particular work activities are excluded, because they are not normal for most people. Thus, a concert pianist with carpal tunnel syndrome in her wrists may still be able to play the piano to an ordinary standard, if not a concert standard. However, the impairment will affect her normal day-to-day activities if also it affects her ability to use a computer keyboard to send emails. Likewise, a man with a back condition may still be able to lift ordinary objects, if not heavy ones for his job. However, his condition will affect his normal day-to-day activities if also it affects his ability to lift ordinary objects out of work.[45]

A slightly different approach is taken in the US where, of course, work *is* a "major life activity" (see above). Instead of ignoring the work aspect, the courts assess if the claimant's impairment precludes her from a range, or class, of jobs. In *Sutton v United Air Lines,*[46] the Supreme Court said that "when the major life activity under consideration is that of working, the statutory phrase 'substantially limits' requires . . . that plaintiffs allege that they are unable to work in a broad class of jobs." The EEOC regulations state "With respect to the major life activity of working . . . the term *substantially limits* means significantly restricted in the ability to perform either a class of jobs or a broad range of jobs in various classes as compared to the average person having comparable training, skills and abilities".[47] It is an "individualised question" in each case.[48] Consequently, in *Burns v Coca-Cola*, a back condition which precluded the plaintiff (with regard to his education and experience) from 50 per cent of jobs in his district, was held to limit one of his major life activities. On the other hand, in *Taylor v Federal Express,*[49] it was held that a worker with a back condition that prevented him from lifting heavy objects could perform a range of daily activities, and who qualified for over 1,400 different types of jobs and over 130,000 actual jobs in the Baltimore-Washington region, did not have a disability. In *Sutton* itself, two seriously short-sighted pilots who could not fly global routes, could nonetheless utilise their skills to work as regional pilots or pilot instructors. The Supreme Court found that their impairment did not substantially limit them in the major life activity of working.[50]

A particular problem arises where a person's capacity to carry out normal day-to-day activities occurs only when at work. In

[45] Guidance, above fn 4, para.D9.
[46] 527 US 471, at 491 (1999). J. O'Connor discusses the issue at paras 489–94.
[47] 29 CFR s.1630.2(j)(3) (2002). See *www.eeoc.gov*, click on "Disability".
[48] *Toyota v Williams* 534 US 184, 198, (Sup Ct 2002).
[49] 429 F 3d 461, at 464 (4th Cir 2005).
[50] 527 US 471, at 493 (1999).

Cruickshank v VAW Motorcast[51] the claimant suffered severe breathing difficulties ("occupational asthma") at work because of the fumes in the works foundry. When away from work, on sick leave, and at the tribunal hearing following his dismissal, the symptoms cleared up. And so, out of work, he could carry out normal day-to-day activities. The EAT held that so long as the symptoms were sufficient to affect day-to-day tasks, it did not matter where this occurred, at work or at home. Thus it held that the claimant had a disability. Accordingly, the new Guidance states: "The effects experienced by a person as a result of environmental conditions, either in the workplace or in another location where a specialised activity is being carried out, should not be discounted simply because there may be a work-related or other specialised activity involved."[52]

(b) Children

Young children are too young to have developed the capacities (listed above, para.11–007) to carry out normal day-to-day activities. Hence, those under six years of age with an impairment are treated as if that impairment has the requisite effect, where normally it would have such an effect on the ability of an older person to carry out normal day-to-day activities.[53]   **11–011**

The Act was extended to cover all education in September 2002.[54] Thus school pupils who meet the definition of disability are protected. The Guidance provides two examples (where the capacity affected is "memory, or ability to concentrate, learn or understand"):

> A 10-year-old girl has learning difficulties. She has a short attention span and has difficulties remembering facts from one day to the next. She can read only a few familiar words and has some early mathematical skills. To record her work in class she needs to use a tape recorder, pictures and symbols.
>
> A 14-year-old boy has been diagnosed as having attention deficit hyperactivity disorder (ADHD). He often forgets his books, worksheets or homework. In class he finds it difficult to concentrate and skips from task to task forgetting instructions. He often fidgets and makes inappropriate remarks in class or in the playground. Sometimes there can be outbursts of temper.[55]

---

[51] [2002] I.C.R. 729, para.28. In *Law Hospital NHS Trust v Rush* [2001] I.R.L.R. 611, the Court of Session held that a nurse's back condition was a disability, despite her being able to perform her work duties.

[52] Guidance, above fn 4, para.D10.

[53] Disability Discrimination (Meaning of Disability) Regulations 1996 SI 1996/1455, reg.6.

[54] Special Educational Needs and Disability Act 2001. See further below, para.11–065.

[55] Guidance, above fn 4, para.D14.

(c) Disfigurements

11–012   There is an exception under the DDA 1995 where the impairment is a "severe disfigurement." Here, the disfigurement need not adversely affect the person's day-to-day activities. It will "be treated as having a substantial adverse effect on the ability of the person concerned to carry out normal day-to-day activities."[56] This exception does not include tattoos or decorative or other (non-medical) piercings.[57] The Guidance suggests severe disfigurements may include: "scars, birthmarks, limb or postural deformation (including restricted bodily development), or diseases of the skin." It also suggests that when assessing whether the disfigurement is "severe", account should be taken of where it is, (e.g. on the back as opposed to the face).[58] This exception is based on a different "social model" philosophy.[59] Disfigurements may not cause any functional impairment, but instead may lead to disadvantage or discrimination because of other people's reaction to the disfigurement.

(3) Long-Term Effects

11–013   According to Sch.1, para.2(1) of the Act, the effect of an impairment has a long-term effect if: (a) it has lasted at least 12 months; or (b) the period for which it lasts is likely to be at least 12 months; or (c) it is likely to last for the rest of the life of the person affected. Sub-paragraph (b) provides for the situation where the effects began less than a year ago, but are likely to continue for at least a year after they began. Sub-paragraph (c) provides for the situation where a person's life expectancy may be shorter than the requisite 12 month period.

The Act also caters for recurring or fluctuating effects. Paragraph 2(2) provides that "Where an impairment ceases to have a substantial adverse effect . . . it is to be treated as continuing to have that effect if that effect is likely to recur." Primarily, this means that intermittent effects will be treated as if they were continuing effects. However, the "12-month rule" must still be met. For instance, where the first episode of a recurring form of depression (bipolar affective disorder) occurred in months one and two of a 13-month period, and the second episode took place in month 13, the effects are treated as having continued for the whole period of 13 months, and would be "long-term" because they recurred beyond 12 months after the first occurrence. On the other hand, where a person suffers two discrete episodes of depression within a ten-month period, triggered by a loss of job and a bereavement respectively, the effects, at this stage, are not "long-term", because they have not yet lasted more than 12 months after the first

---

[56] DDA 1995, Sch.1, para.3.
[57] Disability Discrimination (Meaning of Disability) Regulations 1996 SI 1996/1455, reg.5.
[58] Guidance, above fn 4, para.B21.
[59] See above, para.11–002.

occurrence, and there is no evidence that these episodes are part of an underlying condition of depression which is likely to recur.[60] Things become more complex when trying to meet the 12-month rule by predicting if the effects will recur. Sub-paragraph (b) includes the situation where the effects began, then ceased, but are likely to recur beyond a year from when they first occurred. Any likely recurring effects must again have a *substantial* adverse effect on the person's ability to carry out day-to-day activities. In *Swift v Chief Constable of Wiltshire Constabulary*[61] the claimant's depression caused her substantial concentration and memory problems for an 18 month period. The evidence was that some effects of the depression were likely to recur, such as an occasional panic attack and consequential sleepless night, but these would not have a *substantial* adverse effect, and so the effects were held not to be long-term.

The phrase in para.2(2) *if that effect is likely to recur* suggests the recurring effects must be the same effects as the previous one. This was the view of the EAT in *Swift*, which appeared to base its decision also on the fact the "recurring" effects were different from the original ones. However, the Guidance suggests otherwise. Under the heading "Recurring or fluctuating effects", it states that it is "not necessary for the effect to be the same throughout the period which is being considered . . . other effects on the ability to carry out normal day-to-day activities may develop and the initial effect may disappear altogether."[62] To square this with the wording of Sch.1, para.2(2), *that effect*, should be taken not to refer to the type of effect previously experienced (say concentration or memory problems), but only to the effect being "substantial". Thus the *ratio decidendi* in *Swift* should be confined to a rule that any recurring adverse effects must be substantial.   **11–014**

The EAT has held that the point in time when the assessment of the likelihood of recurrence should be made is at the time of the act complained of, rather than at the time of the hearing, (probably several months later).[63] This reverses earlier decisions, which were influenced by para.B8 of the original Guidance, which provided that account should be taken for the total period that the effect exists, *including anytime after the discriminatory behaviour*. The new Guidance has dropped this final direction in deference to the more

---

[60] Guidance, above fn 4, para.C5.

[61] [2004] I.C.R. 909, para.49–52, EAT.

[62] Guidance, above fn 4, para.C6. Para.B2 of the original Guidance, available to the EAT in *Swift*, was similar: *Guidance on matters to be taken into account in determining questions relating to the definition of disability*, London: HMSO. (ISBN 0-11-270-955-9) Issued on July 25, 1996 under s.3, DDA by the Secretary of State (SI 1996/1996) with effect July 1996.

[63] *Latchman v Reed Business Information* [2002] I.C.R. 1453, para.17, disapproving the contrary view expressed *obiter* in *Greenwood v British Airways* [1999] I.C.R. 969, at 977; *Collet v Diocese of Hallam Trustee* (2001) unreported EAT/1400/00; *Cruickshank v VAW Motorcast Ltd* [2002] I.C.R. 729, paras 22–25.

recent cases.[64] This excludes from the Act the situation where the effects were unlikely to recur at the time of the discriminatory act, but in fact did recur before the tribunal hearing. For instance, a worker takes a month off work because of depression, but recovers to the extent that the depression is unlikely to recur. A few weeks later his application for promotion is rejected because of his sickness record and this triggers a recurrence of the depression. His claim for discrimination will fail because at the time of the alleged discriminatory act the depression was unlikely to recur.[65]

In cases where the tribunal must decide whether the impairment was likely to continue or recur, "likely" means "more probable than not".[66] In *Latchman v Reed Business Information*[67] the risk of the effects (that had lasted about nine months) of depression recurring were assessed at 50 per cent, and so it was not more probable than not that they would recur.

(4) Substantial

11–015   In *Goodwin v The Patent Office*,[68] Morison, J. said that *substantial* means simply "more than minor or trivial" rather than "very large". In *Vicary v British Telecommunications*,[69] the same judge stated that it was not for medical experts the decide whether the effects are substantial: this was a matter for the tribunal.

The Guidance provides some factors that may help decide if the effect is substantial. First, the time taken to carry out an activity. Second, the effects of the impairment should be considered cumulatively, and not in isolation. So several effects, in themselves minor, could cumulate into a substantial effect. Similarly, where a person has more than one impairment, account should be taken of whether the impairments together have a substantial effect overall on the person's ability to carry out normal day-to-day activities.[70] Persons are expected, within reason, to modify their behaviour to prevent or reduce the effects of an impairment, for example, someone with a back problem should avoid extreme activities, such as parachuting. Otherwise, such persons may not be considered as having a disability for the Act. Account should be taken of environmental conditions

---

[64] Guidance, above fn 4, para.C3; original Guidance, above fn 62.
[65] See *Greenwood v British Airways* [1999] I.C.R. 969, where in the event the initial period of depression lasted *over* 12 months, so the claimant was protected as he had a "past disability" (see below, para.11–020). See also *Barker v Westbridge International Ltd* (2000) unreported EAT/1180/98.
[66] Guidance, above fn 4, para.C2
[67] [2002] I.C.R. 1453, EAT.
[68] [1999] I.C.R. 302, at 310, EAT.
[69] [1999] I.R.L.R. 680, at 682, EAT. Applied *Abadeh v BT* [2001] I.C.R. 156, EAT.
[70] In *M v SW School* [2004] EWHC 2586, at paras 13–14, the Special Educational Needs and Disability Tribunal analysed the each of the claimant's vision, mobility and speech difficulties in isolation, and concluded that the effects of each were not substantial. The High Court reversed, holding that the effects of the impairments should be considered as a whole.

that may exacerbate the effect of an impairment. "Factors such as temperature, humidity, lighting, the time of day or night, how tired the person is, or how much stress he or she is under, may have an impact on the effects." For example, rheumatoid arthritis produces particularly bad effects during cold and damp weather.[71]

In *Goodwin* the claimant was dismissed from his post as a patent examiner after complaints from female staff of disturbing behaviour. He is a paranoid schizophrenic and he had auditory hallucinations—that is, he heard voices—which interrupted his concentration. He brought a complaint under the Disability Discrimination Act. The employment tribunal held that he failed to come within the definition of a "disabled person," finding that he was able to "perform his domestic activities without the need for assistance, to get to work efficiently and to carry out his work to a satisfactory standard." The EAT reversed that decision, holding that the tribunal's analysis was too narrow, as it ignored the claimant's capacity to concentrate and communicate, which meant, for instance, he was unable to carry out day-to-day conversion with colleagues. In *Vicary v British Telecommunications*,[72] the claimant had an impairment in her right arm and hand. She suffered pain when doing repetitive light work, for example typing or cutting vegetables, or when she was doing more physical work on a one-off basis, such as shifting a chair at home when sitting down or getting up from a table. The EAT held that these were normal day-to-day activities and that an inability to carry out those functions would "obviously be regarded as a substantial impairment of an ability to carry out normal day-to-day activities."[73]

There are three situations for which the Act makes specific provision on the issue of "substantial".

(a) The Effect of Medical Treatment

The Act stipulates that when assessing if the effects are substantial, the effect of measures that are being taken to treat or correct it should be disregarded. In other words, tribunals must assess the effects *as if* there was no treatment. This does not apply to the correction by glasses or contact lenses of sight impairments.[74] "Measures" include medical treatment and the use of a prosthesis (e.g. an artificial leg) or other aid.[75] In *Kapadia v Lambeth LBC*[76] the EAT held that counselling

11–016

---

[71] Guidance, above fn 4, paras B2–B10.
[72] [1999] I.R.L.R. 680, at 682, EAT. Applied *Abadeh v BT* [2001] I.C.R. 156, EAT.
[73] Contrast the US case *Carr v Publix Super Markets* No 05–12611 (2006 11th Cir) (US App LEXIS 2845), at p.7, where it was held that the plaintiff, who found it impossible, or difficult, to perform certain tasks with his right arm (lifting and operating a cash register), was not limited substantially in his ability to perform manual tasks central to his daily life or otherwise to care for himself.
[74] DDA 1995, Sch.1, para.6.
[75] *ibid.*
[76] [2000] I.R.L.R. 14, affirmed [2000] I.R.L.R. 699, CA.

sessions for a man with depression constituted "medical treatment." In *Carden v Pickerings Europe*[77] the EAT held that plates and pins used for a broken ankle could be an "other aid", even some 20 years after they were inserted, provided that they still corrected or treated what would otherwise be a disability. This "deduced effects" doctrine applies even where the effects are not at all apparent, or completely under control.[78]

In *Goodwin v The Patent Office*[79] Morison, J. suggested that when approaching the question, "The tribunal will wish to examine how the applicant's abilities had actually been affected at the material time, whilst on medication, and then to address their minds to the difficult question as to the effects which they think there would have been but for the medication: the *deduced* effects. The question is then whether the actual and deduced effects on the applicant's abilities to carry out normal day-to-day activities is *clearly more than trivial.*"

11–017 The Act is concerned with measures that "are being taken", and accordingly, where treatment has ceased, a tribunal cannot disregard the treatment.[80] It must judge the effects of the impairment as they are presented. Where the effect of the continuing treatment creates a permanent improvement, that improvement should be taken into account. If the improvement reduces the effects to below being substantial, then the person does not have a disability.[81] The Guidance provides an example of a person treated with a long course of antibiotics for pneumonia, which cures the impairment before the treatment is complete.[82] However, if the improvement is temporary, or it cannot be ascertained whether it is permanent, then the treatment must be disregarded. For instance, a person's depression may improve with psychotherapy, but that person may suffer a relapse should the treatment cease.[83]

In the United States the effect of the impairment must be assessed in its mitigated, rather than untreated or uncorrected, form. This rule applies whether the measures taken are medication, devices, or even the body's own systems. In *Murphy v United Parcel Service*, the plaintiff's hypertension caused by high blood pressure was controlled by medication to the degree that the condition did not significantly restrict his activities. In *Sutton v United Airlines* the plaintiffs had severe myopia, corrected by lenses. And in *Albertson's v Kirkingburg* the plaintiff had sight only in one eye, which corrected by his own subconscious mechanisms. In all three cases

---

[77] [2005] I.R.L.R. 720, EAT.
[78] Guidance, above fn 4, para.B12.
[79] [1999] I.C.R. 302, at 310, EAT.
[80] *Abadeh v BT* [2001] I.C.R. 156, at para.30, EAT.
[81] *ibid.*, at para.31.
[82] Guidance, above fn 4, para.B15.
[83] *Abadeh v BT* [2001] I.C.R. 156, at para.33, EAT

the Supreme Court held that the plaintiffs did not have a disability for the ADA 1990.[84]

(b) Progressive Conditions

By Sch.1, para.8, the Act protects a person with a progressive condition that results in an impairment that has *some* adverse effect (i.e. not substantial), but which is likely to become substantial. Progressive conditions include cancer, systemic lupus erythematosis (SLE), various types of dementia, rheumatoid arthritis, and motor neurone disease.[85] Note that some specified conditions are "deemed" as disabilities under the Act, from the moment they arise (effectively from the point of diagnoses) irrespective of whether there is any adverse effect. These conditions include HIV infection, multiple sclerosis, or cancer, although provision may be made to exclude certain types of cancer.[86]

11–018

Under para.8, a person is protected not from the point of diagnoses, but from when the effects of the condition arise, provided that it is "more likely than not"[87] that at some stage in the future the effects will become substantial. The effect need not be continuous.[88] Any effect can be directly or indirectly caused by the condition, and the predicted effect does not have to be the same as the current effect. In *Kirton v Tetrosyl*[89] the claimant was diagnosed with prostrate cancer. Surgery to treat the cancer resulted in a sphincter deficiency which gave the claimant infrequent (i.e. not substantial) incontinence. The Court of Appeal held that the claimant had now a progressive condition, even though the current impairment was only indirectly caused by the cancer and is different from the likely substantial effects of the cancer.

The requirement for the effects to be "long-term" apply in the normal way.[90] Of course, for some progressive conditions where death is likely to result quickly, the 12-month rule may not apply. In less serious cases the 12 month rule applies, although the period begins when the first effects arise. In *Grimley v Turner & Jarvis Ltd*[91] the claimant was diagnosed with cancer that had an insubstantial adverse effect. About a year later he underwent surgery for this on his kidney, which resulted in a predicted two-month period of substantial adverse effects. The EAT held that the claimant had a progressive condition

---

[84] Respectively 527 US 516, at 521 (1999); 527 US 471, at 482 (1999); 527 US 555, at 565–566 (1999). See generally J. Van Detta "'Typhoid Mary' Meets the ADA: A Case Study of the 'Direct Threat' Standards under the Americans with Disabilities Act" (1999) 22 Harv JL & Pub Policy 849.

[85] Guidance, above fn 4, para.B18.

[86] See above, para.11–002.

[87] *Mowat-Brown v University of Surrey* [2002] I.R.L.R. 235, at para.21, EAT.

[88] Guidance, above fn 4, para.B17.

[89] [2003] I.C.R. 1237.

[90] See above, para.11–013.

[91] (2004) unreported UKEAT/0967/03/ILB.

under para.8, as the effects had lasted over 12 months. It did not matter that the predicted substantial effect was only two months.

(c) Disfigurements

11–019   Severe disfigurements may be considered without more as substantial. See above, para.11–012.

(5) Past Disabilities

11–020   Section 2, DDA 1995, extends the Act's coverage to those who have had a disability in the past. The question of whether or not somebody had a disability is determined under the Act in the normal way, which applies even to those who claim to have had a disability before the Act came into force.

Without s.2 someone who has recovered from a past disability would not be protected. This is particularly important for disabilities that carry a stigma, such as mental illness. And so, for instance, an employer who dismisses a worker upon discovering that she once had a mental illness can be liable under the Act. Schedule 2, modifies Sch.1, para.2, which covers fluctuating effects,[92] so that where in the past the effects cease and unexpectedly recur (i.e. they were not *likely* to recur), the effects will be regarded as continuing.[93]

2. DISABILITY DISCRIMINATION GENERALLY

11–021   The definitions and types of unlawful acts vary slightly across the different fields covered. The principal reason for this is the amendments to the employment field to accord with the Employment Equality Directive 2000/78/EC.

Some unlawful acts remain common the to whole of the Disability Discrimination Act 1995 and broadly follow the scheme of Sex and Race legislation. Victimisation is outlawed by s.55,[94] whilst s.58 provides the same test for the liability of employers or principals for acts of their respective employees or agents.[95] Section 57 prohibits the aiding of unlawful acts.[96]

Most discrimination legislation is symmetrical in nature.[97] This means that a white person may claim under the Race Relations Act 1976, and a man may claim under the Sex Discrimination Act 1975.

---

[92] See above, para.11–013.
[93] See *Greenwood v British Airways*, [1999] I.C.R. 969, EAT, above fn 65.
[94] Discussed Ch.7, p.179. The protection is extended for Pt IV, Ch.1, "Schools". See below, para.11–070.
[95] Discussed Ch.8, para.8–081.
[96] Save as to Pt IV, Ch.1, covering schools. Discussed Ch.5, para.5–028.
[97] See further Ch.1, para.1–005 and Ch.12, para.12–002.

Disability law, including the DDA 1995, aspires to its goal of equality by other (non-symmetrical) means. Rather than giving formal equal rights to persons with or without a disability, it identifies persons with a disability for protection, and (in the case of the duty to make reasonable adjustments) affords persons with a disability *different* treatment (this can be more favourable). For instance, a worker confined to a wheelchair does not want equal treatment in the sense of sharing a staircase. She requires equal *access*, which is achieved by *different* treatment. This approach means that persons without disabilities cannot bring claims under the Act where they consider that they have been treated less favourably than a person with a disability.

This approach inherits a feature of the definition of direct sex **11–022** discrimination. In the same way that direct sex discrimination covers only the claimant's sex,[98] these definitions cover only the claimant's disability. Consequently, two forms of discrimination remain outside the legislation: discrimination on the grounds of *another's* disability and "perceived discrimination." So whilst it is unlawful (religious discrimination) for a line manager to shun a worker for associating with, say, a Muslim, it is not unlawful disability discrimination to shun the worker for associating with a friend with AIDS. By contrast, the Australian Disability Discrimination Act 1992 expressly outlaws discrimination and harassment of a worker on the ground of the disability of an "associate" of that worker.[99] This appears to include a person with a disability who has died.[100] "Perceived discrimination" arises where a person treats another less favourably because he wrongly believes the worker has a disability. For instance, a manager may shun a worker because he wrongly perceives that the worker has AIDS,[101] or because the worker has been wrongly diagnosed as suffering from a mental illness. By contrast the Australian DDA 1992 covers disabilities that are "imputed", whilst the Americans with Disabilities Act 1990 defines disability to include being *regarded* as having a disability and so covers these scenarios.[102] This embraces the "social model" of disability discrimination.[103] However, in the US this provision has been narrowly interpreted. In *Sutton v United Air Lines*[104] the Supreme Court held that United Air Lines, in barring two seriously short-sighted pilots (with corrective lenses, so not prima facie "disabled" under the Act) from global routes, were not

---

[98] See Ch.4, para.4–027.

[99] See e.g. ss.15–18 (employment discrimination), and s.36 (harassment).

[100] This is the view of the Australian Human Rights Commission. See *www.hreoc.gov.au* and click "Disability Rights" and "who are people with a disability".

[101] But unconscious discrimination is unlawful under the DDA: *Williams v YKK (UK) Ltd*, [2003] All E.R. (D) 141 (Mar) EAT (EAT/0408/01 AM, see *www.employmentappeals.gov.uk*).

[102] 42 USC s.12102(2)(c). See B. Doyle, "Employment rights, equal opportunities and disabled persons: the ingredients of reform" (1993) 22 I.L.J. 89, p.93.

[103] See above para.11–002.

[104] *Karen Sutton and Kimberly Hinton v United Air Lines* 527 US 471 (1999), at 489–494.

"regarding" the pilots as a having an impairment, as they allowed them to fly local routes.[105] For employment matters the Employment Equality Directive 2000/78/EC prohibits discrimination simply on the grounds *of disability*, and so covers these two forms of discrimination. So it appears that the employment provisions of the DDA 1995 fall short of the Directive.

3. EMPLOYMENT FIELD

11–023 The employment provisions, contained in Pt II of the Disability Discrimination Act 1995, were heavily amended by the Disability Discrimination Act (Amendment) Regulations 2003,[106] which were passed in response to the Employment Equality Directive 2000/78/EC, and came into force on October 1, 2004. Further amendments were made to the employment provisions by the Disability Discrimination Act 2005, coming into force on December 5, 2005.

(1) Scope
11–024 The original 1995 Act covered employees, contract workers and trade organisations. The Regulations of 2003 removed the previous exclusions of employers with less than 15 workers,[107] employment on ships, planes and hovercraft,[108] fire-fighters, prison officers and specialised police forces.[109] The Regulations extended the coverage to the police, barristers, advocates and their pupils,[110] partnerships,[111] office-holders,[112] qualification bodies, and practical work experience (vocational training).[113] However the armed forces remain outside the scope of the employment provisions.[114] These definitions are much the same as those given in the other discrimination legislation, which are discussed in Ch.8. By another amendment which came into force on October 1, 2004, sections 4G–4K were added to the 1995 Act, extending the coverage of occupational pensions. It is now unlawful for trustees or managers of occupational pension schemes to discriminate against, or harass, members of their schemes.[115] The 2005 Act

---

[105] *Karen Sutton and Kimberly Hinton v United Air Lines* 527 US 471 (1999), at 489–494.
[106] SI 2003/1673.
[107] Disability Discrimination Act 1995 (Amendment) Regulations 2003, SI 2003/1673, reg.7, repealed DDA 1995, s.7.
[108] *ibid.*, reg.27.
[109] *ibid.*, regs 24–26.
[110] *ibid.*, reg.8 inserting ss.7A–7D.
[111] *ibid.*, reg.6 inserting ss.6A–6C.
[112] *ibid.*, reg.6 inserting ss.4C–4F.
[113] *ibid.*, reg.13, inserting ss.14A–14D.
[114] DDA 1995, s.64(7). The exemption is permitted by the Employment Equality Directive 2000/78/EC, Art.3(4).
[115] Disability Discrimination Act 1995 (Pensions) Regulations SI 2003/2770, reg.3.

has added to this, by new sections 15A–C, "members" of locally-electable authorities (i.e. councillors when carrying out official business), which include all local authorities in England, Wales and Scotland and the Greater London Authority.

The Disability Rights Commission has issued two codes of practice for this field, one for employment and occupation, and one for trade organisations and qualification bodies.[116]

In the same way as the other legislation, the Act outlaws discrimination and harassment in recruitment and during employment. Section 4, DDA 1995, directly parallels the equivalent provisions of the other discrimination legislation,[117] making it unlawful to discriminate before someone obtains a job, while they are in employment, and in relation to dismissal.[118] Section 16A, reproduces the provisions elsewhere catering for discrimination, harassment or victimisation after the relationship has come to an end.[119] Although s.16A covers employment matters, it specifically excludes the provisions covering locally-electable authorities (see above). The section came into force on October 1, 2004. Claims arising before that date may succeed on the wording of the pre-existing employment provisions in s.4.[120]

Section 3B[121]provides a uniform free-standing definition of harassment. It covers employment matters and, by s.21A, employment services. Rather like the direct discrimination provisions, it differs slightly in principle from most of the other free-standing definitions (in relation to race, sexual orientation, religion or belief, and age), and resembles the definition for the Sex Discrimination Act 1975. Here the harassment must be related to the *victim's* disability. This excludes harassment on the ground of another's disability and on perceived disability. So for example, harassing a colleague because of a spouse's disability, or in the mistaken belief that the colleague has a disability (e.g. AIDS) will remain lawful under s.3B. According to the Government s.3B is intended to replicate the approach taken to sexual harassment by the EAT in *Driskel v Peninsula Bus Services.*[122] Cases arising before October 1, 2004 may be argued as direct discrimination or disability-related discrimination.

11–025

Discriminatory advertising, and instructions or pressure to discriminate, are outlawed by the DDA 1995[123] in the same way as provided by the Sex Discrimination Act 1975,[124] save that the DDA provisions

---

[116] Respectively, *Code of Practice Employment and Occupation* (2004) London: TSO (ISBN 0 11 703419 3); *Code of Practice Trade Organisations and Qualification Bodies* (2004) London: TSO (ISBN 0 11 703418 5). Available at *www.drc.gov.uk*, click on "The Law".

[117] See Ch.8, paras 8–008 to 8–016.

[118] This includes constructive dismissal: *Meikle v Nottingham CC* [2005] I.C.R. 1, at para.53.

[119] See Ch.8, para.8–017.

[120] *Jones v 3M Healthcare Ltd* [2003] I.C.R. 867, HL. See Ch.8, para.8–017.

[121] Inserted by SI 2003/1673, reg.4, in force October 1, 2004.

[122] [2000] I.R.L.R. 151 EAT. Explanatory Notes to the *pre-consultation draft* Regulations (now SI 2003/1673), para.40. Harassment and *Driskel* are discussed Ch.5, para.5–011.

[123] DDA 1995, ss.16B and 16C respectively, inserted by SI 2003/1673, in force October 1, 2004.

[124] SDA 1975, ss.38 and 39–40 respectively. Discussed Ch.5, paras 5–029 and 5–032.

cover only employment matters. Only the Disability Rights Commission (or when operable the Commission for Equality and Human Rights)[125] can enforce these provisions.

The Act defines three types of employment discrimination, direct discrimination, disability-related discrimination and failure to make reasonable adjustments.

(2) Direct Discrimination

11–026 For employment matters only, direct discrimination is outlawed specifically (from October 1, 2004). Section 3A (5) of the Disability Discrimination Act 1995 provides:

> A person directly discriminates against a disabled person if, on the ground of the disabled person's disability, he treats the disabled person less favourably than he treats or would treat a person not having that particular disability whose relevant circumstances, including his abilities, are the same as, or not materially different from, those of the disabled person.

This closely resembles the definition for direct sex discrimination, and so the general principles of direct discrimination (set out in Ch.4) can be relevant here. On the same lines as sex discrimination, the definition is limited to the claimant's disability. This excludes "perceived" discrimination and discrimination of the ground of another's disability.[126] Unlike disability-related discrimination (below) direct disability discrimination cannot be justified.

The phrase *on the ground of* (in contrast to *related to*) makes this a particularly narrow definition, aimed at facially discriminatory practices.[127] The drafting is attempting to draw a line between the person's disability and the consequences of that disability. Apart from the impairment in question, the comparator must have the same capabilities as the claimant. For instance, an employer may refuse to hire a woman with epilepsy because he believes that she cannot drive safely. The comparator will be someone who cannot drive safely who does not have epilepsy. The refusal to hire was on the ground of her driving capability, and not on the ground of her disability. It would of course be disability-related discrimination under s.3A (1), where the employer has the opportunity to justify the treatment.

11–027 The Government envisaged this definition covering the following instances.[128]

---

[125] See Ch.13, para.13–029 *et seq.*
[126] See above, para.11–022.
[127] The Code of Practice suggests that facially neutral practices may amount to direct discrimination where the practice is a pretext: above fn 116, at para.4.10.
[128] Explanatory Notes to the *pre-consultation draft* Regulations (now SI 2003/1673), para.32.

(a) an employer, on learning that a job applicant has diabetes, summarily rejects the application without giving any consideration of the applicant's circumstances or whether the person concerned would be competent to do the job (with or without a reasonable adjustment);

(b) a disabled employee is refused access to the employer's sports and social club simply on the basis that the club does not allow disabled members, and without any consideration of whether the employee might benefit from membership, and even though they could access the club with a reasonable adjustment;

(c) without any consideration of whether he will be able to work for as many years as other employees, a newly recruited disabled person is required to pay the same contributions to an occupational pension scheme even though he is denied access to ill health retirement benefits available to other members of the scheme.

As in other fields, stereotyping can amount to direct discrimination. For instance an employer may reject an application from a blind person because he wrongly assumed that blind people cannot use a computer.[129] It is possible for an employer to directly discriminate without knowledge of the victim's disability. For instance, the employer may advertise internally for a promotion, stating that the post is not suitable for anyone with a history of mental illness, and exclude, unknowingly, a member of staff with a history of schizophrenia.[130] It is possible also for the employer to directly discriminate by acting on discriminatory factors of which it is unaware. In *Williams v YKK*[131] Elias, J. suggested *obiter* that an unprejudiced manager's decision may be affected, or tainted, by a report made by a prejudiced supervisor. So for instance, a manager who is unaware that a worker's absenteeism was due to her disability, may be influenced to dismiss her by unfavourable opinions delivered by prejudiced colleagues who were aware of her disability. This is direct discrimination because the reason for the treatment is the victim's disability: the basis of prejudiced opinions was disability, rather than absenteeism.[132]

---

[129] Code of Practice above fn 116, at para.4.8.

[130] *ibid.*, at para.4.11.

[131] [2003] All E.R. (D) 141 (Mar), (EAT/0408/01 AM, see *www.employmentappeals.gov.uk*).

[132] *ibid.*, at para.23. In the US, this is known as the "Cat's Paw" theory. See further Ch.4, para.4–021.

(3) Disability-Related Discrimination

11–028   Section 3A (1) of the Disability Discrimination Act 1995 provides:

> . . . a person discriminates against a disabled person if—
>
> (a)   for a reason which relates to the disabled person's disability, he treats him less favourably than he treats or would treat others to whom that reason does not or would not apply, and
> (b)   he cannot show that the treatment in question is justified.

(a) The Comparison and the Reason for the Treatment

11–029   Here, the reason for the less favourable treatment need only be *related* to the disability. Thus if a cafe has a "no dogs" rule, the reason for refusing entry to a blind man with his guide dog relates to his disability.[133] Similarly, a disabled customer who is told to leave the restaurant because she has difficulty eating as a result of her disability is so treated for a reason *related to* her disability. Accordingly, the choice of comparator differs from that under direct discrimination. In these examples the comparator is a person *without* a dog, or *without* an eating difficulty. If it were otherwise, and the comparator were a sighted man *with* a dog, or a person who had difficulty eating for a reason unrelated to a disability (say a coughing fit, or because the food tasted off), the scope of the Act would be drastically reduced. It follows that that the comparison cannot be made until the reason for the treatment is identified. The comparator is a person without that reason.

These points were made in *Clark v TGD Ltd t/a Novacold*.[134] In this case Mr Clark suffered a back injury at work in August 1996 and was diagnosed as having soft tissue injuries around the spine. He was unable to work and absent from September 1996 until his dismissal, in January 1997. In response to Clark's claim for disability-related discrimination Novacold argued that they would have dismissed any person unable to work for that long. The Court of Appeal held that this was using the wrong comparator. The reason for Clark's dismissal was his inability to work, which was related to his disability. Clark should have been compared with a person without his disability who was able to work (the "reason"). Mummery, L.J. noted that this approach would avoid the problems encountered by the courts in their "futile attempts" to identify a hypothetical non-pregnant male comparator for a pregnant woman in sex discrimination cases before

---

[133] Minister of State for Social Security and Disabled People, 253 HC Official Report (6th series) col 150, January 24, 1995.
[134] [1999] I.C.R. 951, at 964–966, CA.

the ECJ decision *Webb v EMO Air Cargo.*[135] It was also consistent with the availability of the justification defence, which is not available for direct discrimination.

There is still some confusion which has led to a string of EAT cases **11–030** which have inadvertently rejected the *Novacold* reasoning. These cases have arisen where an employer invokes a general policy against a person with a disability. In *Hood v London Clubs Management*[136] the claimant's sick pay was withdrawn under a policy to cut sick pay to all workers. The EAT held, apparently applying *Novacold,* that the reason for the treatment was the general policy, and not the claimant's disability (migraines). Therefore the claimant was not treated less favourably than other workers who may have been off sick. This is using wrong comparator. Hood should have been compared with a person without a disability *who could work.* This person would have been paid.[137] As Mummery, L.J. said in *Novacold,* "The reason for his dismissal would not apply to others who are able to perform the main functions of their jobs."[138] Equally, in *Hood,* the reason for the withdrawal of pay would not apply to those who could work. The "sick-pay policy" argument should have been a matter for the defence of justification, not the comparison. Similarly, in *Ministry of Defence Police v Armstrong,*[139] following a period off work relating to her disability, the claimant was not allowed by a general policy to return to her previous duties. The EAT held that "the reason for the refusal was not Mrs Armstrong's disability", but the general policy. The clear error here is the omission of the phrase *related to* (her disability). The logic of these cases is also in conflict with the Code of Practice, which provides the following example of disability-related discrimination: a disabled worker is absent on sick leave for six months. The employer dismisses her in accordance with its general policy of dismissing all staff on sick leave period for six months. The correct comparator is a worker who has *not* taken six months' sick leave.[140]

By contrast, other tribunals have followed *Novacold* more strictly. For instance, in *Summer Bridge Doors v Pickering*[141] the claimant had

---

[135] Case C-32/93 [1994] I.R.L.R. 482, ECJ. See Ch.4, para.4–037 *et seq.*

[136] [2001] I.R.L.R. 719, EAT. See also *R. v Powys CC, Ex p. Hambidge* (No.2) [2000] 2 FCR 69, CA, where in a case on the provision of services, *Novacold* simply was ignored. See below, para.11–046.

[137] Some confusion may have been caused by the distinction in the claimant's pleadings between ordinary pay and sick pay. For the parties it was pay, no matter what the label.

[138] [1999] I.C.R. 951, at 965.

[139] (2004) unreported, UKEAT/0551/03/TM, at para.10. See also *Bank v IBM* (2003) UKEAT/389/03/MAA, at para.32 (available at *www.employmentappelas.gov.uk.* Curiously, in *Meikle v Nottingham CC* [2005] I.C.R. 1, the Court of Appeal accepted the employer's concession that its reduction in sick-pay (in accordance with its general policy) was less favourable treatment relating to the claimant's disability (para.63), without reference to *Hood,* whilst at the same time applying another part of the *Hood* decision, that sick pay is not excluded from the reasonable adjustment duty, (para.60).

[140] Above fn 116, at para.4.30.

[141] (2003) EAT/1088/02 ZT, at paras 30–36. See also *Shrubsole v The Governors of Wellington School* EAT/328/02/DA, at paras 20–21. (Both available at *www.employmentappeals.gov.uk.*)

rheumatoid arthritis, a disability which caused her a weak knee, which in turn caused her to fall with a resulting injury, which led her employer to refuse her work and sick pay. The EAT held that the unfavourable treatment was related to her disability. In *Cosgrove v Caesar & Howie*[142] Ms Cosgrove was dismissed after being off work for a year with depression. The EAT rejected the employer's argument that as it would have dismissed anyone off work for a year it had not treated Ms Cosgrove less favourably. Applying *Novacold* the EAT held that the comparator should have been a person who was not off sick for a year.

(b) Knowledge of the Disability

11–031 In these cases, where the treatment is on the ground of a factor related to the disability, there is no need for the employer to have had knowledge of that disability. Two vivid examples were provided by Lindsay, J. in *Heinz v Kendrick*.[143] First, a postman with a concealed artificial leg may be dismissed for being too slow. Second, a secretary with undeclared dyslexia may be dismissed for "typing hopelessly misspelt letters". The Code of Practice supports this view, giving an example of a woman dismissed for persistent absenteeism (as any worker would be) where the employer was unaware that the reason for her absence was her multiple sclerosis. In all these examples, the employer's act amounts to treatment related to the worker's disability (which may or may not be justified).

(c) Justification of Disability-Related Discrimination

11–032 Section 3A (3), DDA 1995, provides that disability-related less favourable treatment may be justified if "the reason for it is both material to the circumstances of the particular case and substantial".

The employer's ability to justify less favourable treatment is subject to an important proviso. This arises where there is also a duty on the employer to make reasonable adjustments for the claimant (see below), which is likely to occur in most cases.[144] Section 3A (6) provides that if in a case of disability-related discrimination, "a person is under a duty to make reasonable adjustments in relation to a disabled person but fails to comply with that duty, his treatment of that person cannot be justified . . . unless it would have been justified even if he had complied with that duty." This means that it is necessary to consider whether the treatment would still have been justified

---

[142] [2001] I.R.L.R. 653. See further below, para.11–038.
[143] [2000] I.C.R. 491, at para.25, EAT. See also Lord Johnston in *Callaghan v Glasgow CC* [2001] I.R.L.R. 724, at 726, EAT.
[144] See e.g. *per* Pauline Hughes, Head of Legal Services Team, Disability Rights Commission, [2004] 33 I.L.J. 358, at 365.

even if the employer had complied with its duty to make reasonable adjustments. It comes to this: "would a reasonable adjustment have made any difference?" If so, the treatment cannot be justified. In practice this means that where a duty to make reasonable adjustments arises, it must be resolved *before* the question of disability-related treatment.[145] Take, for instance, a case where a job applicant with arthritis is given a typing test. There may arise a reasonable adjustment duty to allow the applicant to use an adapted keyboard. The employer does not afford her this facility (which would have enabled her to type at normal speed) and her typing is too slow. She is not appointed because of this. The employer's refusal to hire was because of the applicant's slow typing speed. But the employer would not be able to justify this disability-related reason because the provision of an adapted keyboard would have made a difference.[146]

Should disability-related discrimination have to be justified, the standard was set by the Court of Appeal in *Jones v Post Office*.[147] In this case, Mr Jones was employed as a mail delivery driver from 1977. He was diagnosed with diabetes and following a heart attack in June 1997, his treatment was switched from tablets to insulin. As a result, and following its medical advice, the Post Office restricted Jones to two-hours per day driving duties. He brought a claim under the DDA. The employment tribunal heard expert evidence for Jones that conflicted with the Post Office's medical advice. This said that the deterioration in Jones' condition signalled by his reliance on insulin made no material difference to the existing risk that he would suffer a hypoglycaemic episode while driving. The tribunal preferred this evidence to the Post Office's expert and found that the Post Office was not justified in restricting Jones' driving. On appeal, this decision was reversed. The Court of Appeal held that it was not for the tribunal to decide such matters.

Pill, L.J. stated that where an employer made a "properly conducted risk assessment" and then acted upon it, the question is whether that act fell within the "range of responses open to a reasonable decision-maker".[148] Arden, L.J. stated that "material" meant that there had to be a "reasonably strong connection" between the reason (the worker's disability) and the "circumstances of the particular case" (presumably here, safe driving). No medical evidence was necessary to decide this point. "Substantial" meant, she continued, that the reason "must carry real weight and thus be of substance." However, employers were not "obliged to search for the Holy Grail." And echoing Pill, L.J.,

11–033

---

[145] See e.g. *per* Lord Roger *Archibald v Fife Council* [2004] I.C.R. 954, at para.32, HL.
[146] Code of Practice above fn 116, at para.6.5.
[147] [2001] I.C.R. 805. For other examples of justification see the Code of Practice (above fn 116), Pt 6.
[148] *ibid.*, at paras 25–26.

the employer must act within the band of responses open to the reasonable employer.[149]

The combined effect of these speeches is that once an employer has made a properly conducted risk assessment, it is free to respond in any way it sees fit, so long as that response is not irrational. This falls short of the standard adopted in other fields of discrimination law for indirect discrimination, which requires challenged measures to be "proportionate", which includes being *necessary* (in other words employers must choose the least discriminatory option in pursuit of their legitimate aim). The apparent basis of this low threshold is evident in both speeches, expressed by Arden, L.J. to be that the Discrimination Disability Act required that the interests of the claimant had to be balanced with those of fellow employees and members of the public.[150] The "balancing" notion has echoes of the *Hampson* balancing test, which in the earlier days of indirect discrimination law also ignored the "necessity" aspect of the justification test.[151] Further, this apparently attractive platitude actually does nothing for the safety of the public. Whilst it gives employers latitude to err on the side of safety, it also provides them freedom to err the other way. For example, an employer's risk assessment may conclude that it is safe for a disabled worker to carry on doing a certain type of work, whereas the worker's own medical advice states the opposite. In this example, the approach in *Jones* compels tribunals to defer to the employer's opinion and to put workers and the public at more risk.

The Court of Appeal's view that tribunals should not substitute their view of the medical evidence for that of the employers contrasts with the established rule that tribunals, *not* experts, decide whether a person has a disability.[152] *Jones* has been criticised also for endowing employers with standards of normal behaviour, which "for many employers includes prejudice and stereotyping—indeed, the DDA Pt II was enacted to tackle precisely this truism."[153]

Nonetheless, *Jones v Post Office* persists for the time being as the standard for justification. Although the threshold is low, employers' reasons are not completely free of judicial scrutiny. There must, at the least, be a properly conducted risk assessment, which will vary with the circumstances. In *Murray v Newham Citizens Advice Bureau*,[154] Mr Murray, whose paranoid schizophrenia was now under medical control, admitted in an interview that he had in the past been imprisoned for stabbing a person. He was not offered the post because the

---

[149] [2001] I.C.R. 805 at paras 37–38 and 39–41. Kay, L.J. agreed with Pill, L.J.

[150] [2001] I.C.R. 805, at para.43. See also Pill, L.J., at para.24.

[151] See Ch.6, para.6–031. See also M. Connolly, "Discrimination Law: Justification, Alternative Measures and Defences Based on Sex" (2001) 30 I.L.J. 311.

[152] *Vicary v BT* [1999] I.R.L.R. 680, at 682, EAT. Applied *Abadeh v BT* [2001] I.C.R. 156, EAT.

[153] J. Davies. "A cuckoo in the nest? A 'range of reasonable responses', justification and Disability Discrimination Act 1995" (2003) 32 I.L.J. 164, at 178.

[154] [2003] I.C.R. 643.

bureau feared he would pose a risk to its clients, but apparently the bureau took no expert advice on this matter. The EAT held that to justify its refusal the bureau had to show that it had made all reasonable inquires into the risk, such as obtaining an opinion from Mr Murray's GP and medical advisors. In *Paul v National Probation Service*,[155] Mr Paul was refused employment because of his chronic depressive illness. The employer based this decision, not on evidence from Mr Paul's consultant psychiatrist, but on a discussion with Mr Paul's GP, who knew little about Mr Paul and his illness and did not comment on his fitness for the job. The EAT, distinguished *Jones v Post Office*, and held that this medical evidence was "plainly in issue" before the tribunal.

(4) The Duty To Make Adjustments
Section 4A (1) of the Disability Discrimination Act 1995 states that: **11–034**

Where—

(a)   a provision, criterion or practice applied by or on behalf of an employer, or

(b)   any physical feature[156] of premises occupied by the employer,

places the disabled person concerned at a substantial disadvantage in comparison with persons who are not disabled, it is the duty of the employer to take such steps as it is reasonable, in all the circumstances of the case, for him to have to take in order to prevent the provision, criterion or practice, or feature, having that effect.

This amended version, in force on October 1, 2004, contained two notable changes from the 1995 original. First, the largely otiose justification defence was removed. Second, the phrase "provision, criterion or practice" replaced "arrangements". Unlike the duty to adjust in some other fields, such as the supply of services, this duty is not anticipatory. It only arises when "triggered" by a job applicant, or existing worker, with a disability.

---

[155] [2004] I.R.L.R. 190, at para.31.
[156] "Physical features" include "steps, stairways, kerbs, exterior surfaces and paving, parking areas, building entrances and exits (including emergency escape routes), internal and external doors, gates, toilet and washing facilities, lighting and ventilation, lifts and escalators, floor coverings, signs, furniture, and temporary or movable items". Code of Practice, above fn 116, para.5.10.

(a)"Provision, Criterion or Practice"

11–035   Prior to October 2004, the duty arose when the employer's "arrangements" (or the physical features of its premises) placed a disabled person at a "substantial disadvantage". The definition of "arrangements" was limited to job offers and "any term, condition or arrangements" on which the employment was afforded.[157] This produced perhaps unforeseen technical difficulties in *Archibald v Fife Council*.[158] Here, the claimant road-sweeper underwent a routine operation on her back. There was a complication leaving her virtually unable to walk and of course unable to do her job. The council offered her the chance to do office-work, but only through competitive interviews. She failed over 100 and eventually was dismissed. She claimed that the council had failed to make reasonable adjustments. The employment tribunal held that the duty did not arise because the "arrangements" only encompassed the office-work arrangements, which did not place Ms Archibald at any disadvantage because of her disability. The Court of Session upheld that decision, but on the different ground that "arrangements" could not include the "fundamental essence of the job". The logic here is that where no adjustments can be made to enable the person to do job in question (road-sweeping), a duty cannot arise.[159] Of course, the outcome defeats the purpose of the Act, which envisages a transfer to other work as a reasonable adjustment.[160] However, the House of Lords, giving a purposive interpretation, stated that the "arrangements" were the job description and the liability to dismissal for a worker who was unable to do the job. Here the job description was to walk and use a broom, and Ms Archibald was dismissed for not being able to do that.[161] Accordingly the House held that the duty was triggered in this case. The new definition "provision, criterion or practice", should if necessary be given an equally generous construction.

(b) When the Duty is Triggered

11–036   The employer's duty is triggered when its provision, criterion or practice, or physical feature of its premises, "places the disabled person concerned at a substantial disadvantage in comparison with persons who are not disabled". The comparison will be relatively straightforward in most cases. However, difficulties have arisen in two particular circumstances: first, where the worker becomes so disabled that she can longer do the job at all, no matter what adjustments were made, and second, where many able-bodied persons also cannot do the job.

---

[157] Section 6(2), prior to October 2004.
[158] [2004] I.C.R. 954, HL.
[159] See [2004] I.R.L.R. 197, at paras 27 and 44 CS.
[160] See now DDA 1995, s.18B (2)(c) and Code of Practice (above fn 116), para.5.18.
[161] [2004] I.C.R. 954, at paras 11, 42 and 62.

First, in *Archibald v Fife Council*[162] (the facts are given above) the council argued that as she could not do the job at all, a proper comparison could not be made: "it was impossible to compare in terms of advantage in a running race a runner and a non-runner".[163] The House of Lords found that she was placed at a disadvantage when compared to others, but the reasoning was not straightforward or unanimous. Lord Rodger found that the comparators should be a limited class of persons, which would vary from case to case, reflecting the variety of scenarios envisaged by the legislation. Further, this class of persons was flexible. For instance, a job applicant may be compared with existing workers (rather than other applicants), or a candidate for promotion may be compared with other candidates who at the time were doing different jobs. In the instant case the comparators should be other road sweepers who were not disabled.[164] In apparent contrast, Baroness Hale stipulated that the comparators were *not* Ms Archibald's fellow road-sweepers, because that merely decides that her disadvantage was caused by her disability. (Her concern here appears to be that upon such an interpretation, no duty on the council to adjust could arise, because there was nothing the council could do to enable Ms Archibald to do the job: it was the disability, and not the council, that caused the disadvantage.) Baroness Hale noted that the Act does not require a like-for-like comparison used in the other discrimination legislation and then virtually abandoned the notion of a comparison, preferring simply to rule that "the duty is triggered where an employee becomes so disabled that she can no longer meet the requirements of her job description."[165]

The second circumstance (where able-bodied persons also cannot do the job) arose in *Smith v Churchills Stairlifts*.[166] Here, Mr Smith had lumbar spondylosis, which prevented him from lifting heavy objects. He was offered a place on a training course, along with nine other candidates, with a view to being appointed to sell radiator cabinets. Between the offer and the start of the training course Churchills decided that their sales team should carry a full-sized radiator cabinet weighing 25 kilograms as a sales aid. Mr Smith was unable to lift the cabinet and his offer was withdrawn. The employment tribunal compared him to members of the population generally and concluded that as most of the population were unable to lift the cabinet, Mr Smith had not been placed at a substantial disadvantage. (In fact one person on the training course dropped out because he could not carry the cabinet.) The Court of Appeal disagreed, echoing Baroness Hale's opinion from *Archibald*, stating that "the proper comparator is readily

---

[162] [2004] I.C.R. 954, HL.
[163] See [2004] I.R.L.R. 197, at para.16, CS.
[164] [2004] I.C.R. 954, at para.42.
[165] *ibid.*, at para.64.
[166] [2006] I.R.L.R. 41, CA. See further below, para.11–039.

identified by reference to the disadvantage caused by the relevant arrangements." Here, the proper comparators were the other nine candidates offered the training course.[167]

(c) Knowledge of the Disability

11–037 Section 4A (3) provides that no duty arises if the employer does not know, and could not reasonably be expected to know, that the person has a disability and is likely to be put at a substantial disadvantage. This is in contrast to direct and disability-related discrimination, where there can be liability without knowledge of the disability.[168] This section will be difficult to apply in cases where the employer acquires partial knowledge of the disability. The difficulty is deciding precisely how much knowledge is required for the duty to arise. The Code of Practice suggests that where a worker displays her (undeclared) depression by sometimes breaking down in tears, a duty arises. By contrast, where an applicant with arthritis merely declares that he cannot type, no duty arises.[169] These examples are helpful in themselves, but offer little more in the way of guidance because in principle they are much the same, the only differences being a matter of degree in the closeness of the relationship and frequency of the signs.

A little more guidance was provided in *Ridout v TC Group*.[170] Here a job applicant declared that she suffered from "photosensitive epilepsy controlled by Epilim" (a rare form of epilepsy). Before her interview she complained about the bright unscreened lighting in the room, and wore sunglasses around her neck. The employer thought that this complaint merely explained her sunglasses and proceeded with the interview, during which Ms Ridout neither used her sunglasses nor stated that she was at a disadvantage. The EAT held that no duty arose. Morison, J. stated that s.4A (3) required tribunals to "measure the extent of the duty if any, against the actual or assumed knowledge of the employer both as to the disability and its likelihood of causing the individual a substantial disadvantage . . ."[171] On the facts of this case, especially Ms Ridout's condition being "very rare", the employer could not be expected to make adjustments without being told in terms that the lighting would disadvantage her.[172]

More generally, Morison, J. commented that it was undesirable that applicants should be forced to "harp on" about their disability during an interview (which will be, of course, before the appointment is made), whilst at the same time it was equally undesirable for

---

[167] [2006] I.R.L.R., at para.39.
[168] See above, respectively para.11–027 and para.11–031.
[169] Code of Practice, above fn 116, at para.5.12.
[170] [1998] I.R.L.R. 628.
[171] *ibid.*, at para.23.
[172] *ibid.*, at para.24.

employers to ask a number of intrusive questions of the applicant about his or her disability: "People must be taken very much on the basis of how they present themselves."[173] This places the emphasis on persons with disabilities, albeit just once, to state in terms their disability and that they may be put at a disadvantage because of it. An approach less likely to produce the undesirable scenarios above, would be that once a disability has been declared the employer asks the applicant what appropriate accommodations are needed. The duty at that stage is to make an inquiry. As the person explains, the duty grows correspondingly.

(d) The Reasonable Adjustment Duty

Although there is little onus on the employer to make inquires in order to trigger the duty (see *Ridout*, above), once that duty is triggered, the employer's duty becomes proactive. In *Cosgrove v Caesar and Howie*[174] Ms Cosgrove, a secretary with a firm of solicitors, went off work for a year with depression. Neither she nor her doctor could suggest any steps that her employer could take to help her back into work. Nonetheless, the EAT held that her employer remained under a duty to take reasonable steps. The duty to make adjustments was on the employer, not the worker. If the employer had turned his mind to the question, he may have considered an alteration of hours, or a gradual return to work, or a transfer to another (less stressful) office.[175] Where the employer does not know what to do, the first step is a proper inquiry.[176] However, where nothing could be done, the employer is under no duty to make an inquiry or consider adjustments.[177]

11–038

The most notable feature of this duty is that it permits employers to treat a person with a disability *more* favourably.[178] This contrasts with the symmetrical model of used in discrimination law elsewhere, which tries to achieve *equal* treatment. In *Archibald v Fife Council*[179] an employment tribunal held that an employer did not breach its duty to make adjustments when failing to waive the "well-established" competitive interview for a transfer to other work. This was because inter alia the EAT incorrectly understood that the Act did not permit more favourable treatment. The House of Lords reversed, holding that in some cases, the duty to make reasonable adjustments not only

---

[173] *ibid.*, at paras 25–26.

[174] [2001] I.R.L.R. 653. See also above, para.11–030.

[175] See also the *Code of Practice*, above fn 116, para.5.24.

[176] *Mid-Staffordshire General Hospital NHS Trust v Cambridge* [2003] I.R.L.R. 566, EAT.

[177] *British Gas Services Ltd v McCaull* [2001] IRLR 60 EAT; *Morison v Key Housing Association* (2004) Unreported EATS/0107/03.

[178] This exception is provided by DDA 1995, s.18D (1).

[179] [2003] All E.R. (D) 13 (Jan) EAT, EATS/0025/02; [2004] I.C.R. 954, HL. See further above, paras 11–035 to 11–036.

permits, but obliges employers to treat a claimant more favourably.[180] In *Archibald*, that could be waiving the normal requirement for a competitive interview. The word "reasonable" means that the duty will be judged objectively. As seen in *Archibald*, possible adjustments are not confined to the job being done by the worker in question. Although the onus falls on the employer, the employer should consider any reasonable suggestions by the worker. This allows for more imaginative solutions. In *Smith v Churchills Stairlifts*[181] (see above) Mr Smith suggested a trial period of selling without the using the heavy radiator cabinet. The employer acted unreasonably when rejecting this suggestion.

11–039   Section 18B(1) provides a detailed guide with factors that may be taken into account when deciding if the adjustments were reasonable:

(*a*)   *the extent to which taking the step would prevent the effect in relation to which the duty is imposed.* The Code of Practice suggests that there is no need to make an adjustment that would have little benefit to the worker. For instance, adapting the stationary cupboard for access, unless distribution of stationery was a significant part of the worker's job.[182]

(*b*)   *the extent to which it is practicable for him to take the step.*

(*c*)   *the financial and other costs which would be incurred by him in taking the step and the extent to which taking it would disrupt any of his activities.* The Code of Practice suggests other factors here: the employee's length of service, level of skill and knowledge, quality of relationships with clients, and the level of the worker's pay. It suggests further that "It would be reasonable for an employer to have to spend at least as much on an adjustment to enable the retention of a disabled person—including any retraining—as might be spent on recruiting and training a replacement."[183]

(*d*)   *the extent of his financial and other resources.*

(*e*)   *the availability to him of financial or other assistance with respect to taking the step.* Here the Code of Practice suggests that the employer may utilise charitable or voluntary schemes, as well as the worker's own input, such as paying her to use her own adapted car for work travel, rather than adapting a company car.[184]

---

[180] [2004] I.C.R. 954, *per* Lord Hope at para.19, Lord Roger at para.30 and more generally, Baroness Hale at para.47.
[181] [2006] I.R.L.R. 41, CA. See further above, para.11–036.
[182] Above, fn 116, para.5.28.
[183] Above, fn 116, para.5.31.
[184] Above, fn 116, para.5.39.

(f)   *the nature of his activities and the size of his undertaking.*
Since October 1, 2004,[185] the Act no longer exempts small
businesses, however, a small business is less likely, for
instance, to have cover for absences enforced by a worker's
disability, or to offer alternative employment.[186]

(g)   *where the step would be taken in relation to a private household, the extent to which taking it would—(i) disrupt that
household, or (ii) disturb any person residing there.* The Code
of Practice suggests that it may be reasonable to communicate with a deaf cleaner by written messages, but not to
provide a dust-free environment at home for a nanny with
severe dust allergy.[187]

The Code of Practice suggests some additional factors, such as the
effect of any adjustment on other workers, or where there are a
number of workers with a similar disability, say all relating to
mobility, it becomes more reasonable to make significant structural
changes to the workplace.[188]

Section 18B(2) of the Act provides the following examples of steps   **11–040**
that may have to be taken:

(a)   making adjustments to premises;

(b)   allocating some of the disabled person's duties to another
person;

(c)   transferring him to fill an existing vacancy;

(d)   altering his hours of working or training;

(e)   assigning him to a different place of work or training;

(f)   allowing him to be absent during working or training hours
for rehabilitation, assessment or treatment;

(g)   giving, or arranging for, training or mentoring (whether for
the disabled person or any other person);

(h)   acquiring or modifying equipment;

(i)   modifying instructions or reference manuals;

(j)   modifying procedures for testing or assessment;

(k)   providing a reader or interpreter;

(l)   providing supervision or other support.

---

[185] SI 2003/1673, reg.7
[186] Above, fn 116, para.5.40.
[187] Above, fn 116, para.5.41.
[188] Above, fn 116, para.5.42.

(5) Employment Discrimination Before October 2004

11–041 There were three significant changes made to the definitions of discrimination on October 1, 2004. Before then, there was no discrete definition of direct discrimination. Such claims had to be drafted as disability-related discrimination, which has a justification defence. Thus potentially, direct discrimination was justifiable. Second, the reasonable adjustment duty could be triggered by the employer's "arrangements" (which was replaced with "provision, criterion or practice"). The narrow statutory definition of "arrangements" caused problems until the House of Lords gave it a liberal interpretation in *Archibald v Fife Council*.[189] So little should turn on that. The third difference is that a failure to make reasonable adjustments was justifiable. The scope for justifying this failure was narrowed considerably in *Collins v Royal National Theatre*[190] where the Court of Appeal held that factors properly relevant to the establishment of the duty and the reasonableness of any adjustments made could not pleaded again to justify a failure. But any other factors will be judged in accordance with *Jones v Post Office*, which includes a subjective element.[191]

4. GOODS, FACILITIES AND SERVICES

(1) Scope

11–042 Part III of the Disability Discrimination Act 1995 covers "discrimination in other areas". The Act's original coverage of the provision of goods, facilities and services fell short of some activities. More recently some of this was cured by the addition of private clubs and *all* services provided by the public sector, which are dealt with on similar terms to the original coverage.

The original coverage, provided by s.19, applies to anyone "concerned with the provision, in the United Kingdom, of services to the public or to a section of the public" (whether for payment or not). In this context "services" includes goods, facilities and services. Section 19(3) states that this includes access to any place where the public are permitted to enter; the use of means of communication and information services; accommodation in a hotel, boarding house or similar; facilities by way of banking or insurance or for grants, loans, credit or finance, entertainment, recreation or refreshment, or employment agencies; or the services of any profession or trade, or any local or other public authority.

Section 19 covers services *to the public*, and so will not include the design and manufacture of goods, unless the service is made directly to the public. So, for instance, a manufacture of tinned food or

---

[189] [2004] I.C.R. 954, HL. See above, para.11–035.
[190] [2004] I.R.L.R. 395, at paras 32–35.
[191] [2001] I.C.R. 805. See above, paras 11–032—11–033.

gardening tools has no obligation under s.19 to make the goods particularly suitable for persons with disabilities. However, if, say, it provides guarantees with goods, or sells goods directly to the public through mail order, then s.19 applies.[192]

Section 21ZA exempts the provision and use of certain types of transport (see further below),[193] but not the range of associated facilities, such as timetable information, waiting rooms, cafes on railway platforms. In *Ross v Ryanair*[194] the Court of Appeal held that both the airport authority and the airline were covered by s.19 for the access from the check-in desk to the aircraft. So where a customer could not walk this distance, a wheelchair had to be provided free of charge. Education is covered by Pt IV of the Act, and is exempt from s.19.[195] However, as with transport, ancillary services, such as access to a building for a parent with her baby, are covered by s.19.[196]

11–043

Under s.19, providers may not discriminate in the standard or terms of the provision, or by refusing "or deliberately not providing" the goods, facilities or services. This is a similar approach to that taken by the sex and race legislation.[197]

Section 19 did not include private clubs, because they are not generally open to the public.[198] Section 21F now outlaws discrimination by private clubs with at least 25 members.[199] In this field, it is unlawful to discriminate against applicants, members, associates, or their guests. In addition, from December 4, 2006, there is a duty to make reasonable adjustments.[200]

The third class of services to be covered by this Part of the Act is those provided by public bodies. From December 4, 2006,[201] s.21B outlaws discrimination in a residual class of public authority functions[202] which are not already covered by other parts of the Act, such as s.19. An example would be a police officer making an arrest.

---

[192] The Code of Practice, Rights of Access: Services and Premises, 2006, expected in force December 4, 2006, para.3.31. Available at *www.drc.gov.uk*, click on "The Law".

[193] See para.11–064.

[194] [2005] 1 W.L.R. 2447, CA. See also *Roads v Central Trains* [2004] EWCA Civ 1541 (s.19 applied to access to railway platform). See also below, para.11–051.

[195] DDA 1995, s.19(5A).

[196] See *Lawrence v Cambridgeshire CC* , [2005] EWHC 3189, below, para.11–049.

[197] SDA 1975 (s.29); RRA 1976 (s.20). See Ch.10, para.10–009.

[198] See the interpretation given to similar provisions in the Race Relations Act 1968: *Charter v RRB* [1973] A.C. 885, HL and *Dockers Labour Club and Institute v RRB* [1976] AC 285, at 297G, HL. See Ch.10, paras 10–010 to 10–011.

[199] Inserted by DDA 2005, s.12, in force December 5, 2005, SI 2005/2774, Art.3.

[200] See SI 2005/3258, reg.6(2) made under DDA 1995, s.21H.

[201] SI 2005/2774 Art.4.

[202] DDA 1995, s.21B (3) exempts: (a) either House of Parliament; (b) a person exercising functions in connection with proceedings in Parliament; (c) the Security Service; (d) the Secret Intelligence Service; (e) the Government Communications Headquarters; and (f) the armed forces when assisting the Government Communications Headquarters.

(2) Discrimination Generally

11–044   For Pt III of the Disability Discrimination Act 1995, there are two types of discrimination: disability-related discrimination and a failure of a duty to make reasonable adjustments. Both types of discrimination have a justification defence, which is discussed separately, further below. There are no specific provisions for direct discrimination or harassment. Direct discrimination is encompassed within disability-related discrimination, which means that, in Pt III, direct discrimination is potentially justifiable. Cases of harassment could fall within disability-related discrimination as providing an inferior service.

(a) Disability-Related Discrimination

11–045   Section 20(1) provides:

> a provider of services discriminates against a disabled person if—
>
> (a)   for a reason which relates to the disabled person's disability, he treats him less favourably than he treats or would treat others to whom that reason does not or would not apply; and
> (b)   he cannot show that the treatment in question is justified.[203]

(a)(i) Less favourable treatment

11–046   This element is discussed in the employment context, above.[204] However, some of the principles require restating in the context of services. First, the asymmetrical nature of this definition means that it does not offend s.20(1) to provide *more* favourable treatment to a person with a disability. Examples may include providing a larger seat (at no extra charge) in a cinema to a customer with a hearing impairment, to accommodate his assistance dog, or allowing free entry to a club for a support worker accompanying a person with a disability.[205]

  Second, the comparison is the same as spelt out in *Clark v TGD Ltd t/a Novacold*.[206] This means that the comparator has neither the claimant's disability *nor* the reason for the treatment. The Code of Practice suggests that, for example it would be unlawful for a club to refuse entry to a person with a severe facial disfigurement. It makes no difference that the club refuses entry many non-disabled persons whom it considers also are not attractive enough for its image. The comparator is a person without the disability *and* without the reason for the treatment, which was the apparent unattractiveness; in other

---

[203] DDA 1995, s.21D and 21G provide materially the same definitions for public authority functions and private clubs respectively.
[204] See under "*(a) The Comparison and the Reason for the Treatment*" above, para.11–029.
[205] Code of Practice, above fn 192, para.5.14.
[206] [1999] I.C.R. 951, at 964–966, CA. See above, para.11–029.

words the comparator is a person attractive enough for the club's image.[207] This principle was ignored by the Court of Appeal in *R. v Powys County Council, Ex p. Hambidge (No.2)*.[208] In this somewhat complex case the council charged for home help by means-testing. To do this it divided the users into three bands. Those in Band A received income support only. Those in Band B, consisting of persons with disabilities, received in addition a disability allowance of £49.50. Those in band C were not poor enough to receive income support. For those in band A, the Council charged nothing, for band B, £32.70 per week, and band C £49.50 per week. Ms Hambidge who fell into band B, compared herself to non-disabled persons in Band A (who were not charged) and argued that the charge was made for a reason related to her disability. The Court of Appeal rejected this argument, holding that the reason for the higher charge was that Ms Hambidge had more money. Laws, L.J. (with whom Aldous and Henry, L.J.J. agreed) stated that "there is no causal link . . . between the rate charged to persons in Band B and their disability. The local authority are . . . indifferent to [Ms Hambidge's] receipt of disability living allowance as such. What concerns them is the level of resources in the hands of those in receipt of care whether or not the presence of disability lies behind the receipt of cash in any particular case."[209] This misses the logic of *Novacold*: when an employer dismisses a worker for long-term absence, it is indifferent to that worker's disability "as such". What concerns the employer is the worker's absence. Laws, L.J. supported his view by comparing Ms Hambidge's treatment with that given to the wealthier persons in band C, who were charged more. But this is irrelevant. The fact that Ms Hambidge was treated more favourably than another with a disability cannot change the fact that the reason for Ms Hambidge's treatment was related to her disability. The matter should have one for justification.

The third principle is that there is no need for the provider to have knowledge of a person's disability. For instance, an assistant at a Jobcentre may refuse to deal with a claimant because she is swearing, which (unknown to the assistant) is a result of her having Tourette's Syndrome. The refusal relates to her disability and is unlawful unless justified.[210]

(b) The Duty to Make Reasonable Adjustments

Providers are bound to consider three ways to make reasonable adjustments. They may change a practice, policy or procedure, or overcome a physical feature, or provide auxiliary aids. The first two are discussed together.

11–047

---

[207] Code of Practice, above fn 192, para.5.9.
[208] [2000] 2 F.C.R. 69.
[209] *ibid.*, at para.24.
[210] Code of Practice, above fn 192, para.5.11.

Section 21(1), DDA 1995 provides that where a provider's practice, policy or procedure makes it impossible or unreasonably difficult for disabled persons to make use of a service, the provider is under a duty to take reasonable steps so that it no longer has that effect. In addition, s.21(2) provides that where a physical feature (for example, one arising from the design or construction of a building or the approach or access to premises) makes it impossible or unreasonably difficult for disabled persons to make use of such a service, the provider is under a duty to take reasonable steps to (a) remove the feature; (b) alter it so that it no longer has that effect; (c) provide a reasonable means of avoiding the feature; or (d) provide a reasonable alternative method of making the service in question available to disabled persons. It can be seen that the formula for physical features is the same, save that the reasonable steps are more specific.

For private clubs and public authority functions the formulas are substantially the same, except that for public authority functions only, there is an additional trigger where the practice, policy or procedure, or physical feature, makes it "unreasonably adverse for disabled persons to experience being subjected to any detriment to which a person is or may be subjected".[211]

Sections 21(1), and 21(2)(d) ("physical feature" duty to provide an alternative) came into force on October 1, 1999.[212] The remaining "physical feature" duties came into force on October 1, 2004.[213] For private clubs and public authority functions the duty to make reasonable adjustments is in force from December 4, 2006.[214]

(b)(i) When the duty is triggered

11–048 The duty is triggered if the provider's practice, policy or procedure, or physical feature, *makes it impossible or unreasonably difficult* for persons with disabilities to make use of such a service. (For public authority functions only, there is the additional *unreasonably adverse* trigger, noted above.)

The duty is to persons with disabilities generally. This means that the duty is anticipatory,[215] (unlike the parallel employment duty). Providers should not wait until a person with a particular disability attempts to use the service. Providers are required to think about and provide for the needs of persons with particular disabilities, such as visual or mobility impairments, although they are not expected to

---

[211] Private clubs: SI 2005/3258, regs 6(1) and 6(2), (made under DDA 1995, s.21H), in force, December 4, 2006; public authority functions: DDA 1995, s.21E (1)–(4), in force December 4, 2006, (SI 2005/2774 Art.4).
[212] SI 1999/1190, Arts 3 and 5(g).
[213] SI 2001/2030, Art.3(a).
[214] Respectively SI 2005/3258, (made under DDA 1995, s.21H); SI 2005/2774, Art.4.
[215] See generally, Code of Practice, above fn 192, paras 6.14 to 6.23.

anticipate the needs for every individual.[216] It is a continuing duty. So providers should keep their practices under review. New adjustments may be necessary based on experiences with people trying to access a service, or when, say, updating equipment, or altering their premises. The anticipatory nature of the duty means that a provider may still be liable even if it does not know that a particular member of the public has a disability. Although the duty is anticipatory, no individual action will arise until a person with a disability finds the service impossible or unreasonable difficult to make use of the service.

This trigger also differs from that given in the employment provisions (*substantial disadvantage*) because no comparison is envisaged. The test simply is whether the person found it unreasonably difficult (or impossible) to use the service. An example arose in *Ross v Ryanair*,[217] where the Court of Appeal held "The long distance between the check-in desk and the departure gate at Stansted Airport makes it unreasonably difficult for disabled persons to make use of the service involved in access to and use of Stansted 'airside'."

The absence of the comparative element was overlooked in **11–049** *Lawrence v Cambridgeshire CC*,[218] a case that centred on Mrs Lawrence's visits to Monkfield Primary School where her eldest son was a pupil. She brought with her another son, Mathew, in a pushchair, who suffered from cerebral palsy. These proceedings arose out of a period when he was under two years' of age. The school operated a "no pushchairs" policy, which meant that whilst signing in her eldest son Mrs Lawrence had to leave Mathew outside for a few moments, or for more lengthy events, she had to carry him in. She complained that that the school should have waived its policy in Mathew's case. The High Court held, first of all, that as any child under two required a pushchair, Mathew's access to the school was "no different" and so the duty did not arise.[219] This is focussing on the children's conditions, rather than the effect of the policy upon them. Effectively, the court is stating that Mathew is no more impaired than a young child without his disabilities. Section 21 does not turn simply on a comparison with persons without a disability. By contrast, in *North v Peterborough CC*[220] the local authority's suspension of its disabled parking bay scheme was found to have made it "impossible" for the claimant to have access to the service. Quite correctly, the county court made no comparison with the parking arrangements for able-bodied drivers.

An alternative holding in *Lawrence* was that although Mrs Lawrence found the policy "unfriendly and unwelcoming" and caused

---

[216] *per* Sedley, L.J., *Roads v Central Trains* [2004] EWCA Civ 1541, at para.11. See also Code of Practice, above fn 192, para.6.19.
[217] [2005] 1 W.L.R. 2447, at para.31, CA. See also above, para.11–043.
[218] [2005] EWHC 3189.
[219] *ibid.*, paras 27–28.
[220] [2004] CLY 2651.

her "stress and irritation", it did not make things unreasonably difficult, as parents of other children had to do the same. Here a comparison with persons without the claimant's disability is a permissible
factor (but not necessarily a determinative one) in deciding what is
(un)reasonable. In other cases carrying a child with a disability could
be a quite different task from carrying one without a disability.

The trigger has been criticised by the Disability Rights Commission
for applying a different and more onerous standard than that used
in the employment provisions, *substantial disadvantage*.[221] The
Commission points out where it is *reasonably* difficult to access the
service, no duty arises, and cited two county court cases to illustrate
this. In *Baggley v Kingston upon Hull Council*[222] a wheelchair user was
placed at the back of a pop concert, where he was unable to see the
performance whenever audience members stood. The judge suggested
obiter that this arrangement did not make it unreasonably difficult for
the claimant to enjoy the concert. In *Appleby v Department for Work
and Pensions*,[223] a deaf claimant at a social security office had to rely
on other claimants to indicate to him when it was his turn, as the
visual indicator was broken and the staff refused to help him. It was
held that it was not unreasonably difficult for him to use the service.

(b)(ii) The reasonable adjustment duty

11–050   The Act does not impose "a minimalist policy of simply ensuring that
some access is available to the disabled".[224] The duty is "to provide
access to a service as close as it is reasonably possible to get to the
standard normally offered to the public at large."[225]

The Code of Practice suggests that the following factors should be
taken into account: effectiveness; practicability; costs of making the
adjustment; disruption; provider's resources; and the availability of
financial or other assistance.[226] These are substantially the same as
those given for the employment duty.[227]

Where the case concerns a physical feature the provider must take
reasonable steps to make any of four specified adjustments. The first
is to remove the feature. This could be removing display units from the
entrance of a shop. The second is altering the feature. This could be a
lowering a bar so that wheelchair users can be served more easily. The
third is to provide a reasonable means of avoiding the feature. This

---

[221] *Disability Equality: Making it Happen*, (2003) DRC, at para.16. For the employment provision, see above, para.11–034 *et seq*.
[222] Kingston upon Hull County Court, claim no. KH101929.
[223] Lambeth County Court, claim no. LB001649.
[224] *per* Sedley, L.J., *Roads v Central Trains* [2004] EWCA Civ 1541, at para.13.
[225] *per* Mynors, Ch, *In re Holy Cross Pershore* [2001] 3 W.L.R. 1521, Consistory Ct (Worcester).
[226] Code of Practice, above fn 192, para.6.25.
[227] See above, para.11–039.

could entail providing a ramp alongside some steps for wheelchair users. The fourth is to provide a reasonable alternative method, say by offering an alternative *suitable* changing room where the original is accessible only by a staircase.[228] The Code of Practice suggests that these should be considered in descending order. An alternative method is the least desirable for the dignity of the person with a disability, as it is not proving the same service.[229]

Physical features include "steps, stairways, kerbs, exterior surfaces **11–051** and paving, parking areas, building entrances and exits (including emergency escape routes), internal and external doors, gates, toilet and washing facilities, public facilities (such as telephones, counters or service desks), lighting and ventilation, lifts and escalators, floor coverings, signs, furniture, and temporary or movable items (such as equipment and display racks). Physical features also include the sheer scale of premises (for example, the size of an airport)".[230]

In *Roads v Central Trains*[231] Thetford station had no facility for wheelchair users to cross to the opposite platform. Mr Roads argued that Central Trains should provide him with a taxi (costing about £50), to drive him round to the opposite platform. Jacob, L.J. suggested strictly *obiter* that the alternative of taking a train in the wrong direction to Ely, where he could cross by wheelchair, and returning on the other line—a journey lasting over an hour—could be a reasonable alternative.[232]

(b)(iii) Auxiliary aids
The third way to make a reasonable adjustment is by providing auxil- **11–052** iary aids. Section 21(4) provides that where an auxiliary aid or service would (a) enable disabled persons to make use of a service or (b) facilitate the use a service, the provider is under a duty to take reasonable steps to provide that auxiliary aid or service.

For private clubs the formulas are substantially the same.[233] For public authority functions, the duty is triggered when an auxiliary aid would (a) enable disabled persons to receive, or facilitate the receiving by disabled persons of any benefit or (b) "reduce the extent to which

---

[228] DDA 1995, s.21(2)(a)–(d). The fourth ("alternative method") came into force on October 1, 1999. The first three came into force on October 1, 2004. The examples are suggested in the Code of Practice, above fn 192, paras 7.47—7.51. For private clubs and public authority functions the methods are substantially the same: respectively, SI 2005/3258, regs 6(1) (a)–(d), (made under DDA 1995, s.21H) all in force December 4, 2006; DDA 1995, s.21E(4)(a)–(d), all in force December 4, 2006, (SI 2005/2774 Art.4).

[229] Code of Practice, above fn 192, para.7.40.

[230] Code of Practice, above fn 192, para.7.45.

[231] [2004] EWCA Civ 1541.

[232] *ibid.*, at para.46. In fact, it was held that this was not a reasonable alternative on the artificial assumption that the taxi was free of charge.

[233] SI 2005/3258, reg.6(3), (made under DDA 1995, s.21H), in force, December 4, 2006.

it is adverse for disabled persons to experience being subjected to any detriment to which a person is or may be subjected".[234] Auxiliary aids are devices or help normally for communicating with persons with hearing or vision impairments. For the former, these include: written information (such as a leaflet or guide); a facility for taking and exchanging written notes; a verbatim speech-to-text transcription service; induction loop systems; subtitles; videos/DVDs/CD-ROMs with BSL interpretation; information displayed on a computer screen; accessible websites; textphones, telephone amplifiers, and inductive couplers; teletext displays; video telephones; audio-visual fire alarms; and qualified BSL interpreters or lip-speakers.[235] For visual impairments, these include: readers; documents in large or clear print, Moon or Braille; information on computer disk or email; information on audiotape; telephone services to supplement other information; spoken announcements or verbal communication; accessible websites; assistance with guiding; audio description services; large print or tactile maps/plans and three dimensional models; and touch facilities (for example, interactive exhibits in a museum or gallery).[236]

(b)(iv) Exemptions to the duty

11–053 Section 21(6), DDA 1995, states that a provider does not have to take any steps which would fundamentally alter the nature of the service in question or the nature of his trade, profession or business.[237] So, for instance, a restaurant need not make a home delivery, unless it already provides such a service; likewise, a high street hairdresser need not make home visits, unless it already provides such a service; and a night club need not brighten its atmospheric lighting to accommodate a customer person with a visual impairment.[238]

Section 21(7) states a provider does not have to take any steps which would cause him to incur expenditure exceeding any prescribed maximum. At the time of writing no such sum had been set.

For public functions only, authorities are not required to take any steps that they have no power to take. For instance, a court could not provide a deaf juror with a sign language interpreter because, by law, no extra people are allowed in the jury room.[239]

11–054 Section 27, DDA 1995, provides an exemption for services, private clubs and public authority functions. This applies where the provider,

---

[234] DDA 1995, s.21E (1)–(4), in force December 4, 2006, (SI 2005/2774 Art.4).

[235] Code of Practice, above fn 192, para.7.22.

[236] Code of Practice, above fn 192, para.7.27.

[237] In force October 1, 1999 (SI 1999/1190, Arts 3, 5(g)). A similar defence is provided for private clubs: SI 2005/3258, reg.14(a), (made under DDA 1995, s.21H) in force December 4, 2006. There is no equivalent for public authority functions.

[238] Code of Practice, above fn 192, para.10.39.

[239] DDA 1995, s.21E(9), in force December 4, 2006, (SI 2005/2774 Art.4). See Code of Practice, above fn 192, para.11.57.

or club, occupies a premises under a lease. The lease may not allow for an alteration to the premises to comply with the reasonable adjustment duty. Here the occupier must seek in writing consent from the landlord, which cannot be unreasonably refused. If a refusal is reasonable, then the occupier is exempt from the duty. However, if consent is not sought a court will ignore any restrictive terms of the lease.[240]

There is a partial exemption where buildings meet some statutory design standards. For some time before the DDA 1995 came into force, design standards have required certain features in new buildings to meet the needs of persons with disabilities. These features may not be enough to meet the requirements of the DDA 1995. Where this is the case, a provider is exempted from removing, altering or adjusting a feature to the building for a period of ten years after its original construction.[241]

There is a further limitation on the duty of private clubs. Where that club meets at a member's private house, that member is under no duty to make any adjustments to any physical features of the house.[242]

(c) Justification

The test for justification applies to both disability-related discrimination and the reasonable adjustments duty. Discriminatory behaviour is justified only if "(a) in the opinion of the provider of services, one or more of the [specified] conditions . . . are satisfied; and (b) it is reasonable, in all the circumstances of the case, for him to hold that opinion."[243] (In addition, for public authority functions only, there is a general justification defence of "a proportionate means of achieving a legitimate aim.")[244]

11–055

This means that the provider, *at the time*, must have held one of the specified reasons in his mind (subjective). Further, it must have been reasonable for him to have relied on that reason (objective). On the issue of reasonableness, a dominant factor in most cases is likely to be the standard of the reasonably competent provider carrying out the same functions. That said, providers of similar services are likely to share a common culture and where that culture is laced with prejudice, conscious or subconscious, or bad practice, courts should not be too deferential to the views of same-service providers.[245]

---

[240] DDA 1995, Sch.4, Pt 2, para.5.
[241] SI 2005/2091, reg.11; for private clubs, SI 2005/3258, reg.12, (both in force from December 4, 2006).
[242] SI 2005/3258, reg.14(b), (made under DDA 1995, s.21H) in force December 4, 2006.
[243] DDA 1995, s.20(3) (services to the public). Section 21G(2)(a) (private clubs) and 21D(3)(a) (public authority functions) are materially the same.
[244] DDA 1995, s.21D(5), in force December 4, 2006, (SI 2005/2774 Art.4).
[245] See the discussion above, para.11–032, of *Jones v Post Office* [2001] I.C.R. 805, which this statutory model reflects.

(c)(i) Specified conditions

11–056 There are two specified conditions for all services. The first is health and safety. Thus, it may be reasonable to refuse persons with certain disabilities entry onto some white-knuckle rides. The second is an incapacity to contract. So it may be reasonable for a bank to refuse a person with senile dementia a mortgage loan because it has sound reasons for believing that the applicant does not understand the nature of the legal agreement and obligations involved.[246]

There are three additional specified conditions for services to the public only. The first is where otherwise the provider would be unable to give the service to the public generally. This could arise where say, a tour guide could not complete the tour for the whole party if he had to cater for a wheelchair-bound customer.[247] The second condition is where the provider presents an inferior service in order to provide it at all. This could arise where, say, a hotel restricts a wheelchair-bound guest to floors only accessible by the lift, even though this guest is confined to inferior rooms and views. The alternative would be to refuse the guest all accommodation. The third condition relates to cost. Providers may charge a customer with a disability more for tailor-made goods, facilities or services, over and above the duty to make reasonable adjustments. The condition could arise where say, a shop supplies a bed specifically made to accommodate the customer's disability. Charging the customer more for this bed than a standard one may be justified.[248]

(c)(ii) Private clubs—additional conditions

11–057 There are three additional conditions available for private clubs, which are parallel to the additional conditions for services to the public. The first is where otherwise the club would be unable to afford others access to a benefit, facility or service. This could arise where, say, a bridge club of a high standard refuses membership to a person whose short-term memory is seriously affected by her disability: if this person could not play competitively, then neither could others in her game.[249] The second condition is where the club offers inferior terms,

---

[246] DDA 1995, ss.20(4)(a)–(b) (services to the public); 21D(4)(a)–(b) (public authority functions) in force December 4, 2006, (SI 2005/2774 Art.4); 21G(3)(a)–(b) (private clubs) in force December 5, 2005 (SI 2005/2774, Art.3). See Code of Practice, above fn 192, paras 8.16–8.22. This mental capacity exemption shall not apply "where another person is acting for a disabled person by virtue of—(a) a power of attorney; or (b) functions conferred by or under Pt 7 of the Mental Health Act 1983; or (c) powers exercisable in relation to the disabled person's property or affairs in consequence of the appointment, under the law of Scotland, of a guardian, tutor or judicial factor." (SI 2005/2901, Pt 2, reg.3; and for private clubs SI 2005/3258, reg.3.)

[247] DDA 1995, s.20(4)(d). See Code of Practice, above fn 192, paras 10–43.

[248] DDA 1995, ss.20(4)(e) and 20(5). See Code of Practice, above fn 192, paras 10–46—10–50.

[249] DDA 1995, s.20G(3)(d). See Code of Practice, above fn 192, para.12–43.

access or any other detriment in order to provide any benefit at all.[250] The third relates to costs. A club may impose costs specifically incurred when providing a tailor-made benefit to a member or guest, over and above the duty to make reasonable adjustments.

(c)(iii) Public authority functions—additional conditions
There are three additional conditions for public authorities. These become increasingly more general. First, the provider can justify disability-related less favourable treatment (but not a failure to make reasonable adjustments) if otherwise it would incur substantial extra costs. For this question regard should be given to the resources of the particular public authority.[251] Thus, a smaller authority may find it easier than a large authority to satisfy this condition. **11–058**

The second condition may apply where discriminating against a person with a disability is *necessary* for the protection of rights and freedoms of others. This condition accommodates the classic case of a clash of rights. For instance, a couple, both terminally ill, may be refused permission to adopt a child because the welfare of the child is likely to prevail and justify the refusal.[252]

The third condition applies where the discriminatory behaviour is "a proportionate means of achieving a legitimate aim." This formula, akin to the *Bilka* test used for indirect discrimination law,[253] means that the authority must show that it is pursuing genuine policy, that discriminatory behaviour is causally linked to achieving this policy, and further, that the behaviour is proportionate. This means that it must be the least discriminatory means of achieving the aim and that the benefit should not outweigh the discriminatory effect. An example would be where a council has a choice of closing one side of a carriageway or the other, in order to make road repairs; it would not be justified in closing the side containing a resident's disabled parking space. Here a less discriminatory alternative exists of closing the opposite side.[254]

5. Sale and Letting of Premises

Premises here is defined as land of any description in the UK, and includes dwelling-houses, office blocks, flats, bed-sits, factory premises, industrial or commercial sites, and agricultural land.[255] The Act outlaws disability-related discrimination in the disposal (sale or **11–059**

---

[250] DDA 1995, s.20G(3)(c).
[251] DDA 1995, s.21D(4)(c). See Code of Practice, above, fn 192, paras 11.50—11.52.
[252] DDA 1995, s.21D(4)(d). See Code of Practice, above, fn 192, paras 11.53.
[253] See Ch.6 para.6–030 and Ch.9, para.9–026, above.
[254] DDA 1995, s.21D(5). See Code of Practice, above, fn 192, paras 11.54—11.56.
[255] DDA 1995, ss.68(1), Code of Practice, above, fn 192, para.14.10.

letting) of remises and, from December 4, 2006, a failure to make reasonable adjustments in the letting of premises.

(1) Disability-Related Discrimination in the Disposal of Premises

11–060 Sections 22 to 24L, DDA 1995, deal with the disposal and management of premises. Sections 22 and 23 follow the format used in the SDA,[256] including the exception for small dwellings.[257] Thus it is unlawful for persons who are selling or letting premises, including in relation to waiting lists, to discriminate. It is also unlawful for someone managing premises to discriminate against occupiers. From December 4, 2006 this applies to commonholders as well.[258] Section 22A provides it is unlawful for a commonhold association to discriminate by withholding a licence or consent for the disposal of an interest in a commonhold unit in favour of, or to, a disabled person or by deliberately not being a party to such a disposal. The discrimination here is limited to disability-related discrimination.

(2) Duty to Make Reasonable Adjustments in the Letting of Premises

11–061 With effect from December 4, 2006, ss.24A–24L impose various reasonable adjustment duties on "controllers of let premises" (landlords and managers) in relation to applicants and lawful occupants.

The new provisions require the controller to take reasonable steps to change a policy, practice or procedure, or term, which makes it impossible or unreasonably difficult for a person with a disability to take a letting, or for an existing occupier with a disability to enjoy the premises or use a benefit or facility conferred with the lease, so that the policy, practice or procedure concerned no longer has that effect.[259] Examples might be allowing a tenant who has mobility difficulties to leave his rubbish in a more accessible place, or allowing an occupier who uses a wheelchair to use an existing accessible entrance at the back of a block of flats even though other tenants cannot use it.[260]

The provisions also require the controller to take reasonable steps to provide an auxiliary aid or service where that would either: enable or facilitate a disabled occupier's enjoyment of the premises or use of any benefit or facility conferred with the letting; or enable or make it easier for a disabled person to take a letting of the premises. The duty applies if: were the auxiliary aid or service not provided, it would be impossible or unreasonably difficult for a disabled person or occupier to enjoy the premises, to make use of any benefit or facility they were

---

[256] Discussed in Ch.10, paras 10–019 to 10–021.
[257] However, the exemption can be limited or ended by statutory instrument: under DDA 2005, s.14, in force December 4, 2006 (SI 2005/2774, Art.4).
[258] Inserted by DDA 2005, Sch.1 para.17, (in force SI 2005/2774, Art.4(f)).
[259] DDA 1995, ss.24D, 24J(3) and (4).
[260] DDA 2005, Explanatory Notes para.144.

entitled to use, or to take a letting.[261] Examples might be a landlord putting correspondence in large print for a visually impaired tenant or provide a clip-on receiver (which vibrates when the door bell rings) for a tenant who has a hearing impairment. However this duty does not extend beyond needs in connection with the premises, such as wheelchair.[262]

These duties can only be triggered by a request from the tenant (or prospective tenant). This means that the duties are not anticipatory.[263] The duties do not extend to the removal or alteration of physical features,[264] the controller's own home,[265] or to "small dwellings.[266] As with the duty in goods, facilities and services, it is possible to justify a failure to make a reasonable adjustment.

(3) Justification

In a similar fashion to s.20, DDA 1995 ("goods, facilities and services," above, para.11–055), justification is limited to specified conditions, where the person believes the condition exists (subjective) and it is reasonable for him to hold that belief (objective). There are five conditions. First the treatment is necessary in order not to endanger the health or safety of any person;[267] second, the person with a disability is incapable of entering into an enforceable agreement, or of giving an informed consent;[268] third in management of premises the treatment (but not eviction) of an existing occupier is necessary in order for the persons with disabilities or the occupiers of other premises forming part of the building to make use of the benefit or facility;[269] fourth,

11–062

---

[261] DDA 1995, ss.24C, 24J(1) and (2).

[262] DDA 2005, Explanatory Notes para.147.

[263] DDA 1995, ss.24C(1), 24D(1) and (2) and 24J(1) and (3).

[264] DDA 1995, ss.24E(1) and 24J(5).

[265] DDA 1995, ss.24B(1) and 24H(1).

[266] DDA 1995, ss.24B(3) and (4), and 24H(3) and (4)). However, the exemption can be limited or ended by statutory instrument: under DDA 2005, s.14.

[267] For example, a landlord may refuse to let a third floor flat to a lone person who has had a stroke resulting in mobility problems, because that person would be unable to negotiate the stairs in safety or use the fire escape or other escape routes in an emergency. On the other hand it is unlikely to be justifiable to refuse a tenancy to a person with AIDS on the basis that the person would be a health risk to other tenants, despite being given government literature confirming AIDS is not a health risk. Code of Practice, above, fn 192, para.17.16.

[268] DDA 1995, 24(3)(b); for limits see SI 2006/887, explained above, fn 246. The owner of a lock-up garage refuses to rent it to a person with a learning disability. Despite the owner attempting to explain that she expects to be paid a weekly rent for the garage, the disabled person appears incapable of understanding the legal obligation involved. The garage owner believes that the disabled person is incapable of entering into an enforceable agreement. This is likely to be a reasonable opinion for the garage owner to hold and the refusal to rent the garage is therefore likely to be justified. However, if the disabled person offers to pay rent monthly in advance, or if his friend is able to act as guarantor for payment of the rent, the refusal to rent the garage is unlikely to be reasonable and would therefore not be justified. *ibid.*, 17.17—17.18.

[269] For example, the management agency of a block of flats may refuse to allow a tenant with mobility difficulties to park by the main entrance because this would obstruct the entrance for other tenants. Similarly, a landlord may refuse to allow a tenant with a learning disability to

where a landlord reasonably refuses to return a deposit because the premises or contents have been damaged for a reason which relates to the disabled person's disability;[270] and fifth, treatment to recover extra costs, save those incurred by complying with the duty to make reasonable adjustments.

In *North Devon Homes Ltd v Brazier*[271] the tenant suffered from paranoid psychosis, which caused her to be "disagreeable and aggressive" She was, accordingly, in breach of her tenancy agreement and as such, s.7, Housing Act 1988, gave a court discretion to grant the landlord possession where it was "reasonable" to do so. The recorder's decision to grant the landlord possession under s.7 was reversed by the High Court. David Steel, J held that the eviction of a persons with disabilities had to be justified according to the DDA 1995, rather than by the standards of the Housing Act.

The condition of health and safety of other tenants was considered in *Manchester City Council v Romano*.[272] Here the council served eviction notices on tenants because their anti-social behaviour, which the tenants claimed was caused by their (mental) impairments. The Court of Appeal applied the two-part test and held that the council believed that eviction was necessary and that this belief was reasonable. Hence the evictions were justified. It was not necessary that the health or safety of others had been damaged, only that it was endangered, although trivial risks should be disregarded. This interpretation, the court held, was compatible with the European Convention on Human Rights, which prevents discrimination in relation to a person's home.[273] In *Rose v Bouchet*[274] a landlord refused short-term accommodation in his guest house to a blind person because a hand rail to some steps was temporarily missing. The sheriff court held that the refusal was justified (on the safety condition) and that the reasonableness of the landlord's decision was to be judged on the facts known to him at the time of the refusal.

(4) Victimisation

11–063 Section 24F extends the Act's general victimisation protection to circumstances where the controller treats a tenant less favourably because the controller has incurred costs in fulfilling his reasonable adjustment duty towards a lawful occupier other than the tenant, (e.g. the tenant's spouse or child).

---

use the shared laundry facilities in a block of flats because, not understanding the instructions, she frequently breaks the washing machines. *ibid.*, para.17.19.
[270] SI 2006/887, reg.3, in force December 4, 2006.
[271] [2003] EWHC 574.
[272] [2004] 4 All E.R. 21.
[273] See Ch.2, para.2–005, above.
[274] [1999] I.R.L.R. 463.

6. TRANSPORT

Activities ancillary to transport services, such as timetables and **11–064**
railway platform access are covered by section 19 (goods, facilities and
services) of the Disability Discrimination Act 1995.[275] However, the
provision of transport, and the services provided to passengers travelling in a vehicle, are exempt from s.19.[276] Further, s.21ZA (2) provides
that it can never be reasonable for a transport provider to alter or
remove a physical feature of a vehicle. Section 21ZA (3) provides the
Secretary of State power to bring certain services within the scope
of s.19.[277]

Part V of the Act allows the Government to set access standards for
buses, coaches, trains, trams and taxis. The Government has produced
regulations on access standards for rail vehicles (SI 1998/2456).
Regulations on access standards for certain buses and coaches, which
are used on local or scheduled services, have applied to new vehicles
from the end of 2000 (SI 2000/1970, as amended). It is now unlawful,
by ss.37 and 37A, for licensed taxis in England and Wales and private
hire vehicles to refuse to carry, or to make any extra charge for,
disabled passengers who are accompanied by a guide or assistance
dog. It is also unlawful to refuse to allow the dog to remain with the
passenger.

7. EDUCATION

(1) Schools

There is three-pronged approach to the needs of school pupils with **11–065**
disabilities. There are planning duties, the Special Educational Needs
(SEN) framework, and the anti-discrimination provisions of the
Disability Discrimination Act 1995. The planning duties require
schools to develop strategies in three main areas: access to the
curriculum, physical environment for access to education and associated services, and communicating information.[278] The SEN framework consists of legislation and guidance creating duties for the
education of children with learning difficulties. The current education
provisions of the DDA 1995, ss.28A–28Q, came into force on

---

[275] See above, para.11–043.
[276] DDA, 1995, s.21ZA, inserted by DDA 2005, s.5 in force June 30, 2005 (SI 2005/1676, Art.2(1)(a)).
[277] See SI2005/3190, reg.3, lifting the exemption on: (a) small passenger and goods hire vehicles; (b) private hire vehicles; (c) public service vehicles; (d) rail vehicles; (e) taxis; (f) break-
down or recovery vehicles; and (g) vehicles deployed on a system using a mode of guided
transport.
[278] DDA 1995, ss.28D–28E; Education (Disability Strategies and Pupils' Educational Records)
(Scotland) Act 2002, ASP 12, s.1.

September 1, 2002.[279] There is also a Code of Practice, issued under s.53A, DDA 1995, by the Disability Rights Commission in 2002.[280]

Section 28A makes it unlawful to discriminate in admissions, exclusions, and the education and its associated services. The discrimination must be either disability-related discrimination or a failure of a duty to take reasonable steps.

(a) Disability-Related Discrimination

11–066 Disability-related discrimination is defined by s.28B(1) in same way as elsewhere in the Act: it is unlawful to treat a pupil less favourably for reason related to his disability, unless it is justified. In education cases, the courts have followed *Clark v TGD Ltd t/a Novacold*[281] and compared the claimant with a person without the particular disability *and* without the reason. In *McAuley Catholic High School v C*[282] a pupil was excluded because of his bad behaviour, which was related to his autistic spectrum disorder. His comparator did not have the disability and was properly behaved. This approach allows scrutiny of the reasons given for the exclusion under the justification element. Of course, where the bad behaviour is unrelated to a pupil's disability, the comparison is with a pupil without the disability but who does behave badly. As with the definition elsewhere, the treatment must be less favourable. So it may not necessarily be discriminatory to give a child home tuition instead of arranging for a school place.[283]

(b) Duty to Take Reasonable Steps

11–067 Section 28C defines the duty to take reasonable steps in much the same way as the employment duty to make reasonable adjustments, save that this duty is anticipatory and there is a justification defence. The duty is to take reasonable steps in the admission arrangements, and in relation to the education and associated services to ensure that persons with disabilities are not placed at a substantial disadvantage in comparison with persons who are not disabled. Although s.28C does not mention exclusions (by contrast with s.28A, above), the reference to "education" embraces taking reasonable steps to avoid exclusion.[284]

---

[279] Inserted by Special Educational Needs and Disability Act 2001, ss.38(1), (5)(a), 42(6), Sch.9, in force (SI 2002/2217, Art.3, Sch.1, Pt 1).

[280] *Code of Practice for Schools* (July 2002), effective from September 1, 2002 (SI 2002/2216). Available at *www.drc.gov.uk*, click on "The Law".

[281] [1999] I.C.R. 951, at 964–966, CA. See above, para.11–029.

[282] [2004] I.C.R. 1563, Q.B.D. See also *R. (T) v Governing Body of OL Primary School* [2005] E.L.R. 522, Q.B.D., at para.6. Contrast the Australian case *Purvis v NSW* 202 ALR 133 (2003), where a pupil who was excluded for his violent behaviour resulting from brain-damage, was compared to a non-disabled but violent pupil. See further above, para.11–006.

[283] *VK v Norfolk CC and the Special Educational Needs and Disability Tribunal* [2005] E.L.R. 342, at para.47, Q.B.D.

[284] *Governing Body of PPC v DS* [2005] EWHC 1036, at para.30.

There are two exemptions from this duty. The first is that there is no duty under s.28C to remove or alter physical features. This is covered by the planning duties. The second exemption is for auxiliary aids,[285] which is covered by the SEN framework (see above).

(c) Justification

There are two ways by which less favourable treatment may be justi-fied. The first—for disability-related discrimination only—allows permitted selection, such as a grammar school selecting pupils by academic ability. If a child with learning difficulties fails an entrance exam, any resulting less favourable treatment can be justified.[286]

11–068

The other way of justification is applicable to both forms of discrimination. Section 28B(7) provides that disability-related discrimination (or "less favourable treatment"), or a failure to make reasonable adjustments, is justified only if the reason for it is both material to the circumstances of the particular case and substantial. The formula is the same used in the employment provisions and so defendants only need to show that their behaviour fell within the "band of reasonable responses".[287] But the scheme, allowing justifi-cation of a failure to make reasonable adjustments, follows the employment provisions before they were amended in October 2004.[288] As with the employment provisions, in a case of less favourable treat-ment, where a duty arises also to make reasonable adjustments, the less favourable treatment cannot be justified if there were reason-able adjustments that should have been made but were not.[289] So where a pupil with Tourette's Syndrome is banned from a school trip because of his abusive swearing, the school cannot justify that ban (amounting to less favourable treatment) unless it has made all reasonable adjustments.

(d) Lack of Knowledge

There is a defence if the school (or responsible body) did not know and could not reasonably have been expected to know, that the person was disabled. This defence is available for both disability-related discrimination and a failure to take reasonable steps, despite the anticipatory nature of the duty.

11–069

---

[285] In *K v Governing Body of a Grammar School* [2006] EWHC 622 it was held that cleaning and changing a pupil with incontinence was an auxiliary service and did not fall within "education or associated service".
[286] DDA 1995, s.28B(6).
[287] *Jones v Post Office* [2001] I.C.R. 805 CA. See above para.11–032.
[288] See "Employment Discrimination Before October 2004" above, para.11–041.
[289] DDA 1995, s.28B(8). For the employment provisions see above, para.11–032.

(e) Victimisation

11–070   The general victimisation provision in s.55 of the Act apply to education as well. However, in addition, the protection applies where the parent does the protected act.[290]

(2) Post-16 Education

11–071   The Employment Equality Directive 2000/78/EC brought about changes in the employment provisions of the DDA 1995. However, employment matters in the Directive cover vocational training, which spreads into the education field. Accordingly, the whole of the post-16 education sector (with some minor exceptions) has been amended to accord with the Directive. This means that in effect, the post-16 education provisions are substantially the same (save for minor exceptions, see below) as the existing employment provisions (as amended October 1, 2004). The amendments were due in force on September 1, 2006. A revised Code of Practice for post-16 education was due at the same time.[291]

The new provisions outlaw discrimination in education services, the conferment of qualifications, admissions and exclusions. In parallel to the employment provisions there are specific definitions for direct discrimination, disability-related discrimination, a duty to make reasonable adjustments (which is not justifiable), advertising, pressure and instructions to discriminate, and relationships that have come to an end, victimisation and harassment.

The definitions depart from the employment provisions and resemble the school ones, (above) in some respects. The duty to make reasonable adjustments includes a duty to provide auxiliary aids. The duty to make adjustments is anticipatory. There are "no knowledge" defences to both a failure to make reasonable adjustments and disability-related discrimination.[292]

8. The Disability Equality Duty for the Public Sector

11–072   See Ch.13, para.13–047.

9. General Exemptions

11–073   Section 59(3) provides that nothing in the Act makes unlawful any act done for the purpose of safeguarding national security. However, for

---

[290] DDA 1995, s.55(3A).
[291] Available at *www.drc.gov.uk*, click on "The Law". At the time of writing this was due to be effected by the Disability Discrimination Act 1995 (Amendment) (Further and Higher Education) Regulations 2006 SI 2006/1771.
[292] See DDA 1995, s.28S(3) and (4).

employment matters only the defence is narrower. Here the act to safeguard national security must be "justified".[293]

Section 59(1), DDA 1995, provides that nothing shall render unlawful any act of discrimination done *under compulsion of*[294] any legislation (made on or after the date the Act was passed), including delegated legislation.

---

[293] DDA 1995, s.59(2A), inserted by 2003/1673, reg.23. This was in response to the parent Employment Equality Directive 2000/78/EC. See further Ch.8, paras 8–029 and 8–046.

[294] See *Hampson v Department of Education and Science* [1991] 1 A.C. 171, HL, discussed above, Ch.8, para.8–047.

CHAPTER 12

POSITIVE ACTION

INTRODUCTION

Positive action (or in the US, "affirmative action") has been defined **12–001**
as "any measure, beyond simple termination of a discriminatory
practice, adopted to correct or compensate for past or present
discrimination or to prevent discrimination recurring in the future".[1]

McCrudden identified five classes of positive action used in
"common parlance"[2]:

Eradicating discrimination. This involves employers taking steps
(e.g. monitoring, regular reviews) to ensure that they are not
discriminating.

---

[1] US Commission on Civil Rights, Statement on Affirmative Action 2 (1977). See generally,
www.usccr.gov.

[2] C. McCrudden, "Rethinking positive action" (1986) 15 I.L.J. 219, pp.223–225. See also "The
Constitututionality of Affirmative Action in the United States: a Note on *Adarand
Constructors Inc v Pena*" (1996) 1 International Journal of Discrimination and the Law, where
the author identifies "at least" three types of affirmative action; D. Oppenheimer,
"Discrimination and affirmative action: an analysis of competing theories of equality and
Weber" 59 NCL Rev 531, who identifies a similar five models (at 534); R. Jenkins "Equal
opportunity in the private sector: the limits of voluntarism", in R. Jenkins and J. Solomos (eds),
Racism and Equal Opportunity Policies in the 1980s, 1987, Cambridge: CUP, pp.113–15.

Facially neutral but purposefully inclusionary polices. Examples would be recruitment from the unemployed, or from particular geographical areas, where say, ethnic minorities may be overrepresented. The danger here, theoretically at least, is that the majority groups could bring an action of indirect discrimination.[3]

Outreach programmes. These are designed to attract qualified candidates from under-represented groups, by bringing job opportunities to the attention of these groups and providing training to help them compete with other applicants. This is to combat what is sometimes called the "pool problem", or more colloquially, the "old boy" or "school tie" network, formed of persons from a close cultural and social background. Typically these pools consist of white middle class males. In many occupations, recruits are drawn from these informal pools.

Preferential treatment in employment. This is reverse discrimination in hiring, promotion or redundancy. Membership of the targeted group may a partial, or the sole, factor in the decision.

Redefining "merit". This alters the qualifications which are necessary to do the job, by including race, gender, sexual orientation or religion as a relevant factor for doing the job properly.

12–002 The irony of the discrimination legislation is that (save for disability) the equal treatment model it employs *prevents* more favourable treatment of those whose disadvantages it seeks to redress. The symmetrical nature of the equal treatment model means that it protects men as well as women, white and black, straight and gay, Christian and Muslim, young and old, even though protecting the former of each of these pairs is not the principal goal of the legislation. The consequence is that an act to favour a principal protected group will disfavour another group. Once this produces a victim, it becomes unlawful discrimination. This means, save for the specified exceptions noted below, positive action is in principle unlawful.

Yet, a common theme of the protected groups is the cause of their present disadvantage is past discrimination. Just as prosperity can tumble down the family heirs, the negative consequences of inferior housing, education, career opportunities, and (particularly in the US) slavery, can spill down the generations. Indeed, a history of prejudice has been the main driving force behind the enactments. Any attempt to redress the effects of past discrimination will breach the equality principle, because it will discriminate against the dominant group, such as men, or whites. Further, positive action is received by the media and public (largely uninformed of this history) as *unfair*, or

---

[3] See *United States v City of Warren, Michigan* 138 F 3d 1083 (6th Cir 1998), where, conversely, an employer advertised in predominantly white areas.

unequal, treatment.[4] Accordingly, politicians and judges have allowed very few exceptions for positive discrimination.

The problem is well illustrated by the British Labour Party's attempts to get more women elected to Parliament. One only had to look, or listen, to proceedings at the Westminster House of Commons, especially a few years' ago, to appreciate its overwhelmingly dominant male culture, and how unrepresentative this was. Yet, in *Jepson and Dyas-Elliott v The Labour Party*[5] the Labour Party's policy of all-women short-lists for parliamentary candidates was held to be unlawful under the Sex Discrimination Act 1975. The effect of the decision was reversed by dedicated legislation, providing a non-symmetrical exception to the equality principle.[6]

The unforgiving nature of the symmetrical rule was emphasised by Balcombe, L.J. in *Lambeth LBC v Commission For Racial Equality*[7] who accepted that the Race Relations Act 1976 permitted certain limited acts of positive action (see below), but was "wholly unpersuaded that one of the two main purposes of the Act is to promote positive action to benefit racial groups." It was illustrated in *ACAS v Taylor*,[8] where ACAS invited its staff to apply for 31 Senior Executive Officer (SEO) posts. This was a nationwide exercise and the first stage was for regional managers to rank the applicants. In Mr Taylor's region, four applicants, three of whom were male, were ranked "B" grade. Mr Taylor was one of these. However, only the female was selected for interview. Nationally, eight out of eight of the "B" grade females, and just six from 16 "B" grade males, were selected for interview. This selection procedure was influenced by the following guidance:

12–003

> "Please remember that more needs to be done to ensure the reality of the claim that ACAS is an equal opportunity employer. For example women make up only 17% of those at SEO level at present and ethnic minorities staff less than 1%. All staff should be considered on their merits as individuals. Where you have any doubts about the fairness of the Annual Reports you should not hesitate to take appropriate action".

The EAT upheld the industrial tribunal's decision that Mr Taylor had been a victim of a policy of positive discrimination and as such had

---

[4] In the 2004 general election, Peter Law resigned from the Labour Party in protest at the selection of a candidate from an all-women short-list. He stood as an independent and overturned the Labour majority of 19,000 votes, winning with a majority of 9,000 (*The Times* April 6, 2004).

[5] [1996] I.R.L.R. 116, IT.

[6] See SDA 1975, s.42A, inserted by the Sex Discrimination (Election Candidates) Act 2002, s.1. The provision will expire at the end of 2015, unless renewed by statutory instrument: s.3, SD(EC)A 2002.

[7] [1990] I.C.R. 768, at 774, CA. See further Ch.8, para.8–045.

[8] EAT/788/97, (Transcript).

suffered direct sex discrimination. Morison, J., noted that the opening sentence of the guidance was "readily capable of being misconstrued" and "capable of leading the unwary into positive discrimination." Save for the general position of the Disability Discrimination Act 1995, the legislation of Great Britain provides only very limited and specific forms of positive action. Otherwise the courts will not tolerate it. The EU legislation *permits* positive action. The ECJ is in the early stages of developing a framework for permissible plans. In the US, the courts have a highly developed framework which allows for positive action, although in some cases positive action may be declared unconstitutional. What follows is a discussion of the situation in each jurisdiction, and a summary of all three.[9]

1. British Law

(1) Sex, Race, Sexual Orientation, Religion or Belief, and Age

12–004 The legislation provides certain limited forms of permissible positive action. These are not the only steps that employers may take. Positive action is only unlawful if it results in an individual (say a white person or a man) becoming the victim of unlawful discrimination.

There are two types of permissible positive action under the legislation, one designed to encourage members of a protected group to apply for the job in question, and the other to equip members of protected groups with the skills to enable them effectively to compete for such jobs.

(a) Training and Encouraging Recruitment—Sex Discrimination Act 1975

12–005 Section 48 covers employers, trade unions and employers' organisations,[10] giving training to *existing* workers or members, or positive encouragement in and beyond the workforce or membership, to take up particular work. In addition, it allows trade unions and employers' organisations (but not employers), to encourage women to become members. Section 47 covers *any person*[11] giving positive encouragement or training to women.

There are two possible triggers to these provisions: first "under-representation" and second, "domestic responsibilities." First, both

---

[9] The whole of one issue of the Journal of Law and Society is dedicated to positive action: (2006) 33(1) J.L.S. 1.

[10] "[A]n organisation of workers, an organisation of employers, or any other organisation whose members carry on a particular profession or trade for the purposes of which the organisation exists." (SDA 1975, s.12.)

[11] Section 47 is not confined to *accredited* training bodies, but a major exception, by s.47(4), is employers acting within s.6 ("applicants and employees", see above, Ch.8, paras 8–002 and 8–008) with the result that s.47 does not apply to apprenticeships.

sections require that either no women, or a comparatively small number of women (doing the work, or holding the post or membership, in question), for a period of one year preceding the action. Under s.47, what matters is the numbers of women across the whole of Great Britain, or an area within Great Britain, doing the kind of work in question. It makes no difference whether there is under-representation in the employment of the particular employer. Section 48 is different, focusing on the issue of whether there is under-representation among women doing the particular job for the particular employer.[12] There is no authority on the meaning in this context of "comparatively small."[13]

Second, permissible gender-specific training under s.47 also can be triggered where a person needs such special training because of time she (or he) has devoted to domestic or family responsibilities to the exclusion of full-time employment (s.47(3)).

(b) Other Activities—Sex Discrimination Act 1975
Section 49 permits trade unions and employers' organisations to reserve, or create, seats on an elected body to "secure a reasonable minimum number" of women on that body. Finally, s.42A,[14] directed at political parties, allows arrangements "adopted for the purpose of reducing inequality in the numbers of men and women elected, as candidates for the party." This applies for elections to the UK, European and Scottish parliaments, as well as the Welsh Assembly and local government.

12–006

(c) Training and Encouraging Recruitment—Race Relations Act 1976
Section 37 parallels s.47 of the SDA 1975, except for two matters. First, when assessing under-representation, it is the proportions, not numbers, that must be compared.[15] Secondly, s.37 does not provide a "domestic responsibility" trigger. Section 38 parallels s.48 of the SDA 1975, except for two matters. As before, the when assessing under-representation, it is the proportions, not numbers, that must be compared. Second, the pool for the comparison can be the workforce or the employer's normal recruitment area.

12–007

---

[12] For discussion of the meaning of under-representation in the context of the Fair Employment (Northern Ireland) Act, see C. McCrudden, "Affirmative action and fair participation: interpreting the Fair Employment Act 1989" (1992) 21 I.L.J. 170, pp.186–90.

[13] See V. Sacks, "Tackling discrimination positively", in B. Hepple and E. Szyszczak (eds), *Discrimination: the Limits of Law*, 1992, London: Mansell, pp.376–78.

[14] Inserted by the Sex Discrimination (Election Candidates) Act 2002, s.1. The provision will "expire" at the end of 2015, unless renewed by statutory instrument: s.3, SD(EC)A 2002. See further, Ch.8, para.8–076.

[15] The formula used in the SDA 1975 is based on an assumption that 50 per cent of Britain's population is female and evenly distributed. A parallel assumption cannot be made for the Race Relations legislation.

The formulas may appear reasonable, but *Hughes v London Borough of Hackney*[16] revealed that in practice it may be difficult to prove under-representation using a comparison with the recruitment area. The background to this case was that 9 per cent of the Council's gardeners were ethnic minority, in comparison to 37 per cent of the borough's population, although only 58 per cent of the Council's recruits were from within the borough. The Council advertised for two parks apprentices, stating:

"Blacks and ethnic minorities are heavily under-represented in the Parks and Open Spaces Services. Where such conditions exist the RRA (section 38) allows an employer to establish extra training opportunities specifically for those groups. We would therefore warmly welcome applications from black and ethnic minority people for the two apprenticeships".

The applicant was rejected by a letter stating that "you cannot be considered for these posts as they are only open to black and ethnic minority people as was indicated in the advertisement." The industrial tribunal upheld his claim of unlawful discrimination for two reasons. First, to prove under-representation, the Council compared the workers with the population of the borough, not, as required by s.38, the normal recruitment area. There was no evidence of where the remaining recruits came from or what percentage of that group were from ethnic minority groups. (The second reason was that s.38 did not extend to restricting job opportunities to particular groups, upholding the distinction made by the Act between encouragement and training on the one hand, and hiring by quota on the other.)

Finally, s.35 provides a defence "for any act done in affording persons of a particular racial group access to facilities or services to meet the special needs of persons of that group in regard to their education, training or welfare . . .". This permits, for example, help with literacy for immigrant groups, special social care arrangements for "cultural reasons",[17] and it has been suggested that it may facilitate preferences for political candidates or posts for racial minorities.[18] Section 36 permits the provision of education or training to people not ordinarily resident in Great Britain and who do not intend to remain afterwards; language schools are the obvious example. However, this exemption applies nowadays only to residual cases, for instance, discrimination purely on the ground of nationality or colour.

---

[16] (1986), unreported, London Central Industrial Tribunal, see 7 EOR 27. Discussed by C. McCrudden, "Rethinking Positive Action" (1986) 15 I.L.J. 219, pp.233–34.

[17] *R. (Stephenson) v Stockton-on-Tees BC* [2004] EWHC 2228, at paras 27–28, reversed on other grounds: [2005] EWCA Civ 960, CA, see further, Ch.10, para.10–026.

[18] A. McColgan, *Discrimination Law, Text Cases and Materials* 2nd edn, 2005, Oxford: Hart, p.135.

It no longer applies to discrimination on grounds of race or ethnic or national origins.[19]

(d) Training and Encouraging Recruitment—Sexual Orientation,
Religion or Belief, or Age
The Sexual Orientation, Religion or Belief, or Age, Regulations[20] **12–008**
follow the scheme set out in s.37 and 38, RRA, or 47 and 48, SDA,
above. The difference is the trigger. Rather than under-representation,
the regulations state that training or encouragement may be given
"where it reasonably appears to the person doing the act that it
prevents or compensates for disadvantages linked to sexual orientation [or religion or belief, or age] suffered by persons doing that or
likely to take up that work".[21] The reason for the change given in
the *pre-consultation* Explanatory Notes to the Sexual Orientation
Regulations (but not the Religion or Belief, or Age, Regulations) is
the difficulty of obtaining statistics. The Government suggested
that "disadvantage" could be under-representation or widespread
harassment.[22]

(2) Disability Discrimination
Unlike the other discrimination legislation, the Disability **12–009**
Discrimination Act 1995 does not take a symmetrical approach. It
affords no protection to those *without* disabilities. As such, positive
discrimination is lawful under the DDA 1995. But there is a constraint
in the public sector. Section 7 of the Local Government and Housing
Act 1989 requires that all local authority workers be appointed on
"merit." Originally, s.7(2) provided an exception related to the 1944
Disabled Persons (Employment) Act, which required that 3 per cent of
workers should be drawn from those registered disabled. This allowed
public sector employers to discriminate in favour of persons with
disabilities. However, the DDA 1995 repealed s.7(2)[23] and replaced it
with the anti-discrimination rules, including the duty to make reasonable adjustments.[24] The position now for local authorities is

---

[19] Race Relations Act 1976 (Amendment) Regulations, SI 2003/1626, reg.34. On residual cases, see further Ch.2, para.2–002.
[20] Respectively, SI 2003/1661; reg.26, SI 2003/1660, reg.25; and SI 2006/1031, reg.29 (in force October 1, 2006).
[21] In the case of trade organisations, such as trade unions, "holding such posts or likely to hold such posts."
[22] The *DTI* (not statutory) Explanatory notes to Employment Equality (Sexual Orientation) Regulations 2003 and the Employment Equality (Religion or Belief) Regulations 2003, at para.155.
[23] DDA, 1995, s.70(4) and Sch.6. See I. Cunningham and P. James, "The DDA—An Early Response from Employers" (1989) 29 Industrial Relations Journal 304.
[24] See now, LGHA 1989, s.7(f). Discussed briefly by Morison, J. in *Hillingdon LB v Morgan* (1999) unreported EAT/1493/98, (see *www.employmentappeals.gov.uk*).

summarised by the Code of Practice, which states that s.7 means a post cannot be advertised as open only to persons with disabilities, although they may be encouraged to apply. In addition, the requirement to appoint on merit does not exclude the duty to make reasonable adjustments and so a person's merit must be assessed after taking into account any such adjustments.[25]

Finally, s.18C, DDA 1995, allows for "supported employment" for "members of a particular group of disabled persons" and for charities to confer benefits on "on one or more categories of person determined by reference to any physical or mental capacity".

2. EC Law[26]

12–010 The European discrimination legislation permits some positive action. Most challenges arriving in the ECJ are to state-run schemes deemed permissible under domestic law, the issue being whether they are permissible under Community law. The EC Treaty, Art.141(4) provides:

> With a view to ensuring full equality in practice between men and women in working life, the principle of equal treatment shall not prevent any Member State from maintaining or adopting measures providing for specific advantages in order to make it easier for the under-represented sex to pursue a vocational activity or to prevent or compensate for disadvantages in professional careers.

The Equal Treatment Directive refers to this formula[27] whilst the Race and Employment Equality Directives substantially restate it,[28] save that the Race Directive it is not limited to employment matters.

There are other pronouncements on the policy of the law which may be used by the ECJ to interpret the legislation.[29] For sex discrim-

---

[25] *Code of Practice Employment and Occupation* (2004) London: TSO (ISBN 0 11 703419 3), at para.13.25 Available at *www.drc.gov.uk*, click on "The Law".

[26] For a discussion of EC positive action law and substantive equality, see C. Barnard and B. Hepple, "Substantive equality", (2000) 59(3) CLJ 562, at pp.576–579.

[27] Council Directive 76/207/EEC, Art.2(8). This replaced Art.2(4) (by Equal Treatment (Amendment) Directive 2002/73/EC, Art.1), which provided: "This Directive shall be without prejudice to measures to promote equal opportunity for men and women, in particular by removing existing inequalities which affect women's opportunities in the areas referred to in Art.1(1) [access to employment, vocational training and promotion, and working conditions]".

[28] Respectively, Council Directive 2000/43/EC, Art.5; Council Directive 2000/78, Art.7(1), qualified by Art.7(2) which provides: "With regard to disabled persons, the principle of equal treatment shall be without prejudice to the right of Member States to maintain or adopt provisions on the protection of health and safety at work or to measures aimed at creating or maintaining provisions or facilities for safeguarding or promoting their integration into the working environment".

[29] Recommendations may used by the ECJ: *Grimaldi v Fonds des maladies professionnelles* Case C-322/88, [1989] E.C.R. 4407. See in this context, e.g. *Lommers v Minister Van Landbouw, Natuurbeheer en Visserij* Case C-476/99, [2002] I.R.L.R. 430.

ination, Declaration No.28 of the Amsterdam Treaty stated that when adopting the measures under Art.141(4) "Member States should, in the first instance, aim at improving the situation of women in working life." The Council Recommendation 84/635/EEC (on the promotion of positive action for women)[30] stated:

> ". . . existing legal provisions on equal treatment, which are designed to afford rights to individuals, are inadequate for the elimination of all existing inequalities unless parallel action is taken by governments, both sides of industry and other bodies concerned, to counteract the prejudicial effects on women in employment which arise from social attitudes, behaviour and structures . . .",

and recommended that member states adopt a positive action policy designed inter alia to encourage "women candidates and the recruitment and promotion of women in sectors and professions, at levels where they are under-represented, particularly as regards positions of responsibility."

The preambles of the Race and Employment Equality Directives suggest that the provisions on positive discrimination "may permit organisations of persons of a particular racial or ethnic origin [or 'a particular religion or belief, disability, age or sexual orientation'] where their main object is the promotion of the special needs of those persons."[31]

In addition, Council Recommendation 1986/379/EEC[32] provides a **12–011** framework for positive action for employment of persons with disabilities, including suggestions and guidelines on: concerted projects, new technology, special training for self-employment, identifying other sectors (such as tertiary services, including tourism and catering, agriculture or horticulture and forestry) which have good prospects and are suitable for people with various disabilities, drawing up special national policies for the re-employment of mentally handicapped workers who lose their jobs because of changes in the character of the employment market, creating more opportunities for part-time employment for disabled workers, and sheltered employment.

The case law so far has concerned only sex discrimination. At first, in *Kalanke*, the ECJ demonstrated a notable lack of enthusiasm for the notion of positive action. In subsequent cases however, the ECJ has taken a less strict line and endorsed a number of positive action programmes, although there are still boundaries.

---

[30] OJ 1984 L 331, p.34.
[31] Respectively, Council Directive 2000/43/EC, Recital 17; Council Directive 2000/78, Recital 23.
[32] OJ 1986 L 225 p.43.

In *Kalanke v Freie Hansestadt Bremen*,[33] a case originating from Germany, the practice was that whenever two candidates were equally qualified, the employer gave preference to the woman (the "tie-break"). This implemented the Bremen public service law, which required this preference where (a) the candidates were equally qualified and (b) where women were under-represented in the relevant post, defined as where women do not make up at least half the staff in the "relevant personnel group". The ECJ held that that this public service law breached the Equal Treatment Directive, stating that the exception for positive action is limited to advantages that improve women's ability to compete in the labour market. The Directive did not permit "an unconditional priority for appointment."[34] Another problem with this programme was that the trigger of under-representation was rather crude. It presumed that as many women as men were economically active, which, because of domestic responsibilities (among other factors) clearly is not the case. There was no attempt to measure the proportion of women in the job market.[35]

12–012   *Kalanke* was distinguished in *Marschall v Land Nordrhein-Westfalen*.[36] The positive action under challenge here stated that where "there are fewer women than men in the particular higher grade post in the career bracket, women are to be given priority for promotion in the event of equal suitability, competence and professional performance, unless reasons specific to an individual [male] candidate tilt the balance in his favour." (This last phrase has become known as a "savings clause.") Like *Kalanke*, this is a "tie-break" rule, except for the savings clause. This distinction allowed the ECJ to hold that this positive action was permissible under the Directive, despite the clause being rather vague. Otherwise, the rule in *Marschall* was just as crude as the one in *Kalanke*, and that the main objection to *Kalanke* (the crudeness of the rule) is now irrelevant.[37]

In *Re Badeck*[38] the ECJ ruled that all five of the following particular systems provided by German local legislation were permissible under the Directive. In the first, *flexible result quota*, sectors and departments set binding targets. A woman will be preferred in any appointment if (a) she is equally qualified as the man, (b) it is necessary to achieve the target, and (c) there are no "reasons of greater legal weight." These "reasons" favoured former employees who left because of family reasons, employees who went part-time for family reasons, former temporary soldiers, seriously disabled persons, and the long-term

---

[33] Case C-450/93, [1996] I.C.R. 314. For comment, see E. Szyszczak, "Positive action after *Kalanke*" (1996) 59 M.L.R. 876.
[34] *ibid.*, at paras 19–22.
[35] These points were made in (1996) 65 E.O.R. 31.
[36] Case C-409/95, [1988] I.R.L.R. 39.
[37] See "Limited positive action allowed" (1998) 77 E.O.R. 38, pp.39–40.
[38] Case C-158/97, [2000] I.R.L.R. 432. See K. Küchhold, "*Badeck*—the third German reference on positive action" (2001) 30 I.L.J. 116.

unemployed. The ECJ approved this because of the "greater legal weight" rule, a savings clause. Unlike *Kalanke*, the preference for women was not "absolute and unconditional."[39]

By the second, *academic flexible result quota*, quotas were applied as above because women were underrepresented amongst universities' temporary research assistants and academic assistants. These quotas reflected the proportion of women among respectively, graduates, or students, in the particular discipline. The ECJ held this to be permissible because there was some relationship between the quota and the "actual fact" of those qualified to do the job, and so there was no fixed "absolute ceiling".[40]

Under the third, *strict training quota,* where women were under-represented on training programmes, half of the places were reserved for women, if enough women applied. The ECJ permitted this because (a) it did not entail "totally inflexibility" because if not enough women applied, more than half the places would go to men; (b) there was no monopoly, other training places were available in the private sector; and (c) this rule only applied to training (as opposed to employment).[41]

12–013

The fourth, *interview quota*, provided that for sectors where women are under-represented, at least as many women as men, or all the women applicants, should be called for interview for a job or training position. Those called had to be suitably qualified for the job. If, for example, only three from seven qualified female applicants are called for interview, then only three men can be called, no matter how many qualified men apply. If, however, all the female applicants are qualified and called, then there is no limit on the number of qualified men who may be called. This was permissible because (a) it was not an "attempt to achieve a final result—appointment or promotion—but afforded qualified women additional opportunities to facilitate their entry into working life and their career", and (b) only qualified candidates could be called to interview.[42]

By the fifth, *quota for collective bodies*, in making appointments to commissions, advisory boards, boards of directors and supervisory boards and other collective bodies, at least half the members should be women. This was permissible because (a) these were non-elected bodies, and (b) since the provision was not mandatory it allowed, to some extent, other criteria to be taken into account.[43]

In *Lommers*[44] the challenged scheme was one set up by a Minister to tackle extensive under-representation of women within his

12–014

---

[39] *ibid.*, paras 26–38.
[40] *ibid.*, paras 39–44.
[41] *ibid.*, paras 45–55.
[42] *ibid.*, paras 56–63.
[43] *ibid.*, paras 64–66.
[44] *Lommers v Minister Van Landbouw, Natuurbeheer en Visserij* Case C-476/99, [2002] I.R.L.R. 430.

Ministry. The scheme provided a limited number of subsidised nursery places only for women, although male workers could use it in emergencies. The ECJ held that this scheme was permissible under the Directive, again the ("emergencies") savings clause being central to the decision.

The limit of the ECJ's post-*Kalanke* tolerance was found in *Abrahamsson and Anderson v Fogelqvist*.[45] In the Swedish university sector just 10 per cent of professors were women. In response legislation was passed to the effect that a woman possessing sufficient qualifications for the post *must* be chosen in preference to a male candidate who would otherwise have been chosen, provided that the difference between their qualifications was not so great that the appointment would be contrary to the requirement of objectivity in the making of appointments. There are two features to this system. First, it is mandatory, with no savings clause. Second, a *lesser-* (rather than just *equally-*) qualified candidate could be selected. The ECJ held that this legislation breached the Directive, holding that the ("objectivity") condition could not be "precisely determined" and could not prevent the mandatory appointment of a lesser- or equally-qualified woman.[46] In other words, the condition did not amount to a savings clause. In answer to a further question the Court stated it would be permissible if "substantially" equally-qualified women could be preferred if there was a savings clause, such as one that took "account of the specific personal situations of all the candidates".[47]

It is clear from these cases that the ECJ has abandoned its strict approach taken in *Kalanke*. From *Marschall and Badeck*, three requirements emerge for positive action to be lawful. First there must be under-representation in the particular sector, department or profession. Second, the woman being preferred must be *equally* qualified to the man.[48] Third, there must be "savings clause." This third ingredient is what the ECJ used to distinguish *Kalanke*. It seems a savings clause may be vague (as in *Marschall*) so long as it prevents a *mandatory* appointment (*Abrahamsson*).

[45] Case C-407/98 [2000] I.R.L.R. 732. See Numhauser-Henning, A, "Swedish Sex Equality Law before the ECJ" (2001) 30 I.L.J. 121.

[46] *ibid.*, paras 44–56.

[47] *ibid.*, para.62.

[48] *Quaere* did the ECJ in *Abrahamson* (*ibid.*) imply it is permissible to give priority to a *lesser-* qualified candidate when suggesting that the candidates could possess "*substantially* equivalent merits,"? (Emphasis supplied.) *Cf Johnson v Transportation Agency, Santa Clara County* 480 US 616 (Sup Ct 1987), below, para.12–018.

3. US Law[49]

In the United States there are two principal ways by which affirmative action may be challenged. The first is under the Federal anti-discrimination employment statute, Title VII (of the Civil Rights Act 1964). Second, public sector programmes are subject to the constitutional right to equal protection under the law.   **12–015**

(1) Title VII
The first thing to note is that Title VII authorises courts to order as a remedy for unlawful discrimination "such affirmative action as may be appropriate, which may include, but is not limited to, reinstatement or hiring of employees, with or without back pay . . . or any other equitable relief as the court deems appropriate."[50] This allows courts to impose affirmative action plans. In *United States v Paradise*[51] the Supreme Court (by a majority of six to three) upheld an order that the Alabama Department of Public Safety hire whites and blacks on a one-to-one ratio until the proportion of black troopers reached 25 per cent, which was roughly the proportion of qualified blacks in the area.   **12–016**

Of course, these can only be made where unlawful discrimination has been proved. Otherwise, "voluntary" affirmative action programmes may be challenged as being contrary to the general anti-discrimination rubric of Title VII. This resembles the position in UK (but not EU) law, where there is no general statutory provision permitting positive action. Thus, the recognition of affirmative action programmes is a matter of judicial activism. In these cases, the starting point for the US courts is to recognise that the symmetrical statutory bar against

[49] See generally W. Eskridge, Jr. and P. Frickey, *Cases and Materials on Legislation, Statutes, and the Creation of Public Policy* 1995, St Paul: West Publishing, pp.67–87; R. Belton *et al Employment Discrimination Law: Cases and Materials on Equality in the Workplace*, 7th edn, 2004, St Paul Thompson West; J.B. White, "What's wrong with our talk about race? On history, particularity, and affirmative action" (2002) 100 (No.7) Michigan Law Review 1927; A.R. Kamp, "The missing jurisprudence of merit" (2002) 11 (No.2/3) Boston University Public Interest Law Journal 141; C. Cunningham, G. Loury and J. Skrentny, "Passing strict scrutiny: using social science to design affirmative action programs" (2002) 90 (No.4) Georgetown Law Journal 835; J. Edwards, *When Race Counts: The Morality of Racial Preference in Britain and America*, 1995, London: Routledge; M. Abram, "Affirmative action: fair shakers and social engineers" (1986) 99 Harv L Rev 1312; A. Goldman *Justice and Reverse Discrimination*, 1979, Princeton: Princeton UP; D. Merritt and B. Reskin, "Sex, race and credentials: the truth about affirmative action in law faculty hiring" (1997) 97 Columbia L Rev 199; M. Duncan, "The future of affirmative action: a jurisprudential/legal critique" (1982) 17 Harv CR CL LR 503; M. Rosenfeld, "Affirmative action, justice and equalities: a philosophical and constitutional appraisal" (1985) Ohio State L.J. 845; R. Colker, "Hypercapitalism: affirmative protections for people with disabilities, illness and parenting responsibilities under US law", (1997) 9 Yale J L & Feminism 213.
[50] S.706(g)(1), USC s.2000e–5(g)(1).
[51] 480 US 149 (1987).

discrimination in Title VII cannot be used to defeat the purpose of the statute:

> "... the very statutory words intended as a spur or catalyst to cause 'employers and unions to self-examine and to self-evaluate their employment practices and to endeavor to eliminate, so far as possible, the last vestiges of an unfortunate and ignominious page in this country's history,' ... cannot be interpreted as an absolute prohibition against all private, voluntary, race-conscious affirmative action efforts to hasten the elimination of such vestiges."[52]

This is in stark contrast to the philosophy of the British judiciary, as it may be recalled, Balcombe, L.J. once pronounced that he was "wholly unpersuaded that one of the two main purposes of the Act is to promote positive action to benefit racial groups."[53]

12–017 The US Supreme Court has developed a three-part analysis for scrutinising a programme for its legality under Title VII. First, the affirmative action must be aimed to remedy traditional patterns of discrimination, such as a conspicuous imbalance in traditionally segregated job categories. Second, it must not unnecessarily trammel, or infringe, the rights of those who do not benefit under the programme. Third, the programme must be temporary, so it can do no more than remedy the problem.

On the first requirement, it not necessary that the imbalance was caused by the employer's past discrimination. So it does not matter if the under-representation was caused by societal factors, (such as a shortage of suitably educated minorities in the relevant job market).[54] For unskilled jobs, the comparison can be with the job market, or *the general population*. However, where a job requires special training, the comparison should be with those in the job market with the relevant qualifications.[55]

In *United Steelworkers of America v Weber*,[56] just 2 per cent of skilled craft workers were black, compared to 39 per cent in the local labour market. An affirmative action plan was devised where training

---

[52] *United Steelworkers of America v Weber* 443 US 193, at 201–203 (Sup Ct 1979), citing *Albemarle Paper v Moody*, 422 US 405, at 418 (Sup Ct 1975).

[53] *Lambeth LBC v Commission for Racial Equality* [1990] I.C.R. 768, at 774, CA. See above para.12–003, and further Ch.8, para.8–045.

[54] "As Justice Blackmun's concurrence made clear, *Weber* held that an employer seeking to justify the adoption of a plan need not point to its own prior discriminatory practices, nor even point to its evidence of an 'arguable violation' on its part." *Johnson v Transportation Agency, Santa Clara County* 480 US 616, at 630, (Sup Ct 1987).

[55] *ibid.*, 480 US 616, at 631–632, (1987). See D. Meyer, "*Note*, finding a 'manifest imbalance': the case for a unified statistical test for voluntary affirmative action under Title VII", (1989) Mich L Rev 1986.

[56] 443 US 193 (1979). See R. Belton, "Discrimination and affirmative action: an analysis of competing theories of equality and *Weber*", 59 NCL Rev 531.

places for craft workers were allocated by seniority, with the proviso that 50 per cent of the new trainees were to be black until the under-representation was redressed. Several whites were refused training places whilst a less senior black was selected. The whites brought a class action alleging the affirmative action plan discriminated on the ground of race, contrary to Title VII. The Supreme Court held that the plan was lawful because (a) it was designed to eliminate traditional patterns of conspicuous racial segregation, (b) it did not unduly impinge on the rights of others because under it no white worker would be dismissed and replaced with a black one, and (c) the plan was temporary.

In *Johnson v Transportation Agency, Santa Clara County*[57] the **12–018** employer identified five job categories where women were under-represented in comparison with the labour market. It settled on a long term-goal to attain a fair representation by including sex as factor in recruitment. Of twelve applicants for the promotion to the post of road dispatcher, seven were qualified to do the job. On the tests, two men top-scored with 75, followed by a woman, on 73. After taking into consideration the test scores, expertise, background, qualifications and the affirmative action plan, the woman was chosen. One of the top-scoring men brought an action of sex discrimination under Title VII. The Supreme Court held that the programme was permissible because (a) there was a manifest under-representation, (b) sex was only one factor in the decision to hire, it was not mandatory to hire women (or engage in "blind hiring" by numbers); (c) the programme did not unduly trammel the rights of men, (the Court noted that the Director was not compelled to choose a woman—he could choose any of the seven qualified applicants, the men kept their existing jobs, and so the "denial of the promotion unsettled no legitimate, firmly rooted expectation"[58] of the male candidates); and (d) although no finishing-date had been specified, it was temporary in nature because its aim was to "attain" fair representation, rather than "maintain" it.

These principles were applied in a school's admissions case, *John Doe (a minor) v Kamehameha Schools*,[59] where a school admitted only native Hawaiians to redress their low levels of educational attainment: they were severely under-represented in professional and managerial positions, and over-represented in low-paid unskilled occupations. It was held unlawful because the absolute rule against non-Hawaiian's unduly trammelled the rights of others. This compares to the ECJ's decision in *Kalanke* (see above para.12–011), where the absence of a savings clause made the hiring of women mandatory.

---

[57] 480 US 616 (1987).
[58] *ibid.*, at 638.
[59] 416 F 3d 1025 (9th Cir 2006).

(2) Constitutional Right to Equal Protection Under the Law

12–019   The United States' Equal Protection Clause of the Fourteenth, and the Fifth, Amendments provides a constitutional guarantee of equal protection of the laws.[60] Under this protection, state or federal actions, including affirmative action plans, may be challenged as unconstitutional. Before looking at affirmative action programmes, a few words are necessary on the judiciary's general approach to constitutional scrutiny. The Supreme Court has identified three classes of protected groups under the Equal Protection Clause: suspect class; quasi-suspect class; and a residual, "normal", class. Suspect classes are entitled to strict scrutiny of the challenged law. This means that the law will only survive if it is suitably tailored to serve a compelling state, or Government, interest.[61] Quasi-suspect classes are entitled to intermediate—or "heightened" scrutiny. Challenged laws will survive this scrutiny if they are "substantially related" to a legitimate state or Government interest.[62] Finally, laws that discriminate against a residual class will be subjected to "normal" scrutiny, which means they must be "rationally related to a legitimate state interest."[63]

It has been held that groups defined by race, alienage [*sic*], national origin,[64] and sexual orientation[65] are suspect classes. Gender[66] and illegitimacy[67] are quasi-suspect classes, whilst age[68] and disability[69] are residual classes. To date, the only constitutional challenges to affirmative action programmes have been based on race, where the courts have applied a strict scrutiny. The case law suggests that lower standards of scrutiny would be applied to other affirmative action plans, such as gender-based programmes. The anomaly is that the primary purpose of the Equal Protection Clause was to end discrimination against former slaves.[70]

12–020   In *Metro Broadcasting v FCC*[71] the challenged programmes were designed to encourage participation by racial minorities in the broadcasting industry. The purpose was *not* to compensate for past discrimi-

---

[60] The equal protection component of the Fifth Amendment imposes precisely the same constitutional requirements on the federal government as the equal protection clause of the Fourteenth Amendment imposes on state governments. See, e.g. *Weinberger v Wiesenfeld*, 420 US 636, at 638 n2 (Sup Ct 1975).

[61] *McLaughlin v Florida*, 379 US 184, at 192 (1964); *Graham v Richardson*, 403 US 365 (1971).

[62] *Mills v Habluetzel*, 456 US 91, at 99 (1982).

[63] *City of Cleburne, Texas v Cleburne Living Center* 473 US 432, at 446 (1985).

[64] *ibid.*, at 440. For the reasoning behind these classifications see Ch.2, para.2–008.

[65] *Watkins v US Army* 875 F 2d 699, at 728 (9th Cir 1989). The case concerned a homosexual. The Court of Appeals did not discuss whether bisexuality would be included.

[66] *Frontiero v Richardson* 411 US 677, at 686 (Sup Ct 1973); *US v Virginia* 518 US 515 (Sup Ct 1996).

[67] *Mathews v Lucas* 427 US 495, at 505 (Sup Ct 1976).

[68] *Massachusetts Board of Retirement v Murgia*, 427 US 307, 313 (Sup Ct 1976).

[69] *Board of Trustees of the University of Alabama v Patricia Garrett* 531 US 356, at 367–368 (Sup Ct 2001); *City Of Cleburne, Texas v Cleburne Living Center* 473 US 432 (Sup Ct 1985).

[70] This point was made by Stevens, J. dissenting in *Adarand Constructors v Pena* 515 US 2000, at 247 (Sup Ct 1995).

[71] *Metro Broadcasting v Federal Communications Commission* 497 US 547 (1990).

nation, but to promote diversification in programming. The Supreme Court held that as it served an "important governmental objective," it was constitutional. However, in *Adarand Constructors v Pena*[72] the Court went back on this, holding that, to be constitutional, an affirmative action programme had to be "narrowly tailored" to serve a *compelling* governmental objective. In other words, it should be subjected to "strict scrutiny." *Adarand* represents the current approach to affirmative action in the United States. In this case the Small Business Act[73] provided that not less than 5 per cent per annum of all government contracts should be awarded to certified small business concerns owned and controlled by socially and economically disadvantaged individuals.[74] A certified company was awarded a sub-contract, despite an uncertified company (Adarand) offering a lower bid. Adarand claimed that the statute discriminated on the ground of race in violation of the Equal Protection Clause of the Fifth Amendment. The Supreme Court remanded the case to be reviewed under "strict scrutiny". For the majority, Thomas, J. offered a more political, rather than technical, explanation, which perhaps does more to explain the majority's decision. Citing the Declaration of Independence ("We hold these truths to be self-evident, that all men are created equal, that they are endowed by their Creator with certain unalienable Rights, that among these are Life, Liberty, and the pursuit of Happiness"), Thomas, J. stated that these affirmative action programmes "undermine the moral basis of the equal protection principle", provoke resentment, "stamp minorities with a badge of inferiority", and may cause a dependence or an entitlement culture. Finally: "In my mind, government-sponsored racial discrimination based on benign prejudice is just as noxious as discrimination inspired by malicious prejudice. In each instance, it is racial discrimination, plain and simple."[75]

The present position is also represented by Powell's, J. speech in the earlier case *Regents of the University of California v Bakke*.[76] Here, a medical school's policy of reserving 16 out of 100 places for minority students was held to be held unlawful. Powell, J. began by stating that "the guarantee of equal protection cannot mean one thing when applied to one individual and something else when applied to a person of another color. If both are not accorded the same protection, then it is not equal."[77]

---

[72] 515 US 200 (1995).

[73] 72 Stat 384, as amended, 15 USC s.631.

[74] Defined respectively as: "those who have been subjected to racial or ethnic prejudice or cultural bias because of their identity as a member of a group without regard to their individual qualities" (*ibid.*, s.8(a)(5), 15 USC. s.637(a)(5)), or "those socially disadvantaged individuals whose ability to compete in the free enterprise system has been impaired due to diminished capital and credit opportunities as compared to others in the same business area who are not socially disadvantaged." (*ibid.*, s.8(a)(6)(A), 15 USC s.637(a)(6)(A)).

[75] 515 US 200, at 240–241 (1995).

[76] 438 US 265 (Sup Ct 1978).

[77] *ibid.*, at 289–290.

The university argued that the programme served four purposes. The first was an interest in "reducing the historic deficit of traditionally disfavored minorities in medical schools and in the medical profession". This was rejected for being "facially invalid" as it was discrimination for its own sake. The second purpose was to remedy "societal discrimination", which Powell, J. observed, was "an amorphous concept of injury that may be ageless in its reach into the past." Unsurprisingly, he rejected this purpose because the programme was not addressed to specific identified discrimination. It also risked placing unnecessary burdens on innocent third parties "who bear no responsibility for whatever harm the beneficiaries of the special admissions program are thought to have suffered." The third purpose was "increasing the number of physicians who will practice in communities currently underserved," was rejected because there was no evidence that minorities were more likely to practise in these communities.

12–021   Powell, J. approved the fourth purpose, "the attainment of a diverse student body", as "constitutionally permissible". His reasoning was rooted in the First Amendment (Freedom of Religion, Press, Expression), reiterating that: "The Nation's future depends upon leaders trained through wide exposure to that robust exchange of ideas which discovers truth out of a multitude of tongues, [rather] than through any kind of authoritative selection". However, he then held that as this "wide exposure" encompasses "a far broader array of qualifications and characteristics of which racial or ethnic origin is but a single though important element", the programme, based *solely* on race, was not necessary (or narrowly tailored) to attain the diversity goal, and so this purpose, ultimately, was rejected.[78] The result (by a majority of five to four) was that the programme was unconstitutional.

Powell's, J. opinion in *Bakke* was endorsed recently by Supreme Court in *Grutter v Bollinger*[79] as the "touchstone constitutional analysis of race-conscious admissions policies."[80] In this case the University of Michigan's Law School included in its admissions policy the School's commitment to diversity, which was to contribute to the Law School's character and the legal profession. It made special reference African-American, Hispanic and Native-American students, who otherwise may not be included in meaningful numbers. Accordingly, the School admitted a "critical mass" of underrepresented minority students. Quotas were not used. Applying *Bakke*, a majority (five to four) held the policy served a compelling interest (diversity) and was narrowly tailored to serve the goal.

---

[78] 438 US 265 at 306–313, citing *Keyishian v Board of Regents*, 385 US 589, at 603 (Sup Ct 1967).
[79] 539 U.S. 306 (2003).
[80] *ibid.*, at 323.

On the same day, the Court handed down its judgment in *Gratz v Bollinger*,[81] rejecting (by a majority of six to three), the University's College of Literature, Science and the Arts' policy of awarding each under-represented minority student 20 points (out of a total of 150) for admission. Candidates awarded over 100 points normally would be admitted. The selection here was too crude and of course not narrowly tailored to serve the goal of diversity.

4. Summary[82]

Of the three jurisdictions examined, only the EU legislation provides an express exception allowing for voluntary positive action. But the absence of such a provision in Title VII has not prevented the US courts from developing framework allowing for plans. They have done this to fulfil the purpose of the statute. This contrasts with the unambitious approach of the UK judiciary, who appear to prefer to leave the matter the Parliament.

12–022

The ECJ's approach, although less mature, has similarities with that of the US Supreme Court under Title VII. There is a likeness between the savings clause principle and the *unduly trammel* doctrine, as both reject plans that make selection of women or minorities mandatory ("blind hiring"). The ECJ has yet to develop any rules for calculating under-representation. So far it has accepted a crude comparison with the general population, which is palatable because women make up about half of any population, if not the job market. A more refined comparison is likely to be demanded by the ECJ when race-based (or other) plans are challenged, where the picture is likely to be more complex. Likewise the ECJ has yet to develop a firm rule that the plan must be temporary, but again, this is likely to come when the facts of a case require it. The further dimension to the US experience is the availability of constitutional challenges in some cases, where the courts appear to be stricter than under Title VII.[83]

---

[81] 539 US 244 (2003).

[82] For comparative studies of affirmative action programmes see: K. Burke, "Fair Employment in Northern Ireland: the role of affirmative action", (1994) 28 Colum J L and Soc Probs 1; M. Chandola Varn, "Affirmative action in India and the US: the untouchable and the black experience", (1992) 3 Ind Int'l & Comp L Rev 101; M. Katz, "Benign preferences: an Indian decision and the *Bakke* case", (1977) 25 Am J Comp L 611; D. Grossman, "Comment, voluntary affirmative action plans in Italy and the US: differing notions of gender equality", (1993) 14 Comp Lab L J 185.

[83] Although in *Johnson v Transportation Agency, Santa Clara County,* 480 US 616, at 649 (Sup Ct 1987) J. O'Connor (concurring) considered that the standards of the "initial inquiry" to be the same. See G. Rutherglen and D. Ortiz, "Affirmative action under the Constitution and Title VII: from confusion to convergence", (1988) 35 UCLA L Rev 467.

CHAPTER 13

ENFORCEMENT OF THE DISCRIMINATION LEGISLATION

INTRODUCTION

The legislation provides two forms of enforcement: individual and strategic. The individual remedies are substantially the same under the legislation and are considered together, save for some differences for Equal Pay claims. The strategic enforcement is entrusted to specialist commissions.   **13–001**

Most actions will be brought in employment tribunals. Those outside employment are brought in the county court or (for Scotland) the sheriff court and proceed "in like manner as any other tort or (in Scotland) in reparation for breach of statutory duty."[1] However, for

---

[1] SDA 1976, s.66(1); RRA 1976, s.57(1); DDA 1995, s.25(1); Religion or Belief Regulations 2003, Sexual Orientation Regulations 2003, reg.31(1); Age Regulations 2006, reg.39(1) (in force October 1, 2006).

courts and tribunals there are some slight variations for damages and the rules on burden of proof differ in cases falling within the ambit of EC discrimination law.

Employment tribunals—formerly known as industrial tribunals—are statutory bodies established to resolve disputes concerning the individual employment relationship.[2] They were established in 1964 and dealt with, inter alia, disputes under the Redundancy Payments Act 1965 and claims of unfair dismissal under the Industrial Relations Act 1971 (redundancy and unfair dismissal is now consolidated in the Employment Rights Act 1996). They also cover employment discrimination claims. This makes sense for no better reason than the facts of many cases give rise to both discrimination and unfair dismissal claims.

There was little planning or forethought as to the way in which the tribunals would operate.[3] In particular, they were established on the assumption that the normal "judicial" adversarial approach would operate, rather than an "administrative" inquisitorial approach.[4] The tribunals were intended to be a cheap, informal and speedy resolution of employment disputes. Yet cases proceed by the traditional process of examination and cross-examination of witnesses, so legal and evidential skills are necessary. Of course, a tribunal panel is limited in the assistance it may give to unrepresented litigants, as it needs to be seen as impartial in the adversarial arena. This is particularly problematic in discrimination cases because this law is highly technical and the facts giving rise to claims are, more often than not, complex and difficult to analyse. This presents a significant drawback for the unrepresented litigant. Nonetheless, the Court of Appeal has made it clear that that employment tribunals should be neither inquisitorial nor proactive.[5]

1. Individual Claims

(1) Burden of Proof

13–002 The shifting burden of proof in cases of indirect discrimination has always been fairly clear from the statutory definition: once the claimant proves a prima facie case, the burden shifts to the defendant to justify the challenged practice.[6] In practice, direct discrimination

---

[2] For a brief history and discussion of employment tribunals, see S. Deacon and G. Morris, *Labour Law,* 4th edn 2005, Oxford: Hart, pp.74–82.

[3] P. Davies and M. Freedland, *Labour Legislation and Public Policy*, 1993, Oxford: Clarendon, pp.161–64.

[4] See J. Clark, "Adversarial and Investigative Approaches to the Arbitral Resolution of Dismissal Disputes: A Comparison of South Africa and the UK" (1999) 28 I.L.J. 319.

[5] *McNicol v Balfour Beatty Rail Maintenance* [2002] I.C.R. 1498, at para.26. For arguments particular to disability discrimination, see Ch.11, para.11–003.

[6] See further, Ch.6, paras 6–006 and 6–029.

has presented more challenging issues of proof. This is because "Very little direct discrimination is today overt or even deliberate."[7] It may be based upon stereotypes, cultural nuances and values, or sub-conscious assumptions or bias. Hence, most of the focus here is on proving direct discrimination.

As discrimination is a civil matter, the traditional rule applies that the burden is on the claimant to prove the case on a balance of probabilities.[8] However, more recently, all cases falling under EC law are subject to a specific rule of a shifting burden. This covers discrimination on the grounds of sex, religion or belief, sexual orientation, age, and racial, or national or ethnic origin (but not purely colour or nationality). The first four categories are confined to employment matters. The specific rule will shift the burden to the defendant once the claimant has proved a prime facie case and will be considered presently. The "traditional" approach still applies to "residual cases",[9] which are of some relevance to the application to more recent cases heard under the new rule.

(a) Residual Cases

The leading authorities are *King v Great Britain-China Centre*[10] and **13–003** *Glasgow CC v Zafar*.[11] The defendant in *King* was an organisation dedicated to fostering closer ties with China. It advertised for a deputy director of the centre, requiring fluent spoken Chinese and personal knowledge of China. Ms King was of Chinese origin who had been educated in Britain and met the requirements. She applied but did not even make the short list.

All eight short-listed candidates were white and the successful candidate was an English graduate in Chinese. None of the five ethnically Chinese applicants had been short-listed. Further, no ethnically Chinese person had ever been employed by the Centre. King brought a claim of direct race discrimination.

The industrial tribunal drew an inference that the defendant had discriminated against King because she did not come from the "same, essentially British, academic background" as the existing staff. The EAT reversed on the basis that the tribunal had placed the burden on

---

[7] *per* Sedley, L.J., *Anya v University of Oxford* [2001] ICR 847, para.11, CA. See also, *Deman v AUT* [2003] EWCA 329, where the Court of Appeal reversed the employment tribunal's and EAT's (EAT/746/99, [2002] All E.R. (D) 162 (Apr)) decisions because the employment tribunal failed to look for sub-conscious discrimination.

[8] "It is sometimes suggested that tribunals see an allegation of discrimination as very serious, almost quasi-criminal in nature, and as a result may, consciously or subconsciously, demand a rather higher standard than the normal balance of probabilities test. See C. Bourn and J. Whitmore, *Anti-Discrimination Law in Britain*, 3rd edn, 1996, London: Sweet & Maxwell, p.116.

[9] See further, Ch.2, para.2–002.

[10] [1992] I.C.R. 516, CA.

[11] [1997] I.R.L.R. 229, CS, [1998] I.C.R. 120, HL.

the defendant to disprove discrimination. The Court of Appeal restored the decision of the industrial tribunal and Neill, L.J. offered the following guidance: [12]

(1) It is for the applicant who complains of racial discrimination to make out his or her case. Thus if the applicant does not prove the case on the balance of probabilities he or she will fail.

(2) It is important to bear in mind that it is unusual to find direct evidence of racial discrimination. Few employers will be prepared to admit such discrimination even to themselves. In some cases the discrimination will not be ill-intentioned but merely based on an assumption that "he or she would not have fitted in".

(3) The outcome of the case will therefore usually depend on what inferences it is proper to draw from the primary facts found by the tribunal. These inferences can include, in appropriate cases, any inferences that it is just and equitable to draw . . . from an evasive or equivocal reply to a questionnaire.[13]

(4) Though there will be some cases where, for example, the non-selection of the applicant for a post or for promotion is clearly not on racial grounds, a finding of discrimination and a finding of a difference in race will often point to the possibility of racial discrimination. In such circumstances, the tribunal will look to the employer for an explanation. If no explanation is then put forward or if the tribunal considers the explanation to be inadequate or unsatisfactory it will be legitimate for the tribunal to infer that the discrimination was on racial grounds. This is not a matter of law, but, as May L.J. put it in *Noone*,[[14]] "almost common sense".

Hence, the Court of Appeal held that the industrial tribunal did not reverse the burden of proof, but made "merely a proper balancing of the factors which could be placed in the scales for and against a finding of unlawful discrimination."

13–004   In *Zafar*, a Scottish employment tribunal found that the claimant had (i) been unfairly dismissed because the dismissal procedure had fallen far below that of the reasonable employer and (ii) been discriminated against on grounds of race. The Court of Session reversed the

---

[12] [1992] I.C.R. 516, at 528–529.
[13] See SDA 1975, s.74(2); RRA 1976, s.65(2); DDA 1995, s.56(3); Religion or Belief Regulations 2003, Sexual Orientation Regulations 2003, reg.33(2); Age Regulations 2006, reg.41(2) (in force October 1, 2006).
[14] *Noone v North West Trains RHA* [1988] I.C.R. 813, CA.

finding of discrimination and Zafar appealed to the House of Lords. Giving judgment for the House, Lord Browne-Wilkinson held that tribunals should ask two questions: (i) was there less favourable treatment? and (ii) if so, was it on grounds of race? He then approved Neill, L.J.'s guidelines (in *King* above). The House of Lords agreed with the Court of Session decision that there had been no racial discrimination: the employer's unreasonable behaviour did not bind a tribunal to make a finding of racial discrimination.

What *King* and *Zafar* have in common is that there was less favourable treatment and each victim belonged to a protected group. Lord Browne-Wilkinson is saying that alone this is not enough for a finding of discrimination on one of the protected grounds, such as race or sex.[15] In *Zafar* that was the sum of the evidence. The additional evidence in *King* was the racial origin of the Centre's staff and those short-listed for interview. This pointed to the less favourable treatment being on the grounds of race. The Centre's failure to explain the less favourable treatment on grounds other than race confirmed this. Combined with the less favourable treatment and the racial origin of the claimant, this was enough to draw an inference of racial discrimination. This demonstrates Neill, L.J.'s fourth guideline (above), that in absence of direct evidence of unlawful discrimination, inferences may be made from circumstantial evidence and the defendant has the burden to refute those inferences with contrary evidence.

In *King*, Neill, L.J. added that "It is unnecessary and unhelpful to introduce the concept of a shifting evidential burden of proof."[16] This contrasts with the new rule (below) and the approach adopted by the courts in the United States. According to the Supreme Court in *McDonnell Douglas Corp v Green*,[17] there is three-stage procedure for disparate treatment (direct discrimination) claims. First, the plaintiff must show that: (a) he belongs to a protected group, (b) he applied and was qualified for a job for which the employer was seeking applicants, (c) he was rejected, and (d) that after the rejection the position remained open. The burden then shifts to the employer to articulate some legitimate non-discriminatory reason for the employer's rejection. The plaintiff may then try to show that the employer's stated reason for rejection was a pretext for the real reason. The formula is varied for dismissal claims.[18] A pretext could be revealed if the employer's reason had never been utilised before, where say, a black

---

[15] This was argued as a point of law by Lord Browne-Wilkinson in *James v Eastleigh BC* [1989] I.R.L.R. 318, at 321, reversed by a bare majority of the House of Lords [1990] I.R.L.R. 288. See further Ch.4, para.4–015.

[16] [1992] ICR 516, at 529.

[17] 411 US 792 (1973).

[18] See e.g. *McKnight v Kimberly Clark Corporation* 149 F 3d 1125, at 1129 (10th Cir 1998), where the first part requires: (1) the plaintiff belonged to a protected group (say aged over 50), (2) and was doing satisfactory work; (3) and was discharged, and (4) his position was filled by a person from a different group (say a younger person).

worker is disciplined for a minor transgression, where in the past no
white workers had been disciplined for similar transgressions.
Statistics of say, the prior hiring practice (*nb King*), may debunk the
stated reason. It has been held in Northern Ireland, however, that no
inference of any kind is raised by the mere fact that the members of
the appointing panel were all of a different religion from a candidate.[19]
The decision may have been in fear of creating an obligation that each
interview panel corresponded to the protected characteristics of each
candidate. There is no recommendation in the Codes of Practice that
the panel should be representative, but the profile of an interview
panel cannot always be excluded as irrelevant to a claim,[20] especially
where the panel's membership was manipulated.[21]

(b) Cases within EC Competence

13–005 The EC derived rule on the burden of proof applies to nearly all
employment tribunal, and some county, or sheriff, court hearings.
Although, as seen above, the issue centres on direct discrimination, the
new rule applies to indirect discrimination,[22] (as well as equal pay
claims).

The new formula provides:[23]

> Where, on the hearing of the complaint, the complainant proves
> facts from which the tribunal could, apart from this section,
> conclude in the absence of an adequate explanation that the
> respondent—
>
> (a) has committed an act of discrimination or harassment
>   against the complainant . . .
>
> the tribunal shall uphold the complaint unless the respondent
> proves that he did not commit, or, as the case may be, is not to be
> treated as having committed,[[24]] that act.

---

[19] *Armagh DC v Fair Employment Agency* [1994] I.R.L.R. 234, NICA.
[20] Issued by the EOC, CRE or DRC. Although the CRE Code includes an employment tribunal
decision implying that a claim may be bought by a white person interviewed by three black
panellists, or *vice versa*. (*Short v Greater London Unison*, Case No. 2301192/98 [2000] DCLD
46. See "Code of practice on racial equality in employment", 2006, CRE, at para.5.7 (ISBN 1
85442 570 6, or *www.cre.gov.uk*, click on "good practice").
[21] See the US case, *Domingo v New England Fish Company* 727 F 2d 1429 at 1435–36 (9th Cir
1984), where the race of those appointed to recruit was a relevant factor.
[22] *Vasiliki Nikoloudi v Organismos Tilepikoinonion Ellados AE* Case C-196/02 [2005] E.C.R.
I-0000, at para.75.
[23] The formula is substantially the same throughout. For employment tribunals (county or sheriff
court): SDA 1976, s.63A, (66A); RRA 1976, s.54A, (57ZA); DDA 1995, s.17A(1C), (25(9));
Religion or Belief Regulations 2003, regs 29, (32); Sexual Orientation Regulations 2003, regs
29, (32); Age Regulations 2006, regs 37, (40) (in force October 1, 2006).
[24] This phrase encompasses liability of employers or principals (see Ch.8, para.8–081), and
aiding unlawful acts (Ch.5, para.5–028).

In *Igen (formally Leeds Careers Guidance) v Wong* [25] the Court of Appeal stated that the new formula meant that parts (1) and (4) of Neill, LJ's guidance in *King* (above) required alteration. The Court of Appeal provided extensive guidance [26]:

13–006

(1) [I]t is for the claimant who complains of sex discrimination to prove on the balance of probabilities facts from which the tribunal could conclude, in the absence of an adequate explanation, that the employer has committed an act of discrimination against the claimant which is unlawful . . .

(2) If the claimant does not prove such facts he or she will fail.

(3) It is important to bear in mind in deciding whether the claimant has proved such facts that it is unusual to find direct evidence of sex discrimination. Few employers would be prepared to admit such discrimination, even to themselves. In some cases the discrimination will not be an intention but merely based on the assumption that "he or she would not have fitted in".

(4) In deciding whether the claimant has proved such facts, it is important to remember that the outcome at this stage of the analysis by the tribunal will therefore usually depend on what inferences it is proper to draw from the primary facts found by the tribunal.

(5) It is important to note the word "could" in [the formula] . . .. At this stage the tribunal does not have to reach a definitive determination that such facts would lead it to the conclusion that there was an act of unlawful discrimination. At this stage a tribunal is looking at the primary facts before it to see what inferences of secondary fact could be drawn from them.

(6) In considering what inferences or conclusions can be drawn from the primary facts, the tribunal must assume that there is no adequate explanation for those facts.

(7) These inferences can include, in appropriate cases, any inferences that it is just and equitable to draw . . . from an evasive or equivocal reply to a questionnaire . . .. [27]

[25] [2005] I.C.R. 931, para.76.

[26] *ibid.*, annexed to judgment. This revised the guidance given in *Barton v Investec* [2003] I.C.R. 1205, at para.25, EAT (for the facts of both cases, see below). It was applied in a case of gender reassignment in *B v BA* [2006] EWCA Civ 132.

[27] See SDA 1975, s.74(2); RRA 1976, s.65(2); DDA 1995, s.56(3); Religion or Belief Regulations 2003, reg.33(2); Sexual Orientation Regulations 2003, reg.33(2); Age Regulations 2006, reg.41(2) (in force October 1, 2006).

(8) Likewise, the tribunal must decide whether any provision of any relevant code of practice is relevant and, if so, take it into account ... This means that inferences may also be drawn from any failure to comply with any relevant code of practice.[28]

(9) Where the claimant has proved facts from which conclusions could be drawn that the employer has treated the claimant less favourably on the ground of sex, then the burden of proof moves to the employer.

(10) It is then for the employer to prove that he did not commit, or as the case may be, is not to be treated as having committed, that act.

(11) To discharge that burden it is necessary for the employer to prove, on the balance of probabilities, that the treatment was in no sense whatsoever on the grounds of sex, since "no discrimination whatsoever" is compatible with the Burden of Proof Directive 97/80/EC.[29]

(12) That requires a tribunal to assess not merely whether the employer has proved an explanation for the facts from which such inferences can be drawn, but further that it is adequate to discharge the burden of proof on the balance of probabilities that sex was not a ground for the treatment in question.

(13) Since the facts necessary to prove an explanation would normally be in the possession of the respondent, a tribunal would normally expect cogent evidence to discharge that burden of proof. In particular, the tribunal will need to examine carefully explanations for failure to deal with the questionnaire procedure and/or code of practice.

13–007 At first glance, it appears that all of this merely consolidates the position set out in *King* and *Zafar*.[30] However, there are two notable alterations, both of which favour the claimant. The first is that once a prima facie case has been established by the claimant, tribunals are *compelled* to find liability, unless the defendant proves there was no unlawful discrimination. In *King* Neill, L.J. stated merely that "it will be legitimate" to find discrimination. Second, the *Wong* guidance emphasised that the defendant's burden is onerous, requiring "cogent" evidence to prove no discrimination *whatsoever*.

---

[28] A breach of the Code does not in itself make a person liable: SDA 56A (1); RRA 1976, s.47(10); DDA 1995, s.53A(8).

[29] This Directive introduced the burden of proof rule into sex discrimination law.

[30] See Simon Brown, L.J., *Nelson v Carillion Services* [2003] I.C.R. 1256, para.26, CA; M. Connolly, "The Burden of Proof Regulations: Change and No Change" [2001] 30 I.L.J. 375.

A theme that persists though is that it is not enough merely to show unfavourable treatment of person belonging to a protected group. In *University of Huddersfield v Wolff*[31] a female lecturer complained that she was rejected for promotion in favour of a male colleague. The EAT held that these facts alone were not enough to raise a prima facie case and shift the burden to the University to show that the difference in treatment was not discriminatory. An exception to this appears to be where there is a lack of transparency in equal pay claims. In *Barton v Investec Henderson Crosthwaite Securities*[32] a City worker's male comparator was paid more and the employer produced no evidence as to the basis for the extra pay. The employment tribunal gave deference to the "vital" culture of discretionary and "unwritten" bonuses, and found that the difference in pay was justified.[33] The EAT held that the tribunal was in error to condone this lack of transparency and that it was for the employer to prove that sex was not a reason for difference in pay. It remains to be seen if this approach spreads beyond equal pay claims, for instance, to discretionary and unwritten promotion and recruitment practices.[34]

Unreasonable treatment as evidence of discrimination was considered under the new formula in *Igen v Wong*. Here, a black worker was treated unreasonably by three supervisors, each white, in disciplinary proceedings. Whilst cautioning against a finding of discrimination merely on unreasonable treatment (see *Zafar*, above), the Court upheld the tribunal's finding of a prima facie case on these facts, (which led to liability under the Race Relations Act 1976). The distinctive aspect of this case was the close involvement of the three white supervisors in the treatment of the black worker.[35]

(2) Commission Assistance

Legal assistance may be provided by the relevant enforcement commission. See further below, paras 13–038 and 13–046.

13–008

(3) Time Limits

The normal rule for employment tribunals is that an application must be presented within three months of the commission of the acts of discrimination alleged. The normal rule for county court or sheriff

13–009

---

[31] [2004] I.C.R. 828, EAT.

[32] [2003] I.C.R. 1205, EAT. See also *Handels-og Kontorfunktionaerernes Forbund i Danmark v Dansk Arbejdsgiverforening (acting for Danfoss)* Case 109/88 [1989] I.R.L.R. 532 and the discussion, Ch.9, para.9–035.

[33] Reported *ibid.*, at para.10.

[34] For a discussion on nepotism and word-of-mouth hiring as indirect discrimination, see Ch.6, paras 6–007—6–011.

[35] [2005] I.C.R. 931, at paras 39–51.

court claims is six months.[36] Different rules apply to equal pay claims (see below) and there a number of extensions in specific cases. [37]

If a claim is out of time, a court or tribunal has discretion to permit a claim "if, in all the circumstances of the case, it considers that it is just and equitable to do so."[38] There are two connected issues with the limitation period. First, identifying when the act of discrimination occurs so to start time running, and second, when it is "just and equitable" to permit a claim to proceed, despite more than three months having elapsed.

(a) When Time Starts Running

13–010 For establishing when the three-month period begins, the legislation provides[39] (a) that where an inclusion of a contractual term amounts to an unlawful act, that act extends throughout the duration of the contract; and (b) any act extending over a period shall be treated as done at the end of that period; and (c) a deliberate omission shall be treated as done when the person in question decided upon it.

Where the discrimination is by a contractual term, the matter is relatively straightforward. The time does not begin to run until the term is removed or the contract ends. So where, for example, an Asian man is employed with an inferior pension entitlement to his white colleagues, the discrimination extends to the duration of the employment contract.[40]

The main area of dispute here falls under para.(b). The issue is a series of separate acts can amount to a single continuing act "extending over a period". If not, only those acts falling within the time limit can be included in the claim (subject to the "just and equitable" discretion, see below). But if a series of acts can be treated as a

---

[36] Respectively SDA 1975, ss.76(1) and (2); RRA 1976, ss.68(1) and (2); DDA 1995, Sch.3, paras 3(1) and 6(1); Religion or Belief Regulations 2003, reg.34(1) and (2); Sexual Orientation Regulations 2003, reg.34(1) and (2); Age Regulations 2006, reg.42(1) and (2) (in force October 1, 2006).

[37] e.g., Where the statutory grievance procedure applies, time may be extended by three months (Employment Act 2002 (Dispute Resolution) Regulations 2004, SI 2004/752, reg.15, see e.g. S. Deacon and G. Morris, *Labour Law*, 4th edn 2005, Oxford: Hart, pp.88–90; for the armed forces, the time limit is six months (SDA 1975 s.76(1)(b), RRA 1976, 68(1)(b), Religion or Belief Regulations 2003, reg.34(1)(b); Sexual Orientation Regulations 2003, reg.34(1)(b); for some education cases, the limit is eight months (SDA 1975, s.76(2A); RRA 1976 s.68(3A), DDA 1995, Sch.3, para.13(2)(b)); where conciliation is sought under the DDA 1995, it is eight months (DDA 1995, Sch.3, para.13(2)(a)).

[38] SDA 1975, s.76(5); RRA 1976, s.68(6); DDA 1995, Sch.3, para.3(2); Religion or Belief Regulations 2003, reg.34(3); Sexual Orientation Regulations 2003, reg.34(3); Age Regulations 2006, reg.42(3) (in force October 1, 2006). The time limit in the grievance procedure (EA 2002, s.32(4)) does not displace this discretion: *BUPA v Cann* [2006] I.R.L.R. 248, EAT.

[39] SDA 1975, s.76(6); RRA 1976, s.68(7); DDA 1995, Sch.3, para.3(3); Religion or Belief Regulations 2003, Sexual Orientation Regulations 2003, reg.34(4); Age Regulations 2006, reg.42(4) (in force October 1, 2006).

[40] *Barclays Bank v Kapur* [1991] 2 A.C. 355, *obiter*, at 367, HL.

single continuing act, they become part of the claim so long as the final act fell within the time limit.

In *Hendricks v Metropolitan Police Commissioner*[41] the Court of Appeal offered some guidance on this question. First, the phrase in the legislation *act extending over a period* is legally "more precise" than expressions such as "institutionalised racism", "a prevailing way of life", a "generalised policy of discrimination", or "climate" or "culture" of unlawful discrimination. But it is not confined to something so formal as a policy, rule, practice, scheme, or regime. What is required is that "the numerous alleged incidents of discrimination are linked to one another and that they are evidence of a continuing discriminatory state of affairs covered by the concept of 'an act extending over a period.'" These acts may continue into a period of absence from work. In addition, evidence of long-past less favourable treatment may still be used to reinforce the current claim. In this case, Joy Hendricks, a black woman police constable, specified nearly 100 acts of sex and race discrimination committed by her employer spanning the whole of her 11-year career. Most were committed in the first five years of service. Her final year of service was spent on long-term stress-related sick leave. The EAT reversed the employment tribunal's decision that the behaviour over the whole 11 years amounted to a continuing act. The EAT took the view that the claimant had to show that the behaviour amounted to a policy of discrimination. The Court of Appeal restored the employment tribunal's decision.

In *Barclays Bank v Kapur*[42] the claimants, East African Asians, had worked in banks in Kenya and Tanzania, before moving to the UK in the early 1970s, where they were employed by Barclays. In contrast to their normal policy, Barclays refused to credit their previous service with the East African banks in calculating their pension entitlement. The claimants could not argue that this was *contractual* discrimination, because the refusal was made before the Race Relations Act 1976 (RRA 1976) came into force. However, the House of Lords held that the refusal was continuing discrimination, rather than a one-off act at the start of their employment, which effectively extended to the duration of their employment. Hence their claim of racial discrimination was not time-barred.

In *Calder v James Finlay Corporation*[43] Mrs Calder requested a mortgage subsidy twice, in March and May 1981. Each time she was refused. She resigned in October and presented a claim of sex discrimination (all male staff had been given mortgage subsidies). The EAT held that the refusal amounted to continuing discrimination as long as she remained in this employment, and so time did not begin to run

13–011

[41] [2003] I.C.R. 530, at paras 48–52.
[42] [1991] 2 A.C. 355.
[43] [1989] I.C.R. 157.

until her resignation. In *Cast v Croydon College*[44] the claimant, after becoming pregnant, was refused permission to return to work after the birth on a part-time basis. Further requests to transfer to a part-time contract were refused and eventually she resigned one month after returning from her maternity leave, and then two months later made a claim of sex discrimination. The Court of Appeal held that the application of a discriminatory policy here amounted to an act extending over a period, so that the effects of the first decision (made before the birth) were continuing.

13–012   There appears to be two circumstances where the courts take a different view of "continuing act". The first is where a single act causes continuing consequences, such as a re-grading or down-grading. This occurred in *Sougrin v Haringey HA*[45] where the Court of Appeal held that as this was not a case where there was a discriminatory "policy" of paying less on racial grounds, the only acts were the re-grading (and rejection of subsequent appeal), which occurred some six months before the claim was submitted. Thus it was out of time. Such cases are extremely difficult to distinguish from *Barclays Bank v Kapur*, and it may be that the more liberal approach signalled in 2002 in *Hendricks* changes matters here. *Hendricks* states that it is not necessary that there is a policy, only a "continuing discriminatory state of affairs". If a single decision results in continuing lower pay, it is arguable that that is a continuing state of affairs.

The second restriction applies to job applicants who are not employees. In *Tyagi v BBC World Service*[46] an existing worker was refused a promotion in April 1997. In relation to this, he presented a claim of racial discrimination in July 1998, after having left the BBC in July 1997. He argued that the BBC had a discriminatory recruitment policy and so he could never get the position he had applied for, and so the alleged discrimination was continuing into the period when he was no longer an employee. The Court of Appeal held that there was no continuing act of discrimination and so his claim was out of time. This restriction is based on the employment provisions of the legislation.[47] For instance, s.4(1), Race Relations Act 1976, applies to the "arrangements" for recruitment or a refusal or omission to offer that employment. None of these, according to the Court of Appeal, are continuing acts. By contrast, s.4(2) applies to employees and the way they are afforded access to opportunities for promotion, transfer or training, or to any other benefits, facilities or services, or by refusing or deliberately omitting to afford him access to them, or any other detriment. All of these can amount to continuing acts. The Court observed that any discriminatory practice in recruitment was

---

[44] [1998] I.C.R. 500.
[45] [1992] I.C.R. 650.
[46] [2001] I.R.L.R. 465.
[47] See Ch.8, paras 8–008 and 8–013.

unlawful under s.28, RRA 1976, which was enforceable only by the Commission for Racial Equality.[48]

In the United States, there is a 180 day time limit for federal Title VII claims (300 days where a claim was first made through a state or local agency). The courts will only consider behaviour preceding that period in "hostile environment" claims (i.e. harassment), where the behaviour "contributed" to the hostile environment within the period.[49]

Paragraph (c) of this provision states that "a deliberate omission shall be treated as done when the person in question decided upon it." This suggests that an employer's deliberate omission to do something is fixed in time and so cannot be a continuing act. This may be so, but the House of Lords in *Barclays Bank v Kapur* afforded para.(c) such a limited scope, that this should matter little. The bank argued that its failure to credit the claimant's previous service was a "deliberate omission" which had to be attributed to the time when the bank "decided upon it", which was when the claimants were first employed. The House of Lords rejected this interpretation, as it could not be squared with the first part of the provision, that an unlawful contractual term continued to have effect for the duration of the contract (see above). Further, this was a "very artificial way" of looking at the facts: "Whenever terms of employment are less favourable it is possible to dress up the complaint as a deliberate omission by saying that the employer 'deliberately omitted' to include the more favourable term in the contract of employment". The House suggested that "deliberate omission" in this context "was included by the draftsman as a sweeping-up provision intended for the protection of employees and addressed to activities peripheral to the employment rather than to the terms of the employment itself and intended to cover a one-off rather than a continuing situation: for example, a deliberate failure to notify a [black] employee of a vacancy for a better job in the company when all his white comparators were invited to apply for the job."[50]

(b) The Meaning of "Just and Equitable"

This discretion is broader than that for unfair dismissal, where a tribunal may extend time only if it was not "reasonably practicable" to present the claim in time.[51] Hence, unfair dismissal cases can offer little guidance on this matter. In *British Coal Corporation v Keeble*[52] the EAT stated that tribunals should adopt as a checklist the factors mentioned in s.33 of the Limitation Act 1980, which provides a broad

---

[48] See below, paras 13–030 and 13–039.

[49] *AMTRAK v Morgan* 536 US 101 (Sup Ct 2002). For "hostile environment" claims, see Ch.5, paras 5–004 to 5–014.

[50] *per* Lord Griffiths, delivering the judgment of the House, [1991] 2 A.C. 355, at pp.367–368.

[51] See e.g. ERA 1996, s.111(2).

[52] [1997] I.R.L.R. 336.

discretion for the Court to extend the limitation period of three years in cases of personal injury and death. However, in *London Borough of Southwark v Afolabi,*[53] Peter Gibson, L.J., in the Court of Appeal, said that a failure to adopt such a checklist was not necessarily an error in law, although it had "utility" in many cases.[54] The wide discretion afforded to a tribunal in discrimination cases was emphasised by the Court of Appeal in *Robertson v Bexley Community Centre (t/a Leisure Link),*[55] stating that a decision should not be reversed unless it was plainly wrong in law. This cuts both ways though, as it prevents an appeal by *either* side unless there was an error in law.

In *Robertson* the claimant trainee was racially abused by his supervisor in April 1999. He complained and the supervisor was disciplined and then went off sick for several months. Upon his return, in October, the supervisor again racially abused the claimant, who resigned the following the day. The employment tribunal held that the claim relating to the abuse in April was out of time and in light of the disciplinary action taken for that, it would not be just and equitable to hear that claim. The Court of Appeal upheld that decision as it was not wrong in law.

13–015   Time may be extended when incorrect legal advice delays the claim. In *British Coal v Keeble,* the claimant was made redundant and paid according to a scheme which was more favourable to men. Her union advised her, incorrectly, that the scheme was lawful, but later counsel's opinion advised her to claim. As a result, her claim was made 22 months after she was made redundant. The EAT allowed her to pursue her claim. In *Hawkins v Ball and Barclays Bank plc,*[56] the claimant presented a claim of sexual harassment five months after the incident, having been advised originally by a solicitor that the incident was trivial. The EAT held that in the circumstances it was just and equitable to permit the claim to proceed.

In *Afolabi* the claimant was interviewed in 1990 for the post of auditor Grade SO2. He was rejected but offered a job at a lower grade, which he took. Nine years later he brought proceedings in relation to a re-grading. For these proceedings he inspected his personnel file, which revealed that in his original interview he been give a very high score. Within three months of inspecting the file, he brought proceedings for racial discrimination in relation to that original interview. The Court of Appeal held, in this "wholly exceptional" case, it was just and equitable to allow the claim to proceed. The Court noted that Mr Afolabi had no reason to inspect his file at an earlier time and no reason to think he had an arguable case before he had seen it. Further,

---

[53] [2003] EWCA Civ 15, CA.
[54] *ibid.*, at para.33. Peter Gibson, L.J. dissented on a separate issue.
[55] [2003] I.R.L.R. 434.
[56] [1996] I.R.L.R. 258.

on the evidence (Southwark Council produced very little on this point), extending the time was equally prejudicial to both parties.

This question arises commonly where the worker awaits the outcome of a grievance or disciplinary procedure before issuing proceedings. In *Aniagwu v London Borough of Hackney,*[57] Morison, J. suggested time should always be extended in this circumstance, saying: "[U]nless there is some particular feature about the case or some particular prejudice which employers can show, every tribunal would inevitably conclude that it is a responsible and proper attitude for someone to seek to redress a grievance through the employer's grievance procedure before embarking on legal proceedings." However, in *Robinson v Post Office*[58] Lindsay, J. in a response later approved by the Court of Appeal,[59] made it clear that delay because of an internal, or "domestic," process, was just one factor in the question.

(4) Time Limits—Equal Pay Claims

Two procedural rules for equal pay claims were challenged as being contrary to Art.119 (now Art.141), EC Treaty, in the cases of *Levez v Jennings*[60] and *Preston v Wolverhampton Healthcare NHS Trust.*[61] The first rule, by s.2(4) of the Equal Pay Act 1970 (EPA 1970), required claims are brought, at the latest, within six months of the termination of employment ("the qualifying date"). The second rule, by s.2(5), was that arrears or damages in respect of unequal pay could only be awarded in respect of the period of two years before the proceedings were instituted; tribunals had no discretion. These rules have now been amended[62] to accord with the judgments of the two cases. The amendments came into force on July 19, 2003.

13–010

(a) The Qualifying Date

Under the new ss.2ZA of the Equal Pay Act the general (six-month) rule still applies, but with three exceptions. The first (s.2ZA (4)) is where a worker is employed on a series of temporary contracts. Before the amendment, she would have to make a claim in respect of each contract. But now, where the series of contracts could be defined by as "stable employment case,"[63] the time limit will not begin to run until the end of the stable employment. The second one, (s.2ZA (5)) arises

13–011

---

[57] [1999] I.R.L.R. 303, EAT.
[58] [2000] I.R.L.R. 804, at paras 29–31, EAT.
[59] *Apelogun-Gabriels v London Borough of London* [2002] I.C.R. 713, at paras 16 and 24.
[60] Case C-326/96, [1999] I.R.L.R. 36, ECJ.
[61] Case C-78/98, [2000] I.C.R. 961.
[62] By The Equal Pay (Amendment) Regulations 2003, SI 2003/1656. Note that slightly different rules apply to the armed forces, EPA 1970, ss.7A(8) and (9), 7AA, 7AB and 7AC.
[63] This does not include the situation where, with no break in employment, the worker changes jobs with different terms: *Newcastle upon Tyne CC v Allan* [2005] I.C.R. 1170, at paras 28–39, EAT.

where, for instance, the employer lies about the pay of a comparator (a "concealment case"). The qualifying date is six months after the claimant discovered (or *ought to* have discovered) the truth. This scenario occurred in *Levez*, below. The third exception (s.2ZA (6)) arises where the woman falls under a disability[64] during the six-month period following employment. The qualifying date is six-months after she ceased to be under a disability. In a case of both concealment *and* disability, the qualifying date is the later of those given by subss.(5) and (6).[65]

(b) Award of Arrears or Damages

13–018 The general thrust of the new ss.2ZB (England and Wales) and 2ZC (Scotland) is to bring the law into line with a claim for breach of contract. So, the arrears date is now six years for England and Wales, and five years for Scotland. In concealment or disability cases, arrears can be claimed for the *whole* period of unequal pay, although, for Scotland, this is limited to a 20 year maximum.[66] These new sections arose from the cases of *Levez* and *Preston.*

In *Levez*, Mrs Levez began work as betting shop manager in February 1991, at £10,000 per annum. In December, her employer falsely told her that another manager, doing like work, earned £10,800 pa, and raised her salary accordingly. In fact the male manager had earned £11,400 pa. On leaving her job in March 1993, Mrs Levez discovered the truth. In September she began proceedings for equal pay, claiming arrears from February 1991. The employer argued that by the then s.2(5), EPA 1970, it was only liable for arrears going back two years from the date the claim was made, that is September 1991. The ECJ held that the general two-year limit imposed by s.2(5) was not of itself incompatible with Community law. However, this limit, so far as it was inflexible and so allowed an employer to profit from its deceit, was incompatible with Community law.

In *Preston,* the ECJ held that s.2(5), in preventing pensionable service to be credited before the two years preceding an initial claim of equal pay, contravened Community Law. When the case returned to the House of Lords,[67] it was held that credit should be backdated to April 8, 1976 (the date when the ECJ held, in *Defrenne v Sabena*[68] that Art.119 (now 141) had direct effect).[69] As noted above, the

---

[64] i.e. a minor or of unsound mind (England and Wales), or under 16 or incapable according to the Adults with Incapacity (Scotland) Act 2000 (EPA 1970, s.11(2A)).

[65] EPA 1970, s.2ZA(7).

[66] EPA 1970, s.2ZC(3).

[67] *Preston v Wolverhampton Healthcare NHS Trust (No.2)*[2001] 2 A.C. 455, at paras 10–12.

[68] *Defrenne v Sabena* Case C-43/75, [1976] I.C.R. 547, ECJ.

[69] This was subject to an employee paying contributions owing for the period for which retroactive membership is claimed: see *Fisscher v Voorhuis Hengelo BV and Stichting Bedrijfspensioenfonds voor de Detailhandel* Case C-128/93, [1995] I.C.R. 635, ECJ.

Government responded to the ECJ judgment by replacing the two-year rule with the six- (or for Scotland, five-) year rule, which brings such claims into line with breach of contract. But the House of Lord's judgment reveals that, in cases of pensions at least, even the amended rule may contravene Community law.

(5) Remedies[70]

Generally, a county or sheriff court can order remedies in their normal way, which of course normally will be damages. Employment tribunals can provide remedies where it considers it "just and equitable" to do so, and may order damages, make a declaration, and make recommendations.

13–019

(a) Damages

The legislation states that all discrimination claims (save for equal pay) should proceed "in like manner as any other tort or (in Scotland) in reparation for breach of statutory duty.[71] This means that successful claimants should be put in the position in which they have been but for the unlawful discrimination. As with tort generally, claimants are under a duty to mitigate their loss.[72] However, compensation is not restricted to foreseeable losses. It should be awarded for losses flowing naturally and directly from the wrong.[73] Further, compensation can be awarded for non-pecuniary losses of psychiatric damage, aggravated damage, and injury to feelings. It is not certain whether exemplary damages are available.

Unlike unfair dismissal, there is no upper limit for compensation in discrimination cases in employment tribunals.[74] In some cases, compensation is not available for indirect discrimination.

13–020

---

[70] See J. Kelly and B. Watt, "Damages in sex harassment cases: a comparative study of American, Canadian and British law" (1996) 16 New York Law School Journal of International and Comparative Law 79.

[71] SDA 1976, ss.65(1)(b) and 66(1); RRA 1976, s.56(1)(b) and 57(1); DDA 1995, s.17A(3); Religion or Belief Regulations 2003, regs 30(1)(b) and 31(1); Sexual Orientation Regulations 2003, regs 30(1)(b) and 31(1); Age Regulations 2006, reg.48(1)(b) and 39(1) (in force October 1, 2006).

[72] Note here the Employment Act 2002 (Dispute Resolution) Regulations 2004, SI 2004/752, which introduced statutory grievance procedures in employment. A failure to follow these before litigation may result in a 10–50 per cent reduction, or increase, in compensation (depending upon which party is at fault).

[73] *Essa v Laing Ltd* [2004] I.C.R. 746 *per* Pill, L.J. at para.37 and Clark, L.J. at para.44. See also Stuart-Smith, L.J. in *Sheriff v Klyne Tugs (Lowestoft) Ltd* [1999] I.C.R. 1170, at paras 17–22, CA.

[74] In *Marshall v Southampton and South West Hampshire AHA (No.2)* Case C-271/91 [1993] I.R.L.R. 445, the ECJ ruled that the (then £11,000) cap breached the Equal Treatment Directive 76/207/EEC. It was lifted by the Sex Discrimination and Equal Pay (Remedies) Regulations 1993 (SI 1993/2798). The cap for race cases was lifted to avoid an anomaly: Race Relations (Remedies) Act 1994. (The cap for unfair dismissal claims stands at February 1, 2006 at £58,400: Employment Rights (Increase of Limits) Order 2005 SI 2005/3352. It is normally raised each February in line with retail prices.)

(a)(i) Pecuniary loss

13–021 Some of calculations necessary were illustrated in *Ministry of Defence v Cannock*,[75] a case concerning many women dismissed from the armed forces because of pregnancy, which was brought under the Equal Treatment Directive 76/207/EEC (at the time the armed forces were excluded from the Sex Discrimination Act 1975). The first feature of the case is that the EAT applied the relevant principles of tort to a claim under EC law. Second, the EAT observed that there was a distinction between these claims and ones for serious personal injury, where there might be loss of a chance ever to work again.[76] The EAT stated that the approach to calculating losses should be neither a finding of fact of what would have happened, nor based simply on what facts are known. The claimants in this case took an "all-or-nothing" strategy, arguing that a tribunal should award compensation based upon for instance (i) whether or not a claimant would have returned to service after the birth; (ii) if so, for how long; and (iii) to what ranks, if any, she would have been promoted during her future service. The MOD argued that the award should be restricted to the known fact of the length of each claimant's commission, which in effect, is a contractual measure. The EAT stated that the correct approach was to assess the "chance" of each the events occurring, and compensate for the loss of chance.[77] It is permissible to use statistics in this assessment. In *Vento v Chief Constable of West Yorkshire*[78] statistics were used showing the percentage of women who in the past had continued to serve in the police force until the age of retirement. By the same reasoning, when a job applicant is rejected because of discrimination, the measure is the loss of the chance to get the job.

Claimants are expected to mitigate their loss in the normal way. So, a victim of a discriminatory dismissal is likely to be under a duty to seek work. In *Cannock*, this may have been reapplying to the services once the "no-pregnancy" rule had been abandoned.[79] In other cases it may mean accepting an offer of reinstatement. A failure to mitigate entitles the tribunal to reduce the award.

For the Court of Appeal in *Ministry of Defence v Wheeler*[80] (another armed forces "pregnancy dismissal" case), it came to this: first, take the sum that the victim would have earned but for the unlawful dismissal, second, deduct from that sum the amount that (in mitigation) she had, or should have, earned elsewhere, and third, apply to that net loss the percentage chance that she would have remained in

---

[75] [1994] I.C.R. 918. See A. Arnull, "EC law and the dismissal of pregnant servicewomen" (1995) 24 I.L.J. 215.
[76] *ibid.*, at 929.
[77] *ibid.*, at 935–938.
[78] [2003] I.C.R. 318, at paras 32–44, CA.
[79] [1994] I.C.R. 918, at 938–940.
[80] [1998] I.C.R. 242, at 246–254, 257, CA.

her pre-dismissal employment. In other words, mitigation should be considered before the question of chance is applied.

(a)(ii) Non-pecuniary loss

Where appropriate, damages may be awarded for psychiatric damage, **13–022** aggravated damage, and (provided specifically by statute) injury to feelings.[81] "Injury to feelings" includes subjective feelings of upset, frustration, worry, anxiety, mental distress, fear, grief, anguish, humiliation, unhappiness, stress, and depression. Compensation for injury to feelings cannot be fixed with any degree of precision. "Translating hurt feelings into hard currency is bound to be an artificial exercise."[82] As Dickson, J. said in *Andrews v Grand & Toy Alberta Ltd*,[83] "There is no medium of exchange for happiness. . . . The monetary evaluation of non-pecuniary losses is a philosophical and policy exercise more than a legal or logical one."

In *Vento v Chief Constable of West Yorkshire Police*[84] Mummery, L.J. offered extensive guidance on calculating the award. He first noted that the older cases were decided before the ceiling on damages was removed, implying that their usefulness as a guide was limited. The guidance divided cases into three bands. The first, for the "most serious cases", (such as a lengthy campaign of discriminatory harassment) should attract awards of £15,000 to £25,000. Only "the most exceptional case" should it exceed £25,000. The middle band, for "serious cases" should be between £5,000 and £15,000. The lowest band, for "less serious cases" should be between £500 and £5,000. Generally awards of less than £500 should not be made as they risk not indicating a proper recognition of the injury.

In this case, Ms Vento won her claim for sex discrimination following a series of bullying which ended with her dismissal for alleged dishonesty. The employment tribunal found that she had "been put through four traumatic years by the conduct of the respondent's officers." It further found that Ms Vento's employer and colleagues acted in a "high-handed manner" by raising questions about her honesty and private life, even after the appeal was decided. The employer made "a cynical offer of reinstatement principally designed to limit the financial damage". None of the relevant officers ever apologised, and when the Deputy Chief Constable eventually

---

[81] "For the avoidance of doubt it is hereby declared that damages in respect of an unlawful act of discrimination or harassment may include compensation for injury to feelings whether or not they include compensation under any other head.": SDA 1976, s.65(4). See also RRA 1976, s.57(4); DDA 1995, s.17A(4); Religion or Belief Regulations 2003, reg.31(3); Sexual Orientation Regulations 2003, reg.31(3); Age Regulations 2006, reg.39(3) (in force October 1, 2006).

[82] *per* Mummery, L.J., *Vento v Chief Constable of West Yorkshire Police* [2003] I.C.R. 318, at para.50.

[83] (1978) 83 DLR (3d) 452 at p.475, Supreme Ct of Canada, cited in *Vento, ibid.*, at para.50.

[84] [2003] I.C.R. 318, at paras 52 and 65.

attempted to apologise he did so unaware of the decisions against him and so spoke "not really knowing for what he was apologising". Overall the employer and its officers were in "institutional denial".

For her non-pecuniary loss, the Court of Appeal awarded Ms Vento £18,000 for injury to feelings, £5,000 aggravated damages and £9,000 for psychiatric damage.

Note that damages for injury to feelings are not available for claims under the Equal Pay Act 1970, which are essentially contractual rather than tortuous.[85]

(a)(iii) Exemplary damages

13–023 Exemplary damages for unlawful discrimination presents a rather confusing story which is still in state of uncertainty. Unlike the pecuniary and non-pecuniary awards discussed above, exemplary damages are not compensatory, but instead are to deter and punish the defendant. Three categories were identified in *Rookes v Barnard*, in 1964.[86] The first is oppressive, arbitrary or unconstitutional behaviour by government servants, who include the police.[87] The second category arises where the defendant calculated that his conduct would make him a profit exceeding any compensation he would have to pay. This can apply to private defendants. The third is where exemplary damages are expressly authorised by statute (at present the discrimination legislation does not do this.)

Accordingly in 1991, in *City of Bradford Metropolitan Council v Arora*,[88] the Court of Appeal upheld an award (under the first category) for £1,000 exemplary damages for a sex and race discrimination claim by an unsuccessful job applicant because of the conduct of the interview process, which included "entirely unnecessary" questions designed "for the purpose of making suggestive, insidious and prejudicial remarks against her". However, in 1993, in *AB v South West Water Services*,[89] the Court of Appeal held that exemplary damages were only available if they had been awarded for the tort in question before *Rookes v Barnard* (the "cause of action" test). Inevitably, this excluded discrimination.[90] Then, in 2001, the House of Lords, in *Kuddus v Chief Constable of Leicestershire Constabulary*,[91] overruled *AB v South West Water Services* and held that exemplary damages depend on the conduct of the public authority (the "conduct" test),

---

[85] *Newcastle upon Tyne CC v Allan* [2005] I.C.R. 1170, EAT. *Quaere*, now that the Equal Treatment Directive covers pay, whether this position can be sustained. See further, Ch.9 paras 9–002 and 9–006.

[86] *Rookes v Barnard* [1964] A.C. 1129, at 1226–1227, HL.

[87] *Cassell v Broome* [1972] A.C. 1027, at 1077–1078, 1130, 1134, HL.

[88] [1991] 2 Q.B. 507.

[89] [1993] Q.B. 507.

[90] *Ministry of Defence v Meredith* [1995] I.R.L.R. 539, EAT, *McConnell v Police Authority of Northern Ireland* [1997] I.R.L.R. 625, NICA.

[91] [2002] 2 A.C. 122.

rather than the cause of action. This resurrects the possibility of exemplary damages for discrimination, although the House in *Kuddus* offered no certainty on the issue. Of those who commented, Lords Hutton and Nicholls said that such awards have a role to play in "outrageous behaviour" (by public authorities) in civil liberties cases.[92] Lord Mackay stated that exemplary damages should not be awarded in discrimination cases unless expressly authorised by statute.[93] Lord Hutton preferred to reserve his opinion on discrimination until the matter came before him.[94]

In *Newcastle upon Tyne CC v Allan,*[95] the President of the EAT, **13–024** Burton, J. suggested *obiter*, that the decision in *Kuddus* "could found an argument" for recovering exemplary damages under the Sex Discrimination Act 1975.

The Law Commission has recommended that exemplary damages are appropriate in some cases of discrimination, where there is "deliberate and outrageous disregard" of the victim's rights, and where "the other remedies awarded would be inadequate to punish the defendant." An example would be an employer ignoring, and effectively conniving in, a campaign of racial harassment.[96] The parent discrimination Directives also suggest that exemplary damages should be available: "The sanctions, which may comprise the payment of compensation to the victim, must be effective, proportionate and *dissuasive*."[97]

It seems, at the least (Lord Mackay's opinion notwithstanding), that exemplary damages in principle (the "conduct" test) should be available against public authorities in discrimination cases. Whether the courts go further remains to be seen.

(a)(iv) Compensation for indirect discrimination

Both the Sex Discrimination Act 1975 and Race Relations Act 1976 **13–025** originally provided that, in the context of indirect discrimination, "no award of damages shall be made if the respondent proves that the requirement or condition was not applied with the intention of treating the claimant unfavourably . . .".[98] As it became clear that this restriction did not comply with EC law,[99] it was reformulated. The first

---

[92] *ibid.*, respectively paras 63 and 75.
[93] *ibid.*, at para.46.
[94] *ibid.*, at para.92.
[95] [2005] I.C.R. 1170, at para.12, EAT.
[96] *Aggravated, Exemplary and Restitutionary Damages*, Law Commission Report No.247, 1997, London: TSO, at pp.4–8 (see *www.lawcom.gov.uk/lc_reports.htm#1997*). This is a general survey into their appropriateness as tort remedies.
[97] Emphasis supplied. 76/207/EEC, Art.8d; 2000/43/EC Art.15; 2000/78/EC, Art.17.
[98] SDA 1975, s.66(3); RRA 1976, s.57(3). See e.g. *Orphanos v QMC* [1985] A.C. 761, HL.
[99] Confirmed in *Draehmpaehl v Urania Immobilien Service ohg* Case C-180/95 [1997] I.R.L.R. 538. The ECJ held that a Member State may not make an award of compensation in a sex discrimination case dependent on showing fault on the part of the employer. See A. McColgan, "Remedies for discrimination" (1994) 23 I.L.J. 226; A. Arnull, "EC law and the dismissal of pregnant servicewomen" (1995) 24 I.L.J. 215.

amendment was for sex discrimination in employment matters in employment tribunals,[100] being covered by the Equal Treatment Directive 76/207/EEC. The new s.65(1B) provided that for cases of unintentional indirect discrimination, compensation is awarded when it is "just and equitable" to do so, *and* the tribunal is satisfied that the power to make a declaration and a recommendation are not in themselves an adequate remedy in the circumstances. The original restriction remains for county or sheriff court hearings.[101] The new formula is repeated in the Sexual Orientation, Religion or Belief, and Age Regulations,[102] and applies to both employment tribunals and county or sheriff court proceedings. This has a lesser significance because the Regulations cover only employment and vocational training. Only rarely will cases arise in the county or sheriff court, such as a claim against a university in respect of vocational training.

Under the Disability Discrimination Act 1995 (DDA 1995), unintentional discrimination is not singled out and so falls under the general approach. Here employment tribunals may give remedies when it is "just and equitable" to do so.[103] The position is the same for those parts of the Race Relations Act 1976 which fall within the competence of the Race Directive 2000/43/EC.[104] But for residual race cases, the original restriction remains.[105]

For those cases with the original restriction, or the reformulated one, the defendant's absence of intention is the trigger. However, for these purposes "intention" has been afforded a broad interpretation. In *JH Walker Ltd v Hussain*[106] the EAT held that these provisions were not concerned with the motive or reason behind the defendant's act, but rather with his awareness of the consequences of his act:

> "[I]ntention" in this context signifies the state of mind of a person who, at the time when he does the relevant act . . .

---

[100] Sex Discrimination and Equal Pay (Miscellaneous Amendments) Regs 1996, SI 1996/438, reg.2(2).

[101] This will require amendment to accord with the Equal Treatment in Goods and Services Directive 2004/113/EC (due in force by December 21, 2007). See generally, Ch.2, para.2–002.

[102] Religion or Belief Regulations 2003, reg.30(2); Sexual Orientation Regulations 2003, reg.30(2); Age Regulations 2006, reg.38(2) (in force October 1, 2006).

[103] See e.g. DDA 1995, s.17A(2).

[104] RRA 1976, s.56(1).

[105] RRA 1976, s.56(3). Residual cases include discrimination based purely on colour, or nationality. See further Ch.2, para.2–002.

[106] [1996] I.C.R. 291, at 299–300. See also Ch.6, para.6–045. Similarly, in *London Underground Ltd v Edwards* [1995] I.C.R. 574, a gender case decided before the change in the law, the EAT held that compensation was payable for indirect discrimination as the employers were aware of the adverse impact of the new rostering arrangements even though they had not been drawn up with the purpose of treating women unfavourably. See further Ch.6, para.6–038.

(a) *wants* to bring about the state of affairs which constitutes the prohibited act of unfavourable treatment on racial grounds; and

(b) *knows* that the prohibited act will follow from his acts.

This approach limits the amount of defendants who could take advantage of this restriction. In *Hussain*, 18 employees were disciplined for taking a day off work to celebrate Eid, a Muslim holy day, in breach of a new rule that holidays could not be taken during the during the company's busiest time. The workers brought a claim of indirect racial discrimination (as the facts arose before the Religion of Belief Regulations 2003). The EAT upheld the award £1,000 compensation to each applicant for injury to feelings. The company was aware that Eid was important to its Muslim workers and the effect of the new rule upon them. The company's motive of promoting business efficiency could not "displace" its knowledge of the consequences of the new rule.

(b) Declaration
A declaration is "an order declaring the rights of the complainant and the respondent in relation to the act to which the complaint relates."[107] This follows a finding in the claimant's favour, but in most cases is accompanied by one or both of the other available remedies, which normally are of more practical significance.

13–026

(c) Recommendations
Where it considers it just and equitable to do so, a tribunal may make "a recommendation that the respondent take within a specified period action appearing to the tribunal to be practicable for the purpose of obviating or reducing the adverse effect on the complainant of any act of discrimination to which the complaint relates."[108] If the employer fails to comply with the recommendation, the tribunal may order compensation.

13–027

This remedy epitomises the individualistic nature of the remedies available. It is limited to making a recommendation affecting the claimant, but not those in the same position. A tribunal cannot order the employer to revise its recruitment and promotion procedures, for instance. Of course, a recommendation for an employer to change its behaviour vis-à-vis the victim may inspire better practice generally, but

---

[107] SDA 1976, s.65(1)(a); RRA 1976, s.56(1)(a); DDA 1995, s.17A(2)(a); Religion or Belief Regulations 2003, reg.30(1)(a); Sexual Orientation Regulations 2003, reg.30(1)(a); Age Regulations 2006, reg.38(1)(a) (in force October 1, 2006).

[108] SDA 1975, s.65(1)(c); RRA 1976, s.56(1)(c); DDA 1995, s.17A92)(c); Religion or Belief Regulations 2003, Sexual Orientation Regulations 2003, reg.31(1)(c); Age Regulations 2006, reg.38(1)(c) (in force October 1, 2006).

the chances of even this effect diminish where the victim was never employed, or is no longer employed, by the defendant.[109]

By contrast, in Northern Ireland Fair Employment Tribunal may make a recommendation "for the purpose of obviating or reducing the adverse effect on *a person other than the complainant* of any unlawful discrimination to which the complaint relates."[110] In the United States, Title VII (the main Federal employment discrimination legislation) authorises a wide range of remedies, including "such affirmative action as may be appropriate, which may include, but is not limited to, reinstatement or hiring of employees, with or without back pay . . . or any other equitable relief as the court deems appropriate."[111] Such orders may go beyond the individual or class complaint, as long as they do not "unnecessarily trammel" the rights of those who do not benefit under the programme.

13–028 The limited potential of the British remedy is revealed in some of the case law. In *Noone v North West Thames RHA (No.2)*,[112] the defendant rejected on racial grounds Dr Noone's job application for the post of consultant microbiologist. The industrial tribunal found in her favour and made a recommendation to the effect that the Health Authority dispense with the statutory procedure of advertising the next consultant microbiologist post, so the field would be narrowed, thus favouring Dr Noone. The Court of Appeal held this was too wide under the power given by the Race Relations Act 1976, because it "set at nought" the statutory hiring procedure. Of course, this being the reason for the decision, it is arguable that the case is not of general application.

In *British Gas v Sharma*,[113] the claimant had been wrongly excluded from a post on racial grounds. An industrial tribunal recommended that the claimant be promoted the next time a suitable vacancy arose. The EAT held that this (a) amounted to positive discrimination and (b) as it was not known when such a vacancy would arise, it could not indicate a "specified period," as required by the legislation. As the purpose was reparation of previous discrimination, the second ground alone is preferable. In *Leeds Rhinos Rugby Club v Sterling*[114] the EAT held that a tribunal could not recommend that a rugby player's contract was renewed simply on the reasoning (no evidence was offered) that following his successful claim for racial discrimination

---

[109] "It seems to be the case that the legislators contemplated the race and sex Commissions following up individual cases to deal with the wider implications, either by promotional work . . . or by use of the formal investigation power." C. Bourn and J. Whitmore, *Anti-Discrimination Law in Britain*, 3rd edn, 1996, London: Sweet & Maxwell, pp.263–64.

[110] Fair Employment and Treatment Order, 1998, Art.39(1)(d) (emphasis supplied).

[111] Section 706(g)(1), USC s.2000e–5(g)(1). See further, Ch.12, para.12–016.

[112] [1988] I.R.L.R. 530, CA.

[113] [1991] I.C.R. 19.

[114] Unreported (2002) EAT/267/01 (Transcript).

other clubs would view him as a trouble maker, and so he was less employable. Finally, in *Irvine v Prestcold*[115] the Court of Appeal held that a recommendation could not include an increase in wages (to compensate for lost promotion) as such matters should be accounted for by compensation.

By contrast, in *Chief Constable of West Yorkshire v Vento*,[116] speaking in the EAT, Wall, J. considered the power to make recommendations "extremely wide". It has been argued that where the victim *would have* got the job but for the discrimination, it is right that the victim should be able jump ahead of the next queue.[117]

2. STRATEGIC ENFORCEMENT OF THE LEGISLATION

The Equality Act 2006 established the Commission for Equality and Human Rights, a new single strategic enforcement body, which is expected to absorb two of the three existing bodies (Equal Opportunities and Disability Rights Commissions), in October 2007, and the third (Commission for Racial Equality), in 2009. It is broader in scope than the original regime, as it embraces the specific legislation for religion or belief, sexual orientation, and age,[118] in addition to sex, race and disability (collectively labelled the "equality enactments"). In addition it has human rights within its remit, which has a general prohibition against discrimination in the securing of those rights.[119] During this transitional period, both the original and new regimes need to be considered.

13–029

(1) The Original Regime[120]
The Equal Opportunities Commission (EOC), the Commission for Racial Equality (CRE) and the Disability Rights Commission (DRC)[121] are the bodies charged both with enforcement of the legislation and with acting in various ways on behalf of their constituencies. There are no bodies representing the sexual orientation, age, or religion or belief legislation, although the Sex Discrimination Act 1975 was amended to bring discrimination on the ground of gender

13–030

---

[115] [1981] I.C.R. 777.

[116] [2002] I.R.L.R. 177, at para.49.

[117] See A. McColgan, *Discrimination Law, Text Cases and Materials* 2nd edn, 2005, Oxford: Hart, p.339.

[118] In force October 1, 2006.

[119] See Ch.2, para.2–004 *et seq.*

[120] For discussion of the structure and functions of the CRE, see C. McCrudden, D. Smith and C. Brown, *Racial Justice at Work: Enforcement of the Race Relations Act 1976 in Employment*, 1991, London: Policy Studies Institute, pp.49–56.

[121] Established by the Disability Rights Commission Act 1999.

reassignment within the competence of the EOC.[122] The statutory duties which all three bodies have in common are to work towards the elimination of discrimination, to promote equality of opportunity, and to keep the working of the legislation under review (this entails making proposals for reform).[123] In addition, the CRE only has the duty to "promote good relations between persons of different racial groups . . ."[124] The DRC in addition may encourage good practice, support and carry out research, and make proposals.

The statutes provide and define a variety of powers for the Commissions. They have powers to issue Codes of Practice, assist individuals to enforce the legislation,[125] and take enforcement action in relation to pressure and instructions to discriminate, discriminatory advertising, and discriminatory practices.[126] The Commissions may also conduct Formal Investigations, with potential legal implications for the subject of the investigation. In addition they have power to deal with persistent discrimination and take judicial review proceedings.

(a) Formal Investigations[127]

13–031 The provisions for Formal Investigations by the EOC and CRE are substantially the same. There is a modified structure for the DRC, which is considered separately below. In most situations the Commissions have no power to institute proceedings directly against a party suspected of discrimination. The legislation provides that the Commissions may conduct Formal Investigations[128] which may lead to the issue of a Non-Discrimination Notice.[129]

Theoretically at least, there are several benefits to this approach, identified by Applebey and Ellis:[130]

> [F]ormal investigations provide the best remedy in five situations:
>
> (1) Cases of "victimless" discrimination . . . where discriminatory attitudes have existed for a long time and are well known so that, for example, women do not apply for jobs . . . and no specific act of discrimination therefore occurs.

---

[122] SDA 1975, s.53(1)(ba), covering employment and vocational training only, reflecting the limited obligation under EC law.

[123] SDA 1975, s.53; RRA 1976, s.43; DRCA 1999, s.2.

[124] RRA 1976, s.43(1)(b).

[125] See below, para.13–038.

[126] See above, Ch.5, para.5–029 *et seq.*

[127] See C. McCrudden, D. Smith and C. Brown, *Racial Justice at Work: Enforcement of the Race Relations Act 1976 in Employment*, 1991, London: Policy Studies Institute, Chs 3 and 4.

[128] SDA 1975, ss.57–61; RRA 1976, ss.48–52; DRCA 1999, s.3 and Sch.3. Formal Investigations by the DRC are discussed below.

[129] SDA 1975, ss.67–70; RRA 1976, ss.58–61.

[130] G. Applebey and E. Ellis, "Formal investigations: the Commission for Racial Equality and the Equal Opportunities Commission as law enforcement agencies" [1984] PL 236, pp.273–75.

(2)   Situations where many people are affected, too many for the courts to handle, and where there would be a waste of resources if everyone had to pursue an individual claim.

(3)   Where the practices are very complicated and require the ascertainment of facts which are beyond the capacity and resources of an individual.

(4)   Where the individual who has been discriminated against is in fact a member of a clearly defined group and the Commission feels it essential to investigate further in the interests of the remaining members of the group.

(5)   Where references are made to the Commissions to investigate matters believed to be in the public interest.

Formal Investigations involve formal and intrusive scrutiny of a named person, with potential legal consequences. The power to launch a Formal Investigation was curtailed by two House of Lords decisions. But the reasons for this are not straightforward.

In the first case, *Hillingdon London BC v CRE*,[131] Hillingdon **13–032** Council were obliged (as any local authority is) to house the homeless, including homeless immigrants arriving at Heathrow Airport, which was within their borough. The Council felt strongly that this should be a responsibility of national government. As a protest a member of the council placed an immigrant family of Asian origin in a taxi and abandoned them outside the doors of the Foreign Office. Meanwhile, the council housed an immigrant family of English origin from Zimbabwe (at the time, Rhodesia). The Commission formed a reasonable suspicion that Hillingdon Council was acting in a discriminatory way when housing arrivals at Heathrow and so decided to embark upon a Formal Investigation. However, the terms of reference stated that the Commission believed that the Council was discriminating when offering accommodation to *the public, or a section of it*. The House of Lords ordered *certiorari* to quash the CRE determination. This was because: (1) s.49(4), Race Relations Act 1976 (RRA 1976), provides that before the Commission can embark upon a "named-person" Formal Investigation it must undertake a "preliminary inquiry." (2) The purpose of the preliminary inquiry is to hear what the person named had to say in response to the Commission's accusations. (3) It follows that if the person named is to be given a genuine opportunity to answer, the Commission cannot "throw the book at him"; thus the accusations must be based upon a (reasonably formed) belief. (4) Accordingly the scope of the Commission's investigatory power is limited to its belief. (5) As the terms of reference expressed a belief ("section of the public") wider than the Commission's actual belief ("arrivals at Heathrow"), the Commission had no power to

---

[131] [1982] A.C. 779.

conduct a Formal Investigation within the terms of reference, and their decision to do so would be quashed.

In the second case, *Re Prestige Group plc*,[132] the Commission launched a "named-person" Formal Investigation into the employment practices of Prestige, even though it had no suspicion that Prestige was practicing any unlawful discrimination. The House of Lords held, applying *Hillingdon*, that s.49(4), RRA 1976, provides that before the Commission can embark upon a Formal Investigation it must have a reasonable belief that those named in the terms of reference have acted unlawfully within the meaning of the RRA 1976.

From these two cases, it would seem that before a commission can embark upon a "named-person" Formal Investigation it must: (a) have a reasonable belief or suspicion that the persons named have contravened the relevant discrimination legislation; (b) hold a "preliminary inquiry" giving the named persons an opportunity to make representations in reply to the accusations; and (c) draw up terms of reference which must be no wider than its actual belief, which must be stated.

13–033   Nine other Formal Investigations by the CRE were abandoned following the *Prestige* decision.[133] Previously, the CRE considered that the RRA 1976 permitted it to make exploratory investigations, i.e. Formal Investigations without any prior suspicion of discrimination. *Hillingdon* can be distinguished from *Prestige* on the ground that in *Hillingdon* the CRE stated an incorrect belief in the terms of reference, whereas in *Prestige* no belief was stated at all. Thus the House of Lords was not bound to follow *Hillingdon* as precedent.

The key to these restrictive decisions lies in the drafting of s.49, RRA 1976.[134] Section 49(1) provides that "the Commission shall not embark upon a Formal Investigation unless the requirements of this section have been complied with." Section 49(2) requires that the Commission draw up "terms of reference." Section 49(4) states that where the terms of reference are confined to persons named in them and the Commission proposes to investigate any act made unlawful under the RRA 1976 which it believes that a "named person" has done, it must inform that person of its belief and afford him the opportunity to make oral or written representations with regard to it. Section 49 appears to state therefore, that before the Commission can embark upon a named-person investigation it must have a "belief" that a person named in the terms of reference has committed an act of unlawful discrimination. And, according to principals of public law, that belief must be a reasonable, or objective, one. However, it would be reasonable to assume that such an important requirement would

---

[132] [1984] I.C.R. 473.

[133] G. Appleby and E. Ellis, "Formal Investigations: the Commission for Racial Equality and the Equal Opportunities Commission as Law Enforcement Agencies" [1984] PL 236, at 264.

[134] The same formula is used in SDA 1975, s.58.

have been more explicit. Section 49(4) *presumes* rather than states the requirement of a belief and it usual practice for Parliament to attach the word "reasonable" to belief or suspicion where it is intended. The explanation is that subs.(4) was inserted into s.49 in error. It was an amendment forced by Lord Hailsham intended to be a new section 50.[135] If the amendment were made as Parliament intended, it would *not* have been a prerequisite to a Formal Investigation. However, prior to *Pepper v Hart*,[136] no court could use Parliamentary debates as a source of statutory interpretation.

In other, less important areas, the courts have made decisions **13–034** favourable to the CRE. In *Home Office v Commission for Racial Equality*,[137] the CRE announced a "general" Formal Investigation into the administration of immigration control, purporting to act under its general aim provided by s.43(1)(a), RRA 1976: "to work towards the elimination of discrimination." The Home Office argued that s.43(1)(a) covered only discrimination under the RRA 1976, and as that Act did not cover immigration, the CRE had no power to investigate it. Woolf, J. held that the CRE had no power to investigate immigration under s.43(1)(a). However, he found it did have such a power under s.43(1)(b) "to promote good race relations generally."[138] In *R. v Commission for Racial Equality, Ex p. Cottrell & Rothon*,[139] the Commission carried out a Formal Investigation into a firm of estate agents (C & R) and produced a report. During the investigations the Commission interviewed C & R's clients. Later the Commission wrote to C & R informing them that, on the basis of their report, it was minded to issue a Non-Discrimination Notice, but not before offering C & R an opportunity to make written and oral representations (as provided by s.58(5)). C & R sent written representations and instructed counsel to make oral representations. At the hearing none of the Commission's witnesses were present. After the hearing the Commission went ahead and served the Non-Discrimination Notice. C & R argued that the hearing was not conducted in accordance with the rules of natural justice (as required by public law) because their counsel had no opportunity to cross-examine the witnesses. It sought an order of *certiorari* to quash the Commission's decision to issue the Non-Discrimination Notice. It was held, in favour of the Commission, as that the procedure was so akin to an administrative one, cross-examination was not necessary.[140]

---

[135] See for instance HL Deb October 4, 1976 cols 1000–1008 and comments of Lord Denning MR in the Court of Appeal in *R. v Commission for Racial Equality, Ex p. Hillingdon LBC* [1982] Q.B. 276, at 285–286.
[136] [1993] A.C. 593, HL.
[137] [1982] Q.B. 385.
[138] *ibid.*, at 396B.
[139] [1980] 3 All E.R. 265, Q.B.D. (Lord Lane C.J. and Woolf, J. (as he then was)).
[140] *ibid.*, at 270*j*.

The Commissions must issue a formal report on their findings from the Formal Investigation. If the evidence discloses unlawful discrimination they may serve a Non-Discrimination Notice.[141] This requires the employer not to commit unlawful discrimination, and where appropriate, to inform the relevant Commission of any changes to practices and procedures have been made to prevent a recurrence.[142] The party subject to the Notice may appeal within six weeks to an employment tribunal, or county or sheriff court, as appropriate.

(b) Disability Rights Commission and Investigations[143]

13–035 The Explanatory Notes to the Disability Rights Commission Act 1999 (DRCA 1999) envisage three types of investigation: a general investigation, and two types of "Named-Person" investigation. The first Named-Person investigation is where the Commission reasonably believes that the person has committed unlawful discrimination. The second can be conducted to monitor whether a person is complying with any requirements in a Non-Discrimination Notice or in an action plan within it, or with any undertakings in a statutory "agreement in lieu of enforcement action" (see below). Before the Commission can embark on any type of investigation Terms of Reference must be drawn up and published. The Commission is empowered to issue a Non-Discrimination Notice, in line with the powers of CRE and EOC. However, a power new to the Disability Rights Commission is that it may "make an agreement in lieu of enforcement action."[144]

A problem from the CRE/EOC legislation remains. As noted above, It was held in *Prestige*[145] that the CRE must have a reasonable belief of unlawful behaviour before it could embark upon a named-person investigation. At the root of that decision was an error in the drafting of the RRA 1976. The error was not repeated in the DRCA 1999. However, the position has not been clarified significantly more than that.

Paragraph 3(1) of Sch.3, states "This paragraph applies where the Commission proposes to investigate in the course of a Formal Investigation (whether or not the investigation has already begun) whether (a) a person has committed an unlawful act . . .". Paragraph 3(3), of Sch.3 provides that "the Commission may not investigate" whether a person named in the Terms of Reference has committed an unlawful act unless (a) it has a reasonable belief, or (b) it is in the course of a Formal Investigation into compliance with a Non-Discrimination Notice or Agreement in Lieu. So para.3(3)(a) suggests

---

[141] SDA 1975, s.67; RRA 1976, s.58.
[142] SDA 1975, s.67(2) and (3); RRA 1976, s.58(2) and (3).
[143] DRCA 1999, s.3 and Sch.3.
[144] DRCA 1999, ss.4 and 5 respectively.
[145] *Commission for Racial Equality v Prestige Group* [1984] I.C.R. 473, HL. See above, para.13–031.

that at the *outset* of most Formal Investigations (that is, where there is no such Notice or Agreement), the Commission must have a reasonable belief of unlawful behaviour by those named. This perhaps contrasts with para.3(1), where the phrase in parenthesis "whether or not the investigation has already begun" suggests that on the one hand, a Named-Person Formal Investigation may begin *without* a reasonable belief of unlawful behaviour; it is the investigation *within* the Formal Investigation, that needs to be supported by a reasonable belief. But this offers little precision on the prerequisites for Named-Person Formal Investigation. Formal Investigations can only be made for a purpose connected with its duties under s.2(1), DDA 1995,[146] such as promoting equalisation of opportunities and encouraging good practice. Logically, the Commission could embark upon a Named-Person Formal Investigation to "encourage good practice" and during that Investigation develop the reasonable belief that there has been unlawful behaviour. Although suggesting otherwise, the Explanatory Notes (see above) do not rule this out expressly.

(c) Persistent Discrimination

After a Non-Discrimination Notice has been issued, or following a tribunal or court finding of unlawful discrimination, the relevant Commission may seek a county court injunction at any time within five years if further acts of discrimination are likely to be committed.[147]

13–036

(d) Judicial Review

The legislation expressly preserves judicial review.[148] In *R v Secretary of State for Employment Ex p. Equal Opportunities Commission*,[149] the House of Lords held that the Commission had *locus standi* to argue that the domestic rules for the qualifying period of unfair dismissal indirectly discriminated against women, contrary to EC law. Following this ruling, it would be difficult to argue that the Commissions did not have a sufficient interest in a case, where their statutory duty is inter alia to work towards the elimination of discrimination. Furthermore, individuals may seek judicial review to challenge state rules that may discriminate against them contrary to EC

13–037

---

[146] See above, para.13–030.
[147] SDA 1975, s.71; RRA 1976, s.62; DRCA 1999, s.6.
[148] SDA 1975, s.62(2); RRA 1976, s.53(2) (does not apply to certain Government appointments: ss.53(4) and 76); DDA 1995, Sch.3, para.2(1); Sexual Orientation regulations 2003, reg.27(2); Religion or Belief, Regulations, 2003, reg.27(2); Age Regulations 2006, reg.35(2) (in force October 1, 2006). Judicial review is not available if a conventional remedy (such as a claim in the county court) is available: *R. v South Bank University, Ex p. Coggeran* [2000] I.C.R. 1342, CA.
[149] [1995] 1 A.C. 1, HL.

law. In *Seymour-Smith*,[150] the challenge was again to the qualifying period for unfair dismissal rights.

(e) Legal Assistance

13–038   The Commissions may provide legal assistance to individual claimants when (a) the case raised a question of principle; or (b) it was unreasonable, having regard to the complexity of the case or the applicant's position in relation to the respondent or other person involved or any other matter, to expect the applicant to deal with the case unaided; or (c) by reason of any other special consideration.[151]

Research has shown that that those granted assistance had a "substantially" better chance of success because (i) a commission tries to select the strongest cases, (ii) it is likely to provide more effective advice and representation, and (iii) it provides moral support, reducing the chances of a fatigued claimant withdrawing. Hence, a commission's decision to support can be critical to the success of a claim, meaning that a commission "retains a dominant and quasi-judicial function."[152]

(2) The New Regime

13–039   The Equality Act 2006 (EA 2006) states that the general duties of Commission for Equality and Human Rights (CEHR) are to exercise its functions "with a view to encouraging and supporting the development of a society in which—(a) people's ability to achieve their potential is not limited by prejudice or discrimination, (b) there is respect for and protection of each individual's human rights, (c) there is respect for the dignity and worth of each individual, (d) each individual has an equal opportunity to participate in society, and (e) there is mutual respect between groups based on understanding and valuing of diversity and on shared respect for equality and human rights."[153]

Its duties specific to "equality and diversity" are that the Commission "shall . . . (a) promote understanding of the importance of equality and diversity, (b) encourage good practice in relation to equality and diversity, (c) promote equality of opportunity, (d) promote awareness and understanding of rights under the equality enactments, (e) enforce the equality enactments, (f) work towards the elimination of unlawful discrimination, and (g) work towards the elimination of unlawful harassment.[154] In addition, the Commission "shall" promote

---

[150] *R. v Secretary of State for Employment Ex p. Seymour-Smith* [2000] 1 All E.R. 857 HL. See further, Ch.6, paras 6–024 and 6–041.

[151] SDA 1975, s.75(1); RRA 1976, s.66(1); DRCA 1999, s.7(2).

[152] C. McCrudden, D. Smith and C. Brown, *Racial Justice at Work: Enforcement of the Race Relations Act 1976 in Employment*, 1991, London: Policy Studies Institute, p.155.

[153] EA 2006, s.3.

[154] EA 2006, s.8.

and encourage "understanding of the importance of good relations" and "good practice in relation to relations" between members of different groups, and between members of groups and others; and work towards enabling members of groups to participate in society. "Groups" means simply those covered by the equality enactments (sex, gender reassignment, race, disability, sexual orientation, religion or belief and age). Its other specific duty is to promote human rights, as defined by the European Convention on Human Rights through the Human Rights Act 1998.[155]

In line with the original regime, the Commission has the power to issue Codes of Practice,[156] give legal assistance to individuals,[157] to take enforcement action in relation to discriminatory advertising, and pressure and instructions to discriminate, and discriminatory practices.[158]

The Government expressly rejected some proposals for other strategic enforcement. The first was that the Commission should be able to bring class actions on behalf of similarly placed "victims". These actions are common in the United States.[159] The Government considered that as these were generally not used in Great Britain, the matter went beyond the introduction of the Commission. The second proposal was that the new Commission should be able to bring hypothetical cases to clarify points of law. This was rejected because "it is very difficult for a court to reach a useful decision in the absence of particular facts" and it is not the practice of the European Court of Justice, the European Court of Human Rights, or the domestic courts.[160]

(a) Inquires and Investigations

The Act provides the Commission with two forms of investigatory power: Inquires and Investigations. Inquires are less serious and cannot, in themselves, lead to legal action by the Commission. By contrast, Investigations can have legal consequences.

13–040

Under s.16, EA 2006, the Commission can launch an Inquiry simply in pursuit of its duties. "These could be thematic (for example

---

[155] See Ch.2, para.2–004 *et seq.*
[156] EA 2006, s.14.
[157] EA 2006, s.28.
[158] EA 2006, s.25. See Ch.5, para.5–029 *et seq.*
[159] Rule 23, Fed R Civ Proc. The requirements are: (i) *numerosity*, claimants so numerous as to make individual claims unruly and impracticable; (ii) *Commonality,* there must common questions of law and fact; (iii) *Typicality*, claims and defences must be typical of the class; (iv) *Representation,* named petitioner can fairly represent the class with competent counsel and no conflict of interest. For other restrictions see *General Telephone Company of the Southwest v Falcon* 457 US 147 (Sup Ct 1982) and D. Piar, "The uncertain future of Title VII class action cases after the Civil Rights Act of 1991", 2001 BYU L Rev 305. See also D. Pannick, *Sex Discrimination Law*, 1985, Oxford: OUP, pp.284–301.
[160] White Paper, "Fairness For All: A New Commission for Equality and Human Rights" 2004, URN 04/1072, London: TSO, at paras 4.40–4.43.

into the causes of unequal outcomes), sectoral (looking at inequality in, for example, the uptake of health screening services or at the employment of disabled people in particular sectors, e.g. the retail sector), or relate to one or more named parties."[161] A "named party" includes individuals, companies and organisations. Before the Inquiry, the Commission must publish its Terms of Reference.[162] Afterwards, it may publish a report, but it cannot state or imply that a person has committed an unlawful act, unless it relates to human rights.

If, during the inquiry, the Commission suspects that person has committed an unlawful act, the inquiry must *not* pursue that suspicion. Instead, the Commission may pursue it using an Investigation.

13–041   For Investigations, s.20, EA 2006, substantially restates the power to make Formal Investigations afforded to the previous Commissions under the legislation and subsequent case law (see above).

Investigations involve formal and intrusive scrutiny of a named person, with potential legal consequences. Three possible triggers allow the Commission to embark on an Investigation. The first is where the Commission has a suspicion that named person has committed an act unlawful under the equality enactments. Under the previous regime the House of Lords held that this suspicion had to be a reasonable one (i.e. objective, not subjective) as a matter of public law principle.[163] The White Paper suggested "Suspicion that unlawful acts may have occurred could be formed by reports to the CEHR from victims of discrimination or harassment, by reports from third parties, or from cases ruled on by courts or tribunals."[164] The Act itself suggests that the suspicion may be based on the results of, or a matter arising during the course of, an Inquiry under s.16. The Commission must draw up and publish terms of reference for the investigation, and these must accord with its suspicion. This was established under the original regime in *Hillingdon London BC v CRE*.[165]

The second and third possibilities for a named investigation are where the Commission decides to ascertain if a person has complied with a requirement imposed by an "unlawful act notice", or with an undertaking given under a statutory "binding agreement" (see below).

(b) Unlawful Act Notices
13–042   If, following an Investigation, the Commission concludes that unlawful discrimination has taken place, it may serve a notice on the named person requiring the discrimination to stop. This may also require the person to draft an action plan designed to avoid repetition

---

[161] Explanatory Notes to the Equality Act 2006, para.56.
[162] EA 2006, Sch.2, para.2.
[163] *Re Prestige Group plc* [1984] I.C.R. 473. See above, paras 13–032—13–033.
[164] White Paper, "Fairness For All: A New Commission for Equality and Human Rights", 2004, URN 04/1072, London: TSO, at para.4.25.
[165] [1982] A.C. 779, HL. see above, paras 13–032—13–033.

or continuation of the unlawful act, which for a period of five years the Commission may monitor and enforce. Named persons subject to an unlawful act notice may appeal within six weeks to an employment tribunal if the allegations fall within its jurisdiction, or to a county or sheriff court for any other acts.[166]

(c) Binding Agreements

Section 23 allows for the Commission to enter an agreement with a person who undertakes to refrain from committing any discrimination and to take, or (or refrain from taking) any specified act, including drafting an action plan. In exchange, the Commission promises not to pursue an Investigation or issue an unlawful act notice. The agreement itself is enforceable. The trigger for this power is where the Commission "thinks" unlawful discrimination has been committed by the person. The Explanatory Notes for to the Equality Act 2006 assume that this means "reason to suspect".[167]

Where the Commission "thinks" that a party to an agreement has failed to comply, or is likely not to comply, with the agreement it may apply to a county court or sheriff for an order of compliance or other specified action.[168]

13–043

(d) Application for Injunction

Under s.24(1), EA 2006, if the Commission "thinks" that a person is likely to commit an unlawful act, it may apply to the county court or sheriff for an injunction or interdict restraining the person from committing the act.

13–044

(e) Judicial Review and other Legal Proceedings

Section 30 provides that the Commission may institute or intervene in legal proceedings in pursuance of its functions. This applies to the Human Rights Act 1998 as well as the equality enactments.

13–045

(f) Legal Assistance

Section 28 of the Equality Act 2006 authorises the Commission to provide legal assistance to "an individual who alleges that he is a victim of behaviour contrary to the equality enactments and who is or may become a party to legal proceedings which relate to the alleged breach of the equality enactments."

13–046

---

[166] EA 2006, ss.21–22.
[167] At para.83.
[168] EA 2006, ss.24(2) and 24(3).

This affords more discretion to the Commission than the original regime (see above, para.13–038), which only permitted assistance when (a) the case raised a question of principle; or (b) it was unreasonable to expect the applicant to deal with the case unaided; or (c) by reason of any other special consideration.

In this section the "equality enactments" includes EC discrimination law. Under this section the Commission may provide legal advice and representation; facilities for the settlement of a dispute; and any other form of assistance.

Section 28(12) authorises the Commission to "support" legal proceedings brought under other domestic legislation (i.e. not the equality enactments) that is either incompatible with or has failed to give effect to Community discrimination law relating to sex, (including reassignment of gender) racial origin, ethnic origin, religion, belief, disability, age or sexual orientation.

(3) Duty of Public Bodies[169]

13–047 The public body duties are in force for race on April 2, 2001[170] and for gender on April 6, 2007.[171] The disability duty is fully in force on December 4, 2006.[172]

The legislation imposes general and specific duties. The general duties for race are (a) to eliminate unlawful discrimination and (b) to promote equality of opportunity[173] and good relations between persons of different racial groups.[174] Under the Sex Discrimination Act 1975, the duties are to eliminate unlawful discrimination and harassment, and (b) to promote equality of opportunity between men and women.[175] Under the DDA 1995, the duties are to "have due regard to" (a) the need to eliminate unlawful discrimination and

---

[169] Outside of England and Wales, the duties are not always confined to sex, race and disability discrimination. The Scottish Parliament may (by Scotland Act 1998) impose an equal opportunities duty local authorities. "Equal Opportunities" means: "the prevention, elimination or regulation of discrimination between persons on grounds of sex or marital status, on racial grounds, or on grounds of disability, age, sexual orientation, language or social origin, or of other personal attributes, including beliefs or opinions, such as religious beliefs or political opinions." (Sch.5, Pt II, para.L2). (See e.g., Housing (Scotland) Act 2001, s.106.) Northern Ireland Act 1998, s.75(1) provides: "A public authority shall in carrying out its functions relating to Northern Ireland have due regard to the need to promote equality of opportunity—(a) between persons of different religious belief, political opinion, racial group, age, marital status or sexual orientation; (b) between men and women generally; (c) between persons with a disability and persons without; and (d) between persons with dependants and persons without." (See e.g. Flags (Northern Ireland) Order 2000.)

[170] SI 2001/566, Art.2(1). For a commentary, see C. O'Cinneide, "The Race Relations (Amendment) Act 2000" [2001] PL 220.

[171] SI 2006/1082, Art.4.

[172] For certain purposes, June 30, 2005 (SI 2005/1676) and December 5, 2005 (SI 2005/2774, Art.3) and for remaining purposes December 4, 2006 (SI 2005/2774, Art.4).

[173] The phrase "equality of opportunity" in the RRA 1976 does not apply to immigration and nationality functions: s.71A, RRA.

[174] RRA 1976, s.71(1).

[175] SDA 1975, s.76A, in force April 6, 2007 (SI 2006/1082, Art.4).

harassment; (b) the need to promote equality of opportunity between disabled persons and other persons; (c) the need to take steps to take account of disabled persons' disabilities, even where that involves treating disabled persons more favourably than other persons; (d) the need to promote positive attitudes towards disabled persons; and (e) the need to encourage participation by disabled persons in public life.[176] In addition to these general duties, specific duties may be specified by statutory instrument.[177]

The Commission has two roles in this. First, it may issue Codes of Practice.[178] Second, it has power to issue compliance notices. If, following an assessment, the Commission "thinks" that a public body has failed in its duties, the Commission may issue a notice requiring compliance. If the Commission "thinks" that the public body is not complying with the notice, the Commission may apply (to the county or sheriff court) for an order requiring compliance.[179]

Alternatively, the Commission can make a statutory agreement with a public authority in respect of a breach of any of a public sector duty in lieu of issuing a public sector duty compliance notice.[180]

---

[176] DDA 1995, s.49A.

[177] RRA 1976, s.71(2) (See e.g. Race Relations Act 1976 (Statutory Duties) Order 2001, SI 3458 requiring certain bodies to publish Race Equality Schemes); SDA 1975, 76B; DDA 1995, s.49D.

[178] Currently RRA 1976, s.71C, (see "Code of Practice on the duty to promote racial equality." (2002) London: CRE (ISBN 1 85442 430 0), issued by the CRE. For a commentary, see (2002) 102 EOR 28. The CRE also has issued four non-statutory Guides in this field); SDA 1975, s.76E; DDA 1995 53A(1C), in force June 30, 2005 (2005 SI 2005/1676, Art.2(1)(c)).

[179] EA 2006, s.32. Until the Commission is operational, the CRE (RRA 1976, 71D and 71E) and DRC (DDA 1995, 49E and 49F) have similar powers.

[180] EA 2006, s.23(5).

INDEX

LEGAL TAXONOMY
FROM SWEET & MAXWELL

This index has been prepared using Sweet and Maxwell's Legal Taxonomy. Main index entries conform to keywords provided by the Legal Taxonomy except where references to specific documents or non-standard terms (denoted by quotation marks) have been included. These keywords provide a means of identifying similar concepts in other Sweet & Maxwell publications and online services to which keywords from the Legal Taxonomy have been applied. Readers may find some minor differences between terms used in the text and those which appear in the index. Suggestions to *sweetandmaxwell.taxonomy@thomson.com*.

(All references are to paragraph number)

411